# Baking

*From my home to yours*

# Baking

*From my home to yours*

## Dorie Greenspan

PHOTOGRAPHS BY ALAN RICHARDSON

HOUGHTON MIFFLIN COMPANY

BOSTON   NEW YORK   2006

*Library of Congress Cataloging-in-Publication Data*

Greenspan, Dorie.
 Baking : from my home to yours / Dorie Greenspan ;
photographs by Alan Richardson.
    p. cm.
 Includes index.
 ISBN-13: 978-0-618-44336-9
 ISBN-10: 0-618-44336-3
 1. Baking.    I. Title.
 TX765.G8155 2006
 641.8'15—dc22          2006003101

Book design by Anne Chalmers
Food styling by Karen Tack
Prop styling by Deb Donahue
Typefaces: Miller, Meta, Bickham Script

Printed in the United States of America

QWV  10  9  8  7  6  5  4  3  2  1

FOR JOSHUA,
my all-time favorite
cookie muncher

# ACKNOWLEDGMENTS

THIS IS MY NINTH COOKBOOK. It is different in almost every way from my previous books, with one grand exception: as with all my other books, I worked with great people.

From the start there was my agent, David Black. David is smart, funny, fiercely supportive and crazy about brownies—a quality not to be underestimated. He is also spot-on about people, and it was David who brought me to Rux Martin, my editor.

I had known Rux and admired her work for years and was thrilled to be working with her. And I can't emphasize the word "with" strongly enough—in Rux I found a true partner, something wonderful and rare in any endeavor. *Baking* is a far better book for having passed under her keen eye.

I was also privileged to work with the remarkable team at Houghton Mifflin, including Michaela Sullivan, who created the cover; Anne Chalmers, who designed the interior; Shelley Berg, who saw the book through production; Jacinta Monniere, who skillfully deciphered editorial hieroglyphs; and Rux's terrific assistant, another brownie lover, Mimi Assad.

That *Baking* is both beautiful and welcoming is thanks to the extraordinary talents of the dream team of food photography: photographer Alan Richardson and his assistant, Roy Galaday; food stylist Karen Tack and her assistant, Ellie Ritt; and prop stylist Deb Donahue. Working with any of them would have been an honor; working with all of them was a gift.

Once again, I was lucky enough to work with Judith Sutton, the best cookbook copy editor on the planet. We've been together on every book I've written, and I hope never to break this streak.

I have an equally long-running streak with *Bon Appétit* magazine and its exceptional editor in chief, Barbara Fairchild. We've worked together happily, creatively and deliciously for fifteen years and I hope we'll be working together for many more years to come. At *Bon Appétit*, I've been made to feel like a treasured member of the family, and I'm incredibly grateful. Extra thanks to Kristine Kidd, who, as director of the test kitchen, encouraged me to develop several recipes that debuted in the magazine and now appear in *Baking*.

I was fortunate to have the unflappable Judith Marshall testing recipes with me in New York. Judith is a gifted baker and a wonderful kitchen companion. We worked as a duo when she was pregnant, and we finished as a trio, with Olivia, her adorable daughter, taking up residence at the end of the kitchen. We're not certain what Olivia will do when she grows up, but we're sure she'll love chocolate.

Special thanks to my pastry SOS team, Pierre Hermé in Paris and Nick Malgieri in New York.

And, as always and for always, my deepest love and greatest thanks to the men who make my life so sweet, my husband, Michael, and our son, Joshua.

# CONTENTS

# Introduction

UNTIL I WAS A JUNIOR IN COLLEGE, my sole cooking experience consisted of burning down my parents' kitchen when I was thirteen, after I tossed frozen French fries into boiling oil and covered the pot. For the next half-dozen years, I remained blissfully clueless about all things culinary. I didn't bake so much as a chocolate chip cookie. But as a nineteen-year-old newlywed, I developed an abundance of curiosity, enthusiasm and, most important, need—our budget didn't allow for dinners out, and it certainly didn't cover store-bought desserts.

To my surprise, I found that I enjoyed cooking and loved baking. In fact, I loved it so much that, years later, when I was finishing a doctorate in gerontology and expecting to find a research job or a quiet spot in a university, I realized that baking was all I really wanted to do. With my husband's encouragement, I decided to trade in academe for an oven, even though most everyone else I knew thought I was nuts.

At my first job interview to become an apprentice pastry chef in New York City, the chef rattled away in French, without asking me if I spoke the language, punctuating his monologue repeatedly with the words "*Je cherche un garçon*"—"I'm looking for a boy." When I pointed out I was not a boy, he said, "Yes, and that is why you will not work in my kitchen."

I did finally beg my way into a couple of great kitchens—all owned by women— and began writing about baking. Eventually I was asked by Julia Child to write *Baking with Julia* and turn what the chefs did on camera during her PBS television series into workable recipes the rest of the world could make at home. One afternoon when we were playing hooky from a prep session, Julia put her arm around my shoulders and said, "We make such a good team because we're really just a pair of home bakers."

I hadn't thought about myself that way, but Julia was right: I *was* a home baker. In all the years I'd spent writing, teaching and explaining the elaborate recipes of pastry chefs, I was still baking crisps, crumbles, kids' cupcakes and the homey desserts of my heart in my own narrow kitchen.

I had become a professional, but I had never stopped enjoying the satisfactions of baking at home. I still love the fragrance of fresh, sweet butter and pure vanilla, the feel of dough, the sound a wooden spoon makes against a pottery mixing bowl, the smell of cookies when they're almost ready to come out of the oven and the remarkable sense of accomplishment every time I make something with my own hands. And I still love simple sweets: chunky cookies that can be packed in lunch boxes, pies for the holiday table, loaf cakes dusted with powdered sugar, Bundt cakes that are good keepers and tall all-American layer cakes, swirled with creamy frosting and big enough to support a battalion of birthday candles.

It's been more than thirty years since I started baking at home, and rarely a day goes by that I don't bake. This book is a record of those years. In some ways, it's a recipe scrapbook, filled just as I would fill a kitchen journal to pass along to our son when he gets ready to start his own home. It's a collection of my favorite recipes, the ones I love and the ones I've shared with my family and friends—a compendium of all that I've learned about home baking. At its heart are the treasured recipes that have proved to do one thing very well—make people happy.

—DORIE GREENSPAN
New York City, 2006

# BREAKFAST
# SWEETS

# MUFFINS, BISCUITS AND SCONES
## A Quick View of Quick Breads

MUFFINS, BISCUITS, scones, coffee cakes and tea loaves, and even crepes, pancakes and waffles, if you want to be precise, are members of that felicitously named family of sweets called quick breads. Whereas traditional breads leavened with yeast require at least one rest period after mixing, quick breads get a fast, exuberant lift from baking powder, a compound that needs not time, but liquid and heat, to work its magic.

THE LEAVENER: I use baking powder for my quick breads. This compound produces a little brigade of bubbles in a batter as soon as it comes in contact with liquid, then it fires its second round of puff power when the oven's heat hits it. To get this power, though, your baking powder must be fresh. While the expiration date on a tin might be a year or so off, I like to replace my baking powder every six months (mark the date on the tin with an indelible pen so you'll know when to toss it)—better safe than flat. If you've got doubts about your powder, stir a teaspoonful into a quarter cup of warm water and check for bubbling, the sign of life.

THE PANS: For the most part, quick breads get their shape from the pans they're baked in (the exceptions are biscuits and scones, which are either rolled and cut or simply dropped). In all cases, the pans should be buttered; in most cases, buttered and floured. To make muffining even quicker, I use paper liners or a silicone muffin pan, either of which obviates the need for prepping the pan and makes cleanup quicker too.

THE TECHNIQUE: It's not just the leavening that's quick in quick breads: they do best when mixed least. For most quick breads, among them almost all muffins, you measure the dry ingredients (usually flour, sugar, baking powder and maybe spices) into a bowl and give them a few turns with a whisk to mix them up and aerate them. Next you put the liquid ingredients (eggs, melted butter or oil and maybe milk) into a large measuring cup with a spout and whisk them until they are blended. Then you pour the liquids over the dry ingredients and gently and swiftly stir them together. No beating and, unless the recipe instructs thoroughness (a rarity), no worrying about lumps and bumps in the batter—most lumps disappear in the baking. This light mixing technique produces quick breads with a lovely open crumb, just the right texture for slather-ons like butter and jam and soft chunky fruit.

# ORANGE BERRY MUFFINS

**THE ORANGE** flavor in these delicate, cakey and generously blueberried muffins is in the background, like a play's prompter—present, but only to encourage the performance of the star. In this case, the blueberries.

For a little extra sparkle, you can sprinkle the tops of the muffins with granulated sugar before sliding them into the oven; for a lot of extra sparkle, sprinkle them with decorating sugar, the coarse sugar that is often used to decorate Christmas cookies.

**SERVING:** The muffins are great warm or at room temperature and they're particularly great split, toasted and spread with butter or jam.

**STORING:** Like all muffins, these are best eaten the day they are made. If you want to keep them, wrap them airtight and pop them into the freezer, where they'll keep for up to 2 months; rewarm in a 350-degree-F oven, if you'd like, or split and toast them.

Grated zest and juice of
1 orange
About ¾ cup buttermilk
2 large eggs
3 tablespoons honey
1 stick (8 tablespoons) unsalted
butter, melted and cooled
⅓ cup sugar
2 cups all-purpose flour

2½ teaspoons baking powder
¼ teaspoon baking soda
¼ teaspoon salt
1 cup blueberries—fresh, preferably,
or frozen (not thawed)

Decorating sugar, for topping
(optional)

**GETTING READY:** Center a rack in the oven and preheat the oven to 400 degrees F. Butter or spray the 12 molds in a regular-size muffin pan or fit the molds with paper muffin cups. Alternatively, use a silicone muffin pan, which needs neither greasing nor paper cups. Place the muffin pan on a baking sheet.

Pour the orange juice into a large glass measuring cup or a bowl and pour in enough buttermilk to make 1 cup. Whisk in the eggs, honey and melted butter.

In a large bowl, rub the sugar and orange zest together with your fingertips until the sugar is moist and the fragrance of orange strong. Whisk in the flour, baking powder, baking soda and salt. Pour the liquid ingredients over the dry ingredients and, with the whisk or a rubber spatula, gently but quickly stir to blend. Don't worry about being thorough—the batter will be lumpy and bubbly, and that's just the way it should be. Stir in the blueberries. Divide the batter evenly among the muffin cups.

Bake for 22 to 25 minutes. If you want to top the muffins with decorating sugar, sprinkle on the sugar after the muffins have baked for 10 minutes. When fully baked, the tops of the muffins will be golden and springy to the touch and a thin knife inserted into the center of the muffins will come out clean. Transfer the pan to a rack and cool for 5 minutes before carefully removing each muffin from its mold.

# CORNIEST CORN MUFFINS

**THESE MUFFINS** have an alluringly old-fashioned look. They're flat, firm-topped and cheerfully yellow, with an equally old-fashioned texture—grainy with small holes running through the crumb—and a wholesome, straight-from-the-farm flavor. They're tangy from the buttermilk and sweet from both the cornmeal (try to find stone-ground) and the corn kernels. You can make these muffins with canned or frozen corn kernels, but if you scrape fresh kernels off the cob, you'll have something even more delightful: because the niblets will get only semisoft in the oven, every bite will offer just a little resistance, a little more "cornfulness" and a lot more pleasure.

If you're using fresh corn kernels, the easiest way to get them off the cob is to cut the cob in half crosswise, then, working with one piece at a time, hold the cob upright in a deep bowl and use a chef's knife to release the kernels from the cob. Position the knife at the base of the niblets and cut straight down the cob, turning the cob after each cut so you can de-kernel it completely. Separate the niblets with your fingers—you'll get about 1 cup from each ear of corn. If no one is around, lean over the sink and suck on the cob—corn juice is famously sweet and very satisfying.

MAKES 12 MUFFINS

**SERVING:** The muffins are great warm or at room temperature and particularly great split, toasted and slathered with butter or jam or both.

**STORING:** Like all muffins, these are best eaten the day they are made. If you want to keep them, wrap them airtight and pop them into the freezer, where they'll keep for about 2 months. Rewarm in a 350-degree-F oven, if you'd like, or split and toast them—do that, and they'll be that much more delicious with butter.

*Playing Around*

**CORNIEST CORN AND HERB MUFFINS:** You can add a slightly savory touch to these sweet muffins by incorporating 1 tablespoon finely chopped fresh thyme or rosemary into the batter. Either stir in the herbs when you mix in the corn kernels or, for a fuller flavor, rub the herbs into the sugar with your fingertips until the sugar is aromatic, then stir the sugar into the bowl with the rest of the dry ingredients.

| | |
|---|---|
| 1 cup all-purpose flour | 3 tablespoons unsalted butter, melted and cooled |
| 1 cup yellow cornmeal, preferably stone-ground | 3 tablespoons corn oil |
| 6 tablespoons sugar | 1 large egg |
| 2½ teaspoons baking powder | 1 large egg yolk |
| ¼ teaspoon baking soda | 1 cup corn kernels (add up to ⅓ cup more if you'd like)—fresh, frozen or canned (in which case, they should be drained and patted dry) |
| ½ teaspoon salt | |
| Pinch of freshly grated nutmeg (optional) | |
| 1 cup buttermilk | |

**GETTING READY:** Center a rack in the oven and preheat the oven to 400 degrees F. Butter or spray the 12 molds in a regular-size muffin pan or fit the molds with paper muffin cups. Alternatively, use a silicone muffin pan, which needs neither greasing nor paper cups. Place the muffin pan on a baking sheet.

In a large bowl, whisk together the flour, cornmeal, sugar, baking powder, baking soda, salt and nutmeg, if you're using it. In a large glass measuring cup or another bowl, whisk the buttermilk, melted butter, oil, egg and yolk together until well blended. Pour the liquid ingredients over the dry ingredients and, with the whisk or a rubber spatula, gently but quickly stir to blend. Don't worry about being thorough—the batter will be lumpy, and that's just the way it should be. Stir in the corn kernels. Divide the batter evenly among the muffin cups.

Bake for 15 to 18 minutes, or until the tops are golden and a thin knife inserted into the center of the muffins comes out clean. Transfer the pan to a rack and cool for 5 minutes before carefully removing each muffin from its mold.

# SAVORY CORN AND PEPPER MUFFINS

• • • • • • • • • • • • • • • • • • • • • • • • • • • • • • • • • • • • • • • • • • • • • • • • • • • • • • • • • • • • • • • • • • • • • •

**SOUTH-OF-THE-BORDER-STYLE** muffins have the spunk, spice and potential to be as good a partner to soup and salad as to huevos rancheros or a mild-mannered four-minute egg. Think of them as mini corn breads—they've got that kind of tight crumb and light crumbliness—and enjoy the cilantro and chiles that give them such a distinctive Southwestern twang. (For a more traditional version of these muffins, see Playing Around.)

1 cup all-purpose flour

1 cup yellow cornmeal, preferably
   stone-ground

3 tablespoons sugar

1 tablespoon baking powder

1½ teaspoons chili powder, or more to
   taste

1 teaspoon salt

½ teaspoon baking soda

¼ teaspoon freshly ground black
   pepper

1 cup buttermilk

1 stick (8 tablespoons) unsalted
   butter, melted and cooled

1 large egg yolk

¼ cup corn kernels (add up to 3
   tablespoons more if you'd like)—fresh
   (see page 4), frozen or canned (in
   which case, they should be drained
   and patted dry)

1 small jalapeño pepper, seeded,
   deveined and finely diced

¼ red bell pepper, seeded, deveined and
   finely diced

2 tablespoons finely chopped fresh
   cilantro

**GETTING READY:** Center a rack in the oven and preheat the oven to 400 degrees F. Butter or spray the 12 molds in a regular-size muffin pan or fit the molds with paper muffin cups. Alternatively, use a silicone muffin pan, which needs neither greasing nor paper cups. Place the muffin pan on a baking sheet.

In a large mixing bowl, whisk together the flour, cornmeal, sugar, baking powder, chili powder, salt, baking soda and black pepper. In a large glass measuring cup or another bowl, whisk the buttermilk, melted butter and egg yolk together until well blended. Pour the liquid ingredients over the dry ingredients and, with the whisk or a rubber spatula, gently but quickly stir to blend. Don't worry about being thorough—the batter will be lumpy, and that's just the way it should be. Stir in the corn kernels, jalapeño, red pepper and cilantro. Divide the batter evenly among the muffin cups.

Bake for about 20 minutes, or until the tops are golden and a thin knife inserted into the center of the muffins comes out clean. Transfer the pan to a rack and cool for 5 minutes before carefully removing each muffin from its mold.

**MAKES 12 MUFFINS**

**SERVING:** These are particularly good served warm and still very good at room temperature. As a morning muffin, they're good with butter; for brunch or supper, try them with red pepper jelly or salsa.

**STORING:** Best served the day they are made, these can be kept covered overnight and split and toasted the next day. They can also be wrapped airtight and frozen for up to 2 months. Rewarm in a 350-degree-F oven, if you'd like, or split and toast them.

*Playing Around*

**PLAIN CORN MUFFINS:** To make muffins that are a little richer and a little less sweet than Corniest Corn Muffins (page 4), omit the chili powder, black pepper, jalapeño, red pepper and cilantro and increase the sugar to ¼ cup.

# CITRUS-CURRANT SUNSHINE MUFFINS

**SMALL, FAIRLY** flat-topped and, as their name suggests, a sunny yellow color, these have a bright, fresh, wake-you-up flavor, the happy result of a mix of fresh orange juice, lemon juice and a dash of lemon extract, which makes the orange flavor even more orangey.

½ cup sugar

Grated zest of 1 orange

2 cups all-purpose flour

2½ teaspoons baking powder

¼ teaspoon baking soda

Pinch of salt

1 cup fresh orange juice

2 tablespoons fresh lemon juice

¼ teaspoon pure lemon extract

1 stick (8 tablespoons) unsalted butter, melted and cooled

2 large eggs

¾ cup moist, plump dried currants

**GETTING READY:** Center a rack in the oven and preheat the oven to 375 degrees F. Butter or spray the 12 molds in a regular-size muffin pan or fit the molds with paper muffin cups. Alternatively, use a silicone muffin pan, which needs neither greasing nor paper cups. Place the muffin pan on a baking sheet.

In a large bowl, rub the sugar and orange zest together with your fingertips until the sugar is moist and the fragrance of orange strong. Whisk in the flour, baking powder, baking soda and salt. In a large glass measuring cup or another bowl, whisk together the orange and lemon juices, lemon extract, melted butter and eggs. Pour the liquid ingredients over the dry ingredients and, with the whisk or a rubber spatula, gently but quickly stir to blend. Don't worry about being thorough—a few lumps are better than overmixing the batter. Fold in the currants. Divide the batter evenly among the muffin cups.

Bake for about 20 minutes, or until the tops are golden and a thin knife inserted into the center of the muffins comes out clean. Transfer the pan to a rack and cool for 5 minutes before carefully removing each muffin from its mold.

**SERVING:** I like these best at room temperature, when their texture is pleasantly chewy. I also like them most with a little swipe of soft sweet butter.

**STORING:** These are at their prime the day they are made, good the following day (just keep them well wrapped overnight) and fine packed airtight and frozen for up to 2 months. Rewarm the muffins in a 350-degree-F oven, if you'd like, or split them, toast them and butter them while they're hot.

# GREAT GRAINS MUFFINS

MADE WITH three different grains and plenty of buttermilk, eggs and maple syrup, these have character, great texture and a heartiness that satisfies without a trace of heaviness. I like to add quartered prunes to the mix, but the muffins are also good with raisins, dried apricots, dried cranberries, a few chopped pecans or nothing additional at all. Ditto when it comes to spreads—they're great with butter, cream cheese, a slice of cheddar, some jam or plain.

MAKES 12 MUFFINS

SERVING: These muffins are great warm or at room temperature.

STORING: Like all muffins, these are best eaten the day they are made, although they're fine the next day, particularly if you split and toast them. If you want to keep them, it's best to wrap them airtight and pop them into the freezer, where they'll keep for up to 2 months. Rewarm in a 350-degree-F oven, if you'd like, or split and toast them.

- 1 cup all-purpose flour
- ⅓ cup whole wheat flour
- ⅓ cup yellow cornmeal
- ⅓ cup old-fashioned oats
- ¼ cup sugar
- 2 teaspoons baking powder
- ¼ teaspoon baking soda
- ¼ teaspoon salt
- 1 cup buttermilk

- ⅓ cup pure maple syrup
- 2 large eggs
- 1 stick (8 tablespoons) unsalted butter, melted and cooled
- ¾ cup quartered moist, plump prunes or other dried fruits (cut up as necessary) and/or chopped nuts (optional)

GETTING READY: Center a rack in the oven and preheat the oven to 400 degrees F. Butter or spray the 12 molds in a regular-size muffin pan or fit the molds with paper muffin cups. Alternatively, use a silicone muffin pan, which needs neither greasing nor paper cups. Place the muffin pan on a baking sheet.

In a large bowl, whisk together the flours, cornmeal, oats, sugar, baking powder, baking soda and salt. In a large glass measuring cup or another bowl, whisk together the buttermilk, maple syrup, eggs and melted butter. Pour the liquid ingredients over the dry ingredients and, with the whisk or a rubber spatula, gently but quickly stir to blend. Don't worry about being thorough—if the batter is a bit lumpy, that's fine. Stir in the fruit or nuts, if you're using them. Divide the batter evenly among the muffin cups.

Bake for 18 to 20 minutes, or until the tops are golden and a thin knife inserted into the center of the muffins comes out clean. Transfer the pan to a rack and cool for 5 minutes, then carefully lift each muffin out of its mold and onto the rack to cool.

# LEMON POPPY SEED MUFFINS

**I CAN** give you four good reasons for wanting to single-handedly polish off a basket of these muffins: their resemblance to your favorite sour cream cake, their surprisingly tender texture, the haunting flavor of the poppy seeds that fleck their crumb and the exhilarating jolt that comes from lots of lemon juice in both the batter and the icing. Need another reason? Bake them with a little blueberry jam or a spot of lemon curd in the center (see Playing Around).

Poppy seeds, like nuts, are naturally oily and therefore prone to rancidity. To guard against spoilage, store them in a tightly sealed container in the freezer, and taste a few before using them to verify their freshness.

MAKES 12 MUFFINS

**SERVING:** These muffins are best at room temperature, served plain or with jam.

**STORING:** Kept in a tightly covered container, the muffins will be fine for a day, although they are at their best the day they are made. Because of the confectioners' sugar icing, they cannot be frozen.

*Playing Around*

**JAM-FILLED LEMON POPPY SEED MUFFINS:** This is an easy variation that tips the balance cakeward for these muffins. Fill the muffin cups with half the batter and top each with a teaspoonful of jam—my preference is blueberry or raspberry jam, lemon marmalade, or even lemon curd—then spoon in the rest of the batter and carry on.

## FOR THE MUFFINS

- ⅔ cup sugar
- Grated zest and juice of 1 lemon
- 2 cups all-purpose flour
- 2 teaspoons baking powder
- ¼ teaspoon baking soda
- ¼ teaspoon salt
- ¾ cup sour cream
- 2 large eggs
- 1 teaspoon pure vanilla extract
- 1 stick (8 tablespoons) unsalted butter, melted and cooled
- 2 tablespoons poppy seeds

## FOR THE ICING

- 1 cup confectioners' sugar, sifted
- 2–3 tablespoons fresh lemon juice

**GETTING READY:** Center a rack in the oven and preheat the oven to 400 degrees F. Butter or spray the 12 molds in a regular-size muffin pan or fit the molds with paper muffin cups. Alternatively, use a silicone muffin pan, which needs neither greasing nor paper cups. Place the muffin pan on a baking sheet.

In a large bowl, rub the sugar and lemon zest together with your fingertips until the sugar is moist and the fragrance of lemon strong. Whisk in the flour, baking powder, baking soda and salt. In a large glass measuring cup or another bowl, whisk the sour cream, eggs, vanilla, lemon juice and melted butter together until well blended. Pour the liquid ingredients over the dry ingredients and, with the whisk or a rubber spatula, gently but quickly stir to blend. Don't worry about being thorough—a few lumps are better than overmixing the batter. Stir in the poppy seeds. Divide the batter evenly among the muffin cups.

Bake for 18 to 20 minutes, or until the tops are golden and a thin knife inserted into the center of the muffins comes out clean. Transfer the pan to a rack and cool for 5 minutes before carefully removing each muffin from its mold. Cool the muffins completely on the rack before icing them.

**TO MAKE THE ICING:** Put the confectioners' sugar in a small bowl and add about 1½ tablespoons of the lemon juice. Stir with a spoon to moisten the sugar, then add enough additional lemon juice, a dribble at a time, to get an icing that is thin enough to drizzle from the tip of the spoon. You can then drizzle lines of icing over the tops of the muffins or coat the tops entirely, the better to get an extra zap of lemon.

# PUMPKIN MUFFINS

**THE BEST** pumpkin muffins in New York are made by Sarabeth Levine, the mistress of Sarabeth's jams and the founder of Sarabeth's restaurants. Her muffins are big and spicy, packed with raisins and topped with sunflower seeds. They're so good they ought to be the standard for all pumpkin muffins in the world. Like the originals, these are a beautiful orange-gold color and have a moist and tender cakey crumb, a gentle spiciness and the hallmark sprinkling of sunflower seeds across their crowns. They are good minutes out of the oven, at room temperature or split and toasted. And while they're luscious on their own, they're even better with a little butter and a lot of orange marmalade or apricot jam.

**SERVING:** Serve these warm or at room temperature, or split and toasted, plain or with butter and jam.

**STORING:** Like all muffins, these are best eaten the day they are made, but they can be wrapped airtight and frozen for up to 2 months. Rewarm in a 350-degree-F oven, or split and toast the muffins before serving.

| | |
|---|---|
| 2 cups all-purpose flour | ¼ cup (packed) light brown sugar |
| 2 teaspoons baking powder | 2 large eggs |
| ¼ teaspoon baking soda | ½ teaspoon pure vanilla extract |
| ¼ teaspoon salt | ¾ cup canned unsweetened pumpkin puree |
| ¾ teaspoon ground cinnamon | |
| ½ teaspoon ground ginger | ¼ cup buttermilk |
| ⅛ teaspoon freshly grated nutmeg | ½ cup moist, plump golden raisins |
| Pinch of ground allspice | ½ cup chopped pecans or walnuts |
| 1 stick (8 tablespoons) unsalted butter, at room temperature | About ⅓ cup unsalted raw sunflower seeds, for topping |
| ½ cup sugar | |

**GETTING READY:** Center a rack in the oven and preheat the oven to 400 degrees F. Butter or spray the 12 molds in a regular-size muffin pan or fit the molds with paper muffin cups. Alternatively, use a silicone muffin pan, which needs neither greasing nor paper cups. Place the muffin pan on a baking sheet.

Whisk together the flour, baking powder, baking soda, salt and spices.

Working with a stand mixer, preferably fitted with a paddle attachment, or with a hand mixer in a large bowl, beat the butter at medium speed until soft. Add both the sugars and continue to beat until light and smooth. One by one, add the eggs, beating for a minute after the eggs are incorporated, then beat in the vanilla. Lower the mixer speed and mix in the pumpkin and buttermilk. With the mixer at low speed, add the dry ingredients in a steady stream, mixing only until they disappear. To avoid overmixing, you can stop the machine early and stir any remaining dry ingredients into the batter using a rubber spatula. Stir in the raisins and nuts. Divide the batter evenly among the muffin cups and sprinkle a few sunflower seeds over the top of each muffin.

Bake for about 25 minutes, or until a thin knife inserted into the center of the muffins comes out clean. Transfer the pan to a rack and cool the muffins for 5 minutes in the pan, then carefully remove each one from its mold and finish cooling on the rack.

# CARROT SPICE MUFFINS

**CARROT MUFFINS**, sometimes called Morning Glories, can be tricky—they should have the spiciness of the all-American carrot cake they're based on, but not the full sweetness, and they should have the cake's moistness, but not its dense, substantial texture. In other words, they should be just like these carrot muffins, which have enough spice and sweetness to keep you coming back for more, but not so much that you think you're eating dessert at the crack of dawn. Because they've got such a great mix of add-ins—along with the carrots, there are coconut, currants and toasted nuts—every bite delivers a different combination of tastes and textures.

| | |
|---|---|
| 2 cups all-purpose flour | 2 large eggs |
| ½ cup sugar | ¾ cup whole milk |
| 1 tablespoon baking powder | 1 teaspoon pure vanilla extract |
| 1½ teaspoons ground cinnamon | 1 cup shredded carrots (about 3, peeled |
| ½ teaspoon ground ginger | and trimmed) |
| ¼ teaspoon baking soda | ½ cup shredded sweetened coconut |
| ¼ teaspoon salt | ⅓ cup moist, plump currants or raisins |
| ⅓ cup (packed) light brown sugar | ⅓ cup pecans or walnuts, toasted, cooled |
| ⅔ cup flavorless oil, such as canola, | and chopped |
| safflower or corn | |

GETTING READY: Center a rack in the oven and preheat the oven to 375 degrees F. Butter or spray the 12 molds in a regular-size muffin pan or fit the molds with paper muffin cups. Alternatively, use a silicone muffin pan, which needs neither greasing nor paper cups. Place the muffin pan on a baking sheet.

In a large bowl, whisk together the flour, sugar, baking powder, cinnamon, ginger, baking soda and salt. Stir in the brown sugar, making certain there are no lumps. In a large glass measuring cup or another bowl, whisk the oil, eggs, milk and vanilla extract together until well combined. Pour the liquid ingredients over the dry ingredients and, with the whisk or a rubber spatula, gently but quickly stir to blend. Don't worry about being thorough—a few lumps are better than over-mixing the batter. Stir in the carrots, coconut, currants and nuts. Divide the batter evenly among the muffin cups.

Bake for about 20 minutes, or until a thin knife inserted into the center of the muffins comes out clean. Transfer the pan to a rack and cool for 5 minutes before carefully removing each muffin from its mold.

MAKES 12 MUFFINS

SERVING: These muffins are delicious warm, but they're even better after they've had at least half an hour to cool. Like many sweets with spice, their flavor intensifies with time.

STORING: These are best the day they are made, but still good (and even a little spicier) 1 day later—just keep them well covered overnight and, if you'd like, give them a quick warm-up in a 350-degree-F oven, or split them and pop them into the toaster. You can also wrap the muffins airtight and freeze them for up to 2 months; re-warm them the same way.

# COFFEE-BREAK MUFFINS

**RATHER THAN** moistening the batter for these muffins with milk, I use a cup of full-bodied coffee. The coffee, reinforced with a spoonful of espresso powder and softened with sugar, half of it caramely brown, turns out a not-very-rich muffin that is exceedingly flavorful and silky, almost puddingish, in texture. Pair the muffins with your morning coffee for an extra shot of caffeine—or go the calm route and make these decaf.

2 cups all-purpose flour

⅓ cup sugar

1 tablespoon instant espresso
  powder

1 tablespoon baking powder

½ teaspoon ground cinnamon

⅛ teaspoon salt

⅓ cup (packed) light brown sugar

1 cup strong coffee, cooled

1 stick (8 tablespoons) unsalted butter,
  melted and cooled

1 large egg

½ teaspoon pure vanilla extract

**MAKES 12 MUFFINS**

**SERVING:** These are delicious warm, but I think they're more flavorful at room temperature. I also think that, as good as they are with butter, they're great on their own.

**STORING:** Wrapped well, these will keep at room temperature overnight; they can be given a quick warm-up in a 350-degree-F oven, or just split and toast them. Wrapped airtight, they can be frozen for up to 2 months. Rewarm in a 350-degree-F oven, if you'd like, or split and toast them.

**GETTING READY:** Center a rack in the oven and preheat the oven to 400 degrees F. Butter or spray the 12 molds in a regular-size muffin pan or fit the molds with paper muffin cups. Alternatively, use a silicone muffin pan, which needs neither greasing nor paper cups. Place the muffin pan on a baking sheet.

In a large bowl, whisk together the flour, sugar, espresso powder, baking powder, cinnamon and salt. Stir in the brown sugar, making certain there are no lumps. In a large glass measuring cup or another bowl, whisk the coffee, melted butter, egg and vanilla extract together until well combined. Pour the liquid ingredients over the dry ingredients and, with the whisk or a rubber spatula, gently but quickly stir to blend. Don't worry about being thorough—a few lumps are better than overmixing the batter. Divide the batter evenly among the muffin cups.

Bake for about 20 minutes, or until a thin knife inserted into the center of the muffins comes out clean. Transfer the pan to a rack and cool for 5 minutes before carefully removing each muffin from its mold.

# ALLSPICE CRUMB MUFFINS

**SLIGHTLY CROWNED** and covered with a tender brown-sugar-and-spice streusel, these muffins have the look and texture of old-fashioned crumb cake and the taste of allspice, a flavor that will probably be unguessable to most of your fellow muffin munchers.

Like mace and nutmeg, allspice is so often used in a supporting role—a pinch here, a speck there—that it's difficult to distinguish it on its own. Dark, round and the size of a pebble, the spice is called Jamaican pepper in some languages (it is not a full-fledged member of the peppercorn family, but it is most commonly grown in Jamaica) and allspice in ours, because it is thought to taste like a combination of spices, specifically cinnamon, nutmeg and clove. For me, the flavor is closest to cloves, but you might get more cinnamon, nutmeg or even pepper—it's the fun of a spice that is so complex.

**MAKES 12 MUFFINS**

**SERVING:** While the fragrance of these muffins makes it almost impossible not to want one straight from the oven, it's better to wait—the flavor of the allspice doesn't really settle in until the muffins have cooled.

**STORING:** These are best the day they are made, but they are good (and even a little spicier) a day later—just keep them well covered overnight and, if you'd like, give them a quick warm-up in a 350-degree-F oven. Alternatively, you can wrap them airtight and freeze them for up to 2 months; reheat in the oven.

FOR THE STREUSEL

- ½ cup all-purpose flour
- ½ cup (packed) light brown sugar
- ½ teaspoon ground allspice
- 5 tablespoons cold unsalted butter, cut into bits

FOR THE MUFFINS

- 2 cups all-purpose flour
- ½ cup sugar
- 1 tablespoon baking powder
- ½ teaspoon ground allspice
- ¼ teaspoon salt
- ¼ cup (packed) light brown sugar
- 1 stick (8 tablespoons) unsalted butter, melted and cooled
- 2 large eggs
- ¾ cup whole milk
- ¼ teaspoon pure vanilla extract
- Grated zest of 1 lemon (optional)

GETTING READY: Center a rack in the oven and preheat the oven to 375 degrees F. Butter or spray the 12 molds in a regular-size muffin pan or fit the molds with paper muffin cups. Alternatively, use a silicone muffin pan, which needs neither greasing nor paper cups. Place the muffin pan on a baking sheet.

TO MAKE THE STREUSEL: Put the flour, brown sugar and allspice in a small bowl and sift them through your fingers to blend. Add the bits of cold butter and toss to coat, then use your fingers to work the butter into the dry ingredients until you've got irregularly shaped crumbs. Set aside in the refrigerator for the moment. (You can make the crumbs up to 3 days ahead and keep them covered in the refrigerator.)

TO MAKE THE MUFFINS: In a large bowl, whisk together the flour, sugar, baking powder, allspice and salt. Stir in the brown sugar, making certain there are no lumps. In a large glass measuring cup or another bowl, whisk the melted butter, eggs, milk and vanilla extract together until well combined. Pour the liquid ingre-

dients over the dry ingredients and, with the whisk or a rubber spatula, gently but quickly stir to blend. Don't worry about being thorough—the batter will be lumpy, and that's just the way it should be. Stir in the lemon zest, if you're using it. Divide the batter evenly among the muffin cups. Sprinkle some streusel over each muffin, then use your fingertips to gently press the crumbs into the batter.

Bake for about 20 minutes, or until the tops are golden and a thin knife inserted into the center of the muffins comes out clean. Transfer the pan to a rack and cool for 5 minutes before carefully removing each muffin from its mold.

# CHOCOLATE–CHOCOLATE CHUNK MUFFINS

**THESE SLIGHTLY** sweet goodies straddle the divide between cupcakes and muffins and can be served as easily for tea as for brunch—although I think any time you can get away with calling chocolate a breakfast food, you should.

¾ stick (6 tablespoons) unsalted
    butter
4 ounces bittersweet chocolate,
    coarsely chopped
2 cups all-purpose flour
⅔ cup sugar
⅓ cup unsweetened cocoa powder,
    sifted

1 tablespoon baking powder
½ teaspoon baking soda
½ teaspoon salt
1¼ cups buttermilk
1 large egg
1 teaspoon pure vanilla extract

MAKES 12 MUFFINS

SERVING: These are delicious warm, served on their own or with some good black cherry jam.

STORING: Wrapped well, these will keep at room temperature overnight; they can be given a quick warm-up in a 350-degree-F oven, or just split and toast them. Wrapped airtight, they can be frozen for up to 2 months. Rewarm in a 350-degree-F oven, if you'd like, or split and toast them.

GETTING READY: Center a rack in the oven and preheat the oven to 375 degrees F. Butter or spray the 12 molds in a regular-size muffin pan or fit the molds with paper muffin cups. Alternatively, use a silicone muffin pan, which needs neither greasing nor paper cups. Place the muffin pan on a baking sheet.

Melt the butter and half the chopped chocolate together in a bowl over a saucepan of simmering water; or do this in a microwave. Remove from the heat.

In a large bowl, whisk together the flour, sugar, cocoa, baking powder, baking soda and salt. In a large glass measuring cup or another bowl, whisk the buttermilk, egg and vanilla extract together until well combined. Pour the liquid ingredients and the melted butter and chocolate over the dry ingredients and, with the whisk or a rubber spatula, gently but quickly stir to blend. Don't worry about being thorough—a few lumps are better than overmixing the batter. Stir in the remaining chopped chocolate. Divide the batter evenly among the muffin cups.

Bake for about 20 minutes, or until a thin knife inserted into the center of the muffins comes out clean. Transfer the pan to a rack and cool for 5 minutes before carefully removing each muffin from its mold.

## Biscuits and Scones
## A How-To for Flakiness

FLAKINESS is the hallmark of great biscuits and scones, the benchmark by which a biscuit or scone maker's skill will be judged. The secret ingredient is fat—mostly fresh, creamy unsalted butter—and the magic technique is something akin to benign neglect.

Butter is my first choice for biscuits and scones because it is delicious. While I can't imagine scones being made with anything other than butter, I concede that good biscuits can be made with shortening.

Whatever fat you choose, the key is to start with it when it's cold and to work it as gently and as minimally as possible, so that when the dough comes together, the fat is still cold. To do this, you should give yourself a head start by cutting the cold butter into small pieces (for biscuits and scones, I cut a stick of butter into 16 bits), then dropping the chunklets into the bowl with the dry ingredients and giving everything a toss or two with your fingers until the butter is coated with the floury mixture.

Now, here comes the benignly neglectful magic technique: be a little lackadaisical about working the butter into the flour. Using your fingertips—always my first choice—or a pastry blender, cut the butter into the dry ingredients quickly but not conscientiously. You want the mixture to resemble a rocky road—there should be some sandy patches, some tiny little pebbly pieces, pieces as slim as flakes and pieces as chubby as peas. Let diversity reign. This is not the time to work everything together until it has the look of finely ground meal. When you've done the job right, you'll have clumps and curds and clearly visible nuggets of butter. It's the water in these higgledy-piggledy bits of butter that, under the heat of the oven, turns to steam and creates air pockets in the dough, pockets that become flaky layers.

Because biscuits and scones are made with baking powder (it's the ingredient that defines them as "quick breads"), they'll rise in the oven no matter what you've done to the dough. In fact, even if you massacre the mixing, you're likely to end with tall, beautiful biscuits and scones. It's only when you break one open and take the first bite that you realize that your gorgeous biscuits have an unpleasant stick-to-the-roof-of-your-mouth texture.

While all biscuits should be flaky, whether they are crusty or soft sided is a matter of personal preference. For crusties (my favorite), place the biscuits on the baking sheet with puff space between each one; for softies, arrange them so that they touch one another.

# BASIC BISCUITS

**HERE'S THE** biscuit you'll make year-round for breakfast, as a sopper-upper for good gravy or, layered with butter and ham, dill and smoked salmon or soft herb-flecked cheese, as a nibble with champagne. It is everything a good biscuit should be: flaky, rich, top-hat high and down-home scrumptious.

**SERVING:** Ideally biscuits should go from oven to table—burned fingers are part of the ritual. These are rich enough to serve plain, but they're so, so good spread with cold sweet butter.

**STORING:** You can keep the biscuits in a plastic bag overnight and give them a quick warm-up in the oven the next day, but you won't recapture their freshly made flakiness.

| | |
|---|---|
| 2 cups all-purpose flour (or 1¾ cups all-purpose flour and ⅓ cup cake flour) | ½ teaspoon salt |
| 1 tablespoon baking powder | ¾ stick (6 tablespoons) cold unsalted butter, cut into 12 pieces |
| 2 teaspoons sugar | ¾ cup cold whole milk |

**GETTING READY:** Center a rack in the oven and preheat the oven to 425 degrees F. Get out a sharp 2-inch-diameter biscuit cutter, and line a baking sheet with parchment or a silicone mat.

Whisk the flour(s), baking powder, sugar and salt together in a bowl. Drop in the butter and, using your fingers, toss to coat the pieces of butter with flour. Quickly, working with your fingertips (my favorite method) or a pastry blender, cut and rub the butter into the dry ingredients until the mixture is pebbly. You'll have pea-size pieces, pieces the size of oatmeal flakes and pieces the size of everything in between—and that's just right.

Pour the milk over the dry ingredients, grab a fork and toss and gently turn the ingredients until you've got a nice soft dough. Now reach into the bowl with your hands and give the dough a quick, gentle kneading—3 or 4 turns should be just enough to bring everything together.

Lightly dust a work surface with flour and turn out the dough. Dust the top of the dough very lightly with flour and pat the dough out with your hands or roll it with a pin until it is about ½ inch high. Don't worry if the dough isn't completely even—a quick, light touch is more important than accuracy.

Use the biscuit cutter to cut out as many biscuits as you can. Try to cut the biscuits close to one another so you get the most you can out of this first round. By hand or with a small spatula, transfer the biscuits to the baking sheet. Gather together the scraps, working them as little as possible, pat out to a ½-inch thickness and cut as many additional biscuits as you can; transfer these to the sheet. (The biscuits can be made to this point and frozen on the baking sheet, then wrapped airtight and kept for up to 2 months. Bake without defrosting—just add a couple more minutes to the oven time.)

Bake the biscuits for 14 to 18 minutes, or until they are puffed and golden brown. Transfer them to a serving basket.

*Playing Around*

**BUTTERMILK BISCUITS:** For a tangier, rich, flaky biscuit, add ¼ teaspoon baking soda to the dry ingredients and replace the whole milk with buttermilk.

## Biscuit Flour

BISCUITS can be made with any of a number of flours or combinations of flours. In the South, the preference is for a soft low-protein, low-gluten pastry flour. The biscuit flour of choice among many Southerners is the venerable White Lily, which is finer and lighter than all-purpose flour. (If you substitute White Lily for all-purpose flour, you'll need to add an additional 2 tablespoons for every cup of all-purpose.) Because I don't often have White Lily flour at hand, I've developed my biscuit recipes to use always-available all-purpose flour or a mixture of 1¾ cups all-purpose flour and ⅓ cup cake flour, which I whisk together with the other dry ingredients.

# SWEET CREAM BISCUITS

**SOFT, RICH** and so satisfyingly mouth-filling, these are more sumptuous than Basic Biscuits (page 21) and more substantial too—the delicious result of trading in the traditional butter and milk for lots of heavy cream. These lend themselves to the usual sweet spreads—honey, jam, butter or any combination thereof—and are good with salty savories, like ham, sausages, bacon or smoked salmon.

2 cups all-purpose flour (or 1¾ cups all-purpose flour and ⅓ cup cake flour)

1 tablespoon baking powder

2 teaspoons sugar

½ teaspoon salt

1–1¼ cups cold heavy cream

**GETTING READY:** Center a rack in the oven and preheat the oven to 425 degrees F. Get out a sharp 2-inch-diameter biscuit cutter, and line a baking sheet with parchment or a silicone mat.

Whisk the flour(s), baking powder, sugar and salt together in a bowl. Pour about 1 cup of the cream over the dry ingredients, grab a fork and start tossing the ingredients together. If necessary, add more cream, a spoonful at a time, until you've got a nice soft dough. Now reach into the bowl with your hands and give the dough a quick, gentle kneading—3 or 4 turns should be just enough to bring everything together.

Lightly dust a work surface with flour and turn out the dough. Dust the top of the dough very lightly with flour and pat the dough out with your hands or roll it with a pin until it is about ½ inch high. Don't worry if the dough isn't completely even—a quick, light touch is more important than accuracy.

Use the biscuit cutter to cut out as many biscuits as you can. Try to cut the biscuits close to one another so you get the most you can out of this first round. By hand or with a small spatula, transfer the biscuits to the baking sheet. Gather together the scraps, working them as little as possible, pat out to a ½-inch thickness and cut as many additional biscuits as you can; transfer these to the sheet. (The biscuits can be made to this point and frozen on the baking sheet, then wrapped airtight and kept for up to 2 months. Bake without defrosting—just add a couple more minutes to the oven time.)

Bake the biscuits for 14 to 18 minutes, or until they are tall, puffed and golden brown. Transfer them to a serving basket.

**MAKES ABOUT 12 BISCUITS**

**SERVING:** Ideally these biscuits should go from oven to table and be served with cold sweet butter.

**STORING:** You can keep the biscuits in a plastic bag overnight and give them a quick warm-up in the oven the next day, but you won't recapture their freshly made flakiness.

# MAPLE-CORNMEAL DROP BISCUITS

THIS IS not the most well-behaved biscuit you'll ever come across—all that sticky maple syrup and slip-through-your-fingers cornmeal produce a dough that's too moist to roll out and cut into neat little rounds. Here you scoop the sweet mixture onto a baking sheet, count the minutes in the oven and enjoy the surprise: a biscuit that's a cross between a featherlight corn bread and a flaky scone, a breakfast or tea sweet that's outrageously good with butter and jam or honey and just as good eaten plain. In fact, if you use tasty, gritty, stone-ground cornmeal, the odds are good you'll want nothing to come between you and its sweet, full flavor.

MAKES ABOUT 12 BISCUITS

SERVING: These biscuits are unusual in that they are delicious hot, warm or at room temperature. At any temperature, they can be served with butter and honey or jam.

STORING: While these are best the day they are made, they can be kept overnight in an airtight container. Warm them briefly in a 350-degree-F oven before serving, or, if you'd like, split them, spread them with a little butter and run them under the broiler.

| | |
|---|---|
| 1 cup all-purpose flour | ¼ teaspoon baking soda |
| 1 cup yellow cornmeal, preferably stone-ground | ¾ stick (6 tablespoons) cold unsalted butter, cut into 12 pieces |
| 1 tablespoon baking powder | ½ cup cold whole milk |
| ½ teaspoon salt | ¼ cup pure maple syrup |

GETTING READY: Center a rack in the oven and preheat the oven to 425 degrees F. Line a baking sheet with parchment or a silicone mat.

Whisk the flour, cornmeal, baking powder, salt and baking soda together in a bowl. Drop in the butter and, using your fingers, toss to coat the pieces of butter with flour. Quickly, working with your fingertips (my favorite method) or a pastry blender, cut and rub the butter into the dry ingredients until the mixture is pebbly. You'll have pea-size pieces, pieces the size of oatmeal flakes and pieces the size of everything in between—and that's just right.

Stir the milk and maple syrup together and pour over the dry ingredients. Grab a fork and toss and gently turn until the ingredients are mostly combined and you've got a very soft dough. Don't worry if the dough doesn't look evenly mixed. Use a tablespoon to scoop 12 mounds of dough onto the baking sheet.

Bake the biscuits for about 15 minutes, or until they are puffed and golden brown (these won't be straight or tall like traditional biscuits). Transfer them to a serving basket.

# PECAN SOUR CREAM BISCUITS

**IN MY** notebook's margins, written next to this recipe in big letters, it says, "TOO GOOD." The biscuits are particularly tender because of the sour cream, subtly caramelish because of the brown sugar and intermittently crunchy because of the chopped pecans.

- 2 cups all-purpose flour (or 1¾ cups all-purpose flour and ⅓ cup cake flour)
- 1 tablespoon baking powder
- ½ teaspoon salt
- ¼ teaspoon baking soda
- ¼ cup (packed) light brown sugar

- 5 tablespoons cold unsalted butter, cut into 10 pieces
- ½ cup cold sour cream
- ¼ cup cold whole milk
- ⅓ cup finely chopped pecans, preferably toasted

MAKES ABOUT 12 BISCUITS

**SERVING:** Ideally these biscuits should go directly from oven to table. They can be enjoyed as is, but they're extra-good spread with cold sweet butter. Because they're sweeter than most biscuits, they're good to keep in mind when you're filling a bread basket for brunch.

**STORING:** You can keep the biscuits in a plastic bag overnight and give them a quick warm-up in the oven the next day, but you won't recapture their freshly made flakiness.

**GETTING READY:** Center a rack in the oven and preheat the oven to 425 degrees F. Get out a sharp 2-inch-diameter biscuit cutter, and line a baking sheet with parchment or a silicone mat.

Whisk the flour(s), baking powder, salt and baking soda together in a bowl. Stir in the brown sugar, making certain there are no lumps. Drop in the butter and, using your fingers, toss to coat the pieces of butter with flour. Quickly, working with your fingertips (my favorite method) or a pastry blender, cut and rub the butter into the dry ingredients until the mixture is pebbly. You'll have pea-size pieces, pieces the size of oatmeal flakes and pieces the size of everything in between—and that's just right.

Stir the sour cream and milk together and pour over the dry ingredients. Grab a fork and gently toss and turn the ingredients together until you've got a nice soft dough. Now reach into the bowl with your hands and give the dough a quick, gentle kneading—3 or 4 turns should be just enough to bring everything together. Toss in the pecans and knead another 2 to 3 times to incorporate them.

Lightly dust a work surface with flour and turn out the dough. Dust the top of the dough very lightly with flour and pat the dough out with your hands or roll it with a pin until it is about ½ inch high. Don't worry if the dough isn't completely even—a quick, light touch is more important than accuracy.

Use the biscuit cutter to cut out as many biscuits as you can. Try to cut the biscuits close to one another so you get the most you can out of this first round. By hand or with a small spatula, transfer the biscuits to the baking sheet. Gather together the scraps, working them as little as possible, pat out to a ½-inch thickness and cut as many additional biscuits as you can; transfer these to the sheet. (The biscuits can be made to this point and frozen on the baking sheet, then wrapped airtight and kept for up to 2 months. Bake without defrosting—just add a couple more minutes to the oven time.)

Bake the biscuits for 14 to 18 minutes, or until they are tall, puffed and golden brown. Transfer them to a serving basket.

# SWEET POTATO BISCUITS

**SOFT AND** creamy-textured, with flaky layers, these biscuits satisfy like cake. Using canned sweet potatoes makes them easy to prepare at a moment's notice. I use canned sweet potatoes packed in light syrup—I just drain the potatoes and mash them with a fork. If you've got leftover cooked sweet potatoes or yams, give them a good mashing, measure out ¾ to 1 cup and you're good to go.

**MAKES ABOUT 18 BISCUITS**

2 cups all-purpose flour

1 tablespoon baking powder

1 teaspoon salt

  Pinch of ground cinnamon or freshly grated nutmeg (optional)

2 tablespoons (packed) light brown sugar

¾ stick (6 tablespoons) cold unsalted butter, cut into 12 pieces

2 15-ounce cans sweet potatoes in light syrup, drained and mashed

**SERVING:** Unlike most biscuits, these are best served after they've had a little time to cool. They are as good at brunch (they're great with salty ham and bacon) as they are at tea (try them with a light cheese spread and/or marmalade). Or have them with butter or jam, fruit butter or fruit compote.

**STORING:** You can keep the biscuits in a plastic bag overnight and give them a quick warm-up in the oven the next day, but you won't recapture their freshly made flakiness.

**GETTING READY:** Center a rack in the oven and preheat the oven to 425 degrees F. Get out a sharp 2- to 2¼-inch-diameter biscuit cutter, and line a baking sheet with parchment or a silicone mat.

Whisk the flour, baking powder, salt and spice, if you're using it, together in a bowl. Add the brown sugar and stir to incorporate it, making sure there are no lumps. Drop in the butter and, using your fingers, toss to coat it with flour. Quickly, working with your fingertips (my favorite method) or a pastry blender, cut and rub the butter into the dry ingredients until the mixture is pebbly. You'll have pea-size pieces, pieces the size of oatmeal flakes and pieces the size of everything in between—and that's just right.

Add the sweet potatoes to the bowl, grab a fork, and toss and gently turn the ingredients until you've got a nice soft dough. Now reach into the bowl with your hands and give the dough a quick, gentle kneading—3 or 4 turns should be just enough to bring everything together.

Lightly dust a work surface with flour and turn out the dough. Dust the top of the dough very lightly with flour and pat the dough out with your hands or roll it with a pin until it is about ½ inch high. Don't worry if the dough isn't completely even—a quick, light touch is more important than accuracy.

Use the biscuit cutter to cut out as many biscuits as you can. Try to cut the biscuits close to one another so you get the most you can out of this first round. By hand or with a small spatula, transfer the biscuits to the baking sheet. Gather together the scraps, working them as little as possible, pat out to a ½-inch thickness and cut as many additional biscuits as you can; transfer these to the sheet. (The biscuits can be made to this point and frozen on the baking sheet, then wrapped airtight and kept for up to 2 months. Bake without defrosting—just add a couple more minutes to the oven time.)

Bake the biscuits for 14 to 18 minutes, or until they are puffed and golden brown. Transfer them to a cooling rack—cooled a bit, they're more sweet potatoey. Give them 10 to 15 minutes on the rack before popping them into a basket and serving.

# CREAM SCONES

**PERFECT FOR** every scone-able occasion from breakfast to tea to midnight nibble, these are also perfect with a tart, chunky citrus marmalade or a bright berry jam.

1 large egg

⅔ cup cold heavy cream

2 cups all-purpose flour

2 tablespoons sugar

1 tablespoon baking powder

¼ teaspoon salt

5 tablespoons unsalted butter, cut into small pieces and chilled

¾ cup moist, plump currants

**SERVING:** Toss these into a basket and bring them to the table with lots of sweet butter and any flavor jam you love.

**STORING:** These are best served soon after they're made. If you want to save them, wrap them airtight as soon as they cool to room temperature and freeze them for up to 2 months. If you've frozen the scones, reheat them in a 350-degree-F oven.

GETTING READY: Center a rack in the oven and preheat the oven to 400 degrees F. Line a baking sheet with parchment or a silicone mat.

Stir the egg and cream together.

Whisk the flour, sugar, baking powder and salt together in a large bowl. Drop in the butter and, using your fingers, toss to coat the pieces of butter with flour. Quickly, working with your fingertips (my favorite method) or a pastry blender, cut and rub the butter into the dry ingredients until the mixture is pebbly. You'll have pea-size pieces, pieces the size of oatmeal flakes and pieces the size of everything in between—and that's just right.

Pour the egg and cream over the dry ingredients and stir with a fork just until the dough, which will be wet and sticky, comes together. Don't overdo it. Still in the bowl, gently knead the dough by hand, or turn it with a rubber spatula 8 to 10 times.

Lightly dust a work surface with flour and turn out the dough. Divide it in half. Working with one piece at a time, pat the dough into a rough circle that's about 5 inches in diameter, cut it into 6 wedges and place it on the baking sheet. (At this point, the scones can be frozen on the baking sheet, then wrapped airtight. Don't defrost before baking—just add about 2 minutes to the baking time.)

Bake the scones for 20 to 22 minutes, or until their tops are golden and firmish. Transfer them to a rack and cool for 10 minutes before serving, or wait for them to cool to room temperature.

# TOASTED ALMOND SCONES

THE TRIPLE-WHAMMY flavor hit here is almonds, almonds and almonds: toasted ground almonds and pure almond extract in the dough and sliced almonds on top.

MAKES 12 SCONES

SERVING: Toss these into a basket and bring them to the table with lots of sweet butter.

STORING: These are best served soon after they're made. If you want to save them, wrap them airtight as soon as they come to room temperature and freeze them for up to 2 months. If you've frozen the scones, re-heat them in a 350-degree-F oven.

1    cup blanched almonds (whole, slivered or sliced), toasted
2    tablespoons sugar
1    large egg
⅓   cup cold heavy cream
¼   cup cold whole milk
⅛   teaspoon pure almond extract
1¾  cups all-purpose flour
1    tablespoon baking powder
¼   teaspoon salt
1    stick (8 tablespoons) cold unsalted butter, cut into small pieces
¼   cup sliced almonds (optional)

GETTING READY: Center a rack in the oven and preheat the oven to 400 degrees F. Line a baking sheet with parchment or a silicone mat.

Divide the toasted almonds in half. Finely grind ½ cup in a food processor or blender with the sugar, taking care not to overgrind the nuts and end up with almond butter. Finely chop the other ½ cup.

Stir the egg, cream, milk and almond extract together.

Whisk the flour, ground almonds and sugar, baking powder and salt together in a large bowl. Drop in the butter and, using your fingers, toss to coat the pieces of butter with flour. Quickly, working with your fingertips (my favorite method) or a pastry blender, cut and rub the butter into the dry ingredients until the mixture is pebbly. You'll have pea-size pieces, pieces the size of oatmeal flakes and pieces the size of everything in between—and that's just right.

Pour the liquid ingredients over the dry ingredients and stir with a fork just until the dough, which will be wet and sticky, comes together. Don't overdo it. Stir in the chopped almonds.

Still in the bowl, gently knead the dough by hand, or turn it with a rubber spatula 8 to 10 times. Turn the dough out onto a lightly floured work surface and divide it in half. Working with one piece at a time, pat the dough into a rough circle that's about 5 inches in diameter, cut it into 6 wedges and top each scone with a few sliced almonds, if you're using them. Place them on the baking sheet. (At this point, the scones can be frozen on the baking sheet, then wrapped airtight. Don't defrost before baking—just add about 2 minutes to the baking time.)

Bake the scones for 20 to 22 minutes, or until their tops are golden and firmish. Transfer to a rack and cool for 10 minutes before serving, or wait for the scones to cool to room temperature.

# OATMEAL NUTMEG SCONES

**THESE ARE** tender and sweet, but not so sweet that you won't want them with jam, and a bit tangy, but not so much that you won't want to try them with cheese, and rather bumpy, lumpy and handmade looking. They're just right for an informal brunch with friends.

1 large egg

½ cup cold buttermilk

1⅔ cups all-purpose flour

1⅓ cups old-fashioned oats

⅓ cup sugar

1 tablespoon baking powder

½ teaspoon baking soda

½ teaspoon salt

¼ teaspoon freshly grated nutmeg

1 stick plus 2 tablespoons (10 tablespoons) cold unsalted butter, cut into small pieces

**MAKES 12 SCONES**

**SERVING:** Toss these into a basket and bring them to the table with lots of sweet butter and any flavor jam you love.

**STORING:** These are best served soon after they're made. If you want to save them, wrap them airtight as soon as they come to room temperature and freeze them for up to 2 months. If you've frozen the scones, reheat them in a 350-degree-F oven.

**GETTING READY:** Center a rack in the oven and preheat the oven to 400 degrees F. Line a baking sheet with parchment or a silicone mat.

Stir the egg and buttermilk together.

Whisk the flour, oats, sugar, baking powder, baking soda, salt and nutmeg together in a large bowl. Drop in the butter and, using your fingers, toss to coat the pieces of butter with flour. Quickly, working with your fingertips (my favorite method) or a pastry blender, cut and rub the butter into the dry ingredients until the mixture is pebbly. You'll have pea-size pieces, pieces the size of oatmeal flakes and pieces the size of everything in between—and that's just right.

Pour the egg and buttermilk mixture over the dry ingredients and stir with a fork just until the dough, which will be wet and sticky, comes together. Don't overdo it.

Still in the bowl, gently knead the dough by hand, or turn it with a rubber spatula 8 to 10 times. Turn the dough out onto a lightly floured work surface and divide it in half. Working with one piece at a time, pat the dough into a rough circle that's about 5 inches in diameter, cut it into 6 wedges and place on the baking sheet. (At this point, the scones can be frozen on the baking sheet, then wrapped airtight. Don't defrost before baking—just add about 2 minutes to the baking time.)

Bake for 20 to 22 minutes, or until their tops are golden and firmish. Transfer them to a rack and cool for 10 minutes before serving, or wait for the scones to cool to room temperature.

*Playing Around*

**FRUITY OATMEAL-NUTMEG SCONES:** Scones in general and these in particular are good with a little fruit mixed into them. Try adding small chunks of banana to the dough before you stir in the egg and buttermilk (cut ½ banana into ½-inch dice). These are also good with about ½ cup diced prunes or small cubes of plump dried apricot added to the dough.

# HONEY-NUT SCONES

**BECAUSE THEY** are made with honey and a mix of white and whole wheat flours, these scones have a hearty, homey warmth, a light sweetness and a touch of the rustic about them. Because they include chopped walnuts, their texture is a bit rougher and slightly more crumbly than that of standard scones. And, for every reason from their ingredients to their looks, these are great for chilly days.

1 large egg

2 tablespoons honey

½ cup cold whole milk

1½ cups all-purpose flour

½ cup whole wheat flour

1 tablespoon baking powder

¼ teaspoon baking soda

¼ teaspoon salt

1 stick (8 tablespoons) cold unsalted butter, cut into small pieces

½ cup chopped walnuts

MAKES 12 SCONES

SERVING: Toss these into a basket and bring them to the table with lots of sweet butter, chunky jam or, if you have some, store-bought pumpkin or prune butter.

STORING: These should really be served the day they're made, preferably shortly after they come from the oven. If you want to save them, wrap them airtight as soon as they cool to room temperature and freeze them for up to 2 months. If you've frozen the scones, re-heat them in a 350-degree-F oven.

GETTING READY: Center a rack in the oven and preheat the oven to 400 degrees F. Line a baking sheet with parchment or a silicone mat.

Stir the egg, honey and milk together.

Whisk the flours, baking powder, baking soda and salt together in a large bowl. Drop in the butter and, using your fingers, toss to coat the pieces of butter with flour. Quickly, working with your fingertips (my favorite method) or a pastry blender, cut and rub the butter into the dry ingredients until the mixture is pebbly. You'll have pea-size pieces, pieces the size of oatmeal flakes and pieces the size of everything in between—and that's just right.

Pour the liquid ingredients over the dry ingredients and stir with a fork just until the dough, which will be wet and sticky, comes together. Don't overdo it. Stir in the chopped walnuts.

Still in the bowl, gently knead the dough by hand, or turn it with a rubber spatula 8 to 10 times. Turn the dough out onto a lightly floured work surface and divide it in half. Working with one piece at a time, pat the dough into a rough circle that's about 5 inches in diameter, cut it into 6 wedges and place on the baking sheet. (At this point, the scones can be frozen on the baking sheet, then wrapped airtight. Don't defrost before baking—just add about 2 minutes to the baking time.)

Bake the scones for about 20 minutes, or until the tops are deeply golden and firmish to the touch. Transfer them to a rack and cool for 10 minutes before serving, or wait for the scones to cool to room temperature.

# APPLE CHEDDAR SCONES

**PUFFY, HAPHAZARDLY** shaped, speckled with dark patches of cheddar cheese and dried apple and packed with as much flavor and texture as possible, these are among my favorite scones. I like them best about 3 minutes out of the oven, when the cheese is still a little melty.

1 large egg

½ cup cold buttermilk

¼ cup cold apple cider or
  unsweetened apple juice

1¾ cups all-purpose flour

⅓ cup yellow cornmeal, preferably
  stone-ground

2 tablespoons sugar

1 tablespoon baking powder

¼ teaspoon baking soda

¼ teaspoon salt

1 stick (8 tablespoons) cold unsalted
  butter, cut into small pieces

¾ cup grated cheddar cheese

½ cup finely diced dried apple

MAKES 12 SCONES

SERVING: Toss these into a basket and bring them to the table with lots of sweet butter and good jam.

STORING: These are best minutes after they're made. If you want to save them, wrap them airtight as soon as they come to room temperature and freeze them for up to 2 months. If you've frozen the scones, reheat them in a 350-degree-F oven.

GETTING READY: Center a rack in the oven and preheat the oven to 400 degrees F. Line a baking sheet with parchment or a silicone mat.

Stir the egg, buttermilk and apple cider together.

Whisk the flour, cornmeal, sugar, baking powder, baking soda and salt together in a large bowl. Drop in the butter and, using your fingers, toss to coat the pieces of butter with flour. Quickly, working with your fingertips (my favorite method) or a pastry blender, cut and rub the butter into the dry ingredients until the mixture is pebbly. You'll have pea-size pieces, pieces the size of oatmeal flakes and pieces the size of everything in between—and that's just right.

Pour the liquid ingredients over the dry ingredients and stir with a fork just until the dough, which will be very wet and sticky, comes together. If there are still some dry ingredients in the bottom of the bowl, stir them in, but try not to overdo the mixing. Stir in the grated cheese and dried apple.

Still in the bowl, gently knead the dough by hand, or turn it with a rubber spatula 8 to 10 times. Then, because the dough is very sticky, the easiest thing to do is to turn it out onto a lightly floured work surface, pat it into a rectangle about ½ inch thick and, using a dough scraper or a chef's knife, cut it into 12 roughly equal pieces; place on the baking sheet. Alternatively, you can just spoon out 12 equal mounds onto the baking sheet. (At this point, the scones can be frozen on the baking sheet, then wrapped airtight. Don't defrost before baking—just add about 2 minutes to the baking time.)

Bake the scones for 20 to 22 minutes, or until their tops are golden and firmish. Transfer them to a rack and cool for 10 minutes before serving, or wait for the scones to cool to room temperature.

# CHESTNUT SCONES

**I'D GUESS** that if you served these scones without mentioning the chestnut flour, no one would be able to tell you what made them so distinctive. The slightly sweet, off-white chestnut flour doesn't have a knock-you-over-the-head kind of flavor, nor does it impart a fragrance or a texture that immediately gives it away. It's a subtle, low-key ingredient whose most striking characteristic is the elegance it brings to everything it touches.

1 large egg

¾ cup cold heavy cream

½ teaspoon pure vanilla extract

1¼ cups all-purpose flour

¾ cup chestnut flour (available in Italian markets and specialty shops)

2 tablespoons sugar

1 tablespoon baking powder

¼ teaspoon salt

1 stick (8 tablespoons) unsalted butter, cut into small pieces and chilled

**GETTING READY:** Center a rack in the oven and preheat the oven to 400 degrees F. Line a baking sheet with parchment or a silicone mat.

Stir the egg, cream and vanilla extract together.

Whisk the flour, chestnut flour, sugar, baking powder and salt together in a large bowl. Drop in the butter and, using your fingers, toss to coat the pieces of butter with flour. Quickly, working with your fingertips (my favorite method) or a pastry blender, cut and rub the butter into the dry ingredients until the mixture is pebbly. You'll have pea-size pieces, pieces the size of oatmeal flakes and pieces the size of everything in between—and that's just right.

Pour the liquid ingredients over the dry ingredients and stir with a fork just until the dough, which will be wet and sticky, comes together. Don't overdo it.

Still in the bowl, gently knead the dough by hand, or turn it with a rubber spatula 8 to 10 times. Turn the dough out onto a lightly floured work surface and divide it in half. Working with one piece at a time, pat the dough into a rough circle that's about 5 inches in diameter, cut it into 6 wedges and place on the baking sheet. (At this point, the scones can be frozen on the baking sheet, then wrapped airtight. Don't defrost before baking—just add about 2 minutes to the baking time.)

Bake the scones for 20 to 22 minutes, or until their tops are golden and firmish. Transfer them to a rack and cool for 10 minutes before serving, or wait for the scones to cool to room temperature.

MAKES 12 SCONES

**SERVING:** Toss these into a basket and bring them to the table with lots of sweet butter and, if you'd like, jam.

**STORING:** These are best served soon after they're made. If you want to save them, wrap them airtight as soon as they come to room temperature and freeze for up to 2 months. If you've frozen the scones, re-heat them in a 350-degree-F oven.

# MORNING CAKES
## AND
### LOAVES

**MEANT FOR BREAKFASTS** and brunches, for lazy
Sundays and holiday weekends, these cakes and breads
make morning meals feel special. And here I have a
confession—I collected them not just for lazy days, but
also for lazy people, specifically lazy me. Most of these
recipes are based on my favorite muffin combinations,
but because they are made in a cake or loaf pan, there's
less prep and more wow: on the show-off scale, cakes
outflash muffins.

Because many of these cakes and sweet breads are
really muffins that have been super-sized, they have a
muffin's open texture, tenderness and light sweetness.
Fruits—among them, blueberry, apple, plum and
mango—take star turns here, but grains—cornmeal
and oatmeal—turn up in quick breads, spicy cardamom
perfumes a crumb-topped coffee cake and there's even a
chocolate loaf.

All get their rise from baking powder, so they should go into
the oven lickety-split. But, unlike their muffiny relatives,
several are good keepers: their larger size helps them retain
their moistness longer. This means you can make them the
night before and look like a hero the next morning. If you do
prepare these ahead, just make sure to cool them completely
before you bundle them up in plastic wrap and tuck them in
for the night.

# BLUEBERRY-BROWN SUGAR PLAIN CAKE

THIS "PLAIN CAKE"—no crumbs, streusel, nuts, icing or filling—is just plain appealing. It's got a soft crumb, a strong streak of caramel brown sugar flavor and the here-and-there surprise of sweet and tart berries. It's a perfect "daylight" cake, good for breakfast, brunch or lunch, and it can easily be a picnic cake, because it's eminently packable.

1⅓ cups all-purpose flour

2 teaspoons baking powder

½ teaspoon ground cinnamon (optional)

⅛ teaspoon plus a pinch of salt

2 large eggs, separated

1 stick (8 tablespoons) unsalted butter, at room temperature

1 cup (packed) light brown sugar

½ cup whole milk

1 pint blueberries—fresh, preferably, or frozen (not thawed)

Confectioners' sugar, for dusting

MAKES ABOUT 15 SERVINGS

SERVING: Once the cake is cool enough to cut, it's cool enough to eat. Give the top another dusting of confectioners' sugar if the first one has settled into the cake, and cut the cake into squares about 2 inches on a side. I like the cake plain, but if you're looking for an accompaniment, look at blueberry jam or a bowl of lightly sweetened sour cream or crème fraîche.

STORING: Well covered, the cake will keep at room temperature for about 3 days. You can wrap the cake airtight and freeze it for up to 2 months, but it really is best fresh.

GETTING READY: Center a rack in the oven and preheat the oven to 375 degrees F. Generously butter an 11-x-7-inch baking pan (a Pyrex pan is great) and place it on a baking sheet.

Whisk together the flour, baking powder, cinnamon, if you're using it, and the ⅛ teaspoon salt.

Working with a stand mixer fitted with the whisk attachment or with a hand mixer in a large bowl, beat the egg whites with the pinch of salt until they form firm, glossy peaks. Gently scrape the whites into a clean bowl if using a stand mixer. Fit the mixer with the paddle attachment, if you have one. (There's no need to clean the mixer bowl.) Put the butter and sugar in the mixer bowl, or in another large bowl if using a hand mixer, and beat on medium speed until creamy. Add the egg yolks and beat 2 minutes more. Reduce the mixer speed to low and add half the dry ingredients, then all of the milk and then the remainder of the dry ingredients, adding each new batch as soon as the previous batch has been incorporated.

Switch to a large rubber spatula and lighten the batter by stirring in about one quarter of the stiffly beaten egg whites. Fold in the rest of the whites, working as gently as you can. Since the cake batter is heavy, it's only natural you'll deflate the whites a little—don't be concerned. Still working with as light a hand as possible, fold in the blueberries, and scrape the batter into the prepared pan.

Bake the cake for 35 to 40 minutes, or until it is golden and a thin knife inserted into the center comes out clean. Transfer the cake to a cooling rack and cool in the pan for about 30 minutes before dusting the top with confectioners' sugar and serving warm.

# APPLE NUT MUFFIN CAKE

**THIS IS** a recipe that gives the lie to the proverb "Haste makes waste." I had measured out all the ingredients for apple nut muffins when my brunch guests arrived, but I hadn't prepped the muffin pan. I grabbed a nonstick silicone baking pan, scraped the batter into it and hurriedly slid the pan into the oven. When I pulled it out, I had a great-looking cake, appealingly rough and rustic and homey, and packed with all the goodness of my old-time muffins—oatmeal, raisins, nuts and, for full, true apple flavor, diced apple and apple cider.

½ cup whole milk

½ cup apple cider or juice (or another
 ½ cup milk)

1 large egg

1 teaspoon pure vanilla extract

½ teaspoon pure almond extract

1 stick (8 tablespoons) unsalted
 butter, melted and cooled

1¾ cups all-purpose flour

½ cup sugar

1 tablespoon baking powder

½ teaspoon baking soda

½ teaspoon ground cinnamon

¼ teaspoon salt

¼ cup (packed) light brown sugar

¾ cup old-fashioned oats

1 medium apple, peeled, cored and cut
 into small dice

½ cup chopped walnuts or pecans

⅓ cup moist, plump raisins

MAKES 8 SERVINGS

**SERVING:** Like muffins, this cake can be served warm or at room temperature. Just cut it into squares and stack the squares on a plate or in a napkin-lined basket. It has enough flavor and more than enough texture to be eaten plain, but, like muffins, it's good with butter, jam, cottage cheese or even thick plain yogurt.

**STORING:** The cake is best eaten the day it is made, but it can be wrapped airtight and frozen for up to 2 months; warm in a 350-degree-F oven before serving.

GETTING READY: Center a rack in the oven and preheat the oven to 400 degrees F. Use an 8-inch square silicone pan, or butter an 8-inch square baking pan, dust the inside with flour, and tap out the excess. Put the pan on a baking sheet.

Whisk together the milk, cider, egg, vanilla and almond extracts and butter.

In a large bowl, whisk together the flour, sugar, baking powder and soda, cinnamon and salt to combine thoroughly. Toss in the brown sugar, making sure there aren't any lumps by running it through your fingers, then add the oats and whisk the dry ingredients a few more times to mix. Switch to a large rubber spatula and stir in the liquid ingredients, stirring just until everything is moistened— as with muffins, less mixing is better than more. Gently stir in the apple, nuts and raisins, and scrape the batter into the prepared pan.

Bake for 30 to 35 minutes, or until the cake is golden brown and a thin knife inserted into the center of the cake comes out clean. Transfer the pan to a rack and cool for a couple of minutes before running a knife around the sides of the pan and unmolding the cake; invert and cool until warm, or to room temperature.

# CARDAMOM CRUMB CAKE

**THERE'S SOMETHING** grown-up and exotic about this plain-looking crumb-topped brunch treat. It's not very sweet, and the bit of espresso powder and generous amount of cardamom in both the crumbs and the cake give it an edge. Cardamom is a spice that can be soft or strong, up-front recognizable or mysteriously unidentifiable, as it is here. This cake is great with a mug of good strong coffee.

MAKES 8 SERVINGS

**SERVING:** Cut the cake into squares and serve warm or at room temperature.

**STORING:** This cake is best served the day it is made. It can be wrapped airtight and frozen for up to 2 months; once it defrosts, it benefits from a quick warm-up in a 350-degree-F oven.

## FOR THE CRUMBS

- ½ cup all-purpose flour
- ½ cup coarsely chopped walnuts
- ⅓ cup sugar
- 1 tablespoon grated orange zest
- ½ teaspoon instant espresso powder
- ½ teaspoon ground cardamom
- ½ stick (4 tablespoons) unsalted butter, cut into 8 pieces, at room temperature

## FOR THE CAKE

- 2 cups all-purpose flour
- 2 teaspoons baking powder
- ¼ teaspoon salt
- 1¼ teaspoons ground cardamom
- 1 teaspoon instant espresso powder
- ⅔ cup sugar
- 2 tablespoons finely grated orange zest
- 1 stick (8 tablespoons) unsalted butter, melted and cooled
- 2 large eggs
- ½ cup whole milk
- ½ cup strong coffee, cooled
- 1½ teaspoons pure vanilla extract

*Playing Around*

I often make just the crumbs and use them to top ice creams and desserts like Chocolate Pudding (page 383), Coffee Caramel Pots de Crème (page 389) or Lemon Cup Custard (page 387). Make the crumbs as directed and refrigerate them for 2 hours. Crumble up the mixture, spread the crumbs out on a baking sheet lined with parchment or a silicone mat and bake in a 350-degree-F oven for about 15 minutes, or until golden and baked through. Let cool. The crumbs can be wrapped airtight and kept at room temperature overnight or frozen for up to 2 months.

**GETTING READY:** Center a rack in the oven and preheat the oven to 400 degrees F. Butter an 8-inch square baking pan, dust the inside with flour and tap out the excess. Put the pan on a baking sheet.

**TO MAKE THE CRUMBS:** Put all the ingredients except the butter in a bowl and toss them together with a spatula just to blend. Add the butter and, using your fingers or the spatula, mix everything together until you've got crumbs of different sizes. It's nice to have a few big pieces, so don't overdo it. Set the crumbs aside. (The crumbs can be made up to 3 days ahead, covered and refrigerated.)

**TO MAKE THE CAKE:** Whisk together the flour, baking powder, salt, cardamom, and espresso powder in a large bowl. Turn the dry ingredients out onto a sheet of wax paper, and put the sugar and zest in the bowl. Rub them together with your fingers until the sugar is moist and the fragrance of orange strong, then return the dry ingredients to the bowl and whisk to blend.

Put the remaining ingredients in another bowl and whisk them to blend. Pour the wet ingredients over the dry and stir—don't beat—to mix. Stir only until you've got an evenly moistened batter. Scrape the batter into the prepared pan and top with a thick, even layer of the crumbs. Pat the crumbs ever so gently into the batter.

Bake for 30 to 35 minutes, or until the cake has risen (it will crown), the crumbs are golden and a thin knife inserted into the center comes out clean.

Transfer to a rack to cool in the pan before serving warm or at room temperature.

You can unmold the cake if you want to, but you'll lose some of the crumbs when you turn it over. I prefer to cut the cake in the pan, taking care not to nick the surface of the pan with my knife. (This is a good job for a plastic or silicone pie server.)

# DIMPLY PLUM CAKE

**A SIMPLE** brown sugar coffee cake flavored with grated orange zest and a pinch of cardamom, this is quick and versatile—you can make it with whatever summer fruit is in your market. That's its practical appeal. Its visual appeal is its honey brown color and the way the plum halves bake into the batter, become jammy and dimple the top of the cake. But the reason to keep making this cake as long as your supply of plums lasts (and later with other fruits; see Playing Around) is its light sweetness and slight spiciness, such a nice contrast to the plums' little bit of tang. It's the kind of cake you'd be happy to have with your first cup of coffee or tea.

**SERVING:** You can serve this cake while it is still warm or wait until it reaches room temperature.

**STORING:** The cake can be kept well wrapped at room temperature for up to 2 days, though its texture will change (not unappealingly) over this time. On day 1, the cake has a somewhat firm, slightly crumbly texture—reminiscent of corn bread; on days 2 and 3, after some time under wraps, it is soft and moist. It does not freeze well.

| | |
|---|---|
| 1½ cups all-purpose flour | 2 large eggs |
| 2 teaspoons baking powder | ⅓ cup flavorless oil, such as canola or |
| ¼ teaspoon salt | safflower |
| Scant ¼ teaspoon ground | Grated zest of 1 orange |
| cardamom (optional) | 1½ teaspoons pure vanilla extract |
| 5 tablespoons unsalted butter, | 8 purple or red plums (in the fall, use |
| at room temperature | Italian prune plums), halved and |
| ¾ cup (packed) light brown sugar | pitted |

GETTING READY: Center a rack in the oven and preheat the oven to 350 degrees F. Butter an 8-inch square baking pan, dust the inside with flour, tap out the excess and put the pan on a baking sheet.

Whisk the flour, baking powder, salt and cardamom, if you're using it, together.

Working with a stand mixer, preferably fitted with a paddle attachment, or with a hand mixer in a large bowl, beat the butter at medium speed until soft and creamy, about 3 minutes. Add the sugar and beat for another 2 minutes. Add the eggs one at a time, beating for a minute after each addition. On medium speed, beat in the oil, orange zest and vanilla. The batter will look very light and smooth, almost satiny. Reduce the mixer speed to low and add the dry ingredients, mixing only until they are incorporated.

Run a spatula around the bowl and under the batter, just to make sure there are no dry spots, then scrape the batter into the pan and smooth the top. Arrange the plums cut side up in the batter—I usually make 4 rows of 4 plum halves each—jiggling the plums a tad just so they settle comfortably into the batter.

Bake for about 40 minutes, or until the top is honey brown and puffed around the plums and a thin knife inserted into the center of the cake comes out clean. Transfer the cake to a rack and cool for 15 minutes—during which time the plums' juice will return to the fruit—then run a knife around the sides of the pan and unmold the cake. Invert and cool right side up.

## Playing Around

This cake works well with several other kinds of fruit. Apricots, peaches, nectarines and cherries are all good. If you'd like, omit the cardamom or substitute another spice. Similarly, you can trade in the orange zest for lemon, lime or even grapefruit. Here are some of my favorite combinations: apricots with orange zest and a teensy pinch of ground star anise; peaches with lemon zest and a little finely chopped fresh basil; nectarines with orange zest; and cherries with lime zest.

# FLIP-OVER PLUM CAKE

**WHO WOULDN'T** want a cake that's got down-home, not-in-the-least-fussy good looks, an unquestionably appealing flavor and a texture that can't decide whether it wants to be a cake or your favorite nursery pudding? It's put together in minutes without any equipment fancier than a couple of bowls and a whisk. Just pour the batter into the pan and top it with fruit. When you pull the cake from the oven, you'll see that the ingredients have flip-flopped and the fruit is bubbling merrily on the bottom and the batter has risen to the top.

**SERVING:** Bring the cake to the table in its baking pan—it's way too soft and creamy to even think about unmolding—and serve it family-style.

**STORING:** The cake is best—and most like pudding—the day it is made, but it can be cooled, covered and refrigerated overnight. Served chilled, it will be firmer but still delicious.

2 pounds ripe but firm plums, preferably Italian prune plums, pitted

1½ cups sugar

1 teaspoon ground cinnamon

¼ teaspoon ground ginger

¼ teaspoon ground coriander

1 cup all-purpose flour

2 teaspoons baking powder

⅛ teaspoon salt

1 cup whole milk

½ teaspoon pure vanilla extract

½ teaspoon pure almond extract

1 stick (8 tablespoons) unsalted butter, cut into 4 pieces

**GETTING READY:** Center a rack in the oven and preheat the oven to 350 degrees F. Have at hand a 9-x-12-inch baking pan, preferably Pyrex or porcelain.

Cut each plum into 4 to 6 pieces and toss into a bowl. Add ½ cup of the sugar, the cinnamon, ginger and coriander, stir the plums around and then let them sit, stirring from time to time, while you prepare the batter. They will give up some juice and a syrup will develop.

Put the remaining 1 cup sugar, the flour, baking powder and salt in another bowl. Whisk to blend, then pour in the milk and extracts and whisk again, so you have a nice smooth batter.

Put the butter in the baking pan and melt it in the oven, about 5 minutes. Remove the pan from the oven.

Give the batter a light whisking and pour it over the hot butter—it will probably set around the edges immediately. Scatter the plums over the batter and drizzle over whatever syrup has accumulated in the bowl.

Bake for 50 to 55 minutes, or until the top is golden and a thin knife inserted into the center of the cake comes out clean. Transfer the cake to a rack and cool in the pan for at least 20 minutes, or let cool to room temperature.

# CORNMEAL AND FRUIT LOAF

**A BIG,** golden, bumpy-topped bread, this begs to be cut into thick farmhouse-style slices. Because of the cornmeal (I like to make this with gritty stone-ground yellow cornmeal) and the fruit, the bread has a natural, rather than a sugary, sweetness. I make it most often with apples—fresh and dried—because they are always at hand in my house, but the cake is also delicious with pears—fresh and dried. And, while it's a good keeper, whether it's just made or slightly stale, I like it toasted.

| | |
|---|---|
| 1 cup buttermilk | 1 tablespoon baking powder |
| 5 tablespoons unsalted butter, melted and cooled | ½ teaspoon baking soda |
| 2 large eggs | ½ teaspoon ground cinnamon (optional) |
| 1¼ cups all-purpose flour | ¼ teaspoon freshly grated nutmeg |
| ¾ cup yellow cornmeal, preferably stone-ground | ¼ teaspoon salt |
| ½ cup sugar | 1 apple or pear, peeled, cored and cut into small dice |
| | ½ cup diced dried apple or pear |

**GETTING READY:** Center a rack in the oven and preheat the oven to 375 degrees F. Butter a 9-x-5-inch loaf pan, dust the inside with flour and tap out the excess. Put the pan on a baking sheet.

Whisk together the buttermilk, melted butter and eggs.

In a large bowl, whisk together the flour, cornmeal, sugar, baking powder, baking soda, cinnamon, if you're using it, nutmeg and salt, making sure they are evenly combined. Switch to a large rubber spatula and stir in the liquid ingredients, stirring just until everything is moistened—as with muffins, less mixing is better than more. Gently stir in the fresh and dried fruit, and scrape the batter into the prepared pan.

Bake for about 1 hour, or until a thin knife inserted into the center of the bread comes out clean. Transfer the pan to a rack and cool for 10 minutes before running a knife around the sides of the pan and unmolding. Invert and cool right side up.

**SERVING:** Served warm or at room temperature, the bread needs nothing more than to be cut into thick slices, but a swipe of apple butter or a little sweet butter is nice too, as is a light toasting.

**STORING:** The bread is best served the day it is baked, but it can be wrapped well and kept at room temperature for a couple of days. If the bread seems a little dry, toast it. Wrapped airtight, the bread can be frozen for up to 2 months.

### Playing Around

**SAVORY CORNMEAL AND FRUIT LOAF:** To give the loaf a more savory touch, reduce the sugar to ⅓ cup, omit the cinnamon and use just a tiny pinch of nutmeg; if you'd like, add coarsely ground or cracked pepper, black or white, to taste (I usually use about ½ teaspoon). For an even more savory bread, crumble 6 strips of well-cooked and very well drained bacon and stir them into the batter when you add the fruit.

# OATMEAL BREAKFAST BREAD

**THERE WAS** a moment in baking—was it the 1980s?—when, in a fat-cutting frenzy, applesauce and prune puree replaced the lion's share of butter in many recipes, especially those for muffins and quick breads. My guess is I built this recipe around the bones of one of those "magic" formulas—my notes aren't so clear, but the addition of applesauce and the presence of oil argue for it. Not that it makes much difference, because in the end it's the taste of this lightly spiced, fruit-speckled, almost pudding-soft bread that counts. Who knows, it might even be good for you.

MAKES 12 SERVINGS

FOR THE TOPPING

¼ cup (packed) light brown sugar

¼ cup chopped walnuts or pecans

¼ teaspoon ground cinnamon

FOR THE BREAD

2 large eggs

1¼ cups unsweetened applesauce

⅓ cup flavorless oil, such as canola or safflower

¼ cup buttermilk or whole milk

1¼ cups all-purpose flour

¾ cup sugar

1½ teaspoons baking powder

¾ teaspoon ground cinnamon

½ teaspoon baking soda

½ teaspoon salt

¼ teaspoon freshly grated nutmeg

Pinch of ground cloves

½ cup diced dried figs, apples or apricots or moist, plump raisins (dark or golden)

1 cup old-fashioned oats

**GETTING READY:** Center a rack in the oven and preheat the oven to 350 degrees F. Butter a 9-x-5-inch loaf pan, dust the inside with flour and tap out the excess. Put the pan on a baking sheet.

**TO MAKE THE TOPPING:** In a small bowl, using your fingers, toss together the sugar, nuts and cinnamon until evenly mixed. Set aside.

**TO MAKE THE BREAD:** Whisk together the eggs, applesauce, oil and buttermilk until well blended.

In a large bowl, whisk together the flour, sugar, baking powder, cinnamon, baking soda, salt, nutmeg and cloves. Remove ½ teaspoon of the mix and toss it with the fruit, just to coat; set aside. Stir the oats into the bowl. Pour the liquid ingredients over the dry and, using a large rubber spatula, stir just until everything is evenly moistened—this is a case in which less is more, so don't overdo the mixing. Scatter the dried fruit over the batter and stir to blend. Scrape the batter into the pan and sprinkle over the topping, tamping it down very lightly with your fingers so it sticks.

Bake for 55 to 65 minutes, or until the bread is beautifully browned and a thin knife inserted into the center comes out clean. Transfer the bread to a rack to cool for about 5 minutes, then run a knife around the sides of the pan and unmold. Invert and cool to room temperature right side up.

**SERVING:** Although you might be tempted to dig into this bread before it cools, don't. The bread is soft when it's at room temperature, but it's too soft when it's warm. So, wait until the bread is fully cooled, then cut it into medium-thin slices and serve with coffee.

**STORING:** Because of the bread's soft texture, it's a good keeper. You can hold it, well wrapped, at room temperature for 3 to 4 days. It can also be frozen for up to 2 months.

# FRESH MANGO BREAD

**THIS IS** a tweaked version of a recipe given to me by my mother's neighbor, Florence Earl. Mrs. Earl, who lives in Florida, made this with mangoes that grew in her yard, but since fresh mangoes are now readily available in markets across the country, even those of us not lucky enough to be able to shake them off a nearby tree can make it quickly and easily.

Mango breads, which are popular in the South, meet the definition of quick breads, but they're really more like loaf cakes than breads. Certainly that's the case with this "bread," which is soft, moist, spiced and abundant with mango and raisins. Mrs. Earl's recipe included chopped nuts, which I omitted. The ginger and lime zest are among my other tweaks.

**SERVING:** As good as this bread is freshly baked, I think it's even better the next day. One day spent wrapped in plastic seems to intensify the fruit and spice flavors. Of course, if you can't wait, don't. Just cut the loaf into thick slices and serve with tea, hot or iced, or coffee.

**STORING:** Wrapped in plastic, the cake will keep for about 4 days at room temperature.

|  |  |
|---|---|
| 3 large eggs | 1 teaspoon ground cinnamon |
| ¾ cup flavorless oil, such as canola or safflower | ¼ teaspoon salt |
| 2½ cups all-purpose flour | ½ cup (packed) light brown sugar |
| 1 cup sugar | 2 cups diced mango (from 1 large peeled and pitted mango) |
| 1 teaspoon baking powder | ¾ cup moist, plump golden raisins |
| 1 teaspoon baking soda | Grated zest of ½ lime |
| 1½ teaspoons ground ginger | |

GETTING READY: Center a rack in the oven and preheat the oven to 350 degrees F. Butter an 8½-x-4½-inch loaf pan, dust the inside with flour and tap out the excess. Put the pan on an insulated baking sheet or on two regular baking sheets stacked one on top of the other. (This extra insulation will keep the bottom of the bread from overbaking.)

Whisk the eggs and oil together.

In a large bowl, whisk together the flour, sugar, baking powder, baking soda, spices and salt. Rub the brown sugar between your palms into the bowl, breaking up any lumps, then stir it in. Pour the wet ingredients over the dry, switch to a sturdy rubber spatula or wooden spoon and mix until blended—the batter will be very thick (really more like a dough than a batter) and not easily mixed, but persevere, it will soon come together. Stir in the mango, raisins and zest. Scrape the batter into the pan and smooth the top with a rubber spatula.

Bake the bread for 1½ hours, or until it is golden brown and a thin knife inserted into the center comes out clean. (If the bread looks as if it's getting too brown as it bakes, cover it loosely with a foil tent.) Transfer the pan to a rack and cool for 5 minutes before running a knife around the sides of the pan and unmolding. Invert and cool to room temperature right side up on the rack.

# COCOA-NANA BREAD

**IN MY** never-ending quest to make chocolate as acceptable as porridge at the breakfast table, I offer this coal-dark morning loaf. It's big and hearty looking, cracked and creviced along the top, with a tight, even crumb and lots of patches of soft melted chocolate bits. At first bite the loaf is chocolate-chocolate, and then the banana flavor kicks in—it's altogether winning and, while it may feel decadent to have it at breakfast, it would be just as winning, if a little less racy, as a P.M. treat.

MAKES 12 SERVINGS

SERVING: I like this bread cut into fairly thick slices, but for more delicate servings, its crumb is close enough to cut it into thin slices without problems. It can be served with yogurt, sour cream or jam or enjoyed as is.

STORING: Wrapped in plastic, the bread will keep for 2 days at room temperature; wrapped airtight, it will keep for up to 2 months in the freezer.

2 cups all-purpose flour

1 cup unsweetened cocoa powder

1½ teaspoons baking powder

½ teaspoon salt

¼ teaspoon baking soda

1 stick (8 tablespoons) unsalted butter, at room temperature

¾ cup sugar

½ cup (packed) light brown sugar

2 large eggs

2 ripe bananas, mashed

¾ cup buttermilk

3 ounces bittersweet chocolate, coarsely chopped, or ½ cup store-bought chocolate chips

GETTING READY: Center a rack in the oven and preheat the oven to 350 degrees F. Butter a 9-x-5-inch loaf pan and place it on an insulated baking sheet or on two regular baking sheets stacked one on top of the other. (This extra insulation will keep the bottom of the bread from overbaking.)

Sift together the flour, cocoa, baking powder, salt and baking soda.

Working with a stand mixer, preferably fitted with a paddle attachment, or with a hand mixer in a large bowl, beat the butter at medium speed for about a minute, until softened. Add the sugars and beat for 2 minutes more. Add the eggs one at a time, beating for a minute after each addition. At this point, the batter may look a little curdled—it's okay. Reduce the mixer speed to low and mix in the mashed bananas. Add the dry ingredients in 3 additions, mixing only until they disappear into the batter. Still on low speed, add the buttermilk, mixing until it is incorporated. Stir in the chopped chocolate. Scrape the batter into the pan.

Bake for 30 minutes. Cover the bread loosely with a foil tent to keep the top from getting too dark, and continue to bake for another 40 to 45 minutes (total baking time is between 70 and 75 minutes), or until a thin knife inserted into the center comes out clean. Transfer the pan to a rack and cool for at least 20 minutes before running a knife around the edges of the bread and unmolding it. Invert and cool to room temperature right side up.

# YEASTED
# TREATS

BAKING WITH yeast is about as close as we nonsorcerers can get to alchemy. There's more than a touch of wizardry in how yeast, patience and heat thoroughly transform a baker's basic ingredients.

Of the factors in the yeast-patience-heat trinity, it's patience that can be most trying: yeast's magic takes time to unfold. And time with yeast is usually measured in hours, not minutes. But when a recipe's directions instruct you to let a dough rise until it's almost doubled in volume, there isn't much in the way of wiggle room if you want to get the best texture, flavor and fragrance. Hurry the yeast, and you'll have a bread that is tight and cramped. The flavor will be inhibited too, since a leisurely rise is also the key to pulling character out of flour. Finally, speed up the process and you'll get the somewhat sharp, beery scent of leftover yeast, yeast that hasn't been fully used in lifting the dough. But if you give the dough the time it needs, you'll have that warm, nutty come-hither fragrance that is one of the great joys of baking bread at home.

While the process of rising bread can't be rushed, it can be slowed and even wrapped around your schedule. Since yeast rises best in a warm environment, and not at all when it is cold, you can put the dough in the refrigerator and send the yeast into a state of suspended animation. Although the dough will rise for about an hour after it is first slipped into the fridge, once it is cold, the rising will stop and the dough can be kept overnight.

Chilling the dough, and arresting its development, puts you in charge of the timetable and makes it easy to have freshly baked bread for brunch. Yes, you'll still have to get up early, but you won't have to stay up all night. Just pull the dough from the refrigerator and give it its final rise. Because the dough is cold, the last rise will be longer, but you can sit back and read the weekend papers while the yeast does its work.

Patience will give you brioche, my favorite bread in the universe. Find the patience to make brioche, and you'll have the key to dozens of other yeasted sweets, among them honey-topped sticky buns, a swirled raisin bread and Kugelhopf, a twisty turban of a coffee cake that will repay you tenfold for any shut-eye lost in its construction.

# GOLDEN BRIOCHE LOAVES

MAKES 2 LOAVES

SERVING: As soon as the loaves cool, they are ready to be sliced thickly and served, toasted or not, with butter and jam.

STORING: Well-wrapped (cooled) loaves will keep overnight at room temperature. If you'd like, you can rewarm the loaves by wrapping them in aluminum foil and heating them for about 15 minutes in a 350-degree-F oven. The loaves can also be wrapped airtight and frozen for up to 2 months; defrost in the wrapping.

"ELEGANT" IS the best word to describe this rich bread, with its golden color, unforgettable texture—pull on a slice and watch how it stretches luxuriously in thin, ever widening lengths (one sign of a superior brioche)—and slightly sweet, fully buttery flavor.

This is the basic recipe for brioche dough, and here it is formed into two loaves, each loaf comprised of four easy-to-pull-apart sections, perfect for serving at breakfast—just add great jam and butter—or for turning into heavenly Sugar-Crusted French Toast (page 60) or, if it lasts long enough to go stale, Bostock (see Playing Around).

As with many yeast doughs, this one works best in larger batches, so please don't downsize the recipe. If you don't need two loaves now, freeze one to enjoy later. Or shape half of the dough into a loaf and use the other half to make Pecan Honey Sticky Buns (page 51) or Brioche Raisin Snails (page 56).

The first time I made brioche, I was taking a baking course and, so that we could get to know its properties, we made the dough by hand, beating everything into silky submission with a wooden spoon. I huffed and puffed harder and longer than I had when I'd run a half-marathon. Thankfully, while bakers of yore had only their energy and a spoon at their disposal, this is not the case nowadays. Today brioche is made with the flick of the switch on a heavy-duty mixer. This is one recipe that should not be made with a hand mixer—in all likelihood, the mixing will wear out the motor. So, either fire up the stand mixer or pull out your sturdiest wooden spoon.

The dough should be made 1 day ahead and then shaped and baked the next.

FOR THE BRIOCHE
- 2 packets active dry yeast
- ⅓ cup just-warm-to-the-touch water
- ⅓ cup just-warm-to-the-touch whole milk
- 3¾ cups all-purpose flour
- 2 teaspoons salt
- 3 large eggs, at room temperature
- ¼ cup sugar
- 3 sticks (12 ounces) unsalted butter, at room temperature but still slightly firm

FOR THE GLAZE
- 1 large egg
- 1 tablespoon water

TO MAKE THE BRIOCHE: Put the yeast, water and milk in the bowl of a stand mixer and, using a wooden spoon, stir until the yeast is dissolved. Add the flour and salt, and fit the mixer with the dough hook, if you have one. Toss a kitchen towel over the mixer, covering the bowl as completely as you can—this will help keep you, the counter and your kitchen floor from being showered in flour. Turn the mixer on and off in a few short pulses, just to dampen the flour (yes, you can peek to see how you're doing), then remove the towel, increase the mixer speed to medium-

low and mix for a minute or two, just until the flour is moistened. At this point you'll have a fairly dry, shaggy mass.

Scrape the sides and bottom of the bowl with a rubber spatula, set the mixer to low and add the eggs, followed by the sugar. Increase the mixer speed to medium and beat for about 3 minutes, until the dough forms a ball. Reduce the speed to low and add the butter in 2-tablespoon-size chunks, beating until each piece is almost incorporated before adding the next. You'll have a dough that is very soft, almost like a batter. Increase the speed to medium-high and continue to beat until the dough pulls away from the sides of the bowl, about 10 minutes.

Transfer the dough to a clean bowl (or wash out the mixer bowl and use it), cover with plastic wrap and leave at room temperature until nearly doubled in size, 40 to 60 minutes, depending upon the warmth of your room.

Deflate the dough by lifting it up around the edges and letting it fall with a slap into the bowl. Cover the bowl with plastic wrap and put it in the refrigerator. Slap the dough down in the bowl every 30 minutes until it stops rising, about 2 hours, then leave the covered dough in the refrigerator to chill overnight.

The next day, butter and flour two 8½-x-4½-inch loaf pans.

Pull the dough from the fridge and divide it into 2 equal pieces. Cut each piece of dough into 4 equal pieces and roll each piece into a log about 3½ inches long. Arrange 4 logs crosswise in the bottom of each pan. Put the pans on a baking sheet lined with parchment or a silicone mat, cover the pans lightly with wax paper and leave the loaves at room temperature until the dough almost fills the pans, 1 to 2 hours. (Again, rising time will depend on how warm the room is.)

GETTING READY TO BAKE: Center a rack in the oven and preheat the oven to 400 degrees F.

TO MAKE THE GLAZE: Beat the egg with the water. Using a pastry brush, gently brush the tops of the loaves with the glaze.

Bake the loaves until they are well risen and deeply golden, 30 to 35 minutes. Transfer the pans to racks to cool for 15 minutes, then run a knife around the sides of the pans and turn the loaves out onto the racks. Invert again and cool for at least 1 hour.

*Playing Around*

BOSTOCK: Bostock, stale brioche spread with almond cream, sprinkled with sliced almonds and baked to a state of puffed and golden deliciousness, was originally a breakfast sweet created by European bakers to make use of their day-old brioche. But the sweet proved so good that bakers now make both brioche and almond cream for the sole purpose of turning these fresh delicacies into bostock. My advice to you is to start with any leftover brioche you have and then, if you love bostock as much as so many Europeans do, consider dedicating one loaf to bostock alone.

To make a single portion of bostock, cut a slice of brioche ½ to ¾ inch thick. Spread the bread with about 3 tablespoons Almond Cream (page 452), leaving a little border bare, and scatter over some sliced almonds, blanched or not. Put the bread on a baking sheet lined with parchment or a silicone mat, and bake in a 350-degree-F oven until the almond cream is puffed and golden brown, 10 to 15 minutes. Serve the bostock warm or at room temperature.

# PECAN HONEY STICKY BUNS

**ANYONE WHO** takes the time to make sticky buns thinks that his or hers are the best. In this regard, I'm just like everyone else. My sticky buns are made from buttery brioche dough, so right off the bat, you know they're special. The dough is spread with more butter and sprinkled with cinnamon and sugar, and then the rolls are left to rise in their sticky glaze. The glaze is very sweet, very sugary and very delicious. It's made of brown sugar, butter, honey and lots of pecans, and when it's baked, the pecans turn into pralines. What's not to like?

If you don't want 15 eat-them-now sticky buns, you can make fewer and freeze the remaining dough. You'll just need to adjust the quantity of glaze. See the instructions for shaping the buns and Storing for more information.

FOR THE GLAZE

- 1 cup (packed) light brown sugar
- 1 stick (8 tablespoons) unsalted butter, cut into 4 pieces
- ¼ cup honey
- 1½ cups pecans (whole or pieces)

FOR THE FILLING

- ¼ cup sugar
- 3 tablespoons (packed) light brown sugar
- 1 tablespoon ground cinnamon
- 3 tablespoons unsalted butter, at room temperature

FOR THE BUNS

- ½ recipe dough for Golden Brioche Loaves (page 48), chilled and ready to shape (make the full recipe and cut the dough in half after refrigerating it overnight)

MAKES 15 BUNS

SERVING: The sticky buns are ready to serve when they have cooled down enough to be enjoyed without fear of burning fingers or tongue. While there is something very special about eating still-warm sticky buns, these are also really good at room temperature.

STORING: Not surprisingly, these are best the day they are made, but, wrapped in plastic, they'll hold overnight. If you've kept the buns, you might want to reheat them briefly in a 350-degree-F oven. While the baked buns cannot be frozen, you can freeze the filled and rolled log of dough or the cut buns—make certain they are wrapped airtight. Defrost the dough or rolls overnight in the refrigerator, then make the glaze, place the buns in the pan of glaze and let rise and bake as directed.

Generously butter a 9-x-13-inch baking pan (a Pyrex pan is perfect for this).

TO MAKE THE GLAZE: In a heavy-bottomed saucepan, bring the brown sugar, butter and honey to a boil over medium-low heat, stirring frequently to dissolve the sugar. Pour the glaze into the buttered pan, evening it out as best you can by tilting the pan or spreading the glaze with a heatproof spatula. Sprinkle over the pecans.

TO MAKE THE FILLING: Mix the sugars and cinnamon together in a bowl. If necessary, in another bowl, work the butter with a spatula until it is soft, smooth and spreadable.

TO SHAPE THE BUNS: On a flour-dusted work surface, roll the chilled dough into a 16-inch square. Using your fingers or a pastry brush, spread the softened butter over the dough. Sprinkle the dough with the cinnamon sugar, leaving a 1-inch strip bare on the side farthest from you. Starting with the side nearest you, roll the dough into a cylinder, keeping the roll as tight as you can. (At this point, you can wrap the dough airtight and freeze it for up to 2 months; see Storing for further

instructions. Or, if you want to make just part of the recipe now, you can use as much of the dough as you'd like and freeze the remainder. Reduce the glaze recipe accordingly.)

With a chef's knife, using a gentle sawing motion, trim just a tiny bit from the ends of the roll if they're very ragged or not well filled, then cut the log into 1-inch-thick buns. (Because you trim the ragged ends of the dough, and you may have lost a little length in the rolling, you will get 15 buns, not 16.) Fit the buns into the pan cut side down, leaving some space between them.

Lightly cover the pan with a piece of wax paper and set the pan in a warm place until the buns have doubled in volume, about 1 hour and 45 minutes. The buns are properly risen when they are puffy, soft, doubled and, in all likelihood, touching one another.

GETTING READY TO BAKE: When the buns have almost fully risen, center a rack in the oven and preheat the oven to 375 degrees F.

Remove the sheet of wax paper and put the pan on a baking sheet lined with parchment or a silicone mat. Bake the sticky buns for about 30 minutes, or until they are puffed and gorgeously golden; the glaze will be bubbling away merrily. Pull the pan from the oven.

The sticky buns must be unmolded minutes after they come out of the oven. If you do not have a rimmed platter large enough to hold them, use a baking sheet lined with a silicone mat or buttered foil. Be careful—the glaze is super-hot and super-sticky.

# BRIOCHE PLUM TART

**THE DOUGH** for this tart is a brioche, but one the French would call skinny or poor—the adjectives having nothing to do with its thickness or its sorry state, but referring instead to the relative paucity of eggs and butter. Because lots of fruit is tucked into the dough, you don't need the usual richness. The dough is pressed into a fluted tart pan, covered with jam, piled high with plums and then baked until it is honey brown, puffed and bubbling. It's beautiful and relatively easy to make—if you've got a stand mixer and a modicum of patience. Since brioche is a yeast dough, you'll have to sit back and relax for a couple of hours while it does the same.

**FOR THE BRIOCHE**

- 1½ teaspoons active dry yeast
- ⅓ cup just-warm-to-the-touch whole milk
- 2 cups all-purpose flour
- 3 tablespoons sugar
  Pinch of salt
- 5 tablespoons unsalted butter, melted and cooled
- 2 large eggs, at room temperature
- 1 teaspoon pure vanilla extract

**FOR THE PLUM FILLING**

- About 14 ripe plums, preferably Italian prune plums (if you use a larger plum, you'll need fewer)
- 2 tablespoons coarsely chopped walnuts or almonds
- 3 tablespoons sugar
- ¼ cup plum jam

**TO MAKE THE BRIOCHE:** Put the yeast and warm milk in the bowl of a stand mixer and stir until the yeast is dissolved. Add the rest of the ingredients to the bowl, and fit the mixer with the dough hook, if you have one. Working on low speed, mix for a minute or two, just to get the ingredients together. Increase the mixer speed to medium and beat for 7 to 10 minutes, stopping a few times to scrape down the bowl and the hook, until the dough is stretchy and fairly smooth. The dough will seem fairly thin, more like a batter than a dough, and it may not be perfectly smooth—that's fine.

Transfer the dough to a clean bowl (or wash out the mixer bowl and use it), cover with plastic wrap and leave it in a warm place until nearly doubled in size, 30 to 40 minutes.

Deflate the dough by lifting it up around the edges and letting it fall with a slap into the bowl. Cover the bowl again with plastic wrap and put it in the refrigerator. Slap the dough down in the bowl every 30 minutes until it stops rising, about 2 hours. Then, if you've got the time, leave the dough in the refrigerator overnight—it will be tastier for the wait.

**SERVING:** Resist the temptation to cut into the tart immediately. Yeast breads and cakes need time to gather themselves before they can deliver the full measure of their delights. Wait until the crust is only just slightly warm to the touch, or until it reaches room temperature, before cutting the tart into wedges. Serve for brunch or when you're taking a late-morning break or having afternoon tea.

**STORING:** This is a have-it-the-day-you-bake-it tart. While you can prepare the brioche dough a day ahead, once baked, it is meant to be eaten.

*Playing Around*

Brioche goes well with other kinds of fruit. While plums are the perfect filler for fall, apricots would be great in summer and apples, pears or even mangoes would be good for winter. If you change the fruit, change the jam on the bottom of the tart too.

TO MAKE THE TART: This tart looks prettiest when it's made in a fluted pan. You can use either a 9-inch metal tart pan with a removable base or a porcelain baking dish, the kind sometimes called a quiche pan. Generously butter the pan.

Press the chilled dough into the bottom of the pan and up the sides—don't worry if it's not even. Cover the pan loosely with plastic wrap and refrigerate for 30 minutes.

While the dough is in the refrigerator, prepare the filling. Halve and pit the plums. If you are using large plums, cut each half into 2 or 3 slices. Set aside. Toss the chopped nuts with the sugar, and set aside.

Remove the tart pan from the fridge and push and press the dough up the sides of the pan. Spoon the jam onto the dough and spread it over the bottom. Arrange the plums cut side down in concentric circles covering the jam. Scatter over the nut mixture, and cover the tart lightly with a piece of plastic wrap. Place the tart on a baking sheet lined with parchment or a silicone mat and let it rest in a warm place for 30 minutes.

Meanwhile, center a rack in the oven and preheat the oven to 425 degrees F.

Uncover the tart and bake for 20 minutes. Cover it loosely with a foil tent to prevent the crust from getting too dark, and continue baking for another 10 minutes, or until the fruit juices are bubbling and the crust is firm and beautifully browned—it will sound hollow when tapped. Transfer the tart to a rack to cool for at least 45 minutes before serving.

EVEN IF I made these three times a day every day, I think there'd still be a clamor for more. There's something about the plump little swirls—the buttery brioche dough, the silky pastry cream, the rum-soaked raisins—that makes them impossibly good and impossible to enjoy in moderation. Minus the fancy fillip of soaking and flaming the raisins in rum (a little step that adds a lot of flavor), these are almost exactly the version I learned to make in my very first baking class.

1 cup moist, plump raisins

3 tablespoons dark rum

1½ teaspoons sugar

Scant ¼ teaspoon ground cinnamon

½ recipe dough for Golden Brioche Loaves (page 48), chilled and ready to shape (make the full recipe and cut the dough in half after refrigerating it overnight)

½ recipe Pastry Cream (page 448)

FOR THE OPTIONAL GLAZE

¾ cup confectioners' sugar, sifted

About 1 teaspoon water

Drop of pure vanilla extract

MAKES ABOUT 12 SNAILS

SERVING: As tempting as it is to grab a hot snail, hot is not the best temperature at which to enjoy these pastries. Like all yeast doughs, brioche needs time to set after coming out of the oven, so serve these when they are warm, not hot, or wait for them to reach room temperature.

STORING: Although these are best the day they are made, they can be wrapped in plastic and kept overnight. If you've kept the snails, you might want to heat them briefly in a 350-degree-F oven. While the baked snails cannot be frozen, you can freeze the filled and rolled log of dough or the cut snails—make certain they are wrapped airtight. Defrost overnight in the refrigerator, then allow them to rise, and bake.

GETTING READY: Line one large or two smaller baking sheets with parchment or silicone mats.

Put the raisins in a small saucepan, cover them with hot water and let them steep for about 4 minutes, until they are plumped. Drain the raisins, return them to the saucepan and, stirring constantly, warm them over low heat. When the raisins are very hot, pull the pan from the heat and pour over the rum. Standing back, ignite the rum. Stir until the flames go out, then cover and set aside. (The raisins and rum can be kept in a covered jar for up to 1 day.)

Mix the sugar and cinnamon together.

On a flour-dusted surface, roll the dough into a rectangle about 12 inches wide and 16 inches long, with a short end toward you. Spread the pastry cream across the dough, leaving a 1-inch strip bare on the side farthest from you. Scatter the raisins over the pastry cream and sprinkle the raisins and cream with the cinnamon sugar. Starting with the side nearest you, roll the dough into a cylinder, keeping the roll as tight as you can. (At this point, you can wrap the dough airtight and freeze it for up to 2 months; see Storing for further instructions. Or, if you do not want to make the full recipe, use as much of the dough as you'd like and freeze the remainder.)

With a chef's knife, using a gentle sawing motion, trim just a tiny bit from the ends if they're very ragged or not well filled, then cut the log into rounds a scant 1 inch thick. Put the snails on the lined baking sheet(s), leaving some puff space between them.

Lightly cover the snails with wax paper and set the baking sheet(s) in a warm place until the snails have doubled in volume—they'll be puffy and soft—about 1 hour and 30 minutes.

GETTING READY TO BAKE: When the snails have almost fully risen, preheat the oven: depending on the number of baking sheets you have, either center a rack in the oven or position the racks to divide the oven into thirds and preheat the oven to 375 degrees F.

Remove the wax paper, and bake the snails for about 25 minutes (rotate the sheets, if you're using two, from top to bottom and front to back after 15 minutes), or until they are puffed and richly browned. Using a metal spatula, transfer the snails to a cooling rack.

IF YOU WANT TO GLAZE THE SNAILS: Put a piece of wax paper under the rack of warm rolls to act as a drip catcher. Put the confectioners' sugar in a small bowl, and stir in the teaspoon of water. Keep adding water drop by drop until you have an icing that falls from the tip of a spoon. Add the vanilla extract, then drizzle the icing over the hot snails.

# RAISIN SWIRL BREAD

HERE'S MY favorite raisin bread, a soft, tender-crumbed, sweet milk bread with delicate swirls of cinnamon sugar and lots of raisins. It makes super toast and spectacular French toast (see Playing Around), and it makes waking up on school days a lot more fun.

While I make the dough for this bread in a mixer using a paddle and then a dough hook, it can be done by hand—you'll need a big mixing bowl, a sturdy wooden spoon and some elbow grease.

### FOR THE BREAD

- 1 packet active dry yeast
- ¼ cup sugar, plus a pinch
- 1¼ cups just-warm-to-the-touch whole milk
- ½ stick (4 tablespoons) unsalted butter, at room temperature
- ¾ teaspoon salt
- 1 large egg
- ¼ teaspoon pure vanilla extract (optional)
- Grated zest of ½ orange (optional)
- Pinch of freshly grated nutmeg (optional)
- 3¾ to 4 cups all-purpose flour

### FOR THE SWIRL

- 1 tablespoon sugar
- 2 teaspoons ground cinnamon
- 2 teaspoons unsweetened cocoa powder (optional)
- 1 cup moist, plump raisins (dark or golden)
- 3 tablespoons unsalted butter, softened to a spreadable consistency

SERVING: While this bread is good just sliced and buttered, it is great toasted. Toasting brings out the sweetness of the loaf and heightens the play between the slightly firm exterior and the soft inside. I also love the bread toasted, buttered and sprinkled with cinnamon sugar or spread with a good thick layer of apricot or black cherry jam.

STORING: Wrapped in plastic wrap, the loaf will keep at room temperature for about 3 days; wrapped airtight, it will keep in the freezer for up to 2 months.

TO MAKE THE BREAD: Put the yeast in a small bowl, toss in the pinch of sugar and stir in ¼ cup of the warm milk. Let rest for 3 minutes, then stir—the yeast may not have dissolved completely and it may not have bubbled, but it should be soft.

Working with a stand mixer, preferably fitted with a paddle attachment, combine the remaining 1 cup milk, the butter and the remaining ¼ cup sugar and mix on low speed for a minute or two. Add the salt, egg and vanilla, if you are using it, as well as the zest and nutmeg, if you're using them, and mix for a minute. In all likelihood, the mixture will look unpleasantly curdly (it will look even worse when you add the yeast). Add the yeast mixture and beat on medium-low speed for 1 minute more.

Turn the mixer off and add 2¾ cups of the flour. Mix on low speed just until you work the flour into the liquids—you'll have a sticky mix. If you've got a dough hook, switch to it now. Add another 1 cup flour, increase the mixer speed to medium and beat the dough for a couple of minutes. If the dough does not come together and almost clean the sides of the bowl, add up to ¼ cup more flour, 1 tablespoon at a time. Keep the mixer speed at medium and knead the dough for about 3 minutes, or until it is smooth and has a lovely buttery sheen. The dough will be very soft, much too soft to knead by hand.

Butter a large bowl, turn the dough into the bowl and cover the bowl tightly with plastic wrap. Put the bowl in a warm place and let the dough rise until it is doubled in size, about 1½ hours.

Scrape the dough onto a large piece of plastic wrap, wrap it and put it in the freezer for 30 minutes to firm enough to be rolled easily. (At this point, you can instead refrigerate the dough overnight if that is more convenient.)

TO MAKE THE SWIRL AND SHAPE THE LOAF: Butter a 9-x-5-inch loaf pan.

Whisk together the sugar, cinnamon and cocoa, if you're using it. Check that the raisins are nice and moist; if they're not, steam them for a minute, then dry them well.

Put the dough on a large work surface lightly dusted with flour, lightly dust the top of the dough and roll the dough into a rectangle about 12 x 18 inches.

Gently smear 2 tablespoons of the butter over the surface of the dough—this is most easily done with your fingers. Sprinkle over the sugar mixture and scatter over the raisins. Starting from a short side of the dough, roll the dough up jelly-roll fashion, making sure to roll the dough snugly. Fit the dough into the buttered pan, seam side down, and tuck the ends under the loaf.

Cover the pan loosely with wax paper and set in a warm place; let the dough rise until it comes just a little above the edge of the pan, about 45 minutes.

GETTING READY TO BAKE: When the dough has almost fully risen, center a rack in the oven and preheat the oven to 375 degrees F. Line a baking sheet with parchment or a silicone mat.

Melt the remaining tablespoon of butter, and brush the top of the loaf with the butter. Put the pan on the baking sheet and bake the bread for about 20 minutes. Cover loosely with a foil tent and bake for another 25 minutes or so, until the bread is golden and sounds hollow when the bottom of the pan is tapped. Transfer the pan to a rack and cool for 5 minutes, then unmold. Invert the bread and cool to room temperature right side up on the rack.

*Playing Around*

SUGAR-CRUSTED FRENCH TOAST: This French toast is luscious with maple syrup, it's even more luscious with fruit—try it with port-poached figs (page 198) or apples sautéed in butter and sugar—and it's most luscious served as the French serve it, for dessert rather than for breakfast. To make the toast, soak six ¾- to 1-inch-thick slices of bread in a mixture of 6 large eggs, 3 large egg yolks, 3½ cups whole milk, ⅔ cup sugar, 1 tablespoon pure vanilla extract and ½ teaspoon salt for about 3 minutes. When the bread is ready, put two large nonstick skillets over medium heat, add 3 tablespoons unsalted butter to each one and melt the butter. Sprinkle each skillet with 2 tablespoons sugar and put 3 slices soaked bread in each one. Cook until the bread is golden brown on the bottom, about 3 minutes. Sprinkle the tops of the bread with sugar—again, using 2 tablespoons sugar for each skillet—and carefully flip the slices over. Add more butter to the pans if needed, and cook for another 3 minutes, or until the undersides are also golden brown. Serve the toast immediately with fruit, syrup, crème fraîche or jam, or with all of them.

# KUGELHOPF

**FOR ANYONE** who comes from Alsace, the northeastern region of France, Kugelhopf, as plain as it is, is a dream food. Part bread, part cake, Kugelhopf is made very much like brioche. In fact, it is almost a brioche, but not a rich one. You won't miss the bit of butter that's left out of the dough, though, because once it's baked, the cake is soaked with melted butter and sprinkled with sugar, so it develops a fine crust.

While, in a pinch, you could make a Kugelhopf in a Bundt pan, it's a treat to make it in the pan designed especially for it. Sometimes called a turk's head or turban, a Kugelhopf pan is fairly slender and has graceful curves (which do, in fact, resemble the wrap of a turban). If you want to be completely authentic, you can look for a heavy pottery Kugelhopf mold from Alsace—you might even find one with painted flowers. Or you can use a silicone turban pan, as I do. It gives me particular pleasure to bake a centuries-old recipe in something so modern.

Like brioche, this dough is best made using a heavy-duty mixer; however, you can succeed in mixing it in a large bowl with a wooden spoon.

MAKES 8 SERVINGS

**SERVING:** If you are not going to serve the cake as soon as it cools, wrap it in plastic without sprinkling it with confectioners' sugar, because it stales quickly. Then sprinkle it with the sugar before serving. Luckily, stale Kugelhopf is delicious cut into thick slices, toasted and spread with butter and marmalade.

**STORING:** The Kugelhopf should be eaten the day it is made or cut and toasted the following day.

**FOR THE CAKE**
- ⅓ cup moist, plump raisins
- Scant 1½ teaspoons active dry yeast
- ⅓ cup just-warm-to-the-touch whole milk
- 1⅔ cups all-purpose flour
- ¼ teaspoon salt
- 2 large eggs
- 1 large egg yolk
- 3 tablespoons sugar
- 1 stick (8 tablespoons) unsalted butter, at room temperature

**FOR THE SOAK**
- ½ stick (4 tablespoons) unsalted butter
- Sugar, for dusting

- Confectioners' sugar, for dusting

**TO MAKE THE CAKE:** Bring a little water to a boil in a small saucepan and toss in the raisins. Turn off the heat and let steep for 2 minutes, then drain the raisins and pat them dry.

Put the yeast and milk in the bowl of a stand mixer and, using a wooden spoon, stir until the yeast is dissolved. Add the flour and salt and stir just to moisten the flour—don't be concerned, the mixture will be shaggy and there may be dry patches.

In a small bowl, beat the eggs and yolk together lightly with a fork. Fit the mixer with the dough hook, if you have one, and, working on low speed, pour in the beaten eggs, mixing until they are incorporated. Add the sugar, increase the mixer speed to medium-high and beat until the dough comes together and smooths out a little, about 5 minutes. Reduce the mixer speed to medium and add the butter in 4 to 6 additions, squeezing each piece to soften it before adding it

and beating until each one is almost fully incorporated before adding the next.

When the butter is blended in, the dough will be very soft. Increase the mixer speed to medium-high and beat, scraping down the sides and bottom of the bowl as needed, until the dough pulls away from the sides of the bowl and climbs up the hook, about 10 minutes. Remove the bowl from the mixer, and stir in the raisins.

Scrape the dough into a clean bowl, cover with plastic wrap and let rise in a warm place until nearly doubled in size, about 1½ hours. (The length of time will depend on the warmth of your room.)

Deflate the dough by lifting it up around the edges and letting it fall back with a slap into the bowl. Cover the bowl again and put it in the refrigerator. Slap the dough down in the bowl every 30 minutes until it stops rising, about 2 hours. Then, if you have the time, let the dough rest in the refrigerator overnight. (The dough can be wrapped tightly and refrigerated for up to 2 days.)

Generously butter a 9-inch Kugelhopf mold (8- to 9-cup capacity) and put the chilled dough in the pan. Cover the pan lightly with buttered parchment or wax paper and let the dough rise in a warm place until it comes almost to the top of the mold, 2 to 3 hours.

GETTING READY TO BAKE: When the dough has almost fully risen, center a rack in the oven and preheat the oven to 375 degrees F.

Remove the paper and bake the Kugelhopf for 10 minutes. Cover the pan loosely with a foil tent and bake for another 15 to 20 minutes, or until the Kugelhopf is golden brown and has risen to the top—or, more likely, over the top—of the pan.

Meanwhile, line a baking sheet with foil and place a rack over it. Remove the Kugelhopf from the oven and unmold it on the rack.

TO SOAK THE CAKE: Melt the butter and gently brush the hot cake with it, allowing the butter to soak into the cake. Sprinkle the hot cake lightly with sugar and cool it to room temperature.

Right before serving, dust the Kugelhopf with confectioners' sugar.

A CACHE
OF COOKIES

# COOKIE JAR COOKIES

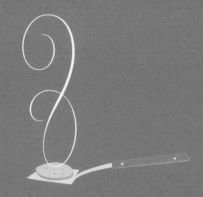

COOKIE JAR COOKIES are the chunky sweets of lunch boxes and afternoon snacks, the grab-'em cookies of kids on the run and the midnight snacks of just about anyone old enough to be up that late. This is the domain of drop cookies, of chocolate chip cookies, of cookies chockablock with nuts and raisins, chips and chopped candies and of cookies hefty enough to dip into ice cream.

These are easy to make and good candidates for baking sessions with children because, other than the measurements, there's almost nothing precise about these sweets. They are either spooned out onto baking sheets or shaped into balls.

What does count is how you bake them. Always start with a cool baking sheet—pull one that's just out of the oven, and your dough will ooze and melt before it bakes. Choose sturdy baking sheets (rimmed, which is what I use, or not) that won't twist or warp under heat. Avoid insulated baking sheets—they bake more slowly than standard sheets and, while they'll never give you burnt bottoms, they usually won't give you beautifully golden ones either. Always line the baking sheet with parchment paper or a silicone mat, which will not only make clean-up easy, but will help the cookies to bake more evenly.

You can be haphazard in how you shape these cookies, but if you use the same amount of dough to shape each one, you'll get another boost in the even-baking department. You'll also get cookies of roughly equal size, so you'll avoid any arguments about who got the biggest one.

In the following recipes, I tell you which cookies like to spread out in the oven and which keep their shape, and how much space to allow between each mound of dough. But even nonspreaders shouldn't be crowded on the baking sheet; all cookies need space so the oven's heat can bake their edges properly.

Don't be in too much of a rush when you bake them either, no matter how eager you are to eat them. Just as it's important not to crowd the dough on the baking sheets, it's important not to crowd the oven in an attempt to reduce the number of batches. If you do, the heat won't circulate evenly around the baking sheets. Some cookies do fine when you bake two sheets at a time and rotate them at the midway point, while others do best when they are baked one sheet at a time in the center of the oven. Curb your impatience and follow my instructions—you'll get better results.

Finally, if the assembled monsters haven't devoured your cookies straight off the cooling racks, you might actually have some to pack into a cookie jar. If that's the case, here's a word of advice: keep crunchy kinds in one jar and the soft, chewy ones in another—mix them up, and you'll end up with a jar full of softies, since crisp cookies are defenseless against moisture from neighbors.

# MY BEST CHOCOLATE CHIP COOKIES

IN THE category of "Great Chocolate Chip Cookies," these get my vote for greatest. They are Toll House cookies' kin, but I think my nips, tucks, tweaks and variations on the classic recipe make them their own kind of wonderful. They're thin and crisp and a bit chewy in the center from just the right mix of sugars—granulated sugar for crispiness and brown sugar for deep caramel flavor.

I've made these cookies with just about every kind of chocolate known to humankind with universally satisfying results, but my all-time favorite way is to chop up premium chocolate, not worrying about cutting it into uniform sizes or shapes. Having chunks, chips and slivers makes the eating more fun, and I love the way the mishmash of shapes looks when the cookies are baked—streaked, marbled, tweedy and totally tempting.

MAKES ABOUT 45 COOKIES

SERVING: These are quintessential cookies-and-milk cookies.

STORING: The cookies can be kept in a cookie jar or sealed container for about 4 days or wrapped airtight and frozen for up to 2 months.

|   |   |
|---|---|
| 2 cups all-purpose flour | ⅔ cup (packed) light brown sugar |
| 1 teaspoon salt (1¼ teaspoons if you really like salt) | 2 teaspoons pure vanilla extract |
| | 2 large eggs |
| ¾ teaspoon baking soda | 12 ounces bittersweet chocolate, chopped |
| 2 sticks (8 ounces) unsalted butter, at room temperature | into chips, or 2 cups store-bought chocolate chips or chunks |
| 1 cup sugar | 1 cup finely chopped walnuts or pecans |

GETTING READY: Center a rack in the oven and preheat the oven to 375 degrees F. Line two baking sheets with parchment or silicone mats.

Whisk together the flour, salt and baking soda.

Working with a stand mixer, preferably fitted with a paddle attachment, or with a hand mixer in a large bowl, beat the butter on medium speed for about 1 minute, until smooth. Add the sugars and beat for another 2 minutes or so, until well blended. Beat in the vanilla. Add the eggs one at a time, beating for 1 minute after each egg goes in. Reduce the mixer speed to low and add the dry ingredients in 3 portions, mixing only until each addition is incorporated. On low speed, or by hand with a rubber spatula, mix in the chocolate and nuts. (The dough can be covered and refrigerated for up to 3 days or frozen. If you'd like, you can freeze rounded tablespoonfuls of dough, ready for baking. Freeze the mounds on a lined baking sheet, then bag them when they're solid. There's no need to defrost the dough before baking—just add another minute or two to the baking time.)

Spoon the dough by slightly rounded tablespoonfuls onto the baking sheets, leaving about 2 inches between spoonfuls.

Bake the cookies—one sheet at a time and rotating the sheet at the midway point—for 10 to 12 minutes, or until they are brown at the edges and golden in the center; they may still be a little soft in the middle, and that's just fine. Pull the sheet from the oven and allow the cookies to rest for 1 minute, then carefully, using a wide metal spatula, transfer them to racks to cool to room temperature.

Repeat with the remainder of the dough, cooling the baking sheets between batches.

## Playing Around

Variations on the basic recipe are both fun and delicious. Try the following, then play around with your own favorite combinations.

COCOA CHOCOLATE CHIP COOKIES: Use 1¼ cups all-purpose flour and ¾ cup unsweetened cocoa powder.

ESPRESSO CHOCOLATE CHIP COOKIES: Add 1½ tablespoons instant espresso powder after you add the vanilla extract.

PEANUT BUTTER CHOCOLATE CHIP COOKIES: Use 1½ sticks (12 tablespoons) unsalted butter and ½ cup peanut butter (you can use chunky or smooth, but it's best not to use natural peanut butter, which will not give you the right texture). Beat them together before adding the sugars. Use salted peanuts instead of walnuts or pecans.

COCONUT CHOCOLATE CHIP COOKIES: Add 1½ cups sweetened shredded coconut, toasted or not, to the dough when you add the chocolate chips and nuts. Why not go all the way and add some raisins or bits of dried apricots too?

## Of Chips and Chops

FOR MOST of my baking life, I depended on chocolate chips and morsels, mini and standard-size, for my cookies. It never occurred to me that I could use anything else. Why would they be called chocolate chip cookies if they didn't have chocolate chips?

Now, however, packaged chips have become my fallback chocolate; I prefer fine-quality bar or block chocolate, which I chop as needed.

Commercially packaged chips (my favorite brand is Guittard's Double Chocolate Chips) are undeniably convenient, melting quickly and easily and keeping their appealing shape when baked. But what they save in convenience, they often lose in flavor and texture.

Unfortunately, the chocolate that is used in big-name supermarket chocolate chips is not of premium quality. Chip chocolate, for the most part, doesn't come from the choicest cacao beans and, when the beans are processed, the chips end up with a very low percentage of cacao.

That's why I chop my own chips and chunks, and I urge you to do the same whenever you're not pressed for time.

# CHOCOLATE CHUNKERS

**THESE FABULOUS**—I mean truly fabulous—cookies are based on the ones I made when I worked at the long-gone Soho Charcuterie and those I made at the still-going-strong Sarabeth's. At the Charcuterie, the cookies were called Chocolate Gobs, and at Sarabeth's, where they continue to be best sellers, they're called Chocolate Chubs. Both of those versions, as well as these, are grandchildren of Maida Heatter's great Mulattoes (in *Maida Heatter's Book of Great Desserts*). They're big, gooey, exceedingly chocolaty—thanks to the unsweetened, bittersweet and milk chocolate as well as cocoa powder in the dough—and exceedingly chunky—thanks to the two different kinds of chopped chocolate pieces, raisins and nuts. Despite their heft, they're serially snackable. You'll never eat just one at a sitting.

A note on the chunks: these cookies are very good made with store-bought chocolate chips, but they are stupendous made with hand-chopped excellent-quality chocolate. Because I think the cookies are worth the time, effort and expense of using really good chocolate for both the dough and the mix-ins, I pull out my best bittersweet chocolate and melt some for the dough, then chop some into generous chunks to stir in right before baking. I also use hand-chopped good-quality milk or white chocolate. Because some hand-chopped pieces will be big and some small, and because some will melt more than others, you'll have a different chocolate treat with each bite.

**MAKES ABOUT 24 COOKIES**

**SERVING:** Serve these with cold milk or hot espresso.

**STORING:** These cookies will keep (I didn't say "stay") in a cookie jar or container for about 4 days. They can be wrapped airtight and frozen for up to 2 months; defrost in their wrapper.

*Playing Around*

THIS is the kind of cookie that's delicious folded into store-bought ice cream or churned into your own-made ice cream. Try breaking up a few cookies and churning them into Cinnamon Ice Cream (page 429).

| | |
|---|---|
| ⅓ cup all-purpose flour | 1 teaspoon pure vanilla extract |
| ¼ cup unsweetened cocoa powder | 6 ounces semisweet chocolate, chopped into chunks, or 1 cup store-bought |
| ½ teaspoon salt | chocolate chips or chunks |
| ¼ teaspoon baking powder | 6 ounces premium-quality milk or white |
| 3 tablespoons unsalted butter, cut into 3 pieces | chocolate, chopped into chunks, or 1 cup store-bought chocolate chips or |
| 6 ounces bittersweet chocolate, coarsely chopped | chunks |
| 1 ounce unsweetened chocolate, coarsely chopped | 1½ cups coarsely chopped nuts, preferably salted peanuts or toasted pecans |
| 2 large eggs, at room temperature | 1 cup moist, plump raisins (dark or golden) or finely chopped moist, |
| ⅔ cup sugar | plump dried apricots |

GETTING READY: Center a rack in the oven and preheat the oven to 350 degrees F. Line two baking sheets with parchment or silicone mats.

Sift together the flour, cocoa, salt and baking powder.

Set a heatproof bowl over a saucepan of simmering water. Add the butter, bittersweet chocolate and unsweetened chocolate and heat, stirring occasionally, just until melted—the chocolate and butter should be smooth and shiny but not so hot that the butter separates. Remove the bowl from the heat and set it on the counter to cool.

Working with a stand mixer, preferably fitted with a paddle attachment, or

with a hand mixer in a large bowl, beat the eggs and sugar together on medium-high speed for about 2 minutes, until they are pale and foamy. Beat in the vanilla extract, then scrape down the bowl. Reduce the mixer speed to low and add the melted butter and chocolate, mixing only until incorporated. With a rubber spatula, scrape down the bowl, then, on low speed, add the dry ingredients. Mix just until the dry ingredients disappear into the dough, which will be thick, smooth and shiny. Scrape down the bowl and, using the rubber spatula, mix in the semi-sweet and milk (or white) chocolate chunks, nuts and raisins—you'll have more crunchies than dough at this point. (The dough can be wrapped in plastic and kept refrigerated for up to 3 days.)

Drop the dough by generously heaping tablespoonfuls onto the baking sheets, leaving about an inch of space between the mounds of dough.

Bake the cookies one sheet at a time for 10 to 12 minutes. The tops of the cookies will look a little dry but the interiors should still be soft. Remove the baking sheet and carefully, using a broad metal spatula, lift the cookies onto a cooling rack to cool to room temperature.

Repeat with the remaining dough, baking only one sheet of cookies at a time and making sure to cool the baking sheets between batches.

If, when the cookies are cooled, the chocolate is still gooey and you'd like it to be a bit firmer, just pop the cookies into the fridge for about 10 minutes.

# CHUNKY PEANUT BUTTER AND OATMEAL CHOCOLATE CHIPSTERS

**THESE ARE** really three great cookies rolled into one. They're chubby, crispy, chunky and crackly topped, perfect for dunking into a big glass of milk, dipping into a bowl of ice cream or keeping company with coffee and super for school bags, picnic baskets and kitchen-counter cookie jars. The oats and chocolate chips make the cookies plenty crunchy, but if you're like me and think tons of crunch is only just enough, you'll opt for a peanut butter that's studded with nuts. (I use Skippy Super Chunk.)

MAKES ABOUT 60 COOKIES

**SERVING:** I can't remember when I actually served these. They're more often plucked from a cookie jar than picked from a platter.

**STORING:** Wrapped airtight or piled into a cookie jar, the cookies will keep at room temperature for about 4 days. Wrapped and frozen, they'll be good for 2 months.

3 cups old-fashioned oats

1 cup all-purpose flour

1 teaspoon baking soda

2 teaspoons ground cinnamon

¼ teaspoon freshly grated nutmeg

¼ teaspoon salt

2 sticks (8 ounces) unsalted butter, at room temperature

1 cup peanut butter—chunky (my choice) or smooth (but not natural)

1 cup sugar

1 cup (packed) light brown sugar

2 large eggs

1 teaspoon pure vanilla extract

9 ounces bittersweet chocolate, chopped into chunks, or 1½ cups store-bought chocolate chips or chunks

## Playing Around

You can substitute soft, moist raisins for the chocolate chunks or just stir in some raisins along with them. If you're really looking for crunch, toss in chopped peanuts too (salted or not). With or without the chocolate chunks, raisins and nuts, these cookies are great with ice cream or around ice cream—think about them the next time you want a chipwich-ish ice cream sandwich.

**GETTING READY:** Position the racks to divide the oven into thirds and preheat the oven to 350 degrees F. Line two baking sheets with parchment or silicone mats.

Whisk together the oats, flour, baking soda, spices and salt.

Working with a stand mixer, preferably fitted with a paddle attachment, or with a hand mixer in a large bowl, beat the butter, peanut butter, sugar and brown sugar on medium speed until smooth and creamy. Add the eggs one at a time, beating for 1 minute after each addition, then beat in the vanilla. Reduce the mixer speed to low and slowly add the dry ingredients, beating only until blended. Mix in the chips. If you have the time, cover and chill the dough for about 2 hours, or for up to 1 day. (Chilling the dough will give you more evenly shaped cookies.)

If the dough is not chilled, drop rounded tablespoonfuls 2 inches apart onto the baking sheets. If the dough is chilled, scoop up rounded tablespoons, roll the balls between your palms and place them 2 inches apart on the sheets. Press the chilled balls gently with the heel of your hand until they are about ½ inch thick.

Bake for 13 to 15 minutes, rotating the sheets from top to bottom and front to back after 7 minutes. The cookies should be golden and just firm around the edges. Lift the cookies onto cooling racks with a wide metal spatula—they'll firm as they cool.

Repeat with the remaining dough, cooling the baking sheets between batches.

I ORIGINALLY named these cookies for their midnight-dark color and their unevenly crackled tops, but many batches later, I've realized that the name describes something else about these sweets—the hour at which you're apt to crave them. And with their double dose of chocolate, their mixture of crunch and chew and their hint of spice, they're the kind of cookies you eat, enjoy and walk away from, only to turn around and come back for more—at lunch, in the afternoon or around midnight.

MAKES ABOUT 50 COOKIES

SERVING: While my son likes to dunk these in milk, I like them with espresso or ice cream.

STORING: Wrapped airtight, the cookies can be kept for about 5 days at room temperature or frozen for up to 2 months.

- 1 stick plus 2 tablespoons (10 tablespoons) unsalted butter, cut into 10 pieces
- 1¼ cups (packed) light brown sugar
- 10 ounces bittersweet chocolate, coarsely chopped
- 2½ cups all-purpose flour
- ½ cup unsweetened cocoa powder
- 1 teaspoon baking soda
- ½ teaspoon salt
- ¼ teaspoon ground cinnamon
- ⅛ teaspoon ground cloves
- 2 large eggs

Put the butter, sugar and chocolate, in that order, into a 2-quart saucepan. Set the pan over low heat and warm the ingredients, stirring occasionally, until melted and smooth. Scrape into the bowl of a stand mixer or another large bowl.

Sift together the flour, cocoa, baking soda, salt, cinnamon and cloves.

Working with the stand mixer, preferably fitted with a paddle attachment, or with a hand mixer on low speed, add the eggs to the chocolate mixture one at a time, beating until they are well blended into the chocolate. With the mixer still on low, add the dry ingredients, mixing just until the dough is smooth and shiny; it will clean the sides of the bowl and form a ball. Turn the dough out onto a work surface and divide it in half. Wrap each piece in plastic wrap and chill for at least 1 hour, or for up to 3 days. (If the dough is solid, leave it on the counter for 30 minutes before proceeding.)

GETTING READY TO BAKE: Position the racks to divide the oven into thirds and preheat the oven to 350 degrees F. Line two baking sheets with parchment or silicone mats.

Working with 1 tablespoon of dough at a time, roll the dough between your palms into firm, shiny balls (if the dough breaks as you work, squeeze and knead it a bit, then reroll it between your palms) and place about 1 inch apart on the baking sheets. Lightly press each one down a tad with your fingertips.

Bake the cookies for 10 to 12 minutes, rotating the baking sheets from top to bottom and front to back at the midway point. The cookies should be delicately firm and crackled across the top. (It's better to under- than overbake.) Remove the sheets from the oven and let the cookies rest on the sheets for 2 minutes, then, using a wide metal spatula, gently transfer the cookies to a rack. Cool to room temperature.

Repeat with the remaining dough, cooling the baking sheets between batches.

*Playing Around*

CHOCOLATE GINGERBREAD CRACKLES: Add ¼ teaspoon ground ginger and a pinch each of ground allspice and coriander with the cinnamon and cloves.

CHOCO-GINGER CRACKLES: Replace the cinnamon and cloves with ¼ teaspoon ground ginger and, after the dough has come together, stir in 2 tablespoons very finely chopped stem ginger (ginger in syrup—available in Asian markets).

# CHOCOLATE OATMEAL DROPS

**THESE HAVE** the look and shape of chocolate-chocolate chip cookies, but not the usual taste or texture. They are deeply and unswervingly chocolaty—closer to the chocolatiness of a brownie than of a cookie. Then there's the texture—a teensy bit crisp at the surface and oatmeal-and-brown-sugar chewy through and through.

MAKES ABOUT 50 COOKIES

SERVING: Excellent with milk, these are also good with coffee.

STORING: Packed in the cookie jar, these will keep for 2 to 3 days; packed in the freezer, they can be kept for up to 2 months.

| | |
|---|---|
| 1½ cups all-purpose flour | 1 tablespoon water |
| ½ cup unsweetened cocoa powder | 1½ cups (packed) light brown sugar |
| ½ teaspoon baking soda | 9 ounces bittersweet chocolate, coarsely chopped |
| ½ teaspoon salt | |
| ½ teaspoon ground cinnamon | 2 large eggs |
| 2 sticks (8 ounces) unsalted butter, cut into 16 pieces | 1½ cups old-fashioned oats |

GETTING READY: Position the racks to divide the oven into thirds and preheat the oven to 350 degrees F. Line two baking sheets with parchment or silicone mats.

Sift together the flour, cocoa, baking soda, salt and cinnamon.

Set a heatproof bowl over a saucepan of simmering water. Put the butter in the bowl and sprinkle over the 1 tablespoon water, then add the brown sugar, followed by the chocolate. Stir occasionally until everything is just melted. Don't let the ingredients get so hot that the butter separates from the sugar and chocolate, and don't be concerned if the mixture looks grainy.

Remove from the heat and whisk in the eggs one at a time; the mixture will look shiny. Whisk in the dry ingredients, stirring only until they disappear into the dough. Stir in the oats. Drop the dough by tablespoonfuls onto the baking sheets, leaving 2 inches between each spoonful.

Bake for about 12 minutes, rotating the sheets from top to bottom and front to back at the midway point, until the cookies are dark around the edges and just slightly soft in the middle. Using a wide metal spatula, transfer the cookies to a rack to cool to room temperature. (If the cookies are difficult to lift from the baking sheet, wait a minute and try again.)

Repeat with the remaining dough, cooling the baking sheets between batches.

# SUGAR-TOPPED MOLASSES SPICE COOKIES

BEWARE THE innocent look of these sugar-topped crackled cookies—they are much more than they seem. Indeed, they are crisp, molasses sweet, big, round, dunkable and, as their name proclaims, spicy. But, in addition to the traditional cookie spices—ginger, cinnamon and allspice—you add a pinch of pepper. With a tiny one, you'll get just a touch of heat; grab a bigger pinch, and you'll produce enough pow to propel these from the cookie jar to the late-night-snack box.

SERVING: These are munchable right out of the cookie jar, but I like to counter the heat of the cookies with the chill of some coffee ice cream—the combo is inspired.

STORING: The cookies will keep for at least 1 week in the cookie jar. Wrapped airtight, they can be frozen for up to 2 months.

2⅓ cups all-purpose flour
2 teaspoons baking soda
½ teaspoon salt
2 teaspoons ground ginger
½ teaspoon ground cinnamon
¼ teaspoon ground allspice
Pinch (small or not so small) of cracked or coarsely ground black pepper

1½ sticks (12 tablespoons) unsalted butter, at room temperature
1 cup (packed) light brown sugar
½ cup molasses (not blackstrap)
1 large egg

About ½ cup sugar, for rolling

Whisk together the flour, baking soda, salt, ginger, cinnamon, allspice and pepper.

Working with a stand mixer, preferably fitted with a paddle attachment, or with a hand mixer in a large bowl, beat the butter on medium speed until smooth and creamy. Add the brown sugar and molasses and beat for 2 minutes or so to blend, scraping down the sides of the bowl as needed. Add the egg and beat for 1 minute more. Reduce the mixer speed to low and add the dry ingredients, mixing until the flour and spices disappear. If some flour remains in the bottom of the bowl, to avoid overbeating the dough, mix in the last of the dry ingredients by hand with a rubber spatula. You'll have a smooth, very soft dough.

Divide the dough in half and wrap each piece in plastic wrap. Freeze for 30 minutes, or refrigerate for at least 1 hour. (The dough can be kept refrigerated for up to 4 days.)

GETTING READY TO BAKE: Center a rack in the oven and preheat the oven to 350 degrees F. Line two baking sheets with parchment or silicone mats.

Put the sugar in a small bowl. Working with one packet of dough at a time, divide it into 12 pieces, and roll each piece into a smooth ball between your palms. One by one, roll the balls around in the bowl of sugar, then place them on one of the baking sheets. Dip the bottom of a glass into the sugar and use it to press down on the cookies until they are between ¼ and ½ inch thick.

Bake the cookies one sheet at a time for 12 to 14 minutes, or until the tops feel set to the touch. Remove the baking sheet from the oven and, if the cookies have spread and are touching, use the edge of a metal spatula to separate them while they are still hot. Transfer the cookies to a rack to cool to room temperature.

Repeat with the second batch of dough.

# PEANUT BUTTER CRISSCROSSES

**THIS RECIPE** is among the classics in my collection, turning out crisp-chewy cookies with the signature crisscrossed lines on their tummies. I make these with crunchy peanut butter, but you can use a smooth butter if that's your preference. As with most recipes, you won't get the texture you want with all-natural peanut butter. Save the stuff from the health food market for sandwiches and midnight munchies.

| | |
|---|---|
| 2½ cups all-purpose flour | 1 cup (packed) light brown sugar |
| 1 teaspoon baking soda | ¾ cup sugar |
| ½ teaspoon baking powder | 2 large eggs |
| ¼ teaspoon salt | 1½ cups chopped salted peanuts |
| Pinch of freshly grated nutmeg | |
| 2 sticks (8 ounces) unsalted butter, at room temperature | About ½ cup sugar, for rolling |
| 1 cup peanut butter—crunchy or smooth (not natural) | |

**GETTING READY:** Position the racks to divide the oven into thirds and preheat the oven to 350 degrees F. Line two baking sheets with parchment or silicone mats.

Whisk together the flour, baking soda, baking powder, salt and nutmeg.

Working with a stand mixer, preferably fitted with a paddle attachment, or with a hand mixer in a large bowl, beat the butter on medium speed for a minute or two, until smooth and creamy. Add the peanut butter and beat for another minute. Add the sugars and beat for 3 minutes more. Add the eggs one at a time, beating for 1 minute after each addition. Scrape down the sides and bottom of the bowl and, on low speed, add the dry ingredients, mixing only until they just disappear. Mix in the chopped peanuts. You'll have a soft, pliable (mushable, actually) dough.

Pour the ½ cup of sugar into a small bowl. Working with a level tablespoonful of dough for each cookie, roll the dough between your palms into balls and drop the balls, a couple at a time, into the sugar. Roll the balls around in the sugar to coat them, then place on the baking sheets, leaving 2 inches between them. Dip the tines of a fork in the sugar and press the tines against each ball first in one direction and then in a perpendicular direction—you should have a flattened round of dough with crisscross indentations.

Bake for about 12 minutes, rotating the sheets from top to bottom and front to back at the midway point. When done, the cookies will be lightly colored and still a little soft. Let the cookies sit on the sheets for a minute before transferring them to cooling racks with a wide metal spatula. Cool to room temperature.

Repeat with the remaining dough, making sure to cool the baking sheets between batches.

**MAKES ABOUT 40 COOKIES**

**SERVING:** Chez moi, these aren't served, they're just piled in the cookie jar, from whence they disappear.

**STORING:** Wrapped well or in a cookie jar, these will keep for about 5 days at room temperature; frozen, they're good for up to 2 months.

*Playing Around*

**COCOA–PEANUT BUTTER CRISSCROSSES:** For a chocolate version, reduce the flour to 2 cups and sift ½ cup unsweetened cocoa powder into the dry ingredients. Use 1 cup chopped salted peanuts and add ⅓ cup finely chopped bittersweet chocolate (or chocolate chips, preferably minis) along with the nuts.

# BUTTERY JAM COOKIES

A CROSS between sturdy cookie jar cookies and more delicate side-of-the-saucer sweets, these chunky jam-laced cookies are surprisingly flaky, like the best biscuits. The thick jam—I like apricot jam, but any marmalade would be good, as would a not-thin raspberry or cherry jam or preserves—gives them a kind of stickiness that I find irresistible. The touch of ginger in the dough acts more like a butter-and-jam booster than another flavor. If you'd like to get a bigger hit from the ginger, try folding in tiny cubes of preserved (stem) or crystallized ginger.

MAKES ABOUT 45 COOKIES

SERVING: These accompany afternoon tea perfectly.

STORING: The cookies can be kept in a sealed container for about 4 days or wrapped airtight and frozen for up to 2 months.

2 cups all-purpose flour

1 teaspoon baking powder

½ teaspoon ground ginger

¼ teaspoon salt

1 stick (8 tablespoons) unsalted
    butter, at room temperature

⅔ cup sugar

1 large egg

2 tablespoons milk

½ teaspoon pure vanilla extract

¼ cup apricot jam (or your flavor of
    choice)

GETTING READY: Position the racks to divide the oven into thirds and preheat the oven to 375 degrees F. Line two baking sheets with parchment or silicone mats.

Whisk together the flour, baking powder, ginger and salt.

Working with a stand mixer, preferably fitted with a paddle attachment, or with a hand mixer in a large bowl, beat the butter on medium speed until creamy and smooth. Add the sugar and beat for a minute. Add the egg and beat for 2 minutes more. The mixture will be satiny. Add the milk and vanilla and beat just to combine. Don't be concerned if the mixture looks curdled, it will even out shortly. Reduce the mixer speed to low, add the jam and beat for 1 minute more. With the mixer still on low, add the dry ingredients and mix only until they are incorporated. You'll have a very thick dough.

Spoon the dough by rounded teaspoonfuls onto the baking sheets, leaving about an inch between mounds.

Bake the cookies for 10 to 12 minutes, rotating the pans from top to bottom and front to back at the midway point. The cookies will be only just firm, fairly pale and browned around the edges. Pull the sheets from the oven and allow the cookies to rest for 1 minute, then carefully transfer them to racks to cool to room temperature.

Repeat with the remainder of the dough, cooling the baking sheets between batches.

# HONEY-WHEAT COOKIES

MAKES ABOUT 36 COOKIES

IF THE mention of wheat germ makes you think of the back-to the-earth movement of the 1970s, you're on to the origin of these cookies. In fact, these are an adaptation of a recipe I pulled out of the *New York Times* and pasted in my notebook during that period. At the time, I'm sure the recipe was featured for its wholesomeness; today I make it often because it's just plain good. The cookies are soft, chewy, sweet from the wheat and tangy from the honey and lemon. They make a great mid-afternoon pick-me-up.

SERVING: With the honey and lemon in the cookies, tea is a natural go-along.

STORING: The cookies will keep at room temperature for about 3 days or wrapped air-tight in the freezer for up to 2 months.

| | |
|---|---|
| 1¾ cups all-purpose flour | 2 teaspoons grated lemon zest |
| 1 cup wheat germ | 1 stick (8 tablespoons) unsalted butter, |
| 1 teaspoon baking powder | at room temperature |
| ¼ teaspoon salt | ½ cup honey |
| ½ cup sugar | 1 large egg |

Whisk together the flour, ½ cup of the wheat germ, the baking powder and salt.

Working in the bowl of a stand mixer or in another large bowl, rub the sugar and lemon zest together with your fingers until the sugar is moist. Add the butter and, using the paddle or whisk attachment or a hand mixer, beat on medium speed for about 2 minutes, until creamy and smooth. Add the honey and beat for another minute or two. Add the egg and beat for about 2 minutes more, until you have a smooth, light, fluffy mixture. Reduce the mixer speed to low and add the dry ingredients in 2 portions, mixing only until each addition disappears. Scrape the dough out onto a large piece of plastic wrap and wrap well. Chill the dough for at least 2 hours, or for up to 2 days.

GETTING READY TO BAKE: Center a rack in the oven and preheat the oven to 350 degrees F. Line two baking sheets with parchment or silicone mats.

Put the remaining ½ cup wheat germ into a bowl. Remove the chilled dough from the fridge and, working with a spoonful of it at a time, roll the dough between your palms into 1-inch balls. Drop each ball into the wheat germ and turn to coat, then place the balls on one of the baking sheets, leaving about 1 inch of space between them (these don't spread much). Use your palm or the bottom of a glass to gently flatten each cookie.

Bake the cookies one sheet at a time, for 10 to 12 minutes, or until they are just firm to the touch. Transfer the cookies to a rack to cool to room temperature.

Repeat with the remaining dough.

MAKES ABOUT 40 COOKIES

IT WOULD be hard to find a more after-schoolish cookie than this one. It's chunky, bumpy, both chewy and crunchy and packed with little surprises—raisins, peanuts, almonds, coconut and, of course, granola. These are great with milk and even good spread with peanut butter or nibbled alongside yogurt. I created them with my son in mind, thinking he and his friends would be happy to come home to a jar crammed to the top with these craggy cookies, but my husband is their biggest fan.

These are best made with granola that doesn't include dried fruit. Often the fruit in packaged granola cereals is too dry and, because it won't soften up in the batter, you can end up with cookies that are hard and dry.

SERVING: Slip these into a lunch box or just pile them onto a plate and have cold milk at hand.

STORING: In a covered cookie jar, these will be fine for about 3 days. If you want to keep them longer, wrap them airtight and freeze them for up to 2 months.

3 cups granola without fruit
¾ cup moist, plump raisins (dark or golden)
½ cup salted peanuts
½ cup slivered almonds
½ cup sweetened shredded coconut
⅓ cup wheat germ
1¾ sticks (14 tablespoons) unsalted butter, at room temperature
¾ cup (packed) light brown sugar
¼ cup sugar
1 large egg
¼ teaspoon salt
1 cup all-purpose flour

GETTING READY: Position the racks to divide the oven into thirds and preheat the oven to 375 degrees F. Line two baking sheets with parchment or silicone mats.

Put the granola in a large bowl and break up any clumps with your fingers. Add the raisins, peanuts, almonds, coconut and wheat germ and mix together.

Working with a stand mixer, preferably fitted with a paddle attachment, or with a hand mixer in a large bowl, beat the butter at medium speed until smooth, about 2 minutes. Add the sugars and beat for another 3 minutes, or until creamy. Add the egg and salt and beat until well blended. Reduce the mixer speed to low and add the flour, mixing only until it is incorporated, then steadily add the granola and fruit. Stop the mixer when most of the granola mix is blended into the batter and finish the job with a sturdy rubber spatula, making sure to get up any bits of dry ingredients left in the bottom of the bowl.

Scoop out rounded tablespoonfuls of dough, pack the scoops between your palms and arrange the mounds on the baking sheets, leaving about 1½ inches between them. Flatten the mounds lightly with your fingertips.

Bake for 10 to 12 minutes, rotating the sheets from top to bottom and front to back at the midway point. The cookies should be golden brown but not firm. Allow them to rest on the sheets for 1 to 2 minutes before transferring them to racks to cool to room temperature.

Repeat with the remaining dough, cooling the baking sheets between batches.

# CHOCOLATE MALTED WHOPPER DROPS

MAKES ABOUT 30 COOKIES

**IF YOU'RE** thinking that these sound like something right out of Willy Wonka's chocolate factory, you're right. They are almost equal parts candy and cookie. The candy part is chunks of chocolate-covered malted milk balls and big chips of chocolate, while the cocoa cookies are soft and lightly flavored with malted milk powder. If Mr. Wonka had a soda fountain, I'd bet these cookies would be on his menu.

**SERVING:** These are wonderful with milk, chocolate milk or malteds, great with ice cream and just as great with strong dark coffee.

**STORING:** These will keep for about 4 days packed in a tin, cookie jar or plastic bags; wrapped airtight, they'll keep for up to 2 months in the freezer.

1¾ cups all-purpose flour

1 cup malted milk powder (or Ovaltine, regular or chocolate-flavored)

¼ cup unsweetened cocoa powder

1½ teaspoons baking powder

¼ teaspoon salt

1 stick plus 3 tablespoons (11 tablespoons) unsalted butter, at room temperature

⅔ cup sugar

2 large eggs

1 teaspoon pure vanilla extract

¼ cup whole milk

2 cups (6 ounces) chocolate-covered malted milk balls (I use Whoppers), coarsely chopped

6 ounces bittersweet chocolate, coarsely chopped, or 1 cup store-bought chocolate chips or chunks

**GETTING READY:** Position the racks to divide the oven into thirds and line two baking sheets with parchment or silicone mats.

Sift together the flour, malted milk powder, cocoa, baking powder and salt.

Working with a stand mixer, preferably fitted with a paddle attachment, or with a hand mixer in a large bowl, beat the butter and sugar together on medium speed for about 3 minutes, until very smooth. Add the eggs one at a time, beating for 1 minute after each addition. Beat in the vanilla; don't be concerned if the mixture looks curdled—it will even out when the dry ingredients are added. Reduce the mixer speed to low and add half the dry ingredients, mixing just until they disappear into the batter. Mix in the milk, then the remaining dry ingredients, mixing only until they are incorporated. The batter will look more like fudge frosting than cookie dough—and that's fine. With the mixer on low, or by hand with a rubber spatula, mix in the malted milk balls and chopped chocolate.

Drop the dough by rounded tablespoonfuls onto the sheets, leaving about 2 inches of space between spoonfuls. Bake for 11 to 13 minutes, rotating the sheets from top to bottom and front to back after 6 minutes. When done, the cookies will be puffed and set but slightly soft to the touch. Let the cookies rest for 2 minutes before using a wide metal spatula to transfer them to racks to cool to room temperature.

Repeat with the remaining dough, cooling the baking sheets between batches.

# CHOCKABLOCK COOKIES

**THIS RECIPE** turns out big, fat cookies loaded—okay, overloaded—with dried fruits, chopped nuts, coconut, oats and chocolate. With so many add-ins, there's not a lot of cookie holding the fruits and nuts together, but what there is is soft, chewy and packed with flavor, because the dough is sweetened with dark, syrupy molasses. But, as full-flavored as these cookies are, they're not of the have-one-and-walk-away variety, so I'd advise you to allow yourself one for each hand.

MAKES ABOUT 30 COOKIES

**SERVING:** These cookies are equally good with milk or coffee.

**STORING:** These will keep for about 4 days in the cookie jar or for up to 2 months wrapped airtight in the freezer.

1½ cups all-purpose flour
¾ teaspoon baking powder
½ teaspoon baking soda
¼ teaspoon salt
½ stick (4 tablespoons) unsalted butter, at room temperature
¼ cup solid vegetable shortening
½ cup sugar
½ cup molasses (not blackstrap)
2 large eggs
1½ cups old-fashioned oats

1 cup coarsely chopped nuts (walnuts, pecans or peanuts are all good)
1 cup coarsely chopped dried fruit (such as apricots, prunes or figs) or 1 cup moist, plump raisins (dark or golden), or a mixture of dried fruit and raisins
12 ounces bittersweet chocolate, coarsely chopped, or 2 cups store-bought chocolate chips or chunks
½ cup sweetened shredded coconut

GETTING READY: Position the racks to divide the oven into thirds and preheat the oven to 325 degrees F. Line two baking sheets with parchment or silicone mats.

Whisk together the flour, baking powder, baking soda and salt.

Working with a stand mixer, preferably fitted with a paddle attachment, or with a hand mixer in a large bowl, beat the butter and shortening together at medium speed until very smooth, about 2 minutes. Add the sugar and beat for another 2 minutes. Pour in the molasses and beat for 1 minute more. Add the eggs one at a time, beating for 1 minute after each addition. Reduce the mixer speed to low and mix in the oats, then add the dry ingredients, mixing only until they disappear into the dough. Toss in the nuts, fruit, chocolate and coconut and turn the mixer on and off quickly a few times to incorporate. Alternatively, you can stir them into the dough with a sturdy rubber spatula. (The dough can be wrapped well and kept chilled for up to 2 days. If you'd like, you can measure out the dough onto a baking sheet, freeze until firm, then put the mounds of dough in a bag and freeze for up to 2 months; bake directly from the freezer, adding a few minutes to the baking time.)

I like to use an ice cream scoop with a 2-tablespoon capacity to divvy up the dough, but you can measure it out by rounded tablespoonfuls. Place the mounds of dough on the baking sheets, leaving about 1½ inches between the mounds.

Bake for 15 to 18 minutes, rotating the pans from top to bottom and front to back at the midway point, until the cookies are golden and just about set. Remove the baking sheets to cooling racks and let the cookies rest on the sheets for about 5 minutes before transferring them to racks to cool to room temperature.

# BROWNIES, BLONDIES, WHITIES AND OTHER BAR COOKIES

BAR COOKIES ARE A BAKER'S BLESSING—you get bunches of cookies for a minimum of work. Unlike cookies that are individually shaped, bar cookies are baked in a pan, the way you'd bake a cake, and shaped simply by cutting.

Without a doubt, the most popular bar cookies are brownies. I'm non-partisan: I love both the gooey, fudgy kind and the chewy, cakey kind, so I've given you recipes for brownies of just about every variety, from those made with one type of chocolate to those made with five. The fun extends to blondies, bar cookies with nuts, coconut, butterscotch drops and chocolate chips; whities—elegant meringue-topped white chocolate brownies studded with raspberries; and a few multistoried bars, like Snickery Squares, layered with dulce de leche and candied peanuts, and Caramel Crunch Bars, with a brown-sugar-shortbread base and a chocolate-toffee top.

For the majority of the recipes, particularly those for the moistest, fudgi-est brownies or the most delicate bar cookies, you should line the pan with foil and butter the foil. The liner gives you an easy way to remove the cookie block from the pan. Once it's removed, you can cut it into bars without fear of nicking and scratching your favorite baking pan.

The most efficient way to line the pan is to tear off a large piece of aluminum foil, turn the pan over, mold the foil against the pan and square the corners (think hospital corners on a bed), then lift the foil up and carefully slip it into the pan. It won't fit perfectly—it never does—but you can quickly press it into shape. Once it's coaxed into place, but-ter the foil, a job best done with a pastry brush slathered with softened butter.

# CLASSIC BROWNIES

**FUDGY BUT** not gooey, intensely chocolaty, dry on top and melty in the middle, these brownies are just about classic. I say "just about" because I make them with a mix of bittersweet and unsweetened chocolate (in true classics, unsweetened chocolate solos) and I like to stir an untraditional half teaspoon of espresso powder into the batter. When the brownies are baked, the coffee flavor is almost imperceptible, but its presence gives the chocolate flavor a turbocharge.

| | |
|---|---|
| 5 tablespoons unsalted butter, cut into 5 pieces | 2 large eggs |
| | 1 teaspoon pure vanilla extract |
| 4 ounces bittersweet chocolate, coarsely chopped | ½ teaspoon instant espresso powder (optional, but really good) |
| 2 ounces unsweetened chocolate, coarsely chopped | ¼–½ teaspoon salt (according to taste) |
| | ⅓ cup all-purpose flour |
| ¾ cup sugar | 1 cup chopped walnuts |

GETTING READY: Center a rack in the oven and preheat the oven to 325 degrees F. Line an 8-inch square baking pan with foil, butter the foil and place the pan on a baking sheet.

Set a heatproof bowl over a saucepan of simmering water. Put the butter in the bowl, top with the chopped chocolates and stir occasionally until the ingredients are just melted—you don't want them to get so hot that the butter separates. Remove the bowl from the pan of water.

With a whisk, stir in the sugar. Don't be concerned when your smooth mixture turns grainy. One by one, whisk in the eggs. Add the vanilla and give the ingredients a vigorous whisking before gently stirring in the espresso, if you're using it, salt and flour; stir only until incorporated. Switch to a rubber spatula and fold in the chopped walnuts.

Scrape the batter into the pan and smooth the top with the spatula.

Bake the brownies for 30 to 33 minutes, or until the top is dull and a thin knife inserted into the center comes out clean. Transfer the pan to a rack and cool the brownies to room temperature.

When the brownies are completely cool, turn out onto a rack, peel away the foil and invert onto a cutting board. Cut into 16 squares, each a scant 2 inches on a side.

MAKES 16 BROWNIES

SERVING: Like all great brownies, these are good eaten out of hand without a bit of embellishment or topped off with whipped or ice cream (coffee ice cream is really good with these), offered either way at room temperature or a bit chilled.

STORING: These are best served within 2 days of baking. If you're going to keep them at room temperature, just cut what you need and keep the remainder wrapped tightly in plastic wrap. To freeze for up to 2 months, wrap the brownies airtight.

# BITTERSWEET BROWNIES

**IF YOU** are a true brownie fan, I can't imagine that you won't fall for this slim (only about ³/₄ inch high), totally bittersweet version, with its very thin crackly crust and its very moist, fudgy-all-the-way-to-the-edges interior, which could almost double as a dense mousse. As with many chocolate desserts, the goodness of this one depends on the excellence of the chocolate. Use a premium-quality bittersweet chocolate—it makes all the difference. (I like to make these with Valrhona Manjari, a chocolate with a subtle spiciness reminiscent of the nuances you find in good wine.)

2 sticks (8 ounces) unsalted butter,
    cut into 16 pieces

9 ounces bittersweet chocolate,
    coarsely chopped

1½ cups sugar

4 large eggs

2 teaspoons pure vanilla extract

1 tablespoon instant espresso powder
    (optional)

½ teaspoon salt

1 cup all-purpose flour

MAKES 32 BROWNIES

**SERVING:** Serve plain, or with whipped cream, crème fraîche (page 459) or ice cream, sprinkled with confectioners' sugar or glazed with ganache (page 276).

**STORING:** These are best served within 2 days of baking. If you're going to keep them at room temperature, just cut what you need and keep the remainder wrapped tightly in plastic wrap. To freeze for up to 2 months, wrap the brownies airtight.

**GETTING READY:** Center a rack in the oven and preheat the oven to 325 degrees F. Line a 9-x-13-inch baking pan with foil, butter the foil and place the pan on a baking sheet.

Set a heatproof bowl over a saucepan of simmering water. Put the butter in the bowl, top with the chopped chocolate and stir occasionally until the ingredients are just melted—you don't want them to get so hot that the butter separates. Remove the bowl from the pan of water.

With a whisk, stir in the sugar. The mixture might get grainy, but it will even out. Whisk in the eggs one by one, then add the vanilla and whisk enthusiastically to smooth the batter. Finally, gently whisk in the espresso powder, if you're using it, salt and flour, stirring only until incorporated. Scrape the batter into the pan and smooth the top with a rubber spatula.

Bake the brownies for just 20 to 22 minutes, or until the top is dull and a thin knife inserted into the center comes out clean. Transfer the pan to a rack and cool the brownies to room temperature.

When they are completely cool, turn out onto a rack, peel away the foil and invert onto a cutting board. Cut into 32 slender rectangles, each roughly 2¼ x 1½ inches.

# RICK KATZ'S BROWNIES FOR JULIA

MAKES 18 BROWNIES

SERVING: Because these are so intensely chocolaty, they are particularly good with espresso.

STORING: These will keep for 2 days at room temperature—cut what you need and keep the remainder covered tightly with plastic wrap. To freeze for up to 2 months, wrap the brownies airtight.

IN 1995, when I was working with Julia Child filming the PBS series *Baking with Julia* and writing the companion book, Boston-based pastry chef Rick Katz was running the prep kitchen in Julia's basement. Working between the washing machine and the dryer, Rick was in charge of getting the recipes of each of the twenty-six visiting chefs ready for their close-ups. An ordinary human would have had his hands full, but superman Rick always found time to make us extra little goodies, among them these very dark, very fudgy brownies. The way he prepares the batter is different from any other brownie recipe I know. Half of the eggs and sugar are mixed in with the chocolate, while the other half are beaten until they double in volume and are as light as a sponge. Whipping the eggs creates the surprisingly creamy, soft and definitively fudgy texture.

1 cup all-purpose flour

1 teaspoon salt

2 sticks (8 ounces) unsalted butter, cut into 16 pieces

4 ounces unsweetened chocolate, coarsely chopped

2 ounces bittersweet chocolate, coarsely chopped

2 cups sugar

1 teaspoon pure vanilla extract

4 large eggs

GETTING READY: Center a rack in the oven and preheat the oven to 350 degrees F. Put a 9-inch square baking pan (I like to use Pyrex for this) on a baking sheet.

Whisk the flour and salt together.

Set a heatproof bowl over a saucepan of gently simmering water, put the butter in the bowl and top with the chopped chocolate. Stir frequently until the ingredients are just melted—you don't want them to get so hot that the butter separates. Add 1 cup of the sugar and whisk gently just to incorporate it, then remove the bowl from the pan of water. Stir in the vanilla and transfer the warm chocolate to a large bowl.

Put the remaining 1 cup sugar into the bowl of a stand mixer or a medium bowl and, using a whisk, stir in the eggs. Switch to a rubber spatula and, little by little, add half of the sugar-egg mixture to the warm chocolate, stirring very gently but without stopping—you don't want the heat of the chocolate to cook the eggs.

With the whisk attachment or with a hand mixer, beat the remaining sugar and eggs on medium-high speed for about 3 minutes, or until they double in volume. Using the spatula and a light touch, fold the whipped eggs into the chocolate mixture, stopping just short of blending them in completely. Sprinkle the dry ingredients over the batter and delicately fold them in, working only until they disappear. Scrape the batter into the pan and smooth the top with the spatula.

Bake for 25 to 28 minutes, or until the top looks dry. Poke a thin knife into the center and take a peek: the brownies should be only just set and still pretty gooey. Transfer the pan to a rack and cool to room temperature.

The brownies are fragile and best cut in the pan. Cut eighteen 1½-x-3-inch bars.

# FRENCH CHOCOLATE BROWNIES

IF THERE were a French Academy of Culinary Correctness (and, knowing the French, there might be), their esteemed members would probably dispute the pedigree of these brownies, but I'm certain their colleagues in the Department of Immigration would grant them a French passport, because these sweets were born in Paris, created the afternoon of a casual dinner party. My thought was to play on the idea of the French chocolate "fondant," a cake known for its chocolatiness and its soft, moist texture. The rum-soaked raisins were a just-for-fun addition.

I baked the cake, cut the portions, centered them on the plates, topped each serving with some softly whipped crème fraîche and waltzed into the dining room, where I was greeted by a chorus of "Oh, brownies—*splendide*." Nicest of all, one of my guests, a Parisian pastry chef, asked for the recipe. With such an endorsement, why would I care that I'd meant my sweet to be a cake? I just called them brownies and have been happy ever since.

MAKES 16 BROWNIES

SERVING: The brownies are good just warm or at room temperature; they're even fine cold. I like these with a little something on top or alongside— good accompaniments are whipped crème fraîche (page 459) or whipped cream, ice cream or chocolate sauce (pages 463 and 464) or, dare I suggest, all three!

STORING: Wrapped well, these can be kept at room temperature for up to 3 days or frozen for up to 2 months.

½ cup all-purpose flour

⅛ teaspoon salt

⅛ teaspoon ground cinnamon

⅓ cup raisins (dark or golden)

1½ tablespoons water

1½ tablespoons dark rum

6 ounces bittersweet chocolate, finely chopped

1½ sticks (12 tablespoons) unsalted butter, cut into 12 pieces, at room temperature

3 large eggs

1 cup sugar

GETTING READY: Center a rack in the oven and preheat the oven to 300 degrees F. Line an 8-inch square baking pan with foil, butter the foil and place the pan on a baking sheet.

Whisk the flour, salt and cinnamon together.

Put the raisins in a small saucepan with the water, bring to a boil over medium heat and cook until the water almost evaporates. Add the rum and let it warm for about 30 seconds, then turn off the heat, stand back and ignite the rum with a long match. Allow the flames to die down, and set the raisins aside.

Put the chocolate in a heatproof bowl and set the bowl over a saucepan of simmering water. Stir occasionally until the chocolate melts. Remove the bowl from the saucepan and add the butter, stirring until it melts. It's important that the chocolate and butter not get very hot. However, if the butter is not melting, you can put the bowl back over the still-hot water for a minute. If you've got a couple of little bits of unmelted butter, leave them—it's better to have a few bits than to overheat the whole.

Working with a stand mixer fitted with the whisk attachment, or with a hand mixer in a large bowl, beat the eggs and sugar until thick and pale, about 2 minutes. Reduce the mixer speed and pour in the chocolate-butter mixture, mixing only until it is incorporated—you'll have a thick, creamy batter. Add the dry ingredients and mix at low speed for about 30 seconds—the dry ingredients won't be completely incorporated. Then finish folding in the dry ingredients by hand with a rubber spatula. Fold in the raisins, along with any liquid remaining in the pan. Scrape the batter into the pan.

Bake for 50 to 60 minutes, or until the top is dry and crackled and a thin knife inserted into the center comes out clean. Transfer the pan to a rack and cool to warm or room temperature.

Carefully lift the brownies out of the pan, using the foil edges as handles, and transfer to a cutting board. Cut into 16 squares, each roughly 2 inches on a side, taking care not to cut through the foil.

# CHIPSTER-TOPPED BROWNIES

**THESE BROWNIES** are topped with a layer of great chocolate chip cookie dough—two all-time favorites baked together in one delicious double-decker.

MAKES 24 BROWNIES

### FOR THE BROWNIE LAYER

- 6 ounces bittersweet chocolate, coarsely chopped
- 3 ounces unsweetened chocolate, coarsely chopped
- 2 sticks (8 ounces) unsalted butter, cut into chunks
- 1⅔ cups sugar
- 4 large eggs
- ½ teaspoon salt
- ½ teaspoon pure vanilla extract
- 1 cup all-purpose flour
- 1 cup walnuts, coarsely chopped

### FOR THE COOKIE LAYER

- 1¼ cups all-purpose flour
- ½ teaspoon baking soda
- ½ teaspoon salt
- 1½ sticks (12 tablespoons) unsalted butter, at room temperature
- ¾ cup (packed) light brown sugar
- ⅔ cup sugar
- 1 large egg
- 1 large egg yolk
- 1 teaspoon pure vanilla extract
- 6 ounces bittersweet chocolate, chopped into chips, or 1 cup store-bought chocolate chips

**SERVING:** Ice cream, whipped cream and crème fraîche are all great accompaniments, as is a generous drizzle of chocolate sauce (pages 463 and 464).

**STORING:** Wrapped well or packed in an airtight container, the bars can be kept at room temperature for 2 days or frozen for up to 2 months.

*Playing Around*

The cookie top can be varied easily by swapping peanut-butter, butterscotch or white chocolate chips for the chopped chocolate. You could even use all of them.

**GETTING READY:** Center a rack in the oven and preheat the oven to 350 degrees F. Butter a 9-x-13-inch baking pan, line it with wax or parchment paper and butter the paper. Put the pan on a baking sheet.

**TO MAKE THE BROWNIE BATTER:** Put both chocolates and the butter in a bowl set over a saucepan of simmering water. Stirring occasionally, heat just until the ingredients are melted, shiny and smooth. If the mixture gets too hot, the butter will separate from the chocolates. Remove the bowl from the heat.

Working with a stand mixer, preferably fitted with a paddle attachment, or with a hand mixer in a large bowl, beat the sugar and eggs on medium-high speed for about 2 minutes, until pale, thick and creamy. Beat in the salt and vanilla extract. Reduce the speed to low and mix in the melted chocolate and butter, mixing only until incorporated. Scrape down the sides of the bowl with a rubber spatula, then, still on low speed, add the flour, mixing only until it disappears into the batter. Using the spatula, fold in the walnuts, and scrape the batter into the prepared pan. Set aside.

**TO MAKE THE COOKIE DOUGH:** Whisk together the flour, baking soda and salt.

Working with the stand mixer in the cleaned bowl or with the hand mixer in another large bowl, beat the butter and both sugars together on medium-high speed until smooth and creamy, about 3 minutes. One at a time, add the egg and the yolk, beating for 1 minute after each addition. Beat in the vanilla. Reduce the mixer speed to low and add the dry ingredients, mixing only until they disappear into the dough. Still on low, mix in the chopped chocolate. Drop the cookie dough by spoonfuls over the brownie batter and, using a spatula and a light touch, spread it evenly over the batter.

Bake for 50 to 55 minutes, or until the cookie top is deep golden brown and firm and a thin knife inserted into the brownie layer comes out with only faint streaks of moist chocolate. Transfer the pan to a rack and cool to room temperature.

When the brownies are completely cool, carefully run a knife between the sides of the pan and the brownies, then invert them onto another rack, remove the paper and turn right side up onto a cutting board. Cut into bars about 2 inches x 1 inch. (You can cut larger bars if you're serving cookie lovers with Texas-size appetites.)

# TRIBUTE-TO-KATHARINE-HEPBURN BROWNIES

AFTER KATHARINE Hepburn died, eulogies came from every quarter, many including stories about her brownies. In an article sent to me by my friend *Bon Appétit* editor in chief Barbara Fairchild, Heather Henderson of St. Paul, Minnesota, recalled wanting to quit her studies at Bryn Mawr. Her father managed to get Miss Hepburn, a Bryn Mawr alum and a neighbor, to intervene. The famous Kate invited both the young woman and her father to her home one afternoon. At tea, Ms. Henderson got a taste of the legendary brownies as well as of the actress's views on education.

In her tribute to the actress, Ms. Henderson wrote, "I'll always be grateful to Miss Hepburn for making me stick it out at Bryn Mawr and for giving me these rules to live by: 1. Never quit; 2. Be yourself and 3. Don't put too much flour in your brownies."

This recipe is a play on the one Miss Hepburn is reported to have used. Since a quick search through my cookbooks uncovered two other brownie recipes credited to Kate, and each was different, I decided it would be fine to add my own little touches. I've kept the essence of Miss Hepburn's recipe—these are thin, soft, very chocolaty brownies made without much flour—but I've added a little cinnamon, some coffee and a quarter pound of chopped fine-quality chocolate. Since the chocolate doesn't firm up much in baking, it makes a soft, gooey brownie even softer and gooier and, to my way of thinking, even yummier. I think Miss Hepburn would approve.

MAKES 16 BROWNIES

SERVING: These are happy being served in all the typical ways—with whipped cream, ice cream or Hot Fudge Sauce (page 465) or paired with a glass of milk to allow for dunking. I think they are best at room temperature, when they are at their moistest, but they are also very good chilled.

STORING: Wrapped well, the brownies will keep for 3 days at room temperature or frozen for up to 2 months.

¼ cup all-purpose flour

½ teaspoon ground cinnamon (optional)

¼ teaspoon salt

1 stick (8 tablespoons) unsalted butter, cut into 8 pieces

½ cup unsweetened cocoa powder

2 teaspoons finely ground instant coffee

2 large eggs, preferably at room temperature

1 cup sugar

1 teaspoon pure vanilla extract

1 cup broken or chopped walnuts or pecans

4 ounces bittersweet chocolate, coarsely chopped

GETTING READY: Center a rack in the oven and preheat the oven to 325 degrees F. Butter an 8-inch square baking pan and line the bottom with parchment or wax paper. Butter the paper, dust the inside of the pan with flour and tap out the excess. Place the pan on a baking sheet.

Whisk the flour, cinnamon, if you're using it, and salt together.

Put the butter in a medium heavy-bottomed saucepan and place the pan over low heat. When the butter starts to melt, sift the cocoa over it and add the instant coffee. Continue to cook, stirring, until the butter is melted and the cocoa and coffee are blended into it. Remove from the heat and cool for about 3 minutes.

Using a whisk or a rubber spatula, beat the eggs into the saucepan one at a time. Next, stir in the sugar and vanilla (don't beat anything too vigorously—you don't want to add air to the batter), followed by the dry ingredients, nuts and chopped chocolate. Scrape the batter into the pan.

Bake for 30 minutes, at which point the brownies will still be gooey but the top will have a dry papery crust. Transfer the pan to a rack and let the brownies cool for at least 30 minutes. (You can wait longer, if you'd like.)

Turn the brownies out onto a rack, peel away the paper and invert onto a cutting board. Cool completely before cutting into 16 squares, each roughly 2 inches on a side.

# QUINTUPLE CHOCOLATE BROWNIES

**THERE'S A** little of every kind of chocolate in these sweet, more-fudgy-than-cakey brownies. Following tradition, the batter is made with unsweetened chocolate, but it's got bittersweet (or semisweet) chocolate, cocoa, milk chocolate chips and a soft white chocolate glaze too. And there are nuts—any kind you'd like, but I hope you'll try salted cashews or peanuts at least once.

MAKES 16 BROWNIES

SERVING: Serve straight up—whipped cream or ice cream is unnecessary with these. Well, a little ice cream is nice—why not?

STORING: The brownies can be put back in their baking pan, wrapped (without touching the glaze) and kept at room temperature for about 3 days or frozen—glaze and all—for up to 2 months.

### FOR THE BROWNIES

½ cup all-purpose flour

¼ cup unsweetened cocoa powder

½ teaspoon salt

1 stick (8 tablespoons) unsalted butter, cut into 8 pieces

3 ounces unsweetened chocolate, coarsely chopped

3 ounces bittersweet or semisweet chocolate, coarsely chopped

2 tablespoons strong coffee

1 cup sugar

3 large eggs

1 teaspoon pure vanilla extract

6 ounces premium-quality milk chocolate, chopped into chips, or 1 cup store-bought milk chocolate chips

1 cup chopped nuts

### FOR THE GLAZE

6 ounces premium-quality white chocolate, finely chopped, or 1 cup store-bought white chocolate chips

⅓ cup heavy cream

GETTING READY: Center a rack in the oven and preheat the oven to 325 degrees F. Line a 9-inch square baking pan with foil, butter the foil and place the pan on a baking sheet.

Sift together the flour, cocoa and salt.

TO MAKE THE BROWNIES: Set a heatproof bowl over a saucepan of simmering water and add, in the following order, the butter, the two chocolates and the coffee. Keeping the pan over low heat, warm just until the butter and chocolates are melted—you don't want the ingredients to get so hot they separate, so keep an eye on the bowl. Stir gently, and when the mixture is smooth, set it aside for 5 minutes.

Using a whisk or a rubber spatula, beat the sugar into the chocolate mixture. Don't beat too vigorously—you don't want to add air to the batter—and don't be concerned about any graininess. Next, stir in the eggs one at time, followed by the vanilla. You should have a smooth, glossy batter. If you're not already using a rubber spatula, switch to one now and gently stir in the dry ingredients, mixing only until they are incorporated. Finally, stir in the milk chocolate chips and the nuts. Scrape the batter into the pan.

Bake for about 35 minutes, or until a thin knife inserted into the center comes out streaked but not thickly coated. Transfer the pan to a cooling rack and let the brownies rest undisturbed for at least 30 minutes. (You can wait longer, if you'd like.)

Turn the brownies out onto a rack, peel away the foil and place it under another rack—it will be the drip catcher for the glaze. Invert the brownies onto the rack and let cool completely.

TO MAKE THE GLAZE: Put the white chocolate in a heatproof bowl. Bring the heavy cream to a boil and pour it over the chocolate. Wait 30 seconds, then, using a rubber spatula, gently stir until the chocolate is melted and the glaze is smooth.

Hold a long metal icing spatula in one hand and the bowl of glaze in the other. Pour the glaze onto the center of the brownies and use the spatula to nudge it evenly over the surface. Don't worry if it dribbles over the edges, you can trim the sides later (or not). Refrigerate the brownies for about 20 minutes to dry the glaze.

Cut into 16 squares, each roughly 2¼ inches on a side.

# GINGER-JAZZED BROWNIES

**IT'S GINGER**, both fresh and dried, that makes these brownies slightly hot. If you want to jazz them up a bit more, glaze the top with a shiny ganache, top each portion with a spoonful of lightly sweetened ginger whipped cream (1 teaspoon ground ginger and 1 cup heavy cream) and finish each serving with a sliver of crystallized ginger.

In order to soften the fresh ginger before mixing it into the batter, I stir a little sugar into the minced ginger and let it sit while I work on the rest of the recipe. If you'd like, you can mince and sugar the ginger the day before.

MAKES 16 BROWNIES

¾ cup all-purpose flour

½ teaspoon salt

½ teaspoon ground ginger

2 tablespoons finely minced peeled fresh ginger

1 cup plus 1½ tablespoons sugar

4 ounces unsweetened chocolate, coarsely chopped

2 ounces bittersweet chocolate, coarsely chopped

1 stick (8 tablespoons) unsalted butter, at room temperature

⅓ cup light corn syrup

½ teaspoon pure vanilla extract

3 large eggs

**GETTING READY:** Center a rack in the oven and preheat the oven to 325 degrees F. Line a 9-inch square baking pan with foil, butter the foil and place the pan on a baking sheet.

Whisk the flour, salt and ground ginger together.

Put the minced fresh ginger and 1½ tablespoons of the sugar in a small bowl, stir and set aside. (If you do this a day ahead, cover the bowl with plastic wrap; if you do it several days ahead, cover and refrigerate.)

Melt the chocolates in a heatproof bowl set over a saucepan of simmering water, or melt them in a microwave oven; keep the heat low so the chocolates do not get very hot. Set aside to cool.

Working with a stand mixer, preferably fitted with a paddle attachment, or with a hand mixer in a large bowl, beat the butter at medium speed until it is smooth and creamy. Beat in the corn syrup, then the remaining 1 cup sugar, and continue to beat for another 2 minutes or so, until the butter is smooth again and the sugar incorporated. Add the vanilla. On medium speed, add the eggs one at a time, beating for 1 minute after each one goes in and scraping down the bowl as needed. Beat for 1 minute more, then reduce the mixer speed to low and add the macerated ginger (and any liquid), then the dry ingredients, mixing only until the flour disappears. Remove the bowl from the mixer and, using a rubber spatula, gently and thoroughly stir in the melted chocolate. Scrape the batter into the pan.

Bake for 30 to 35 minutes, or until the top forms an even sugar crust; a thin knife inserted into the center of the brownies should have streaks of moist, fudgy chocolate on it. Transfer the pan to a rack and cool to room temperature.

When the brownies are completely cool, turn out onto a rack, peel away the foil and invert onto a cutting board. Cut into 16 squares, each roughly 2¼ inches on a side.

**SERVING:** These can be served with a little sweetened whipped cream, vanilla ice cream or cold crème fraîche. Or you can dress them up with a bittersweet ganache glaze (page 276). Embellished or not, these are good with coffee, hot or cold.

**STORING:** Wrapped well, the brownies will keep for 2 days at room temperature (during which time the ginger flavor will become a little more pronounced) or for up to 2 months in the freezer.

*Playing Around*

You can omit the fresh ginger and increase the ground ginger to ¾ teaspoon.

# HONEY-NUT BROWNIES

**WHILE THESE** contain enough chocolate to qualify as brownies, the standout flavor is honey—full, bold and just a touch tangy. Honey is also the ingredient behind their alluring texture—moist, soft and supple. I usually make these with a mixed-blossom honey, but they can be made with a stronger variety: choose one, such as chestnut honey, that has an affinity for chocolate.

- 1 stick (8 tablespoons) unsalted butter, cut into 8 pieces
- 4 ounces bittersweet chocolate, coarsely chopped
- 4 large eggs
- ½ teaspoon salt
- 1 cup honey
- ⅔ cup sugar

- 1 teaspoon pure vanilla extract
- 1 cup all-purpose flour
- 1 cup coarsely chopped nuts, such as pecans, walnuts or toasted almonds

  Cocoa powder or confectioners' sugar, for dusting

MAKES 16 BROWNIES

**SERVING:** Serve, if desired, with lightly sweetened whipped cream or ice cream—I like coffee ice cream with these brownies, but good old vanilla or chocolate or something with spice is also nice.

**STORING:** Wrapped well, the brownies will keep at room temperature for 2 to 3 days (the honey keeps them moist) or in the freezer for up to 2 months.

*Playing Around*

If you'd like to bring up the chocolate flavor a little more and, in the process, make the brownies just a little dressier, allow them to cool, then ice them (see page 212).

**GETTING READY:** Center a rack in the oven and preheat the oven to 325 degrees F. Line a 9-inch square baking pan with foil, butter the foil and place the pan on a baking sheet.

Put the butter and chocolate in a heatproof bowl over a saucepan of simmering water. Heat, stirring occasionally, just until the ingredients are melted—you don't want to overheat the chocolate. Remove the bowl from the heat.

Working with a stand mixer, preferably with a paddle attachment, or with a hand mixer in a large bowl, beat the eggs and salt together on medium-high speed until light and foamy. Add the honey, sugar and vanilla and beat for 2 minutes, or until well blended and smooth. Reduce the mixer speed to low and pour in the chocolate-butter mixture, mixing only until incorporated. Still on low speed, add the flour and mix just until it disappears into the batter. Using a large rubber spatula, fold in the nuts. Scrape the batter into the pan.

Bake for 45 to 50 minutes, or until the brownies have risen, are beautifully brown and a thin knife inserted into the center comes out clean. Transfer the pan to a rack and cool for about 5 minutes.

Turn out onto a rack, peel away the foil and invert onto another rack. Cool to room temperature right side up.

Just before serving, dust the top of the brownies with either cocoa powder or confectioners' sugar or, if you'd like, a little of both. Cut the brownie bar into 16 squares, each roughly 2¼ inches on a side.

# BRRRRR-OWNIES

**WITH SO** much peppermint flavor, these are as frosty as a nor'easter. I created them for our son, Joshua, who keeps York Peppermint Patties in the freezer so that their already mouth-chilling filling turns downright blizzardy.

To get the wonderful, chilly sensation, I borrowed a handful of candy from Joshua's stash, chopped it up and stirred the little nuggets into brownie batter. The result: the chocolate tastes and even feels featherlight—just the thing you'd want on a steamy summer day—but the brownies have depth, moistness, creaminess and fudginess. As my husband said after his first shivery bite, "These are fun!"

| | |
|---|---|
| 5 tablespoons unsalted butter, cut into 5 pieces | 2 large eggs |
| 3 ounces bittersweet chocolate, coarsely chopped | 1 teaspoon pure vanilla extract |
| | Pinch of salt |
| 3 ounces unsweetened chocolate, coarsely chopped | ⅓ cup all-purpose flour |
| | 1 cup (6 ounces) York Peppermint Pattie Bites (or an equal weight of patties), chopped into bits |
| ⅔ cup sugar | |

**MAKES 16 BROWNIES**

**SERVING:** These are even more terrific with vanilla ice cream and chocolate sauce (pages 463 and 464) or Hot Fudge Sauce (page 465).

**STORING:** These are best served within 2 days of baking. If you're going to keep them at room temperature, just cut what you need and keep the remainder wrapped tightly in plastic. To freeze for up to 2 months, wrap the brownies airtight.

**GETTING READY:** Center a rack in the oven and preheat the oven to 325 degrees F. Line an 8-inch square baking pan with foil, butter the foil and place the pan on a baking sheet.

Set a heatproof bowl over a saucepan of gently simmering water. Put the butter in the bowl, top with the chopped chocolates and stir occasionally until the ingredients are just melted—you don't want them to get so hot that the butter separates. Remove the bowl from the pan of water.

With a whisk, stir in the sugar. Don't be concerned when your smooth mixture turns grainy. Whisk in the eggs one by one. Add the vanilla and whisk vigorously to bring the batter together and give it a shine before gently stirring in the salt and flour; stir only until incorporated. Switch to a rubber spatula and fold in the peppermint pieces. Scrape the batter into the pan and smooth the top with the rubber spatula.

Bake the brownies for 30 to 33 minutes, or until the top is dull and a thin knife inserted into the center comes out almost clean. (The tip of the knife may be a touch streaky.) Transfer the pan to a rack and cool to room temperature.

When they are completely cool, turn out onto a rack, peel away the foil and invert onto a cutting board. Cut into sixteen 2-inch squares.

# ESPRESSO CHEESECAKE BROWNIES

**IF, LIKE ME,** you love both brownies and cheesecake and the combination of chocolate and coffee, you'll find these candidates for over-overindulgence. The bottom layer of this triple-decker treat is a bittersweet chocolate brownie, the middle is cheesecake flavored with espresso and marbled with some of the brownie batter and the top is a thin, smooth cover of sweetened sour cream. The flavor combination is impeccable and so is the texture—it's a treat to start with the very soft sour cream topping, bite down to the velvety cheesecake and finish with the firmer but fudgy brownie.

## FOR THE BROWNIES

½ cup all-purpose flour

¼ teaspoon baking powder

   Pinch of salt

5 tablespoons unsalted butter, cut into 5 pieces

4 ounces bittersweet chocolate, coarsely chopped

⅓ cup sugar

2 large eggs

½ teaspoon pure vanilla extract

## FOR THE CHEESECAKE

1½ teaspoons instant espresso powder

1 tablespoon boiling water

8 ounces cream cheese, at room temperature

⅔ cup sugar

½ teaspoon pure vanilla extract

2 large eggs

¼ cup sour cream

1 tablespoon all-purpose flour

## FOR THE TOPPING

1¼ cups sour cream

½ cup confectioners' sugar

MAKES 16 BROWNIES

**SERVING:** Although these are delicious as is, you might want to dust the tops of the bars with cocoa, or even to circle the cold brownies with Hot Fudge Sauce (page 465).

**STORING:** These can be kept covered in the refrigerator for up to 2 days. Because of the sour cream topping, they should not be frozen. However, if you omit the topping, you can wrap the brownies airtight and freeze them for up to 2 months. If, on defrosting, you decide you want a topping, make it, spread it over the brownies and chill to set.

**GETTING READY:** Center a rack in the oven and preheat the oven to 350 degrees F. Butter a 9-inch square baking pan, dust with flour and tap out the excess. Put the pan on a baking sheet.

**TO MAKE THE BROWNIES:** Whisk together the flour, baking powder and salt.

Set a heatproof bowl over a saucepan of simmering water. Put the butter in the bowl, top with the chopped chocolate and stir occasionally until the ingredients are just melted—you don't want them to get so hot that the butter separates. Remove the bowl from the pan of water.

With a whisk, stir the sugar into the chocolate mixture. Add the eggs one at a time, beating well after each addition. Whisk in the vanilla and beat vigorously for a few seconds. With the whisk or a rubber spatula, gently stir in the dry ingredients, mixing only until they disappear into the batter. Set aside while you prepare the cheesecake.

**TO MAKE THE CHEESECAKE:** Dissolve the espresso in the boiling water; set aside to cool to tepid.

Meanwhile, working with a stand mixer, preferably fitted with a paddle attachment, or with a hand mixer in a large bowl, beat the cream cheese on medium speed until completely smooth. Add the sugar and beat for another 3 minutes or so, until well incorporated. Beat in the vanilla and the espresso mixture. Add the eggs one at a time, beating for 1 minute after each addition, then reduce the mixer speed to low and add the sour cream, followed by the flour. The batter will be smooth.

Give the brownie batter a few stirs with a spatula, and pour three quarters of it into the prepared pan. Smooth the brownie layer and pour the cheesecake batter over it, tilting the pan as needed to even the batter. Dot the top of the batter with spoonfuls of the remaining brownie batter, then, using a table knife, swirl the dark batter into the cheesecake batter, taking care not to plunge the knife into the lower brownie layer. The cake looks and tastes best if you swirl sparingly.

Bake for 30 to 35 minutes, or until the brownies pull away from the sides of the pan and the cheesecake layer is beige in the center, lightly browned around the edges and puffed all over. Transfer the pan to a rack and cool to room temperature.

When the brownies are completely cool, refrigerate for at least 2 hours, or until thoroughly chilled.

TO MAKE THE TOPPING: Warm the sour cream and sugar in a saucepan over very low heat, stirring constantly until the sugar is dissolved. Remove from the heat and pour the topping evenly over the cold cheesecake layer.

Return the brownies to the refrigerator and chill for at least 1 more hour, or until the topping is also thoroughly cold.

The easiest way to cut this dessert is to run the knife blade under hot water, wipe it dry and cut the cake into quarters. Remove the quarters from the pan and, again using a warmed-and-dried knife, cut each quarter into 4 pieces.

# BROWNIE BUTTONS

**THESE MINIATURIZED** brownies are a sensational after-school snack, a great half-time munchie or a dainty treat at teatime. To dress them up elegantly, dip the button tops in melted white chocolate and serve them in pretty little paper or foil cups. If snacking is more what you have in mind, skip the glaze and just pile them into a bowl.

Grated zest of ½ orange (optional)

1 teaspoon sugar (optional)

¼ cup plus 2 tablespoons all-purpose flour

Pinch of salt

½ stick (4 tablespoons) unsalted butter, cut into 4 pieces

2½ ounces bittersweet chocolate, coarsely chopped

⅓ cup (packed) light brown sugar

½ teaspoon pure vanilla extract

1 large egg

FOR THE GLAZE (OPTIONAL)

2 ounces white chocolate, finely chopped

MAKES 16 COOKIES

SERVING: Serve these with milk, coffee or even snifters of single-malt Scotch.

STORING: Covered, these will keep at room temperature overnight. If you wrap them air-tight, you can freeze them for up to 2 months, glazed or not.

*Playing Around*

Substitute lemon zest for the orange, or try an equal amount of very finely chopped ginger instead of the zest.

GETTING READY: Center a rack in the oven and preheat the oven to 350 degrees F. Lightly butter two miniature muffin pans, each with a dozen cups, and place them on a baking sheet.

If you're using the orange zest, combine the zest and sugar in a small bowl, rubbing them between your fingertips to blend; set aside. Whisk together the flour and salt.

Melt the butter, chocolate and brown sugar in a medium heavy-bottomed saucepan over very low heat, stirring frequently with a heatproof spatula and keeping an eye on the pan so nothing overheats or burns. When the mixture is smooth, remove from the heat and cool for a minute or two.

Stir the vanilla, egg and the zest, if you're using it, into the chocolate mixture. When the mixture is well blended, add the flour and stir only until it is incorporated. You should have a smooth, glossy batter.

Spoon the batter into 16 of the muffin cups, using about a teaspoon of batter to fill each cup three-quarters full. Put 1 teaspoon of water in each empty cup.

Bake for 14 to 16 minutes, or until the tops of the buttons spring back when touched. Transfer the pans to racks to cool for 3 minutes before carefully releasing the buttons. Cool to room temperature on the racks.

TO MAKE THE OPTIONAL GLAZE: Melt the chocolate in a small heatproof bowl set over a saucepan of simmering water. Stir constantly and don't leave the chocolate for even a minute—white chocolate scorches easily. As soon as the chocolate is smooth, remove from the heat.

One by one, dip the tops of the buttons into the chocolate, twirling the buttons so that you get a little swirl at the center of each one and the excess chocolate drips back into the bowl. Refrigerate the buttons for 15 minutes to set the glaze.

# CHEWY, CHUNKY BLONDIES

CHEWY AND richly butterscotch flavored, just the way blondies should be, and chocolaty, nutty and coconutty too, these have the look of an overgrown Toll House cookie. They've got bumpy tops and incredibly bumpy middles because they are made with more chunky add-ins than batter—a boon for anyone who loves being surprised bite after bite.

2 cups all-purpose flour
¾ teaspoon baking powder
½ teaspoon baking soda
½ teaspoon salt
2 sticks (8 ounces) unsalted butter, at room temperature
1½ cups (packed) light brown sugar
½ cup sugar
2 large eggs

1 teaspoon pure vanilla extract
6 ounces bittersweet or semisweet chocolate, chopped into chips, or 1 cup store-bought chocolate chips
1 cup butterscotch chips or Heath Toffee Bits
1 cup coarsely chopped walnuts
1 cup sweetened shredded coconut

SERVING: Like most brownies, these are good as is and great with ice cream. My favorite accompaniment is coffee ice cream.

STORING: Wrapped well, the blondies will keep for about 3 days at room temperature and for up to 2 months in the freezer.

GETTING READY: Center a rack in the oven and preheat the oven to 325 degrees F. Butter a 9-x-13-inch baking pan and put it on a baking sheet.

Whisk together the flour, baking powder, baking soda and salt.

Working with a stand mixer, preferably fitted with a paddle attachment, or with a hand mixer in a large bowl, beat the butter on medium speed until smooth and creamy. Add both sugars and beat for another 3 minutes, or until well incorporated. Add the eggs one by one, beating for 1 minute after each addition, then beat in the vanilla. Reduce the mixer speed to low and add the dry ingredients, mixing just until they disappear into the batter. Using a rubber spatula, stir in the chips, nuts and coconut. Scrape the batter into the buttered pan and use the spatula to even the top as best as you can.

Bake for about 40 minutes, or until a knife inserted into the center of the blondies comes out clean. The blondies should pull away from the sides of the pan a little and the top should be a nice honey brown. Transfer the pan to a rack and cool for about 15 minutes before turning the blondies out onto another rack. Invert onto a rack and cool the blondies to room temperature right side up.

Cut into 32 bars, each roughly 2¼ x 1½ inches.

# WHITE CHOCOLATE BROWNIES

**WHITE CHOCOLATE,** orange zest and lots of fresh raspberries make these brownies delicious; topping them with meringue makes them glamorous. The cake layer is slender, delightfully dense and both sweet and tart; the meringue is soft and golden. You can call them brownies, but serve them with a swirl of raspberry coulis and they'll be worthy of a black-tie gala.

MAKES 32 BROWNIES

**SERVING:** Dust the squares with additional confectioners' sugar if you think they need it and serve as is or with Raspberry Coulis (page 467).

**STORING:** Kept in the pan and covered lightly with plastic wrap, the brownies can be kept at room temperature overnight. The meringue makes these fragile (and unfreezable). If you omit the meringue, you can wrap the brownies airtight and keep them at room temperature for up to 3 days and frozen for up to 2 months.

### FOR THE BROWNIES
- ⅔ cup all-purpose flour
- ½ cup finely ground almonds
- ½ teaspoon salt
- 1 stick (8 tablespoons) unsalted butter, cut into 8 pieces
- 4 ounces premium-quality white chocolate, coarsely chopped
- 1 cup sugar
- 2 teaspoons grated orange zest

- 4 large eggs
- 1 teaspoon pure vanilla extract
- 1 cup fresh raspberries

### FOR THE MERINGUE
- 3 large egg whites, at room temperature
- Pinch of salt
- ½ cup sugar

- Confectioners' sugar, for dusting

**GETTING READY:** Center a rack in the oven and preheat the oven to 325 degrees F. Butter a 9-x-13-inch pan, line the bottom with parchment or wax paper, butter the paper and dust the bottom and sides of the pan with flour; tap out the excess. Put the pan on a baking sheet.

**TO MAKE THE BROWNIES:** Whisk together the flour, ground almonds and salt.

Set a heatproof bowl over a saucepan of only-just-simmering water. Put the butter in the bowl, top with the chopped chocolate and stir frequently until the ingredients are just melted—you don't want them to get so hot that the butter or the white chocolate separates. (White chocolate is finicky, so don't leave the kitchen while it's over the heat—too much heat and it will fall apart or scorch.) Remove the bowl from the pan of water.

Working in the bowl of a stand mixer or in another large bowl, rub the sugar and orange zest together with your fingers until the sugar is moist and aromatic. Add the eggs and, with the paddle or whisk attachment, or with a hand mixer, beat on medium-high speed for about 3 minutes, or until pale and foamy. Beat in the vanilla. Reduce the mixer speed to low and blend in the melted butter and chocolate. Still working on low, mix in the dry ingredients, stirring only until they disappear into the batter. Scrape the batter into the prepared pan and sprinkle the raspberries evenly over the batter. Set aside while you make the meringue.

**TO MAKE THE MERINGUE:** In the cleaned mixer bowl with the (clean) whisk attachment, or in another large bowl with cleaned beaters, beat the egg whites with the salt on medium speed until they are foamy and just turn opaque. Increase the mixer speed to medium-high and add the sugar in a slow, steady stream. Whip the whites until they form firm but still glossy peaks.

Gently spread the meringue over the brownie batter.

Bake for 30 to 35 minutes, or until the meringue is browned and crackly and the brownies pull away from the sides of the pan. Transfer the pan to a rack and allow to cool to room temperature in the pan.

Cover a cooling rack with a piece of parchment or wax paper, or a silicone baking mat, dust the paper or mat with confectioners' sugar and very gently, so you don't squish the meringue, turn the brownies out onto the rack. Peel away the parchment paper lining and carefully invert the brownies onto a cutting board. Cut into 32 bars, each roughly 2¼ x 1½ inches.

# CARAMEL CRUNCH BARS

ANYONE WITH a passion for caramel and a soft spot for Heath Bars will find these irresistible. From the bottom up, you get a caramel-sweet brown sugar cookie, a slick of chocolate and a shower of toffee bits. I think of these bars as a double treat because, as delicious as they are at room temperature, they are also wonderful frozen—which means they are great for ice cream sandwiches.

Just keep in mind that the cookie layer is really a shortbread and, like all shortbread doughs, the less you work it once the flour is added, the more appealingly crumbly the texture will be.

FOR THE BASE

- 1½ cups all-purpose flour
- 1 teaspoon instant espresso powder or finely ground instant coffee
- ½ teaspoon salt
- ¼ teaspoon ground cinnamon
- 2 sticks (8 ounces) unsalted butter, at room temperature
- ½ cup (packed) light brown sugar

- ¼ cup sugar
- 1 teaspoon pure vanilla extract
- 3 ounces bittersweet or premium-quality milk chocolate, finely chopped

FOR THE TOPPING

- 6 ounces bittersweet or premium-quality milk chocolate, finely chopped
- ¾ cup Heath Toffee Bits

GETTING READY: Center a rack in the oven and preheat the oven to 375 degrees F. Lightly butter a 9-x-13-inch baking pan, line the pan with foil and butter the foil. Put the pan on a baking sheet.

TO MAKE THE BASE: Whisk together the flour, espresso powder, salt and cinnamon.

Working with a stand mixer, preferably fitted with a paddle attachment, or a hand mixer in a large bowl, beat the butter at medium speed until smooth, about 3 minutes. Add the sugars and beat for another 3 minutes, or until the mixture is light and creamy. Beat in the vanilla, then turn off the mixer. Add all the dry ingredients, cover the stand mixer with a kitchen towel (so you and your kitchen don't get showered with flour) and pulse the mixer on and off on low speed about 5 times—at which point a peek at the bowl should reveal that it's safe to turn the mixer to low and mix, uncovered, just until the dry ingredients are almost incorporated. Add the chopped chocolate and mix only until the dry ingredients disappear. If the chocolate isn't evenly mixed, finish the job by hand with a spatula. You'll have a heavy, very sticky dough. Scrape the dough into the buttered pan and, with the spatula and your fingertips, cajole it into a thin, even layer.

Bake for 20 to 22 minutes, or until the base is bubbly—so bubbly you can almost hear it percolating—and puckery. It will look as though it is struggling to pull away from the sides of the pan. Transfer the pan to a rack and turn off the oven.

MAKES ABOUT 54 BARS

SERVING: Serve plain, with a glass of cold milk for the kids and coffee for the grown-ups. Or serve with vanilla ice cream and, if you like, Caramel Sauce (page 466) or Hot Fudge Sauce (page 465)—excessive, but fun.

STORING: Covered, the bars will keep for about 4 days at room temperature; wrapped airtight, they can be frozen for up to 2 months.

*Playing Around*

CARAMEL CRUNCH ICE CREAM BARS: When the kids' birthdays roll around, cut these into large squares, 3 to 4 inches on a side. Working with half of the squares, leaving them frosted side up and working on a baking sheet, spread them with a thick layer of softened ice cream—vanilla (page 428), chocolate (page 430) or cinnamon (page 429). Top with the other half of the bars, frosted side up, and slide them into the freezer to firm up again. If you need to keep them for a while, double-wrap each bar in plastic wrap or aluminum foil.

TO MAKE THE TOPPING: Scatter the chopped chocolate evenly over the top of the hot base and pop the pan back into the oven for 2 to 3 minutes, until the chocolate is soft. Remove from the oven and immediately spread the chocolate over the bars, using an offset spatula or the back of a spoon. Sprinkle the toffee bits over the chocolate and press them down lightly with your fingertips. Place the baking pan on a rack to cool to room temperature.

If, by the time the bars are cool, the chocolate hasn't set, refrigerate them briefly to firm the chocolate.

Carefully lift out of the pan, using the foil edges as handles, and transfer to a cutting board. Trim the edges if they seem a bit thick. Cut about 54 bars, each about 2 inches x 1 inch, taking care not to cut through the foil.

# CHOCOLATE OATMEAL ALMOST-CANDY BARS

I WANTED a fun, kid-in-us-all bar cookie. What I got after playing around in the kitchen is a treat to appeal to the kid in us all if you love peanuts, raisins, fudge and thick, chewy, nut-filled oatmeal cookies. Served cold—which is how I recommend you offer them up—these are like big fat candy bars. When they are chilled, the bottom oatmeal and peanut layer is firm, with lots of chew; the middle layer is like peanut-raisin fudge; and the top layer, a generous smattering of the oatmeal mixture that forms the crust, is pure crunch. Know anyone, young or old, who could turn these down? I can't imagine you'll find a soul—I haven't.

MAKES 32 BARS

SERVING: I think these are best served cold from the fridge, although my husband likes them straight from the freezer, cut into slivers. Before you chill the bars, though, have one—you might find you like them best at room temperature, in which case you're lucky: you can start enjoying them sooner.

STORING: Wrapped well, these will keep for about 4 days at room temperature, 1 week in the refrigerator or up to 2 months in the freezer.

### FOR THE OATMEAL LAYER

- 2½ cups all-purpose flour
- 1 teaspoon baking soda
- 1 teaspoon salt
- ½ teaspoon ground cinnamon
- 2 sticks (8 ounces) unsalted butter, at room temperature
- 2 cups (packed) light brown sugar
- 2 large eggs
- 2 teaspoons pure vanilla extract
- 3 cups old-fashioned oats
- 1 cup salted peanuts, coarsely chopped

### FOR THE CHOCOLATE LAYER

- 1 14-ounce can sweetened condensed milk
- 2 cups (12 ounces) semisweet chocolate chips
- 2 tablespoons unsalted butter
- ¼ teaspoon salt
- 1 teaspoon pure vanilla extract
- 1 cup moist, plump raisins (dark or golden)
- ¾ cup coarsely chopped peanuts, preferably salted

GETTING READY: Center a rack in the oven and preheat the oven to 350 degrees F. Butter a 9-x-13-inch baking pan and place the pan on a baking sheet.

TO MAKE THE OATMEAL LAYER: Whisk together the flour, baking soda, salt and cinnamon.

Working with a stand mixer, preferably fitted with a paddle attachment, or with a hand mixer in a large bowl, beat the butter on medium speed until it is soft and creamy. Add the brown sugar and beat for 2 minutes, then add the eggs one at a time, beating for a minute after each egg goes in. Beat in the vanilla. The mixture should be light and fluffy. Reduce the mixer speed to low and add the dry ingredients, mixing just until they disappear. Still on low speed, or working by hand with a rubber spatula, stir in the oats and chopped peanuts.

Set aside 1½ to 2 cups of the mixture, then turn the remaining dough into the buttered pan. Gently and evenly press the dough over the bottom of the pan. Set aside while you prepare the next layer.

114 BAKING From My Home to Yours

TO MAKE THE CHOCOLATE LAYER: Set a heatproof bowl over a saucepan of simmering water. Put the condensed milk, chocolate chips, butter and salt in the bowl and stir occasionally until the milk is warm and the chocolate and butter are melted. Remove the bowl from the pan of water and stir in the vanilla, raisins and peanuts.

Pour the warm chocolate over the oatmeal crust, then scatter the remaining oatmeal mixture over the top. Don't try to spread the oatmeal, and don't worry about getting the topping even—this is fun, remember?

Bake for 25 to 30 minutes, or until the topping is golden brown and the chocolate layer is dull and starting to come away from the sides of the pan. Transfer the baking pan to a rack and cool for about 2 hours.

Run a blunt knife between the edges of the cake and the pan, and carefully turn the cake out onto a rack. Turn right side up, then refrigerate for at least 1 hour before cutting.

Cut into 32 rectangles, each roughly $2^{1}/_{4}$ x $1^{1}/_{2}$ inches.

# APPLESAUCE SPICE BARS

**DON'T PASS** these up because they seem too simple and old-fashioned. They are homey, true, but they're also irresistibly good, the kind of sweet you can serve to both little kids and know-it-all adults. The batter is mixed quickly and easily in a saucepan, as is the brown sugar glaze, and the finished bars are good keepers— but storing them will probably not be an issue because I can't think of any time, from after school to midnight, when they wouldn't be just right.

**MAKES 32 BARS**

**SERVING:** Serve with coffee, tea, milk or mulled cider. These are also awfully good with a little scoop of ice cream.

**STORING:** Kept in a covered container, the bars will be fine for about 3 days at room temperature. Because of the glaze, they cannot be frozen.

### FOR THE BARS

- 1¼ cups all-purpose flour
- 1 teaspoon baking powder
- ¼ teaspoon baking soda
- 1 teaspoon ground cinnamon
- ¼ teaspoon ground allspice
- ¼ teaspoon salt
- 1 stick (8 tablespoons) unsalted butter
- 1 cup (packed) light brown sugar
- 2 large eggs
- ½ cup unsweetened applesauce
- 1 teaspoon pure vanilla extract
- 1 tablespoon applejack, brandy or dark rum (optional)
- 1 baking apple, such as Rome or Cortland, peeled, cored and finely diced or chopped
- ½ cup plump, moist raisins (dark or golden)
- ½ cup chopped pecans

### FOR THE GLAZE

- 2½ tablespoons heavy cream
- ⅓ cup (packed) light brown sugar
- 2½ tablespoons unsalted butter
- 1 teaspoon light corn syrup
- ½ teaspoon pure vanilla extract

**GETTING READY:** Center a rack in the oven and preheat the oven to 350 degrees F. Butter a 9-x-13 inch baking pan, line the bottom with parchment paper, butter the paper and dust the inside of the pan with flour. Tap out the excess flour and put the pan on a baking sheet.

**TO MAKE THE BARS:** Whisk together the flour, baking powder, baking soda, spices and salt.

In a medium heavy-bottomed saucepan, melt the butter over low heat. Add the brown sugar and stir with a whisk until it is melted and the mixture is smooth, about 1 minute. Remove the pan from the heat.

Still working in the saucepan, whisk in the eggs one at a time, mixing until they are well blended. Add the applesauce, vanilla and applejack, if you're using it, and whisk until the ingredients are incorporated and the mixture is once again smooth. Switch to a rubber spatula and gently stir in the dry ingredients, mixing only until they disappear, then mix in the apple, raisins and nuts. Scrape the batter into the prepared pan and smooth the top with a rubber spatula.

Bake for 23 to 25 minutes, or until the bars just start to pull away from the sides of the pan and a knife inserted into the center comes out clean. Transfer the baking pan to a rack and let the cake cool while you make the glaze.

TO MAKE THE GLAZE: In a small saucepan, whisk together the cream, sugar, butter and corn syrup. Put the pan over medium heat and bring the mixture to a boil, whisking frequently. Adjust the heat so that the glaze simmers, and cook, whisking frequently, for 5 minutes. Remove the pan from the heat and stir in the vanilla.

Turn the bars out onto a rack, remove the paper and invert the bars onto another rack, so they are right side up. Slide the parchment paper under the rack to serve as a drip catcher, grab a long metal icing spatula and pour the hot glaze over the bars, using the spatula to spread it evenly over the cake. Let them cool to room temperature before you cut them.

Cut into 32 rectangles, each about $2\frac{1}{4}$ x $1\frac{1}{2}$ inches.

# PEANUTTIEST BLONDIES

**MADE WITH** peanut butter and bolstered with lots of salted peanuts and chocolate chips, these blondies are big, firm, sweet, satisfying and definitely members-in-good-standing of the chewy branch of the brownie family. They're real kid fare, great with milk, malteds or hot chocolate, and so good with ice cream.

1 cup all-purpose flour

½ teaspoon baking powder

½ teaspoon ground cinnamon

¼ teaspoon baking soda

¼ teaspoon salt

½ cup peanut butter—crunchy (my preference) or creamy (not natural)

5 tablespoons unsalted butter, at room temperature

¾ cup sugar

¾ cup (packed) light brown sugar

2 large eggs

½ teaspoon pure vanilla extract

1 cup coarsely chopped salted peanuts

6 ounces semisweet or premium-quality milk chocolate, coarsely chopped, or 1 cup store-bought chocolate chips (I like mini semisweet chips for these)

**SERVING:** Serve these plain or with ice cream. They're especially good with coffee.

**STORING:** Wrapped well, the blondies will keep for about 3 days at room temperature or for up to 2 months in the freezer.

**GETTING READY:** Center a rack in the oven and preheat the oven to 350 degrees F. Line a 9-inch square pan with foil, butter the foil and put the pan on a baking sheet.

Whisk together the flour, baking powder, cinnamon, baking soda and salt.

Working with a stand mixer, preferably fitted with a paddle attachment, or with a hand mixer in a large bowl, beat the peanut butter and butter together on medium speed until smooth. Add both the sugars and beat for 1 to 2 minutes, until well incorporated into the butter. Add the eggs one at time, beating for 1 minute after each egg goes in. Beat in the vanilla extract. Reduce the mixer speed to low and add the dry ingredients, mixing only until they disappear into the dough; the dough will be thick. Add the peanuts and chocolate and give the mixer a few turns to stir them into the dough. If the chunky ingredients aren't mixed in after a few seconds, just finish the job with a sturdy spatula—don't overmix the dough. Scrape the dough into the prepared pan.

Bake the blondies for 40 to 50 minutes, or until they turn a deep honey brown and a thin knife inserted into the center comes out clean. Transfer the pan to a rack and cool to room temperature.

When it is completely cool, carefully lift the blondies out of the pan, using the foil edges as handles, and turn them out onto a rack. Peel away the foil and invert onto a cutting board. Use a long knife to cut into 16 bars, each roughly 2¼ inches on a side.

# SNICKERY SQUARES

I LIKE to think of these as classy Snickers, a made-at-home, slimmer, sleeker version of the beloved candy bar. The squares are composed of a buttery short-bread base, a layer of smooth caramel dulce de leche mixed with crunchy candied salted peanuts (like the ones you get in Cracker Jacks) and a top coat of dark chocolate sprinkled with crushed candied peanuts. All the pieces are simple and each is tasty on its own, but put them together, and you get something much better than the individual components.

MAKES 16 SQUARES

SERVING: The squares can be served at room temperature or chilled. I like to serve them with ice cream—vanilla (page 428), chocolate (page 430), coffee or cinnamon (page 429).

STORING: Covered, these will keep for 2 days at room temperature. Wrapped well, they'll hold for 5 days in the refrigerator or for up to 2 months in the freezer.

FOR THE CRUST

1 cup all-purpose flour

¼ cup sugar

2 tablespoons confectioners' sugar

¼ teaspoon salt

1 stick (8 tablespoons) unsalted butter, cut into small pieces and chilled

1 large egg yolk, lightly beaten

FOR THE TOPPING

7 ounces bittersweet chocolate, coarsely chopped

½ stick (4 tablespoons) unsalted butter, cut into 8 pieces, at room temperature

FOR THE FILLING

⅓ cup sugar

3 tablespoons water

1½ cups salted peanuts

About 1½ cups store-bought dulce de leche

GETTING READY: Center a rack in the oven and preheat the oven to 350 degrees F. Butter an 8-inch square pan and put it on a baking sheet.

TO MAKE THE CRUST: Toss the flour, sugar, confectioners' sugar and salt into a food processor and pulse a few times to combine. Toss in the pieces of cold butter and pulse about 12 times, until the mixture looks like coarse meal. Pour the yolk over the ingredients and pulse until the dough forms clumps and curds—stop before the dough comes together in a ball.

Turn the dough into the buttered pan and gently press it evenly across the bottom of the pan. Prick the dough all over with a fork and slide the sheet into the oven.

Bake the crust for 15 to 20 minutes, or until it takes on just a little color around the edges. Transfer the pan to a rack and cool to room temperature before filling.

TO MAKE THE FILLING: Have a parchment- or, better yet, a silicone mat–lined baking sheet at the ready, as well as a long-handled wooden spoon (you'll be cooking sugar that will climb to over 300 degrees F, so you'll want to keep as far away

from it as possible) and a medium (about 2-quart) heavy-bottomed saucepan. (If you're new to caramelizing, take a minute to read Caramelize, page 477.)

Put the sugar and water in the saucepan and cook over medium-high heat, stirring, until the sugar dissolves. Keeping the heat fairly high, continue to cook the sugar, without stirring, until it just starts to color. (If sugar splatters onto the sides of the saucepan, wash down the splatters with a pastry brush dipped in cold water.) Toss in the peanuts and immediately start stirring. Keep stirring, to coat the peanuts with the sugar. Within a few minutes, they will be covered with sugar and turn white—keep stirring until the sugar turns back into caramel. When the peanuts are coated with a nice deep amber caramel, remove the pan from the heat and turn the nuts out onto the baking sheet, using the wooden spoon to spread them out as best you can. Cool the nuts to room temperature.

When they are cool enough to handle, separate the nuts or break them into small pieces. Divide the nuts in half. Keep half of the nuts whole or in biggish pieces for the filling, and finely chop the other half for the topping.

Spread the dulce de leche over the shortbread base and sprinkle over the whole candied nuts or the big pieces.

TO MAKE THE TOPPING: Melt the chocolate in a heatproof bowl set over a saucepan of barely simmering water or in a microwave oven, using a low power setting. Remove the chocolate from the heat and gently stir in the butter, stirring until it is fully blended into the chocolate.

Pour the chocolate over the dulce de leche, smoothing it with a long metal icing spatula, then sprinkle over the finely chopped candied peanuts. Slide the pan into the refrigerator to set the topping, about 20 minutes; if you'd like to serve the squares cold, keep them refrigerated for at least 3 hours before cutting.

Cut into 16 bars, each roughly 2½ inches on a side.

# SIDE-OF-
THE-SAUCER
COOKIES

HERE ARE COOKIES that are comfortable alongside tea, coffee, a flute of champagne, a glass of sherry or a snifter of something fine, aged and strong, like single-malt Scotch, Kentucky straight bourbon or a little cognac. In this collection you'll find dainty madeleine shells, rugelach roll-ups, meringues as billowy as cumulus clouds, shortbreads, buttery French sablés, crunchy Italian biscotti and nut balls that disappear in two polite-size bites. These are the cookies that are often served as after-dessert desserts in chic restaurants.

Being a side-of-the saucer cookie is less a question of procedure than of presentation—they're the kind of cookies you'd put on a pedestal, a doily or your "good" china.

Cookies like these are not difficult to make, but several take a bit more TLC than bar or cookie jar cookies. Save them for an afternoon when you are looking forward to fussing a bit, when you've got the time to mold, roll or even fry dough—as you will with Mrs. Vogel's Scherben. You can also save them for a time when you want to show off. While making madeleines is no different from making a basic sponge cake—it's the shell-shaped pans, not you, that form the cookies so precisely—they've got an ooh-là-là factor sponge cakes can't touch.

# Shortbreads and Sablés

**WHAT YOU** call the fabulously buttery, slightly gritty, tender, sandy-textured cookies that are so right with tea or coffee may depend on where you live. In France, the cookies are known as *sablés, galettes* or *palets;* in Scotland, they're shortbread; and here, at home, they are shortbread, sand tarts or simply butter cookies.

At their most elemental and traditional, shortbreads and their kin are made of butter, sugar—either granulated or confectioners', or a combination of the two—and flour. And, although some recipes have an egg or two, or maybe just yolks, it's not the eggs that define the cookies, it's the other ingredients and, most important, how you handle them.

Here's all you need to know to get perfectly crumbly shortbread or sablés every time.

Use fresh butter that is soft, but not at all greasy—if your butter is sitting in an oily puddle, it's gone too soft and your sablés won't have their characteristic sandiness.

Don't beat the butter (or the butter, sugar and eggs) so enthusiastically that the mixture is light and fluffy. You don't want to beat air into this dough, because it would cause the cookies to puff as they bake in the oven and sink as they cool on the counter.

Be soft and gentle when you blend in the flour. This is the make-or-break step in the process. With the word "sandy" singing in your head, add the flour all at once and mix it only until it disappears into the dough. To guard against overmixing, you can mix in the last of the flour by hand.

Shape the dough as the recipe directs and then make sure to give it a good, long chill; it will improve the flavor of the cookies and help them keep their shape under the oven's heat. Try to refrigerate the dough for at least 2 hours, but know that longer is better.

Cool the cookies completely before you serve them. As seductive as the smell of warm butter, sugar and flour is, the cookies taste better when they reach room temperature.

# ESPRESSO-CHOCOLATE SHORTBREAD COOKIES

**I NEVER** tire of the satisfying combination of espresso and chocolate and am always pleased when I think of another way to use it. Stirring some instant espresso into a classic shortbread dough and then adding bits of bittersweet chocolate transforms a traditional cookie into a modern treat with an edge.

If you're new to making shortbread, take a look at the pointers on page 124.

- 1 tablespoon instant espresso powder
- 1 tablespoon boiling water
- 2 sticks (8 ounces) unsalted butter, at room temperature
- ²⁄₃ cup confectioners' sugar
- ½ teaspoon pure vanilla extract

- 2 cups all-purpose flour
- 4 ounces bittersweet chocolate, finely chopped, or ¾ cup store-bought mini chocolate chips

- Confectioners' sugar, for dusting (optional)

MAKES 32 COOKIES

**SERVING:** The obvious choice is the best choice for these cookies—coffee is the perfect match.

**STORING:** These cookies can be packed airtight and kept at room temperature for up to 4 days or frozen for up to 2 months. (If you think you're going to be freezing them, it's best not to dust them with confectioners' sugar, which gets gloppy in the freezer.)

Dissolve the espresso in the boiling water, and set aside to cool to tepid.

Working with a stand mixer, preferably fitted with a paddle attachment, or with a hand mixer in a large bowl, beat the butter and confectioners' sugar together on medium speed for about 3 minutes, until the mixture is very smooth. Beat in the vanilla and espresso, then reduce the mixer speed to low and add the flour, mixing only until it disappears into the dough. Don't work the dough much once the flour is incorporated. Fold in the chopped chocolate with a sturdy rubber spatula.

Using the spatula, transfer the soft, sticky dough to a gallon-size zipper-lock plastic bag. Put the bag on a flat surface, leaving the top open, and roll the dough into a 9-x-10½-inch rectangle that's ¼ inch thick. As you roll, turn the bag occasionally and lift the plastic from the dough so it doesn't cause creases. When you get the right size and thickness, seal the bag, pressing out as much air as possible, and refrigerate the dough for at least 2 hours, or for up to 2 days.

**GETTING READY TO BAKE:** Position the racks to divide the oven into thirds and preheat the oven to 325 degrees F. Line two baking sheets with parchment or silicone mats.

Put the plastic bag on a cutting board and slit it open. Turn the firm dough out onto the board (discard the bag) and, using a ruler as a guide and a sharp knife, cut the dough into 1½-inch squares. Transfer the squares to the baking sheets and carefully prick each one twice with a fork, gently pushing the tines through the cookies until they hit the sheet.

Bake for 18 to 20 minutes, rotating the sheets from top to bottom and front to back at the midway point. The shortbreads will be very pale—they shouldn't take on much color. Transfer the cookies to a rack.

If you'd like, dust the cookies with confectioners' sugar while they are still hot. Cool the cookies to room temperature before serving.

*Playing Around*

**OATMEAL SPICE SHORTBREADS:** Omit the espresso, boiling water and chopped chocolate. Reduce the flour to 1½ cups, and whisk it together with ²⁄₃ cup old-fashioned oats, ¾ teaspoon ground cinnamon, ½ teaspoon ground ginger, ¼ teaspoon freshly grated nutmeg and ⅛ teaspoon ground cloves. Once the butter and confectioners' sugar are well beaten, add the vanilla, then the dry ingredients, mixing only until they are incorporated.

# BROWN SUGAR–PECAN SHORTBREAD COOKIES

MAKES 32 COOKIES

**AS SOFT** and buttery and appealing as shortbread can be, but just a tad sweeter because of the pecans and a little more caramely because of the brown sugar, these will make pecan-sandy fans smile. (See page 124 for pointers on making shortbread.)

| | |
|---|---|
| 1½ cups all-purpose flour | ¾ cup (packed) light brown sugar |
| ¼ cup cornstarch | ½ cup finely ground pecans |
| ¼ teaspoon salt | |
| Pinch of ground cloves | Confectioners' sugar, for dusting |
| 2 sticks (8 ounces) unsalted butter, at room temperature | (optional) |

SERVING: These are good with tea or coffee, but they're also a good go-along for ice cream.

STORING: Packed in a covered container, these will keep for about 4 days at room temperature; wrapped airtight, they can be frozen for up to 2 months.

Sift together the flour, cornstarch, salt and cloves.

Working with a stand mixer, preferably fitted with a paddle attachment, or with a hand mixer in a large bowl, beat the butter and brown sugar together on medium speed for about 3 minutes, until the mixture is very smooth. Reduce the mixer speed to low and add the dry ingredients, mixing only until they disappear into the dough. Don't work the dough much once the flour is incorporated. Add the pecans and give the mixer a couple of turns, just to get the nuts into the dough.

Using a rubber spatula, transfer the soft, sticky dough to a gallon-size zipper-lock plastic bag. Put the bag on a flat surface, leaving the top open, and roll the dough into a 9-x-10½-inch rectangle that's ¼ inch thick. As you roll, turn the bag occasionally and lift the plastic from the dough so it doesn't cause creases. When you get the right size and thickness, seal the bag, pressing out as much air as possible, and refrigerate the dough for at least 2 hours, or for up to 2 days.

**GETTING READY TO BAKE:** Position the racks to divide the oven into thirds and preheat the oven to 350 degrees F. Line two baking sheets with parchment or silicone mats.

Put the plastic bag on a cutting board and slit it open. Turn the firm dough out onto the board (discard the bag) and, using a ruler as a guide and a sharp knife, cut the dough into 1½-inch squares. Transfer the squares to the baking sheets and carefully prick each one twice with a fork, gently pushing the tines through the cookies until they hit the sheet.

Bake for 18 to 20 minutes, rotating the sheets from top to bottom and front to back at the midway point. The shortbreads will be very pale—they shouldn't take on much color. Transfer the cookies to a rack.

If you'd like, dust the cookies with confectioners' sugar while they are still hot. Cool the cookies to room temperature before serving.

# SALT AND PEPPER COCOA SHORTBREADS

**TO CALL** these buttery shortbreads slice-and-bake icebox cookies is to describe them accurately—and shortchange them shamefully. These are, indeed, cookies that are put together quickly, rolled into logs and chilled in the refrigerator, ready to be sliced, baked and served at a moment's notice. But just because they are simple to make doesn't mean they are simple in any other way. Because of their tender texture and the subtle play between the chocolate (which makes the cookies fudgy), the salt (which heightens the chocolate quotient) and the black pepper (which sparks the entire mix), these little shortbread coins turn out to be quite sophisticated, although not above being paired with a glass of milk.

As with most slice-and-bake cookies, the logs of dough can be kept refrigerated for a few days or frozen for a few months. And the recipe can be doubled or tripled, if you want to have cookies today and logs tucked away for tomorrow. (See page 124 for tips on making shortbread.)

MAKES ABOUT 24 COOKIES

**SERVING:** Not surprisingly, these are excellent with espresso. Equally unsurprisingly, they are great with ice cream, especially vanilla (page 428), chocolate (page 430) and Unbelievably Good Chocolate Blueberry (page 433).

**STORING:** The cookies will keep for 4 to 5 days at room temperature in a tin; wrapped airtight, they can be frozen for up to 2 months.

| | |
|---|---|
| 1½ cups all-purpose flour | 1 large egg yolk |
| ½ cup unsweetened cocoa powder | ¾ teaspoon fleur de sel or ½ teaspoon |
| 2 sticks (8 ounces) unsalted butter, | fine sea salt |
| at room temperature | ½ teaspoon coarsely ground black pepper |
| ⅔ cup confectioners' sugar | 1 teaspoon pure vanilla extract |

Sift the flour and cocoa together.

Working with a stand mixer, preferably fitted with a paddle attachment, or with a hand mixer in a large bowl, beat the butter on medium-low speed until soft and smooth. Add the confectioners' sugar and continue to beat until the butter is satiny. Add the yolk, salt, pepper and vanilla and beat until the mixture is once again smooth. Add the flour-cocoa mixture in 3 additions, beating on low speed only until each addition is incorporated.

Turn the dough out onto a work surface and gather it together. Divide it in half and roll each half into a log that is 1 to 1¼ inches thick and about 6 inches long. I find it's easiest to flatten each piece with your fingertips into a thick rectangle, then to roll the piece up into a log. Roll the log back and forth under your palms to get a good shape and to stretch it to length. It's kid's play, but pay attention—if you don't check the solidity of your log by feeling it around the middle, you could end up with one that's hollow in the center. It's not fatal, but neither is it attractive: a hollow center results in holes in your cookies. Once the logs are formed, wrap them in plastic wrap, twisting the ends of the plastic firecracker-style to tighten the rolls, and refrigerate for at least 4 hours. (The cookie logs can be refrigerated for up to 4 days or wrapped airtight and frozen for about 2 months. If you freeze the logs, you can cut and bake the rounds frozen—just add a couple of minutes to the baking time.)

*Playing Around*

If you want to fancy up the cookies a bit and, at the same time, give your guests a hint of what's in store, brush each round of dough with a little egg wash (1 egg beaten with 1 teaspoon of water) and sprinkle a teensy bit of cracked black pepper and a few grains of fleur de sel (or even pretzel salt) in the center before baking.

GETTING READY TO BAKE: Position the racks to divide the oven into thirds and preheat the oven to 350 degrees F. Line two baking sheets with parchment or silicone mats.

Using a thin-bladed knife, cut the logs into $\frac{1}{2}$-inch-thick rounds and place the rounds on the baking sheets, leaving at least 1 inch between the rounds.

Bake for 14 to 16 minutes, rotating the baking sheets from top to bottom and front to back at the 7-minute mark; the cookies should feel reasonably firm to the touch. Remove the baking sheets from the oven and transfer the cookies to a rack to cool to room temperature.

# CORNMEAL SHORTBREAD COOKIES

**THESE CLASSIC**, buttery, rich shortbread cookies have a textural twist—an appealing tickle-your-tongue roughness that comes from using a bit of cornmeal. I like to make them a little thinner than most shortbread and bake them just a little longer and just a little darker—all in the service of crunch. (See page 124 for pointers on making shortbread.)

MAKES 32 COOKIES

**SERVING:** Tea is the traditional—and the perfect—mate for these.

**STORING:** Kept in a covered container, these will keep for about 4 days at room temperature; wrapped airtight, they can be frozen for up to 2 months.

| | | |
|---|---|---|
| 1½ | cups all-purpose flour | Grated zest of 1 lemon |
| ¼ | cup cornstarch | 2 sticks (8 ounces) unsalted butter, |
| ½ | teaspoon salt | at room temperature |
| ½ | cup yellow cornmeal | 1 teaspoon pure vanilla extract or |
| ⅔ | cup sugar | ½ teaspoon pure almond extract |

Sift the flour, cornstarch and salt together into a bowl, then whisk in the cornmeal.

Working in the bowl of a stand mixer or another large bowl, rub the sugar and zest together with your fingers until the sugar is moist and aromatic. Fit the mixer with the paddle attachment or the whisk, or use a hand mixer. Add the butter and extract to the bowl and beat on medium speed for about 3 minutes, or until the mixture is very smooth. Reduce the mixer speed to low and add the dry ingredients, mixing only until they just disappear into the dough. Don't work the dough much once the flour is incorporated.

Using a rubber spatula, transfer the soft, sticky dough to a gallon-size zipper-lock plastic bag. Put the bag on a flat surface, leaving the top open, and roll the dough into a 9-x-10½-inch rectangle that's ¼ inch thick. As you roll, turn the bag occasionally and lift the plastic from the dough so it doesn't cause creases. When you get the right size and thickness, seal the bag, pressing out as much air as possible, and refrigerate the dough for at least 2 hours, or for up to 2 days.

GETTING READY TO BAKE: Position the racks to divide the oven into thirds and preheat the oven to 350 degrees F. Line two baking sheets with parchment or silicone mats.

Put the plastic bag on a cutting board and slit it open. Turn the firm dough out onto the board (discard the bag) and, using a ruler as a guide and a sharp knife, cut the dough into 1½-inch squares. Transfer the squares to the baking sheets and carefully prick each one twice with a fork, gently pushing the tines through the cookies until they hit the sheet.

Place the baking sheets in the oven and immediately lower the oven temperature to 300 degrees F. Bake the shortbreads for 25 to 30 minutes, rotating the sheets from top to bottom and front to back at the midway point. The shortbreads should be set and only just tinged golden. Transfer the cookies to racks to cool to room temperature.

# SABLÉS

SABLÉS, RICH, tender shortbread cookies, are as popular in France as chocolate chip cookies are in America. And for several good reasons: the pure flavor of butter, the cookie's key player; a paradoxical but paradisical texture—the cookie is both crumbly and melt-in-your-mouth tender; and it has an anytime rightness that makes it as perfect with a tall glass of milk, a bowl of ice cream or a basket of berries as it is on a petits fours tray in France's grandest restaurants. I learned to make sablés in Paris working with some of the city's best pâtissiers, and this master recipe is based on what they taught me—the Playing Around variations are my American riffs on their standard.

The dough for sablés is shaped into logs and then sprinkled with sugar before it is sliced and baked. During the year, I coat the logs with sparkly white decorating sugar. When the holidays come around, I double the recipe and go mad with color, sprinkling some of the logs with brilliant red sugar, some with green and some with a rainbow mix. Trimmed in color and packed in festive tins, these make terrific Christmas cookies.

If you're new to sablés, take a look at the pointers on page 124 before you set to work.

MAKES ABOUT 50 COOKIES

SERVING: Serve these with anything from lemonade to espresso.

STORING: The cookies will keep in a tin at room temperature for about 5 days. If you do not sprinkle the sablés with sugar, they can be wrapped airtight and frozen for up to 2 months. Because the sugar will melt in the freezer, the decorated cookies are not suitable for freezing.

2 sticks (8 ounces) unsalted butter, at room temperature

½ cup sugar

¼ cup confectioners' sugar, sifted

½ teaspoon salt, preferably fine sea salt

2 large egg yolks, at room temperature

2 cups all-purpose flour

Decorating (coarse) sugar

Working with a stand mixer, preferably fitted with a paddle attachment, or with a hand mixer in a large bowl, beat the butter at medium speed until smooth and very creamy. Add the sugars and salt and beat until well blended, about 1 minute. The mixture should be smooth and velvety, not fluffy and airy. Reduce the mixer speed to low and beat in the egg yolks, again beating until the mixture is homogenous.

Turn off the mixer. Pour in the flour, drape a kitchen towel over the stand mixer to protect yourself and the counter from flying flour and pulse the mixer at low speed about 5 times, a second or two each time. Take a peek—if there is still a lot of flour on the surface of the dough, pulse a couple more times; if not, remove the towel. Continuing at low speed, mix for about 30 seconds more, just until the flour disappears into the dough and the dough looks uniformly moist. (If most of the flour is incorporated but you've still got some in the bottom of the bowl, use a rubber spatula to work the rest of the flour into the dough.) The dough will not clean the sides of the bowl, nor will it come together in a ball—and it shouldn't. You want to work the dough as little as possible. What you're aiming for is a soft, moist, clumpy (rather than smooth) dough. Pinch it, and it will feel a little like Play-Doh.

Scrape the dough out onto a smooth work surface, gather it into a ball and divide it in half. Shape each piece into a smooth log about 9 inches long: it's easiest to work on a piece of plastic wrap and use the plastic to help form the log. Wrap the logs well and refrigerate them for at least 3 hours, preferably longer. (The dough can be kept in the refrigerator for up to 3 days or frozen for up to 2 months.)

GETTING READY TO BAKE: Center a rack in the oven and preheat the oven to 350 degrees F. Line two baking sheets with parchment or silicone mats.

Remove a log of dough from the refrigerator, unwrap it and place it on a piece of parchment or wax paper. Whisk the egg yolk until it is smooth, and brush some of the yolk all over the sides of the dough—this is the glue—then sprinkle the entire surface of the log with decorating sugar.

Trim the ends of the roll if they're ragged, and slice the log into $1/3$-inch-thick cookies. (You can make these as thick as $1/2$ inch or as thin as—but no thinner than—$1/4$ inch.) Place the rounds on the baking sheets, leaving an inch of space between them.

Bake one sheet at a time for 17 to 20 minutes, rotating the baking sheet at the midway point. When properly baked, the cookies will be light brown on the bottom, lightly golden around the edges and pale on top; they may feel tender when you touch the top gently, and that's fine. Remove from the oven and let the cookies rest a minute or two before carefully lifting them onto a rack with a wide metal spatula to cool to room temperature.

Repeat with the remaining log of dough, making sure the baking sheets are cool before you bake the second batch.

*Playing Around*

**LEMON SABLÉS:** Working in a small bowl, using your fingers, rub the grated zest of 1 to 1½ lemons (depending on your taste) into the granulated sugar until the sugar is moist and very aromatic, then add this and the confectioners' sugar to the beaten butter. (Sablés can also be made with orange or lime zest; vary the amount of zest as you please.)

**PECAN SABLÉS:** Reduce the amount of flour to 1½ cups, and add ½ cup very finely ground pecans to the mixture after you have added the sugars. (In place of pecans, you can use ground almonds, hazelnuts or walnuts.) If you'd like, instead of sprinkling the dough logs with sugar, sprinkle them with very finely chopped pecans or a mixture of pecans and sugar.

**SPICE SABLÉS:** Whisk 1½ teaspoons ground cinnamon, ½ teaspoon ground ginger and ¼ teaspoon freshly grated nutmeg into the flour.

**PARMESAN SABLÉS:** For savory sablés that are ideal with aperitifs, omit both the granulated and confectioners' sugar and add ¾ cup (2¼ ounces) very finely grated Parmesan to the beaten butter. These are fine plain, but the logs can also be brushed with beaten egg yolk and sprinkled with finely chopped almonds. If you love salt, press a few grains of fleur de sel gently into the top of each sablé before slipping the baking sheet into the oven.

**WHEN I** was a kid, the main street in our neighborhood boasted a bakery every two blocks. We always had freshly made bread from the baker closest to our house and almost as often a box of butter cookies from the baker farthest away. My mother would always ask for an assortment, which meant we ended up with too many of those pink-and-green marzipan cookies and not enough of the linzers, buttery, lightly spiced sandwich cookies filled with raspberry jam that peeked through a little cutout on the top. These were the ones I liked best.

This recipe is not a duplicate of the cookie of my childhood, but it is inspired by it and it brings back childhood memories. I've made these cookies a bit spicier than the originals—I like that extra zing—and I make the peekaboo cutouts only when I'm in the mood to fuss a bit. The rolling out, which is a cinch, can be done just as soon as the malleable dough is made.

MAKES ABOUT 50 COOKIES
(OR 25 SANDWICH COOKIES)

**SERVING:** These are best served with espresso topped with whipped cream. They're also awfully good served with a big bowl of chocolate ice cream.

**STORING:** The cookies will keep at room temperature for about 3 days and can be frozen for up to 2 months—skip the sugar-dusting if you're going to freeze the cookies.

| | |
|---|---|
| 1½ cups finely ground almonds, hazelnuts or walnuts | 1 stick (8 tablespoons) unsalted butter, at room temperature |
| 1½ cups all-purpose flour | ½ cup sugar |
| 1½ teaspoons ground cinnamon | ½ cup raspberry jam or strained apricot jam plus 1 teaspoon water (optional) |
| ¼ teaspoon salt | |
| Scant ¼ teaspoon ground cloves | |
| 1 large egg | Confectioners' sugar, for dusting |
| 2 teaspoons water | |

Whisk together the ground nuts, flour, cinnamon, salt and cloves. Using a fork, stir the egg and water together in a small bowl.

Working with a stand mixer, preferably fitted with a paddle attachment, or with a hand mixer in a large bowl, beat the butter and sugar together at medium speed until smooth, about 3 minutes, scraping down the bowl as needed. Add the egg mixture and beat for 1 minute more. Reduce the speed to low and add the dry ingredients, mixing only until they disappear into the dough. Don't work the dough much once the flour is incorporated. If the dough comes together but some dry crumbs remain in the bottom of the bowl, stop the mixer and finish blending the ingredients with a rubber spatula or your hands.

Divide the dough in half. Working with one half at a time, put the dough between two large sheets of wax paper or plastic wrap. Using your hands, flatten the dough into a disk, then grab a rolling pin and roll out the dough, turning it over frequently so that the paper doesn't cut into it, until it is about ¼ inch thick. Leave the dough in the paper and repeat with the second piece of dough. Transfer the wrapped dough to a baking sheet or cutting board (to keep it flat) and refrigerate or freeze it until it is very firm, about 2 hours in the refrigerator or about 45 minutes in the freezer. The rolled-out dough can be wrapped airtight and stored in the refrigerator for up to 3 days or in the freezer for up to 2 months. Just thaw the dough enough to cut out the cookies and go on from there.

*Playing Around*

**CHOCOLATE-FILLED LINZER SABLÉS:** To fill the cookies with chocolate, put 6 ounces finely chopped bittersweet chocolate in a heatproof bowl. Bring ⅓ cup heavy cream to a boil. Pour the cream over the chocolate; let stand briefly. With a whisk, gently stir until you have a smooth, glossy ganache. Stir in 1 tablespoon of room-temperature unsalted butter. Chill the ganache briefly to bring it to spreading consistency.

Place about ½ teaspoon of the ganache in the center of half of the cookies and sandwich with the remaining cookies. Under the theory that more is better, there's no reason not to use both chocolate and jam to fill the cookies. Spread half the cookies with a thin layer of jam, top with about ½ teaspoon of the ganache and sandwich with the remaining cookies.

**GETTING READY TO BAKE:** Center a rack in the oven and preheat the oven to 375 degrees F. Line two baking sheets with parchment or silicone mats.

Peel off the top sheet of wax paper from one piece of dough and, using a 2-inch round cookie cutter—a scalloped cutter is nice for these—cut out as many cookies as you can. If you want to have a peekaboo cutout, use the end of a piping tip to cut out a very small circle from the centers of half the cookies. Transfer the rounds to the baking sheets, leaving a little space between the cookies. Set the scraps aside—you can combine them with the scraps from the second disk and roll and cut more cookies.

Bake the cookies one sheet at a time for 11 to 13 minutes, or until the cookies are lightly golden, dry and just firm to the touch. Transfer the cookies to a rack to cool to room temperature.

Repeat with the second disk of dough, making sure to cool the baking sheets between batches. Gather the scraps of dough together, press them into a disk, roll them between sheets of wax paper or plastic wrap and refrigerate until firm, then cut and bake.

IF YOU'D LIKE TO MAKE SANDWICH COOKIES: Place the jam in a small saucepan or in a microwaveable bowl and stir in the 1 teaspoon water. Bring to a boil over low heat or in the microwave. Let the jam cool slightly, then turn half of the cookies flat side up and place about 1/2 teaspoon of the jam in the center of each cookie; sandwich with the remaining cookies.

Just before serving, dust the cookies lightly with confectioners' sugar.

## What Goes Round Stays Round

**SLICE-AND-BAKE** cookies made from logs of dough
are the simplest in the baker's repertory.

The easiest way to keep the log of dough round while stowing it in the fridge or freezer is to chill it inside a cardboard tube left from a roll of paper toweling—slit the tube so it's easy to wrap it around the dough. (I learned this trick from food stylist Jeanne Voltz.) When you're slicing the log, the easiest way to prevent losing that nice roundness is to give the log a quarter turn each time you slice off a circle of dough.

Of course, no matter how careful you are about keeping everything round, some doughs just don't toe the line and go raggedy in the oven. If this happens, just call them "rustic."

**I ONCE** said I thought these cookies, the brainchild of the Parisian pastry chef Pierre Hermé, were as important a culinary breakthrough as Toll House cookies, and I've never thought better of the statement. These butter-rich, sandy-textured slice-and-bake cookies are members of the sablé family (see page 124 and page 137 for pointers). But, unlike classic sablés, they are midnight dark—there's cocoa in the dough—and packed with chunks of hand-chopped bittersweet chocolate. Perhaps most memorably, they're salty. Not just a little salty, but remarkably and sensationally salty. It's the salt—Pierre uses fleur de sel, a moist, off-white sea salt—that surprises, delights and makes the chocolate flavors in the cookies seem preternaturally profound.

When I included these in *Paris Sweets,* they were called Korova Cookies and they instantly won fans, among them my neighbor Richard Gold, who gave them their new name. Richard is convinced that a daily dose of Pierre's cookies is all that is needed to ensure planetary peace and happiness.

**MAKES ABOUT 36 COOKIES**

**SERVING:** The cookies can be eaten when they are warm or at room temperature—I prefer them at room temperature, when the textural difference between the crumbly cookie and the chocolate bits is greatest—and are best suited to cold milk or hot coffee.

**STORING:** Packed airtight, the cookies will keep at room temperature for up to 3 days; they can be frozen for up to 2 months.

| | |
|---|---|
| 1¼ cups all-purpose flour | ¼ cup sugar |
| ⅓ cup unsweetened cocoa powder | ½ teaspoon fleur de sel or ¼ teaspoon fine sea salt |
| ½ teaspoon baking soda | |
| 1 stick plus 3 tablespoons (11 tablespoons) unsalted butter, at room temperature | 1 teaspoon pure vanilla extract |
| | 5 ounces bittersweet chocolate, chopped into chips, or a generous ¾ cup store-bought mini chocolate chips |
| ⅔ cup (packed) light brown sugar | |

Sift the flour, cocoa and baking soda together.

Working with a stand mixer, preferably fitted with a paddle attachment, or with a hand mixer in a large bowl, beat the butter on medium speed until soft and creamy. Add both sugars, the salt and vanilla extract and beat for 2 minutes more.

Turn off the mixer. Pour in the dry ingredients, drape a kitchen towel over the stand mixer to protect yourself and your kitchen from flying flour and pulse the mixer at low speed about 5 times, a second or two each time. Take a peek—if there is still a lot of flour on the surface of the dough, pulse a couple of times more; if not, remove the towel. Continuing at low speed, mix for about 30 seconds more, just until the flour disappears into the dough—for the best texture, work the dough as little as possible once the flour is added, and don't be concerned if the dough looks a little crumbly. Toss in the chocolate pieces and mix only to incorporate.

Turn the dough out onto a work surface, gather it together and divide it in half. Working with one half at a time, shape the dough into logs that are 1½ inches in diameter. Wrap the logs in plastic wrap and refrigerate them for at least 3 hours. (The dough can be refrigerated for up to 3 days or frozen for up to 2 months. If you've frozen the dough, you needn't defrost it before baking—just slice the logs into cookies and bake the cookies 1 minute longer.)

**GETTING READY TO BAKE:** Center a rack in the oven and preheat the oven to 325 degrees F. Line two baking sheets with parchment or silicone mats.

Using a sharp thin knife, slice the logs into rounds that are ½ inch thick. (The rounds are likely to crack as you're cutting them—don't be concerned, just squeeze the bits back onto each cookie.) Arrange the rounds on the baking sheets, leaving about 1 inch between them.

Bake the cookies one sheet at a time for 12 minutes—they won't look done, nor will they be firm, but that's just the way they should be. Transfer the baking sheet to a cooling rack and let the cookies rest until they are only just warm, at which point you can serve them or let them reach room temperature.

## A Cookie Comes Full Circle

NOT LONG AGO, I was invited to speak to a group of French-American women at a luncheon being hosted by one of the members in her Manhattan apartment. The lunch, prepared by the family's private chef, was light, colorful, delicious and so French that for a few hours, I forgot I was in New York. I spoke after the main course, before dessert, and when I was just minutes into my little talk, the hostess emerged from the kitchen with a plate of cookies, walked up to me and said, "You must try one of these immediately—they're our favorite cookies, and they're so fabulous because the chef puts salt in them!" One look and I was pretty sure they were World Peace Cookies; one taste and I knew. But what was I supposed to say? Was I supposed to admit that I knew the cookies and that the recipe was probably mine? I didn't think so, so I said, "These are great," then turned to the audience and told them they were in for a treat.

When I finished my talk, the hostess asked if I'd like to go into the kitchen to meet the chef. Of course I would. I walked into the kitchen, stretched out my hand and said, "What a terrific lunch. Thank you." Then I introduced myself.

The chef, who had no idea I was going to be there, was flustered and repeatedly apologized for having served me my own recipe. "Stop apologizing," I almost shouted. "You have no idea how exciting this is!" And it was exciting. It was a joy to know that something I liked so much had made other people happy. That the feeling had come full circle made it even more joyful.

IF ONLY the dough for these quite sophisticated little rounds didn't have to chill, you could go from craving to nibbling in 20 minutes flat. After all, it's quick to make—it comes together in a food processor in about 5 minutes. It's also quick to shape—it's rolled into logs in under 5 minutes. And it's quick to bake—3 minutes to slice and just 7 minutes in the oven. But there is that chilling period. Since these are classic slice-and-bake refrigerator cookies, they need a few hours in the fridge to firm up. Think of it as time to decide whether you'll serve these mildly spiced, slightly chewy, almond-flecked chocolate cookies plain, dipped into melted chocolate, dotted with raspberry jam or alongside coffee ice cream.

MAKES ABOUT 40 COOKIES

SERVING: Offer these up as is with coffee, tea or ice cream. Or, if you'd like to dress them up, dip them up to their mid-points in melted chocolate, or—this is my favorite—serve them with a pot of great-quality raspberry jam, so everyone at the table can spoon a dollop onto each cookie.

STORING: The cookies can be kept in a tin for about 4 days.

| | |
|---|---|
| 1½ cups all-purpose flour | ¾ cup sugar |
| ½ cup blanched almonds (whole, sliced or slivered) | 1 stick (8 tablespoons) unsalted butter, at room temperature |
| 3 tablespoons unsweetened cocoa powder | ½ teaspoon pure vanilla extract |
| ½ teaspoon baking powder | 1 large egg |
| ⅛ teaspoon ground allspice or cloves | 2 ounces bittersweet chocolate, melted and cooled |
| Pinch of salt | |

Put the flour, almonds, cocoa, baking powder, spice and salt in a food processor and pulse, scraping down the sides of the bowl as necessary, until the almonds are finely ground. Turn the ingredients out onto a sheet of wax paper.

Put the sugar and the butter into the processor and whir for a minute, then scrape the bowl and process for another 15 seconds; the butter and sugar should be smoothly blended. Add the vanilla and egg and process for 30 seconds, then scrape and process for another 30 seconds. Add the chocolate and pulse to blend. Finally, add the dry ingredients and pulse until they are fully incorporated. You'll have a soft, fudgy, very malleable dough. Scrape it out onto a work surface.

Divide the dough in half and roll each piece into a log 7 to 8 inches long and 1 inch in diameter. Once the logs are formed, wrap them in plastic wrap, twisting the ends of the plastic firecracker-style to tighten the rolls. Refrigerate for at least 4 hours. (The logs can be wrapped airtight and refrigerated for up to 4 days or kept frozen for up to 2 months; slice and bake the frozen logs without defrosting—just add a minute or two to the baking time.)

GETTING READY TO BAKE: Center a rack in the oven and preheat the oven to 375 degrees F. Line two baking sheets with parchment or silicone mats.

Using a thin knife, cut the logs into ⅓-inch-thick rounds and place the rounds on the baking sheets, leaving at least 1 inch between rounds.

Bake the cookies one sheet at a time for 7 minutes, or until the cookies are slightly puffed and their tops look dry. Transfer the sheet to a rack and wait 1 minute before carefully lifting the still-fragile cookies onto a rack to cool to room temperature.

*Playing Around*

CHOCOLATE SPICE ICE CREAM SANDWICHES: I like using these cookies as the "bread" for ice cream sandwiches because their texture, firm but a little crumbly, and their flavor, gently spiced, hold up when chilled. You can make very elegant petit four–style ice cream sandwiches by keeping the cookies at their 1-inch diameter. Just spread the bottoms of half the cookies with softened ice cream, mounding the ice cream about ¼ inch thick, use the other half of the batch as toppers and freeze the sandwiches on a lined baking sheet until firm; wrap airtight when frozen. Or, after you've made the dough, form it into logs with a chubby 2- or 3-inch diameter. Whichever size you make, fill the sandwiches with premium-quality or—better yet—homemade ice cream, choosing coffee, chocolate (page 430), vanilla (page 428) or something exotic, like Honey-Peach Ice Cream (page 437).

# LENOX ALMOND BISCOTTI

**WHEN TONY** Fortuna, the owner of Lenox, one of my favorite restaurants in New York City, gave me this recipe for his biscotti, I stopped making any other almond biscotti and started making these in double batches—twice a week. They are perfect—crunchy but not rock solid, dippable, dunkable and eminently munchable, as good with breakfast café au lait as with late-night herbal tea. They're great with ice cream, fruit salad, mousses and puddings too. *Mille grazie,* Tony.

These lend themselves to many variations, and additions (see Playing Around).

MAKES ABOUT 30 COOKIES

**SERVING:** These are good with just about anything—including themselves. Eat one, and you'll want another.

**STORING:** Because they are dry and they're fine if they get even drier, the biscotti will keep at room temperature, covered or not, for about a week. They can be frozen, but I rarely store them that way—mostly because they rarely last long enough to get wrapped up for long-term storage.

| | |
|---|---|
| 1½ cups all-purpose flour | 1 cup sugar |
| 1½ teaspoons baking powder | 2 large eggs |
| ¼ teaspoon salt | 1½ teaspoons pure almond extract |
| ½ cup yellow cornmeal | ¾ cup sliced almonds, blanched |
| 1 stick (8 tablespoons) unsalted | or unblanched |
| butter, at room temperature | |

**GETTING READY:** Center a rack in the oven and preheat the oven to 350 degrees F. Line a baking sheet with parchment or a silicone mat.

Whisk the flour, baking powder and salt together. Add the cornmeal and whisk again to blend.

Working with a stand mixer, preferably fitted with a paddle attachment, or with a hand mixer in a large bowl, beat the butter and sugar together at medium speed for 3 minutes, until very smooth. Add the eggs and continue to beat, scraping down the bowl as needed, for another 2 minutes, or until the mixture is light, smooth and creamy. Beat in the almond extract. Reduce the mixer speed to low and add the dry ingredients, mixing only until they are incorporated. You'll have a soft stick-to-your-fingers dough that will ball up around the paddle or beaters. Scrape down the paddle and bowl, toss in the almonds and mix just to blend.

Scrape half the dough onto one side of the baking sheet. Using your fingers and a rubber spatula or scraper, work the dough into a log about 12 inches long and 1½ inches wide. The log will be more rectangular than domed, and bumpy, rough and uneven. Form a second log with the remaining dough on the other side of the baking sheet.

Bake for 15 minutes, or until the logs are lightly golden but still soft and springy to the touch. Transfer the baking sheet to a rack and cool the logs on the baking sheet for 30 minutes.

If you turned off the oven, bring it back up to 350 degrees F.

Using a wide metal spatula, transfer the logs to a cutting board and, with a long serrated knife, trim the ends and cut the logs into ¾-inch-thick slices. Return the slices to the baking sheet—this time standing them up like a marching band—and slide the sheet back into the oven.

Bake the biscotti for another 15 minutes, or until they are golden and firm. Transfer them to racks and cool to room temperature.

## *Playing Around*

I'll get you started with some suggestions for varying these biscotti, but I know you'll have several of your own—just look in your cupboard for ideas.

**DRIED FRUIT BIS-COTTI:** Add about ⅓ cup dried fruit, such as raisins, dried cherries, cranberries, apricots (chopped) or currants, to the dough. If you'd like an extra shot of flavor, flame the fruit with port, kirsch, dark rum or amaretto (see page 92 for instructions on how to steep and flame dried fruit).

**SPICED BISCOTTI:** Whisk some spice into the flour mixture: ground cinnamon, ginger, cardamom or even black pepper. For cinnamon and ginger, use ½ to 1 teaspoon; for cardamom, ½ teaspoon; and for black pepper, ½ to 1 teaspoon. Start with the lesser amount, then make to-taste adjustments on the next batch. If you choose to add ginger, you could also add very small pieces of stem ginger in syrup (available at Asian markets and in the Asian foods sections of some supermarkets).

**ANISETTE BISCOTTI:** Many traditional biscotti are flavored with anise, and these can be too. For the best results, grind the aniseed (start with 1½ teaspoons and, if you want, increase or decrease the amount in your next batch) in a food processor or blender with the sugar.

**NUTTY BISCOTTI:** Substitute walnuts, pecans, hazelnuts or chopped macadamia nuts for the almonds or, following the theory that more is merrier, make the biscotti with a combination of nuts.

**LEMON OR ORANGE BISCOTTI:** Rub the grated zest of 2 lemons or 1 orange into the sugar before beating the butter and sugar together.

# CHOCOLATE BISCOTTI

MAKES ABOUT 40 COOKIES

**MY DEAR** and wonderful New York neighbor Richard Gold gave me this recipe. He got it from Thelma Labensky, a woman I've never met but whom I now consider a miracle worker, since her biscotti have been known to turn grouches into grinners (at least for the few minutes they're eating her cookies). Thelma's biscotti are cocoa-and-espresso dark and liberally speckled with chopped almonds and small chunks of semisweet chocolate. And, of course, they're crunchy.

| | |
|---|---|
| 2 cups all-purpose flour | 2 large eggs, lightly beaten |
| ½ cup unsweetened cocoa powder | 1 teaspoon pure vanilla extract |
| 2 tablespoons instant espresso powder | 1 cup chopped almonds, blanched or unblanched |
| ¾ teaspoon baking soda | 4 ounces bittersweet chocolate, coarsely chopped, or ¾ cup store-bought mini chocolate chips |
| ½ teaspoon baking powder | |
| 1 teaspoon salt | |
| ¾ stick (6 tablespoons) unsalted butter, at room temperature | Sugar, for dusting |
| 1 cup sugar | |

**GETTING READY:** Center a rack in the oven and preheat the oven to 350 degrees F. Line a baking sheet with parchment or a silicone mat.

Sift together the flour, cocoa, espresso powder, baking soda, baking powder and salt.

Working with a stand mixer, preferably fitted with a paddle attachment, or with a hand mixer in a large bowl, beat the butter and sugar together on medium speed until pale, about 2 minutes; the mixture may be crumbly. Scrape down the sides of the bowl, add the eggs and vanilla and beat for another 2 minutes; don't worry if the mixture looks curdled. Reduce the mixer speed to low and mix in the dry ingredients in 3 additions, mixing only until a dough forms. Scrape down the sides of the bowl. Mix in the chopped nuts and chocolate, then turn the dough out onto a work surface and knead in any dry ingredients that might have escaped mixing.

Divide the dough in half. Working with one half at a time, roll the dough into 12-inch-long logs. Flatten both logs with the palm of your hand, so that they are ½ to 1 inch high, about 2 inches across and sort of rectangular, then carefully lift the logs onto the baking sheet. Sprinkle each log with a little sugar.

Bake the logs for about 25 minutes, or until they are just slightly firm. The logs will spread and crack—and that's just fine. Remove the baking sheet from the oven, put it on a cooling rack and cool the logs for about 20 minutes. (Leave the oven on.)

Working with one log at a time, using a long serrated knife, cut each log into slices between ½ and ¾ inch thick. Stand the slices up on the baking sheet—you'll have an army of biscotti—and bake the cookies again, this time for just 10 minutes.

Transfer the biscotti to a rack to cool.

**SERVING:** You can serve these with coffee—espresso, cappuccino, lattes or plain-old-poured-from-the-pot coffee—red wine, milk or ice cream. Or, if you stick them in a cookie jar and leave them on the counter, they'll just about serve themselves.

**STORING:** By their very nature, biscotti are good keepers. They'll keep in a cookie jar or an open basket for a week or more. Wrapped airtight, they can be frozen for up to 2 months.

*Playing Around*

**CHOCOLATE-CHERRY BISCOTTI:** As impossible as it seems, these are even more irresistible than the original version. Add ⅓ cup chopped dried cherries to the dough along with the almonds and chocolate.

**WHITE CHOCOLATE-DIPPED BISCOTTI:** Have a baking sheet lined with a silicone baking mat or a sheet of parchment or wax paper at hand. Gently melt 12 ounces finely chopped white chocolate or 2 cups store-bought white chocolate chips in a heatproof bowl over a saucepan of simmering water, and scrape the chocolate into a narrow heatproof container. One by one, dip the biscotti into the chocolate, coating them to their midpoints. Lay the biscotti on the mat or paper, and when they are all dipped, slide them into the refrigerator for about 15 minutes to set the white chocolate.

# COCONUT BUTTER THINS

**THERE WAS** a moment when I thought I shouldn't include these because they are so fragile—but they're too good not to share. They are like shortbread cookies in their preparation and melt-in-your-mouth butteriness, but once they're slid into the oven, they become more wafery and lacy. Because they also contain coconut and chopped macadamia nuts, they've got a bit of bump and crunch.

MAKES 32 COOKIES

**SERVING:** Save these for an after-dessert dessert, so they'll be the last taste you have with your last sip of coffee or tea.

**STORING:** Wrapped well, these will keep for about 3 days at room temperature or for up to 2 months in the freezer.

| | |
|---|---|
| 1½ cups all-purpose flour | 2 sticks (8 ounces) unsalted butter, |
| ¼ cup cornstarch | at room temperature |
| ¼ teaspoon salt | 1½ teaspoons pure vanilla extract |
| Pinch of ground coriander | ⅔ cup sweetened shredded coconut |
| ⅔ cup sugar | ½ cup finely chopped macadamia nuts |
| Grated zest of 1 lime | (don't be afraid to use salted nuts) |

Whisk together the flour, cornstarch, salt and coriander.

If you want to get a little more flavor out of the lime zest, put the sugar and zest in the mixer bowl and, using your fingertips, work the zest into the sugar until the sugar is moist and the mixture fragrant.

Working with a stand mixer, preferably fitted with a paddle attachment, or with a hand mixer in a large bowl, beat the butter, sugar and zest on medium speed for about 3 minutes, or until smooth. Beat in the vanilla extract. Reduce the mixer speed to low and add the flour mixture, mixing only until the dry ingredients disappear. Add the coconut and nuts and pulse to incorporate them. There will probably be some dry ingredients in the bottom of the bowl—don't work them in with the mixer, just reach into the bowl and knead them in.

Transfer the soft, sticky dough to a gallon-size zipper-lock bag. Put the bag on a flat surface, leaving the top open, and roll the dough into a 9-x-10½-inch rectangle that's ¼ inch thick. As you roll, turn the bag occasionally and lift the plastic from the dough so it doesn't cause creases. When you get the right size and thickness, seal the bag, pressing out as much air as possible, and refrigerate the dough for at least 2 hours or for up to 2 days.

GETTING READY TO BAKE: Position the racks to divide the oven into thirds and preheat the oven to 325 degrees F. Line two baking sheets with parchment or silicone mats.

Put the plastic bag on a cutting board and slit it open. Turn the dough out onto the board (discard the bag), and, using a ruler as a guide and a sharp knife, cut it into 32 squares, each roughly 1½ inches on a side. Transfer the squares to the baking sheets, leaving about 2 inches between them, and carefully prick each one twice with a fork, gently pushing the tines through the cookies to the sheet.

Bake for 18 to 20 minutes, rotating the sheets from top to bottom and front to back at the midway point. The shortbreads will be very pale—they shouldn't take on much color. Transfer the cookies to a rack and cool to room temperature.

MAKES ABOUT
FIFTY 2-INCH COOKIES

**THESE ARE** my rendition of my grandmother's sugar cookies, the ones she used to make for us every week, sprinkling the tops of the cookies earmarked for my brother and me with cinnamon sugar and the tops of those meant for our parents with poppy seeds. Actually this recipe is a composite of grandmother recipes, from mine and my husband's (with an Aunt Bertha recipe tossed in for good measure), all of which were written on small recipe cards and fingerprint-stained long before they came to me.

The cookies are crisp, buttery (but not soft buttery, like their cousins in the shortbread family) and basic—literally, meaning they can be the base for several variations. You can stir zest into the dough or add chopped nuts, shredded coconut or grated chocolate. You can roll out the dough and cut it with cutters plain or fancy, or you can even turn it into the world's easiest cookie, the slice-and-bake. (See Playing Around for a few ideas.) And the cookies take nicely to frosting, icing or glazing.

**SERVING:** My grandmother always served these with lemon tea.

**STORING:** The cookies will keep at room temperature in a tin for up to 1 week. Wrapped well, they can be frozen for up to 2 months.

| | |
|---|---|
| 2 cups all-purpose flour | 1 large egg |
| ½ teaspoon salt | 1 large egg yolk |
| ½ teaspoon baking powder | 1 teaspoon pure vanilla extract |
| 1 stick plus 2 tablespoons (10 tablespoons) unsalted butter, at room temperature | |
| 1 cup sugar | Sugar or cinnamon sugar, for dusting (optional) |

Whisk the flour, salt and baking powder together.

Working with a stand mixer, preferably fitted with a paddle attachment, or with a hand mixer in a large bowl, beat the butter at medium speed for a minute or so, until smooth. Beat in the sugar and continue to beat for about 2 minutes, until the mixture is light and pale. Add the egg and yolk and beat for another minute or two; beat in the vanilla. Reduce the mixer speed to low and steadily add the flour mixture, mixing only until it has been incorporated—because this dough is best when worked least, you might want to stop the mixer before all the flour is thoroughly blended into the dough and finish the job with a rubber spatula. When mixed, the dough will be soft, creamy and malleable.

Turn the dough out onto a counter and divide it in half. If you want to make roll-out cookies, shape each half into a disk and wrap in plastic. If you want to make slice-and-bake cookies, shape each half into a chubby sausage (the diameter is up to you—I usually like cookies that are about 2 inches in diameter) and wrap in plastic. Whether you're going to roll or slice the dough, it must be chilled for at least 2 hours. (Well wrapped, the dough can be refrigerated for up to 3 days or frozen for up to 2 months.)

### Playing Around

My grandmother never toyed with her plain recipe, but my husband's grandmother would add the grated zest of 1 lemon or 1 orange to the dough, and you can too—for the most flavor, rub the zest into the sugar, before adding it to the butter, until the sugar is moist and aromatic. For a lightly spiced cookie, add ½ to 1 teaspoon, depending on your taste, ground cinnamon, ginger, allspice or cardamom. You can also play with the cookie's topping, giving the cookies a dusting of decorating sugar before they go into the oven or making a confectioners' sugar and lemon juice (or water) icing (use about ¾ cup sugar and about 1 tablespoon liquid, or enough to get the right consistency) to spread on them after they've cooled.

GETTING READY TO BAKE: Center a rack in the oven and preheat the oven to 350 degrees F. Line two baking sheets with parchment or silicone mats.

If you are making roll-out cookies, working with one packet of dough at a time, roll out the dough between sheets of plastic wrap or wax paper to a thickness of $1/4$ inch, lifting the plastic or paper and turning the dough over often so that it rolls evenly. Lift off the top sheet of plastic or paper and cut out the cookies—I like a 2-inch round cookie cutter for these. Pull away the excess dough, saving the scraps for rerolling, and carefully lift the rounds onto the baking sheets with a spatula, leaving about $1^1/2$ inches between the cookies. (This is a soft dough and you might have trouble peeling away the excess or lifting the cutouts; if so, cover the dough, chill it for about 15 minutes and try again.) After you've rolled and cut the second packet of dough, you can form the scraps into a disk, then chill, roll, cut and bake.

If you are making slice-and-bake cookies, use a sharp thin knife to slice the dough into $1/4$-inch-thick rounds, and place the rounds on the baking sheets, leaving about $1^1/2$ inches of space between the cookies.

Bake the cookies one sheet at a time for 9 to 11 minutes, rotating the sheet at the midpoint. The cookies should feel firm, but they should not color much, if at all. Remove the pan from the oven and dust the cookies with sugar or cinnamon sugar, if you'd like. Let them rest for 1 minute before carefully lifting them onto a rack to cool to room temperature.

Repeat with the remaining dough, cooling the baking sheets between batches.

# COTTAGE CHEESE PUFFLETS

**I FOUND** this recipe written in my first kitchen scrapbook, with no hint as to where it came from. The only note on the page was the word "delicious" printed in red.

I remember making the cookies often the first few years of my marriage, and I remember they were addictively munchable. Then the book got buried on a high-up shelf. When I liberated it just a couple of years ago, I made the pufflets again and discovered they'd aged beautifully: they're still the winners they were decades ago—proof, once more, that goodness is timeless.

The dough for these tender little pastry triangles, based on cottage cheese and butter, is softly flaky, mildly tangy and interesting enough to stand on its own. If you wanted, you could just cut out tiny squares of the dough and bake them as is. But by dropping a spoonful of jam in the center of each square and folding them over into triangles, you create a twice-as-good cookie.

The original recipe called for mixing the dough by hand with a wooden spoon, but it's faster, easier and better made in a food processor.

MAKES ABOUT FORTY-EIGHT
2¼-INCH COOKIES

SERVING: These are lovely with either coffee or tea.

STORING: The pufflets are really best eaten the day they are made. The dough loses its characteristic lightness and flakiness over the course of a day and night.

| | |
|---|---|
| 2 sticks (8 ounces) unsalted butter, at room temperature | 1 teaspoon pure vanilla extract |
| 2 tablespoons sugar | 1⅔ cups all-purpose flour |
| ¼ teaspoon salt | About ¼ cup thick preserves, marmalade or jam (your choice) |
| 8 ounces (about ¾ cup) cottage cheese | Confectioners' sugar, for dusting |

Put the butter, sugar and salt in a food processor and process, scraping down the sides of the bowl a couple of times, for 2 minutes, or until the butter is completely creamy. Add the cottage cheese and vanilla and process for another 2 minutes, again scraping the bowl once or twice. The mixture will be velvety, more like whipped cream cheese than cottage cheese. Add the flour, pulsing only until it is thoroughly blended into the dough.

Scrape the dough out of the bowl and onto a piece of plastic wrap. Shape the dough into a rectangle or square, pat it down, cover it completely and refrigerate it for at least 3 hours, or for up to 3 days. (The dough can be wrapped airtight and frozen for up to 2 months; defrost, still wrapped, overnight in the refrigerator.)

GETTING READY TO BAKE: Center a rack in the oven and preheat the oven to 400 degrees F. Line two baking sheets with parchment or silicone mats.

To roll out the dough, you can work either between sheets of wax paper or plastic wrap or on a lightly floured surface.

Cut the dough in half. Working with one half at a time, roll the dough to a thickness of a scant ⅛ inch. Because you are going to be cutting the dough into squares, it's best to roll it into a rectangular or square shape. If at any time the dough seems too soft to roll, pop it into the refrigerator for a quick chill.

Using a cookie cutter, a paring knife or a pastry wheel, cut the dough into 2- to 3-inch squares. (I use a 2¼-inch square cookie cutter.) Put a dab of jam on one square of dough, just off center, and, with a wet finger, moisten the edges of the dough. Fold the dough over to enclose the jam and form a triangle, pressing lightly to seal the edges. Repeat with the remaining squares and line the pufflets up on the baking sheets, spacing them about ½ inch apart. Poke a minute steam hole in the center of each. (You can roll, fill and shape the pufflets, freeze them on a tray, then, when they are frozen, transfer them to an airtight container. The pufflets can be baked straight from the freezer—no need to defrost—just add another 2 minutes or so to the baking time.)

Bake the pastries one sheet at a time for 10 to 12 minutes, or until puffed, firm and beautifully golden. Transfer the pufflets to a rack, dust with confectioners' sugar and cool to warm or room temperature before serving.

Repeat with the remaining dough, cooling the baking sheets between batches.

MAKES 32 COOKIES

**SOMETIME DURING** the first year of my marriage, I visited my mother-in-law in her kitchen. There she was, listening to the radio, whistling (she is a formidable whistler) and rolling cream cheese dough around raisins and nuts to form the crescent-shaped cookies known as rugelach. I was spellbound—I'd had no idea that rugelach could be made at home. As far as I knew, rugelach, like ketchup or ships-in-bottles, were made only in laboratories. But here was my mother-in-law shaping the cookies with ease. And a short time later, there I was, eating them with ease. These cookies weren't like the rugelach my mother bought every week at the local German bakery—they were much better. I was so excited I asked for the recipe.

My mother-in-law wrote it out in her precise hand on a 3-x-5 index card. And, as she wrote, she told me that this recipe was not exactly the same as the one her mother used, that it had come from Mrs. Strauss, her next-door neighbor, and that she was sure I'd have no problem making the cookies as long as I didn't overmix the dough.

She was right. I was a newcomer to the world of baking, but I had no problem with the dough, the only potentially tricky part of the process.

Since then, I've made rugelach countless times, but nowadays my dough is even more foolproof because I make it in a food processor. I've also made a few other changes to the recipe. While my mother-in-law's rugelach were filled with cinnamon-sugared nuts, mine also include a slick of jam, some currants and a handful of chopped chocolate. This is a very old recipe, and I have no doubt that everyone who has made it has added or subtracted a little bit to make it her own—and my mom-in-law, Mrs. Strauss, and I expect you to do the same.

**SERVING:** Tea is traditional, but we drink coffee with rugelach. These are pretty and, even with their jam-and-fruit filling, not overly sweet, and they are even good with sparkling wine.

**STORING:** The cookies can be kept covered at room temperature for up to 3 days or wrapped airtight and frozen for up to 2 months.

FOR THE DOUGH

- 4 ounces cold cream cheese, cut into 4 pieces
- 1 stick (8 tablespoons) cold unsalted butter, cut into 4 pieces
- 1 cup all-purpose flour
- ¼ teaspoon salt

FOR THE FILLING

- ⅔ cup raspberry jam, apricot jam or marmalade
- 2 tablespoons sugar
- ½ teaspoon ground cinnamon

- ¼ cup chopped nuts (I prefer pecans, but you can use walnuts or almonds)
- ¼ cup plump, moist dried currants
- 4 ounces bittersweet chocolate, finely chopped, or ⅔ cup store-bought mini chocolate chips

FOR THE GLAZE

- 1 large egg
- 1 teaspoon cold water
- 2 tablespoons sugar, preferably decorating (coarse) sugar

**TO MAKE THE DOUGH:** Let the cream cheese and butter rest on the counter for 10 minutes—you want them to be slightly softened but still cool.

Put the flour and salt in a food processor, scatter over the chunks of cream cheese and butter and pulse the machine 6 to 10 times. Then process, scraping

down the sides of the bowl often, just until the dough forms large curds—don't work it so long that it forms a ball on the blade.

Turn the dough out, gather it into a ball and divide it in half. Shape each half into a disk, wrap the disks in plastic wrap and refrigerate for at least 2 hours, or up to 1 day. (Wrapped airtight, the dough can be frozen for up to 2 months.)

TO MAKE THE FILLING: Heat the jam in a saucepan over low heat, or do this in a microwave, until it liquefies. Mix the sugar and cinnamon together.

Line two baking sheets with parchment or silicone mats. (Silicone baking mats are great for rugelach.)

TO SHAPE THE COOKIES: Pull one packet of dough from the refrigerator. If it is too firm to roll easily, either leave it on the counter for about 10 minutes or give it a few bashes with your rolling pin.

On a lightly floured surface, roll the dough into an 11- to 12-inch circle. Spoon (or brush) a thin gloss of jam over the dough, and sprinkle over half of the cinnamon sugar. Scatter over half of the nuts, half of the currants and half of the chopped chocolate. Cover the filling with a piece of wax paper and gently press the filling into the dough, then remove the paper and save it for the next batch.

Using a pizza wheel or a sharp knife, cut the dough into 16 wedges, or triangles. (The easiest way to do this is to cut the dough into quarters, then to cut each quarter into 4 triangles.) Starting at the base of each triangle, roll the dough up so that each cookie becomes a little crescent. Arrange the roll-ups on one baking sheet, making sure the points are tucked under the cookies, and refrigerate. Repeat with the second packet of dough, and refrigerate the cookies for at least 30 minutes before baking. (The cookies can be covered and refrigerated overnight or frozen for up to 2 months; don't defrost before baking, just add a couple of minutes to the baking time.)

GETTING READY TO BAKE: Position the racks to divide the oven into thirds and preheat the oven to 350 degrees F.

TO GLAZE: Stir the egg and water together, and brush a bit of this glaze over each rugelach. Sprinkle the cookies with the sugar.

Bake the cookies for 20 to 25 minutes, rotating the sheets from top to bottom and front to back at the midway point, until they are puffed and golden. Transfer the cookies to racks to cool to just warm or to room temperature.

# CAFÉ VOLCANO COOKIES

**LIGHT, BUMPY**, nutty and completely higgledy-piggledy-shaped, these cratered meringue nuggets are just the cookie to reach for with your last coffee of the afternoon or your last spoonful of ice cream at night. They are featherweight but packed with flavor, and I love the way they disappear in your mouth—quickly, so quickly and fizzily that if they didn't have nuts, you'd think you were eating espresso Pop Rocks.

- 1 cup blanched almonds (whole, sliced or slivered), coarsely chopped
- 1 cup walnuts, coarsely chopped
- 2 large egg whites, at room temperature
- 1 cup sugar
- 2 teaspoons instant espresso powder

**MAKES ABOUT 36 COOKIES**

**SERVING:** Offer these just as they are, with espresso, hot coffee or ice cream.

**STORING:** Kept in a cool, dry place at room temperature (they should never be refrigerated), the cookies will hold up for about 3 days. As with all meringues, humidity will make them go soggy and sticky.

**GETTING READY:** Position the racks to divide the oven into thirds and preheat the oven to 350 degrees F. Line two baking sheets with parchment or silicone mats.

Spread the chopped almonds and walnuts out on one of the baking sheets and toast the nuts in the oven. They will need 10 minutes or less to turn golden brown, so keep a close eye on them and stir them at least twice. When the nuts are toasted, remove them—with the liner—from the baking sheet and cool the sheet. Transfer the nuts to a plate, then reline the sheet and use it to bake the cookies.

Put all the ingredients, including the nuts, in a medium heavy-bottomed saucepan. Set it over medium heat and stir constantly with a silicone or wooden spatula until the ingredients are just warm to the touch. Remove from the heat.

Drop the batter by slightly rounded teaspoonfuls onto the baking sheets, leaving about an inch of space between the mounds.

Bake the cookies for about 20 minutes, rotating the pans from top to bottom and front to back at the midway point. When properly baked, the cookies will be puffed, cratered, shiny and dry. Remove the cookies from the oven and let them remain on the sheets for 5 minutes before gently prying them from the liners and transferring them to racks to cool to room temperature.

*Playing Around*

**CHOCOLATE-DIPPED VOLCANO COOKIES:** In the pastry shops of France and Italy, cookies of this type are often given a dip in tempered chocolate—the slightly firm chocolate shell makes a nice contrast to the airy meringue. You can get a similar effect by simply dipping the cookies into melted chocolate, transferring them to a parchment- or silicone-lined sheet and popping them into the refrigerator for about 10 minutes to set the chocolate. Because melted chocolate doesn't dry with the same shiny finish as tempered chocolate, you might want to dust the cookies with cocoa powder just before serving—it will camouflage your shortcut.

# COCOA ALMOND MERINGUES

IN PARIS, where meringues are so popular they could be their own food group, meringue puffs are sometimes called *rochers,* or rocks. And indeed, spooned out rather than neatly piped, these small cookies have the rough, craggy surface of stone nuggets. Their interiors are wonderfully chewy and their flavor a bit caramelish, slightly nutty and quite chocolaty. It's surprising how much chocolate flavor a small amount of cocoa and a handful of chopped chocolate can deliver.

1 cup confectioners' sugar, plus extra for dusting

⅓ cup finely ground almonds

¼ cup unsweetened cocoa powder

4 large egg whites, at room temperature

Pinch of salt

½ cup sugar

½ teaspoon pure vanilla extract

⅓ cup very finely chopped bittersweet chocolate or finely chopped store-bought chocolate chips

MAKES ABOUT 30 COOKIES

SERVING: Serve these just as they are with coffee or with ice cream.

STORING: The meringues must be kept in a cool, dry environment or they will become unpleasantly soft and sticky. Store them in an airtight tin or uncovered in a basket at room temperature.

*Playing Around*

If you'd like, you can omit the chopped chocolate or replace it with an equal amount of sweetened shredded coconut, toasted chopped almonds or pecans.

GETTING READY: Position the racks to divide the oven into thirds and preheat the oven to 300 degrees F. Line two baking sheets with parchment or silicone mats.

Sift together the confectioners' sugar, ground almonds and cocoa.

Working with a stand mixer fitted with the whisk attachment or with a hand mixer in a large dry bowl (make sure the bowl is impeccably clean and dry), whip the egg whites and salt on medium speed until the whites are opaque. Increase the speed to medium-high and continue to whip as you add the sugar about 1 tablespoon at a time. Then whip until the whites are firm and hold stiff peaks—they should still be very shiny. Beat in the vanilla, and remove the bowl from the mixer. With a large rubber spatula, quickly but gently fold in the dry ingredients, followed by the chopped chocolate. The whites will inevitably deflate as you fold in the dry ingredients—just try to work rapidly and use a light touch, so you deflate them as little as possible.

Drop the meringue by tablespoonfuls onto the baking sheets, leaving about 2 inches between the mounds. Dust the tops of the meringues very lightly with confectioners' sugar.

Bake for 10 minutes, then, without opening the oven door, reduce the oven temperature to 200 degrees F and bake for 1 hour more. Remove the baking sheets from the oven and allow the meringues to stand in a cool, dry place (not the refrigerator) until they reach room temperature.

Carefully peel the meringues off the parchment or silicone lining.

# PECAN POWDER PUFFS

MAKES ABOUT 32 COOKIES

**I LEARNED** to make these tender confectioners'-sugar-coated cookies shortly after I was married, and I wrote the recipe down with the name Pecan Powder Puffs. As I became more familiar with baking, I noticed that the same cookies were sometimes called Pecan Balls and, more often, Mexican Wedding Cakes.

You can make these cookies with a mixer or by hand, but I've found that using a food processor—a tool I didn't have when I first made them—is ideal. The dough is best when it's mixed least, and the processor allows you to get the mixing done super-quickly. And, just as you can change the method of mixing the dough, you can also change the nut that gives the cookies their base flavor. Feel free to use almonds or walnuts in place of the pecans, and to add a pinch or two of spice to the mix, if the spirit so moves you.

| | |
|---|---|
| 1 cup pecans | 1 stick (8 tablespoons) unsalted butter, |
| ¼ cup sugar | at room temperature |
| 1 cup minus 1 tablespoon all-purpose | 1 teaspoon pure vanilla extract |
| flour | |
| ¼ teaspoon salt | Confectioners' sugar, sifted, for rolling |
| Pinch of ground cinnamon | |
| (optional) | |

Put the pecans and 1 tablespoon of the sugar in a food processor and process in very short pulses until the nuts are pulverized. Scrape the nuts into a bowl, add the flour, salt and cinnamon, if you're using it, and whisk to combine.

Put the butter in the processor and process, scraping down the sides of the bowl as needed, until the butter is smooth and creamy. Add the remaining 3 tablespoons sugar and the vanilla and process for 30 seconds or so to blend. Pour in the pecan-and-flour mixture and, using short pulses, process only until it is worked into the dough. You want to process the dough as little as possible—the less you work the dough, the lighter and more appealingly crumbly the cookies will be. Scrape the dough out of the bowl onto plastic wrap, gather it together and form it into a ball. Wrap and chill for at least 2 hours, or for up to 2 days.

GETTING READY TO BAKE: Center a rack in the oven and preheat the oven to 350 degrees F. Line two baking sheets with parchment or silicone mats.

Remove the dough from the fridge. Using a small spoon, break off marble-size pieces, then roll each piece of dough between your palms to form a smooth ball and place the balls on the baking sheets; there's no need to leave much space between the balls.

Bake the cookies one sheet at a time for 12 to 15 minutes, or until they are lightly golden and almost firm. Gently transfer them to a rack to cool to room temperature.

Just before serving, roll the cookies in the confectioners' sugar and toss them gently from hand to hand to shake off the excess sugar.

SERVING: Don't forget to have plenty of napkins nearby—the confectioners' sugar has a way of sticking to fingers and lips.

STORING: These cookies are really best the day they are made. You can keep them in a closed container for a day or two, but they'll need another confectioners' sugar dusting. You can also freeze them for up to 2 months; re-sugar before serving.

*Playing Around*

It's a natural jump from Pecan Powder Puffs to puffs based on finely ground walnuts or almonds, or even cocoa and nuts.

WALNUT POWDER PUFFS: Use walnuts instead of pecans and, instead of the optional cinnamon, flavor the cookies with a pinch of allspice and a tiny pinch of ground cloves.

ALMOND POWDER PUFFS: Use almonds instead of pecans, reduce the vanilla extract to ½ teaspoon and add ⅛ teaspoon pure almond extract.

COCOA-NUT PUFFS: You can use pecans, walnuts or almonds for these. Reduce the flour to ¾ cup and add 3 tablespoons unsweetened cocoa powder, sifted, to the dry ingredients. If you want, roll the cooled puffs in the confectioners' sugar, then dust them with sifted cocoa.

# MRS. VOGEL'S SCHERBEN

**THESE FRIED** dough cookies are crisp, firm, fun and a little messy too—one bite and they crack, sending a shower of sugar and cookie every which way. It's impossible to be neat with these, and after a bite, you won't care.

My friend Michael Vogel, who has loved these cookies since childhood, gave me this recipe, explaining that it was handed down from his grandmother, who first made these for him, to his mother, a gifted baker who used to call them *schneeballen,* or snowballs. Snowballs is a sweet name, but, even as a kid, Michael didn't think it was descriptive enough. He would have opted for "snowflakes," because the cookies are rolled thin, cut into zigzag-edged strips and fried until they blister, bubble, curl and crinkle, then coated with sugar—very snowflake-ish.

By the time Michael got around to asking his mother for the recipe, she was ninety years old, but she was still baking regularly. She gave him the recipe—and permission to pass it along to me—after she'd made batches of them for a big Thanksgiving dinner. To Michael's delight, as his mother was reciting the recipe, she called them *scherben,* which means shards in German, a name Michael declared perfect—even better than "snowflakes." Whether they're *schneeballen* or *scherben,* they might be recognized as *bugnes* by les Français, as *merveilles* by anyone Swiss and as plain old fried dough by Americans from various parts of the country. They are a fairly universal sweet—easy, economical and delicious. Pretty, too.

Just a word about that messy sugar coating—it's essential. The dough itself has just a tad of sugar in it, so it's the final dusting that gives it its needed sweetness. Be generous.

MAKES ABOUT 36 COOKIES

**SERVING:** Scherben are at their very, very best eaten as soon as they are cool enough to bite into. This is easier to do than you'd think, since as soon as you start frying these, whoever is in your house will come into the kitchen and grab cookies whether you've given the go-ahead or not. However, they are also terrific a few hours later.

**STORING:** These are meant to be eaten the day they are made. If you must keep them (or if there are any left to keep), store them, uncovered, in a tin in a cool, dry place. Don't refrigerate them—they'll get soggy.

| | |
|---|---|
| 1 tablespoon unsalted butter, at room temperature | 3–4 tablespoons hot water |
| Big pinch of sugar | Cinnamon sugar and confectioners' sugar, for dusting |
| Little pinch of salt | |
| 1 large egg, at room temperature | Flavorless oil, such as canola or sunflower, for deep frying |
| 1 cup all-purpose flour | |
| ¼ teaspoon baking powder | |

Working in a medium bowl with a wooden spoon or a large rubber spatula, beat the butter, sugar and salt until smooth and creamy. Add the egg and beat—the mixture will look curdled, but that's okay. Mix the flour and baking powder together and pour them into the bowl, then stir until most of the flour is moistened. The dough will look like coarse, clumpy meal. Add 3 tablespoons hot water and continue to stir until the dough comes together. If you've still got dry portions, sprinkle over a little more water. Keep stirring—you'll have a moist dough that might be a bit shaggy.

Reach into the bowl and knead the dough just until it smooths out and comes together. Gather the dough into a ball, wrap it in plastic and chill for at least 1 hour. (The dough can be kept in the refrigerator overnight if it's more convenient.)

Line a baking sheet with plastic wrap. Cut the dough in half. Working with one half at a time, on a well-floured surface, and keeping both sides of the dough floured, roll the dough into a very thin rectangle—try to make it about 12 x 8 inches, but don't worry if it's not the right size or if it's lopsided; scherben can be any size, any shape. If you keep the work surface well floured and turn the dough, so it's not sticking and so you're rolling on both sides, you'll find that it is very easy to roll and that you can roll it paper thin. Mark off 1-inch strips with a ruler and cut the strips with a pastry wheel or pizza cutter—using a zigzag pastry wheel makes pretty cookies. Cut the strips crosswise in half, then, using a small knife, cut a lengthwise slit about 1½ inches long in each strip. Place the strips on the lined baking sheet and cover them with another piece of plastic wrap. Roll and cut the other half of the dough and lay those cookies over the first batch. Cover with plastic and refrigerate for at least 1 hour. (If it's more convenient, these can stay in the fridge for a day.)

GETTING READY TO FRY: Line a baking sheet with a triple thickness of paper towels and put it close to the stove. Fill one sugar duster or strainer with cinnamon sugar and another with confectioners' sugar. Pour at least 4 inches of oil into a deep saucepan (or use an electric deep-fryer) and heat the oil to 350 degrees F, as measured on a deep-fat-frying thermometer.

Drop 4 to 6 strips into the pan (don't crowd the pan) and fry until the undersides are golden, then turn and fry the other sides; each batch will take 2 to 3 minutes. Lift the cookies out of the oil on a perforated skimmer, allowing excess oil to drip back into the pan, then turn the cookies out onto the baking sheet to drain. Put in another batch to fry, and while they are frying, turn the cookies that are draining so the other sides can drain. Then, while the cookies are still hot and slightly damp from the oil, dust both sides with cinnamon sugar. Continue until all the dough is fried.

Just before serving, dust the scherben with confectioners' sugar.

# SOUR CREAM CHOCOLATE CAKE COOKIES

I CALL these "cake cookies" because they are cakey soft and have a tiny spongy crumb. They are not deeply chocolaty, not very rich and, to be honest, they look more handmade than handsome (they are thin and plain), but they are unfailingly happy-making. I can't think of a time when I, or anyone else, took one cookie and didn't go back for another. Part of the appeal is the texture, to be sure, but who would walk away from the tangy-sweet combination of sour cream and chocolate? Or the fun of coming upon a few plump currants?

SERVING: The cinnamon, chocolate and cream in these call out for coffee, but they're just as good served with ice cream.

STORING: Because these are so soft, they are best stored loosely stacked in a tin with wax paper between the layers. They can be kept at room temperature for about 4 days or packed airtight and frozen for about 2 months.

2¼ cups all-purpose flour

2 tablespoons unsweetened cocoa powder

1 teaspoon baking soda

½ teaspoon salt

¼ teaspoon ground cinnamon
    Pinch of freshly grated nutmeg

½ stick (4 tablespoons) unsalted butter, at room temperature

1¼ cups (packed) light brown sugar

½ cup sugar

2 large eggs

1 teaspoon pure vanilla extract

2 ounces unsweetened chocolate, melted and cooled to tepid

1 cup sour cream

½ cup plump, moist dried currants or raisins (dark or golden)

GETTING READY: Position the racks to divide the oven into thirds and preheat the oven to 375 degrees F. Line two baking sheets with parchment or silicone mats.

Whisk together the flour, cocoa, baking soda, salt, cinnamon and nutmeg.

Working with a stand mixer, preferably fitted with a paddle attachment, or with a hand mixer in a large bowl, beat the butter on medium speed until it is creamy and smooth. Add the sugars and beat for 2 minutes or so, then add the eggs one by one. Beat for another minute—the mixture should be smooth and satiny. Reduce the mixer speed to low and mix in the vanilla extract and melted chocolate. With the mixer still on low speed, add the dry ingredients and the sour cream alternately, adding the dry ingredients in 3 batches and the sour cream in 2 (begin and end with the dry ingredients). Mix only until the ingredients are incorporated and the batter is smooth, then mix in the currants.

Drop the batter by heaping teaspoonfuls onto the baking sheets, making certain to leave 2 inches between the spoonfuls.

Bake for 12 to 15 minutes, rotating the sheets from top to bottom and front to back at the midway point. The cookies will puff, spread and round themselves out in baking. They're done when they are set on top but still springy to the touch. Pull the sheets from the oven and let the cookies rest for 1 minute, then, using a wide metal spatula, carefully transfer them to a rack. Cool to room temperature.

Repeat with the remaining batter, making sure to cool the baking sheets between batches.

# DULCE DE LECHE DUOS

JUST A few years ago, I would have had to give an explanation of what dulce de leche is and where to find it or, more likely, how to make it. Today the thick, butterscotchish, toffee-like spread made from slowly cooked sweetened milk can be found in ice cream and yogurt and, best of all, in jars—ready-to-use dulce de leche is now a supermarket staple. These cookies, flavored with ready-made filling, are round and flatish, crisp on the outside and soft, almost cakey and just a little chewy in their skinny centers. Sandwich them with more dulce de leche and you double the pleasure.

SERVING: These are good served with café con leche, café au lait, cappuccino or just plain coffee and milk.

STORING: Packed in a sealed container, the sandwich cookies will keep at room temperature for about 4 days; they can be frozen for up to 2 months.

| | |
|---|---|
| 2½ cups all-purpose flour | ¾ cup store-bought dulce de leche, |
| 1 teaspoon baking soda | plus more for filling |
| ¼ teaspoon salt | ¾ cup (packed) light brown sugar |
| 2 sticks (8 ounces) unsalted butter, | ½ cup sugar |
| at room temperature | 2 large eggs |

GETTING READY: Position the racks to divide the oven into thirds and preheat the oven to 350 degrees F. Line two baking sheets with parchment or silicone mats.

Whisk together the flour, baking soda and salt.

Working with a stand mixer, preferably fitted with a paddle attachment, or with a hand mixer in a large bowl, beat the butter at medium speed until soft. Add the ¾ cup dulce de leche and both sugars and continue to beat until light and fluffy, about 3 minutes. Add the eggs one at a time, beating for 1 minute after each addition. Don't be concerned if the mixture looks a little curdled—it will smooth out when the flour mixture goes in. Reduce the mixer speed to low and add the dry ingredients, mixing only until they disappear into the batter.

Spoon the dough onto the baking sheets, using a heaping teaspoon of dough for each cookie and leaving 2 inches between them.

Bake the cookies for 10 to 12 minutes, rotating the pans from top to bottom and front to back at the midway point. The cookies should be honey brown with a light sugar crust, but they will still be soft, so remove the sheets from the oven but don't touch the cookies for another minute or two. Then, using a wide metal spatula, transfer the cookies to a rack to cool to room temperature.

Repeat with the remaining dough, making sure you cool the baking sheets before spooning the dough onto them.

When the cookies are completely cool, spread the flat bottoms of half the cookies with a small amount of dulce de leche, and sandwich with the flat sides of the remaining cookies.

*Playing Around*

CHOCOLATY DULCE DE LECHE DUOS: You can add a touch of chocolate flavor to these sandwiches in one of two ways. Either melt some bittersweet chocolate (semisweet is too sweet) and spread the bottoms of all the cookies with the chocolate before sandwiching them with dulce de leche, or replace the dulce de leche filling with Bittersweet Ganache (page 453) or chocolate ice cream (in which case, of course, you'll have to store the duos in the freezer).

# GINGERED CARROT COOKIES

**HERE'S A** delicious case of trying to make one thing and ending up with another. I wanted to make the cookie equivalent of carrot cake, and I included all my favorite carrot cake ingredients—among them, coconut, raisins and pecans, and just one of the usual carrot cake spices, ginger. But when I baked my first batch, I realized I'd undercalculated the amount of carrots: you could see the perky orange shreds peeping out of the bumpy cookies, but you couldn't really distinguish their taste. Surprisingly, though, this was just fine. Fewer carrots mean more room for the other ingredients to make their flavors—and textures—known. And the texture of the cookies is worth noting—soft, chewy and not unlike a scone. All things considered, these turned out to be a very tasty miscalculation.

**MAKES ABOUT 32 COOKIES**

**SERVING:** These are so good with morning coffee—good with afternoon tea too.

**STORING:** The cookies can be kept in a covered container at room temperature for about 4 days or packed airtight and kept frozen for up to 2 months.

2 cups all-purpose flour

1 teaspoon baking powder

½ teaspoon salt

1 teaspoon ground ginger

    Pinch of freshly grated nutmeg

1½ sticks (12 tablespoons) unsalted
    butter, at room temperature

⅔ cup sugar

⅓ cup (packed) light brown sugar

1 large egg

½ teaspoon pure vanilla extract

1 cup shredded carrots (about 3, peeled
    and trimmed)

1 cup sweetened shredded coconut

1 cup moist, plump raisins (dark or
    golden)

½ cup coarsely chopped pecans,
    preferably toasted

**GETTING READY:** Position the racks to divide the oven into thirds and preheat the oven to 375 degrees F. Line two baking sheets with parchment or silicone mats.

Whisk together the flour, baking powder, salt, ginger and nutmeg.

Working with a stand mixer, preferably fitted with a paddle attachment, or with a hand mixer in a large bowl, beat the butter on medium speed until creamy and smooth. Add the sugars and beat for 2 minutes or so, then add the egg and beat for another minute. Reduce the mixer speed to low and beat in the vanilla. Continuing on low speed, add the dry ingredients in 2 or 3 batches and beat only until they just disappear into the mix. You'll have a very thick dough, and you might be tempted to overbeat it to incorporate the flour—don't. Mix in the carrots, coconut, raisins and pecans.

Spoon the dough onto the baking sheets in heaping tablespoonfuls, leaving about an inch of space between them; these don't spread much.

Bake for 16 to 18 minutes, rotating the sheets from top to bottom and front to back at the midway point. The cookies should be light brown and only just firm on top. Carefully transfer the cookies to racks to cool to room temperature.

# KIDS' THUMBPRINTS

**I'VE ALWAYS** been a fan of jelly-bellied thumbprint cookies, those little sweets you roll into a ball and hollow out in the center with a poke of your finger. The cookies are good, but it's the stuff that goes into the thumbprint that I'm always after—jelly or jam, the redder the better. These are even more friendly to kids than most because they're peanut butter cookies rolled in crunchy roasted peanuts.

The prints are made by a child's thumb. If you're above the age of eight or so, you'll probably have to use your pinky to hollow out the centers—or borrow a kid for your cookie-making session.

**MAKES ABOUT 60 COOKIES**

**SERVING:** Just pile these on a plate and let the kids have at them.

**STORING:** Covered, these will keep for about 4 days at room temperature; packed airtight, they'll keep for up to 2 months in the freezer.

- 1½ sticks (12 tablespoons) unsalted butter, at room temperature
- ½ cup peanut butter—crunchy (my choice) or smooth (not natural)
- ½ cup (packed) light brown sugar
- ¼ cup sugar
- 1 teaspoon pure vanilla extract
- 1 large egg, separated

- 1⅔ cups all-purpose flour
- 1 large egg white
- 1½ cups roasted peanuts (salted or unsalted), finely chopped
- About ¾ cup jam or jelly (cherry, raspberry, strawberry and blueberry are particularly good)

*Playing Around*

**MELTED CHIP THUMB-PRINTS:** For a chocolate version of this treat, omit the jam and fill the cookies' hollows with chips—chocolate, peanut butter, butterscotch or a combination thereof—before baking. Each cookie will only take a chip or two, but you'll know they're there.

**GETTING READY:** Position the racks to divide the oven into thirds and preheat the oven to 375 degrees F. Line two baking sheets with parchment or silicone mats.

Working with a stand mixer, preferably fitted with a paddle attachment, or with a hand mixer in a large bowl, beat the butter, peanut butter and sugars together on medium speed until very light and fluffy, 3 to 4 minutes. Add the vanilla and egg yolk and continue to beat until well blended. Reduce the mixer speed to low and add the flour, mixing only until it is incorporated.

Put the 2 egg whites in a small bowl and beat them with a fork until slightly frothy. Put the chopped nuts in another bowl.

Working with a teaspoonful of dough at a time, roll the dough between your palms to form small balls, turn the balls in the egg whites until they are completely coated, and then drop them into the nuts and roll to coat. Place the cookies 2 inches apart on the baking sheets. Steadying each cookie with the thumb and a finger of one hand, use the pinkie of your other hand (or the end of a wooden spoon) to poke a hole in the center of each cookie. Be careful not to go all the way down to the baking sheet.

Bake for 15 to 18 minutes, rotating the sheets from top to bottom and front to back at the midway mark. The cookies should be lightly golden. Using a wide metal spatula, transfer the cookies to a rack.

Repeat with the remaining dough, cooling the baking sheets before baking the next batch.

Put the jam or jelly in a small saucepan and bring it to a boil, stirring, over low heat (or bring the jam to a boil in a microwave oven). Using a small spoon, fill each thumbprint with hot jam. Allow the cookies—and especially the jam—to cool to room temperature, at which point the jam will form a shiny, nonsticky finish.

**WHY SHOULD** the kids have all the fun? These thumbprint cookies have a soft, crumbly, very buttery shortbread texture and two grown-up ingredients—hazelnuts and raspberry jam. Hazelnuts and raspberry are my favorite combination, but you could trade in the hazelnuts for walnuts (or even milder almonds) and the raspberry jam for apricot jam or orange marmalade.

1¾ cups finely ground hazelnuts

1¾ cups all-purpose flour

2 sticks (8 ounces) unsalted butter, at room temperature

½ cup sugar

1 teaspoon pure vanilla extract

½ teaspoon pure almond extract

Confectioners' sugar, for dusting

About 1 cup raspberry jam (or the jam or marmalade of your choice)

**MAKES ABOUT 60 COOKIES**

**SERVING:** These are pretty enough to be served on the top tier of an old-fashioned teatime cake or cookie server. They are also fun enough to be piled on a plate and grabbed at whim.

**STORING:** Wrapped well, the cookies will be fine for 3 days at room temperature or for up to 2 months in the freezer.

GETTING READY: Position the racks to divide the oven into thirds and preheat the oven to 350 degrees F. Line two baking sheets with parchment or silicone mats.

Whisk together the ground nuts and flour.

Working with a stand mixer, preferably fitted with a paddle attachment, or with a hand mixer in a large bowl, beat the butter and sugar together on medium speed until light and fluffy, 3 to 4 minutes. Add the extracts and beat to blend. Reduce the mixer speed to low and gradually add the nut-flour mixture, mixing only until it is incorporated into the dough.

Working with a teaspoonful of dough at a time, roll the dough between your palms to form small balls and place the balls 2 inches apart on the baking sheets. Steadying each cookie with the thumb and a finger of one hand, use the pinkie of your other hand (or the end of a wooden spoon) to poke a hole in the center of each cookie. Be careful not to go all the way down to the baking sheet.

Bake for 15 to 18 minutes, rotating the sheets from top to bottom and front to back at the midway point. The cookies should be only slightly colored—they may even look underdone, which is fine: they should not be overbaked. When the cookies are baked, remove the baking sheets from the oven and let the cookies rest on the sheets for 2 minutes before transferring them to cooling racks with a wide metal spatula and sifting confectioners' sugar over them.

Repeat with the remaining dough, remembering to cool the baking sheets before baking the next batch.

Bring the jam to a boil in a small saucepan over low heat, or bring to a boil in a microwave oven; remove from the heat. Fill the indentations of all the cookies with enough of the hot jam to come level with the tops. Cool to room temperature.

# TRADITIONAL MADELEINES

**MADELEINES ARE** among the most recognizable pastries in the French repertoire because of their look: they are made in scallop-shaped molds from which they emerge ridged on one side, plump and full-bellied on the other and golden. That they are among the best known is thanks to Marcel Proust, who immortalized them in his novel *Remembrance of Things Past.* Everyone seems to know the story of Proust's narrator dipping the cookie into his tea and having the first taste bring back a flood of childhood memories. With that short entry, Proust and the madeleine gained such celebrity that even people who've never tasted the cookie refer to it with confidence as a touchstone. Yet when you take away all the literary allusions and all the romance, what you're left with is a tea cake that deserves to be famous for its deliciousness alone.

The madeleine is a beautiful, if somewhat plain, cookie made from the kind of batter you'd use for a sponge cake. What distinguishes it is its lightness; its texture—the tiny-bubbled crumb is *très raffiné;* and its flavor, a delicate mix of lemon, vanilla and butter.

This recipe is for a classic madeleine like the one I learned to make in Paris—it's the kind that would make Proust happy. But there are other kinds of madeleines, madeleines Proust might not approve of but that would please most everyone else. When you're ready for a different take on the classic, try Mini Madeleines (page 172), Earl Grey Madeleines (page 169) and the far-from-traditional Fluff-Filled Chocolate Madeleines (page 170). I don't even want to imagine what Proust would think of those!

Just to set the record straight, while it's Proust who gets all the credit for making madeleines a household name, the honor really belongs to King Stanislas Leszczynski of Poland, who, in the eighteenth century, tasted a tea cake made by a local woman in Commercy, France. He was so delighted with the cookie that he named it after the baker, Madeleine.

MAKES 12 LARGE
OR 36 MINI COOKIES

SERVING: Serve the cookies when they are only slightly warm or when they reach room temperature, with tea or espresso.

STORING: Although the batter can be kept in the refrigerator for up to 2 days, the madeleines should be eaten soon after they are made. You can keep them overnight in a sealed container, but they really are better on day 1. If you must store them, wrap them airtight and freeze them; they'll keep for up to 2 months.

| | |
|---|---|
| ⅔ cup all-purpose flour | 2 teaspoons pure vanilla extract |
| ¾ teaspoon baking powder | ¾ stick (6 tablespoons) unsalted butter, |
| Pinch of salt | melted and cooled |
| ½ cup sugar | |
| Grated zest of 1 lemon | Confectioners' sugar, for dusting |
| 2 large eggs, at room temperature | |

Whisk together the flour, baking powder and salt.

Working in a mixer bowl, or in a large bowl, rub the sugar and lemon zest together with your fingertips until the sugar is moist and fragrant. Add the eggs to the bowl. Working with the whisk attachment, or with a hand mixer, beat the eggs and sugar together on medium-high speed until pale, thick and light, 2 to 3 minutes. Beat in the vanilla. With a rubber spatula, very gently fold in the dry ingredients, followed by the melted butter. Press a piece of plastic wrap against the surface of the batter and refrigerate it for at least 3 hours, or for up to 2 days. This long chill period will help the batter form the hump that is characteristic of

madeleines. (For convenience, you can spoon the batter into the madeleine molds, cover and refrigerate, then bake the cookies directly from the fridge; see below for instructions on prepping the pans.)

GETTING READY TO BAKE: Center a rack in the oven and preheat the oven to 400 degrees F. Butter 12 full-size madeleine molds, or up to 36 mini madeleine molds, dust the insides with flour and tap out the excess. Or, if you have a nonstick pan (or pans), give it a light coating of vegetable cooking spray. If you have a silicone pan, no prep is needed. Place the pan(s) on a baking sheet.

Spoon the batter into the molds, filling each one almost to the top. Don't worry about spreading the batter evenly, the oven's heat will take care of that. Bake large madeleines for 11 to 13 minutes, and minis for 8 to 10 minutes, or until they are golden and the tops spring back when touched. Remove the pan(s) from the oven and release the madeleines from the molds by rapping the edge of the pan against the counter. Gently pry any recalcitrant madeleines from the pan using your fingers or a butter knife. Transfer the cookies to a rack to cool to just warm or to room temperature.

If you are making minis and have more batter, bake the next batch(es), making certain that you cool, then properly prepare the pan(s) before baking.

Just before serving, dust the madeleines with confectioners' sugar.

# EARL GREY MADELEINES

I'VE PUT the key elements of Proust's famously documented experience of dipping a madeleine into tea together for this recipe. The technique for infusing the melted butter with the taste and aroma of tea is an ingenious one I learned from the tea masters at Mariage Frères in Paris. I've since used it to create madeleines with other flavors (see Playing Around).

| | |
|---|---|
| 5 tablespoons unsalted butter | ⅓ cup sugar |
| 2 tablespoons Earl Grey tea leaves | Grated zest of ½ lemon |
| ¾ cup all-purpose flour | 2 large eggs, at room temperature |
| ½ teaspoon baking powder | 2 tablespoons honey |
| Pinch of salt | 2 teaspoons pure vanilla extract |

To flavor the butter with the tea, melt the butter in a small saucepan over low heat or in a microwave oven. Stir in the tea and allow it to infuse for 15 minutes.

Line a small sieve with a double layer of damp cheesecloth, then strain the butter into a small bowl; discard the tea leaves.

Whisk together the flour, baking powder and salt.

Put the sugar and lemon zest in a mixer bowl or in another large bowl and, using your fingertips, work the zest into the sugar until the mixture is fragrant.

Working with a mixer fitted with the whisk attachment or with a hand mixer in a large bowl, beat the eggs, sugar and zest together until pale and thick, 2 to 3 minutes. Add the honey and vanilla and beat for 1 minute more. Switch to a rubber spatula and gently fold in the dry ingredients. When they are incorporated, fold in the butter. Press a piece of plastic wrap against the surface of the batter and refrigerate for at least 3 hours or for up to 2 days. This long chill will help the batter form the hump that is characteristic of madeleines. (For convenience, you can spoon the batter into the madeleine molds, cover and chill, then bake the cookies directly from the fridge; see below for instructions on prepping the pans.)

GETTING READY TO BAKE: Center a rack in the oven and preheat the oven to 400 degrees F. Butter 12 full-size madeleine molds, dust the insides with flour and tap out the excess. Or, if you have a nonstick madeleine pan, give it a light coating of vegetable cooking spray. If you have a silicone pan, there is no prep needed. Place the pan on a baking sheet.

Spoon the batter into the molds—don't worry about leveling the batter, the oven's heat will take care of that.

Bake for 12 to 14 minutes, or until the madeleines are golden and the tops spring back when touched. Remove the pan from the oven and release the madeleines from the mold by rapping the edge of the pan against the counter. Gently pry any recalcitrant madeleines from the pan using your fingers or a butter knife.

Transfer the cookies to a rack to cool to just warm or to room temperature.

MAKES 12 COOKIES

SERVING: While they have an entire tea service baked right into them, there's still nothing better than having these madeleines alongside a cup of fragrant Earl Grey tea.

STORING: Although the batter can be kept in the refrigerator for up to 2 days, the madeleines should be eaten soon after they are made. You can keep them overnight in a sealed container, but they really are better on day 1. If you must store them, wrap them airtight and freeze them; they'll keep for up to 2 months.

## Playing Around

LAVENDER MADELEINES: Replace the tea with 1 tablespoon edible lavender.

ROSEMARY-ORANGE MADELEINES: Replace the tea with 1½ tablespoons finely chopped fresh rosemary and, instead of the lemon zest, rub the zest of ½ orange into the sugar. And, if you'd like, when the madeleines come out of the oven, sprinkle them very lightly with orange-flower water.

SPICED MADELEINES: Omit the tea and whisk ½ teaspoon ground cinnamon, a small pinch of freshly grated nutmeg and a teeny pinch of ground ginger in with the flour.

# FLUFF-FILLED CHOCOLATE MADELEINES

**HERE'S A** madeleine for the nonliterary set. It's a true French madeleine, but it's made with chocolate, filled with Marshmallow Fluff and finished off with a bittersweet chocolate glaze. This madeleine is more like a Hostess cupcake than a French national treasure and, as such, more likely to be chased by a mug of cocoa than a cup of tea.

MAKES 12 COOKIES

SERVING: Coffee of every variety, milk, and hot chocolate are all good companions.

STORING: Although the batter can be kept in the refrigerator for a couple of days, the madeleines should be eaten soon after they are made. However, wrapped airtight, they can be frozen—even after they've been filled and frosted—for up to 2 months. And stale madeleines, as Proust would be the first to tell you, are good for dunking.

### FOR THE MADELEINES

- ⅔ cup all-purpose flour
- ¼ cup unsweetened cocoa powder
- ½ teaspoon baking powder
  Pinch of salt
- 2 large eggs, at room temperature
- ½ cup sugar
- ½ teaspoon pure vanilla extract
- ¾ stick (6 tablespoons) unsalted butter, melted and cooled

Marshmallow Fluff, for filling and frosting

### FOR THE DIP

- 4 ounces bittersweet chocolate, finely chopped
- ½ cup heavy cream
- 1½ tablespoons unsalted butter, at room temperature

*Playing Around*

Use the same poke-and-pipe technique to fill the madeleines with raspberry jam, lemon curd—homemade (page 462) or store-bought—or Nutella.

**TO MAKE THE MADELEINES:** Sift the flour, cocoa, baking powder and salt together.

Working with a stand mixer fitted with the whisk attachment or with a hand mixer in a large bowl, beat the eggs and sugar together until pale and slightly thickened, about 3 minutes. Beat in the vanilla extract, then switch to a rubber spatula and gently fold in the sifted dry ingredients, followed by the melted butter. Put a piece of plastic wrap directly against the surface of the batter and refrigerate for at least 3 hours or for up to 2 days. Chilling the batter gives you a better chance of getting the characteristic hump on the back of the cookies.

**GETTING READY TO BAKE:** Center a rack in the oven and preheat the oven to 400 degrees F. Generously butter 12 full-size madeleine molds, dust the insides with flour and tap out the excess. Butter and flour or spray the pan even if it is nonstick; skip this step if you are using a silicone pan. Place the pan on a baking sheet.

Spoon the batter into the molds.

Place the pan in the oven and immediately lower the oven temperature to 350 degrees F. Bake the cookies for 13 to 15 minutes, or until they feel springy to the touch. Remove the pan from the oven and rap one side of the madeleine pan against the counter—the plump little cakes should come tumbling out. Gently pry any reluctant cookies out with your fingers or a butter knife. Cool to room temperature on a rack.

**TO FILL THE MADELEINES:** Fit a small pastry bag with a small plain tip and spoon the fluff into the bag. Use the point of the tip to poke a hole in the rounded (plain) side of each madeleine, and pipe enough fluff into each cookie to fill it—stop when the fluff reaches the top of the cake. (You'll use only a bit of fluff.)

**TO MAKE THE DIP:** Put the chocolate in a small deep heatproof bowl. Bring the heavy cream to a full boil, then pour it over the chocolate. Wait for 1 minute, then gently whisk the cream into the chocolate: start at the center and slowly work your way out in concentric circles until you have a smooth, shiny mixture. Gently whisk in the butter.

Line a small baking sheet with wax paper. One by one, hold a madeleine at its narrow end and dip it into the chocolate, then lift it up, let the excess chocolate drip back into the bowl and place smooth side down on the wax paper. Slide the baking sheet into the refrigerator to set the glaze, about 15 minutes. (You'll have more ganache than you need, but making a larger quantity produces a better ganache. The leftover dip can be covered and refrigerated for 1 week or frozen for up to 1 month.)

If you'd like, pipe a little squiggle of fluff on the top of each madeleine once the chocolate is set.

# MINI MADELEINES

**WITH THIS** recipe in your possession, you have the power to make the world around you a happier place, since it is impossible to eat these baby madeleines and not smile. The recipe, given to me by my friend Rica Allanic, turns out tiny traditionally shell-shaped cookies, untraditionally sweetened with brown sugar and honey. They are ineffably light and tender and as poppable as potato chips.

⅔ cup all-purpose flour

1 teaspoon baking powder

Pinch of salt

2 large eggs, at room temperature

6 tablespoons sugar

1 tablespoon (packed) light brown sugar

⅛ teaspoon pure vanilla extract

Grated zest of ½ lemon

¾ stick (6 tablespoons) unsalted butter, melted and cooled

1 teaspoon honey

Confectioners' sugar, for dusting

**SERVING:** These are at their most delectable straight from the oven. Just give the warm cakes their dusting of confectioners' sugar, pile them in a basket or put them on a plate and bring them to the table.

**STORING:** If you are not going to eat the madeleines immediately, you must at least eat them the day you make them. They are not meant for keeping, even if they are good for dunking when they are a bit stale.

Whisk together the flour, baking powder and salt.

In a medium bowl, whisk together the eggs and sugars until smooth. Whisk in the dry ingredients, followed by the vanilla and lemon zest. Gently whisk in the melted butter and, finally, the honey. You'll have a thick, smooth, shiny batter. Press a piece of plastic wrap against the surface of the batter and refrigerate for at least 30 minutes or up to 2 days. (For convenience, you can spoon the batter into the madeleine molds, cover and chill, then bake the cookies directly from the fridge; see below for instructions on prepping the pans.)

GETTING READY TO BAKE: Center a rack in the oven and preheat the oven to 425 degrees F. Generously butter up to three mini madeleine pans, dust the insides with flour and tap out the excess. Or, if you have nonstick pans, just spray the interiors with vegetable cooking spray. If you've got silicone pans, they can be used just as they are. Put the pan(s) on a baking sheet.

Fill each little madeleine mold with about a teaspoon of batter; the molds should be about three-quarters full. Don't worry about leveling the batter—it will do it by itself in the oven.

Bake the cookies for 8 to 10 minutes, or until they are puffed and golden brown around the edges. Remove the sheet from the oven and give the madeleine pan(s) a hearty rap against the counter. Gently pry out any cakes that don't want to leave their nests with your fingers or a butter knife. You can serve the madeleines immediately or put them on a rack to cool.

Repeat with any remaining batter, making certain to cool and rebutter and flour or respray the pan(s).

Just before serving, dust the madeleines with confectioners' sugar.

# TRANSLUCENT MAPLE TUILES

MAKES ABOUT 48 COOKIES

**TUILES ARE** a classic French cookie, named for and curved like the *tuiles*, or tiles, that line the rooftops of country homes, particularly those in Provence. In its homeland, a tuile is apt to take a supporting rather than a lead role. You might find a tuile alongside a bowl of ice cream or chocolate mousse, on top of a custard or on a plate with other little cookies served after the main dessert, with coffee. It's a nice way to serve these fragile, ultrathin cookies, but it's not the only way. I think they are just right in the afternoon with a cup of tea and perfect as an all-by-themselves dessert when the meal has been sumptuous.

However you decide to offer these, there's no question they'll be welcomed, since they are a particularly unusual (and delicious) member of the tuile family. Rather than being made with the traditional flour-white-sugar-and-almond batter, they are made with brown sugar, maple syrup and very little flour, which means they emerge from the oven looking like caramelized circles of golden, honeycombed stained glass. They are amazingly elegant for something so simple.

Because the dough keeps in the refrigerator for up to 1 week and because the cookies bake so quickly, you can really make these on demand, baking only as many tuiles as you want at the moment. Similarly, you can curve them or not.

SERVING: These are ready to serve as soon as they are set. I like to use a long narrow plate to serve the curved cookies and to line them up with their curves slightly overlapping, so they look like a chorus line of pet turtles.

STORING: If your kitchen isn't too humid, you can keep these overnight on a lined baking sheet—don't cover them, just let them breathe. Unfortunately, they cannot be frozen.

½ stick (4 tablespoons) unsalted butter, at room temperature

¼ cup (packed) brown sugar

¼ cup pure maple syrup

⅓ cup plus 1 tablespoon all-purpose flour, sifted

In a small bowl, using a sturdy rubber spatula or a hand mixer, beat the butter, brown sugar and maple syrup together until light in color and texture. Gently stir in the flour, mixing only until it is incorporated. Cover the bowl, pressing a piece of plastic wrap against the surface of the batter, and refrigerate for at least 3 hours, or for up to 1 week.

GETTING READY TO BAKE: Position the racks to divide the oven into thirds and preheat the oven to 400 degrees F. Have two unlined baking sheets at hand and, if you want to curve the cookies into their traditional tile shape, a rolling pin or a slender bottle.

Roll small scoops of dough between your palms to form balls the size of small cherries or hazelnuts, and put the balls 2 inches apart on the unbuttered baking sheets.

Bake for about 7 minutes, or until the cookies spread and are golden colored and honeycombed. Immediately remove the baking sheets from the oven, let the cookies rest a few seconds and then, using a wide metal spatula, lift them from the sheets: the best way to do this is to carefully work the spatula under a cookie edge, then push the spatula beneath the cookie with a quick jerk. If the cookie crumples a bit, as it might, don't worry—it will straighten out on the rolling pin or rack. For

curved cookies, moving with alacrity, lay the cookies, a few at a time, over the rolling pin. Transfer the cookies to a rack after they have set—under a minute—or, if you want flat cookies, just cool them on a rack. If the cookies cool and stick stubbornly to the baking sheet, slide the sheet into the oven for another minute to warm them.

If you are making another batch of cookies, make certain the baking sheets are clean and cool.

CAKES
OF ALL KINDS

# BUNDTS, TUBES AND TURBANS

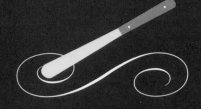

THAT CAKES MADE IN BUNDT, tube and turban-shaped pans have been popular for decades and that they are now more popular than ever is proof positive that bakers are ingenious and resourceful—who wouldn't take to a cake that's easy to make, good tasting and great looking thanks to no extra effort on the part of the baker? With these cakes, beauty is automatic—it's conferred by the shape of the pan.

Whether you are using the plainest tube pan, an old-fashioned Kugelhopf pan with the look of a spiraled turban (in fact, in some places the pan is called a Turk's turban) or any of the increasingly whimsical Bundt pans, you get a big, beautiful cake that can stand on its own as a centerpiece sweet.

Because these pans are large, usually at least 9 inches in diameter, and hold 10 cups or more of batter, the cakes you make in them are long-baking and emerge from the oven with a fine, deeply golden crust. Since the pans' nooks and crannies are responsible for the cakes' eye appeal, be sure to give the pans a good buttering before the batter goes in. I find the easiest way to butter pans, particularly intricately patterned ones, is to use a pastry brush generously coated with softened butter.

And though I often recommend putting your cake pans on a baking sheet, you should never put a tube pan on a sheet. Do this, and you'll defeat the purpose of the tube, which is to allow heat to come up through the center of the pan and to bake the batter from both the middle and the sides.

A final piece of advice: When it's time to test for doneness, don't even think about using a measly toothpick. Big, tall cakes need big, long testers. Grab a slender paring knife and insert it into the center of the cake, making sure that it goes halfway down the pan. If the knife comes out clean, you can be certain your cake is fully baked.

I've given you a collection that ranges from my jazzed-up take on the classic sour cream Bundt and my favorite, and almost infinitely variable, coconut turban to cakes that are laced with fruit, enlivened by spice or marbled. They are all big, all beautiful and all good keepers—and all good looking even after they've been cut into.

# BROWN SUGAR BUNDT CAKE

**LIGHT BROWN** sugar is a prime player in this fragrant Bundt's soft, tender texture and comforting taste. I like the combination of pear and prune, but the cake is so welcoming you can trade the prunes in for raisins or dried currants, dried pears, pieces of dried apricot or chopped nuts, and you can swap the pears for apples—the brown sugar will pull everything together. If you have time, wrap the cake well and leave it on the counter to ripen the flavors for a day before serving.

2¼ cups all-purpose flour

½ cup ground hazelnuts or walnuts (or ¼ cup more all-purpose flour)

1 teaspoon baking powder

½ teaspoon baking soda

¼ teaspoon salt

2 sticks (8 ounces) unsalted butter, at room temperature

2 cups (packed) light brown sugar

3 large eggs, at room temperature

1½ teaspoons pure vanilla extract

¼ teaspoon pure almond extract (only if you're using ground nuts)

1 cup buttermilk, at room temperature

2 medium pears, peeled, cored and cut into ¼-inch dice

½ cup moist, plump prunes, snipped into ¼-inch pieces, or ½ cup moist, plump raisins (dark or golden)

Confectioners' sugar, for dusting

**GETTING READY:** Center a rack in the oven and preheat the oven to 350 degrees F. Butter a 9- to 10-inch (12-cup) Bundt pan, dust the inside with flour and tap out the excess. If your pan is not nonstick, dust the interior of the pan with flour, then tap out the excess. (If you've got a silicone Bundt pan, there's no need to butter or flour it.) Don't place the pan on a baking sheet—you want the oven's heat to circulate through the Bundt's inner tube.

Whisk together the flour, nuts, baking powder, baking soda and salt.

Working with a stand mixer, preferably fitted with a paddle attachment, or with a hand mixer in a large bowl, beat the butter and sugar together at medium speed until light and fluffy, about 3 minutes. Add the eggs one at a time, beating for 1 minute after each addition. Beat in the vanilla and the almond extract, if you're using it. Reduce the mixer speed to low and add the flour mixture and the buttermilk alternately—add the flour in 3 additions and the buttermilk in 2 (begin and end with the dry ingredients). Mix only until the ingredients are incorporated and scrape down the bowl as needed. With a rubber spatula, stir in the pears and prunes. Scrape the batter into the pan and smooth the top with the spatula.

Bake for 60 to 65 minutes, or until a thin knife inserted deep into the center of the cake comes out clean. (If the cake looks as if it's browning too fast, cover the top loosely with a foil tent.) Transfer the cake to a rack and cool for 10 minutes before unmolding, then cool to room temperature on the rack.

When you're ready to serve, dust the top of the cake with confectioners' sugar.

MAKES 12 SERVINGS

**SERVING:** For me, brown sugar is a go-with-tea ingredient.

**STORING:** Not surprisingly, this is a good keeper. It will keep for about 5 days wrapped well and at room temperature—it's really better the day after it is baked than it is on bake day—and it can be frozen for up to 2 months; defrost still wrapped.

*Playing Around*

**BROWN SUGAR–NUT BUNDT CAKE:** For a nuttier cake, use 2 cups all-purpose flour and ¾ cup ground nuts—hazelnuts, walnuts or almonds. Decrease the vanilla extract to 1¼ teaspoons, and use the almond extract. Omit the pears and prunes and stir in 1 cup chopped toasted nuts—use the same nut as the one you ground.

MAKES 12 SERVINGS

**ESSENTIALLY A** walnut cake that is part vanilla and part mocha (both good go-with-walnut flavors), this is beautiful, particularly if you pour in all the white batter, cover it with the dark batter and marble it minimally, so that you end up with a chocolate gingko leaf pattern in the center.

| | |
|---|---|
| 2¼ cups all-purpose flour | ¼ cup coffee, hot or cold |
| ½ cup finely ground walnuts | 1 teaspoon finely ground instant coffee |
| 1 teaspoon baking powder | or instant espresso powder |
| 1 teaspoon salt | 1¾ cups sugar |
| 2 sticks plus 2 tablespoons | 4 large eggs, preferably at room |
| (9 ounces) unsalted butter, | temperature |
| at room temperature | 2 teaspoons pure vanilla extract |
| 3 ounces bittersweet chocolate, | 1 cup whole milk, at room temperature |
| coarsely chopped | |

**GETTING READY:** Center a rack in the oven and preheat the oven to 350 degrees F. Butter a 9- to 10-inch (12-cup) Bundt pan, dust the inside with flour and tap out the excess. (If you've got a silicone Bundt pan, there's no need to butter or flour it.) Don't place the pan on a baking sheet—you want the oven's heat to circulate through the Bundt's inner tube.

Whisk together the flour, ground walnuts, baking powder and salt.

Set a heatproof bowl over a saucepan of gently simmering water. Put 2 tablespoons of the butter, cut into 4 pieces, into the bowl, along with the chocolate, coffee and instant coffee. Heat the mixture, stirring often, until the butter and chocolate are melted and everything is smooth and creamy—keep the heat low so that the butter and chocolate don't separate. Remove the bowl from the heat.

Working with a stand mixer, preferably with a paddle attachment, or with a hand mixer in a large bowl, beat the remaining 2 sticks butter and the sugar at medium speed for about 3 minutes—you'll have a thick paste; this won't be light and fluffy. Beat in the eggs one by one, beating well after each addition. The mixture should look smooth and satiny. Beat in the vanilla extract. Reduce the mixer speed to low and add the dry ingredients and the milk alternately, adding the dry mixture in 3 portions and the milk in 2 (begin and end with the dry ingredients).

Scrape a little less than half the batter into the bowl with the melted chocolate and, using a rubber spatula, stir to blend thoroughly.

If you want to go for the gingko pattern, scrape all of the white batter into the pan and top with the chocolate. If you want a more marbled pattern, alternate spoonfuls of light and dark batter in the pan. When all the batter is in the pan, swirl a table knife sparingly through the batters to marble them.

Bake for 65 to 70 minutes, or until a thin knife inserted deep into the center of the cake comes out clean. Transfer the Bundt pan to a rack and let cool for 10 minutes before unmolding, then cool the cake completely on the rack.

**SERVING:** If you are going to serve this as a tea- or coffee-break cake, just slice and serve. However, if you'd like to turn it into a substantial dessert, add a scoop of ice cream and a drizzle of Hot Fudge Sauce (page 465). A few candied walnuts (page 469) wouldn't hurt.

**STORING:** Because this cake is so buttery and moist, it is an excellent keeper. Wrapped well, it will keep at room temperature for about 5 days (and, if it stales a bit, it will still be delicious lightly toasted); packed airtight, it can be frozen for up to 2 months.

# NUTTY, CHOCOLATY, SWIRLY SOUR CREAM BUNDT CAKE

**ONE OF** the nice things about having baked for so many years is being able to see sweets come into fashion, go out of fashion and come back again. That's the case with this sour cream cake. I saw it come into fashion in the 1970s (although it may have been fashionable—and then unfashionable—well before), fall out of favor and make a comeback recently.

I've seen lots of versions with variations on the amount of flour or butter or number of eggs, but they are all essentially the same: a fairly fine-grained Bundt cake with the characteristic tang of sour cream and the equally characteristic roundness of butter. Most have something swirled through them, usually in the middle and usually a mixture of cinnamon and sugar, sometimes with a few nuts chopped in for fun.

My version is traditional, but I've toyed with it slightly over the decades and have gone heavy on the swirls. The mixture I layer into the cake has the classic cinnamon-sugar base and chopped nuts, but it's also got raisins or currants and big bits of bittersweet chocolate.

When you taste this cake, you will understand why classics become classics.

**MAKES 12 SERVINGS**

**SERVING:** This cake is good the day it is made, but, like many pound cake–ish cakes, it's even better the day after. The cake can be dusted with the confectioners' sugar to show off its curves, if you like, and cut into not-so-thin slices to be served with coffee or tea. I think the cake is just fine solo— no sauce, no whipped cream, no ice cream—however, it is aw- fully nice with a big spoonful of marmalade or berry jam.

**STORING:** Wrapped well, the cake will keep for about 4 days at room temperature or up to 2 months in the freezer.

### FOR THE SWIRL

- ½ cup sugar
- ½ cup chopped walnuts or pecans
- 2 ounces bittersweet chocolate, finely chopped, or ⅓ cup mini chocolate chips
- ⅓ cup plump, moist raisins (dark or golden) or dried currants
- 2½ teaspoons ground cinnamon
- Pinch of freshly grated nutmeg
- Pinch of salt

### FOR THE CAKE

- 2 cups all-purpose flour
- 1 teaspoon baking powder
- ½ teaspoon salt
- 1¾ cups sugar
- Grated zest of 1 orange
- 2 sticks (8 ounces) unsalted butter, at room temperature
- 2 large eggs
- 1½ teaspoons pure vanilla extract
- 1 cup sour cream

Confectioners' sugar, for dusting (optional)

**GETTING READY:** Center a rack in the oven and preheat the oven to 350 degrees F. Butter a 9- to 10-inch (12-cup) Bundt pan, dust the interior with flour and tap out the excess. (If you've got a silicone Bundt pan, there's no need to butter or flour it.) Don't place the Bundt pan on a baking sheet—you want the oven's heat to circu- late freely through the Bundt's inner tube.

**TO MAKE THE SWIRL:** Put all the ingredients in a bowl and stir to mix.

**TO MAKE THE CAKE:** Whisk together the flour, baking powder and salt.

Working in the bowl of a stand mixer or in another large bowl, rub the sugar and zest together with your fingers until the sugar is moist and aromatic. Add the butter. With the paddle or whisk attachment or with a hand mixer, beat on medium speed for 4 minutes. Add the eggs one at a time, beating for 1 minute after each egg goes in. Beat in the vanilla. Reduce the mixer speed to low and mix in the sour cream. Still working on low, add the dry ingredients and mix only until they disappear into the batter.

Give the batter a last stir or two with a rubber spatula (just to make sure all the dry ingredients are properly incorporated), then scoop about one third of the batter into the Bundt pan. Evenly sprinkle on half of the swirl mixture, then spoon in the rest of the batter. Make a shallow indentation with the back of the spoon in the center of the ring of batter and fill it with the remaining swirl mixture, then cover the mixture lightly with the batter on the sides of the indentation—the batter probably won't cover the mixture completely, and that's fine.

Bake for 60 to 65 minutes, or until a thin knife inserted deep into the center of the cake comes out clean. Transfer the pan to a rack and let the cake rest for 10 minutes before unmolding it onto the rack to cool to room temperature.

Just before serving, dust the cake with confectioners' sugar, if desired.

# DOUBLE APPLE BUNDT CAKE

**IF YOU'RE** struck by the urge to pin a big blue ribbon on this cake right before you serve it, I'll understand. It looks, smells and tastes as though it would take first prize in a country fair—even if expert farmhouse bakers had made all the other entries. The cake is very moist, thanks to the addition of apple butter and grated fresh apples, which melt into the batter during baking. It's fine served with just a dusting of confectioners' sugar, but it's even nicer with a simple icing. If you have the time, don't ice or dust the cake the day you bake it; instead, wrap it well in plastic wrap and let it sit at room temperature overnight. This little rest will give the flavors time to blend fully.

I start making this cake in the early fall, when the first crop of apples turns up in the farmers' markets, and tuck away the recipe only when the temperature starts to climb and I can be sure summer is on its way.

2 cups all-purpose flour

2 teaspoons baking powder

½ teaspoon baking soda

½ teaspoon ground cinnamon

¼ teaspoon freshly grated nutmeg

¼ teaspoon ground ginger

¼ teaspoon salt

1¼ sticks (10 tablespoons) unsalted
    butter, at room temperature

1½ cups sugar

2 large eggs

1 cup store-bought apple butter—
    spiced or plain

2 medium apples, peeled, cored and
    grated

1 cup pecans or walnuts, chopped

½ cup plump, moist raisins (dark or
    golden)

Confectioners' sugar, for dusting
    (optional)

**FOR THE ICING (OPTIONAL)**

⅓ cup confectioners' sugar

About 2 tablespoons fresh orange
    or lemon juice

**MAKES 12 SERVINGS**

**SERVING:** Leave the cake plain, ice it or dust it with the confectioners' sugar and cut it into slices about ¼ inch thick and serve, figuring 2 slices per person, with cream or ice cream, or, better yet, with homemade applesauce. To make your own applesauce, make the filling from the Normandy Apple Tart (page 304)—double the recipe so you'll have enough for everyone, and maybe a tad left over.

**STORING:** Wrapped well, the cake will keep for up to 4 days at room temperature and for up to 2 months in the freezer.

---

**GETTING READY:** Center a rack in the oven and preheat the oven to 350 degrees F. Butter a 9- to 10-inch (12-cup) Bundt pan. If your pan is not nonstick, dust the interior of the pan with flour, then tap out the excess. (If you've got a silicone Bundt pan, there's no need to butter or flour it.) Don't place the pan on a baking sheet—you want the oven's heat to circulate through the Bundt's inner tube.

Whisk together the flour, baking powder, baking soda, spices and salt.

Working with a stand mixer, preferably fitted with a paddle attachment, or with a hand mixer in a large bowl, beat the butter and sugar on medium speed, scraping the bowl as needed, for 3 minutes, or until the mixture is smooth, thick and pale. Add the eggs one at a time, beating for about 1 minute after each addition; you'll have a light, fluffy batter. Reduce the mixer speed to low and beat in the apple butter—don't worry if it curdles the batter. Still on low, add the grated apples and mix to completely blend. Add the dry ingredients, mixing only until they disappear into the batter. Using a rubber spatula, fold in the nuts and raisins. Turn the batter into the Bundt pan and smooth the top of the batter with the rubber spatula.

Bake for 50 to 55 minutes, or until a thin knife inserted deep into the center of the cake comes out clean. Transfer the pan to a rack to cool for 5 minutes before unmolding and cooling the cake to room temperature. If possible, once the cake is completely cool, wrap well in plastic and let it stand overnight at room temperature to ripen the flavors.

If you're not going to ice the cake, you can dust it with confectioners' sugar just before serving.

TO MAKE THE OPTIONAL ICING: Put the sugar in a small bowl and stir in a squirt or two of either orange or lemon juice. Keep adding the juice a little at a time until you have an icing that falls easily from the tip of a spoon. Drizzle the icing over the top of the cake, letting it slide down the curves of the cake in whatever pattern it makes. Let the cake stand until the icing dries, a matter of minutes, before slicing.

**NAME YOUR** favorite it-tastes-like-Thanksgiving flavor, and you'll find it here: pumpkin, cranberry, apples, pecans and the fall-winter spices cinnamon, nutmeg and ginger. The only thing that might be missing is maple syrup, and there's no reason you can't add it by mixing a little into some whipped cream and topping each serving with a fat spoonful. Or, make a maple icing to drizzle down the cake's sides (see Playing Around). Like all Bundts, this one has convenience and generosity on its side. It's essentially a one-bowl cake that bakes up ready to serve and ready for a crowd.

| | |
|---|---|
| 2 cups all-purpose flour | 2 large eggs, at room temperature |
| 2 teaspoons baking powder | 1 teaspoon pure vanilla extract |
| ½ teaspoon baking soda | 1¼ cups canned unsweetened pumpkin |
| 2 teaspoons ground cinnamon | puree |
| ¼ teaspoon freshly grated nutmeg | 1 large apple, peeled, cored and finely |
| Pinch of salt | chopped |
| 1½ teaspoons grated fresh ginger (or | 1 cup cranberries, halved or coarsely |
| 1 teaspoon ground ginger) | chopped |
| 1¼ sticks (10 tablespoons) unsalted | 1 cup pecans, coarsely chopped |
| butter, at room temperature | |
| 1 cup sugar | Confectioners' sugar, for dusting |
| ½ cup (packed) light brown sugar | |

GETTING READY: Center a rack in the oven and preheat the oven to 350 degrees F. Butter a 9- to 10-inch (12-cup) Bundt pan. (If you've got a silicone Bundt pan, there's no need to butter it.) Don't place the pan on a baking sheet—you want the oven's heat to circulate freely through the Bundt's inner tube.

Whisk together the flour, baking powder, baking soda, cinnamon, nutmeg, salt and ground ginger, if you're using it (not the grated ginger).

Working with a stand mixer, preferably fitted with a paddle attachment, or with a hand mixer in a large bowl, beat the butter and both sugars together at medium speed until light and fluffy. Add the eggs one at a time, and beat for 1 minute after each addition. Beat in the vanilla. Reduce the mixer speed to low and add the pumpkin, chopped apple and grated ginger, if you're using it—don't be concerned if the mixture looks curdled. Still on low speed, add the dry ingredients, mixing only until they are incorporated. With a rubber spatula, stir in the cranberries and pecans. Scrape the batter into the pan and smooth the top with the rubber spatula.

Bake for 60 to 70 minutes, or until a thin knife inserted into the center of the cake comes out clean. Transfer the cake to a rack and cool for 10 minutes before unmolding, then cool to room temperature on the rack.

Just before bringing the cake to the table, dust it with confectioners' sugar.

MAKES 12 SERVINGS

SERVING: Because of the apples, cranberries and nuts, this cake doesn't lend itself to being cut into dainty slices—and that's just as well: you really want to get a mouthful, the better to appreciate the cake's many flavors. It needs no embellishments if you're serving it as an afternoon treat, but it is nice with softly whipped cream or a scoop of ice cream. For brunch, toast the cake lightly and spread it with a little salted butter and/or a slick of pure maple syrup.

STORING: Wrapped well, the cake will keep at room temperature for up to 5 days, at which point it will be perfect for toasting; or freeze for up to 2 months.

*Playing Around*
**MAPLE SYRUP ICING:** To make a maple-flavored icing for the cake, sift 6 tablespoons confectioners' sugar into a bowl. Stir in 2 tablespoons maple syrup. Add more maple syrup little by little, until you have an icing that runs nicely off the tip of the spoon—you might need another ½ tablespoon syrup to get the right consistency. Put the cooled cake on a sheet of wax paper and drizzle the icing from the tip of the spoon over it. Let the icing set for a few minutes before serving.

# MILK CHOCOLATE MINI BUNDT CAKES

APART FROM being adorable—how can one-to-a-person baby Bundts be anything but?—these cakes are flavorful and easy to make. They've got a light, lovely, mild chocolate crumb, a mid-level swirl of sugared walnuts and a top glaze of dark chocolate. They have everything the big-size Bundts have, in Lilliputian proportions.

These cakes are made in a pan that has 6 miniature molds. Constructed like a 6-cup muffin pan, mini Bundt pans are available in kitchenware shops.

MAKES 6 SERVINGS

**FOR THE SWIRL**

¾ cup chopped walnuts or pecans

2 teaspoons unsweetened cocoa powder

2 teaspoons sugar

**FOR THE CAKE**

1 cup all-purpose flour

½ teaspoon baking powder

¼ teaspoon salt

1 stick (8 tablespoons) unsalted butter, at room temperature

⅓ cup sugar

1 large egg

½ teaspoon pure vanilla extract

½ cup whole milk

7 ounces premium-quality milk chocolate, melted and cooled

**FOR THE GLAZE**

2 ounces bittersweet chocolate, finely chopped

2 teaspoons light corn syrup

1 tablespoon chopped toasted walnuts or pecans (optional)

GETTING READY: Center a rack in the oven and preheat the oven to 350 degrees F. Generously butter a 6-mold mini Bundt pan.

TO MAKE THE SWIRL: Toss the nuts, cocoa and sugar together in a small bowl.

TO MAKE THE CAKE: Whisk together the flour, baking powder and salt.

Working with a stand mixer, preferably fitted with a paddle attachment, or with a hand mixer in a large bowl, beat the butter and sugar together on medium speed until smooth, about 3 minutes, scraping down the bowl as needed. Add the egg and beat for 1 minute more, then beat in the vanilla. Don't be concerned if the mixture looks curdled—it will smooth out soon. Reduce the mixer speed to low and add half the flour mixture, mixing only until it is incorporated. Add the milk, and when it is blended into the batter, add the remaining flour mixture, again mixing just to incorporate. Finally, add the melted chocolate and mix to blend.

Fill each of the mini Bundt molds with a little batter, then divide the swirl ingredients evenly among the molds and top off the Bundts with the remaining batter.

Bake for 20 to 22 minutes, or until a thin knife inserted into the centers of the cakes comes out clean. Transfer the pan to a rack and allow the cakes to rest for 5 minutes, then invert them onto the rack and let them cool to room temperature.

SERVING: Have fun with these. Bring them to the table stacked in a pyramid or serve them on individual plates with some whipped cream—maybe even whipped cream topped with chocolate shavings (page 471)—or circle each cake with chocolate sauce. Because milk chocolate is so mild, these cakes can be served with milk or hot cocoa or with steaming strong espresso.

STORING: Wrapped well, the cakes will keep for 2 days at room temperature or for up to 2 months in the freezer; thaw them in their wrappings. If the glaze dulls, as it undoubtedly will, just give it a shot of hot air from a hairdryer.

*Playing Around*

You can make small changes in this cake with ease. If you'd like a buttermilk chocolate cake, replace the whole milk with buttermilk and whisk ⅛ teaspoon baking soda into the dry ingredients. If you'd like to play around with the swirl, try substituting teensy bits of dried fruit or chopped-up brittle for the nuts. You can replace the nutty swirl with jam, or even skip the swirl completely and go for a totally cake cake. As for the glaze, the cake will be good, just less chocolaty, if you finish it with a dusting of confectioners' sugar or a drizzle of icing made by adding a few drops of water to a little confectioners' sugar.

**TO MAKE THE GLAZE:** Melt the chocolate in a heatproof bowl over a saucepan of water or in a microwave oven (which I think is more convenient for such a small quantity of chocolate). Stir in the corn syrup. Using a small offset metal spatula or a table knife, spread the shiny glaze over the tops of the Bundts, then scatter the nuts, if you're using them, over the glaze. Let the glaze set at room temperature; it will take about 15 minutes.

# CLASSIC BANANA BUNDT CAKE

**MY FRIEND** Ellen Einstein, who, with her husband, Dan, owns Sweet Sixteenth Bakery in Nashville, gave me this recipe for her favorite banana cake, an American standard. It's dense, moist and extremely banana-y—the tangy sour cream accentuates the flavor of the banana.

3 cups all-purpose flour

2 teaspoons baking soda

½ teaspoon salt

2 sticks (8 ounces) unsalted butter, at room temperature

2 cups sugar

2 teaspoons pure vanilla extract

2 large eggs, preferably at room temperature

About 4 very ripe bananas, mashed (you should have 1½–1¾ cups)

1 cup sour cream or plain yogurt

**GETTING READY:** Center a rack in the oven and preheat the oven to 350 degrees F. Generously butter a 9- to 10-inch (12-cup) Bundt pan. (If you've got a silicone Bundt pan, there's no need to butter it.) Don't place the pan on a baking sheet— you want the oven's heat to circulate through the Bundt's inner tube.

Whisk the flour, baking soda and salt together.

Working with a stand mixer, preferably fitted with a paddle attachment, or with a hand mixer in a large bowl, beat the butter until creamy. Add the sugar and beat at medium speed until pale and fluffy. Beat in the vanilla, then add the eggs one at a time, beating for about 1 minute after each egg goes in. Reduce the mixer speed to low and mix in the bananas. Finally, mix in half the dry ingredients (don't be disturbed when the batter curdles), all the sour cream and then the rest of the flour mixture. Scrape the batter into the pan, rap the pan on the counter to de-bubble the batter and smooth the top.

Bake for 65 to 75 minutes, or until a thin knife inserted deep into the center of the cake comes out clean. Check the cake after about 30 minutes—if it is browning too quickly, cover it loosely with a foil tent. Transfer the cake to a rack and cool for 10 minutes before unmolding onto the rack to cool to room temperature.

If you've got the time, wrap the cooled cake in plastic and allow it to sit on the counter overnight before serving—it's better the next day.

**MAKES 14 SERVINGS**

**SERVING:** Cut the cake into thick slices and serve with coffee, tea or a slurpable mocha milkshake.

**STORING:** Wrapped airtight, the cake will keep at room temperature for up to 5 days or in the freezer for up to 2 months.

## Playing Around

**LEMONY WHITE ICING:** Sift ¾ cup confectioners' sugar into a bowl and squeeze in enough fresh lemon juice (start with 2 teaspoons and add more by drops) to make an icing thin enough to drizzle down the Bundt's curves.

# SIMPLE ROUNDS,
# SQUARES AND LOAVES

THESE ARE CAKES you can make on the spur of the moment because the ingredients are usually on hand, cakes you can make when you don't have much time for baking and cakes you can serve with ease whether you're looking to top off a school night family dinner or a casual weekend meal with friends.

Some get their zing from fruit: you'll find an easy cake with figs and lots of honey, one with apple and coconut, a banana cake that lets you have it your way—you can mix and match ingredients to your heart's content— and a shortbread sandwich cake filled with a cranberry marmalade that's a Thanksgiving classic at my house. You'll find nut cakes (I love the simplicity of Ingela's Swedish Visiting Cake, which is baked and served in a skillet) and chocolate cakes (don't miss Jacqueline Picard's Almost-Fudge Gâteau, an elegant cake that's made as easily as brownies) and loaf cakes galore.

I make loaf cakes a lot because they are versatile, homey and keepable— make one on Friday, and you'll have great nibbles all weekend. While you've got my beloved recipe for French Yogurt Cake in this section and Rum-Drenched Vanilla Cakes that pull off the trick of being at once both plain and sophisticated, the lion's share of these recipes are for pound cakes and marbled loaves. In each case, I've given you a basic recipe and many, many variations, because with cakes like these, you have the opportunity to add your own touches and make sweets that can become "house specials." Please read Pound Cake Pointers (page 220) for additional instructions on mixing and baking and Marbling Made Easy (page 229) for some ideas on blending batters.

# BLUEBERRY CRUMB CAKE

IT'S EASY to get attached to this light, tender cake with its walnut-studded crumb topping. It's also easy to find an occasion to serve it—breakfast, brunch, lunch, dinner or snacktime will do. The dominant flavor here is the berries. Don't be tempted to increase the amount of walnuts in the topping—scarcity makes them even more delightful.

MAKES 8 SERVINGS

SERVING: Like all good coffee cakes, this needs nothing but coffee—or tea.

STORING: Best served the day it is made, the cake can be wrapped well and kept overnight at room temperature.

*Playing Around*

This batter works well with almost any kind of berry (except strawberries—they're too watery) in place of or with the blueberries, as well as with slices or cubes of soft fruits, such as peeled peaches or nectarines, apricots or plums.

### FOR THE CRUMBS

- 5 tablespoons unsalted butter, at room temperature
- ¼ cup sugar
- ⅓ cup (packed) light brown sugar
- ⅓ cup all-purpose flour
- ¼ teaspoon salt
- ½ cup chopped walnuts

### FOR THE CAKE

- 1 pint (2 cups) blueberries (preferably fresh, or frozen, not thawed)
- 2 cups plus 2 teaspoons all-purpose flour

- 2 teaspoons baking powder
- ½ teaspoon baking soda
- ¼ teaspoon salt
- ¼ teaspoon ground cinnamon
- ⅛ teaspoon freshly grated nutmeg
- ⅔ cup sugar
  Grated zest of ½ lemon or ¼ orange
- ¾ stick (6 tablespoons) unsalted butter, at room temperature
- 2 large eggs, at room temperature
- 1 teaspoon pure vanilla extract
- ½ cup buttermilk

GETTING READY: Center a rack in the oven and preheat the oven to 350 degrees F. Butter an 8-inch square pan (Pyrex is great for this) and put it on a baking sheet.

TO MAKE THE CRUMBS: Put all the ingredients except the nuts in a food processor and pulse just until the mixture forms clumps and curds and holds together when pressed. Scrape the topping into a bowl, stir in the nuts and press a piece of plastic against the surface. Refrigerate until needed. (Covered well, the crumb mix can be refrigerated for up to 3 days.)

TO MAKE THE CAKE: Using your fingertips, toss the blueberries and 2 teaspoons of the flour together in a small bowl just to coat the berries; set aside. Whisk together the remaining 2 cups flour, the baking powder, baking soda, salt, cinnamon and nutmeg.

Working in the bowl of a stand mixer or in another large bowl, rub the sugar and zest together with your fingertips until the sugar is moist and aromatic. Add the butter and, with the paddle or whisk attachment, or with a hand mixer, beat the sugar with the butter at medium speed until light, about 3 minutes. Add the eggs one by one, beating for about 1 minute after each addition, then beat in the vanilla extract. Don't be concerned if the batter looks curdled—it will soon smooth out. Reduce the mixer speed to low and add the flour mixture and the buttermilk alternately, the flour in 3 parts and the buttermilk in 2 (begin and end with the dry

ingredients). You will have a thick, creamy batter. With a rubber spatula, gently
stir in the berries.

Scrape the batter into the buttered pan and smooth the top gently with the
spatula. Pull the crumb mix from the refrigerator and, with your fingertips, break
it into pieces. There's no need to try to get even pieces—these are crumbs, they're
supposed to be lumpy and bumpy and every shape and size. Scatter the crumbs
over the batter, pressing them down ever so slightly.

Bake for 55 to 65 minutes, or until the crumbs are golden and a thin knife inserted into the center of the cake comes out clean. Transfer the cake to a rack and
cool just until it is warm or until it reaches room temperature.

MAKES 10 SERVINGS

**I HAVE** a friend who, having grown up on the sweets of Austria and Hungary, always tells me he likes "dry" cakes. By this, he doesn't mean anything overbaked, stale or crumbly. What he has in mind is something like a pound cake or a plain coffee cake, one without frosting or fuss, without too much going on—in other words, the kind of cake that is always right with coffee or tea, one that is welcome just about any time of day, one that you might cut a slice from each time you pass it on your way through the kitchen. This is one of those cakes. Moist, plain but very satisfying in its purity and flavorful in a well-mannered way, it will quickly shrink as slice after slice is cut and nibbled at whim.

The cake gets its coconut flavor from unsweetened coconut milk, shredded dried coconut (sweetened or not, toasted or not) and a spoonful of vanilla extract, which seems to deepen the coconut flavor. It could have a bit of dark rum, a touch of spice or even some zest added to it—see Playing Around for some ideas.

| | |
|---|---|
| 2 cups all-purpose flour | 2 cups sugar |
| 1 teaspoon baking powder | 1 teaspoon pure vanilla extract |
| Pinch of salt | 2 teaspoons dark rum (optional, but so |
| 1 cup canned unsweetened coconut | good) |
| milk (stir well before measuring) | ¾ cup shredded coconut (unsweetened or |
| ½ stick (4 tablespoons) unsalted | sweetened), toasted or not |
| butter, cut into 4 pieces | |
| 4 large eggs, preferably at room | |
| temperature | |

**GETTING READY:** Center a rack in the oven and preheat the oven to 350 degrees F. Butter a 9- to 10-inch (10- to 12-cup) Kugelhopf or Bundt pan, or use an unbuttered silicone pan. Don't place the pan on a baking sheet—you want the oven's heat to circulate through the inner tube.

Sift the flour, baking powder and salt together.

Pour the coconut milk into a small saucepan, add the butter and heat until the milk is hot and the butter melted. Remove from the heat, but keep warm.

Working with a stand mixer fitted with the whisk attachment or with a hand mixer in a large bowl, beat the eggs and sugar at medium-high speed until pale, thick and almost doubled in volume, about 3 minutes. Beat in the vanilla and the rum, if you're using it. Reduce the mixer speed to low and add the dry ingredients, scraping down the sides of the bowl as needed and stopping just when the flour disappears.

**SERVING:** This is a great cake with tea, but it's also wonderful with coffee. (I love it with cappuccino or, on the opposite end of the coffee spectrum, with espresso.) It's a good dunker, and as it gets a little stale, it becomes an even better one. When it's a bit stale, it's really good lightly toasted, cut into finger-shaped pieces and dipped, biscotti-style, in vin santo. If you want to dress this cake up a little, serve it with a spoonful of Lemon Cream (page 461) mixed with a bit of sour cream or crème fraîche (page 459), or toast the cake and top it with ice cream and chocolate sauce (pages 463 and 464) or Raspberry Coulis (page 467).

**STORING:** Wrapped in plastic, the cake will keep at room temperature for up to 4 days, longer if you decide to toast it. It can be packed airtight and kept in the freezer for up to 2 months.

Keeping the mixer on low, add the coconut, mixing only until it is blended, then steadily add the hot milk and butter. When the mixture is smooth, stop mixing and give the batter a couple of turns with a rubber spatula, just to make certain that any ingredients that might have fallen to the bottom of the bowl are incorporated. Pour the batter into the pan and give the pan a few back-and-forth shakes to even the batter.

Bake for 60 to 65 minutes, or until the cake is golden brown and a thin knife inserted deep into the center comes out clean. Transfer the cake to a rack and cool for 10 minutes before unmolding onto the rack to cool to room temperature.

## Playing Around

It's easy to make either subtle or substantive changes to this cake, for instance:

**COCONUT LEMON TEA CAKE:** Rub the grated zest of 1 lemon into the sugar before beating it with the eggs; add the juice of ½ lemon to the coconut milk and butter.

**COCONUT LIME TEA CAKE:** Rub the grated zest of 2 limes into the sugar before beating it with the eggs; add the juice of 1 lime to the coconut milk and butter. Keep the dark rum or replace it with Malibu coconut rum.

**COCONUT ORANGE TEA CAKE:** Rub the grated zest of ½ orange into the sugar before beating it with the eggs; add the juice of ¼ orange to the coconut milk and butter.

*Note:* With any of the citrus variations, if you want to really bring out the citrus flavor, you can add a drop or two—not more—of the corresponding pure citrus oil.

**COCONUT SPICE TEA CAKE:** Coconut is a good partner to several spices, so if you want to add another flavor to the cake, try sifting in any of the following with the flour: 1¼ teaspoons ground coriander, 1 teaspoon ground ginger, ¾ teaspoon ground cardamom, ¼ teaspoon ground cinnamon or 1 teaspoon crushed Szechwan peppercorns.

**COCONUT SESAME TEA CAKE:** Right before pouring the batter into the pan, gently fold in ½ cup toasted regular sesame seeds or, if you like them and can find them, ½ cup toasted black sesame seeds.

# SWEDISH VISITING CAKE

**THE FIRST** time my friend Ingela Helgesson came to see us, she arrived with this cake on a flowered platter, explaining that it was the cake that her mother and her friends always brought to one another. Ingela also said her mother used to claim that you could start making it when you saw guests coming up the road and have it ready by the time they were settling down for coffee. That's only a slight exaggeration.

The cake is thin and light with a golden sugar crust and an interior that is soft, chewy, moist and reminiscent of cakes made with almond paste. Although it's amply satisfying in its plainness, I upped the flavor just a little by adding vanilla and almond extract.

Ingela does what her mom did—she bakes the cake in a greased 9-inch cast-iron skillet. That gives the cake a great bottom crust, to say nothing of authenticity. However, if you haven't got an old-fashioned skillet, you can use a well-buttered cake or pie pan.

MAKES 8 TO 10 SERVINGS

SERVING: The cake is good eaten warm or at room temperature. Either way, it is meant to be cut into small wedges and eaten sans forks—this is a finger cake.

STORING: The cake is an excellent keeper. Well wrapped, it will keep for about 5 days at room temperature or for up to 2 months in the freezer.

| | |
|---|---|
| 1 cup sugar, plus a little more for sprinkling | ½ teaspoon pure almond extract (optional) |
| Grated zest of 1 lemon | 1 cup all-purpose flour |
| 2 large eggs | 1 stick (8 tablespoons) unsalted butter, melted and cooled |
| ¼ teaspoon salt | About ¼ cup sliced almonds (blanched or not) |
| 1 teaspoon pure vanilla extract (optional) | |

**GETTING READY:** Center a rack in the oven and preheat the oven to 350 degrees F. Butter a seasoned 9-inch cast-iron skillet or other heavy ovenproof skillet, a 9-inch round cake pan or even a pie pan.

Pour the sugar into a medium bowl. Add the lemon zest and blend the zest into the sugar with your fingers until the sugar is moist and aromatic. Whisk in the eggs one at a time until well blended. Whisk in the salt and the extracts, if you're using them. Switch to a rubber spatula and stir in the flour. Finally, fold in the melted butter.

Scrape the batter into the skillet and smooth the top with the rubber spatula. Scatter the sliced almonds over the top and sprinkle with a little sugar. If you're using a cake or pie pan, place the pan on a baking sheet.

Bake the cake for 25 to 30 minutes, or until it is golden and a little crisp on the outside; the inside will remain moist, even, as Ingela says, "slightly damp." Remove the skillet from the oven and let the cake cool for 5 minutes, then run a thin knife around the sides and bottom of the cake to loosen it. You can serve the cake, warm or cooled, directly from the skillet or turned out onto a serving plate.

GROWN IN climates that bring to mind the word "sultry," figs conjure sun and heat and sensuality. But the fig has an autumnal side too, reminding us of warm months while it heralds shorter days and cooler nights. This cake plays to the fruit's affinity for fall and chill-weather foods like cornmeal, honey and ruby port. The buttery cake is a moist, appealing round, sweetened with honey and distinguished by the addition of yellow cornmeal. The honey and cornmeal provide a somewhat Italianate base for the fruit, which is lightly poached in port and honey before it is pressed into the batter. And there's a bonus—once the figs are poached, the remaining syrup is boiled for a few minutes and becomes a lovely sauce. Sauced, the cake jumps from an everyday treat to a company dessert.

**MAKES 8 TO 10 SERVINGS**

SERVING: Offer wedges of the cake topped with the port sauce (which can be warmed, if you'd like). Whipped cream or ice cream alongside would be even lovelier.

STORING: Wrapped well, the cake will keep at room temperature for 2 days.

| | |
|---|---|
| ¾ cup ruby port | ¼ cup sugar |
| 1 cup honey | Grated zest of ½ lemon |
| 2 thin slices lemon | 1½ sticks (12 tablespoons) unsalted butter, |
| 16–20 fresh figs, stemmed and halved | cut into 6 pieces, at room |
| 1½ cups all-purpose flour | temperature |
| ½ cup yellow cornmeal | 3 large eggs, preferably at room |
| 2 teaspoons baking powder | temperature |
| ¼ teaspoon salt | 1 teaspoon pure vanilla extract |

FOR THE FIGS AND SAUCE: Stir the port and ½ cup of the honey together in a small saucepan. Toss in the lemon slices and bring to a boil over medium heat. Lower the heat, add the figs, cover the pan and cook for 4 to 6 minutes, or until the figs are soft but not falling apart. Using a slotted spoon, transfer the figs to a bowl.

Raise the heat just a little and cook the poaching liquid for another 10 to 15 minutes, or until slightly thickened; the syrup should coat a metal spoon. Remove the pan from the heat and set the sauce aside.

GETTING READY TO BAKE: Center a rack in the oven and preheat the oven to 350 degrees F. Butter a 9-inch springform pan. Line the bottom with parchment paper, butter the paper and dust the inside of the pan with flour, tapping out the excess. Put the pan on a baking sheet lined with parchment or a silicone mat.

TO MAKE THE CAKE: Whisk together the flour, cornmeal, baking powder and salt.

Put the sugar and grated zest in the bowl of a stand mixer or another large bowl, and rub them together with your fingertips until the sugar is moist, grainy and aromatic. Toss in the butter. With the paddle or whisk attachment or with a hand mixer, beat the butter and sugar together on medium speed until creamy, about 3 minutes. Add the eggs one by one, beating for 1 minute after each addition. Pour in the remaining ½ cup honey, add the vanilla extract and beat for another 2 minutes. The mixture may look curdled and not so pretty—keep mixing, it will get better soon. Reduce the mixer speed to low and add the dry ingredients, mixing only until they are incorporated; you'll have a fairly thick batter. Scrape the

batter into the prepared pan and jiggle the pan from side to side a few times to even the batter, then scatter the poached figs over the top.

Bake for 55 to 60 minutes, or until the cake is puffed and golden brown and a knife inserted into the center comes out clean. Transfer the cake to a rack and cool for 10 minutes before running a blunt knife around the edges and releasing the sides of the pan. Cool the cake to slightly warm or to room temperature before serving it with the sauce.

SOMETIMES, WHEN you're really lucky, everything can go wrong and you still end up with a winner. I'd found a recipe for a polenta and ricotta cake in a little recipe pamphlet that had come with one of my French food magazines. The idea of ricotta and cornmeal caught my attention, and because I had all the ingredients at hand, I thought I'd try it immediately. It wasn't until I looked at the ingredients measured out on my counter that I started to have my doubts. The recipe called for a lot of polenta and no flour—wouldn't it be heavy? And there were no eggs—wouldn't it be dry? No butter—wouldn't it be drier still? So I started reworking the recipe, adding flour and honey and eggs and butter and, just for the fun of it, dried figs and grated lemon zest too. While wholesale rigmaroling rarely works in baking, for reasons unknown—perhaps the well wishes of the kitchen gods—this recipe turned out to be perfect.

The cake is compact but very moist, with a tiny unexpected crunch running through it. This phantom-crust crunch is just the right match to the crunch of the seeds in the dried figs. You can definitely taste the honey in the cake (it's got an almost citrusy edge), but the ricotta is elusive—even if its signature tang and smoothness are there. This cake is even better the day after it's been made—honey cakes do well with a ripening rest.

MAKES 8 SERVINGS

SERVING: Serve the cake when it is still slightly warm or wait until it reaches room temperature, my preference. Honey cakes are good with tea, and this one's no exception. While I like the cake plain, it's very good with a little softly whipped cream that's lightly sweetened with honey.

STORING: Wrapped in plastic, the cake will keep for about 5 days at room temperature. In fact, it will be even better after it's had a day's rest. The cake can also be frozen for up to 2 months; defrost in its wrapper.

*Playing Around*

For a cake that's even more reminiscent of a Mediterranean sweet, toss the figs with a pinch or three of crushed fresh thyme leaves or minced fresh rosemary.

---

About 16 moist, plump dried
    Mission or Kadota figs, stemmed
1 cup medium-grain polenta or yellow
    cornmeal
½ cup all-purpose flour
1 teaspoon baking powder
¼ teaspoon salt
1 cup ricotta
⅓ cup tepid water
¾ cup sugar

¾ cup honey (if you're a real honey lover,
    use a full-flavored honey such as
    chestnut, pine or buckwheat)
Grated zest of 1 lemon
1 stick (8 tablespoons) unsalted butter,
    melted and cooled, plus 1 tablespoon,
    cut into bits and chilled
2 large eggs

---

GETTING READY: Center a rack in the oven and preheat the oven to 325 degrees F. Butter a 10½-inch fluted tart pan with a removable bottom and put it on a baking sheet lined with parchment or a silicone mat.

Check that the figs are, indeed, moist and plump. If they are the least bit hard, toss them into a small pan of boiling water and steep for a minute, then drain and pat dry. If the figs are large (bigger than a bite), snip them in half.

Whisk the polenta, flour, baking powder and salt together.

Working with a stand mixer fitted with the whisk attachment or with a hand mixer in a large bowl, beat the ricotta and water together on low speed until very smooth. With the mixer at medium speed, add the sugar, honey and lemon zest and beat until light. Beat in the melted butter, then add the eggs one at a time, beating until the mixture is smooth. Reduce the mixer speed to low and add the dry ingredients, mixing only until they are fully incorporated. You'll have a sleek, smooth, pourable batter.

Pour about one third of the batter into the pan and scatter over the figs. Pour in the rest of the batter, smooth the top with a rubber spatula, if necessary, and dot the batter evenly with the chilled bits of butter.

Bake for 35 to 40 minutes, or until a thin knife inserted into the center of the cake comes out clean. The cake should be honey brown and pulling away just a little from the sides of the pan, and the butter will have left light-colored circles in the top. Transfer the cake to a rack and remove the sides of the pan after about 5 minutes. Cool to warm, or cool completely.

# FAR BRETON

MAKES 8 SERVINGS

**SERVING:** The *far* is best at room temperature—that's when it is most puddingish—so try to serve it soon after you've un-molded it. It should be served plain with just the dusting of confectioners' sugar.

**STORING:** I think the *far* is best on the day it is made, but it can be kept in the refrigerator for a day and served either chilled or at room temperature.

**LUCK COMES** in many forms. Many years ago it came in the form of Marie-Cecile Noblet, our French au pair. Not only was she terrific with Joshua, our son, and a delight to have in our home, but she could cook. She came from Brittany and, as young as she was when she came to live with us, she had spent a few years working with her father, a chef and hotelier, so whenever the baby didn't need us, we'd dash to the kitchen and cook together. Marie-Cecile was a natural cook—she could feel her way around almost any dish—and although she arrived without a single written recipe, she cooked and baked with ease and remarkable precision. She called it cooking *au pif*—cooking by following her nose.

*Au pif* was how Marie-Cecile made her Far Breton, a custardy cake beloved in Brittany but just about unknown here. Based on a crepe batter, the *far* is simple in every way—the batter is whirred together in a blender, given an overnight rest, then mixed with dried fruit and baked. Marie-Cecile made her *far* with prunes, but I can't remember whether she steeped them or not (she probably plumped them over steaming water) and, of course, because she made the cake *au pif*, there is no recipe to refer to. So, in the spirit of *au pif*-ness, I offer you my recipe for *far* made with prunes and raisins (although you could use dried apricots or cherries or any of the fruits in combination), and I offer you a steeping choice: Earl Grey tea (a great companion to prunes) or Armagnac (an equally great, if stronger, companion).

| | |
|---|---|
| 3 large eggs | ¾ cup all-purpose flour |
| 2 cups whole milk | 1 cup pitted prunes |
| ½ cup sugar | ⅓ cup dark raisins |
| ¼ teaspoon pure vanilla extract | 1 cup hot tea, such as Earl Grey, or ¼ cup |
| ⅛ teaspoon salt | Armagnac plus ¼ cup water |
| 5 tablespoons unsalted butter, melted and cooled | Confectioners' sugar, for dusting |

**UP TO 1 DAY AHEAD:** Put the eggs, milk, sugar, vanilla, salt and melted butter in a blender or food processor and whir for 1 minute to blend. Add the flour and pulse the batter several times. Pour the batter into a pitcher, cover and refrigerate for at least 3 hours, or, preferably, overnight.

Meanwhile, for tea-soaked fruit, put the fruit in a heatproof bowl and pour over the hot tea. When the tea cools to room temperature, cover. For Armagnac-soaked fruit, put the fruit and water in a small saucepan over medium heat. Cook until the water almost evaporates, then turn off the heat and pour the Armagnac evenly over the fruit. Stand back, ignite the alcohol with a long match and wait until the flames die out before pouring the fruit and syrup into a heatproof bowl. When the fruit is cool, cover it and set aside.

GETTING READY TO BAKE: Center a rack in the oven and preheat the oven to 375 degrees F. Butter an 8-x-2-inch round cake pan, line the bottom with parchment or wax paper, butter the paper and dust the pan with flour, tapping out the excess. Put the pan on a baking sheet.

Remove the batter from the refrigerator and whisk to reblend it, then rap the pitcher against the counter to break the top bubbles. Pour the batter into the pan and drop in the fruit, trying to distribute it fairly evenly; discard whatever soaking syrup remains.

Bake for 50 to 60 minutes, or until the top of the cake is puffed and brown and a thin knife inserted into the center comes out clean. Transfer the pan to a cooling rack and cool to room temperature.

The *far* is fragile (its fragility is part of what makes it so delicious) and it takes a little extra TLC to unmold it. So that the custard is not cut by the wires of the cooling rack, cover the rack with a piece of parchment or wax paper, and dust the paper with confectioners' sugar. Have a serving plate at hand. Run a blunt knife gently between the cake and the sides of the pan and turn the cake out onto the prepared rack. Don't leave it on the rack any longer than necessary—quickly and gently invert it onto the serving plate.

Just before serving, dust the cake with confectioners' sugar.

# LOTS-OF-WAYS BANANA CAKE

MAKES 8 TO 16 SERVINGS,
DEPENDING ON WHETHER
YOU SERVE A SINGLE- OR
DOUBLE-DECKER CAKE

**THE INSPIRATION** to bake a banana cake always seems to strike when a bunch of bananas are mottling on the counter. But just because you've got the fruit doesn't mean you have all the other stuff you need, which is why I created this amazingly flexible cake. No coconut? Skip it. No brown sugar? Use white. No coconut milk? Use milk, buttermilk, sour cream or yogurt. You can serve the cake as a single layer or a double (the recipe makes two layers), plain, frosted, filled or frosted and filled. Take a look at Playing Around for some ideas.

If you make the cake with the ingredients listed first below, you'll get a consistency that isn't heavy but not featherweight either. It has enough substance to chew on, but it's light enough to entice you to go back for a second serving . . . or a third.

**SERVING:** See Playing Around for a bunch of suggestions.

**STORING:** Wrapped airtight, the cakes will keep for about 4 days at room temperature or for up to 2 months in the freezer.

2⅔ cups all-purpose flour

1¼ teaspoons baking soda

½ teaspoon salt

½ teaspoon freshly grated nutmeg

1½ sticks (12 tablespoons) unsalted butter, at room temperature

1 cup (packed) light brown sugar (or granulated sugar)

¾ cup sugar

2 large eggs, preferably at room temperature

1½ teaspoons pure vanilla extract

2 tablespoons dark rum or Malibu coconut rum (optional)

About 4 very ripe bananas, mashed (you should have 1½–1¾ cups)

½ cup canned unsweetened coconut milk, regular (stir well before measuring) or "lite" (or whole milk, buttermilk, sour cream or plain yogurt)

1 cup sweetened shredded coconut, preferably toasted (or an equal amount of moist, plump dried fruit, such as currants, raisins, chopped apricots, cranberries, blueberries or halved cherries, or a combination of coconut and dried fruit)

GETTING READY: Center a rack in the oven and preheat the oven to 350 degrees F. Butter two 9-x-2-inch round cake pans, dust the insides with flour and tap out the excess. Put the pans on a baking sheet.

Whisk the flour, baking soda, salt and nutmeg together.

Working with a stand mixer, preferably fitted with a paddle attachment, or with a hand mixer in a large bowl, beat the butter until creamy. Add the sugars and beat at medium speed for a couple of minutes, then add the eggs one at a time, beating well after each addition, followed by the vanilla and rum. You'll have a beautiful satiny batter. Now lower the speed and add the bananas—the batter will curdle, but that's fine; it will come together as you add the remaining ingredients. Still on low speed, add the dry and liquid ingredients alternately, adding the flour mixture in 3 portions and the coconut milk in 2 (begin and end with the dry ingredients). Mix just until everything is incorporated. Switch to a rubber spatula and gently stir in the coconut. Divide the batter evenly between the two pans.

Bake for about 45 minutes, or until the cakes are a deep golden brown. They should start to pull away from the sides of the pans and a thin knife inserted into their centers will come out clean. Transfer the cakes to a cooling rack and cool for 5 minutes, then unmold and invert onto another rack to cool to room temperature right side up.

## Playing Around

**FROSTING:** To frost one layer or to fill and frost both layers, consider
Sweetened whipped cream to which you've added vanilla, a splash of dark rum or Malibu coconut rum and toasted coconut
Marshmallow frosting (page 247)
Chocolate Whipped Cream (page 457) and, just for fun, a crown of chocolate shavings (page 471)
Bittersweet Ganache (page 453)

**RUM SYRUP:** If you like the flavor of rum, you can douse the cakes with rum syrup as soon as they come out of the oven (see page 226 for the syrup recipe—give these cakes the same treatment you'd give the Rum-Drenched Vanilla Cakes).

**ONE-LAYER CAKE:** Serve just one layer, lightly sprinkled with confectioners' sugar or cocoa powder, and accompany it with lightly whipped cream and/or ice cream (chocolate, coconut, vanilla or coffee) and/or Hot Fudge Sauce (page 465).

**GRAND BANANA SUNDAE:** You can cut one cake into small cubes and make a sundae. Toss the pieces of cake with some cubes of fresh banana and a little rum and top with ice cream, hot fudge sauce and whipped cream. Why not go all the way and add some toasted coconut too?

# CRANBERRY UPSIDE-DOWNER

MAKES 6 TO 8 SERVINGS

**I CAN'T** recall exactly when I created this cake, but I do remember it was for Thanksgiving. I wanted something simple and festive to end the big meal and this was perfect. Because I buy lots of bags of cranberries in October and November (when they're plentiful) and keep them in my freezer, I've got berries enough to make this cake all winter long for dinner desserts as well as for Sunday morning brunches.

1 cup all-purpose flour

1 teaspoon baking powder

1 teaspoon ground cinnamon

¼ teaspoon salt

1¾ sticks (14 tablespoons) unsalted
    butter, at room temperature

1 cup minus 2 tablespoons sugar

¼ cup chopped walnuts or pecans

2 cups cranberries—fresh or frozen (if
    frozen, do not thaw)

2 large eggs

1 teaspoon pure vanilla extract or
    ½ teaspoon pure almond extract

⅓ cup whole milk

⅓ cup red currant jelly, for glazing
    the cake

**GETTING READY:** Center a rack in the oven and preheat the oven to 350 degrees F. Put an 8-x-2-inch round cake pan on a baking sheet.

Whisk together the flour, baking powder, cinnamon and salt.

Melt 6 tablespoons of the butter in a small saucepan. Sprinkle in 6 tablespoons of the sugar and cook, stirring, until the mixture comes to a boil. Pour this evenly over the bottom of the cake pan, then scatter over the nuts and top with the cranberries, smoothing the layer and pressing it down gently with your fingertips. (If you've used frozen berries and they've caused the butter to congeal, don't worry—everything will melt in the oven.) Set aside.

Working with a stand mixer, preferably fitted with a paddle attachment, or with a hand mixer in a large bowl, beat the remaining stick (8 tablespoons) of butter on medium speed until smooth. Add the remaining ½ cup sugar and continue to beat until pale and creamy, about 3 minutes. Add the eggs one at a time, beating for 1 minute after each addition and scraping down the bowl as needed. Pour in the vanilla. Reduce the mixer speed to low and add half of the dry ingredients, mixing only until they disappear into the batter. Mix in the milk, then the rest of the dry ingredients. Spoon the batter over the cranberries and smooth the top with a rubber spatula.

Bake for 40 to 45 minutes, or until the cake is golden and a thin knife inserted into the center of the cake comes out clean. Remove it from the oven and run a blunt knife between the sides of the pan and the cake. Carefully turn the cake out onto a serving platter. If any of the berries stick to the pan—as they might—just scrape them off with a table knife and return them to the cake.

Warm the jelly in a small saucepan over low heat, or do this in a microwave oven. Gently brush the glaze over the hot cake.

**SERVING:** When the situation allows, I like to serve this cake about 20 minutes out of the oven, when it is still warm. However, it's more than fine at room temperature—even the following day. It's always good with vanilla ice cream or sweetened whipped cream.

**STORING:** The cake is best served the day it is made, but it can be covered and kept at room temperature overnight. Because of the berry topping, it's not a good candidate for freezing.

*Playing Around*

**SUMMERY PEACH UPSIDE-DOWNER:** When the season changes, make this cake with a peach topping. Omit the nuts and cranberries. Slice 3 large peeled and pitted peaches and arrange them in rings on top of the melted butter and sugar. If you'd like, toss in a few raspberries for color. Bake as directed, but allow the cake to rest for at least 30 minutes before serving so that the juices—and there'll be plenty—have a chance to settle into the cake. If you want to glaze the cake, use strained apricot jam or even apple or quince jelly.

MAKES 8 TO 10 SERVINGS

**CRANBERRIES ARE** an underrated culinary treasure. They get the center stage for a couple of hours on Thanksgiving, then they're pretty much forgotten. Tsk, tsk. But they're worth stocking up on to have them on hand for muffins, cakes (page 206), galettes (page 364) and this simple and beautiful sweet.

Part cake, part torte and even part bar cookie, this dessert has two elements: a double layer of shortbread and a filling of fresh cranberry and orange jam. Because the shortbread is very rich, it bakes to a lovely golden color and makes a really pretty frame for the brilliant red jam. The texture of the cake is soft and a tad chewy, the flavors are sweet and sharp at the same time and the look, like the taste, is both homey and sophisticated, as is often the case with simple desserts.

A word on size: For a feast, you'll want a bigger cake—no problem: double the recipe and make it in a 9-x-13-inch pan. If rolling out such a long piece of the soft dough seems a little daunting, just roll it out one quarter at a time (that is, do half of each layer at a time) and then pinch the pieces together. Because the dough is soft and really more a cake than a pastry dough, it will puff and bake together nicely.

**SERVING:** Serve the cake at room temperature, as is or with a big scoop of ice cream.

**STORING:** Tightly wrapped, the cake will keep for up to 4 days at room temperature or for up to 2 months in the freezer.

### FOR THE JAM FILLING
- 1 large navel orange
- About ¼ cup orange juice
- 1 12-ounce bag cranberries, fresh or frozen (not thawed)
- About 1 cup sugar

### FOR THE CAKE
- 2½ cups all-purpose flour
- 1 teaspoon baking powder
- Pinch of salt
- 1 stick plus 5 tablespoons (13 tablespoons) unsalted butter, at room temperature
- 1 cup plus 2 teaspoons sugar
- 1 large egg
- 1 large yolk
- 1 teaspoon pure vanilla extract

**TO MAKE THE JAM FILLING:** Grate the zest of the orange into a medium heavy-bottomed saucepan. Slice off the peel, removing the white, cottony pith that sticks to the fruit, and slice between the membranes to release the orange segments. Cut the segments into ¼-inch-wide pieces and toss these into the pan. Working over a measuring cup, squeeze the juice from the membranes—if you have ¼ cup, great; if not, add enough additional orange juice (or water) to make ¼ cup—and pour it into the pan.

Put the cranberries in the pan, stir in ¾ cup of the sugar, set the pan over medium heat and bring to a boil, stirring frequently. Cook, stirring almost constantly, until the cranberries pop and your spoon leaves tracks, about 5 minutes. Scrape the jam into a bowl and taste it—if it's too tart, add more sugar to taste. Cool to room temperature. (The filling can be made up to 2 weeks ahead and stored in an airtight container in the refrigerator.)

TO MAKE THE CAKE: Whisk together the flour, baking powder and salt.

Working with a stand mixer, preferably fitted with a paddle attachment, or with a hand mixer in a large bowl, beat the butter on medium speed until soft and smooth. Add 1 cup of the sugar and continue to beat until it dissolves into the butter. Reduce the mixer speed to low and add the egg and yolk, beating until they too are absorbed. Beat in the vanilla. Add the flour mixture, mixing only until it is incorporated; since this is a delicate dough, one that should not be overbeaten, you might want to finish mixing in the flour by hand using a sturdy spatula. You'll have a thick dough, one that is quite malleable.

Turn the dough out onto a smooth work surface and gather it together into a ball, then divide it in half and pat each half into a disk. Wrap the disks in plastic and refrigerate them for 15 to 30 minutes. (At this point, the dough can be refrigerated overnight; set it out at room temperature for about 20 minutes before proceeding.)

GETTING READY TO BAKE: While the dough is chilling, center a rack in the oven and preheat the oven to 350 degrees F. Lightly butter a 9-inch springform pan (preferably nonstick) and place it on a baking sheet lined with parchment or a silicone mat.

Work with one piece of dough at a time. For the bottom layer, either roll the dough to size between two pieces of plastic wrap—it's an easy dough to roll—and lay it in the pan, or put the dough in the pan and press it lightly and evenly across the bottom with your fingertips. Spread the cranberry filling over the dough.

Unwrap the second piece of dough, but leave it on the piece of plastic. Press and/or roll it until it is just the diameter of the pan. Carefully lift the dough and invert it in onto the filling, lift off the plastic and use your fingers to even it as necessary so that it covers the filling. Brush the top of the cake very lightly with water and sprinkle with the remaining 2 teaspoons sugar.

Bake for 35 to 40 minutes, or until the top of the cake is lightly golden and a thin knife inserted into the center comes out clean. Transfer the pan to a cooling rack and cool for about 20 minutes, then run a blunt knife around the cake, remove the sides of the pan and let cool to room temperature.

*Playing Around*

It's easy to enjoy this cake over the course of the year by swapping the cranberry jam for your favorite seasonal fillings. For instance:

FALL SHORTBREAD CAKE: Replace the cranberry filling with a slender middle layer of caramelized apples (see page 408), thinly sliced apples tossed in sugar and spices (such as ground cinnamon, allspice, ginger and/or nutmeg), thick applesauce (page 304), spiced apple butter or a thin layer of store-bought apple butter topped with one of applesauce.

ANYTIME SHORTBREAD CAKE: Replace the cranberry jam with about 2 cups of your favorite chunky fruit preserves or citrus marmalade.

# CINNAMON SQUARES

**THIS IS** a simple cake in every way. You mix it in minutes by hand and bake it in an ordinary square pan (I use a nonstick Baker's Secret pan from the supermarket), first spreading half of the cinnamon batter into the pan, adding chocolate bits and a mixture of cinnamon, sugar and instant espresso, then the rest of the batter. The cake gets a delicious and equally simple frosting, a melt of chocolate and butter. It's pretty enough in a homey way, but there's something about the softness of the cake, the warmth of its cinnamon flavor, the way the swirl of cinnamon, sugar, chocolate and coffee melts into the cake and that really good frosting that makes it as good at a brunch as it is as a midnight snack.

### FOR THE CAKE

- 1¼ cups plus 2 tablespoons sugar
- 1 tablespoon plus 2½ teaspoons ground cinnamon
- 1½ teaspoons instant espresso powder
- 1¾ cups all-purpose flour
- 2 teaspoons baking powder
  Pinch of salt
- ¾ cup whole milk
- 2 large eggs
- ½ teaspoon pure vanilla extract
- 1 stick plus 2 tablespoons (10 tablespoons) unsalted butter, melted and cooled
- 3 ounces bittersweet chocolate, finely chopped, or ½ cup store-bought mini chocolate chips

### FOR THE FROSTING

- 6 ounces bittersweet chocolate, finely chopped
- 2½ tablespoons unsalted butter, cut into 4 pieces

**MAKES 9 SERVINGS**

**SERVING:** Serve the cake as is or, if you'd like, with whipped cream, crème fraîche or sour cream.

**STORING:** Wrapped in plastic, the cake will keep at room temperature for 2 days. It can be frozen for up to 2 months, but it's best to put the cake in the freezer unwrapped and then, when the frosting is firm, to wrap it airtight; defrost, still wrapped, overnight in the refrigerator.

### *Playing Around*

**CAPPUCCINO SQUARES:** If you like the cappuccino flavor combination of coffee and cinnamon, you can easily switch the balance in this recipe by adding a jolt of coffee flavor to the batter. Just mix 1 tablespoon instant espresso into the milk and warm the milk in a microwave oven until it is hot enough to dissolve the coffee. Cool the milk and carry on.

**GETTING READY:** Center a rack in the oven and preheat the oven to 350 degrees F. Butter an 8-inch square baking pan and line the bottom with parchment or wax paper. Place the pan on a baking sheet.

**TO MAKE THE CAKE:** Stir 2 tablespoons of the sugar, 2½ teaspoons of the cinnamon and the espresso together in a small bowl.

In a large bowl, whisk together the flour, the remaining 1¼ cups sugar, the baking powder, salt and the remaining 1 tablespoon cinnamon. In another bowl, whisk together the milk, eggs and vanilla. Pour the liquid ingredients over the flour mixture and gently whisk until you have a homogenous batter. Now, using the whisk or a rubber spatula, fold in the butter with a light touch, just until the butter is absorbed. You'll have a smooth, satiny batter.

Scrape half of the batter into the pan and smooth the top. Sprinkle the chocolate over the batter and dust with the cinnamon-sugar mixture. Cover with the rest of the batter and smooth the top again.

Bake for 35 to 40 minutes, or until the cake is puffed and beginning to pull away from the sides of the pan; a thin knife inserted into the center will come out clean. Transfer the cake to a cooling rack and let it rest for 15 minutes before unmolding it onto another rack. Peel off the paper, invert it onto the first rack, and cool to room temperature right side up.

TO MAKE THE FROSTING: Put the chocolate and butter in a heatproof bowl and fit the bowl over a saucepan of simmering water. Cook, stirring gently and often, just until they melt. Be careful not to overheat the mixture so much that it thins out; the chocolate should be smooth, very shiny, thick and spreadable. (If it thins, leave the frosting at room temperature for a bit, until it thickens a little.)

Using an offset metal icing spatula or a table knife, spread the frosting in generous sweeps and swirls over the top of the cake. Allow the frosting to set at room temperature, then cut the cake into 9 squares, each about 2½ inches on a side.

**IF YOU'RE** longing for Christmas, this cake can help you fool yourself into believing St. Nick is almost on the rooftop. Packed with fresh, candied and ground ginger, spices, molasses and a little chocolate, it is moist, mildly spicy and just a teensy bit hot from the ginger. It's a hearty, high square with a wonderfully solid look, and it's topped with a swath of bittersweet icing.

### FOR THE CAKE

- 2 tablespoons finely chopped peeled fresh ginger
- 1 tablespoon sugar
- 2 cups all-purpose flour
- 1 teaspoon baking soda
- 2 teaspoons ground ginger
- ¾ teaspoon ground cinnamon
- ¼ teaspoon ground cloves
- 1 stick plus 3 tablespoons (11 tablespoons) unsalted butter, at room temperature
- ¾ cup (packed) light brown sugar
- 3 large eggs
- ½ cup molasses (not blackstrap)
- 6 ounces bittersweet chocolate—2 ounces melted and cooled, 4 ounces finely chopped
- 1 cup buttermilk
- 1 tablespoon finely chopped stem ginger in syrup (available in Asian markets and some supermarkets; optional)

### FOR THE ICING

- 3 ounces bittersweet chocolate, coarsely chopped
- 1 tablespoon strong coffee
- 3 tablespoons unsalted butter, at room temperature
- 3 tablespoons confectioners' sugar

**GETTING READY:** Center a rack in the oven and preheat the oven to 350 degrees F. Butter a 9-inch square baking pan and put it on a baking sheet.

**TO MAKE THE CAKE:** Put the fresh ginger and sugar in a small bowl, stir and set aside.

Whisk the flour, baking soda and spices together.

Working with a stand mixer, preferably fitted with a paddle attachment, or with a hand mixer in a large bowl, beat the butter and brown sugar together at medium speed until light and fluffy, about 3 minutes. Add the eggs one at a time, beating for 1 minute after each egg goes in. Don't worry if the mixture looks curdled at this stage. Pour in the molasses and beat until smooth. Reduce the mixer speed to low and add the melted chocolate, along with the sugared ginger, if you're using it. Still on low speed, add the dry ingredients in 3 additions and the buttermilk in 2 (begin and end with the dry ingredients), mixing the batter only as much as needed to blend the ingredients. Fold in the chopped chocolate and the ginger in syrup. Pour the batter into the pan.

Bake for about 40 minutes, or until the cake starts to pull away from the sides of the pan and a thin knife inserted into the center comes out clean. Don't be concerned if the cake has domed and cracked—it will settle down as it cools. Transfer the cake to a rack and cool for 10 minutes, then unmold the cake. Turn right side up to cool to room temperature before icing the cake. (The edges of the cake might be quite brown, but don't fret—you can trim them after you ice the cake.)

---

MAKES 9 SERVINGS

**SERVING:** Serve the gingerbread as is or with whipped cream, crème fraîche (a great accompaniment) or Ginger-Infused Whipped Cream (see Playing Around).

**STORING:** Gingerbread is a good keeper. You can wrap it and keep it at room temperature for about 3 days or freeze it, icing and all, for up to 2 months.

*Playing Around*

**GINGER-INFUSED WHIPPED CREAM:** Bring 1 cup heavy cream and 8 dime-size slices of peeled fresh ginger almost to a boil in a saucepan, or do this in a microwave. Remove from the heat, cover and let the cream steep for an hour or so, then refrigerate the cream for at least 2 hours (it can stay overnight, if that suits you better). Strain the cream, discard the ginger and whip the cream until it holds soft peaks. Fold in sifted confectioners' sugar to taste.

**GINGERBREAD FRUIT CAKE:** To make this cake even more Christmasy, when you add the chopped chocolate and ginger in syrup, also fold in 1 to 2 tablespoons finely chopped best-quality candied orange peel and about ½ cup brandy- or rum-flamed raisins (see page 92).

TO MAKE THE ICING: Set a heatproof bowl over a pan of simmering water, put the chocolate and coffee in the bowl, and stir occasionally until the chocolate is melted. Remove the bowl and, using a small whisk, stir in the butter 1 tablespoon at a time. Sift the confectioners' sugar over the chocolate and stir in. Transfer the bowl to a counter and let the icing sit for about 10 minutes.

Put the gingerbread, still on the rack, on a piece of wax paper or foil (the drip catcher). Pour the icing onto the center of the cake and use a long metal spatula to spread the icing evenly over the top. Allow the icing to set for 30 minutes (you can hurry it along by chilling the cake briefly). If the edges of the cake are overbaked, now's the time to trim them. Then cut the gingerbread into 9 even pieces.

# APPLE-COCONUT FAMILY CAKE

**THE TASTES** in this light, moist cake are coconut, a hint of cinnamon and the sweetness of apples, all of which put you in mind of early fall. Our friend Michael Vogel aptly calls it a "family" cake.

- 1 cup plus 2 tablespoons all-purpose flour
- 2 teaspoons baking powder
- ¼ teaspoon baking soda
- ¼ teaspoon ground cinnamon
  Pinch of salt
- 3 apples (I use Golden Delicious), peeled and cored
- 2 large eggs, preferably at room temperature

- ½ cup plus 2 teaspoons sugar
- ½ cup plain yogurt
- 6 tablespoons flavorless oil, such as canola or grapeseed
- 1 tablespoon dark rum
- 2 teaspoons pure vanilla extract
- 1 cup shredded coconut, preferably unsweetened

About ½ cup apple jelly, for glaze

MAKES 8 SERVINGS

**SERVING:** The cake can be served warm or at room temperature. While it is great as is, it's scrumptious with a little whipped cream.

**STORING:** This cake is a good keeper. Wrapped well, it will keep at room temperature for about 4 days. Because of the apples and glaze, it isn't a good candidate for freezing.

*Playing Around*

**COCONUT-NUT FAMILY CAKE:** Keep the coconut in the cake, but add ½ cup ground pecans or walnuts and an equal amount of the same nut, finely chopped. This double-nut cake is just as good made with slices of pineapple or pears as it is with apples.

**GETTING READY:** Center a rack in the oven and preheat the oven to 350 degrees F. Butter a 9-inch springform pan and place it on a baking sheet lined with parchment or a silicone mat.

Whisk together the flour, baking powder, baking soda, cinnamon and salt.

Cut 2 of the apples into a small dice, cover with plastic wrap and set aside. Cut the third apple from blossom to stem into slices about ¼ inch thick; cover.

In a large bowl, whisk the eggs and ½ cup of the sugar together for a minute. Whisk in the yogurt, oil, rum and vanilla and whisk for about a minute, until smooth. Still using the whisk, or switching to a rubber spatula, fold in the flour mixture, followed by the coconut and the diced apple.

Scrape the batter into the pan and jiggle the pan from side to side a couple of times to even the batter. Arrange the sliced apples in an attractive pattern over the top of the cake—I like to make a sunburst pattern—and sprinkle the apples with the remaining 2 teaspoons sugar.

Bake for 45 to 50 minutes, or until the apples and cake are golden and a thin knife inserted into the center comes out clean. Transfer the springform pan to a rack, and cool the cake for 20 minutes or so.

Meanwhile, make the glaze. Warm the apple jelly with a splash of water just until it liquefies.

Once the cake has cooled for 20 minutes, run a knife around the edges of the cake and release the sides of the pan. Using a pastry brush, give the top of the cake a generous gloss of glaze.

# CHOCOLATE-CHOCOLATE CUPCAKES

**SURE, YOU** could serve these to three-year-olds, but I think everyone would be happier if you waited until your audience was grown-up enough to appreciate the cupcakes' dark, close crumb, the very dark and not very sweet chocolate flavor and the elegance of the glaze, a ganache that is ever so slightly firm on the outside and satiny soft beneath.

MAKES 12 CUPCAKES

### FOR THE CUPCAKES

- 1 cup all-purpose flour
- ¼ cup unsweetened cocoa powder
- ¼ teaspoon baking powder
- ¼ teaspoon baking soda
- ¼ teaspoon salt
- 1 stick (8 tablespoons) unsalted butter, at room temperature
- ¾ cup sugar
- 1 large egg
- 1 large egg yolk
- ½ teaspoon pure vanilla extract
- ½ cup buttermilk
- 2 ounces bittersweet chocolate, melted and cooled

### FOR THE GLAZE

- 3 ounces bittersweet chocolate, coarsely chopped
- 1 tablespoon confectioners' sugar, sifted
- 2 tablespoons cold unsalted butter, cut into 6 pieces

**SERVING:** These can be served as a kids' treat for adults (you can even speckle the ganache with sprinkles, jimmies or dragées when it's still fluid), but I like to give them a bit of glam and serve them on plates with cake forks. I also like to serve crème fraîche (page 459) and chocolate shavings (page 471) on the side. Oh, and these look lovely with a pretty birthday candle smack-dab in the center.

**STORING:** The cakes will keep in a well-sealed tin overnight. They can also be wrapped airtight—glazed or unglazed—and frozen for up to 2 months.

*Playing Around*

**FILLED CUPCAKES:** Before glazing the cakes, you can fill the centers of these with storebought Marshmallow Fluff, Bittersweet Ganache (page 453), Nutella or jelly. Just fit a pastry bag with a tip you can plunge into the bottom of the cake, fill the bag with the goody of your choice, plunge and squeeze away.

**GETTING READY:** Center a rack in the oven and preheat the oven to 350 degrees F. Fit the 12 molds in a regular-size muffin pan with paper muffin cups (my preference), or butter them, dust them with flour and tap out the excess. Alternatively, you can use a silicone muffin pan, which needs neither paper cups nor greasing. Place the muffin pan on a baking sheet and set it aside.

**TO MAKE THE CUPCAKES:** Whisk together the flour, cocoa, baking powder, baking soda and salt.

Working with a stand mixer, preferably fitted with a paddle attachment, or with a hand mixer in a large bowl, beat the butter at medium speed until soft and creamy. Add the sugar and beat for about 2 minutes, until it is blended into the butter. Add the egg, then the yolk, beating for 1 minute after each addition and scraping down the sides and bottom of the bowl with a rubber spatula as needed. Beat in the vanilla, then reduce the mixer speed to low and add half the dry ingredients, mixing only until they disappear. Scrape down the bowl and add the buttermilk, mixing until incorporated, then mix in the remaining dry ingredients. Scrape down the bowl, add the melted chocolate and mix it in with the rubber spatula. Divide the batter evenly among the muffin molds.

Bake for 22 to 25 minutes, or until the tops of the cakes are dry and springy to the touch and a knife inserted into their centers comes out clean. Transfer the

muffin pan to a rack and let the cakes cool for 5 minutes before unmolding them. Cool to room temperature on the rack before glazing.

TO MAKE THE GLAZE: Melt the chocolate in a heatproof bowl over a saucepan of simmering water. Transfer the bowl to the counter and let stand for 5 minutes.

Using a small whisk or rubber spatula, stir the confectioners' sugar into the chocolate, followed by the pieces of cold butter. The glaze may be very thin at this point, or it might be perfectly spreadable. If it is too thin to spread or use as a dip (I often dip the tops of the cakes into the ganache, then give the cakes a little twirl as I pull them out, so they have a squiggle of glaze in the center), stir it over ice water for a few seconds—really, less than a minute. With a small metal icing spatula, give each cupcake a crown of shiny ganache, and let the glaze set at room temperature (or in the fridge if you're in a hurry). If the glaze loses its gloss and you miss it, give the tops of the cakes a puff of hot air from a hairdryer right before serving.

# ALMOST-FUDGE GÂTEAU

**WHEN GREAT** chefs want help creating great restaurants, they call my Parisian friend Hélène Samuel. Hélène has worked with the best of the best and has even opened her own restaurant, Delicabar. But for all the restaurant work she does, until recently, she barely made anything more than a bowl of pasta for herself, because she didn't have a stove at home. Like many Parisians, Hélène had two burners, a microwave and no oven. Then, in a recent flurry of redecoration, she bought new furniture and—ta-dah—an oven. After that, there was no stopping her. For the first few weeks, she made this chocolate cake from a recipe given to her by her cousin, Jacqueline Picard, every day. She'd sit cross-legged in front of the window of her miraculous new stove, watching the beaten egg whites puff the chocolate batter up the sides of the pan. "I've given up television," she said. "I watch my oven instead."

In classic French style, this cake is plain looking but profoundly flavorful, moist, pleasantly dense and definitively chocolate—just the thing for all oven owners.

MAKES 10 SERVINGS

SERVING: The cake is delicious with a little crème fraîche, but it's also good with whipped cream, ice cream of almost any goes-with-chocolate flavor or on its own.

STORING: Wrapped airtight, the cake, glazed or plain, will keep for about 3 days at room temperature or for 2 months in the freezer.

5 large eggs

9 ounces bittersweet chocolate, coarsely chopped

1 cup sugar

5 tablespoons unsalted butter, cut into chunks

2 tablespoons coffee or water

⅓ cup all-purpose flour

Pinch of salt

**FOR THE GLAZE (OPTIONAL)**

4 ounces bittersweet chocolate, coarsely chopped

½ cup heavy cream

2 teaspoons light corn syrup

GETTING READY: Center a rack in the oven and preheat the oven to 350 degrees F. Butter a 9-inch springform pan, line the bottom with parchment paper, butter the paper, dust the inside of the pan with flour and tap out the excess. Place the pan on a baking sheet lined with parchment or a silicone mat.

Separate the eggs, putting the whites in a mixer bowl or other large bowl and the yolks in a small bowl.

Set a heatproof bowl over a saucepan of simmering water and add the chocolate, sugar, butter and coffee. Stir occasionally until the chocolate and butter are melted; the sugar may still be grainy, and that's fine. Transfer the bowl to the counter and let the mixture sit for 3 minutes.

Using a rubber spatula, stir in the yolks one by one, then fold in the flour.

Working with the whisk attachment of the mixer or a hand mixer, beat the egg whites with the pinch of salt until they hold firm but glossy peaks. Using the spatula, stir about one quarter of the beaten whites into the batter, then gently fold in the rest. Scrape the batter into the pan and jiggle the pan from side to side a couple of times to even the batter.

Bake for 35 to 45 minutes, or until the cake has risen evenly (it might rise around the edges and you'll think it's done, but give it a few minutes more, and the center will puff too) and the top has firmed (it will probably be cracked) and doesn't shimmy when tapped; a thin knife inserted into the center should come out just slightly streaked with chocolate. Transfer the pan to a cooling rack and let the cake rest for 5 to 10 minutes.

Run a blunt knife gently around the edges of the cake and remove the sides of the pan. Carefully turn the cake over onto a rack and remove the pan bottom and the parchment paper. Invert the cake onto another rack and cool to room temperature right side up. As the cake cools, it may sink.

TO MAKE THE OPTIONAL GLAZE: First, turn the cooled cake over onto another rack so you'll be glazing the flat bottom, and place the rack over a baking sheet lined with parchment or wax paper to catch any drips.

Put the chocolate in a small heatproof bowl.

Melt the chocolate over a pan of simmering water or in a microwave oven— the chocolate should be just melted and only warm, not hot. Meanwhile, bring the cream to a boil in a small saucepan. Pour the hot cream over the chocolate and stir very gently with a rubber spatula until the mixture is smooth and shiny. Stir in the corn syrup.

Pour the glaze over the cake and smooth the top with a long metal icing spatula. Don't worry if the glaze drips unevenly down the sides of the cake—it will just add to its charms. Allow the glaze to set at room temperature or, if you're impatient, slip the cake into the refrigerator for about 20 minutes. If the glaze dulls in the fridge, just give it a little gentle heat from a hairdryer.

# Pound Cake Pointers

**POUND CAKE** is a baker's basic, whether served unadorned or as the base for an ice cream sundae or a tumble of juicy berries. A brunch sweet, a teatime nibble or an end to dinner, it can even be toasted and buttered when all that remains is an inch or two of a slightly stale loaf.

Pound cake gets its name from the proportions in the classic recipe: a pound of butter, a pound of flour, a pound of sugar and a pound of eggs. The fine, tight, tiny-bubble moist crumb of a pound cake can be described only as elegant. The same is true of the cake's light golden crust.

And then there's the taste. Pound cake's primary flavor comes from butter. For this reason, you should try to rustle up the best butter you can when you're baking pound cake.

Cookbook author Elizabeth Alston and I organized a butter tasting for members of The Baker's Dozen East, a group of professional and home bakers. During the tasting, we sampled more than a dozen butters and then we tasted pound cakes, each made with a different one. The two cakes the seventy bakers liked the most were the cakes made with Echiré, an excellent French butter, and the terrific butter from the Vermont Butter and Cheese Company, both cultured butters with above-average butterfat content (these butters are available at many specialty markets). What was interesting about the taste test was the fact that, despite the pounds of eggs, sugar and flour, the quality of the butter made an important difference. (To find out more about cultured butter, see page 475.)

Of course, once you've got great ingredients, you've got to do right by them. And with pound cake, doing right means taking the time to let the ingredients warm and to mix the batter properly. Here are a few pointers for pound cake perfection:

In order to get the fine-grained texture that is the hallmark of a pound cake, have all the ingredients at room temperature; warmed ingredients blend more homogeneously than cold ones.

Because there is only a touch of baking powder in the recipe, the cake rises primarily on egg power. It's the air that is beaten into the eggs that gives the cake its lift, and warm eggs beat to greater volume than chilled ones do.

The butter must be at room temperature, but it shouldn't be so soft that it is oily and shapeless. (If you use either Echiré or Vermont Butter and Cheese butter, you'll find that even if the butter is left on the counter for hours in a warm room, it will not get oily or collapse.)

While you can mix pound cake batter by hand—as our forebears did—a mixer is the tool of choice, because you want to blend the butter and sugar as thoroughly as possible. Don't skimp on the beating time—give the butter and sugar a good 5-minute beat, and you'll be rewarded with the characteristic fine crumb.

Add the eggs one at a time, and give each egg at least a 1-minute beat—2 minutes is better.

Once the last egg goes into the mixing bowl, the beating is over. The next step is to blend the flour into the batter, and this has to be done gently. You can do it with the mixer, keeping the speed at the lowest setting, or you can choose to incorporate the flour by hand, folding it into the batter with a sturdy rubber spatula. Either way, the mixing time should be short—as soon as the flour is in, stop.

Because pound cake needs a long bake in a moderate oven, I like to put the cake on an insulated baking sheet or on two stacked regular baking sheets—the insulation keeps the bottom of the cake from baking too quickly and from getting too brown. Whether or not you opt for insulation, you should keep an eye on the loaf as it bakes because the top can get dark well before the loaf is baked through. If that's the case, cover the cake loosely with a foil tent.

A cracked top is a characteristic of a pound cake and one I find endearing. I don't mind a haphazard crack, but for those of you who prize precision, here's a little trick I learned from Pierre Hermé: After the cake has been in the oven for 10 minutes and the top has developed the slightest, lightest start of a crust, dip a dough scraper in melted butter and plunge the scraper lengthwise into the center of the cake. This will encourage the cake to form its crack along the scraper's straight line.

# PERFECTION POUND CAKE

**THIS RECIPE** for a textbook-perfect pound cake comes from cookbook author and friend Elizabeth Alston. It is based on an old family recipe, and it turns out a cake with the fresh-from-the-farm flavor of butter and eggs, a moist, closely knit crumb and a soft crust that cuts beautifully whether you're slicing it thick (so it can be a base for ice cream or syrupy fruits) or thin (so you can serve it plain or with a little jam). The cake can be made with all-purpose or cake flour—use cake flour, and the crumb will be even more delicate and just a touch more tender. And, as with many butter-rich cakes, this one is not just a good keeper, it actually improves with time, its taste and texture becoming even better after ripening. Let the cake cool completely, wrap it tightly in plastic wrap and leave it on the counter overnight.

Before you dive into making pound cake, take a look at the pointers on page 220.

MAKES 12 SERVINGS

**SERVING:** I like to cut the cake into rather thin slices and serve 2 or 3 slices to a person, offering some chunky fruit jam on the side. Sliced thicker, the cake is a terrific base for fruit and ice cream.

**STORING:** Wrapped well, the cake will keep for 5 to 7 days at room temperature (stale cake is great toasted) or up to 2 months in the freezer.

| | |
|---|---|
| 2 cups all-purpose flour or 2¼ cups cake flour | 1 cup sugar |
| 1 teaspoon baking powder | 4 large eggs, at room temperature |
| ¼ teaspoon salt | 1 teaspoon pure vanilla extract |
| 2 sticks (8 ounces) unsalted butter, at room temperature | |

**GETTING READY:** Center a rack in the oven and preheat the oven to 325 degrees F. Butter a 9-x-5-inch loaf pan or an 8½-x-4½-inch loaf pan. Put the pan on an insulated baking sheet or on two regular baking sheets stacked one on top of the other.

Whisk together the flour, baking powder and salt.

Working with a stand mixer, preferably fitted with a paddle attachment, or with a hand mixer in a large bowl, beat the butter and sugar on high speed until pale and fluffy, a full 5 minutes. Scrape down the bowl and beater and reduce the mixer speed to medium. Add the eggs one at a time, beating for 1 to 2 minutes after each egg goes in. As you're working, scrape down the bowl and beater often. Mix in the vanilla extract. Reduce the mixer speed to low and add the flour, mixing only until it is incorporated—don't overmix. In fact, you might want to fold in the last of the flour, or even all of it, by hand with a rubber spatula. Scrape the batter into the buttered pan and smooth the top.

Put the cake into the oven to bake, and check on it after about 45 minutes. If it's browning too quickly, cover it loosely with a foil tent. If you're using a 9-x-5 pan, you'll need to bake the cake for 70 to 75 minutes; the smaller pan needs about 90 minutes. The cake is properly baked when a thin knife inserted deep into the center comes out clean.

Remove the cake from the oven, transfer the pan to a rack and let rest for 30 minutes.

Run a blunt knife between the cake and the sides of the pan and turn the cake out, then turn it right side up on the rack and cool to room temperature.

## Playing Around

Pound cake lends itself to variations minor and major. You can add vanilla or almond extract to the batter (½ teaspoon will do it) or rub the grated zest of 1 lemon or ½ orange into the sugar before you beat the sugar with the butter. Or think about:

**MARBLED POUND CAKE**: After the batter is fully mixed, transfer half of it to another bowl and gently blend in 4 ounces bittersweet chocolate, melted and cooled. Alternate large spoonfuls of the light and dark batters in the pan, then run a kitchen knife in a zigzag pattern through the batters to marble them. For more tips on marbling, see page 229.

**COCOA POUND CAKE**: Reduce the amount of flour to 1⅔ cups all-purpose or 1¾ cups cake flour and sift ½ cup unsweetened cocoa with the flour, baking powder and salt.

# FRENCH YOGURT CAKE WITH MARMALADE GLAZE

**IT'S RARE** to be invited to a French person's house for dinner and have a baked-at-home dessert. Most French people don't bake, because they don't have to—no matter where you are, a pâtisserie with wonderful cakes is just minutes away. But I don't think there's a home cook in France who doesn't make this moist yogurt cake, a delightful cross between pound cake and sponge cake. Every time I mention it to a French friend, he or she says, "Oh, I make it all the time" or "That's the cake my mother used to make" or "That's the cake I make for my kids' birthdays." The primary reason the French make this cake is that it's delicious, but there are other reasons too, among them the indisputable fact that the cake is absolutely foolproof and shamelessly easy.

Unlike just about every other cake in France, the ingredients for this cake are measured in the yogurt container, rather than being weighed out. Since our yogurt containers are not the same size, I've adapted the recipe to American standard measuring cups. The measurements are now different, but the cake remains foolproof. And like many pound cakes, it will be better the day after it is made.

1 cup all-purpose flour

½ cup ground almonds (or, if you'd prefer, omit the almonds and use another ½ cup all-purpose flour)

2 teaspoons baking powder

Pinch of salt

1 cup sugar

Grated zest of 1 lemon

½ cup plain yogurt

3 large eggs

¼ teaspoon pure vanilla extract

½ cup flavorless oil, such as canola or safflower

**FOR THE GLAZE**

½ cup lemon marmalade, strained

1 teaspoon water

MAKES 8 SERVINGS

SERVING: In France, this cake is usually served with a little sweetened crème fraîche, but it lends itself to other toppings as well. Fresh soft fruit, like sliced peaches or plums, is a natural with it, as are berries with a touch of sugar. And, because the cake is plain and just a little tangy from the yogurt, it pairs happily with Lemon Cream (page 461) or Lemon Curd (page 462) and is delicious with chocolate mousse or chocolate sauce (pages 463 and 464).

STORING: Wrapped well, the cake keeps at room temperature for at least 4 days. If you do not glaze the cake, you can wrap it airtight and freeze it for up to 2 months; it's best not to freeze the glazed cake.

**GETTING READY:** Center a rack in the oven and preheat the oven to 350 degrees F. Generously butter an 8½-x-4½-inch loaf pan and place the pan on a baking sheet.

Whisk together the flour, ground almonds, if you're using them, baking powder and salt.

Put the sugar and zest in a medium bowl and, with your fingertips, rub the zest into the sugar until the sugar is moist and aromatic. Add the yogurt, eggs and vanilla and whisk vigorously until the mixture is very well blended. Still whisking, add the dry ingredients, then switch to a large rubber spatula and fold in the oil. You'll have a thick, smooth batter with a slight sheen. Scrape the batter into the pan and smooth the top.

Bake for 50 to 55 minutes, or until the cake begins to come away from the sides of the pan; it should be golden brown and a thin knife inserted into the center will come out clean. Transfer the pan to a rack and cool for 5 minutes, then run a blunt knife between the cake and the sides of the pan. Unmold, and cool to room temperature right side up on the rack.

TO MAKE THE GLAZE: Put the marmalade in a small saucepan or a microwave-safe bowl, stir in the teaspoon of water and heat until the jelly is hot and liquefied. Using a pastry brush, gently brush the cake with the glaze.

## *Playing Around*

**LAYERED AND ROUND FRENCH YOGURT CAKE:** For a cake that's just a little dressy—a cake like the ones my French friends make for their children's birthdays—make the cake in a buttered 9-x-2-inch round cake pan, baking it for 35 to 40 minutes. When the cake is cool, use a serrated knife to cut it horizontally into two layers. You can fill and frost the cake with whatever strikes your fancy, but it's lovely filled with Lemon Cream (page 461) or spread with jam or curd and frosted with sweetened whipped cream. Or turn the cake into a strawberry shortcake: Spread the cut layer with strawberry jam, cover it with sweetened whipped cream and top with cut berries. Place the remaining layer atop the berries, and finish the cake with clouds of whipped cream and a circle of big, beautiful whole berries.

**RIVIERA YOGURT CAKE:** Replace the whole-milk yogurt with the same quantity of thick strained yogurt. (To strain, line a sieve with a double thickness of dampened cheesecloth, add the yogurt, put over a bowl, cover and refrigerate overnight.) I use Total Greek Yogurt with 2% fat, which doesn't need to be strained. Substitute olive oil for the vegetable oil. And, to complete the Riviera flavors, add ½ tablespoon finely minced fresh rosemary or 1 tablespoon finely minced fresh mint to the bowl when you are rubbing the sugar and zest together.

**THE TEXTURE** of this cake is so perfect—the crumb so soft, even and tightly knit—that you could mistake it for a Sara Lee pound cake. That's high praise in my book: I've always loved Sara Lee's compact, tiny-bubble crumb and the way slices of the cake are simultaneously firm and supple. But what you get here is a flavor Sara Lee can never deliver, one that depends on using the very best vanilla you can find. The first choice is a pair of moist, pliable vanilla beans. You get the truest flavor from beans and, if you follow the nifty technique of rubbing the pulp of the beans into the sugar, you'll get maximum results. If you use extract, you'll still produce an excellent cake, but you've got to use pure extract. As for the rum—it should be high-quality, dark and strong (see page 492).

Make the syrup as soon as you slide the cakes into the oven to bake—that way, it will have time to cool.

MAKES ABOUT 16 SERVINGS

**SERVING:** If you've got the time, wrap the completely cooled cakes in plastic wrap and let them sit on the counter overnight—the flavor really develops with a leisurely rest. The cake is lovely with a cup of tea and ideal with any juicy fruit, particularly fresh berries.

**STORING:** Wrapped airtight, the cakes will keep for 4 days at room temperature. If you do not drench the cakes with the rum syrup, you can keep them, well wrapped, in the freezer for up to 2 months; soaked cakes are best not frozen.

**FOR THE CAKES**

- 2⅔ cups all-purpose flour
- 2½ teaspoons baking powder
- Pinch of salt
- 2⅓ cups sugar
- 2 plump, moist vanilla beans, split lengthwise, seeds scraped out and reserved, or 1½ tablespoons pure vanilla extract
- 6 large eggs, preferably at room temperature
- ⅔ cup heavy cream
- 2½ tablespoons dark rum
- 1 stick plus 7 tablespoons (15 tablespoons) unsalted butter, melted and cooled

**FOR THE SYRUP**

- ⅓ cup water
- ¼ cup sugar
- ¼ cup dark rum

**GETTING READY:** Center a rack in the oven and preheat the oven to 350 degrees F. Butter two 8½-x-4½-x-2½-inch loaf pans, dust the insides with flour and tap out the excess. (Even if the pans are nonstick, it's a good idea to butter and flour them.) Place the pans on an insulated baking sheet or on two regular sheets stacked one on top of the other.

Sift the flour, baking powder and salt together.

Put the sugar and the pulp from the vanilla beans, if using them, in a large bowl and, working with your fingers, rub them together until the sugar is moist and thoroughly imbued with the fragrance of vanilla. (If you are using vanilla extract, add it later, after you've added the eggs.) Add the eggs and whisk them into the sugar, beating until they are thoroughly incorporated. Whisk in the extract, if you're using it, then whisk in the cream, followed by the rum. Continuing with the whisk or switching to a large rubber spatula, gently stir in the dry ingredients in 3 or 4 additions; the batter will be smooth and thick. Finish by folding in the melted butter in 2 or 3 additions. Pour the batter into the pans, smoothing the tops with a rubber spatula.

Bake for 55 to 60 minutes, or until a knife inserted into the center of the cakes comes out clean. (As soon as the cakes go into the oven, make the syrup.) After about 30 minutes in the oven, check the cakes for color—if they are browning too quickly, cover them lightly with foil tents.

MEANWHILE, MAKE THE SYRUP: Stir the water and sugar together in a medium saucepan over medium heat until the sugar melts, then bring to a boil. Remove the pan from the heat and stir in the rum. Pour the syrup into a heatproof bowl and let cool.

When the cakes test done, transfer them to a wire rack to cool for 5 minutes before unmolding them and turning them right side up on the rack. Place the rack over a baking sheet lined with wax paper and, using a thin skewer, cake tester or thin-bladed sharp knife, poke holes all over the cakes. Brush the cakes all over with the syrup, working slowly so that the cakes sop it up. Leave the cakes on the rack to cool to room temperature.

## Playing Around

Made without the rum, this recipe produces two beautiful pound cakes that can be eaten plain, toasted and spread with butter and jam or used as the base of a dress-up cake. If you'd like to add another flavor to the cake, think about the following:

**LEMON LOAF CAKES:** Use only ½ vanilla bean (or 1½ teaspoons pure vanilla extract), and rub the grated zest of 2 lemons into the sugar. In addition, you can add 2 thick strips of lemon zest to the pan when you heat the water and sugar for the syrup. You can even replace all or part of the rum in the syrup with lemon juice, if you want additional tartness.

**ORANGE LOAF CAKES:** Follow the changes for the Lemon Loaf Cakes, but rub the zest of 1 large orange into the sugar. If you want a cake with a purer orange flavor, substitute 2 tablespoons Grand Marnier for the rum in the cake batter or, with or without the rum, add ½ teaspoon pure orange extract or ⅛ teaspoon orange oil to the batter.

**CANDIED GINGER LOAF CAKES:** Very finely cut-up bits of moist stem ginger in syrup (found in Asian markets and the specialty foods sections of some supermarkets) are a hot-sweet addition to the vanilla, lemon or orange cakes. Stir 3 to 4 tablespoons of the ginger bits, depending on your taste, into the batter before pouring it into the pans. For a fully gingered cake, whisk 1 tablespoon ground ginger into the dry ingredients. Serve this loaf without the syrup soak or, if you'd like, brush the warm loaf lightly with some of the syrup from the preserved ginger.

# DATE-NUT LOAF

**WHEN I** was a kid, date-nut loaves were very popular: both date-nut bread, which was like raisin bread, and date-nut quick bread, more like cake than real bread. This loaf falls into the cake camp. More specifically, it falls into the camp of those cakes that are fine the day they are made, even better the day after and, a day later, much better lightly toasted and spread with butter, jam, honey or cream cheese.

MAKES ABOUT 10 SERVINGS

2 cups all-purpose flour

2 teaspoons baking powder

¼ teaspoon salt

2 sticks (8 ounces) unsalted butter, at room temperature

3 ounces cream cheese, at room temperature

¾ cup (packed) light brown sugar

4 large eggs

1 teaspoon pure vanilla extract

¼ teaspoon pure almond extract

1 cup soft pitted dried dates, each cut into 8 pieces

1 cup walnuts, coarsely chopped

**GETTING READY:** Center a rack in the oven and preheat the oven to 325 degrees F. Butter a 9-x-5-inch loaf pan, dust the inside with flour and tap out the excess. Put the pan on an insulated baking sheet or two regular sheets stacked one on top of the other.

Whisk together the flour, baking powder and salt.

Working with a stand mixer, preferably fitted with a paddle attachment, or with a hand mixer in a large bowl, beat the butter and cream cheese on medium speed until very smooth, about 2 minutes. Add the sugar and beat until the mixture is light and fluffy, another 3 minutes or so. Add the eggs one at a time, beating for 1 minute after each addition, then beat in the extracts. The batter may look curdled—don't worry, it will come together in a minute. Reduce the mixer speed to low and mix in the dry ingredients, mixing only until they are incorporated. Using a rubber spatula, fold in the dates and nuts. Turn the batter into the pan.

Bake for 40 minutes. Cover the top of the cake loosely with a foil tent and bake for another 40 minutes or so (total baking time is about 1 hour and 20 minutes), until the top is honey brown, bumpy and cracked and a thin knife inserted into the center of the cake comes out clean. Transfer the cake to a rack and cool about 10 minutes before unmolding, then cool to room temperature right side up on the rack.

**SERVING:** Although the cake is fine served as soon as it cools, it really benefits from a day's ripening. Wrap the cake in plastic wrap and, if you have the time and patience, keep it at room temperature for a day before slicing and serving—toasted or not.

**STORING:** Well wrapped, the cake will keep for about 5 days at room temperature or up to 2 months in the freezer.

*Playing Around*

If you want to change the dried fruit or the kind of nuts, go ahead. One of my favorite variations is a prune and walnut loaf—I like the sweet-tart flavor of the prunes with brown sugar and cream cheese. For the same reasons, dried apricots are a good alternative.

## Marbling Made Easy

EVER SINCE I can remember, marble cakes have been magical to me. Even now, hundreds of homemade marble cakes later, I continue to find the intricate patterns fascinating—and delightfully idiosyncratic. Although I now know how easy it is to get a beautiful dark-and-light design, it's impossible to get the same pattern twice, which I think is part of the fun.

While a marble cake must have contrasting dark and light areas, there's no rule that says the dark must be chocolate and the white must be vanilla, even if this is one of the most sublime combinations in the universe. Some of my favorite duos are on page 231, but I hope you'll feel free to marble your own favorite twosomes. Just divide the batter in half and add your flavorings: spices; ground nuts; fresh or dried fruit, finely diced or pureed; chocolate of any kind; extracts; or even food coloring. As long as you avoid the extremes—a batter that is either runny or heavy-as-dough thick—you should be just fine.

The key to marbling is restraint—mix the dark and light with abandon, and you'll end up with a monochromatic cake and a mush of flavors. The most effective method of marbling is the simplest: drop spoonfuls of dark and light batter randomly into the pan, then plunge a table knife deep into the batter and zigzag the knife through the batter, making only about 6 or 8 zigs and zags. It's so much fun you might want to swiggle your way back—don't.

A fussier technique takes only a minute longer and usually produces a more regular pattern (although nothing is certain with marble cakes). This method involves spooning the batter out in long alternating rows or, if the pan is round, in rings (or piping it, if you want to be really fussy). So, for instance, you'd make a first layer of three rows or rings—light, dark, light—then a second layer on top of it—this time dark, light, dark. After the batter is spooned into the pan, you use the same swiggling motion, with perhaps fewer zigs and zags.

Then there's always the technique from the it's-anyone's-guess-what-you'll-get school of marbling, in which you either pour in the dark batter and top it with the light, or make three layers of batter, light on top and bottom, dark in between, or vice versa, then do your zigging and zagging.

# BASIC MARBLED LOAF CAKE

•••••••••••••••••••••••••••••••••••••••••••••••••••••••••••••••••••••••••••••••••••••••••••••••

**HERE IS** a recipe that just begs to be fiddled with—in fact, I created it just so that I could fiddle with it. It's a fine plain cake that gets better when you use it as the base for a two-tone, two-flavor marble cake. In Playing Around, I've given you the recipes for some of my favorite marbling combinations, and I hope you'll make them, but I also hope you'll come up with combinations of your own: there's nothing better than having a homemade cake that's truly a house special.

|   |   |
|---|---|
| 2 cups plus 2 tablespoons all-purpose flour | 1 cup sugar |
| 1¼ teaspoons baking powder | 4 large eggs |
| ½ teaspoon salt | ½ teaspoon pure vanilla extract |
| 1½ sticks (12 tablespoons) unsalted butter, at room temperature | ½ cup whole milk |
|  | Choice of flavorings (see Playing Around) |

**GETTING READY:** Center a rack in the oven and preheat the oven to 325 degrees F. Butter an 8½-x-4½-x-2½-inch loaf pan, dust the inside with flour and tap out the excess. Place the pan on an insulated baking sheet or on two regular baking sheets stacked one on top of the other.

Whisk together the flour, baking powder and salt.

Working with a stand mixer, preferably fitted with a paddle attachment, or with a hand mixer in a large bowl, beat the butter on medium speed until smooth, about 3 minutes. Add the sugar and beat for another 2 to 3 minutes. Add the eggs one at a time, beating well after each addition. Don't be concerned if the batter curdles and stays curdled—it will be fine. Beat in the vanilla. Reduce the mixer speed to low and alternately add the flour mixture in 3 additions and the milk in 2 (begin and end with the dry ingredients), mixing only until each addition is incorporated.

At this point, you are ready to divide the batter, add your selected flavorings and marble the batters (see page 229 for tips). Scrape the batter into the pan.

Bake the cake for 1 hour and 20 to 30 minutes, or until a thin knife inserted deep into the center comes out clean. If the cake looks as if it's getting too brown during its bake, cover it loosely with a foil tent. Transfer the cake to a cooling rack and let it rest for about 15 minutes before unmolding, then cool the cake to room temperature right side up on the rack.

MAKES ABOUT 8 SERVINGS

**SERVING:** Cut the cake into slices either thin or thick and serve as is, or with whipped cream or ice cream or even ice cream and a sauce.

**STORING:** Wrapped well, the cake will keep at room temperature for up to 4 days or in the freezer (wrapped airtight) for up to 2 months.

**230 BAKING** From My Home to Yours

## Playing Around

Here are the recipes for some of my favorite marble loaves:

**TRADITIONAL MARBLE LOAF**: Divide the batter in half and stir 4 ounces bittersweet chocolate, melted and cooled, into one half and keep the other half plain.

**BLACK-AND-WHITE CHOCOLATE MARBLE LOAF**: Divide the batter in half and stir 4 ounces high-quality white chocolate, melted and cooled, into one portion and 4 ounces bittersweet chocolate, melted and cooled, into the other.

**PEPPERMINT MARBLE LOAF (MY FAVORITE)**: Divide the batter in half and stir 4 ounces high-quality white chocolate, melted and cooled, and ¼ teaspoon pure peppermint extract into one portion and 4 ounces bittersweet chocolate, melted and cooled, into the other. Because the peppermint is such a surprise, I like to leave the white batter as intact as possible by marbling the batters only a little.

**CARDAMOM AND COFFEE MARBLE LOAF**: Divide the batter in half and stir 1 teaspoon ground cardamom into one portion. Dissolve 2½ teaspoons instant coffee powder in 1 tablespoon boiling water and stir this into the other portion.

**CHOCOLATE AND ORANGE MARBLE LOAF**: Divide the batter in half and stir 4 ounces bittersweet chocolate, melted and cooled, into one portion and the grated zest of 1 orange and ¼ teaspoon pure orange extract or a few drops of orange oil into the other.

ONE PART chocolate, one part rummy banana and all parts delicious. There's a fair amount of nutmeg in the batter for this cake, but its flavor isn't obvious with the first bite—it takes a few seconds to emerge.

1⅓ cups all-purpose flour

1 teaspoon baking powder

½ teaspoon salt

¼ teaspoon freshly grated nutmeg

1½ ripe bananas, peeled

   Squirt of fresh lemon juice

   Grated zest of ½ lemon

1 tablespoon dark rum

3 ounces bittersweet chocolate, finely chopped

1 stick plus 2 tablespoons (10 tablespoons) unsalted butter, at room temperature

⅔ cup (packed) light brown sugar

⅓ cup sugar

4 large eggs

1 teaspoon pure vanilla extract

½ cup whole milk

MAKES ABOUT 8 SERVINGS

SERVING: This cake is good cut thick or thin, served plain or with some ice cream. It's very good with coffee or tea and especially good with chocolate milk, hot or cold.

STORING: Wrapped in plastic wrap, the cake will keep for 4 to 5 days at room temperature; wrapped airtight, it will keep for up to 2 months in the freezer.

*Playing Around*

If you'd like to add a little more texture to the cake as well as another flavor, add ⅓ cup chopped toasted pecans to either of the batters.

GETTING READY: Center a rack in the oven and preheat the oven to 325 degrees F. Butter an 8½-x-4½-x-2½-inch loaf pan, dust the inside with flour and tap out the excess. Place the pan on an insulated baking sheet or on two regular baking sheets stacked one on top of the other.

Whisk together the flour, baking powder, salt and nutmeg.

In a small bowl, mash the bananas with the lemon juice and zest, then stir in the rum.

Melt the chocolate and 2 tablespoons of the butter together in a microwave oven or in a heatproof bowl set over a saucepan of gently simmering water.

Working with a stand mixer, preferably fitted with a paddle attachment, or with a hand mixer in a large bowl, beat the remaining stick (8 tablespoons) of butter at medium speed until creamy, about 3 minutes. Add the sugars and beat for another 2 to 3 minutes, until light and smooth. Add the eggs one at a time, beating well after each addition, then beat in the vanilla. The batter will look curdled, and it will continue to look curdled as you add ingredients. Reduce the mixer speed to low and add half the flour mixture, mixing only until it is just incorporated. With the mixer running, pour in the milk, and when it is blended, add the remaining dry ingredients. Scrape down the bowl and mix in the mashed bananas. The batter will look even lumpier.

Pour a little less than half the batter into the bowl with the melted chocolate and stir to blend. Drop alternating spoonfuls of both batters into the prepared pan (or follow any of the marbling techniques on page 229), then, using a table knife, swirl the batters together, taking care not to overdo it.

Bake for 1 hour and 20 to 30 minutes, or until a knife inserted deep into the center of the cake comes out clean. Check after 30 minutes and if the cake starts to brown too much, cover it loosely with a foil tent. Transfer the cake to a cooling rack and let it rest for about 15 minutes before unmolding, then cool the cake to room temperature right side up on the rack.

# A FEW FABULOUS CHEESECAKES

ALONG WITH CHOCOLATE CHIP COOKIES, apple pie and brownies, one dessert never wanes in popularity, gaining countless more devotees each year: the all-American cheesecake.

I say "all-American" because cheesecakes have a long and luscious lineage in Europe—in Germany and Austria, where they're made with the native equivalents of cottage, pot or farmer cheeses, and in Italy, where ricotta is the cheese of choice. Here the cheesecakes we dig into with delight are the super-creamy cakes made with thoroughly American cream cheese. Sometimes dense, sometimes light, always smooth, almost velvety, and always unabashedly rich, American cheesecakes take pride of place at the coolest restaurants and sell out at corner delis. They are equal-opportunity pleasers.

And they're easy to make at home—in fact, to my mind, they're always better homemade. If you're new to cheesecakes, here are a few pointers.

USE A SPRINGFORM PAN: Good cheesecakes, even dense ones, are soft, somewhat fragile and not the type of cake you can turn out of a pan. The beauty of a springform pan is its removable sides, perfect for this kind of creamy concoction. Lift away the sides, and leave the cake on the pan's base for serving.

PREBAKE THE CRUST: Most cheesecakes sit in or on a crumb crust. Although the crust will bake with the cake, don't skip the quick 10-minute prebaking—it's what gives the crumbs their nice crunch. For the best results, mix the ingredients for the crust, pat them into the pan and slide the pan into the freezer while you preheat the oven.

MIX LIKE MAD: So that the finished cake has the flawlessly smooth texture that is the hallmark of a great cheesecake, the batter must be completely smooth. Whether you are working with a mixer or a food processor, make sure to blend the batter until it is not just lump-free but satiny—any lumps in the batter will not disappear during baking.

COOL THE CAKE: Never rush a cheesecake to the table. Cooling and then chilling it is as important a step in its preparation as baking.

UNMOLD IT WITH CARE: It's not exactly surgery, but removing the sides of the springform can be a delicate operation. My preferred method is to run a blunt knife around the cake and then to warm the sides of the pan with a hairdryer. Using a hairdryer beats dunking the pan into a sinkful of warm water—no seeps, no drips—and you have lots more control. If the sides of the cake have softened a tad during the heat spell, smooth them with an icing spatula and chill the cake briefly before serving.

# TALL AND CREAMY CHEESECAKE: A BASIC

**NOT REALLY** a New York cheesecake—there's no lemon (although there could be)—this is an all-American cheesecake of the big, beautiful, lush and creamy variety, the kind that causes gasps of delight when you bring it to the table and sighs of satisfaction when you and your guests savor bite after bite. It's also a cheesecake you can customize. You can make the cake milder or tangier by using all heavy cream or all sour cream, or a combination of the two. You can add fruits or nuts, swirls of chocolate or drops of extract. You'll find some suggestions in Playing Around, including one of my all-time favorites, the Coco-Nut Cheesecake, but if you're a cheesecake lover, you'll find your own quickly.

MAKES 16 SERVINGS

SERVING: The easiest way to cut cheesecake is to use a long, thin knife that has been run under hot water and lightly wiped. Keep warming the knife as you cut slices of the cake.

STORING: Wrapped well, the cake will keep for up to 1 week in the refrigerator or for up to 2 months in the freezer. It's best to defrost the still-wrapped cheesecake overnight in the refrigerator.

### FOR THE CRUST

- 1¾ cups graham cracker crumbs
- 3 tablespoons sugar
- Pinch of salt
- ½ stick (4 tablespoons) unsalted butter, melted

### FOR THE CHEESECAKE

- 2 pounds (four 8-ounce boxes) cream cheese, at room temperature
- 1⅓ cups sugar
- ½ teaspoon salt
- 2 teaspoons pure vanilla extract
- 4 large eggs, at room temperature
- 1⅓ cups sour cream or heavy cream, or a combination of the two

TO MAKE THE CRUST: Butter a 9-inch springform pan—choose one that has sides that are 2¾ inches high (if the sides are lower, you will have cheesecake batter left over)—and wrap the bottom of the pan in a double layer of aluminum foil.

Stir the crumbs, sugar and salt together in a medium bowl. Pour over the melted butter and stir until all of the dry ingredients are uniformly moist. (I do this with my fingers.) Turn the ingredients into the springform pan and use your fingers to pat an even layer of crumbs over the bottom of the pan and about halfway up the sides. Don't worry if the sides are not perfectly even or if the crumbs reach slightly above or below the midway point on the sides. Put the pan in the freezer while you preheat the oven. (The crust can be covered and frozen for up to 2 months.)

Center a rack in the oven, preheat the oven to 350 degrees F and place the springform on a baking sheet. Bake for 10 minutes. Set the crust aside to cool on a rack while you make the cheesecake.

Reduce the oven temperature to 325 degrees F.

TO MAKE THE CHEESECAKE: Put a kettle of water on to boil.

Working with a stand mixer, preferably fitted with a paddle attachment, or with a hand mixer in a large bowl, beat the cream cheese at medium speed until soft and creamy, about 4 minutes. With the mixer running, add the sugar and salt and continue to beat for another 4 minutes or so, until the cream cheese is light. Beat in the vanilla. Add the eggs one by one, beating for a full minute after each addition—you want a well-aerated batter. Reduce the mixer speed to low and mix in the sour cream and/or heavy cream.

Put the foil-wrapped springform pan in a roasting pan that is large enough to hold the pan with some space around it.

Give the batter a few stirs with a rubber spatula, just to make sure that there is nothing left unmixed at the bottom of the bowl, and scrape the batter into the springform pan. The batter will reach the rim of the pan. (If you have a pan with lower sides and have leftover batter, you can bake the batter in a buttered ramekin or small soufflé mold.) Put the roasting pan in the oven and pour enough boiling water into it to come halfway up the sides of the springform pan.

Bake the cheesecake for 1 hour and 30 minutes, at which point the top should be browned (and perhaps cracked) and may have risen just a little above the rim of the pan. Turn off the oven and prop the oven door open with a wooden spoon. Allow the cheesecake to luxuriate in its water bath for another hour.

After 1 hour, carefully pull the setup out of the oven, lift the springform pan out of the roaster—be careful, there may be some hot water in the aluminum foil—and remove the foil. Let the cheesecake come to room temperature on a cooling rack.

When the cake is cool, cover the top lightly and refrigerate for at least 4 hours; overnight is better.

At serving time, remove the sides of the springform pan—I use a hairdryer to do this (see page 234)—and set the cake on a serving platter.

## Playing Around

Here are a few ideas for varying both the crust and the filling—you can create your own riffs on this basic as well.

**CHOCOLATE CRUST:** Replace the graham cracker crumbs with chocolate wafer crumbs. Depending on what filling you're using, you might want to add a pinch of cinnamon, nutmeg or ginger (or a little of all three) to the mix.

**GINGERSNAP CRUST:** Replace the graham cracker crumbs with gingersnap cookie crumbs.

**GRAHAM-COCONUT CRUST:** I like to use this crust with the Coco-Nut Cheesecake (below). Add ½ cup toasted shredded sweetened coconut to the graham cracker mix.

**GRAHAM-NUT CRUST:** Add ½ cup toasted and finely chopped nuts—almonds, pecans, walnuts or even macadamias—to the graham cracker mix.

**LEMON CHEESECAKE:** Add the grated zest of 2 lemons, the juice of 1 lemon and ½ teaspoon pure lemon extract to the batter.

**LIME CHEESECAKE:** Add the grated zest of 2 limes, the juice of both limes and, if you have it, ⅛ teaspoon pure lime oil to the batter.

**ORANGE CHEESE-CAKE:** Add the grated zest of 1 orange, the juice of the orange and ½ teaspoon pure orange extract to the batter.

**BLACK-AND-WHITE CHEESECAKE:** Add 4 ounces bittersweet chocolate, melted and cooled, to one third of the batter. Now you've got a choice: To make a Marbled Black-and-White Cheesecake, pour all of the vanilla batter into the springform pan, dollop the top of the batter with the chocolate and use a table knife to swirl the dark batter through the white. To make a Layered Black-and-

White Cheesecake, pour half of the white batter into the pan and spread it evenly with a spatula, then top with the chocolate batter, spreading it to the edges of the pan, and finish with the remaining white batter. Both of these are great served with a drizzle of chocolate sauce (pages 463 and 464).

**BLACK, WHITE AND MORE CHEESECAKE:** You can even go a little further with the Black-and-White Cheesecake by flavoring the chocolate mixture with cinnamon or espresso or both, by adding ¼ teaspoon pure peppermint extract to the chocolate batter or ½ teaspoon to the vanilla batter or by folding finely chopped nuts into either batter.

**BERRY CHEESECAKE:** Pour half of the batter into the pan, drop in about 1 cup fresh raspberries, blueberries or a combination of berries (except strawberries—they're too watery), and top with the

remaining batter (you may have a little batter left over). Alternatively, you can very gently fold about 1 cup small berries into the batter, taking care not to crush the berries—and color the batter.

**COCONUT CHEESE-CAKE:** Use the Graham-Coconut Crust for this. Follow the directions for the basic cheesecake, but use the following ingredients: 1½ pounds (three 8-ounce boxes) cream cheese, 1 cup sugar, ½ teaspoon salt, 1 teaspoon pure vanilla extract, ½ teaspoon pure almond extract, 3 eggs, 1 cup sour cream or heavy cream or a combination, 1 cup finely chopped toasted blanched almonds and 1 cup toasted shredded coconut.

# BROWN SUGAR–APPLE CHEESECAKE

**WHEN I** called this cheesecake "substantial," a friend said I was being redundant, since, according to her, being substantial is a characteristic built into a cheesecake's DNA. I don't believe that. Some cheesecakes are actually very light, and some are not just substantial, they're downright heavy and meant to be just that. This cheesecake is a textural middle-of-the-roader with great-tasting surprises: the butterscotch-colored cheesecake is a triple-cream combo—cream cheese, sour cream and heavy cream; it's flavored with brown sugar, apple cider and cinnamon; and, almost best of all, it's got a layer of soft, caramelish browned-in-butter apples. Like all cheesecakes, this one should be served well chilled, yet because of the brown sugar and cinnamon, the apples and the gingersnap crust, I think of it as a cozy dessert to serve on frosty fall nights.

MAKES ABOUT 16 SERVINGS

**SERVING:** If you'd like, you can brush the top of the cake with a little warm apple jelly to give it a shine or dust it with confectioners' sugar.

**STORING:** Tightly covered, the cheesecake will keep in the refrigerator for 3 days or in the freezer for up to 1 month. But it's always best to freeze cakes without a jelly glaze (which can get gloppy if frozen). To defrost, leave the cake in its wrapper and allow it to defrost in the refrigerator overnight.

FOR THE CRUST

- 30 gingersnaps (or a scant 2 cups graham cracker crumbs)
- 2 tablespoons light brown sugar
- ½ teaspoon ground cinnamon (optional)
- ½ stick (4 tablespoons) unsalted butter, melted

FOR THE APPLES

- ½ stick (4 tablespoons) unsalted butter
- 3 large Golden Delicious or Fuji apples, peeled, cored and cut into eighths
- 2 tablespoons (packed) light brown sugar

FOR THE FILLING

- 1½ pounds (three 8-ounce packages) cream cheese, at room temperature
- ¾ cup (packed) light brown sugar
- 6 tablespoons sugar
- 3 tablespoons apple cider
- 2 teaspoons pure vanilla extract
- 2 teaspoons ground cinnamon
- 3 large eggs
- ¾ cup sour cream
- ⅓ cup heavy cream

- Apple jelly, for glazing, or confectioners' sugar, for dusting (optional)

TO MAKE THE CRUST: Butter the bottom and sides of a 10-inch springform pan.

Put the gingersnaps in a food processor and whir until you have crumbs; you should have a scant 2 cups. (If you are using graham cracker crumbs, just put them in the processor.) Pulse in the sugar and cinnamon, if you're using it, then pour over the melted butter and pulse until the crumbs are moistened. Turn the crumbs into the springform pan and, using your fingertips, firmly press them evenly over the bottom and up the sides of the pan as far as they'll go. Put the pan in the freezer while you preheat the oven. (The crust can be covered and frozen for up to 2 months.)

Center a rack in the oven and preheat the oven to 350 degrees F.

Remove the pan from the freezer and wrap the bottom tightly in aluminum foil, going up the sides. Place the pan on a baking sheet and bake for 10 minutes, or until the crust is set and lightly browned. Transfer to a rack to cool while you make the apples and filling. Leave the oven at 350 degrees F.

**TO MAKE THE APPLES:** Melt 2 tablespoons of the butter in a large nonstick skillet over medium-high heat. When the foam subsides, toss in half of the apple slices and cook, turning once, until they are golden brown, about 3 minutes. Sprinkle the apples with 1 tablespoon of the sugar and cook them, turning, just until coated, another minute or so. Scrape the apples onto a plate, wipe out the skillet and repeat with the remaining apples. Let the apples cool while you make the filling.

**GETTING READY TO BAKE:** Have a roasting pan large enough to hold the spring-form pan at hand. Put a kettle of water on to boil.

**TO MAKE THE FILLING:** Working with a stand mixer, preferably fitted with a paddle attachment, or with a hand mixer in a large bowl, beat the cream cheese on medium speed, scraping down the bowl often, for about 4 minutes, or until it is velvety smooth. Add the sugars and beat for another 2 minutes. Beat in the cider, vanilla and cinnamon. Reduce the speed to low and beat in the eggs one by one, beating for 1 minute after each egg goes in. Finally, beat in the sour cream and heavy cream, beating just until the batter is smooth.

Pour about one third of the batter into the baked crust. Drain the apples by lifting them off the plate with a slotted spoon or spatula, and spoon them into the pan. Cover with the remaining batter and, if needed, jiggle the pan to even the top. Place the springform in the roasting pan and pour in enough boiling water to come halfway up the sides of the springform pan.

Bake the cheesecake for 1 hour and 30 to 45 minutes, covering the cake loosely with a foil tent at the 45-minute mark. The cake will rise evenly and crack around the edges, and it should be fully set except, possibly, in the very center—if the center shimmies, that's just fine. Gently transfer the cake, still in the pan, to a cooling rack and let it cool to room temperature, then refrigerate it for at least 6 hours; overnight would be better.

Run a blunt knife around the edges of the pan to loosen the crust, open the pan's latch and release and remove the sides.

*Playing Around*

**APPLE-BUTTER CHEESE-CAKE:** An easy way to get deep apple flavor without using apples is to spread a layer of store-bought apple butter (use 1 to 1½ cups) over the baked crust before you pour in the cheesecake filling. (I like to use spiced apple butter for this cake.) Or pour in the cheese-cake batter, dot the top of the filling with about ¾ cup apple butter and, using a table knife, marble the apple butter into the batter. Since the apple butter is heavier than the batter, the dollops of butter will quickly sink into the batter, in which case, you'll have to continue to do your swirling on faith—just zigzag the knife as you would normally.

# HIDDEN BERRY CREAM CHEESE TORTE

MAKES 8 SERVINGS

SERVING: This torte can be served at cool room temperature, when it is very soft and creamy, but I think its texture improves with an hour in the refrigerator, and it is still thoroughly delightful served cold.

STORING: Wrapped well, the torte will keep in the refrigerator for up to 2 days.

WHILE TRYING to think how to describe this torte, I did what I always do: I grabbed a pencil and paper and a slice. Only after I'd put down my pencil and picked up my third (granted, skinny) slice of torte did I realize that my research had crossed the line into something bordering on greed. Oh, the hazards of cookbookery. And oh, the delight of something so smooth, creamy, soothing and satisfying.

Now here's the rub—I'm still not sure how to best explain this little treat. The straight description from the bottom up is: a sweet vanilla butter cookie crust, then a layer of berry jam and, the topmost treat, the hard-to-explain, easy-to-make cheesecake part, which is a mixture of cream cheese and cottage cheese that bakes to a thin, velvety layer that inspires triple indulgences.

### FOR THE CRUST

- 1¾ cups all-purpose flour
- ½ cup sugar
- ¼ teaspoon salt
- 1½ sticks (12 tablespoons) unsalted butter, cut into small pieces and chilled
- 2 large egg yolks
- 1 teaspoon pure vanilla extract

### FOR THE FILLING

- ⅓ cup thick berry or cherry jam
- 9 ounces cream cheese, at room temperature
- 8 ounces (1 cup) cottage cheese, at room temperature
- ¾ cup sugar
- ¼ teaspoon salt
- Pinch of ground cinnamon
- Pinch of freshly grated nutmeg
- 2 large eggs, preferably at room temperature

Confectioners' sugar, for dusting (optional)

GETTING READY: Butter a 9-inch springform pan, dust the inside with flour and tap out the excess. Place on a baking sheet lined with parchment or a silicone mat.

TO MAKE THE CRUST: Put the flour, sugar and salt in a food processor and pulse just to blend. Toss in the pieces of butter and pulse until the mixture resembles coarse meal. Stir the egg yolks and vanilla together with a fork, and, still pulsing the machine, add them and continue to pulse until the dough comes together in clumps and curds—restrain yourself, and don't allow the dough to form a ball.

Turn the dough out onto a work surface. If you want to roll the dough, gather it into a ball, wrap it in plastic wrap and refrigerate it for about 20 minutes before rolling. (I like to roll this, and all sweet crusts, between sheets of plastic wrap.) Or simply press the dough into the pan. The dough should come about 1½ inches up the sides of the springform. Refrigerate for at least 30 minutes.

Center a rack in the oven and preheat the oven to 375 degrees F.

Fit a piece of buttered aluminum foil against the crust, covering it completely. Fill the crust lightly with rice, dried beans or pie weights and slide the sheet into

the oven. Bake the crust for 20 minutes, then carefully remove the foil and weights and bake for another 5 minutes or so—you don't want the crust to get too brown. Transfer to a rack to cool while you make the filling.

Lower the oven temperature to 350 degrees F.

TO MAKE THE FILLING: Stir the jam, and spread it over the bottom of the crust—it's okay to do this while the crust is still warm.

Put the cream cheese and cottage cheese into the food processor and process, scraping down the sides of the bowl a few times, for 2 minutes, until you've got a smooth, satiny mix. Add the sugar, salt and spices and process for another 30 seconds. With the machine running, add the eggs and process, scraping the bowl as needed, for a final minute. Pour the filling over the jam.

Bake the cake for 60 to 70 minutes, or until the filling is uniformly puffed and no longer jiggly. Gently transfer the springform pan to a cooling rack and allow the torte to cool to room temperature, during which time the filling will collapse into a thin, elegant layer.

Run a blunt knife between the crust and the sides of the pan, then open and remove the sides of the springform. If the sides of the crust extend above the filling and you don't like this look, very gently saw off the excess crust using a serrated knife. Chill the torte slightly or thoroughly before serving and, if you'd like, dust the top with confectioners' sugar.

# LOW AND LUSH CHOCOLATE CHEESECAKE

**A CLARION** call to pleasure, this is elegantly low and seductively lush. Oh, and it's push-button easy to make.

MAKES 8 SERVINGS

### FOR THE CRUST
- 1½ cups graham cracker crumbs
- 2 tablespoons sugar
- ¼ teaspoon ground cinnamon
- 3 tablespoons unsalted butter, melted

### FOR THE FILLING
- 1½ pounds (three 8-ounce packages) cream cheese, at room temperature
- ½ cup sugar
- 3 large eggs, preferably at room temperature
- 1 teaspoon pure vanilla extract
  Pinch of salt
- 4 ounces bittersweet chocolate, melted and slightly cooled

**GETTING READY:** Center a rack in the oven and preheat the oven to 350 degrees F. Butter an 8½- or 9-inch springform pan and put the pan on a baking sheet lined with parchment or a silicone mat.

**TO MAKE THE CRUST:** Stir the crumbs, sugar and cinnamon together in a medium bowl. Pour over the melted butter and stir until all of the dry ingredients are uniformly moist. (I do this with my fingers.) Turn the crumbs into the pan and, with your fingers, press the crumbs evenly over the bottom of the pan and as far up the sides as they'll go. Freeze the crust for about 10 minutes.

Bake for 10 minutes, only until the crust is lightly set and just tinged with color. Cool on a rack or refrigerate while you make the filling. Keep the oven at 350 degrees F.

**TO MAKE THE FILLING:** Cut each bar of cream cheese into quarters and toss the pieces into a food processor, along with the sugar. Process, scraping down the bowl 2 or 3 times, for a full 2 minutes. You'll see how dramatically the cream cheese changes; it will look like white velvet at the end of its beating. Add the eggs, vanilla and salt and give the batter 4 longish pulses, then scrape down the bowl and pulse 2 more times. Pour in the chocolate and pulse and scrape a few times to blend the batter well.

Remove the bowl from the processor and rap it hard on the counter a couple of times to de-bubble the batter. Scrape the batter into the cooled crust.

Bake the cheesecake for 35 to 40 minutes if you are using a 9-inch pan or 45 to 50 minutes if you are using an 8½-inch pan. The top should be puffed and set, but if you tap the pan gently, the center of the cake will still be a little shaky—that's just fine. Transfer the pan to a cooling rack and allow the cheesecake to cool to room temperature, then refrigerate for at least 8 hours or for up to 3 days.

Run a blunt knife between the crust and sides of the pan, then open and remove the sides of the springform.

**SERVING:** While it really needs no embellishment, the cake is extra-great with a little drizzle of Hot Fudge Sauce (page 465). If you're a fan of chocolate-and-fruit combinations, you might want to serve it with some fruit coulis or puree—raspberry (page 467) is a natural, but apricot, orange and blueberry are good too.

**STORING:** Wrapped well, the cheesecake will keep in the refrigerator for up to 3 days. It can be frozen for up to 2 months; defrost, still wrapped, overnight in the refrigerator.

## Playing Around
**CAPPUCCINO SWIRL CHOCOLATE CHEESECAKE:** Make a cinnamon-espresso syrup by whisking together 1½ tablespoons sugar, 1 tablespoon instant espresso powder and ¼ teaspoon ground cinnamon and mixing in 2 tablespoons boiling water. Cool to tepid or to room temperature. Spoon about one third of the batter into a measuring cup with a spout and stir in the syrup. Pour the remaining batter into the crust, then pour over the cappuccino batter, pouring so that it creates a swirl pattern in the chocolate. For good measure, take a table knife and give the 2 batters a few extra swirls.

# CELEBRATION CAKES

EVEN AN ORDINARY WEDNESDAY would seem like Christmas if Bill's Big Carrot Cake, with six layers of cake and a coconut and cream cheese frosting, showed up for dinner. And who wouldn't think New Year's Eve had come early if the sleek, smoothly glazed Chocolate Caramel Chestnut Cake, with its incredible caramel-tinged ganache filling, were marched to the table?

Truth is, as often as I bake—which is just about daily—I don't make these cakes on an ordinary Wednesday. It's not that they're difficult to make, but because most of them have a couple of components, they do take time.

Here's the good news, though: most of these can be made in stages, and some even months in advance, packed into the freezer and pulled out the night before the party. If scheduling is a priority, the make-ahead information in each recipe will help you plan.

In general, cake layers can be prepared at least a day ahead. Cool the layers completely, wrap them very well in plastic wrap and, unless otherwise instructed, keep them at room temperature. If a cake has a syrup to brush over its layers, the syrup too can be made ahead and refrigerated, as can some of the fillings and frostings.

Assembling a cake has less to do with baking than it does with architecture—it is really a construction project. In general, before you begin frosting, scan the tops of the layers at eye level and, if they have risen in the center and are crowned, even them by slicing off the rounded portions with a long serrated knife and a gentle sawing motion. If you like, you can put the cake on a cardboard cake round (it provides a sturdy bottom and makes moving the cake easier) and place the round on a decorator's turntable, a lazy Susan or a serving plate. (If you are using a plate, you can protect it from dribbles of frosting by covering the edges with four strips of wax or parchment paper.) Dip a long metal icing spatula—or a table knife—into the filling and put a dab of it between the cardboard and the cake to "glue" the two together.

NOW, divide the filling into the portions you'll need by drawing a line with the spatula to section off what you'll need for each layer and, if the filling is also the frosting, what you'll need to cover the cake. Scoop up the allotted amount and spackle it evenly over the layer, stopping just a ¼ inch or so from the edges. If the filling is very light, like whipped cream, or very loose, like jam, leave a broader bare space, because it will spread when the weight of the next layer presses on it.

CONTINUE building the cake like this, arranging the top layer so that its flattest side is up. Use a pastry brush to brush away any cake crumbs, and then set to work on the frosting. If you've got a frosting like buttercream that you want to keep smooth, give the whole cake a very thin coating of it—this is called a crumb coat, because it seals in any stray crumbs—then refrigerate the cake for about 30 minutes to set the frosting before continuing.

FROST the sides of the cake first, allowing the frosting to come up a little over the top of the cake. When you're ready to do the top, put almost all of the remaining frosting in the center (leaving a little in the bowl for touch-ups) and start spreading it evenly over the layer. When you get to the edges, where the excess from the sides of the cake is ruffled up, use the spatula to pull that in and to smooth it into the frosting on the top. While the frosting is still soft, pull away the protective sheets of paper, if you used them. If there's anything you want to sprinkle over the top of the cake or press into the sides, now's the time to do it, while the frosting is still soft. If it needs to set, leave the cake at room temperature or slide it into the refrigerator, depending on the recipe.

Even if you are making a cake that should be eaten the day it is assembled, you'll want to set it aside for a few hours so that the assorted components can settle into a whole. I like to give the elements at least 2 hours (more is better). Not only will the flavors be more cohesive, but the layers will have had time to attach themselves to one another, and you'll be able to cut impressively clean wedges just like a pro.

# DEVIL'S FOOD WHITE-OUT CAKE

I'VE SOMETIMES thought that if my mother had been a baker (she wasn't), and if she had ever made me this cake (which she didn't), it would have been my childhood favorite. This is a dig-into kind of cake, not one meant to be cut daintily or eaten with restraint. The three layers are devilishly dark and chocolaty, chocolaty, chocolaty, from cocoa, bittersweet chocolate and semisweet chocolate. Freshly made or at room temperature, they are moist and a little fluffy; chilled, they're still moist, but denser and firmer, very much like a super-fudgy brownie. While the layers could be filled and frosted with almost any thick frosting, my favorite is a billowy, sweet marshmallow one. The flavor and texture are perfect, and the cake looks spectacular when it's generously fluffed and when one of the coal-dark layers is broken into crumbs and pressed into the frosting. Finished like that, it makes a grand birthday cake, whether it's for a kid's birthday or a celebration calling for twenty or more candles.

MAKES 12 SERVINGS

SERVING: I think the cake is best at room temperature or just cool, but many people prefer it cold (the texture of the cake becomes fudgier after it has been refrigerated). No matter the temperature, the cake is so pretty it should be cut at the table, so bring it out on a platter and cut it into generous wedges using a serrated knife and a sawing motion.

STORING: The frosted cake can be stored in the refrigerator for up to 2 days; let it stand at room temperature for 30 minutes before serving, or longer if you have the time.

## FOR THE CAKE

- 1⅓ cups all-purpose flour
- ½ cup unsweetened cocoa powder
- ¾ teaspoon baking soda
- ½ teaspoon baking powder
- ¼ teaspoon salt
- 1¼ sticks (10 tablespoons) unsalted butter, at room temperature
- ½ cup (packed) light brown sugar
- ½ cup sugar
- 3 large eggs, at room temperature
- 1 teaspoon pure vanilla extract
- 2 ounces bittersweet chocolate, melted and cooled
- ½ cup buttermilk or whole milk, at room temperature
- ½ cup boiling water
- 4 ounces semisweet or milk chocolate, finely chopped, or ⅔ cup store-bought mini chocolate chips

## FOR THE FILLING AND FROSTING

- ½ cup egg whites (about 4 large)
- 1 cup sugar
- ¾ teaspoon cream of tartar
- 1 cup water
- 1 tablespoon pure vanilla extract

GETTING READY: Center a rack in the oven and preheat the oven to 350 degrees F. Butter two 8-x-2-inch round cake pans, dust the insides with flour, tap out the excess and line the bottoms with parchment or wax paper. Put the pans on a baking sheet.

TO MAKE THE CAKE: Sift together the flour, cocoa, baking soda, baking powder and salt.

Working with a stand mixer, preferably fitted with a paddle attachment, or with a hand mixer in a large bowl, beat the butter on medium speed until soft and creamy. Add the sugars and continue to beat for another 3 minutes. Add the eggs one by one, beating for 1 minute after each addition. Beat in the vanilla; don't be concerned if the mixture looks curdled. Reduce the mixer speed to low and mix in the melted chocolate. When it is fully incorporated, add the dry ingredients alternately with the buttermilk, adding the dry ingredients in 3 additions and the milk in 2 (begin and end with the dry ingredients); scrape down the sides of the bowl as needed and mix only until the ingredients disappear into the batter. At this point, the batter will be thick, like frosting. Still working on low speed, mix in the boiling water, which will thin the batter considerably. Switch to a rubber spatula, scrape down the bowl and stir in the chopped chocolate. Divide the batter evenly between the two pans and smooth the tops with the rubber spatula.

Bake for 25 to 30 minutes, rotating the pans at the midway point. When fully baked, the cakes will be springy to the touch and a thin knife inserted into the centers will come out clean. Don't worry if the tops have a few small cracks. Transfer the cake pans to a rack and cool for about 5 minutes, then run a knife around the sides of the cakes, unmold them and peel off the paper liners. Invert and cool to room temperature right side up. (The cooled cake layers can be wrapped airtight and stored at room temperature overnight or frozen for up to 2 months.)

When you are ready to fill and frost the cake, inspect the layers. If the cakes have crowned, use a long serrated knife and a gentle sawing motion to even them. With the same knife, slice each layer horizontally in half. Set 3 layers aside and crumble the fourth layer; set the crumbs aside.

TO MAKE THE FILLING AND FROSTING: Put the egg whites in a clean, dry mixer bowl or in another large bowl. Have a candy thermometer at hand.

Put the sugar, cream of tartar and water in a small saucepan and stir to combine. Bring the mixture to a boil over medium-high heat, cover the pan and boil for 3 minutes. Uncover and allow the syrup to boil until it reaches 242 degrees F on the candy thermometer. While the syrup is cooking, start beating the egg whites.

When the syrup is at about 235 degrees F, begin beating the egg whites on medium speed with the whisk attachment or with a hand mixer. If the whites form firm, shiny peaks before the syrup reaches temperature, reduce the mixer speed to low and keep mixing the whites until the syrup catches up. With the mixer at medium speed, and standing back slightly, carefully pour in the hot syrup, pouring it between the beater(s) and the side of the bowl. Splatters are inevitable—don't try to scrape them into the whites, just carry on. Add the vanilla extract and keep beating the whites at medium speed until they reach room temperature,

about 5 minutes. You should have a smooth, shiny, marshmallowy frosting. Although you could keep it in the fridge in a pinch, it's really better to use it right now.

TO ASSEMBLE THE CAKE: Put a bottom layer cut side up on a cardboard cake round or on a cake plate protected by strips of wax or parchment paper. Using a long metal icing spatula, cover the layer generously with frosting. Top with a second layer, cut side up, and frost it. Finish with the third layer, cut side down, and frost the sides and top of the cake. Don't worry about smoothing the frosting—it should be swirly. Now, cover the entire cake with the chocolate cake crumbs, gently pressing the crumbs into the filling with your fingers.

Refrigerate the cake for about 1 hour before serving. (If it's more convenient, you can chill the cake for 8 hours or more; cover it loosely and keep it away from foods with strong odors.)

STICK A bright-colored Post-it to this page, so you'll always know where to turn for a just-right cake for any celebration. The original recipe was given to me by my great dear friend Nick Malgieri, of baking fame, and since getting it, I've found endless opportunities to make it—you will too. The cake is snow white, with an elegant tight crumb and an easygoing nature: it always bakes up perfectly; it is delicate on the tongue but sturdy in the kitchen—no fussing when it comes to slicing the layers in half or cutting tall, beautiful wedges for serving; and, it tastes just as you'd want a party cake to taste—special. The base recipe is for a cake flavored with lemon, layered with a little raspberry jam and filled and frosted with a classic (and so simple) pure white lemony hot-meringue buttercream, but because the elements are so fundamental, they lend themselves to variation (see Playing Around), making the perfect cake not just perfect, but also versatile.

MAKES 12 TO 14 SERVINGS

SERVING: The cake is ready to serve as soon as it is assembled, but I think it's best to let it sit and set for a couple of hours in a cool room—not the refrigerator. Whether you wait or slice and enjoy it immediately, the cake should be served at room temperature; it loses all its subtlety when it's cold. Depending on your audience, you can serve the cake with just about anything from milk to sweet or bubbly wine.

STORING: The cake is best the day it is made, but you can refrigerate it, well covered, for up to 2 days. Bring it to room temperature before serving. If you want to freeze the cake, slide it into the freezer to set, then wrap it really well—it will keep for up to 2 months in the freezer; defrost it, still wrapped, overnight in the refrigerator.

FOR THE CAKE

2¼ cups cake flour
1 tablespoon baking powder
½ teaspoon salt
1¼ cups whole milk or buttermilk (I prefer buttermilk with the lemon)
4 large egg whites
1½ cups sugar
2 teaspoons grated lemon zest
1 stick (8 tablespoons) unsalted butter, at room temperature
½ teaspoon pure lemon extract

FOR THE BUTTERCREAM

1 cup sugar
4 large egg whites
3 sticks (12 ounces) unsalted butter, at room temperature
¼ cup fresh lemon juice (from 2 large lemons)
1 teaspoon pure vanilla extract

FOR FINISHING

⅔ cup seedless raspberry preserves, stirred vigorously or warmed gently until spreadable
About 1½ cups sweetened shredded coconut

GETTING READY: Center a rack in the oven and preheat the oven to 350 degrees F. Butter two 9-x-2-inch round cake pans and line the bottom of each pan with a round of buttered parchment or wax paper. Put the pans on a baking sheet.

TO MAKE THE CAKE: Sift together the flour, baking powder and salt.

Whisk together the milk and egg whites in a medium bowl.

Put the sugar and lemon zest in a mixer bowl or another large bowl and rub them together with your fingers until the sugar is moist and fragrant. Add the butter and, working with the paddle or whisk attachment, or with a hand mixer, beat at medium speed for a full 3 minutes, until the butter and sugar are very light. Beat in the extract, then add one third of the flour mixture, still beating on medium speed. Beat in half of the milk-egg mixture, then beat in half of the remaining dry ingredients until incorporated. Add the rest of the milk and eggs,

beating until the batter is homogeneous, then add the last of the dry ingredients. Finally, give the batter a good 2-minute beating to ensure that it is thoroughly mixed and well aerated. Divide the batter between the two pans and smooth the tops with a rubber spatula.

Bake for 30 to 35 minutes, or until the cakes are well risen and springy to the touch—a thin knife inserted into the centers should come out clean. Transfer the cakes to cooling racks and cool for about 5 minutes, then run a knife around the sides of the cakes, unmold them and peel off the paper liners. Invert and cool to room temperature right side up. (The cooled cake layers can be wrapped airtight and stored at room temperature overnight or frozen for up to 2 months.)

**TO MAKE THE BUTTERCREAM:** Put the sugar and egg whites in a mixer bowl or other large heatproof bowl, fit the bowl over a pan of simmering water and whisk constantly, keeping the mixture over the heat, until it feels hot to the touch, about 3 minutes. The sugar should be dissolved, and the mixture will look like shiny marshmallow cream. Remove the bowl from the heat.

Working with the whisk attachment or with a hand mixer, beat the meringue on medium speed until it is cool, about 5 minutes. Switch to the paddle attachment if you have one, and add the butter a stick at a time, beating until smooth. Once all the butter is in, beat the buttercream on medium-high speed until it is thick and very smooth, 6 to 10 minutes. During this time, the buttercream may curdle or separate—just keep beating and it will come together again. On medium speed, gradually beat in the lemon juice, waiting until each addition is absorbed before adding more, and then the vanilla. You should have a shiny, smooth, velvety, pristine white buttercream. Press a piece of plastic against the surface of the buttercream and set aside briefly.

**TO ASSEMBLE THE CAKE:** Using a sharp serrated knife and a gentle sawing motion, slice each layer horizontally in half. Put one layer cut side up on a cardboard cake round or a cake plate protected by strips of wax or parchment paper. Spread it with one third of the preserves. Cover the jam evenly with about one quarter of the buttercream. Top with another layer, spread with preserves and buttercream and then do the same with a third layer (you'll have used all the jam and have buttercream left over). Place the last layer cut side down on top of the cake and use the remaining buttercream to frost the sides and top. Press the coconut into the frosting, patting it gently all over the sides and top.

*Playing Around*

Since lemon is such a friendly flavor, feel free to make changes in the preserves: other red preserves—cherry or strawberry—look especially nice, but you can even use plum or blueberry jam.

**FRESH BERRY PARTY CAKE:** If you will be serving the cake the day it is made, cover each layer of buttercream with fresh berries—use whole raspberries, sliced or halved strawberries or whole blackberries, and match the preserves to the fruit. You can replace the coconut on top of the cake with a crown of berries or use both coconut and berries. You can also replace the buttercream between the layers with fairly firmly whipped sweetened cream and then either frost the cake with buttercream (the contrast between the lighter whipped cream and the firmer buttercream is nice) or finish it with more whipped cream. If you use whipped cream, you'll have to store the cake in the refrigerator—let it sit for about 20 minutes at a cool room temperature before serving.

**CANDIED LEMON PARTY CAKE:** Make a batch of candied lemon slices (page 468) to slip between the layers. Spread each of the bottom 3 layers of the cake with preserves or marmalade, then buttercream; pat some lemon slices dry, slice them into small pieces and arrange them in a single layer over each layer of buttercream. Omit the coconut, or not, and finish the top of the frosted cake with lemon slices or with one decoratively twisted candied lemon slice in the center.

BILL'S BIG CARROT CAKE
(RECIPE ON PAGE 254)

# BILL'S BIG CARROT CAKE

THIS IS the cake our late friend the talented jeweler Bill Bartholomew used to bring to our house for holiday dinners. Carrot cake was once so popular that it was hard not to think of it as ubiquitous; it was also hard to find a great one. This one is. The recipe is more than thirty years old, but it is still perfect. It's not overly spicy, and it has texture from the grated carrots, shredded coconut, chopped nuts and raisins or, my current preference, dried cranberries. You'll have enough of the classic lemony cream cheese frosting to fill the three layers and cover the sides and top, but I prefer to leave the sides bare and fill each layer so generously that the frosting ripples out around the edges when I put the next layer on. (The photograph is on the previous page.)

## FOR THE CAKE

- 2 cups all-purpose flour
- 2 teaspoons baking powder
- 2 teaspoons baking soda
- 2 teaspoons ground cinnamon
- ¾ teaspoon salt
- 3 cups grated carrots (About 9 carrots; I grate them in a food processor fitted with a shredding blade)
- 1 cup coarsely chopped walnuts or pecans
- 1 cup shredded coconut (sweetened or unsweetened)
- ½ cup moist, plump raisins (dark or golden) or dried cranberries
- 2 cups sugar
- 1 cup canola or safflower oil
- 4 large eggs

## FOR THE FROSTING

- 8 ounces cream cheese, at room temperature
- 1 stick (8 tablespoons) unsalted butter, at room temperature
- 1 pound (3¾ cups) confectioners' sugar, sifted
- 1 tablespoon fresh lemon juice or ½ teaspoon pure lemon extract
- ½ cup shredded coconut (optional)

  Finely chopped toasted nuts and/or toasted shredded coconut, for topping (optional)

MAKES 10 SERVINGS

SERVING: The cake can be served as soon as the frosting is set. It can also wait, at room temperature and covered with a cake keeper, overnight. The cake is best served in thick slices at room temperature and, while it's good plain, it's better with vanilla ice cream or even some Lemon Curd (page 462) with a little whipped cream folded in.

STORING: Covered, the cake will keep at room temperature for 2 to 3 days. It can also be frozen. Freeze it uncovered, then, when it is firm, wrap airtight and freeze for up to 2 months; defrost, still wrapped, in the refrigerator overnight.

GETTING READY: Position the racks to divide the oven into thirds and preheat the oven to 325 degrees F. Butter three 9-x-2-inch round cake pans, flour the insides and tap out the excess. Put two pans on one baking sheet and one on another.

TO MAKE THE CAKE: Whisk together the flour, baking powder, baking soda, cinnamon and salt. In another bowl, stir together the carrots, chopped nuts, coconut and raisins.

Working with a stand mixer, preferably fitted with a paddle attachment, or with a hand mixer in a large bowl, beat the sugar and oil together on medium speed until smooth. Add the eggs one by one, and continue to beat until the batter is even smoother. Reduce the speed to low and add the flour mixture, mixing only until the dry ingredients disappear. Gently mix in the chunky ingredients. Divide the batter among the baking pans.

Bake for 40 to 50 minutes, rotating the pans from top to bottom and front to back at the midway point, until a thin knife inserted into the centers comes out clean; the cakes will have just started to come away from the sides of the pans. Transfer the cakes to cooling racks and cool for about 5 minutes, then run a knife around the sides of the cakes and unmold them. Invert and cool to room temperature right side up. (The cakes can be wrapped airtight and kept at room temperature overnight or frozen for up to 2 months.)

TO MAKE THE FROSTING: Working with the stand mixer, preferably fitted with a paddle attachment, or with a hand mixer in a large bowl, beat the cream cheese and butter together until smooth and creamy. Gradually add the sugar and continue to beat until the frosting is velvety smooth. Beat in the lemon juice or extract.

If you'd like coconut in the filling, scoop out about half of the frosting and stir the coconut into this portion.

TO ASSEMBLE THE CAKE: Put one layer top side up on a cardboard cake round or a cake plate protected by strips of wax or parchment paper. If you added the coconut to the frosting, use half of the coconut frosting to generously cover the first layer (or cover generously with plain frosting). Use an offset spatula or a spoon to smooth the frosting all the way to the edges of the layer. Top with the second layer, this time placing the cake top side down, and frost with the remainder of the coconut frosting (or more plain frosting). Top with the last layer, right side up, and frost the top—and the sides, if you want—of the cake. Finish the top with swirls of frosting. If you want to top the cake with toasted nuts or coconut, sprinkle them on now, while the frosting is soft.

Refrigerate the cake for 30 minutes, just to set the frosting before serving.

# COCOA-BUTTERMILK BIRTHDAY CAKE

**WHETHER YOU'RE** celebrating your baby's first birthday or your great-grandfather's ninety-fifth, if you've got an audience with a yen for chocolate, here's your best-bet cake. It's classically American, with layers that are made with cocoa and buttermilk. They're tender, light and happy to be matched with just about any frosting. My favorite accompaniment for this cake is the Chocolate-Malt Buttercream, a soft, sweet chocolate frosting with just a hint of malt flavor and a slight tickle of sugar on the tongue, but you can choose from several other fill-and-frost possibilities (see Playing Around).

## FOR THE CAKE

- 2 cups all-purpose flour
- ½ cup unsweetened cocoa powder
- ½ teaspoon baking powder
- ½ teaspoon baking soda
- ½ teaspoon salt
- 2 sticks (8 ounces) unsalted butter, at room temperature
- 1½ cups sugar
- 2 large eggs
- 2 large egg yolks
- 1 teaspoon pure vanilla extract
- 1 cup buttermilk
- 4 ounces bittersweet chocolate, melted and cooled (optional)

## FOR THE CHOCOLATE MALT BUTTER-CREAM

- 6 ounces bittersweet chocolate, coarsely chopped
- ⅓ cup (packed) light brown sugar
- ¼ cup malted milk powder
- 1 tablespoon unsweetened cocoa powder
- ¼ cup boiling water
- 2 sticks (8 ounces) unsalted butter, at room temperature
- Pinch of salt
- ¾ teaspoon pure vanilla extract
- 2¼ cups confectioners' sugar, sifted

MAKES 8 SERVINGS

**SERVING:** Serve the cake at room temperature, so that the cocoa layers are soft and tender and the frosting is creamy. It's great with coffee and milk, but it's also good with green tea.

**STORING:** The cake can be refrigerated overnight, and it can also be frozen. Freeze it uncovered, then, when it is solid, wrap it airtight. Transfer the cake to the refrigerator to thaw, still wrapped, overnight. Bring the cake to room temperature before serving.

### Playing Around

Try a marshmallow frosting (page 247), a meringue buttercream (page 250), a ganache (page 270) or some whipped cream—plain (page 456), chocolate (page 457) or coffee (page 456).

**GETTING READY TO BAKE:** Center a rack in the oven and preheat the oven to 350 degrees F. Butter two 9-x-2-inch round cake pans, dust the insides with flour, tap out the excess and line the bottoms with rounds of parchment or wax paper. Put the pans on a baking sheet.

**TO MAKE THE CAKE:** Whisk together the flour, cocoa, baking powder, baking soda and salt.

Working with a stand mixer, preferably fitted with a paddle attachment, or with a hand mixer in a large bowl, beat the butter on medium speed until soft and creamy. Add the sugar and beat for about 2 minutes, until it is thoroughly blended into the butter. Add the eggs one at a time, then the yolks one by one, beating for 1 minute after each addition and scraping down the sides and bottom of the bowl as needed. Beat in the vanilla. Reduce the mixer speed to low and add the dry ingredients alternately with the buttermilk; add the dry ingredients in 3 portions and the buttermilk in 2 (begin and end with the dry ingredients); mix only until each new batch is blended into the batter. Scrape down the bowl and, if you want, add the melted chocolate, folding it in with a rubber spatula. Divide the batter between the cake pans.

Bake for 26 to 30 minutes, or until the cakes feel springy to the touch and start to pull away from the sides of the pans. Transfer the cakes to racks and cool for about 5 minutes, then run a knife around the sides of the cakes, unmold them and peel off the paper liners. Invert and cool to room temperature right side up. (Once the layers are cooled, they can be wrapped airtight and left at room temperature overnight or kept frozen for up to 2 months.)

TO MAKE THE BUTTERCREAM: Melt the chocolate with half the brown sugar in a heatproof bowl set over a saucepan of simmering water. Remove from the heat.

Whisk the malt powder and cocoa together in a small bowl, pour over 3 tablespoons of the boiling water and whisk until smooth. Whisking the melted chocolate gently, gradually pour in the hot malt-cocoa mixture and stir to blend—it should be dark, smooth and glossy; set aside.

Working with the stand mixer, preferably fitted with the paddle attachment, or with a hand mixer in a large bowl, beat the butter on medium speed until soft and fluffy, about 2 minutes. Add the remaining brown sugar and beat for 2 to 3 minutes more, until well blended. Beat in the salt and vanilla extract, then reduce the mixer speed to low. Scrape in the chocolate mixture and mix until smooth. Still working on low speed, gradually add the confectioners' sugar. When all the sugar is in, increase the mixer speed to medium and beat for a couple of minutes. Lower the speed and add the remaining tablespoon of boiling water, then increase the speed and give the frosting another quick spin. It will be light and should be thick enough to use immediately. If it doesn't hold its shape, beat it just a bit more.

TO ASSEMBLE THE CAKE: Place one layer top side up on a cardboard round or a cake plate protected by strips of wax or parchment paper. Frost the top of the layer, and cover with the second layer, top side down. Frost the sides and top of the cake, either smoothing the buttercream for a sleek look or using a spatula, knife or spoon to swirl it for a more exuberant look.

Refrigerate the cake for at least 1 hour (or for up to 1 day, if that's more convenient) to set the frosting, then bring it to room temperature before serving.

THIS ONE
FOR BAANBSIS

**IT WOULD** be hard to imagine a time, a place or an audience for which this cake wouldn't be right. It's got good looks, good flavors and good manners—it knows how to get along with everyone from those who search for understatement to those who search for sophistication.

The yellow buttermilk cake is filled with alternating layers of white chocolate whipped cream and dark chocolate pastry cream. When the cake is cut, its look is simple and symmetrical. In a way, so is its taste.

FOR THE CAKE

- 2 cups cake flour
- 2 teaspoons baking powder
- 1/8 teaspoon baking soda
- 1/4 teaspoon salt
- 1 1/4 sticks (10 tablespoons) unsalted butter, at room temperature
- 1 cup sugar
- 3 large eggs
- 1 large egg yolk
- 1 teaspoon pure vanilla extract
- 3/4 cup buttermilk

FOR THE DARK CHOCOLATE CREAM

- 2 cups whole milk
- 4 large egg yolks
- 6 tablespoons sugar

- 3 tablespoons cornstarch, sifted
- 1/4 teaspoon salt
- 7 ounces bittersweet chocolate, melted
- 2 1/2 tablespoons unsalted butter, cut into 5 pieces, at room temperature

FOR THE WHITE CHOCOLATE WHIPPED CREAM

- 6 ounces premium-quality white chocolate (such as Valrhona Ivoire or Guittard), finely chopped
- 1 1/2 cups heavy cream

Chocolate shavings or curls (see page 471), dark or white or a combination, for decoration (optional)

MAKES 10 SERVINGS

SERVING: Remove the cake from the fridge about 20 minutes before serving. Use a serrated knife and a gentle sawing motion to cut it. Though the cake is particularly good with coffee or tea, it also goes well with a sweet or sparkling dessert wine.

STORING: While both the dark chocolate cream and white chocolate cream can be made ahead and kept tightly covered in the refrigerator, once assembled, the cake is best after about 3 hours in the fridge. However, it can be refrigerated overnight—just cover it loosely and keep it away from foods with strong odors.

GETTING READY: Center a rack in the oven and preheat the oven to 350 degrees F. Butter two 9-x-2-inch round cake pans, dust the insides with flour, tap out the excess and line the bottoms of the pans with parchment or wax paper. Put the pans on a baking sheet.

TO MAKE THE CAKE: Sift together the cake flour, baking powder, baking soda and salt.

Working with a stand mixer, preferably fitted with a paddle attachment, or with a hand mixer in a large bowl, beat the butter on medium speed until soft and creamy. Add the sugar and beat for another 3 minutes. Add the eggs one by one, and then the yolk, beating for 1 minute after each addition. Beat in the vanilla; don't be concerned if the mixture looks curdled. Reduce the mixer speed to low and add the dry ingredients alternately with the buttermilk, adding the dry ingredients in 3 additions and the milk in 2 (begin and end with the dry ingredients); scrape down the sides of the bowl as needed and mix only until the ingredients disappear into the batter. Divide the batter evenly between the two pans and smooth the tops with a rubber spatula.

Bake for 28 to 30 minutes, rotating the pans at the midway point. When fully baked, the cakes will be golden and springy to the touch and a thin knife inserted into the centers will come out clean. Transfer the cakes to a rack and cool for about 5 minutes, then unmold, remove the paper and invert to cool to room temperature right side up on the rack.

TO MAKE THE DARK CHOCOLATE CREAM: Bring the milk to a boil.

Meanwhile, in a large heavy-bottomed saucepan, whisk the egg yolks with the sugar, cornstarch and salt until thick and well blended. Whisking without stopping, drizzle in about ¼ cup of the hot milk—this will temper, or warm, the yolks so they won't curdle—then, still whisking, add the remainder of the milk in a steady stream. Put the pan over medium heat and, whisking vigorously, constantly and thoroughly (make sure to get into the edges of the pan), bring the mixture to a boil. Keep at a boil, still whisking, for 1 to 2 minutes. Remove the pan from the heat.

Whisk in the melted chocolate, and let stand for 5 minutes. Then whisk in the pieces of butter, stirring until they are fully incorporated and the chocolate cream is smooth and silky. Press a piece of plastic wrap against the surface of the cream to create an airtight seal and refrigerate the cream until chilled, or for up to 3 days. Or, if you want to cool the cream quickly, put the bowl with the cream into a larger bowl filled with ice cubes and cold water and stir the cream occasionally until it is thoroughly chilled, about 20 minutes.

TO MAKE THE WHITE CHOCOLATE WHIPPED CREAM: Put the white chocolate in a heatproof bowl and put the bowl over a saucepan of gently simmering water. Stir frequently to melt the chocolate evenly. Meanwhile, bring ½ cup of the heavy cream to a boil.

When the white chocolate is melted, remove the bowl from the pan. Pour the hot cream into the melted chocolate and let it sit for a minute. Using a small spatula, stir the chocolate gently until it is smooth. Let it sit on the counter until it reaches room temperature—it can't be the least bit warm when you add it to the whipped cream.

Working with the stand mixer with the whisk attachment or with a hand mixer in a large bowl, beat the remaining 1 cup heavy cream only until it holds the softest peaks. Turn the machine to high, add the cooled white chocolate all at once and continue to beat until the whipped cream holds firm peaks. Turn the whipped cream into a bowl, press a piece of plastic wrap gently against the surface to create an airtight seal and refrigerate for at least 2 hours, or up to 6 hours.

TO ASSEMBLE THE CAKE: If the tops of the cake layers have crowned, use a long serrated knife and a gentle sawing motion to even them. Slice each layer horizon-

tally in half. Place one layer cut side down on a cardboard cake round or on a cake plate protected by strips of wax or parchment paper.

Remove the dark and white chocolate creams from the refrigerator and whisk each of them vigorously to loosen and smooth them. With a long metal icing spatula, spread enough dark chocolate cream (about 1 cup) over the cake layer to cover it completely. Top the cream with another cake layer, cut side up, and cover this layer with white chocolate whipped cream, making the white layer about the same thickness as the dark layer. Cover with a third layer, cut side up, and cover with another cup or so of the dark chocolate cream. (You'll have some dark chocolate cream left over—use it as a dip for madeleines or sablés.) Top with the final layer of cake, cut side down, and frost the sides and top with the remaining white chocolate whipped cream. If you'd like to decorate the top with chocolate shavings or curls, do it now.

Refrigerate for at least 3 hours, or overnight.

# GOOEY CHOCOLATE CAKES

**IT'S BEEN** more than ten years since the molten chocolate cake won the hearts of just about every pastry chef here and in France. There doesn't seem to be a chocolate lover on either side of the ocean who hasn't savored this cake: small, dark and warm, with a lava-like runny center, sophisticated, easily dress-upable and, best of all, truly easy to make. In fact, it's one of few restaurant desserts that can be made at home with foolproof results, even if you're not a star baker.

The most important rule to remember in making these individual cakes is to use not only the best chocolate you can find, but the chocolate you most love to eat, since that's the ingredient you will taste.

Usually these cakes are made in individual ramekins, but with all the ramekins stacked in my cupboard, I couldn't come up with six that were the right size. Then I discovered that disposable aluminum foil muffin pans are ideal. I buy the kind that have six cups and come two pans to a package. I also wash them in the dishwasher and re-use them.

MAKES 6 SERVINGS

**SERVING:** These should be served as soon as they are put on plates. The cakes are not meant to be served alone—they need something to play off their warm, gooey, sooooooo choco-laty interior. Ice cream is the most obvious choice and, to my mind, the best in terms of tex-ture and, of course, tempera-ture. Any chocolate-friendly fla-vor will be good. Circling the cake with Crème Anglaise (page 451) is another good idea and, for those for whom too much is not enough, circling the cakes with crème anglaise and run-ning a ring of Bittersweet Chocolate Sauce (page 463) through the custard is an even better idea.

**STORING:** Although the whole point of a warm, runny cake is to eat it when it is warm and runny, the cake is still deli-cious, but different, the follow-ing day. If you wrap the cooled cakes in plastic wrap and keep them at room temperature, the next day the texture of the cen-ter of the cake (the part that was once gooey) will remind you of ganache. Eating the cake will be like enjoying a bonbon: it will be firm on the outside and creamy within.

| | |
|---|---|
| ⅓ cup all-purpose flour | 1 stick (8 tablespoons) unsalted butter, |
| 3 tablespoons unsweetened cocoa |    cut into 8 pieces |
|    powder | 2 large eggs, at room temperature |
| ¼ teaspoon salt | 1 large egg yolk, at room temperature |
| 5 ounces bittersweet chocolate, | 6 tablespoons sugar |
|    4 ounces coarsely chopped, | |
|    1 ounce very finely chopped | |

**GETTING READY:** Center a rack in the oven and preheat the oven to 400 degrees F. Butter (or spray—it's easier) 6 cups of a regular-size muffin pan, preferably a dis-posable aluminum foil pan, dust the insides with flour and tap out the excess. Put the muffin pan on a baking sheet.

Sift the flour, cocoa and salt together.

Set a heatproof bowl over a saucepan of gently simmering water, put the coarsely chopped chocolate and the butter in the bowl and stir occasionally over the simmering water just until they are melted—you don't want them to get so hot that the butter separates. Remove the bowl from the pan of water.

In a large bowl, whisk the eggs and yolk until homogenous. Add the sugar and whisk until well blended, about 2 minutes. Add the dry ingredients and, still using the whisk, stir (don't beat) them into the eggs. Little by little, and using a light hand, stir in the melted chocolate and butter. Divide the batter evenly among the muffin cups and sprinkle the finely chopped chocolate over the batter.

Bake the cakes for 13 minutes. Transfer them, still on the baking sheet, to a rack to cool for 3 minutes. (There is no way to test that these cakes are properly baked, because the inside remains liquid.)

Line a cutting board with a silicone baking mat or parchment or wax paper, and, after the 3-minute rest, unmold the cakes onto the board. Use a wide metal spatula to lift the cakes onto dessert plates.

*Playing Around*

Like many chocolate cakes, these can be flavored. You can add a teaspoon of instant espresso powder to the bowl with the chocolate and butter as it melts, or add a very small amount (about ⅛ teaspoon) of orange oil or pure peppermint extract to the batter. Or you can pop something into the center of the cakes. While I don't like to add another texture to the cakes, that doesn't mean you can't. You can fill the muffin cups halfway and drop cocoa nibs (see page 479), very finely chopped toasted nuts, brittle bits or even a few white, butterscotch or peanut butter chips into the center, then finish filling the cakes.

CARAMEL-PEANUT-TOPPED
BROWNIE CAKE
(RECIPE ON PAGE 264)

# CARAMEL-PEANUT-TOPPED BROWNIE CAKE

**IT'S FUNNY** to be at a table full of articulate adults all grinning and nodding as they merrily eat their way to second helpings of this scrumptious cake. Is it the dense, dark, very chocolaty cake—a little sticky and a little chewy in the way good fudgy brownies often can be—that makes them so happy? Or is it the topping—a layer of soft, stretchy, sweet, gooey caramel (like the inside of a Rollo candy) pebbled with lots of salted peanuts? "Yum" is all I can ever get out of them.

Depending on just how much caramel you put on top of your cake, the recipe may give you more than you'll need, but it's tricky to work with smaller amounts of sugar. Here's my suggestion: Don't reduce the quantities. Make the recipe as is and then, if you've got some left over, use it to make caramel sauce—see Playing Around. (The photograph is on the previous page.)

### FOR THE CAKE

- 1 cup all-purpose flour
- 1 teaspoon baking soda
- ¼ teaspoon salt
- 1 stick (8 tablespoons) unsalted butter, cut into 8 pieces
- 5 ounces bittersweet chocolate, coarsely chopped
- 3 large eggs
- ½ cup (packed) light brown sugar
- ¼ cup sugar
- 3 tablespoons light corn syrup
- ½ teaspoon pure vanilla extract

### FOR THE TOPPING

- 2 cups sugar
- ½ cup water
- 1½ tablespoons light corn syrup
- ⅔ cup heavy cream
- 2 tablespoons unsalted butter, at room temperature
- 1 cup salted peanuts

**GETTING READY:** Center a rack in the oven and preheat the oven to 350 degrees F. Butter an 8-inch round springform pan, dust the inside with flour, tap out the excess and line the bottom of the pan with a piece of parchment or wax paper. Put the pan on a baking sheet lined with parchment or a silicone mat.

**TO MAKE THE CAKE:** Whisk the flour, baking soda and salt together.

Set a heatproof bowl over a saucepan of gently simmering water, put the butter and chocolate in the bowl and heat, stirring occasionally, until the ingredients are just melted—you don't want them to get so hot that the butter separates. Remove the bowl from the heat.

In a large bowl, whisk the eggs and sugars together until well blended. Whisk in the corn syrup, followed by the vanilla. Whisk in the melted butter and chocolate. Still working with the whisk, gently stir in the dry ingredients, mixing only until they are incorporated. You will have a thick, smooth, shiny batter. Pour the batter into the pan and jiggle the pan a bit to even out the batter.

Bake the cake for 40 to 45 minutes, or until a thin knife inserted into the center comes out almost clean (you might find some moist crumbs clinging to the

**MAKES 10 SERVINGS**

**SERVING:** I think the cake needs something cold and white as an accompaniment, so I serve it with ice cream, whipped cream or crème fraîche. My husband likes it with chocolate ice cream, my son prefers coffee ice cream and one friend goes for banana sorbet.

**STORING:** Wrapped, the cake will keep at room temperature for 1 to 2 days. The cake itself, without the topping, can be wrapped airtight and frozen for up to 2 months, but once you put the topping on, the freezer is no longer an option.

*Playing Around*

**CARAMEL SAUCE:** You may have about ½ cup of caramel left over. (If you have more or less, just adjust the amount of cream you use for this sauce.) Melt the caramel, either in a microwave oven, heating it for short intervals, or in a heatproof bowl over a saucepan of simmering water. Bring about 1 cup heavy cream to a boil in a medium saucepan. Add the caramel, stirring to mix—I use a silicone spatula for this job—then let the sauce boil vigorously for 3 minutes, during which time it will bubble up, so stand clear. Pull the pan from the heat and pour the sauce into a clean canning jar or other container that can handle high heat. Cool the sauce to room temperature before covering and storing it in the refrigerator. Warmed just a little, the sauce is spectacular over ice cream.

blade). Transfer the pan to a rack and cool the cake for 15 minutes, then run a blunt knife between the cake and the pan and remove the sides of the pan. During baking, the cake probably will have puffed to the top of the pan; don't be concerned if it sinks a little or if it develops a little crater in the center. Cool the cake to room temperature.

When the cake is completely cool, invert it, remove the base of the pan and peel off the paper. Wash and dry the springform pan, and return the cake to it right side up. Refasten the sides around the cake.

TO MAKE THE TOPPING: Put the sugar, water and corn syrup in a medium heavy-bottomed saucepan, stir just to combine the ingredients and then put the pan over medium-high heat. Heat, without stirring, until the caramel turns deep amber, 5 to 10 minutes, depending on the size of your saucepan and the intensity of the heat. As the sugar is caramelizing, wipe down any splatters on the sides of the pan with a pastry brush dipped in cold water. To test the color of the caramel, drop a bit on a white plate. Don't be timid about the color—if it's too pale, it won't have much taste.

Lower the heat a bit and, standing back from the saucepan—the caramel will bubble and spatter—add the cream and butter. When the spatters are less vehement, stir to calm down the caramel and dissolve any lumps. Stir in the peanuts, and pour the caramel and peanuts into a 1-quart Pyrex measuring cup or a heat-proof bowl.

You've probably got more caramel than you need, but you want to get all the peanuts on the cake, so spoon the peanuts out of the hot caramel and onto the cake. After you've done that, pour or spoon on enough caramel to cover all the nuts. You'll have a layer about ¼ inch high (give or take a bit). Allow the topping to set at room temperature—about 20 minutes—before serving. Keep the leftover caramel at room temperature and then make caramel sauce or, when it's cool, refrigerate it until you are ready to make the sauce; see Playing Around.

At serving time, you should be able to just run a blunt knife between the caramel and the pan and simply remove the sides of the springform. If this isn't the case, hit the sides with some hot air from a hairdryer or wrap the sides in a towel moistened with hot water. Bring the whole cake to the table on a platter, so that you can get some "oohs."

# TIRAMISU CAKE

**THERE WAS** a time in the 1990s when probably the only way to avoid tiramisu would have been to go to Antarctica—and even then you might not be sure it wouldn't turn up. It was introduced to the public by Tom Hanks and Meg Ryan in the movie *Sleepless in Seattle,* and that it remains beloved is a testament not to celebrity endorsement or the power of mass media, but to the fact that it is so good.

At its most basic, the dessert, which is, in some ways, like a British trifle, is composed of ladyfingers dipped in espresso; a mascarpone cream flavored with Marsala or triple sec or some combination of liqueurs; and a dusting of cocoa powder. I decided to turn it into a cake. The base is a yellow cake, which has the same adaptability and accepting nature as ladyfingers. I soak the layers in an espresso syrup, fill them with a mascarpone cream and frost the cake with that same cream flavored with espresso. Following tradition, I dust the top of the cake with cocoa, but I also tuck some small chunks of chocolate into the filling.

Just in case you are wondering, *tiramisú* means pick-me-up, as in "It's four o'clock in the afternoon, and I sure could use a pick-me-up." Should you find yourself in such a state at any hour, I think you'd be happy to pick yourself up with this.

**MAKES 10 SERVINGS**

**SERVING:** The cake is best when it is cool, not cold, so give it about 20 minutes at room temperature before serving. Cut with a serrated knife and a gentle sawing motion. Serve with that other pick-me-up, coffee, or, better yet, espresso.

**STORING:** Once chilled, the cake can be wrapped lightly and kept in the refrigerator overnight.

## FOR THE CAKE

- 2 cups cake flour
- 2 teaspoons baking powder
- ⅛ teaspoon baking soda
- ¼ teaspoon salt
- 1¼ sticks (10 tablespoons) unsalted butter, at room temperature
- 1 cup sugar
- 3 large eggs
- 1 large egg yolk
- 1½ teaspoons pure vanilla extract
- ¾ cup buttermilk

## FOR THE ESPRESSO EXTRACT

- 2 tablespoons instant espresso powder
- 2 tablespoons boiling water

## FOR THE ESPRESSO SYRUP

- ½ cup water
- ⅓ cup sugar
- 1 tablespoon amaretto, Kahlúa or brandy

## FOR THE FILLING AND FROSTING

- 1 8-ounce container mascarpone
- ½ cup confectioners' sugar, sifted
- 1½ teaspoons pure vanilla extract
- 1 tablespoon amaretto, Kahlúa or brandy
- 1 cup cold heavy cream
- 2½ ounces bittersweet or semisweet chocolate, finely chopped, or about ½ cup store-bought mini chocolate chips

Chocolate-covered espresso beans, for decoration (optional)

Cocoa powder, for dusting

GETTING READY: Center a rack in the oven and preheat the oven to 350 degrees F. Butter two 9-x-2-inch round cake pans, dust the insides with flour, tap out the excess and line the bottoms of the pans with parchment or wax paper. Put the pans on a baking sheet.

TO MAKE THE CAKE: Sift together the cake flour, baking powder, baking soda and salt.

Working with a stand mixer, preferably fitted with a paddle attachment, or with a hand mixer in a large bowl, beat the butter on medium speed until soft and creamy. Add the sugar and beat for another 3 minutes. Add the eggs one by one, and then the yolk, beating for 1 minute after each addition. Beat in the vanilla; don't be concerned if the mixture looks curdled. Reduce the mixer speed to low and add the dry ingredients alternately with the buttermilk, adding the dry ingredients in 3 additions and the milk in 2 (begin and end with the dry ingredients); scrape down the sides of the bowl as needed and mix only until the ingredients disappear into the batter. Divide the batter evenly between the two pans and smooth the tops with a rubber spatula.

Bake for 28 to 30 minutes, rotating the pans at the midway point. When fully baked, the cakes will be golden and springy to the touch and a thin knife inserted into the centers will come out clean. Transfer the cakes to a rack and cool for about 5 minutes, then run a knife around the sides of the cakes, unmold them and peel off the paper liners. Invert and cool to room temperature right side up.

TO MAKE THE EXTRACT: Stir the espresso powder and boiling water together in a small cup until blended. Set aside.

TO MAKE THE SYRUP: Stir the water and sugar together in a small saucepan and bring just to a boil. Pour the syrup into a small heatproof bowl and stir in 1 tablespoon of the espresso extract and the liqueur or brandy; set aside.

TO MAKE THE FILLING AND FROSTING: Put the mascarpone, sugar, vanilla and liqueur in a large bowl and whisk just until blended and smooth.

Working with the stand mixer with the whisk attachment or with a hand mixer, whip the heavy cream until it holds firm peaks. Switch to a rubber spatula and stir about one quarter of the whipped cream into the mascarpone. Fold in the rest of the whipped cream with a light touch.

TO ASSEMBLE THE CAKE: If the tops of the cake layers have crowned, use a long serrated knife and a gentle sawing motion to even them. Place one layer right side up on a cardboard round or a cake plate protected with strips of wax or parchment paper. Using a pastry brush or a small spoon, soak the layer with about one third of the espresso syrup. Smooth some of the mascarpone cream over the layer—use about 1¼ cups—and gently press the chopped chocolate into the filling. Put the second cake layer on the counter and soak the top of it with half the remaining espresso syrup, then turn the layer over and position it, soaked side down, over the filling. Soak the top of the cake with the remaining syrup.

For the frosting, whisk 1 to 1½ tablespoons of the remaining espresso extract into the remaining mascarpone filling. Taste the frosting as you go to decide how much extract you want to add. If the frosting looks as if it might be a little too soft to spread over the cake, press a piece of plastic wrap against its surface and refrigerate it for 15 minutes or so. Refrigerate the cake too.

With a long metal icing spatula, smooth the frosting around the sides of the cake and over the top. If you want to decorate the cake with chocolate-covered espresso beans, press them into the filling, making concentric circles of beans or just putting some beans in the center of the cake.

Refrigerate the cake for at least 3 hours (or for up to 1 day) before serving—the elements need time to meld.

Just before serving, dust the top of the cake with cocoa.

CHOCOLATE CARAMEL CHESTNUT CAKE
(RECIPE ON PAGE 270)

# CHOCOLATE CARAMEL CHESTNUT CAKE

........................................................................

**WHEN** *Bon Appétit* magazine chose to feature this recipe in its holiday issue, I imagined enclaves of chestnut lovers cheering—at last, the nut that has favored status around the world was being honored in America. It's odd, but chestnuts fare better in song here than they do at the table. With the exception of chestnut stuffing, there are few great American chestnut dishes, and even fewer great American chestnut desserts. This lavish cake offers up chestnuts' repertoire of tastes and textures: sweet and smooth in the cake, mild and pleasantly crumbly sprinkled between the layers and faintly woodsy and toothsome on top. Except for the fact that I love this dessert for its taste, I'd be tempted to say that the reason to make it is because it's just not polite to eat the cake's filling, a truly fabulous chocolate caramel ganache, straight out of a bowl.

The ganache is best if refrigerated overnight. The glaze needs a 4-hour rest and the cake, if it's been seriously chilled, needs serious time on the counter to come to room temperature—serve it cold, and you won't get the full measure of pleasure from the ganache—so plan ahead. (The photograph is on the previous page.)

MAKES 16 SERVINGS

**SERVING:** This cake must be served at room temperature— serve it cold, and you'll lose the subtle play of flavors and textures. Bring the whole cake to the table—it's too gorgeous to hide in the kitchen—and cut it into squares with a serrated knife.

**STORING:** Because every element of the cake can be made ahead, you can work on it in stages. The filled and glazed cake can be kept in the refrigerator for a day, but add the chestnut garnish right before serving.

## FOR THE GANACHE

- 9 ounces premium-quality milk chocolate (such as Valrhona or Guittard), finely chopped
- 3 ounces bittersweet chocolate, finely chopped
- 6 tablespoons sugar
- 2 tablespoons water
- 1 cinnamon stick
- 1 cup plus 2 tablespoons heavy cream
- ¼ teaspoon salt
- 2¼ sticks (10 ounces) unsalted butter, at room temperature

## FOR THE CAKE

- 2 cups cake flour
- 2 teaspoons baking powder
- 1 teaspoon salt
- 2 sticks (8 ounces) unsalted butter, at room temperature
- 1¼ cups (packed) light brown sugar
- 4 large eggs, separated
- 2 teaspoons pure vanilla extract

- 1 cup store-bought sweetened chestnut spread with vanilla (available in specialty markets and many supermarkets)
- ¼ cup whole milk

## FOR THE SYRUP

- ¼ cup brandy
- 2 tablespoons (packed) brown sugar

  About 24 jarred peeled whole chestnuts (about 7 ounces; available in specialty markets and many supermarkets), 12 coarsely chopped, the rest left whole

## FOR THE GLAZE

- 8 ounces bittersweet chocolate, finely chopped
- 1 cup heavy cream
- ¼ cup sugar
- ¼ cup water

  Edible gold dust (optional; available at bakers' supply shops)

TO MAKE THE GANACHE: Put the milk and bittersweet chocolates in a heatproof bowl.

Put the sugar, water and cinnamon stick in a medium heavy-bottomed saucepan, stir, place over medium-low heat and cook, stirring, until the sugar dissolves. Increase the heat, bring to a boil and boil, without stirring, until the caramel turns a deep amber color, brushing down the sides of the pan with a wet pastry brush to remove any sugar crystals and swirling the pan from time to time. (Depending on the size of your pan, it will take between 5 and 7 minutes for the caramel to color properly.) Stand back and add the cream and salt—the mixture will bubble furiously and it might seize, but it will smooth out as you heat it. With the caramel at a boil, whisk it for another minute, or until it is smooth, then pull the pan from the heat and discard the cinnamon stick.

Pour the hot caramel over the chocolate and gently stir until the chocolate is melted and the ganache is smooth. Let stand, stirring occasionally, until it is completely cool, about 1 hour.

Working with a stand mixer, preferably fitted with a paddle attachment, or with a hand mixer in a large bowl, beat the butter until smooth and fluffy. Add the chocolate ganache to the butter in 4 additions, beating on low just until smooth. Scrape the ganache into a container, cover and refrigerate overnight. (The ganache can be made ahead and refrigerated for up to 3 days.)

GETTING READY TO BAKE: Center a rack in the oven and preheat the oven to 350 degrees F. Butter a 2-inch-high 9-inch square pan, dust the inside with flour, tap out the excess and line the bottom of the pan with parchment paper. Put the pan on a baking sheet.

TO MAKE THE CAKE: Sift together the flour, baking powder and salt.

Working with a stand mixer, preferably with a paddle attachment, or with a hand mixer in a large bowl, beat the butter at medium speed until smooth and light. Add 1 cup of the brown sugar and beat for about 2 minutes. Add the egg yolks one by one, beating after each addition until well blended. Beat in the vanilla extract, chestnut spread and milk. Reduce the mixer speed to low, add the dry ingredients and gently mix them in. If using a stand mixer, scrape the batter into a large bowl and thoroughly wash and dry the mixer bowl.

Working in the clean mixer bowl with the whisk attachment or in another large bowl with the hand mixer (and clean beaters), beat the egg whites until they form soft peaks. Add the remaining 1/4 cup brown sugar and beat until the peaks are stiff but not dry. Using a large rubber spatula, fold the egg whites into the chestnut batter in 3 additions. Scrape the batter into the pan.

Bake for about 48 minutes, until the cake is golden on top and a thin knife inserted into the center comes out clean. Transfer the cake to a cooling rack and run a knife around the cake to loosen it from the sides of the pan. Let cool to room temperature in the pan. (The cooled cake can be covered and kept at room temperature overnight.)

TO MAKE THE SYRUP: Stir the brandy and brown sugar together in a small bowl until the sugar dissolves.

TO ASSEMBLE THE CAKE: Cut an 8-inch cardboard square for a base for the cake. Turn the cake out onto the rack and peel off the parchment paper. Using a long serrated knife and a gentle sawing motion, cut the cake horizontally into 3 layers.

Place one layer cut side up on the cardboard. Brush it with half the brandy syrup, spread it with 1 cup of the ganache and sprinkle over half the chopped chestnuts. Top with a second layer, cut side up, and repeat with the remaining brandy syrup, another cup of ganache and the remaining chopped chestnuts. Put the last layer on top, cut side up, and spread the remaining ganache over the sides and top of the cake. Refrigerate the cake while you make the glaze.

TO MAKE THE GLAZE: Put the chocolate in a heatproof bowl.

Bring the cream, sugar and water to a boil in a medium saucepan, stirring until the sugar dissolves. Remove the pan from the heat, pour the cream over the chocolate and wait 1 minute, then whisk very gently, in ever-increasing circles, until the chocolate is melted and the glaze is smooth. Leave the glaze at room temperature until it is thick, but still pourable, a state it may take up to 4 hours to reach.

TO FINISH THE CAKE: Put a cooling rack over a piece of wax paper (the drip catcher) and put the chilled cake on the rack. Pour the glaze over the cake and, using a long metal icing spatula, spread the glaze smoothly across the top of the cake and over the sides. Refrigerate the cake until the glaze sets.

To decorate the cake, brush the 10 to 12 whole chestnuts with gold dust, if you're using it. Arrange the chestnuts in a diagonal line across the top of the cake.

# BERRY SURPRISE CAKE

**ONE OF** the great pleasures of my New York City childhood was clutching a handful of coins, walking to the luncheonette about ten blocks from home and buying a charlotte russe. Charlotte russe, a sweet rarely seen these days, and certainly not at corner luncheonettes, was originally made of ladyfingers and custard, whipped cream and perhaps some fruit. The charlotte russe of my youth was a mixture of sponge cake, fruit or jam and gobs of whipped cream, topped by an unnaturally red cherry. But its real appeal was its packaging—the dessert came in a cardboard cylinder with a pointy rick-rack border. First you ate the swirls of whipped cream that extended at least a mile above the cardboard rim, then—and this was the best part—you pushed the round of cardboard on the bottom and, in a feat of brilliant engineering, the cake rose up so you could eat every last bit of it. You could even lick the base, as I did, and so did everyone else I knew.

This cake doesn't have any moving parts, but the fact that it's made by hollowing out a place in the center of the baked cake for some cream and berries is reminiscent of the spirit of charlotte russe.

The container for this surprise is a sturdy génoise, a whole-egg sponge cake that will hold up when you cut out its center and excavate a cozy nest for the filling. The filling, a mixture of cream cheese and heavy cream, is very simple to make, but because of the tang of the cream cheese, it tastes complex and is awfully good with red berries. Most of the time I use raspberries as the surprise, but strawberries or a combination of berries is also fine. Naturally the cake is finished with whipped cream.

## FOR THE CAKE

- ⅔ cup all-purpose flour
- ¾ teaspoon baking powder
- Pinch of salt
- 4 large eggs
- ⅔ cup sugar
- 1 teaspoon pure vanilla extract
- 2 tablespoons unsalted butter, melted and cooled

## FOR THE SYRUP

- ⅓ cup water
- 3 tablespoons sugar
- 1 tablespoon kirsch, Chambord, framboise or raspberry syrup

## FOR THE FILLING

- 6 ounces cream cheese, at room temperature
- ½ cup plus ⅔ cup heavy cream
- 1 tablespoon sugar
- 1½ teaspoons pure vanilla extract

## FOR THE TOPPING

- 1 cup cold heavy cream
- 3 tablespoons confectioners' sugar, sifted
- 1 teaspoon pure vanilla extract
- 1–1½ pints fresh raspberries, for filling and topping

**GETTING READY:** Center a rack in the oven and preheat the oven to 350 degrees F. Butter a 3-inch-high 8-inch springform pan, dust the inside with flour, tap out the excess and line the bottom with parchment paper. Put the pan on a baking sheet lined with parchment or a silicone mat.

**SERVING:** Cut the cake at the table using a serrated knife. It can be served just as it is or you can drizzle a little Raspberry Coulis (page 467) over each slice.

**STORING:** While you can bake the cake up to 1 day ahead and keep it wrapped at room temperature (a day-old cake is a bit easier to cut than a fresh cake), or freeze it well wrapped for up to 2 months, once the cake is assembled, it is best to serve it the same day.

## Playing Around

The filling is so good you might want to use it without the cake. If so, just mix some fruit in a bowl, add sugar to it, or not, and splash the fruit with a little liqueur (eaux-de-vie, liqueurs such as Chambord or brandies like kirsch are really good with soft fruits) if you'd like. Spoon the fruit into pretty bowls or glasses—everything looks good in champagne flutes—and top with the cream filling.

TO MAKE THE CAKE: Sift together the flour, baking powder and salt.

Place the eggs and sugar in the bowl of a mixer or another large heatproof bowl and whisk to blend. Put the bowl in a skillet with an inch or two of simmering water and continue to whisk until the sugar dissolves completely and the mixture is just warm to the touch, about 3 minutes. Remove the bowl from the heat and whisk in the vanilla.

Working with a stand mixer fitted with the whisk attachment or with a hand mixer, beat on medium speed for about 5 minutes, until the mixture almost triples in volume and forms a ribbon that holds its shape for about 10 seconds when the beater is lifted.

Switch to a large rubber spatula, sift over half the dry ingredients and fold them in gently—don't overmix, you'll have another chance to gather up any recalcitrant ingredients. Fold in the cooled melted butter, then sift over the remaining dry ingredients and very gingerly fold them in. The beautifully beaten eggs are fragile and must be treated like the divas they are. Check that you don't have a puddle of melted butter at the bottom of the bowl—a frequent hazard—then scrape the batter into the pan and jiggle the pan gently to even it.

Bake the cake for 30 to 33 minutes, or until the top is springy to the touch and the sides are starting to pull away from the pan. (A thin knife inserted into the center would come out clean, but it would also deflate the still-fragile cake a little.) Transfer the cake to a rack and let it sit for 5 minutes, then run a blunt knife between the cake and the pan and remove the sides of the pan. Invert the cake and remove the base of the pan and peel off the paper, then invert again and cool to room temperature right side up. (When cool, the cake can be wrapped and kept at room temperature overnight—it will cut a little more easily if it rests—or wrapped airtight and frozen for up to 2 months.)

TO MAKE THE SYRUP: Stir the water and sugar together in a small saucepan, bring to a boil and boil for 1 minute. Pour the syrup into a heatproof bowl. Stir in the liqueur, and let the syrup come to room temperature.

TO MAKE THE FILLING: Working with a stand mixer, preferably fitted with a paddle attachment, or with a hand mixer in a large bowl, beat the cream cheese at medium speed until soft, smooth and fluffy. While beating, gradually add ½ cup of the cream, the sugar and vanilla and continue to beat until the cream is absorbed and the cheese is smooth. Scrape the mixture into a medium bowl.

Pour the remaining ⅔ cup cream into the bowl you beat the cream cheese in (there's no need to wash it) and, using the whisk attachment or the hand mixer, whip the cream until it holds firm peaks. Stir about one quarter of the whipped cream into the cream cheese mixture, then fold in the rest. There's no need to wash the bowl—you'll be using it for the topping.

**TO MAKE THE TOPPING:** Just before you are ready to assemble the cake, whip the cream until it holds medium peaks. Add the sugar and vanilla and continue to whip until the cream holds firm peaks. Cover the cream and refrigerate it.

**TO ASSEMBLE THE CAKE:** Using a serrated knife, slice off the top ½ inch of the cake and set this layer aside. If it crumbles—that can happen to the best of us— just save the pieces. With the knife, sketch a circle on top of the cake that is ½ inch in from the edges of the cake. Cut down through the outline, stopping between ¼ and ½ inch from the bottom. Using the knife and your fingers, carefully pull out the cake within this circle, leaving the little nest that will house your surprise. (You can eat the cake you cut out with coffee.) Transfer the cake nest to a platter or a cardboard round.

Brush the inside of the cake with some of the syrup, discarding what remains, and spoon a thin layer of the filling over the bottom. Toss in ½ pint of the berries— more if you'd like—and cover with the remaining filling. Lift the reserved top layer onto the cake and press it down gently to form the cake. If all you have are scraps, fret not: just arrange them over the top of the cake and press them gently to recon struct a layer.

Using a long metal icing spatula, frost the top and sides of the cake with the topping. Finish with some raspberries, placing the berries carefully around the top of the cake or piling them up in the center. Refrigerate the cake for at least 1 hour (or for up to 6 hours) before serving.

IF YOU can push a button, you can make this fabulous cake. It's made in the food processor and fifteen minutes is all the time it takes to get the simple batter into the oven. The cake is stylishly slim and typically European in that it is a true torte, a slender cake based on ground nuts rather than flour. Bittersweet chocolate, ground almonds and amaretti, crunchy sweet almond macaroons from Italy, give it its distinctive flavor.

My favorite amaretti for this cake are Amaretti di Saronno from D. Lazzaroni & Co., which come wrapped in pairs and packed in beautiful red tins (which, once empty, make great storage bins). I also like Lazzaroni's mini cookies, called amarettini. Both are available at specialty shops, Italian markets and some supermarkets. That said, I've used just about every other brand available in markets all over the country and never made a torte I didn't love.

If you'd like to make individual tortes, see Playing Around.

6 large double Amaretti di Saronno or 18 mini amarettini (see above)

¾ cup almonds (blanched or not; whole, sliced or slivered)

1 stick (8 tablespoons) unsalted butter, at room temperature

½ cup sugar

3 large eggs, at room temperature

4 ounces bittersweet chocolate, melted and cooled

FOR THE GLAZE

4 ounces bittersweet chocolate, finely chopped

½ cup heavy cream

2 tablespoons sugar

2 tablespoons water

FOR THE ALMOND WHIPPED CREAM (OPTIONAL)

¾ cup heavy cream

½ teaspoon pure almond extract

1½ teaspoons confectioners' sugar

1 or 2 amaretti or amarettini, crumbled, or a few spoonfuls of toasted sliced almonds, for decoration

MAKES 8 SERVINGS

SERVING: This cake is best served at room temperature, and in slender slices. If you don't want to serve the whipped cream, pair the cake with crème fraîche (page 459), vanilla or coffee ice cream, Arborio rice pudding (page 412) or chocolate mousse.

STORING: Wrapped well (although the wrapping will smudge the glaze), the torte can be kept in the refrigerator for up to 2 days—bring it to room temperature before serving. Wrapped airtight, it can be frozen for up to 2 months.

GETTING READY: Center a rack in the oven and preheat the oven to 350 degrees F. Butter an 8-x-2-inch round cake pan, line the bottom with parchment or wax paper and butter the paper. Dust the inside of the pan with flour, tap out the excess and put the pan on a baking sheet lined with parchment or a silicone mat.

Put the amaretti and almonds in a food processor and pulse to grind them finely and evenly. Turn out onto a piece of wax paper and set aside.

Put the butter, sugar and eggs into the processor and process for about 3 minutes, until the batter is very smooth and has a satiny sheen. Stop to scrape down the sides of the bowl as needed so the ingredients blend evenly. Pour in the amaretti and almonds and the melted chocolate and pulse just until they are thoroughly incorporated. Turn the batter into the prepared pan and smooth the top with a rubber spatula.

Bake for 25 to 30 minutes, or until a thin knife inserted into the center of the cake comes out almost clean—streaky is more what you're looking for. The cake will dome slightly and the top will look dry; it might even crack—don't worry. Transfer the cake to a rack to cool for 15 minutes.

Run a knife around the sides of the pan and unmold the cake onto the rack. The cake will be very thin. Peel off the paper liner, invert the cake and cool to room temperature right side up.

When you are ready to glaze the cake, put the cake, still on the rack, over a sheet of wax paper (the drip catcher).

TO MAKE THE GLAZE: Put the chopped chocolate in a 2-cup Pyrex measuring cup or in a bowl with a spout.

Stir the cream, sugar and water together in a small saucepan, and bring to a boil over medium heat. Pour the cream over the chocolate and wait for 1 minute, then, using a small rubber spatula, gently stir until the glaze is smooth, blended and shiny. Pour the glaze over the top of the cake and, with a long metal icing spatula, spread it over the top, allowing it to spill over the sides of the cake; then smooth the glaze over the sides. Refrigerate the cake for about 30 minutes to set the glaze.

TO MAKE THE OPTIONAL ALMOND WHIPPED CREAM: Working with a stand mixer fitted with the whisk attachment or with a hand mixer in a medium bowl, whip the cream on medium-low speed until it holds soft peaks. Beat in the almond extract. Sift the confectioners' sugar into the bowl and fold it into the cream with a rubber spatula.

Slice the cake and top each slice with a spoonful of almond whipped cream, if you have it, and a sprinkling of crushed amaretti or toasted almonds.

*Playing Around*

I like to use this cake as the base of a hot fudge sundae. Top each wedge of cake with a fat scoop of ice cream (Cherry Garcia is great), cover with Bittersweet Chocolate Sauce (page 463) and top with a respectable amount of whipped cream, some toasted almonds and, if you're the old-fashioned type, a maraschino cherry.

**INDIVIDUAL TORTES**: Prepare four 4-inch round cake pans, divide the batter among the pans and bake for about 25 minutes. If you need to make more servings, the recipe is easily doubled.

# Chocolate Armagnac Cake: The Back Story

**MY VERY** first day at my very first job in a professional kitchen was as scary as the start of kindergarten. After all, I was a writer used to working alone in my bedroom, often in fuzzy slippers. It started off well enough.

I arrived early, got a nice greeting, a white jacket, an apron I could wrap around myself three times, a cup of coffee and the ultimate compliment from one of the owners as she breezed through the kitchen. She stopped next to me for a second, asked if I was new and said, "How chic—a thin pastry chef."

Magic words. Maybe I'd be one yet.

For the first couple of months, everything chugged along merrily. People seemed open and friendly. I loved the two things that were mine to do each morning: Chocolate Chunkers (see page 70) and chocolate whisky-raisin cakes. But, after a while, after the excitement, the newness and the pride of being in a real kitchen wore off, I was a little . . . bored. "If I'm bored making the same desserts every day," I mused, "then the customers upstairs must be just as bored eating them."

The beloved and on-the-menu-all-the-time recipe that I was most tired of was for the chocolate almond cake shot through with whisky-soaked raisins. So, one day I swapped the whisky raisins for prunes soaked in Armagnac.

When the owner called me up to her office that afternoon, she told me how good the cake was and that it had caused quite a to-do in the dining room. I was thrilled.

She continued. Since the cake had been on the menu from opening day, since the menu read "Chocolate Whisky-Raisin Cake" and since the servers didn't have a clue that a sorcerer's apprentice had done away with both the whisky and the raisins and, to top it off, replaced them with prunes, the world's most misunderstood fruit, the staff had a lot of unhappy diners on their hands.

I apologized—profusely. I promised not to do it again.

Madame la Boss assured me that, indeed, I would never do it again, at least not in her establishment, because I was fired.

"Fired?"

"Fired!"

It was incomprehensible. This woman was credited with putting together the most innovative restaurant in New York at the time.

"Tell me again," I said. "Why are you firing me?"

"You're fired for creative insubordination!"

I was miserable for weeks; I'd been done in by prunes. But in the end I came to be rather proud of myself. Wasn't creativity a good thing?

Perhaps I'd have a future after all.

# CHOCOLATE ARMAGNAC CAKE—THE CAKE THAT GOT ME FIRED

**THIS CAKE** is an intensely chocolaty chocolate cake made with ground pecans and chunks of prunes soaked in fabulously aromatic Armagnac. The cake is a variation on a restaurant's specialty, which was made with ground almonds and whisky-soaked raisins (see Playing Around). That cake, in turn, was a slight variation on a cake created by Simone Beck, a French cook best known in America as one of Julia Child's co-authors on *Mastering the Art of French Cooking*. I lost my job because of improvising on this cake (page 278), but I got to keep the recipe—a trade-off I now consider ample.

### FOR THE CAKE

- ⅔ cup finely ground pecans (or walnuts)
- ¼ cup all-purpose flour
- ¼ teaspoon salt
- 12 plump, moist prunes, pitted if necessary and cut into bits
- ¼ cup plus 3 tablespoons water
- ¼ cup Armagnac (or cognac, brandy or Scotch whisky)
- 7 ounces bittersweet chocolate, coarsely chopped
- 1 stick (8 tablespoons) unsalted butter, cut into 4 pieces
- 3 large eggs, separated
- ⅔ cup sugar

### FOR THE GLAZE

- 3 ounces bittersweet chocolate, coarsely chopped
- 3 tablespoons confectioners' sugar
- 3 tablespoons unsalted butter, at room temperature

MAKES 8 SERVINGS

**SERVING:** The cake should be served at room temperature—chill it, and you'll diminish its flavor and compact its texture. That said, there are lots of people, my husband included, who like the cake cold, because then it becomes more fudgy. Cream, whipped or ice, is a welcome accompaniment.

**STORING:** The cake can be kept at room temperature for a day or wrapped well and refrigerated for up to 3 days; bring it to room temperature before serving.

*Playing Around*

**CHOCOLATE WHISKY CAKE:** The original cake by Simone Beck featured raisins and Scotch, rather than prunes and Armagnac. If you'd like to use that combination, put ¼ cup raisins and ¼ cup Scotch whisky in a covered jar and shake the jar a few times. Let the raisins steep for at least 3 hours (or for up to 1 day), turning the jar upside down and then right side up from time to time. When you add the raisins to the batter, add whatever whisky remains as well.

**GETTING READY:** Center a rack in the oven and preheat the oven to 375 degrees F. Butter an 8-inch springform pan, fit the bottom of the pan with a round of parchment or wax paper and butter the paper. Dust the inside of the pan with flour and tap out the excess. Put the pan on a baking sheet lined with parchment or a silicone mat.

**TO MAKE THE CAKE:** Whisk together the nuts, flour and salt.

Put the prunes and ¼ cup of the water in a small saucepan over medium heat and cook, being careful not to scorch the fruit, until the water almost evaporates. Pull the pan from the heat and pour in the Armagnac, stand back and set it aflame. When the flames die out, transfer the fruit and any remaining liquid to a bowl and let cool. (If it's more convenient, you can flame and steep the prunes up to 1 day ahead. Pack the prunes and their liquid into a covered jar and keep at room temperature.)

Combine the chocolate, butter and the remaining 3 tablespoons water in a heatproof bowl, set it over a pan of simmering water and stir occasionally until the chocolate and butter are melted; or do this in a microwave oven. Remove the

chocolate from the heat just as soon as it is melted and not very hot—you don't want the chocolate and butter to separate.

In a large bowl, whisk the egg yolks and sugar together until thick and pale, about 2 minutes. Switch to a rubber spatula and, one by one, stir in the chocolate and butter mixture, the nut mixture, and the prunes with any liquid.

Working with a stand mixer fitted with the whisk attachment or with a hand mixer in a large bowl, beat the egg whites until they hold firm, glossy peaks. Stir about one quarter of the beaten whites into the chocolate mixture, then gently fold in the remaining whites. Turn the batter into the pan.

Bake the cake for 28 to 32 minutes, or until it is puffed, firm on top and starting to come ever so slightly away from the sides of the pan; a thin knife inserted into the center will come out streaky—the cake should not be wet, but you don't want it to be completely dry. Transfer the cake to a rack and let it cool for about 10 minutes, then carefully remove the sides of the pan. Invert the cake, pull off the paper and turn right side up to cool to room temperature. The cake should be absolutely cool before you glaze it.

GETTING READY TO GLAZE: If the cake has crowned, use a long serrated knife and a gentle sawing motion to even the top. Turn the cake over onto a cooling rack— you want the very flat bottom of the cake to be the top. Put a piece of wax paper or foil under the cooling rack to serve as a drip catcher.

TO MAKE THE GLAZE: Melt the chocolate in a heatproof bowl over a pan of gently simmering water, or in a microwave oven. Remove it from the heat and, using a small spatula, stir in the sugar, then the butter, a bit at a time, stirring until you have a smooth glaze.

Have a long metal icing spatula at hand. Pour the glaze over the top of the cake, allowing the excess to run down the sides, and use the spatula to smooth the top of the cake if necessary—usually the glaze is a self-spreader—and to even it around the sides of the cake. Let the glaze set at room temperature or, if you want to speed it up, slide the cake into the refrigerator for about 20 minutes. If you'd like the glaze to be more like a frosting, let it cool until it is thick enough to spread, then swirl it over the cake.

# PEANUT BUTTER TORTE

........................................................................................................

**PEANUT BUTTER** may be quintessential kid stuff, but I can think of few PB sweets that are meant for kids only. Certainly I never once fooled myself into thinking I was creating this dessert for the younger set alone. The crust is made from crushed Oreos; the filling is a cream cheese and peanut butter mousse; the crunchies in the mousse are a spiced mix of peanuts and chocolate; the shiny glaze is bittersweet chocolate ganache; and it's all topped off with a dusting of salted peanuts. School bake sale or celebratory supper with friends? Your choice.

**MAKES 6 TO 8 SERVINGS**

**SERVING:** I like to serve the torte with strong espresso, but it lends itself to being paired with black tea, hot cocoa or even a not-too-thick not-too-sweet coffee milk shake.

**STORING:** Well covered, the torte will keep in the refrigerator for about 2 days; just make sure to keep it away from foods with strong odors.

| | |
|---|---|
| 1¼ cups finely chopped salted peanuts (for the filling, crunch and topping) | ½ stick (4 tablespoons) unsalted butter, melted and cooled |
| 2 teaspoons sugar | Small pinch of salt |
| ½ teaspoon instant espresso powder (or finely ground instant coffee) | 2½ cups heavy cream |
| ¼ teaspoon ground cinnamon | 1¼ cups confectioners' sugar, sifted |
| Pinch of freshly grated nutmeg | 12 ounces cream cheese, at room temperature |
| ½ cup mini chocolate chips (or finely chopped semisweet chocolate) | 1½ cups salted peanut butter—crunchy or smooth (not natural; I use Skippy) |
| 24 Oreo cookies, finely crumbled or ground in a food processor or blender | 2 tablespoons whole milk |
| | 4 ounces bittersweet chocolate, finely chopped |

GETTING READY: Center a rack in the oven and preheat the oven to 350 degrees F. Butter a 9-inch springform pan and place it on a baking sheet lined with parchment or a silicone mat.

Toss ½ cup of the chopped peanuts, the sugar, espresso powder, cinnamon, nutmeg and chocolate chips together in a small bowl. Set aside.

Put the Oreo crumbs, melted butter and salt in another small bowl and stir with a fork just until the crumbs are moistened. Press the crumbs evenly over the bottom and up the sides of the springform pan (they should go up about 2 inches on the sides). Freeze the crust for 10 minutes.

Bake the crust for 10 minutes, then transfer it to a rack and let it cool completely before filling.

Working with a stand mixer fitted with the whisk attachment or with a hand mixer in a large bowl, whip 2 cups of the cream until it holds medium peaks. Beat in ¼ cup of the confectioners' sugar and whip until the cream holds medium-firm peaks. Scrape the cream into a bowl and refrigerate until needed.

Wipe out (no need to wash) the bowl, fit the stand mixer with the paddle attachment if you have one, or continue with the hand mixer, and beat the cream cheese with the remaining 1 cup confectioners' sugar on medium speed until the cream cheese is satiny smooth. Beat in the peanut butter, ¼ cup of the chopped peanuts and the milk.

Using a large rubber spatula, gently stir in about one quarter of the whipped cream, just to lighten the mousse. Still working with the spatula, stir in the crunchy peanut mixture, then gingerly fold in the remaining whipped cream.

Scrape the mousse into the crust, mounding and smoothing the top. Refrigerate for at least 4 hours, or overnight; cover with plastic wrap as soon as the mousse firms.

TO FINISH THE TORTE: Put the chopped chocolate in a heatproof bowl and set the bowl over a saucepan of simmering water. Leave the bowl over the water just until the chocolate softens and starts to melt, about 3 minutes; remove the bowl from the saucepan.

Bring the remaining ½ cup cream to a full boil. Pour the cream over the chocolate and, working with a rubber spatula, very gently stir together until the ganache is completely blended and glossy.

Pour the ganache over the torte, smoothing it with a metal icing spatula. Scatter the remaining ½ cup peanuts over the top and chill to set the topping, about 20 minutes.

When the ganache is firm, remove the sides of the springform pan; it's easiest to warm the pan with a hairdryer, then remove the sides, but you can also wrap a kitchen towel dampened with hot water around the pan and leave it there for 10 seconds. Refrigerate until ready to serve.

I HAD a Black Forest cake in mind when I was creating this mini extravaganza, but I got carried away. Instead of envisioning sedate chocolate layers filled and frosted with whipped cream and studded with cherries, I became intrigued with the possibility of intensifying the chocolate in the cake and went deep into fudgy-brownie land. I made the cherries a part of the cake rather than an accessory to the filling. In fact, I did away with the filling entirely and gave the whole kit and caboodle a little kick by tossing in some coarsely ground black pepper. Given that I'd gone so far, whipped cream frosting seemed way too tame. I opted for topping the torte with a light, airy but creamy mascarpone mousse. In the end, it was just right.

MAKES 12 SERVINGS

SERVING: Depending on when you are serving the cake, it would be nice to serve it with a small glass of cold kirsch.

STORING: The assembled cake can be kept covered in the refrigerator for 1 day.

### FOR THE BROWNIE LAYER

- ¾ cup all-purpose flour
- ¼ cup unsweetened cocoa powder
- 1 teaspoon (or up to 2 teaspoons, to taste) coarsely ground black pepper
- ¼ teaspoon salt
- 1 cup dried tart cherries
- ¼ cup water
- ¼ cup kirsch
- 3 tablespoons cherry preserves
- 1½ sticks (12 tablespoons) unsalted butter, cut into chunks
- 11 ounces bittersweet or semisweet chocolate, coarsely chopped
- 1½ cups sugar
- 4 large eggs, at room temperature
- ¼ teaspoon pure vanilla extract

### FOR THE MOUSSE

- 3 ounces cream cheese, at room temperature
- ⅓ cup sugar
- 1 teaspoon pure vanilla extract
- Pinch of salt
- 1½ cups (12 ounces) mascarpone cheese
- ¾ cup cold heavy cream

Unsweetened cocoa powder, for dusting

*Playing Around*

CHERRY CHEVRONS: The idea for this decoration was suggested to me by Kristine Kidd, *Bon Appétit* magazine's food editor. The technique is a nifty one, used by pros to give a dressy look to everything from fancy cakes to the raspberry coulis poured around a dessert on an individual plate. You'll need one 12-ounce jar of cherry preserves (not jam). This is more preserves than you need, but it's hard to work with a smaller amount. Puree the preserves in a food processor until smooth, and spoon them into a small resealable plastic bag or a small piping bag fitted with a small plain tip. If you are using the plastic bag, cut off enough of one corner to make a ⅛-inch opening. Pipe the preserves in parallel lines across the mousse, leaving 1 inch of space between each line. Then, starting 1 inch in from one side, drag the tip of a toothpick across the lines in one direction. Next, 1 inch in from the first line, drag the toothpick back in the opposite direction. Continue, alternating the direction every time, to form a zigzag chevron pattern.

GETTING READY: Center a rack in the oven and preheat the oven to 350 degrees F. Butter a 9-inch springform pan and line the bottom with parchment or wax paper. Put the pan on a baking sheet lined with parchment or a silicone mat.

TO MAKE THE BROWNIE LAYER: Whisk together the flour, cocoa, pepper and salt.

Put the cherries and water in a small saucepan over medium heat and bring to a boil. When the water is almost evaporated, add the kirsch and bring it to a boil. Boil for 1 minute, then stand back and carefully ignite the kirsch. When the flames die, stir in the preserves and boil until the mixture thickens, about 3 minutes. Remove the pan from the heat and set aside to cool.

Put the butter and 7 ounces of the chopped chocolate in a heatproof bowl and set the bowl over a pan of gently simmering water. Heat, stirring occasionally, until the butter and chocolate are just melted. Stir in ½ cup of the sugar, and remove the bowl from the heat.

Working with a stand mixer, preferably fitted with a paddle attachment, or with a hand mixer in a large bowl, beat the eggs, the remaining 1 cup sugar and the vanilla extract until pale and thick, about 5 minutes. Switch to a large sturdy spatula and gently mix in the melted chocolate. Still using the spatula, fold in the dry ingredients, followed by the cherries and the remaining 4 ounces of chopped chocolate. Turn the batter into the springform pan and smooth the top with a rubber spatula.

Bake the brownie cake for about 55 minutes, or until the top is dry—it may be slightly cracked, but that's okay—and the cake is just starting to pull away from the sides of the pan. If you stick a thin knife into the center, it should come out streaked with some moist (not wet) batter attached. Transfer the pan to a cooling rack and let the cake cool for 15 minutes, then loosen the brownie by running a blunt knife between the cake and the pan and remove the sides of the pan. Cool the cake completely on the base of the pan.

When the cake is cool, invert it onto a rack and remove the base of the pan and the parchment paper. Wash and dry the pan and return the cake to it. Refasten the sides around the cake. (The cake can be made ahead; wrap it well and store it in the refrigerator for up to 1 day. Or wrap it airtight and keep it in the freezer for up to 2 months; defrost it in the wrapper.)

TO MAKE THE MOUSSE: Working with the stand mixer, preferably fitted with a paddle attachment, or with a hand mixer in a large bowl, beat the cream cheese, sugar, vanilla extract and salt together on medium-high speed, scraping the bowl as needed, until very smooth. Reduce the mixer speed to low, add the mascarpone and mix just until it is smooth. Add the cream and beat only until it is blended—don't overbeat; you want a light, smooth mousse. Pour the mousse over the brownie and tilt and jiggle the pan to even the mousse.

Slip the cake into the refrigerator and refrigerate for at least 4 hours (or overnight) to set the mousse.

Remove the sides of the springform and let the cake sit at room temperature for about 20 minutes before serving. Dust the top of the cake with cocoa powder just before serving.

THIS IS my kind of cake: it looks fussed over and yet it takes no more time, effort or talent to make than a batch of brownies. At heart, it's a very dark chocolate loaf cake with a tight crumb and a sour cream tang, two layers of jam and a chocolate-and-sour-cream frosting that is thick, shiny, soft and lick-the-bowl good. The cake can be frosted in swirls and whorls and served with birthday candles and glasses of milk, or it can be given a leveling swish with a spatula so the look is sleek and sophisticated.

### FOR THE CAKE

- 1½ cups all-purpose flour
- ½ cup unsweetened cocoa powder
- 1 teaspoon baking powder
- ¼ teaspoon baking soda
- ¼ teaspoon salt
- 2 sticks (8 ounces) unsalted butter, at room temperature
- 1⅓ cups sugar
- 2 large eggs
- 1 cup sour cream

- ⅓ cup best-quality red raspberry or cherry jam, for the filling
- 1 teaspoon water

### FOR THE FROSTING

- 5 ounces semisweet chocolate, coarsely chopped
- ½ cup sour cream, at room temperature

MAKES 12 SERVINGS

SERVING: The cake is ready to be served as soon as it is frosted, but I like to wait about an hour, until the frosting develops the slightest little crust; the frosting underneath the crust will still be soft and velvety. (If you refrigerate the cake, the frosting will get firmer.) Serve the cake with a bit of whipped cream and, if you'd like, a pitcher of the Smooth and Tangy Chocolate Sauce (see Playing Around).

STORING: The frosted cake can be lightly covered and kept at room temperature overnight or refrigerated for up to 2 days; bring it to room temperature before serving. It can also be frozen. Freeze unwrapped until firm, then wrap airtight and keep in the freezer for up to 2 months; thaw, fully wrapped, overnight in the refrigerator.

GETTING READY: Center a rack in the oven and preheat the oven to 350 degrees F. Butter a 9½-x-5-inch loaf pan, dust the inside with flour and tap out the excess. Place the pan on an insulated baking sheet or on two regular baking sheets stacked on top of one another.

TO MAKE THE CAKE: Sift together the flour, cocoa, baking powder, baking soda and salt.

Working with a stand mixer, preferably fitted with a paddle attachment, or with a hand mixer in a large bowl, beat the butter and sugar together at medium speed for about 3 minutes, or until very light and fluffy. Add the eggs one at a time, beating for 1 minute after each one goes in. Reduce the mixer speed to low and mix in the sour cream. Still working on low speed, add the dry ingredients and mix only until they disappear into the batter. Give the batter a last stir with a sturdy rubber spatula and scrape the batter into the pan.

Bake for 60 to 70 minutes, or until a knife inserted into the cake comes out clean. If, after about 45 minutes, the cake looks as if it's browning too quickly, cover it loosely with a foil tent. Transfer the pan to a cooling rack and let the cake rest for about 5 minutes before turning it out onto the rack. Cool to room temperature upside down.

**TO FILL THE CAKE:** Bring the jam and water to a boil over low heat or in a microwave oven. Stir to smooth it, and keep at hand.

The top of the cake will become the bottom layer, so if it is uneven and your cake rocks a bit on the counter, turn it right side up and use a long serrated knife to level it. Using the serrated knife, cut the cake into 3 even layers. Put the first layer (originally the top of the cake) cut side up on a long serving plate and spread half of the jam over it. Cover with the middle layer and spread that layer with the remaining jam. Lift the top layer into place, cut side down. Use a small pastry brush to chase away any crumbs on the top or sides of the cake.

**TO MAKE THE FROSTING:** Fit a heatproof bowl into a pan of gently simmering water, add the chocolate and warm, stirring occasionally, until the chocolate is melted. Still working over the hot water, stir in the sour cream. Don't be concerned if the cream tightens—just keep stirring gently and the frosting will become smooth and glossy.

Remove from the heat and cover the sides and top of the cake with the still-warm frosting.

*Playing Around*

**SMOOTH AND TANGY CHOCOLATE SAUCE:** If you want to serve the cake with a sauce that is perfectly matched to it, double the frosting recipe and use half for the frosting and the other half to make a sauce. For the sauce: Bring about 1 cup whole milk (it's hard to give an exact amount because the consistency of the sauce will be up to you) almost to a boil. Put the bowl of extra frosting back over the pan of hot water and gently whisk in the hot milk a little at a time, adding as much as you want to get the desired consistency. The sauce is ready to use when it is as thick or thin as you'd like and perfectly smooth. You can make the sauce in advance and keep it covered in the refrigerator for up to 3 days; just warm it gently before serving.

MAKES 8 SERVINGS

IN AN effort to wrest the ice cream cake genre from the under-ten set, I offer this thoroughly grown-up rendition, a five-layer cake in which three bands of chocolate ganache alternate with layers of raspberry ice cream. I use my own quick raspberry ice cream for the filling—store-bought vanilla ice cream swirled with frozen berries and flavored with a little raspberry liqueur—but any ice cream that goes with chocolate, store-bought, homemade or fiddled with, will go with this cake. See Playing Around for some of my favorite combinations.

The ice cream is mixed in a food processor. If yours isn't big enough to accommodate a quart of ice cream, make the filling in two batches.

The active work time on this torte is minimal, but the waiting around is considerable. You've got to wait 15 to 30 minutes for each layer of the torte to freeze before you can top it with the next layer, so plan ahead.

**SERVING:** The torte can be served plain, with whipped cream, with chocolate sauce or with a little Raspberry Coulis (page 467).

**STORING:** Wrapped well, the torte will keep in the freezer for up to 1 month.

| | |
|---|---|
| 1¾ sticks (14 tablespoons) unsalted butter, cut into pieces | 1 tablespoon framboise (raspberry eau-de-vie), Chambord or other raspberry liqueur (optional) |
| 9 ounces bittersweet chocolate, coarsely chopped | 1 quart premium-quality vanilla ice cream |
| ½ cup sugar | |
| 8 large eggs | |
| 1 10-ounce package frozen raspberries in syrup, thawed | 1 pint fresh raspberries, for decorating (optional) |

GETTING READY: Oil or lightly spray (with vegetable cooking oil) an 8- or 8½-inch springform pan.

Put the butter and chocolate in a heatproof bowl, set the bowl over a saucepan of simmering water and warm the ingredients, stirring occasionally, until they are melted. Be gentle with the heat—you don't want the butter and chocolate to separate. Transfer the bowl to the counter, whisk in the sugar and let the mixture cool for about 5 minutes.

Whisk the eggs into the chocolate mixture one at a time, whisking well after each addition. Rap the bowl against the counter to de-bubble the ganache, and pour one third of it into the springform pan. Freeze for at least 30 minutes to set the ganache. Press a piece of plastic wrap against the surface of the remaining ganache and keep it on the counter.

When the first layer of ganache is set, start making the raspberry ice cream. Puree the raspberries in a food processor. Add the liqueur, if you're using it, and pulse to incorporate. Spoon the ice cream into the processor and pulse just until it is blended with the puree—don't process so long that the ice cream melts.

Spread half the ice cream over the ganache layer, return the springform to the freezer and freeze for at least 15 minutes. Scrape the remaining ice cream into a bowl, cover it with a piece of plastic wrap and put it in the freezer. Don't wash the processor yet—you might need to soften the ice cream again.

When the raspberry layer is set, pour half of the remaining ganache over it. Return the pan to the freezer for another 30 minutes.

*Playing Around*

I'm sure you'll have your own ideas about ice cream flavors to layer with the truffle cream, but here are a few of my favorites to get you thinking. Not surprisingly, the chocolate is great with vanilla, whether it's plain vanilla or vanilla with chocolate chips or fudge swirl. Sometimes I beat some cocoa nibs (see page 479) into vanilla ice cream. Beating cocoa nibs into coffee ice cream is also great. (I usually sprinkle some nibs over the top of the torte too.) Strawberry ice cream is good, and you can use fresh strawberries and even a little crème fraîche as the decoration. At Christmas, it's fun to make this torte with peppermint ice cream (or mint chocolate chip) and decorate the top with a shower of crushed red and white candy canes or peppermint candies. For a very sophisticated torte, I layer the truffle cream with Burnt Sugar Ice Cream (page 432)—it's as grown-up as ice cream gets. The decoration of choice is shattered nut brittle.

TO MAKE THE PASTRY: Bring the water, milk, butter, sugar and salt to a boil in a medium saucepan over medium-high heat. Add the flour all at once and mix it in with a wooden spoon, then keep stirring energetically until the dough comes together in a shiny mass. The bottom of the pan will be covered with a thin film of flour. Cook the dough for another 1 to 2 minutes, stirring constantly, then transfer the hot dough to the bowl of a stand mixer or another large bowl.

Working with a stand mixer, preferably fitted with a paddle attachment, or with a hand mixer, beat in 3 of the eggs one at a time, beating until each is fully incorporated before adding the next. Whisk the remaining egg in a small bowl and very gradually add enough of the beaten egg to form a dough that is thick, shiny and silky.

Spoon the warm dough into the pastry bag, position the tip above the outline of the circle and pipe a ring of dough about 1 inch thick. Pipe a second ring of dough inside the first ring and just touching it. Pipe a third ring of dough on top of the circle where the first and second rings of dough meet. If you have any extra dough, pipe out as many cream puffs as you can or use the dough to make a few éclairs. (The cream puff dough must be piped out as soon as it is mixed. However, if you'd like, you can pipe out the ring and freeze it for up to 2 months before baking it; don't defrost it, just add about 10 minutes to the baking time.)

Bake for 15 minutes. Reduce the oven temperature to 375 degrees F.

Bake the ring for another 20 to 25 minutes (total baking time is 35 to 40 minutes), or until it is puffed, brown and firm. Transfer the baking sheet to a rack and let the ring cool completely.

TO MAKE THE CREAM: Bring 1⅓ cups cream and the mint leaves to a boil in a medium saucepan. Pull the pan from the heat, cover and let steep for 1 hour, then pour into a bowl and refrigerate until cold, about 3 hours.

Strain the cream into a measuring cup and add as much additional chilled cream as needed to measure 1⅓ cups.

Use a serrated knife and a very gentle sawing motion to slice off the top of the pastry ring in one piece; pull out and discard any soft dough from the inside of the base. Carefully place the pastry ring base on a platter.

Working with a stand mixer fitted with the whisk attachment or with a hand mixer in a medium bowl, whip the cream and ¼ cup of the sugar until the cream holds firm peaks. Stir the remaining 2 tablespoons of sugar into the crème fraîche and, using a rubber spatula, gently fold the crème fraîche into the mint whipped cream. Taste the cream, and if you'd like a stronger mint flavor, add a drop or two of extract.

Spoon the mint cream into a clean pastry bag and pipe large rosettes into the base, keeping the rosettes close to one another. Pipe a second row of rosettes on top of the first row, piping the top rosettes between the bottom rosettes. Refrigerate the base while you make the glaze.

TO MAKE THE GLAZE: Melt the chocolate with the cream and corn syrup in a small heatproof bowl set over a saucepan of simmering water, stirring until the glaze is melted and smooth.

Using a small icing spatula, spread the glaze over the top circle of pastry. Sprinkle the toasted nuts over the glaze, and press them down gently. Carefully set the ring on top of the base—don't press down, you want the top to rest lightly on the whipped cream—and refrigerate the cake for at least 1 hour before serving. (Covered lightly and kept away from food with strong odors, the ring can be refrigerated for up to 8 hours.)

# COCONUT-ROASTED PINEAPPLE DACQUOISE

DACQUOISE IS the name given to both a meringue pastry—usually two disks of nut meringue (originally almond meringue) sandwiching a cream (originally coffee buttercream)—and the meringues themselves. But when you take the first bite, etymological considerations disappear and sighs take their place. In this rectangular dacquoise, the nut pastry is coconut and almond and the filling is creamy white chocolate ganache and roasted pineapple.

SERVING: The dacquoise is meant to be served cold. Because it is sweet, it should be served with something that will play off its sweetness, such as espresso.

STORING: The dacquoise's elements—the meringue, pineapple and ganache—can all be made ahead, and the assembled dacquoise should be chilled before serving. A word of caution about the meringue layers: Keep them away from moisture. Humidity will make the meringues sticky.

### FOR THE DACQUOISE

- 1 cup unsweetened shredded coconut (available in health food stores)
- ½ cup slivered almonds
- ⅔ cup plus 1½ cups confectioners' sugar
- 2 tablespoons cornstarch
- 8 large egg whites, at room temperature
- 1 teaspoon cream of tartar

### FOR THE PINEAPPLE

- 1 large (4¼-pound) ripe pineapple, peeled, quartered lengthwise, cored and each quarter cut crosswise into ⅛-inch-thick wedges
  Confectioners' sugar

### FOR THE GANACHE

- 14 ounces premium-quality white chocolate (such as Valrhona Ivoire or Guittard), finely chopped
- 3 cups heavy cream

  About 1 cup sweetened shredded coconut, lightly toasted, for decorating

GETTING READY: Position the racks to divide the oven into thirds and preheat the oven to 225 degrees F. Using two pieces of parchment paper, draw three rectangles (two on one sheet, one on the other), each 12 x 6 inches. Turn the sheets over (making sure the outlines show) and use them to line two baking sheets.

TO MAKE THE DACQUOISE: Put the coconut, almonds, ⅔ cup of the confectioners' sugar and the cornstarch in a food processor and pulse until finely ground.

Working with a stand mixer fitted with the whisk attachment or with a hand mixer in a large bowl, beat the egg whites and cream of tartar at medium-high speed until soft peaks form. Beat in the remaining 1½ cups confectioners' sugar, ½ cup at a time, then beat until the meringue is thick and glossy and holds firm peaks. Using a large rubber spatula, very gently fold in the coconut mixture.

Spoon one third of the meringue (about 2½ cups) onto each outlined rectangle. Using a long metal icing spatula, spread the meringue into smooth, even layers.

Bake the meringues for 3 hours, rotating the sheets from top to bottom and front to back after 1½ hours. The meringues should be golden and crisp to the touch. Let cool completely on the baking sheets on racks. (The meringues can be made 1 day ahead and kept lightly covered with wax paper at room temperature— as long as the room is dry.)

FOR THE PINEAPPLE: Preheat the broiler and place the rack about 4 inches beneath the heat. Line two large rimmed baking sheets with foil.

Place the pineapple wedges between a double thickness of paper towels and pat dry.

Arrange the pineapple wedges on the baking sheets in a single layer and sift just enough confectioners' sugar over them to coat them lightly. Broil the fruit, one sheet at time, for 6 to 8 minutes, or until the pineapple is slightly charred in spots—turn the sheets as needed for even cooking. Cool on the sheets.

FOR THE GANACHE: Put the white chocolate in a large bowl. Bring the cream to a boil, then pour it over the chocolate. Let it rest for 1 minute, then whisk until the ganache is smooth. Press a piece of plastic wrap against the surface of the ganache to create an airtight seal and chill, stirring occasionally, until it is very cold, about 3 hours.

When the ganache is thoroughly chilled and you are ready to assemble the dacquoise, beat the ganache with a mixer (use the whisk attachment or a hand mixer) until it is light and fluffy, but don't overbeat—it should be just on the verge of mounding.

TO ASSEMBLE THE DACQUOISE: Set out a serving plate or cut a 12-x-6-inch piece of cardboard. Place 1 meringue rectangle flat side down on the plate or cardboard and, using a long metal icing spatula, spread ¾ cup of the ganache thinly over it. Cover the ganache with a single layer of pineapple wedges (about 24 wedges in 3 rows of 8). Repeat with another meringue, more ganache and more pineapple. Top with the third meringue, and cover the sides and top of the cake with the remaining ganache. Press the toasted coconut onto the sides of the cake. Arrange the remaining pineapple decoratively over the top of the cake.

Refrigerate the dacquoise for at least 4 hours, or up to 6 hours, before serving.

# PIES AND TARTS
## Warm and Cold,
## Fruity and Nutty,
## Creamy and Crunchy

# APPLES
# LOTS OF WAYS

IF I WERE FORCED TO CHOOSE only one fruit to have in my baker's kitchen, my hands-down choice would be apples: various, versatile and good with just about any kind of pastry, from flaky dough for pies to buttery dough for tarts.

As you look through this collection, you'll find a tall double-crusted apple pie and a thin apple tart; simple constructions, like an apple tartlet composed of apples, puff pastry and little else; an unbeatable tarte Tatin; and a Normandy tart, in which apples turn up as both a thick sweet sauce and a thin pinwheel of slices.

Make any of these and you'll find that changing the variety of apples you use will give each dessert a different taste and sometimes a different texture. Happily, you can mix and match, but you'd be hard-pressed to make a mistake. My first choice is always based on what tastes good to me, then I think about what I'm going to make. Because I like sweet apples that have a touch of tartness to them, I often pick Fujis, Braeburns, Jonagolds or Gingergolds for pies, or Winesaps when they're available. All these will keep their shape when baked and, if you mix them up, give you a little textural play as well.

For applesauce, I reach for softer apples, like Empires or even McIntoshes, and when I'm working from old recipes like Russian Grandmothers' Apple Pie-Cake, I go for Romes or Cortlands, the kinds of apples my grandmother would have found in her local market. The Rome is a little tart and keeps its shape nicely, while the Cortland is softer, juicier and a bit sweeter. Because both have been cultivated since the nineteenth century, they're right for almost any heirloom recipe.

Granny Smiths are a fine choice when tartness is what you're after. However, I rarely use them nowadays, because most are too tart and too dry. The good ones, when you find them, are juicy and have a teensy touch of sweetness mingled with their characteristic tang.

One of my favorite apples, especially for French apple tarts, is one that's not usually a baker's first pick: Golden Delicious. When I was first learning to bake, my instructors, mostly French chefs working in America, always made their tarts with these apples, which tasted to them most like the apples they used at home.

But I toss all habits and preferences to the wind when I'm at a farmers' market, where heirloom varieties are available. Then, I just tell the farmer what I'm making, buy whatever he recommends and relish the anticipation of tasting something new.

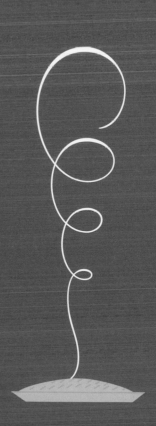

# ALL-AMERICAN, ALL-DELICIOUS APPLE PIE

**YOU HAVE** to be careful about what you say when the subject is an icon, and can there be anything more iconic in America than apple pie? So that I err on the side of understatement and don't make pronouncements that will get me into trouble with the apple pie police, I'll say only that this pie is PDG, or pretty darn good, and leave it to you, after you've made it and savored it, to say more. There's nothing surprising about the pie—which should be true of all things iconic—except how wonderfully well all the usual suspects come together. The double crust is remarkably flaky and tasty (not just a container for the filling, it has its own star qualities), and the apples are sweetened and only lightly spiced, mixed with a bit of tapioca, so their juices thicken a little, and dotted with butter, because butter really does make everything better. When the pie is pulled from the oven, the top crust is deeply golden and the juices from the apples are bubbling up through its cutouts. It is picture perfect.

I like to use a mix of apples for pie, combining sweet apples with tart ones, and crisp apples with apples that have a softer texture. I also like to use big apples, not because they taste better than small ones, but because they're easier to peel, you need to peel fewer of them and they make faster work of getting to the fun part—digging into the pie.

Good for Almost Everything Pie
 Dough for a double crust (page
 442), chilled
4 pounds (about 6 very large) apples
¾ cup sugar
 Grated zest of 1 lemon
2 tablespoons quick-cooking tapioca
½ teaspoon ground cinnamon
⅛–¼ teaspoon freshly grated nutmeg
¼ teaspoon salt

2 tablespoons graham cracker crumbs
 (or dry bread crumbs)
2 tablespoons cold unsalted butter,
 cut into bits

FOR THE GLAZE (OPTIONAL)
 Milk or heavy cream
 Decorating (coarse) or granulated
 sugar

GETTING READY: Butter a 9-inch deep-dish pie plate (I use a Pyrex pie plate). If you want to use a standard 9-inch pie plate, just reduce the amount of filling by about one quarter.

Working on a well-floured surface (or between wax paper or plastic wrap), roll out one piece of the dough to a thickness of about ⅛ inch (see page 441 for more details on rolling pastry crust). Fit the dough into the buttered pie plate and trim the edges to a ½-inch overhang. Roll the other piece of dough into a ⅛-inch-thick circle and slip it onto a baking sheet lined with parchment or a silicone mat. Cover both the circle and the crust in the pie plate with plastic wrap and refrigerate for about 20 minutes, while you preheat the oven and prepare the filling. (If it's more convenient, the crusts can be well covered and kept refrigerated overnight.)

MAKES 6 TO 8 SERVINGS

SERVING: The pie is ready to serve when it is only slightly warm or at room temperature; it should never be served hot—the texture of the crust will be off if the pie is too hot. Because this is an all-American pie, it should be served with your favorite all-American ice cream. Of course, depending on what part of America you come from, you might think the favorite accompaniment is cheddar cheese—in which case, you should serve the pie warm and top each wedge with a nice slice of cheese.

STORING: Like all pies, this is best the day it is made. If you want to make the pie ahead, the best thing to do is to freeze it unbaked. Assemble the pie—but don't brush the crust with milk or sprinkle it with sugar—and stow it in the freezer. When it is firm, wrap it well and keep it for up to 2 months. When you want to bake the pie, just unwrap it, put it on a baking sheet lined with parchment or a silicone mat and bake without thawing it. Of course, it will take more time to bake than a just-assembled pie, but the taste will be just as good.

GETTING READY TO BAKE: Center a rack in the oven and preheat the oven to 425 degrees F.

Peel, core and slice the apples. You've got a choice for slicing: you can cut each apple in half and then slice each half crosswise or lengthwise into slices about $1/4$ inch thick, or you can cut the apple into chunks about $1/4$ to $1/2$ inch on a side. In either case, put the apples into a large bowl and add the sugar, lemon zest, tapioca, cinnamon, nutmeg and salt. Toss everything together really well—I do this with my hands. If you've got a little time, let the mix sit for about 5 minutes, until juice starts to accumulate in the bottom of the bowl.

Remove the pie plate and top crust from the refrigerator and put the pie plate on a baking sheet lined with parchment or a silicone mat. Sprinkle the crumbs evenly over the bottom of the crust—this will help keep it from getting too soggy (some sog is inevitable)—and then turn the apples and their juices into the crust. The apples will heap over the top of the crust. Pat them into an even mound. Dot the apples with the bits of cold butter.

Very lightly moisten the rim of the bottom crust with water, then center the top crust over the apples. (If the crusts—top and bottom—are still very cold and in danger of cracking when you work with them, let them sit at room temperature for about 5 minutes.) Either fold the overhang from the top crust under the bottom crust and crimp the crust attractively, or press the top crust against the bottom crust and trim the overhang from both crusts even with the rim of the pie plate. If you've pressed and trimmed the crust, use the tines of a fork to press the two crusts together securely.

Use a sharp paring knife to cut about 6 slits in the top crust. I always use the wide end of a piping tip to cut a circle out of the center of the crust as a steam vent. If you'd like, brush the top crust with a little milk or cream and sprinkle it with sugar.

Bake the pie for 15 minutes. Lower the oven temperature to 375 degrees F, and bake the pie for another 50 to 60 minutes (total baking time is between 65 and 75 minutes), or until the crust is gorgeously browned and the juices bubble up through the top crust. After about 40 minutes in the oven, if the top crust looks as if it's browning too quickly, cover the pie loosely with a foil tent.

Transfer the pie to a rack and let it rest until it is only just warm or until it reaches room temperature.

*Playing Around*

It's easy to make little changes to the pie: You can add raisins or nuts, or both, to the filling. You can change the spices—omit the cinnamon and nutmeg and use ¼ teaspoon ground cardamom, or ½ to 1 teaspoon ginger (ground or freshly grated), instead. You can mix pears in with the apples, or make an all-pear or even a pear and quince pie. Once you've got the form down pat, it's easy to customize the filling—just taste before you bake.

NORMANDY APPLE TART
(RECIPE ON PAGE 304)

IF THERE were a French Johnny Appleseed, he'd have come from Normandy, France's apple basket. Many of the best apple tarts were created in that region, including this one, which always does the area proud. It's simple but elegant, boasting nothing more than applesauce topped with slices of browned-at-the-edges apples. There are few ways as lovely to show off an apple's goodness.

I make my own applesauce for this tart, and I urge you to do the same, especially since making it is easy and you'll get a wonderful flavor and texture. It's best to use apples that are mealier than those you'd want to eat out of hand. Apples like Empire, Cortland and McIntosh are good for the sauce, but not so good for the top layer, where you want a firmer apple, like a Golden Delicious. But if you don't have the time to start from scratch, you can still make a terrific tart—just use premium-quality store-bought applesauce, preferably unsweetened, so you can sweeten it to taste. If you like, add a little vanilla. The applesauce I make is smooth and moderately thick—it mounds softly on a spoon. If the sauce you buy seems thin to you, just simmer it for a few minutes to thicken it slightly. (The photograph is on the previous page.)

MAKES 6 SERVINGS

SERVING: The tart can be served when it is only just warm or when it reaches room temperature, and it should be served with exactly what the Normans would choose to serve with it—crème fraîche, another of Normandy's specialties. You can sweeten the crème fraîche lightly if you'd like, or serve it straight up, cold and tangy.

STORING: Although the applesauce can be made ahead, as with all tarts, this one is best served the day it is made, preferably within a few hours of being made.

### FOR THE APPLESAUCE

- 2 pounds (about 6 medium) apples, preferably red apples such as Empire, Cortland or McIntosh
- ¼ cup water, or more
- 1 tablespoon (packed) light brown sugar
- 1–4 tablespoons sugar (optional)
- ½ teaspoon pure vanilla extract (optional)

### FOR THE CRUST

- 1 9-inch tart shell made with Sweet Tart Dough (page 444), partially baked and cooled

### FOR THE TOPPING

- 2 medium apples (preferably firm Golden Delicious apples, not the mealy type of apples you used for the applesauce)
- 1 large egg, beaten with ½ teaspoon water, for egg wash

### FOR THE GLAZE (OPTIONAL)

- About ⅓ cup apple jelly
- 1 teaspoon water

*Playing Around*

You can make the same tart using pears. Make certain the ones for the sauce are fully ripe, maybe even overripe. If your pears are hard and without aroma, pop them into a paper bag and keep them on the counter for a day or two.

TO MAKE THE APPLESAUCE: If you have a food mill, a nifty gadget that separates peel and pits from fruit as it purees and strains, or if you don't mind pushing a little harder on a conventional strainer, don't bother peeling and coring the apples, just cut them into chunks and toss them into a 2- to 3-quart heavy-bottomed saucepan. (I like to leave the skin on the apples because it gives the applesauce a rosier color.) Otherwise, peel and core the apples before cutting them up. Stir in the water and brown sugar, cover the pan and put it over medium-low heat. Don't go far from the stove, because applesauce has a way of bubbling up. Stir the apples from time to time to keep them from scorching, and if the water is boiling away quickly, add more by driblets. When the apples are soft enough to be mashed with a spoon—15 to 20 minutes—remove the pan from the heat and pass the apples through a food mill, or press them through a sturdy strainer, into a bowl.

If the applesauce seems thin (if liquid accumulates around the edges), return the sauce to the pan and cook, stirring constantly, for a few minutes, until the sauce is just thick enough to sit up on a spoon. Remove the pan from the heat and return the sauce to the bowl. Taste the sauce, adding granulated sugar if you think it needs it (traditionally the applesauce for this tart was not very sweet) and vanilla, if you want it. Press a piece of plastic wrap against the surface, and refrigerate until no longer warm. (The applesauce can be made up to 4 days ahead and refrigerated, tightly covered.)

GETTING READY TO BAKE: Center a rack in the oven and preheat the oven to 400 degrees F.

Fill the tart shell almost to the top of the rim with the applesauce and put the pan on a baking sheet lined with parchment or a silicone mat.

TO MAKE THE TOPPING: Peel the apples, cut them in half and remove the cores. Cut each apple half lengthwise in half again and then, still working lengthwise, cut about 7 slices from each of the quarters. (The slices will be very thin.) Arrange the slices in slightly overlapping concentric circles on the applesauce, starting at the edge and laying them down so their tips are against the crust. You will probably have enough room for only 2 circles and some artfully arranged snippets of apple in the center. (If another arrangement appeals to you more, go for it.) Using a pastry brush, paint the egg wash over the sliced apples.

Bake the tart for about 50 minutes—it will look as though the applesauce and apples have risen a bit. The apples should be golden, a little burnt around the edges and soft enough to be pierced easily with the tip of a knife. If you'd like to enhance the color around the edges of the apples, run the tart under the broiler just until you get the color you're after. Transfer the pan to a cooling rack.

TO MAKE THE OPTIONAL GLAZE: If you want to glaze the tart, an easy and very professional touch, bring the jelly and the water to a boil. When the jelly is liquefied, brush a thin layer over the top of the tart with a pastry brush. Return the pan to the rack and cool the tart until it is just warm or at room temperature.

**TOURTE IS** the French term for a covered tart, and it wasn't until after I created this sweet that I realized I had created a *tourte*. What I had in mind when I went into the kitchen to start baking was a slimmed-down apple pie, something not quite so generous as the all-American favorite, not so high, not so fully packed and not so rustic looking. What I ended up with was a trim, sleek but still come-hithery double-crusted tart with the warmth and appeal of an applesauce cookie. The crust is made from almond sugar cookie dough and, if it were cooked down just a tad longer, the filling, which is spiced, spiked with cider and smoothed with browned butter, could be a grandmother's best applesauce.

A double recipe of Sweet Tart Dough
    with Nuts (page 444)

FOR THE FILLING

2 pounds (about 5 medium) tart-
    sweet apples, peeled, cored and
    cut into 2-inch chunks
⅓ cup (packed) light brown sugar
2 tablespoons apple cider, apple juice
    or water

Pinch of freshly grated nutmeg
3 tablespoons unsalted butter
½ teaspoon pure vanilla extract
⅓ cup ground almonds
¼ cup moist, plump raisins (dark or
    golden; optional)
Pinch of ground cinnamon, freshly
    grated nutmeg, allspice and/or salt
    (optional)

**SERVING:** This is a winner topped with crème fraîche or plain vanilla ice cream.

**STORING:** Tarts are best served the day they are made, but this one is good served chilled the next day.

*Playing Around*

**TOURTELY PEAR TART:** You can change the tourte easily by substituting an equal quantity of pears for the apples. Instead of apple cider or juice, use water, and, at the end, toss in a splash of Poire Williams or pear eau-de-vie. You can replace the ground almonds with ground hazelnuts.

**TO MAKE THE CRUST:** Butter a 9-inch fluted tart pan with a removable bottom. Divide the almond tart dough in half. Wrap one half and refrigerate it. Press the remaining soft dough over the bottom and up the sides of the tart pan, allowing the dough to extend just a bit above the rim. Butter a piece of aluminum foil and press it, buttered side down, lightly against the crust. Refrigerate for at least 2 hours.

When the second packet of dough is chilled enough to roll, place it between two sheets of wax paper or plastic wrap and roll it into a circle that is between ⅛ and ¼ inch thick. Using a pot lid as a guide, cut the dough into a 10-inch circle. Use the wide end of a piping tip or a sharp knife to cut a small circle (a steam vent) out of the center. Slide the dough onto a cutting board or a baking sheet, cover with plastic wrap and refrigerate until needed.

**TO BAKE THE CRUST:** Position a rack in the center of the oven and preheat the oven to 400 degrees F.

Put the tart pan on a baking sheet lined with parchment or a silicone mat. Fill the foil-covered crust with dried beans, rice or pie weights and bake for 20 minutes. Remove the foil and weights and bake for another 5 to 10 minutes, or until just lightly browned. Transfer the tart pan to a rack and cool to room temperature.

TO MAKE THE FILLING: Put the apples, brown sugar, cider and nutmeg in a medium saucepan over medium heat, cover and bring to a boil. Check the heat—you want the mixture to stay at a medium bubble—and continue to cook, still covered, for about 10 minutes, or until the apples are so soft you can almost, but not quite, mash them with the back of a spoon. While they're cooking, stay close by—the mixture has a tendency to boil over. Remove the cover and, stirring constantly, cook until the liquid evaporates, about 5 minutes more. Scrape the filling into a bowl, and wipe out the pan.

Put the butter in the pan and set the pan over medium-high heat. Cook until the butter boils and turns a deep golden brown. Don't walk away—the time between brown and burned is quick. When the butter is brown and smells nutty, stir it into the apples, along with the vanilla, almonds and raisins, if you're using them. Taste the applesauce and decide if you want to add the additional spices and/or salt. Press a piece of plastic wrap against the surface of the applesauce and cool. (The applesauce can be made up to 2 days ahead and refrigerated.)

GETTING READY TO BAKE: Center a rack in the oven and preheat the oven to 425 degrees F. Place the tart pan on a baking sheet lined with parchment or a silicone mat.

Fill the crust with the applesauce and smooth the surface. Lightly moisten the edges of the crust with water and place the chilled top crust over the tart. If the top crust is very cold and therefore a little brittle, let it stand at room temperature for about 5 minutes before proceeding. When the crust is still cool but pliable, run a rolling pin over the top crust to seal the tart; trim off the excess dough.

Bake the tart for 20 minutes. Lower the oven temperature to 350 degrees F and cover the tart loosely with a foil tent. Continue to bake for another 20 to 25 minutes (total baking time is 40 to 45 minutes), or until the crust is golden. Transfer the tart to a rack and cool until just warm or at room temperature before serving.

# Grandma's Apple Cake

WHEN I was a kid, we never had apple pie or apple tarts. We had what we called apple cake, although we always called it Grandma's Apple Cake, because she was the only person who made it.

It was a weekly treat, and the dough Grandma used was her everything dough, from which she also made cookies and turnovers. Each weekend she came to visit with a care package in tow. It always included jars of her rich, deeply golden chicken soup, with glistening little pools of fat that bobbed on the surface; a box of everything-dough cookies; and apple cake wrapped in a shoe box (I never thought to wonder how she came up with a new box each week) lined with several layers of brown paper cut from grocery bags. The cake was cut into diamond shapes, the layers separated by sheets of wax paper.

I remember two things vividly: that no matter how many layers of brown paper and sheets of wax paper Grandma used, the rich dough and soft apples made little ring marks on the outside of the box, and that as soon as Grandma got settled, she'd hand the cake to my brother and say, "I made this just for you." My brother took her at her word and never shared a bit of it with any of us. The only way I ever got a piece was to swipe it!

After my grandmother's death, I started asking around the family to see if anyone had Grandma's recipe. I turned up two similar versions and set to work trying to re-create my childhood delight, but nothing I made ever tasted right to me. Each time, I'd call my mother, who has never baked a thing in her life but who was in the house when Grandma baked, and she'd add another little piece to the recipe. "Grandma used to grate her apples and squeeze them dry between her palms," my mother would remember, "and she would use the apple juice as the liquid in the dough." So I'd try that. Then my mother would remember that Grandma would make the cake in a sheet pan. Later, she'd call and say maybe it was a roasting pan. At some point, I gave up.

Then, just a couple of years ago, after I gave a cooking demonstration in Syracuse, New York, a young woman, Melissa Hellman, came up to tell me that she was going to Paris and asked if I might have any restaurant recommendations for her. Before I even had a chance to send her a single suggestion, Melissa sent me an advance thank-you, a copy of her Grandma Honey's apple cake recipe, which her Aunt Vicki had transcribed. I knew immediately that this was going to be as close as I was ever going to come to my grandmother's recipe.

In fact, the recipes were different in fundamental ways. My grandmother grated her apples; Grandma Honey didn't. Mine used apple juice in her dough; Grandma Honey used lemon juice, a nice tenderizer. My grandmother made her cake in a big rectangular baking pan; Grandma Honey made the cake in a deep-dish pie pan, so it looked more like a bumpy, rustic, thick-crusted pie. But it was almost a full year later when I realized the most important difference: my grandmother used oil in almost all her baking, including the dough for her apple cake; Grandma Honey used butter. I reworked the dough to make it with oil and was surprised to find that I liked Grandma Honey's more.

Melissa's grandmother is much younger than my grandmother would have been, and the recipes show the difference between Old World cooks and New, the first making do with what was available and affordable and the others baking with what is best.

I've gratefully adopted Grandma Honey's recipe as my family's official Russian grandmother's apple cake, but it was touch-and-go with my mom. I cut her a piece, handed her a fork and waited. Bite one: no comment. Bite two: "No, it's not Grandma's." Bite three: "It's better than Grandma's—really."

Thank you, Melissa.

**THIS RECIPE** was given to me by Melissa Hellman, a young woman who attended one of my cooking classes, and the story behind it is almost as delicious as the dessert itself (see page 308). Although it is made like a pie—two layers of crust enveloping a layer of apples—both my grandmother and Melissa's called it a cake. And, in fact, it is like a cake because the dough is soft, thick and sweet and so are the apples. This dough is also perfect for old-fashioned butter cookies that can be rolled out or made as slice-and-bakes (see Playing Around).

**MAKES 18 SERVINGS**

**FOR THE DOUGH**

- 2 sticks (8 ounces) unsalted butter, at room temperature
- 1 cup sugar
- 2 large eggs
- 1 tablespoon baking powder
- ½ teaspoon salt
- Juice of 1 lemon
- 3¼–3½ cups all-purpose flour

**FOR THE APPLES**

- 10 medium apples, all one kind or a mix (I like to use Fuji, Golden Delicious and Ida Reds; my grandmother probably used dry baking apples like Cortland and Rome)
- Squirt of fresh lemon juice
- 1 cup moist, plump raisins (dark or golden)
- ¼ cup sugar
- 1¼ teaspoons ground cinnamon

Sugar, preferably decorating (coarse) sugar, for dusting

**SERVING:** I cut this into rectangles, each about 3 x 2 inches, but you might want to cut diamond shapes, as my grandmother did, or squares. Whatever you do, don't be too dainty—it's not that kind of dessert. I always serve this plain and with tea, but, of course, it's good with ice cream and just as good with coffee.

**STORING:** Wrapped well, the cake will keep in the refrigerator for up to 4 days. It will get softer and just a touch soggy, but it's still awfully nice. Keep it on the counter for a little while before serving, just to take the chill off it. The cake can be wrapped airtight and frozen for up to 2 months, but if you want to freeze it, it's better to freeze it unbaked and then bake it (without thawing) about 10 minutes longer.

**TO MAKE THE DOUGH:** Working with a stand mixer, preferably fitted with a paddle attachment, or with a hand mixer in a large bowl, beat the butter and sugar together on medium speed until smooth, about 2 minutes. Add the eggs and continue to beat until the mixture is light and fluffy, about 3 minutes more. Reduce the mixer speed to low, add the baking powder and salt and mix just to combine. Add the lemon juice—the dough will probably curdle, but don't worry about it. Still working on low speed, slowly but steadily add 3¼ cups of the flour, mixing to incorporate it and scraping down the bowl as needed. The dough is meant to be soft, but if you think it looks more like a batter than a dough at this point, add the extra ¼ cup flour. (The dough usually needs the extra flour.) When properly combined, the dough should almost clean the sides of the bowl.

Turn the dough out onto a work surface, gather it into a ball and divide it in half. Shape each half into a rectangle. Wrap the dough in plastic wrap and refrigerate for at least 2 hours, or for up to 3 days. (The dough can be wrapped airtight and frozen for up to 2 months; defrost overnight in the refrigerator.)

**TO MAKE THE APPLES:** Peel and core the apples and cut into slices about ¼ inch thick; cut the slices in half crosswise if you want. Toss the slices in a bowl with a little lemon juice—even with the juice, the apples may turn brown, but that's fine—and add the raisins. Mix the sugar and cinnamon together, sprinkle over the apples and stir to coat evenly. Taste an apple and add more sugar, cinnamon and/or lemon juice if you like.

GETTING READY TO BAKE: Center a rack in the oven and preheat the oven to 375 degrees F. Generously butter a 9-x-12-inch baking pan (Pyrex is good) and place it on a baking sheet lined with parchment or a silicone mat.

Remove the dough from the fridge. If it is too hard to roll and it cracks, either let it sit at room temperature for about 15 minutes or give it a few bashes with your rolling pin to get it moving. Once it's a little more malleable, you've got a few choices. You can roll it on a well-floured work surface or roll it between sheets of plastic wrap or wax paper. You can even press or roll out pieces of the dough and patch them together in the pan—because of the baking powder in the dough, it will puff and self-heal under the oven's heat. Roll the dough out until it is just a little larger all around than your pan and about ¼ inch thick—you don't want the dough to be too thin, because you really want to taste it. Transfer the dough to the pan. If the dough comes up the sides of the pan, that's fine; if it doesn't, that's fine too.

Give the apples another toss in the bowl, then turn them into the pan and, using your hands, spread them evenly across the bottom.

Roll out the second piece of dough and position it over the apples. Cut the dough so you've got a ¼- to ½-inch overhang and tuck the excess into the sides of the pan, as though you were making a bed. (If you don't have that much overhang, just press what you've got against the sides of the pan.)

Brush the top of the dough lightly with water and sprinkle sugar over the dough. Using a small sharp knife, cut 6 to 8 evenly spaced slits in the dough.

Bake for 65 to 80 minutes, or until the dough is a nice golden brown and the juices from the apples are bubbling up through the slits. Transfer the baking pan to a cooling rack and cool to just warm or to room temperature. You'll be tempted to taste it sooner, but I think the dough needs a little time to rest.

*Playing Around*

APPLE TURNOVERS: Roll out the dough until it is a little thinner than ¼ inch and cut it into circles 4½ to 5 inches in diameter. Fill each one with 1 to 2 tablespoons of the apple filling (I chop the apples when I'm using them in a small turnover) or substitute another fruit filling, apple butter and apple chunks or some great preserves. Brush the edges of each dough circle with a little water, fold over the dough to make a half-circle pocket and use the tines of a fork to seal the edges. Transfer to a baking sheet lined with parchment or a silicone mat and cut a steam slit in the top of each turnover. Bake in a 375-degree-F oven for about 20 minutes, or until the dough is golden brown and you can smell the sweet filling. Cool to room temperature before serving.

*Playing Around*

RUSSIAN DEEP-DISH APPLE PIE CAKE: Build the dessert in a buttered 9-inch deep-dish pie pan. After the dough is mixed, divide it and shape it into disks. Use one half of the dough to line the pie pan, leaving a ½-inch overhang. For the filling, use just 8 apples, a squirt of fresh lemon juice, ¾ cup raisins, 3 tablespoons sugar and 1 teaspoon ground cinnamon.

Roll the dough out into a circle for the top and place it over the filling. Trim it to a ½-inch overhang, press the top and bottom crust overhangs together and fold them under, so that they are flush with the edge of the pie. Cut some steam slits, brush the crust with water and sprinkle with sugar. Bake for 50 to 60 minutes. The pie might need more time, but check early.

RUSSIAN BUTTER COOKIES: Roll the dough out to a thickness of about ⅛ inch, cut the cookies and brush them with an egg wash—use a fork to lightly beat 1 egg with 1 teaspoon water. Or shape the dough into logs and refrigerate for 2 hours or more, then slice into ¼-inch-thick cookies.

Sprinkle the cookies with sugar (regular or decorating), poppy seeds,

cinnamon sugar or finely chopped nuts mixed with cinnamon sugar. Arrange on a sheet lined with parchment or a silicone mat and bake in a 350-degree F oven for about 12 minutes, or until set. Transfer to cooling racks to cool to room temperature.

**FEW DESSERTS** are more storied than the tarte Tatin, which became a universal darling after the Tatin sisters, French innkeepers, famously forgot to line a pan with crust before they put in the apples and started baking. Rather than begin again, in a flash of thrift and ingenuity, they decided to put the crust on top and serve the tart upside down. For reasons I've never understood, tarte Tatin has a reputation for being a bear to bake. Not so. It's a forgiving recipe, emerging from the oven with its prettily placed apples glazed with caramel and perched on a golden pastry ring. In fact, the tart is so loosey-goosey in its construction that I can give you only a rough guess on the number of apples you'll need. You'll figure it out as you go along, and after you've made the tart once, you probably won't even need a recipe to make it again.

1   sheet (about 8 ounces) frozen puff
    pastry (preferably all-butter; see
    Note, page 315) thawed, or Good
    for Almost Everything Pie Dough
    for a single crust (page 442),
    chilled, or Sweet Tart Dough (page
    444), chilled

1   stick (8 tablespoons) unsalted butter
¾   cup sugar
    About 8 sweet firm apples, such as Fuji,
    Gala or Golden Delicious, peeled,
    cored and quartered

GETTING READY: Center a rack in the oven and preheat the oven to 375 degrees F. Choose a 9- or 10-inch ovenproof skillet—I like cast iron—or, if you've got one, a tarte Tatin pan. Line a baking sheet with parchment or a silicone mat. You'll also need a large rimmed serving plate for the tart.

Working on a floured surface (if you are using puff pastry) or between wax paper or plastic wrap, roll the dough out until it is about ⅛ inch thick (it can be thicker, if you'd like). Using a paring knife, cut the dough into a circle that is 1 inch larger than the diameter of the pan you're using. Prick the dough all over with the tines of a fork and transfer it to the baking sheet. Cover the dough and refrigerate it while you work on the apples.

Put the skillet over medium heat and add the butter. When it melts, tilt the pan so that the sides have a thin coating of melted butter (or do this with a pastry brush). Sprinkle the sugar over the butter. Remove from the heat.

Fit a layer of apples into the skillet, putting the apples into the pan rounded side down and making concentric circles. What's important here is to pack in the apples—because they will shrink as they cook, you want to make sure they are snug in the pan. When you've got a tight single layer, cut the remaining apple quarters in half and strew them over the first layer. (You might have to cut more apples to get a fairly even layer here, or you might have apple quarters left over.) Don't worry about making this layer beautiful—no one will see it, but it will give the finished tart a little height.

Put the pan over medium heat and cook—staying close by—until the sugar turns a deep caramel color. You'll see it bubbling up the sides of the pan, but if you

MAKES 6 SERVINGS

SERVING: Much as you might like to, you cannot serve the tart straight from the oven to the adoring crowd—the caramelized sugar is dangerously hot. Let the tart sit for at least 10 minutes or let it sit longer, until it is only just warm, before serving, then serve it with some unsweetened crème fraîche.

STORING: While you can get the dough ready early in the day and even caramelize the apples about 1 hour ahead, once this tart is made, you can do right by it only by serving it within the hour.

*Playing Around*

While apples are the standard, the technique of caramelizing the fruit and topping it with pastry can be used with pears, mangoes (yes, mangoes—they make a great Tatin, just make sure to choose firm fruit) or quinces. The Tatin technique is also good for soft summer fruits like apricots and (peeled) peaches, but be gentle in that case: It's best to cook the butter and sugar in the skillet without the fruit. When the caramel is the color you want, remove the pan from the heat and cool the mixture. Arrange the fruit in the pan, cover it with the pastry and bake.

need a clearer view, you can gently push an apple aside. To get the color you want without burning the sugar, you may have to lower the heat after a while. Count on 15 minutes, more or less, to get the color. Transfer the skillet to the baking sheet.

Take a last look at the fruit and, if you see gaps, mounds or valleys, gently nudge the fruit into place with a wooden spoon. Remove the pastry from the fridge and center it over the fruit, loosely tucking in any overhang (it's okay if you have a double layer of dough around the edges), or not—the oven's heat will shrink the pastry to size.

Bake for 30 to 40 minutes, or until the pastry is baked through and, if you used puff pastry, puffed.

Now, here's the only tricky part: Cover the skillet with the large rimmed serving plate and, acting quickly and confidently (and making sure you're wearing good oven mitts), turn the tart out onto the platter and remove the pan. If any of the apples have stuck to the pan—it happens to the best of us—gently lift them off the pan with an icing spatula and press them gently back onto the tart.

Let cool for at least 10 minutes before serving.

# ALSATIAN APPLE TART

**THIS TART** was a revelation. It was among the early batches of desserts I was taught to make when I began learning how to prepare French pastry, and the first time I made it at home, I was thrilled: it tasted just like the apple-custard tarts I had eaten in France. To me, it seemed remarkable, if not downright unbelievable, that I, a beginning baker, working in the middle of New York City, could make something with flavor and texture authentic enough to transport me to the world capital of pastry. It was the encouragement I needed to keep baking.

For all the pleasure this tart delivers, it is really quite basic, comprising a terrific crust (I like to use the Sweet Tart Dough with Nuts), thick slices of sweet apples and a vanilla-flavored mix of eggs, cream and sugar that is poured over the apples and, under heat, transformed into a soft custard. It is both comforting and elegant, and a reason to be grateful to the bakers of Alsace, the northeastern region of France, credited with creating this treat.

**SERVING:** Resist the temptation to eat this tart when it is warm—it really needs time to come together and to have the apple juices beat a retreat back into the apples.

**STORING:** Serve this tart soon after it is made, and certainly on the same day; keep it longer, and it will get soggy.

- 1 pound medium-size firm sweet apples, such as Golden Delicious
- 1 9-inch tart shell made with Sweet Tart Dough (page 444) or Sweet Tart Dough with Nuts (page 444), partially baked and cooled
- ¾ cup heavy cream
- 6 tablespoons sugar
- 1 large egg
- 1 large egg yolk
- ¾ teaspoon pure vanilla extract

About ⅓ cup apple jelly plus 1 teaspoon water, for glazing, or confectioners' sugar, for dusting

*Playing Around*

This tart is good made with pears. Make sure to pat them dry with paper towels before you lay them into the crust—pears are juicier than apples and their juices can slow the setting of the custard. When summer rolls around, the tart is also good with peaches, which must be peeled, as well as with apricots. If you use apricots, add ¼ teaspoon pure almond extract to the custard—it will reinforce the fruit's flavor—and glaze the tart with apricot jam. With round fruits, like apricots and peaches, you can, if you'd like, forego the slicing and just halve and pit the fruit, then lay the halves into the crust rounded side up.

**GETTING READY:** Center a rack in the oven and preheat the oven to 375 degrees F. Put the tart pan on a baking sheet lined with parchment or a silicone mat.

Peel the apples, cut them in half from top to bottom and remove the cores. Cut the apple halves lengthwise into thick slices (about ¼ to ½ inch thick)—you'll probably get about 12 slices from each—and lay them in the tart shell, arranging them in overlapping concentric circles and mounding a few slices in the center. If the apples stick up above the rim of the crust, so much the better.

In a 1-quart measuring cup with a spout (for convenience), whisk together the cream, sugar, whole egg, yolk and vanilla, and pour the mixture over the apples. (If you had big apples or lots of them, you might not use all the custard—don't force it; the custard should come just below the crust's rim).

Bake the tart for 50 to 55 minutes, or until the apples can be easily pierced with the tip of a knife and the custard is set. (If a knife inserted into the custard comes out clean, it's done.) Transfer the tart to a rack and allow it to cool to just a tad above room temperature or to room temperature.

If you want to glaze the tart, bring the jelly and water to a boil. Using a pastry brush or, better yet, a pastry feather (custard is delicate) and a light touch, cover the top of the tart with the hot jelly. If the apples and custard have separated, use the glaze to fill in the cracks. If you are not glazing the tart, just dust the top generously with confectioners' sugar.

# TARTE FINE

**IN FRANCE**, *tarte fine* is a chic, slender tart made from a slim layer of puff pastry topped with paper-thin slices of apple. In this country, it is often called apple pizza, a name that aptly describes the tart's looks, but not its elegance. In the end, the name is thoroughly unimportant—it's the taste and texture that mean something, and this tart gets a perfect score on those counts.

The tart is an easy treat to put together on short notice, since all it requires is store-bought puff pastry, a couple of apples, an egg, sugar and 15 minutes or less of active cutting and arranging.

The tart can be made with any sweet but lightly acidic apple, but I always make it with firm Golden Delicious apples, because they are most like the apples used for a *tarte fine* in France.

Note: Pepperidge Farm puff pastry sheets are available in every supermarket across the country. However, I can't encourage you enough to search out an all-butter puff pastry at a local specialty store. If the store doesn't carry frozen all-butter puff pastry, perhaps it will order it for you. The pastry I buy—which is so good I stopped making puff pastry at home—is made by Dufour Pastry.

MAKES 6 SERVINGS

**SERVING:** Unlike other tart doughs, puff pastry is delicious eaten hot and better warm than at room temperature. Cut the tart into thirds, then cut the thirds in half. Serve each portion with a scoop of vanilla ice cream or a spoonful of crème fraîche.

**STORING:** You should serve the tart within 1 hour—max—of pulling it out of the oven.

| | |
|---|---|
| 3 medium-size firm sweet apples, preferably Golden Delicious | 2 teaspoons milk or heavy cream |
| Squirt of fresh lemon juice | 1 large egg, beaten with about ½ teaspoon water, for egg wash |
| 1 sheet (about 8 ounces) frozen puff pastry, preferably all butter (see above), thawed | 3–4 teaspoons sugar |
| | ⅓ cup apricot jam, for glazing |

**GETTING READY:** Center a rack in the oven and preheat the oven to 400 degrees F.

Peel the apples, slice them in half lengthwise and core them. Cut the apple halves in half again and cut about 7 lengthwise slices from each quarter. Put the slices into a bowl and toss them with the lemon juice.

On a sheet of parchment paper or a silicone baking mat, roll the sheet of puff pastry out into a rectangle that is about 9½ x 10½ inches. If the dough is warm, cover it with a piece of plastic wrap and refrigerate it for about 20 minutes. If it's still cool, just lift the paper or mat and place it on a baking sheet. Arrange the apple slices in slightly overlapping rows on the pastry, making sure to leave a border of ¼ to ½ inch bare. Brush the borders lightly with the milk or cream, then brush the egg wash over the apple slices. Sprinkle the apples and the borders with the sugar.

Bake the tart for 30 to 35 minutes, or until the pastry is puffed and golden around the edges and the apples are soft and brown at the borders. Remove from the oven. If you want the edges of the apples to be even darker, you can run the tart under the broiler; be very careful not to overbake the pastry border. (To avoid burning the edges, you can cover the perimeter of the tart with aluminum foil.)

Boil the jam with a smidgen of water until it liquefies, then brush the glaze over the apples (if the jam has any chunks of apricot in it, avoid them).

Serve the tart hot or warm.

*Playing Around*

If you'd like a sweeter tart, before you arrange the apple layer, scatter 2 tablespoons butter, cut into bits, over the pastry rectangle and sprinkle over 2 tablespoons sugar. Omit the egg wash, and once the apples are in place, brush them with 3 to 4 tablespoons melted butter and sprinkle with about 3 tablespoons sugar. Bake and glaze the tart as directed.

THE RECIPE for these small sour cream turnovers filled with apple came from a notebook from my early baking days. I don't know where I got the recipe, and, since I didn't date it, I can't be sure of when I got it either.

The dough is a little miracle. It's quickly made and thoroughly chilled, then, to encourage it to puff, it's rolled and folded over like a business letter. However, thanks to the acidity of the sour cream, this dough is more tender than puff pastry—and it's also a whole lot faster and simpler to make and much easier to work with. For the dough to be workable and for it to achieve its maximum puff in the oven, though, it does need to be refrigerated for several hours.

MAKES ABOUT 16 TURNOVERS

SERVING: These are good with strong coffee or, at the opposite end of the spectrum, a mild tisane.

STORING: The dough is at its flakiest and the apples most tender soon after they are baked. The baked turnovers don't take to refrigerating or freezing.

### FOR THE DOUGH

- 1 cup sour cream
- ½ cup sugar
- 4 cups all-purpose flour
- 1 teaspoon salt
- 3 sticks (12 ounces) cold unsalted butter, cut into small pieces

### FOR THE FILLING

- 1 tablespoon all-purpose flour
- ½ cup sugar
- ¼ teaspoon ground cinnamon
- 4 Fuji or Granny Smith apples, peeled, cored and cut into small chunks
- 3 tablespoons cold unsalted butter, cut into small bits

- 1 large egg, beaten with 1 teaspoon water, for egg wash
- Sugar, for dusting

*Playing Around*

Feel free to change the fruit filling at will and with the seasons. The turnovers are lovely with (peeled) pears, plums or (peeled) peaches. They're also wonderful with bits of apricots, fresh raspberries or a mix of raspberries and blueberries. Or use a mix of soft or cooked dried fruits and nuts, or even just a spoonful of jam. Mixing a thick jam or marmalade with some chopped nuts and bits of soft dried fruits is a good idea too.

TO MAKE THE DOUGH: Stir the sour cream and sugar together; set aside.

Whisk the flour and salt together in a large bowl, then toss the butter bits over the flour. Working with a pastry blender, two knives or your fingers (I'm a finger blender), cut the butter into the ingredients until the mixture resembles coarse meal. Don't worry about being thorough—it's better to have an uneven mix than an overworked dough. Switch to a fork and, using a lifting and tossing motion, gently stir in the sour cream. The dough will be very soft.

Divide the dough in half. Put each half on a piece of plastic wrap and use the plastic to shape each piece into a rectangle (don't worry about size or precision). Wrap the dough and refrigerate it for at least 1 hour, or for up to 2 days.

Remove one piece of dough from the fridge and roll it into a rectangle about 9 x 18 inches. The dough is easiest to work with if you roll it between sheets of wax paper or plastic wrap—if you want to roll it traditionally, make sure to flour the rolling surface. Fold the dough in thirds, like a business letter, wrap it and refrigerate it. Repeat with the second piece of dough, and refrigerate the dough for at least 2 hours, or up to 1 day.

TO MAKE THE FILLING: Whisk the flour, sugar and cinnamon together in a large bowl. Add the apples and toss to coat.

GETTING READY TO BAKE: Position the racks to divide the oven into thirds and preheat the oven to 375 degrees F. Line two baking sheets with parchment or silicone mats.

Roll out one piece of dough to a thickness of about ⅛ inch, and cut out 4½-inch rounds with a large cutter or the edge of a tartlet pan. Repeat with the second piece of dough. If you'd like, you can gather the scraps together, chill them and make additional turnovers. (The turnovers made from scraps will taste good, but they won't be as pretty and light as the first-rounders.) You'll get 7 or 8 rounds from each piece of dough.

Place 1 to 2 tablespoons apples in the center of each round and dot with the butter. Moisten the edges of each round with a little water and fold the turnovers in half, sealing the edges by pressing them together with the tines of a fork. Use the fork to poke steam holes in each turnover, and transfer the turnovers to the baking sheets. (At this point, the turnovers can be frozen; wrap them airtight when they are firm and store them for up to 2 months. Bake them without defrosting, adding a few minutes to their time in the oven.)

Brush the tops of the turnovers with a little of the egg wash and sprinkle each one with a pinch of sugar. Bake for about 20 minutes, rotating the baking sheets from top to bottom and front to back after 10 minutes. When done, the turnovers will be puffed, firm to the touch and golden. Gently transfer them to racks and cool to room temperature.

# PARISIAN APPLE TARTLET

**THIS APPLE** tartlet was inspired by the kinds of small pastries I often see people in Paris eating out of hand as they leave their favorite bakeries. Sometimes the tartlets are made a little bigger than this one, sometimes a little smaller; sometimes the dough almost covers the fruit, sometimes not; and sometimes there's a little glaze over the tartlet and sometimes there isn't. While the tartlet is never complicated, I've pared my version of it down to the barest essentials: a round of puff pastry, half a sweet apple, a sprinkle of brown sugar and a pat of butter. It is abundantly satisfying to eat and almost embarrassingly simple to make. Because preparing this is just a matter of assembling the ingredients, I've given you the recipe for a single tartlet—you can multiply it endlessly and you won't need a calculator to do the math.

MAKES ONE 4-INCH TARTLET

**SERVING:** You've got a choice: you can wrap the tartlet in a piece of waxy paper and eat it standing up, pretending you're walking the cobblestoned streets of Paris, or you can put it on a proper plate with proper cutlery and serve it as an elegant finish to a meal.

**STORING:** The tartlet should be served soon after it is baked and certainly on the day it is made.

*Playing Around*

Use this simple construction to make a pear, plum, apricot, peach or even a mango tartlet.

---

1   ⅛-inch-thick 4-inch circle cold puff pastry (preferably all-butter; see Note, page 315)

½   firm sweet apple, such as a Golden Delicious or Fuji, peeled and cored

Light brown sugar

1   teaspoon cold butter, cut into 3 pieces

---

**GETTING READY:** Center a rack in the oven and preheat the oven to 400 degrees F. Line a baking sheet with parchment paper or a silicone mat and put the pastry circle on the sheet.

Cut the apple half into 4 chunks and center the chunks on the pastry circle. Sprinkle the apple with 1 to 2 teaspoons brown sugar—depending on how much sweetness you want—and dot with the bits of butter.

Bake the tartlet for about 25 minutes (the time will vary depending on how your apple bakes), until the pastry is deeply browned and puffed up around the apple and the apple can be easily pierced with the tip of a knife.

Transfer the baking sheet to a rack and let the tartlet cool—it's great just a little warm and equally good at room temperature.

# A QUINTET OF
# FALL HOLIDAY PIES

FOR ALL THE YEARS I've known my mother-in-law, I still can't predict what she'll say about almost anything—except my invitation to Thanksgiving dinner. Every year I ask her if she'll be coming to our house, and every year she says the same thing: "I wouldn't miss your pumpkin pie!"

Holiday dinner is about the pie. Always was. Always will be. And that's good news for those of us who bake: it means we've got the culinary last word. To make that last word memorable, here are five of my favorite holiday pies: two pumpkin pies, one with sour cream, the other with caramelized sugar; one pumpkin-pecan combo; one pecan pie with chocolate and coffee; and a big double-crusted pie spotlighting butternut squash, pumpkin's next-of-kin. This is my Thanksgiving repertoire, but no one complains when one or the other of these turns up for Christmas.

While none of the pies is difficult to make, any can be a problem on Thanksgiving Day, when you've got a turkey just about living in the oven. Here are a few hints for baking holiday pies under what I think of as battle-front conditions:

• Roll ahead. You can have the pie dough rolled out and fitted into buttered pie plates, ready and waiting for you in the freezer, for up to 2 months. You don't even need to defrost the crusts—just give them a few extra minutes in the oven.

• Partially bake the crusts. If you can do this early in the day, before the turkey goes into the oven, so much the better. However, because you're going to bake the crusts again with filling, you can do the partial bake the night before and keep the crusts at room temperature.

• Get a head start on the pumpkin fillings. You can make the fillings for both the pumpkin pies, as well as the pumpkin layer of the Thanksgiving Twofer Pie,

the night before and keep them in the refrigerator. You can assemble the entire squash pie up to 2 months ahead, freeze it and bake it directly from the freezer.

• Be prepared. Have all the ingredients for the fillings measured out so that as soon as the oven is free, you're set to go.

• Double up. Desperate times call for desperate measures, so when space and time are tight, I bake the stuffing, sweet potatoes and green bean casserole at the same time as the pies. The pies may be delicate, but the fixings are usually flexible, so I just set the oven to the temperature needed for the sweets and let the savories come along for the ride.

# THANKSGIVING TWOFER PIE

**WITH THIS** pie, you get two Thanksgiving Day favorites for the effort of one: pumpkin and pecan—pumpkin on the bottom and pecan more or less on top. Although you pour the pecan filling over the pumpkin, the two meld in the oven into a combo-filling, creamy on the bottom, sweet and crunchy (but not typically pecan pie soft) on top. It's so good that it may create its own Thanksgiving tradition. "Pumpcan" pie, anyone?

**SERVING:** Add any of the usual pumpkin and/or pecan pie toppings, such as vanilla ice cream or lightly sweetened whipped cream, and you're good to go.

**STORING:** Not surprisingly, this pie is best served the day it is made. And even though I think it is best served warmish or at room temperature, you don't have to follow my advice—my husband doesn't: he likes his Twofer chilled.

1 9-inch single crust made with Good for Almost Everything Pie Dough (page 442), partially baked and cooled

### FOR THE PUMPKIN FILLING

1 cup canned unsweetened pumpkin puree
⅔ cup heavy cream
½ cup (packed) light brown sugar
1 large egg
1 large egg yolk
2 teaspoons dark rum
½ teaspoon pure vanilla extract
½ teaspoon ground cinnamon
¼ teaspoon ground ginger
¼ teaspoon salt

### FOR THE PECAN FILLING

½ cup light or dark corn syrup
¼ cup (packed) light brown sugar
2 tablespoons unsalted butter, melted and cooled
1 large egg
1 large egg yolk
½ teaspoon pure vanilla extract
¼ teaspoon ground cinnamon
⅛ teaspoon salt
1½ cups (about 7 ounces) pecan halves or pieces

**GETTING READY:** Center a rack in the oven and preheat the oven to 450 degrees F. Put the pie plate on a baking sheet lined with parchment or a silicone mat.

**TO MAKE THE PUMPKIN FILLING:** Put all the ingredients in a food processor and pulse and process, scraping down the sides of the bowl as needed, for 2 minutes. Leave the filling in the processor for the moment.

**TO MAKE THE PECAN FILLING:** In a medium bowl, with a whisk, beat all of the ingredients except the pecans together until smooth.

**TO ASSEMBLE:** Give the pumpkin filling one last quick pulse, then remove the bowl from the machine, rap it on the counter to de-bubble the batter and pour the filling into the piecrust. Top the pumpkin filling evenly with the nuts, then pour over the pecan filling mixture. Use your finger to poke down any pecans that float to the top and aren't covered with filling.

Bake the pie for 10 minutes. Reduce the oven temperature to 300 degrees F and bake the pie for another 35 to 40 minutes (total baking time is 45 to 50 minutes), or until it is evenly puffed and a thin knife inserted into the center comes out clean. Transfer the pie to a cooling rack and let it stand until it is just warm or until it reaches room temperature.

# CARAMEL PUMPKIN PIE

....................................................................

**THERE'S NOTHING** wishy-washy about this dark-as-chocolate pumpkin pie. It's got a big, bold personality—burnt sugar makes the filling memorable. Really dark caramel, sugar cooked until it smokes, is an assertive flavor, bordering on bitter and not a bit timid about making itself known in any dessert. Here, paired with pumpkin, caramel shows off shamelessly—and deliciously. The filling includes all the traditional elements of the holiday staple: pumpkin, cream, eggs and spices, with some vanilla and rum tossed in too. But because part of the sugar is caramelized before it is added to the filling, everything about the pie changes. The first time I served it, a couple of people raved, then asked, "What is this?"

MAKES 6 TO 8 SERVINGS

**SERVING:** There are two camps of pumpkin pie eaters: those who like their pie at room temperature and those who like it chilled. I thought I was a room-temp gal until I nibbled the chilled leftovers the next day and thought, "Nope, I really like it cold." You'll have to decide for yourself.

**STORING:** This pie is best served the day it is made but just slightly less than best the day after. If you're going to hold the pie for a day, cover and chill it.

*Playing Around*

**STREUSELED CARAMEL PUMPKIN PIE:** To add a little crunch to this dessert, bake the pie for 10 minutes, then scatter chunks of almond streusel (page 346) over the top and finish baking.

1 9-inch single crust made with Good for Almost Everything Pie Dough (page 442), partially baked and cooled

1 cup sugar

¾ cup heavy cream

2 tablespoons dark rum, cognac or apple cider

2 tablespoons unsalted butter, cut into 4 pieces

1 cup canned unsweetened pumpkin puree

1¼ teaspoons ground cinnamon

¾ teaspoon ground ginger

Pinch of freshly grated nutmeg

Tiny pinch of ground allspice

Pinch of salt

1½ teaspoons pure vanilla extract

2 large eggs

Lightly sweetened whipped cream, for serving

**GETTING READY:** Center a rack in the oven and preheat the oven to 350 degrees F. Place the pie plate on a baking sheet lined with parchment or a silicone mat.

Sprinkle ½ cup of the sugar evenly over the bottom of a large nonstick skillet. Place the skillet over medium-high heat and, staying close by, cook until the sugar melts and starts to color. Once you see a little color, gently swirl the skillet so that the sugar colors evenly. Cook the sugar, without stirring, until it turns deep amber—almost mahogany. The sugar will bubble up and foam and soon it will start to smoke. It is very dramatic, and it might make you think you've gone too far, but you want a dark (though not burned black) color; the darker the sugar, the fuller the flavor. When the bubbles have gone from foamy to big and fat, you will probably have reached the right color. To check the color, drop a bit of the caramelized sugar on a white plate.

Lower the heat to medium, stand back and pour the cream into the skillet. The sugar will bubble and hiss and, if the cream was cold, it may even clump. Just continue to cook, stirring, and it will even out. Add the rum and butter and cook just until the caramel is smooth. Pour the caramel into a heatproof pitcher or bowl and cool it for about 15 minutes.

## A Passion for Pumpkin

I'VE GOT a penchant for pumpkin. And in hopes of making a few con-
verts, I want to mention my top three reasons for loving it.

First, I love its easygoing compatibility: if the vegetable were getting its kindergarten report card, it would get an A for "playing well with others." Being a team
player—and a good carrier for sweetness and spice—is one of pumpkin's greatest
virtues and one of the reasons it's so great to bake with.

Then there's its smooth texture. Smooth pureed unsweetened pumpkin
blends perfectly with butter and cream, sweet or sour, and lends moistness (but
not heaviness) to everything it is added to.

Finally, there's the convenience factor. Here's where I confess that the pumpkin of my passion doesn't come from the patch, but right off the supermarket
shelves. I always use canned puree (not pie filling, which is already spiced) and
always have a couple of cans in the cupboard, because a craving can strike long
after—or long before—the proverbial frost is on the proverbial pumpkin.

Working with a whisk in a large bowl, beat the pumpkin to break it up and
smooth it. Add the remaining ½ cup sugar and beat to blend. Whisk in the spices,
salt, vanilla and eggs, beating until the mixture is smooth. Whisk in the caramel.
Rap the bowl against the counter a few times to de-bubble the filling, then pour
the filling into the crust.

Bake for 45 to 50 minutes, or until the filling is puffed and set—tap the pan
gently and the filling won't jiggle. A thin knife inserted into the center of the pie
will come out clean—it will also leave a gash in the filling, but you'll be covering it
with whipped cream.

Transfer the pie to a rack and cool to room temperature, or cool and refrigerate (see Serving). When you are ready to serve, spread the lightly whipped cream
over the top of the pie. If you'd like a dressier look, whip the cream until it is firm,
put it into a piping bag fitted with a star tip and pipe rosettes over the surface of
the pie. Alternatively, you can pipe the cream in a lattice pattern.

# SOUR CREAM PUMPKIN PIE (OR TART)

LIKE ALL good Thanksgiving cooks, I make pumpkin pie for the holiday. But I also make it throughout the fall and winter for no other reason than that it is so good. As all pumpkin pies should be, this one is slip-through-your-teeth smooth and lavishly rich and creamy, and it is also spiced like eggnog and spiked with dark rum. On Turkey Day, I make this pie as a pie, but at other times I pour the filling into a fluted tart shell—just changing the shape transforms the dessert from a homey all-American classic into a classy dinner-party finisher. You'll have filling left over if you make a tart rather than a pie—use it to make mini tartlets; bake the minis at 400 degrees F for 10 to 15 minutes.

MAKES 6 TO 8 SERVINGS

SERVING: Pumpkin pie and whipped cream are naturals, and if you've tested the pie's doneness with a knife, you might want to serve the whipped cream as a cover-up. I like this pie chilled, but others are fans of it at room temperature—decide for yourself.

STORING: Like most pies, this one is best served the day it is made. However, you can make the pie early in the day and keep it refrigerated until needed.

- 1 9-inch single crust made with Good for Almost Everything Pie Dough (page 442), partially baked and cooled, or one 9-inch tart shell made with Sweet Tart Dough (page 444), partially baked and cooled
- 2 cups canned unsweetened pumpkin puree
- 3 large eggs, at room temperature
- 1 cup (packed) light brown sugar
- 2 tablespoons unsalted butter, melted and cooled

- 1½ cups heavy cream
- ⅓ cup sour cream
- 1½ teaspoons ground cinnamon
- 1½ teaspoons ground ginger
- Pinch of ground cloves
- Pinch of freshly grated nutmeg
- Pinch of salt
- 3 tablespoons dark rum
- 2 teaspoons pure vanilla extract

- Lightly sweetened lightly whipped cream, for topping

*Playing Around*

PUMPKIN-BANANA PIE: Years ago I had a very unusual and lovely variation on this pie, created by the legendary Provençal chef Roger Vergé, and I've been making it from time to time ever since. Line the bottom of the pie or tart shell with sliced bananas (cut them on the bias and don't make them too thin—a scant ¼ inch is good) and pour the custard over the fruit; bake as directed.

GETTING READY: Center a rack in the oven and preheat the oven to 450 degrees F. Line a baking sheet with parchment or a silicone mat and put the pie plate (or tart pan) on it.

Put all of the filling ingredients in a food processor and process for 2 minutes, stopping to scrape down the sides of the bowl once or twice. Alternatively, you can whisk the ingredients together vigorously in a mixing bowl. Rap the work bowl or mixing bowl against the counter to burst any surface bubbles, and pour the filling into the crust.

Bake for 10 minutes, then reduce the oven temperature to 300 degrees F and continue to bake for 35 to 45 minutes longer (20 to 25 minutes for a tart), or until a knife inserted close to the center comes out clean. If you don't want to create a slash in your masterpiece, tap the pan gently—if the custard doesn't jiggle, or only jiggles a teensy bit in the very center, it's done. Transfer the pie (or tart) to a rack and cool to room temperature.

# MY FAVORITE PECAN PIE

MAKES 8 SERVINGS

**IF THERE** were a dictionary of desserts, I'd bet that when you looked up pecan pie, the first adjective you'd find used to describe it would be "sweet." There's just about universal agreement that if a pecan pie isn't sweet, it's not a pecan pie. But to me, most pecan pies are just too sweet to be enjoyable. Because one bite delivers such a big burst of sugar, I find myself putting the pie aside and therefore depriving myself of all its other pleasures—the crust, the sensation of coming upon a meaty pecan embedded in jiggly filling and the fun of lingering over dessert, my favorite course, and making it last as long as possible.

Because my husband likes pecan pie—a lot—I made it often, and each time I tweaked the recipe searching for my personal best, a pie sweet enough to merit full pecan pie–hood, but balanced enough to make it fully satisfying. Decreasing the amount of sugar and corn syrup helps, of course, as does adding a little salt and a pinch of spice. But what really did it for me was the addition of espresso powder and bittersweet chocolate. Not a lot, but enough to keep the sugar from being the first, strongest, longest and most memorable flavor in the pie. In fact, in this pie, you even taste the pecans.

**SERVING:** Pecan pie is good at any temperature, and different at each one. It's softest and most puddingish eaten warm (about 45 minutes out of the oven), most flavorful eaten at room temperature and most candy-like when it is chilled. At any temperature, it's good with ice cream—vanilla, chocolate or coffee would be my choices.

**STORING:** Once cooled to room temperature, the pie can be covered and refrigerated for 1 day.

*Playing Around*

If all you want is a great plain pecan pie, omit the cinnamon, espresso and chocolate. If you want a sweeter pie, increase the amount of corn syrup to 1 cup.

- 1 9-inch single crust made with Good for Almost Everything Pie Dough (page 442), partially baked and cooled
- ¾ cup light corn syrup
- ½ cup (packed) light brown sugar
- 3 tablespoons unsalted butter, melted and cooled
- 3 large eggs, preferably at room temperature
- 2 teaspoons instant espresso powder
- 1 teaspoon pure vanilla extract
- ½ teaspoon ground cinnamon
- ¼ teaspoon salt
- 1½ cups (about 7 ounces) pecan halves or pieces
- 3 ounces bittersweet chocolate, coarsely chopped

**GETTING READY:** Position a rack in the lower third of the oven and preheat the oven to 425 degrees F. Put the pie plate on a baking sheet lined with parchment or a silicone mat.

In a large bowl, whisk the corn syrup and brown sugar together until smooth. Whisk in the melted butter, then add the eggs one at a time, beating until you have a smooth, foamy mixture. Add the espresso powder, vanilla, cinnamon and salt and give the batter a good mix. Rap the bowl against the counter a couple of times to pop any bubbles that might have formed, then stir in the pecans and chocolate. Turn the filling into the crust.

Bake the pie for 15 minutes. Meanwhile, make a foil shield for the crust by cutting a 9-inch circle out of the center of an 11- or 12-inch square of aluminum foil.

Lower the oven temperature to 350 degrees F. Place the foil shield on top of the piecrust—the filling will be exposed, the crust covered by the foil. Bake the pie for another 15 to 20 minutes (total baking time is 30 to 35 minutes), or until it has puffed (the middle and the edges should be fairly evenly puffed), is beautifully browned and no longer jiggles when tapped. Transfer the pie plate to a rack, remove the shield and cool to room temperature.

# DEPTHS-OF-FALL BUTTERNUT SQUASH PIE

**LIKE MOST** people, I've got my lazy spots, and squash is one of them. I love winter squash in just about every guise, but I just can't stand peeling it. With all the great kitchen gear I've got, I've never found a gizmo that makes removing the hard shell of a butternut squash easy—I think squash-peeling cooks should get hazardous-duty pay. You can be sure I was one of the first in line at the supermarket when peeled, ready-to-cook squash arrived.

My guess is that marketers expected us to carry the squash home, pop it into the microwave and serve it as a side dish. But it turns out to be perfect for this hearty double-crusted pie, in which the squash is tossed with pears and dried fruit, orange zest and juice, some nuts and a restrained amount of spice and allowed to hold on to its earthy, forthright flavor. This makes a surprising pie—not at all like the traditional pies made with butternut's first cousin, pumpkin—and one that I can imagine (minus the orange, perhaps) might have been just right on the Pilgrims' harvest table.

MAKES 8 SERVINGS

**SERVING:** This is a go-with-ice-cream pie. Try it with vanilla or cinnamon ice cream.

**STORING:** This pie is really best served the day it is made. If you must keep it overnight, store it covered in the refrigerator and bring it to room temperature or warm it for a few minutes in a 350-degree-F oven before serving.

|  |  |
|---|---|
| Good for Almost Everything Pie Dough for a double crust (page 442), chilled | ½ cup (packed) light brown sugar |
|  | 1 teaspoon ground cinnamon |
| 1¼ pounds (about 2 cups) cubed (1-inch), peeled ready-to-cook butternut squash | ¼ teaspoon freshly grated nutmeg |
|  | Grated zest of ½ orange |
| 2 ripe pears, peeled, cored and cut into ½-inch cubes | 2 tablespoons fresh orange juice |
|  | ⅓ cup coarsely chopped walnuts |
| ½ cup moist, plump dried fruit, such as cranberries, raisins (dark or golden) or finely diced apples or pears | 2 tablespoons plain dry bread crumbs |
|  | Sugar, for dusting |

**TO MAKE THE PIECRUST:** Working on a well-floured surface (or between wax paper or plastic wrap), roll out one piece of the dough to a thickness of about ⅛ inch (see page 441 for more details on rolling pastry crust). Fit the dough into a buttered 9-inch pie pan and trim the edges to about a 1-inch overhang. Roll the other piece of dough into a circle that's about ⅛ inch thick and about 11 inches in diameter, and slip it onto a baking sheet lined with parchment. Cover and refrigerate both until needed. (Wrapped well, the crusts can be refrigerated overnight or frozen for up to 2 months.)

**GETTING READY TO BAKE:** Position a rack in the lower third of the oven and preheat the oven to 400 degrees F.

Cook the squash in a microwave oven for 6 minutes, or until almost cooked through. (Alternatively, you can steam the squash.) Pat the squash dry and toss it into a large bowl.

Add the remaining filling ingredients to the bowl and turn them gently with a large rubber spatula to blend. Let the filling sit for 5 minutes or so, just long enough to give the sugar time to melt, then gently mix again.

Remove the pie plate and top crust from the refrigerator and put the pie plate on a baking sheet lined with parchment or a silicone mat. Spoon the filling into the bottom crust and level the top. Brush the rim of the bottom crust with a little water and center the rolled-out top crust over the pie—if the top crust is too cold and not pliable, let it sit for a couple of minutes. Using your fingertips, press the top crust gently against the bottom. Either fold the overhang from the top crust under the bottom crust and crimp the crust attractively, or press the top crust against the bottom crust and trim the overhang from both crusts even with the rim of the pie plate. If you've pressed and trimmed the crust, use the tines of a fork to press the two crusts together.

Using a small sharp knife, cut 4 slits in the top crust, and cut a circle out of the center of the crust using the wide end of a pastry tip. (If you have time, refrigerate the pie for about 30 minutes. The pie can also be wrapped airtight and frozen for up to 2 months; bake directly from the freezer, adding about 10 minutes to the baking time.)

Brush the top of the pie lightly with water and dust with a little sugar. Bake the pie for 55 to 60 minutes, or until it is deeply golden and the filling is bubbling up through the center hole. Check the pie at 40 minutes—if it is already pretty brown, cover it loosely with a foil tent. Transfer the pie to a rack to cool to just warm or to room temperature.

# CREAMY PIES AND TARTS

ANYONE INTERESTED in understanding the culinary differences between America and France has only to look at what each country does with a crust and some creamy filling. On our side of the Atlantic, we're likely to turn these ingredients into a teeter-tottery tall pie with more topping than filling—slice one, and you get wedges as high as they are wide. Go to France, and you can't scare up a cream pie, but you'll be overwhelmed by the number of tarts, all of which will be slender and chic and few of which will be topped—if there's whipped cream, it will be only a dollop served on the side; if there's meringue, it will be a thin, smooth layer. Yet, different as they are, the creamy pies and tarts from both cultures share two important traits: their flavors are unfailingly attention-grabbing and their textures downright sexy.

So that you can taste the differences for yourself, I've pulled together my favorite recipes from both countries. Representing the Stars and Stripes are a banana and a chocolate cream pie, a version of a coconut cream pie in a French tart shell and a pie that goes the traditional Key lime pie one better: beneath the lime filling sits a layer of coconut cream reminiscent of a Mounds bar. Holding up the French tricolor are three chocolate tarts—one all chocolate, one with a soft, peanutty caramel base and one with raspberries—and an assortment of powerfully flavorful citrus tarts.

These pies and tarts have big personalities and soft textures that require a modicum of coddling. So that they can deliver what they promise, here are a few pointers.

• Bake the crusts fully. A well-baked golden brown crust has more taste than an underbaked one and more texture too—the better baked the crust, the livelier the contrast with the soft, creamy filling.

• With the exception of the French chocolate tarts, cream pies and tarts should be enjoyed cold. Take that into consideration when you plan your baking and serving time.

• Whether you've made your filling ahead or filled the crust in advance, make sure the delicate creams are tightly covered in the refrigerator and kept far away from any foods with strong odors.

• If you can, assemble the pie or tart as close as possible to serving time. While the fully assembled dessert can be refrigerated—and the filling should be refrigerated—if you can pull off serving a cold filling in a room-temperature crust, you'll enjoy the differences in temperature as well as in texture.

• Even if you've filled your pie or tart ahead of time, try to swirl on the topping at the last minute—whipped cream and meringue are both better freshly made.

# THE MOST EXTRAORDINARY FRENCH LEMON CREAM TART

**THE FILLING** in this tart is everything. It is the lemon cream I learned to make from Pierre Hermé, and it is the ne plus ultra of the lemon world. The tart is basic—a great crust, velvety lemon cream—and profoundly satisfying. It is also profoundly play-aroundable. You can add a fruit topping (circlets of fresh raspberries are spectacular with this tart) or a layer of fruit at the bottom; you can finish the tart with meringue; or you can serve it with anything from whipped cream to raspberry coulis.

1 cup sugar
 Grated zest of 3 lemons
4 large eggs
¾ cup fresh lemon juice (from 4–5 lemons)
2 sticks plus 5 tablespoons (10½ ounces) unsalted butter, cut into tablespoon-size pieces, at room temperature

1 9-inch tart shell made with Sweet Tart Dough (page 444), Sweet Tart Dough with Nuts (page 444) or Spiced Tart Dough (page 447), fully baked and cooled

MAKES 8 SERVINGS

SERVING: It's a particular pleasure to have this tart when the cream is cold and the crust is at room temperature. A raspberry (page 467) or other fruit coulis is nice, but not necessary; so is a little crème fraîche. I know it sounds odd to offer something as rich as crème fraîche with a tart like this, but it works—because the lemon cream is so light and so intensely citric, it doesn't taste or feel rich.

STORING: While you can make the lemon cream ahead, once the tart is constructed, it's best to eat it the day it is made.

GETTING READY: Have an instant-read thermometer, a strainer and a blender (first choice) or food processor at hand. Bring a few inches of water to a simmer in a saucepan.

Put the sugar and zest in a large heatproof bowl that can be set over the pan of simmering water. Off the heat, rub the sugar and zest together between your fingers until the sugar is moist, grainy and very aromatic. Whisk in the eggs, followed by the lemon juice.

Set the bowl over the pan and start stirring with the whisk as soon as the mixture feels tepid to the touch. Cook the lemon cream until it reaches 180 degrees F. As you whisk—you must whisk constantly to keep the eggs from scrambling—you'll see that the cream will start out light and foamy, then the bubbles will get bigger, and then, as it gets closer to 180 degrees F, it will start to thicken and the whisk will leave tracks. Heads up at this point—the tracks mean the cream is almost ready. Don't stop whisking or checking the temperature, and have patience—depending on how much heat you're giving the cream, getting to temp can take as long as 10 minutes.

As soon as it reaches 180 degrees F, remove the cream from the heat and strain it into the container of the blender (or food processor); discard the zest. Let the cream stand, stirring occasionally, until it cools to 140 degrees F, about 10 minutes.

Turn the blender to high (or turn on the processor) and, with the machine going, add the butter about 5 pieces at a time. Scrape down the sides of the container as needed as you incorporate the butter. Once the butter is in, keep the machine going—to get the perfect light, airy texture of lemon-cream dreams, you must continue to blend the cream for another 3 minutes. If your machine protests and gets a bit too hot, work in 1-minute intervals, giving the machine a little rest between beats.

Pour the cream into a container, press a piece of plastic wrap against the surface to create an airtight seal and refrigerate for at least 4 hours or overnight. (The cream will keep in the fridge for 4 days or, tightly sealed, in the freezer for up to 2 months; thaw it overnight in the refrigerator.)

When you are ready to assemble the tart, just whisk the cream to loosen it and spoon it into the tart shell. Serve the tart, or refrigerate until needed.

## Of Lemon Cream and Pierre Hermé

I AM THANKFUL to Pierre Hermé, France's king of pastry, for many things, chief among them his friendship—we have written two books together—and his lemon cream. When we were just beginning work on our first book, Pierre explained the cream to me. In his typical fashion, he spoke softly, explained thoroughly and added just the meekest editorial comment: "It is nice," he said, with a sly little gone-in-a-flash smile. I immediately put two stars next to the recipe, a note to myself to try it right away.

At first glance, you would think that the lemon cream is just another version of lemon curd—the ingredients are almost identical. What's different is how they are treated, and it makes an enormous difference in the taste and texture.

In a curd, the eggs, lemon juice, sugar and butter are cooked together until they thicken. The result is silky, lemony and, above all, unmistakably rich and buttery. In Pierre's lemon cream, the eggs, lemon juice and sugar—but not the butter—are cooked together until they thicken, just like curd. The mixture is then poured into a blender and allowed to cool for a few minutes. Then the butter is added, in pieces, and the cream is whipped around for a few minutes. Here's the genius—instead of melting as it does in curd, the butter emulsifies (just as oil does in mayonnaise), so that the resulting texture is velvety and deceptively light. It is a stroke of culinary magic.

Like curd, lemon cream is a utility player. It can be spread on toast, used as a filling for cakes and pies, spooned over fruit desserts or just eaten off the spoon when no one is peeking. And it can also be played around with, which is what I've done to create the Creamiest Lime Cream Meringue Pie (page 337) as well as the Fresh Orange Cream Tart (page 334).

# FRESH ORANGE CREAM TART

I FIND it odd that as often as orange juice is used in cakes and as often as orange zest is added to desserts, it's rare to discover a tart that gives orange center stage. A cousin of the Most Extraordinary French Lemon Cream Tart and Creamiest Lime Cream Meringue Pie (pages 331 and 337), this one has all the family's best traits: it's boldly flavored, extravagantly smooth, just as extravagantly rich and, for all its richness, surprisingly light. If you'd like to underline the drama of the tart and make it even more festive, construct it in a square tart pan and top it with a few slices of startlingly red blood oranges. Made that way, the tart is perfect for Christmas.

**FOR THE ORANGE FILLING**

1 cup sugar

Grated zest of 3 oranges

Grated zest of 1 lemon

4 large eggs

Scant ¾ cup fresh blood-orange juice or Valencia orange juice

3 tablespoons fresh lemon juice

1¼ teaspoons unflavored gelatin

1 tablespoon cold water

2¾ sticks (11 ounces) unsalted butter, cut into tablespoon-size pieces, at cool room temperature

1 9-inch tart shell (round or square) made with Sweet Tart Dough (page 444) or Sweet Tart Dough with Nuts (page 444), fully baked and cooled

3 orange segments, for decoration

⅓ cup quince or apple jelly mixed with ½ teaspoon of water, for glazing

GETTING READY: Have an instant-read thermometer, a strainer and a blender (first choice) or food processor at hand. Bring a few inches of water to a simmer in a saucepan.

Put the sugar and orange and lemon zest in a large heatproof bowl that can be set over the pan of simmering water. Off the heat, rub the sugar and zests together between your fingertips until the sugar is moist, grainy and very aromatic. Whisk in the eggs, followed by the orange and lemon juice.

Set the bowl over the pan and start stirring with the whisk as soon as the mixture feels tepid to the touch. You want to cook the cream until it reaches 180 degrees F. As you whisk—you must whisk constantly to keep the eggs from scrambling—you'll see that the cream will start out light and foamy, then the bubbles will get bigger and then, as it gets closer to 180 degrees F, it will start to thicken and the whisk will leave tracks. Heads up at this point—the tracks mean the cream is almost ready. Don't stop whisking or checking the temperature, and have patience—depending on how much heat you're giving the cream, getting to temp can take as long as 10 minutes.

SERVING: The tart should be served cold and needs nothing more than dark espresso or champagne.

STORING: While the orange cream can be made ahead, the tart should be served on the day it is assembled.

*Playing Around*

**COOKIE-TOPPED ORANGE CREAM TART:** For a more unusual presentation, I often make a double recipe of tart dough, then use the second batch of dough to make small thin cookies. Roll the dough out to a thickness of about ⅛ inch and use a cookie cutter (one with a diameter of less than 2 inches) to cut out any shape cookie you want. I'm partial to stars, but plain circles look pretty and polka-dottish. Brush the cookies with a little egg wash (1 egg beaten with a splash of water) and sprinkle with decorating (coarse) sugar, if you'd like. Bake the cookies in a 350-degree-F oven for 13 to 15 minutes—they should remain pale. When the cookies are cool, place them in any pattern that pleases you over the top of the tart. If you decide to cookie-top the tart, you should leave off the fresh orange slices and you can omit the jelly glaze, or not. If you want to glaze the tart, apply the glaze and then add the cookies.

As soon as it reaches 180 degrees F, remove the cream from the heat and strain it into the container of the blender (or food processor); discard the zest.

Soften the gelatin in the cold water, then dissolve it by heating it for 15 seconds in a microwave oven (or do this in a saucepan over extremely low heat). Add the gelatin to the filling and pulse once just to blend, then let the filling cool to 140 degrees F, about 10 minutes.

Turn the blender to high (or turn on the processor) and, with the machine going, add the butter about 5 pieces at a time. Scrape down the sides of the container as needed as you incorporate the butter. Once the butter is in, keep the machine going—to get the perfect light, airy texture, you must continue to blend the cream for another 3 minutes. If your machine protests and gets a bit too hot, work in 1-minute intervals, giving the machine a little rest between beats.

Pour the cream into a container, press a piece of plastic wrap against the surface and refrigerate for at least 4 hours. (The cream can be refrigerated, tightly covered, for up to 5 days or frozen for up to 2 months; thaw overnight in the fridge.)

When you are ready to construct the tart, whisk the cream vigorously to loosen it. Spread the cream evenly in the crust. Arrange the orange segments in the center of the tart and prepare the glaze: bring the jelly and water to a boil. Use a pastry brush or pastry feather to lightly spread the jelly over the orange segments and cream. Serve now or refrigerate the tart until needed.

**TWICE IN** my life I have fallen hard for tarts made from whole lemons. The first was by New York chef Daniel Boulud, the second was one from the Rollet-Pradier pâtisserie in Paris. Both times, what won me over was the bright, fresh, powerfully puckery flavor of the lemon—all of it, zest, pulp and juice. This tart, baked in a tender almond crust, combines the best of those two versions and has a filling that is almost like a thick lemon jelly: tangy, sweet, soft and instantly habit-forming. It's quite stylish in its simplicity.

MAKES 8 SERVINGS

1½ lemons, scrubbed and dried

1½ cups sugar

1 large egg, at room temperature

2 large egg yolks, at room temperature

1½ tablespoons cornstarch

½ cup heavy cream

½ stick (4 tablespoons) unsalted butter, melted and cooled

1 9-inch tart shell made with Sweet Tart Dough with Nuts (page 444), partially baked and cooled

Whipped cream, crème fraîche (page 459) or Faux Crème Fraîche (page 460), for topping, or confectioners' sugar, for dusting

**SERVING:** The tart can be served at room temperature or chilled. I like to give each serving a spoonful of whipped cream or crème fraîche, but it's really not necessary—a dusting of confectioners' sugar suffices nicely.

**STORING:** If you want to serve the tart at room temperature, you should try to serve it the day it is made. If you want to serve it chilled, let it cool to room temperature, then cover it lightly with plastic wrap and slide it into the fridge; it will keep for up to 2 days (although the crust will go a little soft, I think you'll still enjoy the tart).

**GETTING READY:** Center a rack in the oven and preheat the oven to 325 degrees F. Place the tart pan on a baking sheet lined with parchment or a silicone mat.

Slice the whole lemon in half and pull out the seeds from it and the half lemon, then cut the lemons into small pieces.

The filling is best made in a blender, but if what you've got is a food processor, you can use it—just take care to work the ingredients until they are smooth and to scrape down the sides of the bowl often. Put the lemons and sugar in the blender or processor and pulse, blend and scrape down the sides until you have a smooth mix. Add the remaining filling ingredients and pulse and blend until the filling is homogeneous. Rap the bowl on the counter several times to de-bubble the filling as much as possible, and pour it into the partially baked crust.

Very carefully—the tart shell will be full—transfer the baking sheet to the oven. Bake for 20 minutes, then increase the oven temperature to 350 degrees F and bake the tart for an additional 25 to 30 minutes (total baking time is 45 to 50 minutes). Don't be alarmed when the filling starts to bubble up. (It might even bubble over the edge of the tart—that's okay.) When the tart is properly baked, it should be set, although perhaps still shaky in the center, and most of the top will have formed a light sugary crust.

Transfer the tart pan to a cooling rack and let it cool to room temperature. Chill it, if you'd like, before serving with the cream or a dusting of confectioners' sugar.

*Playing Around*

**TARTEST LEMON TART BRÛLÉE:** For a shiny sugar-crackle topping, refrigerate the tart until it is fully chilled, then sprinkle the top with granulated sugar—I work in patches—and, using a blowtorch (see page 475), burn the sugar until it melts and shines. Serve as soon as the sugar settles down.

# CREAMIEST LIME CREAM MERINGUE PIE

**THE LOOK** of this pie is sumptuous, its texture silky and its lime-ginger flavor big, bright and sassy. While I'm happy to have a lemon meringue pie any time of year, I save this pie for summer because, as fresh as lime and ginger taste on their own, when they're mixed together, they turn uber-zingy and so cool you'd think they'd been in the deep freeze. It may be an illusion, but one you'll be happy to play along with on a sweltering day.

FOR THE FILLING

- 1 cup sugar
- Grated zest of 3 limes
- 4 large eggs, preferably at room temperature
- ¾ cup fresh lime juice (from about 6 limes)
- A 1-inch chunk of fresh ginger, peeled and finely grated
- 2 teaspoons cornstarch
- 2½ sticks (10 ounces) unsalted butter, cut into tablespoon-size pieces, at room temperature

- 1 9-inch graham cracker crust (page 235), fully baked and cooled, or a single crust made with Good for Almost Everything Pie Dough (page 442), fully baked and cooled

FOR THE MERINGUE

- 4 large egg whites, at room temperature
- ½ cup sugar

MAKES 8 SERVINGS

SERVING: The pie is best served chilled and in generous wedges.

STORING: I think meringue-topped pies are at their best the day they are made. Kept longer, the risk of weepy meringue gets higher.

*Playing Around*

**GINGERED LIME AND MANGO MERINGUE PIE:** Peel a ripe mango, cut it into small cubes and sprinkle with a little fresh lime juice. Spread about one third of the lime cream into the crust, top with the diced mango and cover with the remaining cream. Chill and finish with meringue as directed. Or omit the meringue and top the pie with long, elegant slices of mango and a gloss of quince or apple jelly: boil about ¼ cup jelly with ½ teaspoon water, then brush the glaze over the pie.

GETTING READY: Have an instant-read thermometer, a strainer and a blender (first choice) or a food processor at hand. Bring a few inches of water to a simmer in a saucepan.

Put the sugar and zest into a heatproof bowl that can be set over the pan of simmering water. Off the heat, rub the sugar and zest between your fingertips for a few minutes, until the sugar is moist and the fragrance of lime is strong. Whisk in the eggs, then whisk in the juice, ginger and cornstarch.

Set the bowl over the pan and start stirring with the whisk as soon as the mixture feels tepid to the touch. Cook the lime cream until it reaches 180 degrees F. As you whisk—you must whisk constantly to keep the eggs from scrambling—you'll see that the cream will start out light and foamy, then the bubbles will get bigger, and then, as it gets closer to 180 degrees F, it will start to thicken and the whisk will leave tracks. Heads up at this point—the tracks mean the cream is almost ready. Don't stop whisking or checking the temperature, and have patience—depending on how much heat you're giving the cream, getting to temp can take as long as 10 minutes.

As soon as it reaches 180 degrees F, remove the cream from the heat and strain the cream into the container of the blender (or food processor); discard the zest. Let it cool until it reaches 140 degrees F, about 10 minutes.

Turn the blender to high speed (or turn on the processor) and add the butter a few pieces at a time. Scrape down the sides of the container as needed as you in-

corporate the butter. After all the butter is in, continue to blend the cream for another 3 minutes. If you find the machine is getting really hot, work in 1-minute intervals, giving the machine a little rest between beats.

Pour the cream into a container, press a piece of plastic wrap against the surface and refrigerate the cream for at least 4 hours, or overnight. (The cream can be packed airtight and frozen for up to 2 months; thaw overnight in the refrigerator.)

TO FINISH THE PIE WITH MERINGUE: Preheat the broiler.

Whisk the cream to loosen it and spoon it into the pie shell. Place the pie plate on a baking sheet.

Working in a clean dry mixer bowl with the clean whisk attachment, or in a large bowl with a hand mixer, whip the egg whites at medium speed until opaque. With the mixer running, add the sugar in a slow stream and continue to beat until the whites are glossy and form firm peaks.

Spread the meringue over the lime filling, swirling it if you'd like. Make sure the meringue comes all the way to the edges of the crust, because it will shrink when it bakes.

Run the pie under the broiler until the meringue is golden and the tips are dark brown. (Or, if you've got a blowtorch, use it to brown the meringue.) Remove the pie from the oven and let it cool for about 15 minutes, then refrigerate for at least 3 hours before serving.

MY PARENTS lived in Florida for decades and they vacationed there for decades before that. I don't think there was ever a time when we kids were young that they didn't come back with boxes of chocolate-coated coconut patties. I'm sure the coconut filling was supposed to be soft and chewy, as in a Mounds bar, but it was always a little dry (sorry to tell you now, Mom). Yet the candies still hold a sweet spot in my memory, and I thought of them when I started to make a Key lime pie.

What I did was put a layer of sweet (but not exceedingly so), soft, chewy coconut in the bottom of the traditional graham cracker crust and cover it with the classic Key lime filling (lime juice, sweetened condensed milk and eggs). Then when I made the meringue for the topping, I folded some coconut into it, so the pie is symmetrical—coconuttily speaking.

Of course you can make your own graham cracker crust for this pie, but I always use a store-bought one.

MAKES 6 SERVINGS

SERVING: If the pie has been frozen long enough to be firm, let it sit at room temperature for about 30 minutes. You want it to be cold but not frozen. Serve with espresso—dark and strong.

STORING: Covered and kept away from foods with strong odors, the pie can be refrigerated for about 8 hours.

1 9-inch graham cracker crust (page 235), fully baked and cooled, or a store-bought crust

1⅓ cups heavy cream

1½ cups shredded sweetened coconut

4 large eggs, separated

1 14-ounce can sweetened condensed milk

½ cup fresh Key (or regular) lime juice (from about 5 regular limes)

¼ cup sugar

GETTING READY: Center a rack in the oven and preheat the oven to 350 degrees F. Put the pie plate on a baking sheet lined with parchment or a silicone mat.

Put the cream and 1 cup of the coconut in a small saucepan and bring it to a boil over medium-low heat, stirring almost constantly. Continue to cook and stir until the cream is reduced by half and the mixture is slightly thickened. Scrape the coconut cream into a bowl and set it aside while you prepare the lime filling.

Working with a stand mixer, preferably fitted with a paddle attachment, or with a hand mixer in a large bowl, beat the egg yolks on high speed until thick and pale. Reduce the mixer speed to low and beat in the condensed milk. Still on low, add half of the lime juice. When it is incorporated, add the remaining juice, again mixing until it is blended. Spread the coconut cream in the bottom of the graham cracker crust, and pour over the lime filling.

Bake the pie for 12 minutes. Transfer the pie to a cooling rack and cool for 15 minutes, then freeze the pie for at least 1 hour.

TO FINISH THE PIE WITH MERINGUE: Preheat the broiler.

Put the 4 egg whites and the sugar in a medium heavy-bottomed saucepan and heat over medium-low heat, whisking all the while, until the whites are hot to the touch. Transfer the whites to a stand mixer fitted with the whisk attachment, or use a hand mixer in a large bowl, and beat the whites at high speed until they

reach room temperature and hold firm peaks. Using a rubber spatula, fold the remaining ½ cup coconut into the meringue.

Spread the meringue over the top of the pie, and run the pie under the broiler until the top of the meringue is golden brown. (Or, if you've got a blowtorch, you can use it to brown the meringue.) Return the pie to the freezer for another 30 minutes or for up to 3 hours before serving.

**FOR YEARS** I made this pie by filling my favorite crust with bananas, my best vanilla pastry cream and swirls of whipped cream. Then, not so long ago, I made three tiny changes—I swapped the white sugar in the pastry cream for brown, added a smidgen of spice and stirred sour cream into the topping—and the time-treasured pie went from great to sublime.

MAKES 8 SERVINGS

**FOR THE CUSTARD**

2 cups whole milk

6 large egg yolks

½ cup (packed) light brown sugar, pressed through a sieve

⅓ cup cornstarch, sifted

½ teaspoon ground cinnamon

⅛ teaspoon freshly grated nutmeg

Pinch of salt

1 teaspoon pure vanilla extract

3 tablespoons cold unsalted butter, cut into bits

3 ripe but firm bananas

1 9-inch single crust made with Good for Almost Everything Pie Dough (page 442), fully baked and cooled

**FOR THE TOPPING**

1 cup cold heavy cream

2 tablespoons confectioners' sugar, sifted

1 teaspoon pure vanilla extract

2 tablespoons sour cream

**SERVING:** I like to serve the pie as soon as it is assembled, when the pastry cream and whipped cream are cold but not really chilled and the crust has not been refrigerated. I think this is when the pie is at its best—but, trust me, it will still be wonderful if you serve it from the fridge. For me, this is a go-with-coffee pie.

**STORING:** The pastry cream can be made ahead, and you can keep the assembled pie in the fridge for a few hours, but you really must eat it the day it is made—no hardship.

**TO MAKE THE CUSTARD:** Bring the milk to a boil.

Meanwhile, in a large heavy-bottomed saucepan, whisk the yolks together with the brown sugar, cornstarch, cinnamon, nutmeg and salt until well blended and thick. Whisking without stopping, drizzle in about ¼ cup of the hot milk—this will temper, or warm, the yolks so they won't curdle—then, still whisking, add the remainder of the milk in a steady stream. Put the pan over medium heat and, whisking constantly (make sure to get into the edges of the pan), bring the mixture to a boil. Boil, still whisking, for 1 to 2 minutes before removing from the heat.

Whisk in the vanilla extract. Let stand for 5 minutes, then whisk in the bits of butter, stirring until they are fully incorporated and the custard is smooth and silky. You can either press a piece of plastic wrap against the surface of the custard to create an airtight seal and refrigerate the custard until cold or, if you want to cool the custard quickly—as I always do—put the bowl into a larger bowl filled with ice cubes and cold water and stir occasionally until the custard is thoroughly chilled, about 20 minutes. (If it's more convenient, you can refrigerate the custard, tightly covered, for up to 3 days.)

When you are ready to assemble the pie, peel the bananas and cut them on a shallow diagonal into ¼-inch-thick slices.

Whisk the cold custard vigorously to loosen it, and spread about one quarter of it over the bottom of the piecrust—it will be a thin layer. Top with half of the banana slices. Repeat, adding a thin layer of pastry cream and the remaining bananas, then smooth the rest of the pastry cream over the last layer of bananas.

TO MAKE THE TOPPING: Working with a stand mixer fitted with the whisk attachment or with a hand mixer in a large bowl, beat the cream until it just starts to thicken. Beat in the confectioners' sugar and vanilla and continue to beat until the cream holds firm peaks. Switch to a rubber spatula and gently fold in the sour cream.

TO FINISH: Spoon the whipped cream over the filling and spread it evenly to the edges of the custard. Serve, or rcfrigerate until needed.

# TOASTED-COCONUT CUSTARD TART

**I'D DESCRIBE** this as a classic, but lots of people who don't like classic coconut custard pies love this tart, which strays from tradition in three ways. For starters, it's a tart not a pie, so the balance between coconut filling and whipped cream topping is different—the filling, usually grabbing the lion's share of a mouthful, goes just about halvsies with the topping. Second, the filling has more flavor than the classic, and it's also got a good hit of dark rum and a pinch of coriander. Finally, the shortbread-like crust adds a little crunch and some buttery goodness: don't make it too thin—you want it to play an important role.

MAKES 6 TO 8 SERVINGS

SERVING: Serve with espresso.

STORING: While the custard can be made in advance, once the tart is assembled, it's best to serve it the same day.

FOR THE CUSTARD

- 2 cups whole milk
- ½ cup sugar
- 6 large egg yolks
- ⅓ cup cornstarch, sifted
- Pinch of salt
- Pinch of ground coriander
- 2 tablespoons dark rum
- 1 teaspoon pure vanilla extract
- 3½ tablespoons cold unsalted butter, cut into small pieces
- 1 cup shredded sweetened coconut, lightly toasted

- 1 9-inch tart shell made with Sweet Tart Dough (page 444), fully baked and cooled

FOR THE TOPPING

- 1 cup very cold heavy cream
- 3 tablespoons confectioners' sugar, sifted
- 1 teaspoon dark rum
- ½ teaspoon pure vanilla extract

- Toasted sweetened shredded coconut (optional)

**TO MAKE THE CUSTARD:** Bring the milk to a boil.

Meanwhile, in a large heavy-bottomed saucepan, whisk the sugar together with the yolks, cornstarch, salt and coriander until well blended and thick. Whisking without stopping, drizzle in about ¼ cup of the hot milk—this will temper, or warm, the yolks so they won't curdle—then, still whisking, add the remainder of the milk in a steady stream. Put the pan over medium heat and, whisking constantly (make sure to get into the edges of the pan), bring the mixture to a boil. Boil, whisking, for 1 to 2 minutes before removing the pan from the heat.

Whisk in the rum and vanilla extract. Let sit for 5 minutes, then whisk in the bits of butter, stirring until they are fully incorporated and the custard is smooth and silky. Finally, stir in the toasted coconut. You can either press a piece of plastic wrap against the surface of the custard to create an airtight seal and refrigerate the custard until cold or, if you want to cool the custard quickly—as I always do— put the bowl into a larger bowl filled with ice cubes and cold water and stir occasionally until the custard is thoroughly chilled, about 20 minutes. (If it's more convenient, you can refrigerate the custard, tightly covered, for up to 3 days.)

To assemble the tart, whisk the cooled custard vigorously to loosen it, then scrape it into the crust.

TO MAKE THE TOPPING: Working with a stand mixer fitted with the whisk attachment or with a hand mixer in a large bowl, whip the cream until it holds medium peaks. Add the confectioners' sugar and beat until the cream holds firm peaks. Whip in the rum and vanilla.

TO ASSEMBLE THE TART: Spoon the whipped cream over the tart and spread it evenly to the edges of the custard. If you'd like, sprinkle the top of the cream with coconut.

# CRUNCHY AND CUSTARDY PEACH TART

A RIPE peach is one of nature's great gifts and, when presented with such a bounty, I'm never sure what to do—savor it immediately or put it in a tart? When I'm grown-up enough to practice a little restraint, I make this tart. The peaches are fanned into a sweet almond crust and surrounded by a simple custard that has just a splash of almond extract, its only flavoring and the one that brings out the nuances of a good peach. Then, just for fun and a bit of crunch, I scatter over a little almond streusel. If summer isn't your favorite time of year, this tart could make you reconsider the season.

MAKES 6 TO 8 SERVINGS

SERVING: I like this tart with nothing more than a dusting of confectioners' sugar, but after all these years of making it, I still can't decide what temperature really shows it off best. It's good when it's only a tad warm, good at room temperature and good cold. My advice: keep eating until you decide.

STORING: The tart can be refrigerated overnight; cover it to protect it from drying and from odors.

FOR THE STREUSEL

2 tablespoons all-purpose flour
2 tablespoons (packed) light brown sugar
2 tablespoons chopped almonds
2 tablespoons cold unsalted butter, cut into pieces

1 9-inch tart crust made with Sweet Tart Dough with Nuts (page 444), partially baked and cooled

FOR THE FILLING

3 large ripe peaches, peeled (see page 367), halved and pitted
½ cup heavy cream
1 large egg
¼ cup sugar
⅛ teaspoon pure almond extract

Confectioners' sugar, for dusting

TO MAKE THE STREUSEL: Working with your fingertips, blend all the ingredients together in a small bowl until evenly combined. Cover the streusel tightly with plastic wrap and refrigerate it until needed. (Wrapped well, the streusel can be refrigerated for up to 2 days.)

GETTING READY TO BAKE: Center a rack in the oven and preheat the oven to 425 degrees F. Place the tart pan on a baking sheet lined with parchment or a silicone mat.

TO MAKE THE TART: Slice 5 of the peach halves crosswise. The best way to do this is to place each peach half cut side down on a cutting board and slice it crosswise into thin slices, keeping the sliced half intact. Then lift each half on a spatula, press down on the half lightly to fan it just a bit and place it in the crust, with the edge of the outer peach slice almost touching the edge of the crust, so you have 5 peach "spokes" and an empty space in the center. Trim the remaining unsliced peach half so it will fit into the center of the tart and, using the tip of your knife, cut a little tic-tac-toe pattern in the center of the peach. Set aside while you make the creamy filling.

Whisk the cream, egg, sugar and almond extract together in a small bowl. When blended, rap the bowl on the counter to knock out the air bubbles, and pour the filling over and around the peaches.

Bake the tart for 10 minutes. Lower the oven temperature to 375 degrees F, and bake the tart for another 20 minutes, at which point you should add the streusel.

Remove the streusel from the refrigerator and, using your fingers, break it up into small bits. Carefully pull the baking sheet to the front of the oven (if you can manage to get the streusel onto the tart without removing the tart from the oven and jostling the delicate filling, so much the better, but pull it out completely if it's easier) and sprinkle the streusel evenly over the creamy parts of the tart.

Bake for another 20 to 25 minutes (total baking time is 50 to 55 minutes), or until the filling is set and the streusel is golden. Remove the tart from the oven and transfer the pan to a rack to cool until barely warm or at room temperature.

Just before serving, dust with confectioners' sugar.

# FOLD-OVER PEAR TORTE

HERE ARE the mechanics of this dessert: a springform pan is lined with pie dough and filled with cut pears, chopped dried apricots and a rich cream, then, before it is slid into the oven, the edges of the dough are folded down. What you end up with is a tall, golden roly-poly dessert that is a happy mix of the rustic and the accomplished.

Because of the pears in the filling, this is a fall-into-winter dessert. Yet when my son first tasted it, he said, "It's so summery." That may have been wishful thinking on his part, since there was snow outside our windows, but I understood what he meant—the fruit is surrounded by a cream and egg custard that's so deeply flavored with vanilla and almond as to produce, almost magically, a warmed-by-the-sun sensation.

MAKES 6 TO 8 SERVINGS

SERVING: Make sure to allow the torte to cool to room temperature before cutting—it needs time to set. Dust the top with the confectioners' sugar before bringing it to the table and slicing it into portions.

STORING: Although you can fit the crust into the pan and keep it covered in the refrigerator for up to 2 days or frozen for up to 2 months, the torte is best eaten the day it is made.

Good for Almost Everything Pie Dough for a single crust (page 442), chilled

FOR THE FILLING
- ⅓ cup all-purpose flour
- ¼ teaspoon baking powder
- Pinch of salt
- 3 large ripe but firm pears
- Squirt of fresh lemon juice (grate the zest first)
- Grated zest of ½ lemon
- ½ cup finely diced moist, plump dried apricots (about 10 Turkish apricots) or an equal amount of moist, plump golden raisins

- ⅓ cup chopped walnuts
- 2 large eggs
- ½ cup sugar
- 1 tablespoon dark rum
- 2 teaspoons pure vanilla extract
- ½ teaspoon pure almond extract
- 2 tablespoons unsalted butter, melted and cooled
- 1 cup heavy cream

Confectioners' sugar, for dusting

Roll the pie dough between sheets of plastic wrap, wax paper or in a rolling slip-cover into a 14-inch round (see page 441 for more details on rolling pastry crust). Slip the dough, still between its wraps, onto a baking sheet and refrigerate for about 20 minutes.

Generously butter an 8-inch springform pan. Remove the dough from the fridge, pull off the top piece of plastic, wax paper or the slipcover and turn the round of dough over onto the springform pan. Now—this can be a bit tricky—gently push the dough down into the pan so that it is flat against the bottom. Begin to press the sides of the dough against the sides of the pan. This is best done by turning the pan on its side and then turning the pan as you work on the dough. The dough will pleat a bit—that's okay—and it might even crack. If it cracks, carefully press the cracks together. Cover and return the pan to the refrigerator while you preheat the oven and make the filling.

GETTING READY TO BAKE: Center a rack in the oven and preheat the oven to 400 degrees F. Line a baking sheet with parchment or a silicone mat.

TO MAKE THE FILLING: Whisk together the flour, baking powder and salt.

Peel and core the pears, then cut them into 1/4-inch cubes. Put them in a bowl and toss with the lemon juice to keep them from darkening. Stir in the zest, apricots and nuts.

Working with a stand mixer, preferably fitted with a paddle attachment, or with a hand mixer in a large bowl, beat the eggs and sugar together on medium-high speed until they thicken, about 3 minutes. Reduce the mixer speed to low and add the rum and the extracts. Still on low, add the dry ingredients, mixing only until they are incorporated. Finally, add the butter, followed by the cream, mixing only until the batter is homogeneous.

Remove the springform pan from the refrigerator and place it on the baking sheet. Spoon the fruit into the pan, then pour in the batter, stopping when you've got about 1/2 to 1 inch of crust extending above the batter. Depending on how thin your crust was rolled, how you fitted it into the pan and/or how much fruit you have, you may have more batter than you've got room for—don't overfill the crust. Using your fingertips, carefully push the crust down over the filling—don't fold the top down, just push it toward the center in a ruffle. There should be space between the filling and the crust; the filling will rise to fill it.

Put the torte in the oven, lower the oven temperature to 350 degrees F and bake for 60 to 70 minutes, or until the crust is beautifully browned and a knife inserted into the custard comes out clean. Peek after 40 minutes and tent the torte loosely with aluminum foil if it looks as if it's getting too brown. Transfer the springform pan to a cooling rack and allow the torte to cool to room temperature.

Run a blunt knife between the cooled torte and the pan, then remove the sides of the pan. Dust with confectioners' sugar just before serving.

# BANANA-COCONUT ICE CREAM PIE

THIS IS a cool pie with warm flavors. The buttery crust is made with coconut and cookies, and the ice cream filling gets its tropical taste from bananas and rum. The flavor is yours to go crazy with—add some chocolate chunks if you'd like, or maybe some rum-flamed raisins (page 92). While the pie's a natural in summer, it's even more fun in winter, when a taste of sunshine is almost as good as the real thing.

MAKES 8 SERVINGS

FOR THE CRUST
- 1 stick (8 tablespoons) unsalted butter
- 2 cups sweetened shredded coconut
- 5 butter cookies, such as LU Petit Beurre or shortbread, crushed into crumbs (about ½ cup)

- 1 ripe but firm banana

FOR THE FILLING
- 2 very ripe bananas
- 2 teaspoons fresh lemon juice
- 2 tablespoons dark rum
- 1 pint premium-quality chocolate ice cream

FOR SERVING
- 1 ripe but firm banana
- 1 teaspoon fresh lemon juice

**SERVING:** Once the top banana is in place, the pie is ready to be served. It can be served plain, but, in keeping with the tropical theme, some sweetened whipped cream would be nice—or even whipped cream flavored with a splash of dark rum.

**STORING:** Without the banana decoration, the pie can be wrapped airtight and frozen for up to 2 months; serve right from the freezer.

*Playing Around*

In addition to whatever add-ins you might want to include, you can also change the flavor of the ice cream. I sometimes make this pie with vanilla ice cream and it's delicious, but then the filling is not a pure color—the bananas have a tendency to turn the ice cream a little dark. This never bothers me.

TO MAKE THE CRUST: Butter a 9-inch deep-dish pie plate.

Melt the butter in a medium heavy skillet over medium heat. Add the coconut and cook, stirring without stopping, until golden brown. Remove the pan from the heat and stir in the cookie crumbs. Turn the mixture into the pie plate and press it over the bottom and up the sides. Freeze for 30 minutes. (If you'd like, once the dough is frozen, you can wrap the pie plate and keep it in the freezer for up to 2 months.)

Cut the firm banana into thin slices and arrange the slices over the crust.

TO MAKE THE FILLING: Cut the bananas into chunks and toss them into a food processor along with the lemon juice and rum. Process until you have a smooth puree, scraping down the bowl as needed, about 20 seconds. Add the ice cream and pulse the machine on and off in quick spurts, scraping down the sides of the bowl as needed, about 8 times, or just until the ingredients are blended—don't process so long that the ice cream melts.

Scrape the ice cream into the piecrust and smooth the top with a rubber spatula. Cover the pie with plastic wrap and freeze it for at least 4 hours. (If you want to keep the pie longer, wrap it airtight and freeze for up to 2 months.)

When you are ready to serve, slice the firm banana into very thin rounds, toss the slices with the lemon juice (to keep them from blackening) and arrange the rounds in decorative circles on top of the pie.

# TARTE NOIRE

**WHILE THIS** is one of the most sophisticated tarts in a Parisian pastry chef's repertoire, it is also the simplest—and the darkest, sleekest and chicest too. It has only two components—a sweet shortbread crust and a slender layer of bittersweet chocolate ganache. Made with fine chocolate (the only kind you should use for a ganache) and served at room temperature, when the texture of the filling resembles the center of a fine bonbon and the contrast between the soft ganache and the butter-rich crust is marked, the tart becomes an exemplar of understated elegance. It is infallibly pâtisserie perfect.

Because the ganache is made with just chocolate, cream and butter, the flavor of whatever chocolate you choose will be the same from the time you chop it into bits to the time you taste it in the tart. For this reason, you should use only chocolate you enjoy eating out of hand. I like to make the tart with Valrhona Manjari or Guittard Sur del Lago, both bittersweet chocolates.

FOR THE FILLING

- 8 ounces bittersweet chocolate, finely chopped
- 1 cup plus 2 tablespoons heavy cream
- ½ stick (4 tablespoons) unsalted butter, cut into 4 pieces, at room temperature
- 1 9-inch tart shell made with Sweet Tart Dough (page 444) or Chocolate Shortbread Tart Dough (page 446), fully baked and cooled

Put the chopped chocolate in a heatproof bowl and have a whisk or a rubber spatula at hand.

Bring the cream to a boil, then pour half of it over the chocolate and let it sit for 30 seconds. Working with the whisk or spatula, very gently stir the chocolate and cream together in small circles, starting at the center of the bowl and working your way out in increasingly larger concentric circles. Pour in the remainder of the cream and blend it into the chocolate, using the same circular motion. When the ganache is smooth and shiny, stir in the butter piece by piece. Don't stir the ganache any more than you must to blend the ingredients—the less you work it, the darker, smoother and shinier it will be. (The ganache can be used now, refrigerated or even frozen for later; see Storing.)

Pour the ganache into the crust and, holding the pan with both hands, gently turn the pan from side to side to even the ganache. Refrigerate the tart for 30 minutes to set the ganache, then remove the tart from the fridge and keep it at room temperature until serving time.

MAKES 8 SERVINGS

**SERVING:** Purists will want to enjoy the tart at room temperature and au naturel. Having gone to pains to use great chocolate for the tart, you might want to show it off solo. However, like all good things chocolate, the tart is lovely with just a little lightly whipped very sparingly sweetened cream. I wouldn't serve this with ice cream—the contrast between the thick room-temperature filling and the frozen ice cream would be too jarring.

**STORING:** The tart should be served the day it is made. However, the ganache can be made ahead and kept in the refrigerator for up to 2 days. When you are ready to use it, allow it to come to room temperature, then heat it gently in a microwave oven, using 5-second spurts of heat and checking on its progress vigilantly, until it is pourable. Or you can put the bowl of ganache in a larger bowl of hot water and stir every 10 seconds until it can be poured. You can even freeze the ganache, tightly covered, for up to 2 months. Thaw it overnight in the refrigerator, bring it to room temperature and then warm it in a microwave oven or bowl of hot water until it is pourable.

# CHOCOLATE CREAM TART

........................................................................................................

MAKES 8 SERVINGS

**EXCEPT THAT** it's made with the best bittersweet chocolate I can lay my hands on and baked in a dark chocolate shortbread crust, this tart's next of kin is the chocolate cream pie of roadside diners. In my rendition, the cream (made from my favorite French recipe for pastry cream) is thick, dark and velvety; the whipped cream is only lightly sweetened and the share of chocolate shavings is more generous than any greasy spoon would offer. In its simple cloak of black and white, the tart reminds me of an early Christian Dior creation.

**SERVING:** I like to serve this tart on its own and chase it with espresso or cold milk.

**STORING:** Although you can bake the tart crust and make the chocolate cream ahead, and you can even refrigerate the cream-filled tart for up to 6 hours, once the tart has its whipped cream crown, it's best to serve it within 2 hours.

### FOR THE FILLING
- 2 cups whole milk
- 4 large egg yolks
- 6 tablespoons sugar
- 3 tablespoons cornstarch, sifted
- ¼ teaspoon salt
- 7 ounces bittersweet chocolate, melted
- 2½ tablespoons unsalted butter, cut into pieces, at room temperature

- 1 9-inch Chocolate Shortbread Tart Dough (page 446), fully baked and cooled

### FOR THE TOPPING
- ½ cup cold heavy cream
- 1½ tablespoons confectioners' sugar, sifted
- ¼ teaspoon pure vanilla extract

  Chocolate shavings or curls (page 471), for decoration or cocoa powder, for dusting

TO MAKE THE FILLING: Bring the milk to a boil.

Meanwhile, in a large heavy-bottomed saucepan, whisk the yolks together with the sugar, cornstarch and salt until well blended and thick. Whisking without stopping, drizzle in about ¼ cup of the hot milk—this will temper, or warm, the yolks so they won't curdle—then, still whisking, add the remainder of the milk in a steady stream. Put the pan over medium heat and, whisking constantly (make sure to get into the edges of the pan), bring the mixture to a boil. Keep at a boil, still whisking, for 1 to 2 minutes, then remove the pan from the heat.

Whisk in the melted chocolate. Let sit for 5 minutes, then whisk in the bits of butter, stirring until they are fully incorporated and the custard is smooth and silky. You can press a piece of plastic wrap against the surface of the custard to create an airtight seal and refrigerate the custard or, if you want to cool the custard quickly—as I always do—put the bowl into a larger bowl filled with ice cubes and cold water and stir the custard occasionally until it is thoroughly chilled, about 20 minutes. (If it's more convenient, you can keep the custard, tightly covered, in the refrigerator for up to 3 days.)

When you are ready to assemble the tart, whisk the chocolate cream vigorously to loosen it and to bring back its velvety texture. Spoon the cream into the tart shell, stopping just short of the crust's rim (you may have some left over)—you want to leave room for the topping. Smooth the top and, if you are not serving the tart immediately, press a piece of plastic wrap against the cream and refrigerate the tart until needed (or for up to 6 hours).

TO MAKE THE TOPPING: Working with a stand mixer fitted with the whisk attachment or with a hand mixer in a large bowl, beat the cream until it just starts to thicken. Beat in the confectioners' sugar and vanilla and continue to beat until the cream holds firm peaks.

Spread the whipped cream over the tart and smooth it with a metal icing spatula or, if you prefer swirls, go for them. Serve the tart now or refrigerate it for up to 2 hours before serving. When you are ready to serve the tart, scatter chocolate shavings or curls over the top or, if you'd prefer, lightly dust the top with cocoa powder.

*Playing Around*

CHOCOLATE COCONUT CREAM PIE: By mixing and matching a few of the elements, you can have an almost completely different dessert. Trade in the chocolate tart shell for a fully baked 9-inch pie shell made with Good for Almost Everything Pie Dough (page 442). Before you fill the shell with chocolate cream, add a layer of coconut cream: To make the coconut layer, put 1⅓ cups heavy cream and 1 cup sweetened shredded coconut in a small saucepan and bring to a boil over medium-low heat, stirring almost constantly. Continue to cook and stir until the cream is reduced by half and the mixture is slightly thickened. Scrape the coconut cream into a bowl and cool to room temperature before spreading it over the bottom of the crust and covering it with the chocolate cream. For the topping, whip 1 cup heavy cream with 3 tablespoons confectioners' sugar, 1 tablespoon dark rum (optional) and 1 teaspoon pure vanilla extract. Swirl it over the top of the pie and cover the whipped cream with toasted coconut or with chocolate shavings, or a combination of the two.

# SOFT CHOCOLATE AND RASPBERRY TART

**AFTER THIS** tart has baked and cooled just a little, the chocolate filling takes on the lovable characteristics of pudding, becoming soft and creamy and seductively slithery, and the flavor of the berries intensifies. I use a mixture of dark and milk chocolates because I think a milder blend is better with berries. If you prefer, you can make it with all dark chocolate; using all milk chocolate would set the balance askew.

MAKES 8 SERVINGS

3 ounces bittersweet chocolate, finely chopped

2 ounces premium-quality milk chocolate, finely chopped

½ cup heavy cream

½ stick (4 tablespoons) unsalted butter, cut into 4 pieces

2½ tablespoons sugar

2 large eggs, at room temperature

1 large egg yolk, at room temperature

1 cup (a 6-ounce container) fresh raspberries

1 9-inch tart shell made with Sweet Tart Dough with Nuts (page 444), fully baked and cooled

**SERVING:** There are some people who like this tart ever so slightly warm, but the flavor and texture don't really come into their own until the tart is cooled to room temperature. Serve it cold and it will lose its lovely creaminess. Whatever temperature ends up being your favorite, do serve the tart with whipped cream or crème fraîche.

**STORING:** This tart is best served the day it is made. In fact, it's really best just a few hours out of the oven, if you can swing that.

**GETTING READY:** Center a rack in the oven and preheat the oven to 300 degrees F. Put the tart pan on a baking sheet lined with parchment or a silicone mat.

Set a heatproof bowl over a pan of gently simmering water, add the bittersweet and milk chocolates and heat, stirring occasionally, until they are melted. Remove the bowl from the heat.

Meanwhile, bring the cream and butter just to a boil.

Pour the cream-butter mixture over the chocolate and let it stand for 30 seconds. Working with a whisk or a rubber spatula, gently stir the liquid into the chocolate—start stirring in the center of the bowl and work your way out in ever-widening circles. When the mixture is smooth, stir in the sugar, then the eggs and finally the yolk. Rap the bowl against the counter to break any bubbles that might have formed.

Scatter the berries over the bottom of the crust, then pour the chocolate ganache over them.

Bake the tart for about 30 minutes—the filling should not jiggle if you tap the pan and a knife inserted into the center of the tart should come out a little streaky. Transfer the tart pan to a rack and cool to room temperature before serving.

*Playing Around*

Try the tart with blackberries or blueberries, but not with strawberries—they're too watery. The tart is also good with cherries, either fresh cherries or bottled small cherries packed in heavy syrup. I like to use slightly sour *griottes* (French cherries) or *amarene* (Italian cherries). Both are available at specialty stores. If you use cherries in syrup, drain them and pat dry before use.

# CHOCOLATE-CRUNCHED CARAMEL TART

A MIX of posh and pop (okay, the balance tips toward posh), this bittersweet chocolate ganache tart has a hidden layer of creamy, soft caramel full of honey-roasted peanuts straight from the supermarket shelf. As plebian as the nuts may be, they add just the right amount of sugar and salt to the caramel and just enough crackle and crunch to keep this very polished tart from taking itself too seriously.

I'm a fan of Trader Joe's honey-roasted peanuts, but Planters are fine too. Also, if you'd prefer, you can stud the caramel with plain roasted peanuts (the caramel will be a little saltier—if you like, you can rub off some of the salt on the nuts before chopping them), toasted walnuts, toasted pecans or, for a very European take on the tart, toasted and skinned hazelnuts.

MAKES 8 SERVINGS

SERVING: The tart should be served at room temperature so that the caramel is soft and stretchy and the chocolate is luxuriously smooth and ready to melt instantly on your tongue.

STORING: While the tart should be served the day it is made, the ganache can be made ahead and refrigerated for up to 2 days. When you are ready to use it, allow it to come to room temperature, then heat it gently in a microwave oven, using 5-second spurts of heat and checking on its progress vigilantly, until it is pourable. You can even freeze the ganache, tightly covered, for up to 2 months. Thaw it overnight in the refrigerator, bring it to room temperature and then warm it in a microwave oven or over a bowl of hot water until it is pourable.

### FOR THE CARAMEL

Scant ½ cup heavy cream
½ cup sugar, sifted
1 tablespoon light corn syrup
2 tablespoons salted butter, cut into 4 pieces, at room temperature
Pinch of salt if you are not using salted butter

### FOR THE GANACHE

8 ounces bittersweet chocolate, finely chopped
1 cup plus 2 tablespoons heavy cream
½ stick (4 tablespoons) unsalted butter, cut into 4 pieces, at room temperature
¾ cup honey-roasted peanuts, coarsely chopped (see above for other choices)
1 9-inch tart shell made with Sweet Tart Dough (page 444), fully baked and cooled

GETTING READY: Because you have to work quickly once the sugar caramelizes, you should have all the ingredients for the caramel measured out and at hand before you start. Also have a medium heatproof bowl at hand to hold the hot caramel.

TO MAKE THE CARAMEL: Bring the heavy cream to a boil.

Meanwhile, put a medium skillet, preferably nonstick, over medium heat and sprinkle in about 3 tablespoons of the sugar. When it melts, stir it with a wooden spatula or a fork and sprinkle over another 3 tablespoons. When that sugar is melted, add the remaining 2 tablespoons sugar—the sugar in the pan may already have started to color, and that's fine. Stir in the corn syrup and boil the syrup until it reaches a deep caramel color—it will probably begin to smoke, and that's normal.

Stand back from the skillet and stir in the butter and salt, if you're using it. The caramel will bubble furiously and may spatter, so make sure you're away from the action. When the butter is in, add the warm cream—the caramel will bubble furiously again. Lower the temperature just a tad and let the caramel boil for just

2 minutes. (If you want to check on a thermometer, the caramel should be at 226 degrees F.)

Pour the seething caramel into the heatproof bowl and set it aside while you make the ganache.

TO MAKE THE GANACHE: Put the chopped chocolate in a heatproof bowl and have a whisk or a rubber spatula at hand.

Bring the cream to a boil, then pour half of it over the chocolate and let it sit for 30 seconds. Working with the whisk or spatula, very gently stir the chocolate and cream together in small circles, starting at the center of the bowl and working your way out in increasingly larger concentric circles. Pour in the remainder of the cream and blend it into the chocolate, using the same circular motion. When the ganache is smooth and shiny, stir in the butter piece by piece. Don't stir the ganache any more than you must to blend the ingredients—the less you work it, the darker, smoother and shinier it will be.

Cover the ganache with a piece of plastic wrap, pressing the plastic against the surface of the chocolate to create an airtight seal. Set aside at room temperature for the moment. (If it's more convenient, the ganache can be refrigerated or even frozen for future use; see Storing.)

TO ASSEMBLE THE TART: Using a small rubber spatula, stir the peanuts into the caramel. If the caramel has cooled and is too thick to spread easily, gently warm it in a microwave oven using 3-second heat spurts. (Or you can just hold the heatproof bowl about 10 inches above the burner on your range—keep it over the heat for a couple of seconds, then check the caramel's consistency and repeat if necessary.)

Spread the caramel over the bottom of the tart shell; you'll have a thin layer. Refrigerate the tart for 15 minutes to set the caramel.

Check the ganache. If it has thickened and is no longer pourable, warm it in 3-second spurts in a microwave oven or over direct heat (see the hints for warming caramel, above). Rap the bowl to break any surface bubbles, pour the ganache over the caramel and jiggle the tart pan to even it.

Refrigerate the tart for 30 minutes—no longer—then keep it at room temperature until serving time.

# COFFEE ICE CREAM TART

**THIS TART** can't help it if it has an undemanding nature: it's the quintessential convenience food, yet it's every bit as wonderful as its more time-consuming, fussy relatives. Composed of an easy press-in almond crust and a filling of tweaked store-bought ice cream, it's fail-proof and incredibly patient—it will stay in the freezer for months, making it a sure bet that on the day that you're desperate for a dessert but don't have a second to spare you'll be rewarded with a double joy: a tart that pleases everyone and the feeling of having triumphed when the odds were against you.

MAKES 8 SERVINGS

SERVING: The tart is more than fine just the way it is, but it's also delicious with a little chocolate sauce (pages 463 and 464).

STORING: Once the chocolate decoration is set, the tart can be wrapped airtight and kept in the freezer for up to 2 months.

### FOR THE CRUST

- 1 cup (4 ounces) toasted slivered or sliced blanched almonds
- ¾ cup all-purpose flour
- ⅓ cup (packed) light brown sugar
- ½ teaspoon freshly grated nutmeg
  Pinch of salt
- ½ stick (4 tablespoons) cold unsalted butter, cut into 4 pieces
- 1 large egg
- ¼ teaspoon pure almond extract
- 2 ounces bittersweet chocolate, finely chopped

### FOR THE FILLING

- 1 cup (4 ounces) toasted slivered or sliced blanched almonds
- 1 quart premium-quality coffee ice cream
- ½ teaspoon pure almond extract or 1 tablespoon amaretto
  Pinch of freshly grated nutmeg

- 2 ounces bittersweet chocolate, chopped, for decoration

*Playing Around*

You can fill the tart with chocolate or vanilla ice cream if you'd like, giving it the same almond treatment, or not, or you can make it really summery and fill it with a berry or peach ice cream (see pages 434 and 437 for some ideas). You can replace the almonds with hazelnuts (in that case, use the almond extract) or peanuts (skip the almond extract or amaretto). It's a recipe that lends itself to variations without end.

**TO MAKE THE CRUST:** Lightly butter a 10- or 11-inch fluted tart pan and line a baking sheet with parchment or a silicone mat.

Put the almonds, flour, sugar, nutmeg and salt in a food processor and pulse for about 10 seconds, or until the nuts are coarsely chopped. Toss in the pieces of butter and pulse until the dough resembles coarse meal. Add the egg and extract and continue to pulse until the dough forms clumps and large curds, about 10 seconds. Turn the dough out into the tart pan and wipe out the processor. (You'll use it for the filling.)

Press the dough evenly over the bottom and up the sides of the tart pan. Freeze for 30 minutes. (If you'd like, once the dough is frozen, you can wrap the tart pan and keep it in the freezer for up to 2 months.)

**GETTING READY TO BAKE:** Center a rack in the oven and preheat the oven to 400 degrees F.

Butter a piece of aluminum foil and press it, buttered side down, snugly into the tart pan; put the tart pan on the baking sheet. Bake the shell for 20 minutes, then remove the foil. If the crust has puffed, press it down with the back of a fork. Bake the crust for another 8 minutes or so, or until it is firm and golden. Transfer the pan to a cooling rack.

Scatter the chopped chocolate over the bottom of the hot crust and use a small icing spatula (or a pastry brush) to spread it even. Cool the crust to room temperature.

**TO MAKE THE FILLING:** Put the almonds in the processor and pulse and process until they form a paste, a minute or two. Add the ice cream, extract or amaretto and the nutmeg and pulse the machine on and off in quick spurts, scraping down the sides of the bowl as needed, about 8 times, or until the ingredients are just blended—don't process so long that the ice cream melts. Scrape the ice cream into the tart shell and smooth the top. Put the tart in the freezer for at least 30 minutes.

**TO DECORATE THE TART:** Melt the chocolate in a microwave oven or in a bowl over a pan of hot water. If you like, put the chocolate in a small piping bag fitted with a very small plain tip (the kind used for writing) and pipe a lattice or a series of zig-zags across the top of the tart. Or, for a more abstract look, dip the tines of a fork into the chocolate and drizzle the chocolate free-form.

Slide the tart into the freezer to set the chocolate, about 5 minutes, then cover and freeze for at least 4 hours.

# FRUIT PIES
# AND TARTS

FRUIT AND DOUGH are the proverbial marriage made in heaven, their compatibility so complete it's hard to conjure up a combination that doesn't produce a smile and the desire for a second helping.

At its most basic, a fruit pie or tart is just fruit and dough, give or take some sugar, spice or maybe a little butter. Part of what is so enormously attractive about these pastries is their variability: with most of the recipes, you can change the fruit with the seasons. When summer rolls around, I make a point of keeping crusts in the freezer so that I can produce pies and tarts at a moment's notice. I roll out the dough, fit it into the pan and freeze it, then wrap it airtight. When it's time, I bake the crust directly from the freezer, no defrosting necessary.

Each of the three doughs that form the base of the pies and tarts in this section produces a perfect crust, whether you're a pro or a first-timer. Because putting together and rolling out pie dough can be intimidating for the neophyte—it certainly was for me when I started making pies—I wanted to create a great-tasting dough that is easy to prepare and a snap to roll. I worked on my Good for Almost Everything Pie Dough for many years, tweaking and toying with it until I got what I wanted. The dough is quickly made in a food processor, and I use it for everything from single- and double-crusted pies to rustic free-form galettes.

With a sweet, rich buttery flavor and the texture of a shortbread cookie, the Sweet Tart Dough makes the quintessential crust for fruit tarts. Amazingly, it's both foolproof and just about technique-free: it too is made in a food processor. But keep in mind that the dough needs to be well chilled, preferably frozen, before it is baked and it is best when it is fully baked—don't remove it from the oven until it is golden brown.

The easiest of all doughs is store-bought puff pastry, which welcomes fruit, encourages innovation and rises to startling heights in the oven. While you can turn puff pastry into a pie or tart shell, its lightness, butteriness and eponymous puff are shown to their greatest advantage when you use the dough free-style. Roll out a piece, arrange some fruit over it, dot with butter, sprinkle with sugar and slide it into the oven.

# DOUBLE-CRUSTED BLUEBERRY PIE

**HERE'S A** classic summer treat, one that always reminds my husband of the trip he made to the bakery for his mom when he was eight years old. His mission was to buy a blueberry pie (his favorite) and to bring it home so it could be served after supper. He went to the bakery (Ebinger's) and watched as the counterwoman in her white apron and little white cap put the pie in a cardboard box, then tied it up with a length of red-and-white string she pulled from a huge spool and cut with a little snipper, which all the servers wore as pinkie rings.

Balancing the pie on the palms of his hands, Michael headed home, walking slowly and taking good care of his delicious package. And then he stumbled, and when he did, the box took a spin and landed bottom up. What was a kid to do? Being resourceful, Michael did what anyone would have done; he opened the box, righted the pie and ate all the blueberries. Then he slipped the string back around the box and finished his walk home. Whenever I think of the mishap, it's easy for me to imagine Michael sitting cross-legged on the sidewalk, scooping up filling, licking his fingers and being sorry he had had the little accident, but letting nothing about it detract from the pleasure of eating blueberry pie on a warm afternoon.

This pie is good enough to make lasting memories, with or without any accompanying drama. Its filling is full-flavored and juicy without being thin, and the bottom crust is prevented from turning soggy by a layer of dry bread crumbs. I bet you'll make it over and over during berry season.

MAKES 6 TO 8 SERVINGS

**SERVING:** The ideal way to serve this pie is at room temperature, but some pie people like it warm and some like it chilled. Everyone seems to like it with ice cream. Vanilla's the classic, but it's luscious with Blueberry–Sour Cream Ice Cream (page 434) or Unbelievably Good Chocolate Blueberry Ice Cream (page 433).

**STORING:** The pie is best served the day it is made, but it can be wrapped lightly and refrigerated, then served chilled or reheated (put it in a 350-degree-F oven for about 20 minutes).

*Playing Around*

If you're lucky enough to have an herb garden, think about adding some finely chopped or thinly shredded lemon verbena or peppermint leaves to the filling. A scant tablespoonful is just enough to give a little extra flavor to the mix.

|  |  |
|---|---|
| Good for Almost Everything Pie Dough for a double crust (page 442), chilled | Squirt of fresh lemon juice, or a little more, to taste |
| 2½ pints fresh blueberries | ¼ cup dry bread crumbs (you can use packaged unseasoned crumbs) |
| 1 cup sugar, or a little more, to taste, plus more for dusting |  |
| ½ cup all-purpose flour | 1 large egg, beaten with 1 teaspoon water, for egg wash |
| Pinch of salt | Sugar, for dusting |
| Coarsely grated zest of ½ lemon |  |

**GETTING READY:** Butter a 9-inch pie plate (I use a standard Pyrex pie plate).

Working on a well-floured surface (or between wax paper or plastic wrap), roll out one piece of the dough to a thickness of about ⅛ inch (see page 441 for more details on rolling pastry crust). Fit the dough into the buttered pie plate and trim the edges to a ½-inch overhang. Roll the other piece of dough into a ⅛-inch-thick circle and place it on a baking sheet lined with parchment or a silicone mat. Cover both the circle and the pie plate with plastic wrap and refrigerate while you preheat the oven and prepare the filling.

**GETTING READY TO BAKE:** Position a rack in the lower third of the oven and preheat the oven to 425 degrees F.

Put the berries in a large bowl and gently stir in the sugar, flour, salt, zest and juice; let sit for about 5 minutes. Taste the filling and add more sugar and/or lemon juice, if needed.

Remove the pie shell and top crust from the refrigerator. Sprinkle an even layer of the bread crumbs over the bottom of the shell. Give the filling a last stir and turn it into the crust.

Using your fingertips, moisten the rim of the bottom crust with a little cold water. Center the top crust over the filling and gently press the top crust against the bottom. Either fold the overhang from the top crust under the bottom crust and crimp the edges attractively or press the top crust against the bottom crust and trim the overhang from both crusts even with the rim of the pie plate. If you've pressed and trimmed the crust, use the tines of a fork to press the two crusts together securely. Using a small sharp knife, cut 4 slits in the top crust and cut a circle out of the center, then lift the plate onto the baking sheet. (If you have time, refrigerate the pie for about 30 minutes. The pie can also be wrapped airtight and frozen for up to 2 months. Glaze and sugar it before you put it in the oven and add at least 15 minutes to the baking time.)

Brush the top crust with the egg wash, then sprinkle the crust with a little sugar—just to give it sparkle.

Bake the pie for 30 minutes. Reduce the oven temperature to 375 degrees F, and bake the pie for another 30 minutes or so (total baking time is about 1 hour), or until the crust is a beautiful golden brown and the filling is bubbling up through the slits. If the crust seems to be browning too quickly, make a loose foil tent for the pie.

Transfer the pie to a rack and let it cool—and settle—for at least 30 minutes before serving.

# CRANBERRY LIME GALETTE

**BY ITS** very nature, a galette is rustic and not meant to be perfect. It's a round of pie dough folded over the edges of a filling, and what makes it so charming are its pleats, bends and wrinkles. The glistening cranberry filling in this galette is gorgeous and luscious. It's a mix of tart, spicy cranberries, ginger and lime and soft, mellow brown sugar, apples and raspberry jam, and it teeter-totters delightfully between sweet and puckery. On the practical side, the galette is both festive enough to serve at a dinner party and easy enough to make for a weekday meal (and, as beautiful as it is, it can be made ahead, frozen and baked on demand). I created it for a Thanksgiving dinner, fell in love with it and serve it all through the fall and winter.

I find it unwieldy to make the galette any larger than about 9 inches in diameter. If you've got more than six people around the table, double the recipe and make two galettes.

MAKES 6 SERVINGS

**SERVING:** The galette is so beautiful that it should be brought to the table uncut, but before you present it, give it its dusting of confectioners' sugar. While this is good with ice cream or sweetened whipped cream, it is outstanding with White Chocolate Whipped Cream (page 458).

**STORING:** The galette is best served the day it is made, preferably shortly after it has come from the oven. If it has had to wait, you can reheat it for 10 minutes in a 350-degree-F oven.

|  |  |
|---|---|
| Good for Almost Everything Pie Dough for a single crust (page 442), chilled | ⅓ cup moist, plump dried cranberries (optional) |
| 3 tablespoons ground nuts (walnuts, almonds, pecans or skinned hazelnuts) | ¾ cup (packed) light brown sugar |
| | A 1½-inch piece of fresh ginger, peeled and finely chopped |
| 3 tablespoons dry bread crumbs (store-bought unseasoned crumbs are fine) | Grated zest of 1 lime |
| | Juice of ½ lime |
| | 3 tablespoons raspberry jam or jelly |
| 2 cups cranberries, fresh or frozen (if frozen, thaw and pat dry) | Decorating (coarse) or granulated sugar, for dusting |
| 1 medium apple, peeled, cored and cut into ½-inch chunks | Confectioners' sugar, for dusting |

*Playing Around*

**CRANBERRY ORANGE GALETTE:** If you'd like a filling that's a little less edgy but no less enticing, replace the lime zest and juice with orange zest and juice (use the zest from ½ orange and 1 to 2 tablespoons juice) and replace the raspberry jam with good-quality orange marmalade.

**GETTING READY:** Center a rack in the oven and preheat the oven to 400 degrees F. Line a baking sheet with parchment (see below) or a silicone mat.

To make it easier to move the pie dough onto the baking sheet, roll it between sheets of parchment (in which case, you can use one of the rolling sheets to line the baking sheet) or wax paper or plastic wrap. Alternatively, work on a well-floured surface, taking care to keep the dough moving by turning it and flouring the surface often.

Roll the dough into a large ⅛-inch-thick circle. Using a pastry wheel or a paring knife, trim the dough to a 13-inch diameter. Transfer the dough to the baking sheet and keep it covered in the refrigerator while you make the filling.

Mix together the nuts and bread crumbs.

Toss together all the remaining ingredients (except the decorating and confectioners' sugars for dusting) in a bowl, stirring just to mix.

Remove the crust from the refrigerator. Using a cake pan or pot lid as a template and the tip of a blunt kitchen knife as a marker, gently trace a 9-inch circle in

the center of the dough—this is the area for the filling. Sprinkle the center circle with the nut and crumb mixture and top with the filling. Now gently lift the unfilled border of dough up and onto the filling: as you lift the dough and place it on the filling, it will pleat. Brush the dough very lightly with a little water, then sprinkle it with a teaspoon or two of decorating or granulated sugar.

Bake the galette for 35 to 40 minutes, or until the crust is brown, the cranberries have popped and the filling is bubbling. Place the baking sheet on a rack to cool for 10 minutes.

Very carefully slide a small baking sheet or a cake lifter under the galette and slip the galette onto a rack to cool. Serve the galette when it is just warm or when it has reached room temperature, lightly dusted with confectioners' sugar.

# SUMMER FRUIT GALETTE

**MAKES 6 SERVINGS**

**I MADE** this galette for the first time when I had a basket of ripe apricots on the counter. Because just having the ripe apricots was a treat (their season is fleeting), I started building them a minimalist home. It began with a circle of soft, flaky pie dough. I was about to lay the apricots directly on the dough when I thought I should have a little something to absorb the abundance of juice from the fruit. So I brushed the dough with a little jam and added graham cracker crumbs. After the fruit had baked through to tender, the galette looked a little ragged, which is how my minimalist structure got one last addition, some quickly stirred up custard.

Having made something so easy and so terrific, I soon found other fruits and jams to tuck into the same crust—peaches and plums and rhubarb too.

Think of this recipe as a base from which you can work, but, depending on the juiciness and size of your fruit, you'll have to decide on how much or how little of the crumbs and custard you'll need. That's what happens when Mother Nature is your baking partner.

What flavor of jam you use depends on what you like and what you think will go with the fruit you choose. My favorite with apricots, peaches, plums, berries, pears or apples is ginger preserves, a kind of marmalade found in most supermarkets.

**SERVING:** The galette tempts you to top each wedge with something creamy—whipped cream, crème fraîche, vanilla ice cream, even a little Greek yogurt, but I usually resist that temptation and serve it with nothing more than the sprinkling of confectioners' sugar.

**STORING:** Enjoy the galette the day it is made, preferably within hours of baking it.

Good for Almost Everything Pie Dough for a single crust (page 442), chilled

2–3 tablespoons jam or marmalade (see above)

About 2 tablespoons graham cracker crumbs

Fresh summer fruit: about 10 apricots, 8 to 10 nectarines, 8 ripe but firm peaches, 8 to 10 firm plums or 2 stalks rhubarb

Decorating (coarse) or granulated sugar, for dusting

**FOR THE CUSTARD**

3 tablespoons unsalted butter, melted and cooled

⅓ cup sugar

1 large egg

¼ teaspoon pure vanilla extract

Confectioners' sugar, for dusting

**GETTING READY:** Center a rack in the oven and preheat the oven to 425 degrees F. Line a baking sheet with parchment (see below) or a silicone mat.

To make it easier to move the pie dough onto the baking sheet, roll the dough between sheets of parchment paper (in which case, you can use one of the rolling sheets to line the baking sheet) or wax paper or plastic wrap. Alternatively, work on a well-floured surface, taking care to keep the dough moving by turning it and flouring the surface often.

Roll the dough into a large ⅛-inch-thick circle. Using a pastry wheel or a paring knife, trim the dough to a 13-inch diameter. Using a cake pan or a pot lid as a template and the tip of a blunt kitchen knife as a marker, lightly trace a 9-inch circle in the center of the dough—this is the area for the filling.

With the back of a spoon or a small offset spatula, spread some of the jam over the circle—how much you use will depend on how much jam flavor you want. Sprinkle over the crumbs, adding a little more than 2 tablespoons if you think you've got particularly juicy fruit. Put a piece of plastic wrap or wax paper over the dough and refrigerate it while you prepare the fruit.

Wipe the apricots, nectarines or plums clean with a damp towel and cut in half; discard the pits. Blanch peaches for 10 seconds in a pot of boiling water, transfer them to a bowl of ice water to cool, then slip off the skins. Halve and pit the peaches or peel rhubarb to remove the strings, and cut into 1- to 2-inch pieces.

Arrange the fruit on the dough, cut side down if using stone fruits, then gently lift the unfilled border of dough up and onto the filling. As you lift the dough and place it on the filling, it will pleat. If you're not in a rush, freeze the galette for 15 minutes to give the crust a rest.

Brush the dough very lightly with a little water, then sprinkle it with a teaspoon or two of sugar. Bake the galette for 25 minutes, or until the crust is brown and the fruit soft.

MEANWHILE, MAKE THE CUSTARD: Whisk together the melted butter, sugar, egg and vanilla in a bowl; set aside until needed.

Remove the baking sheet from the oven (leave the oven on), and carefully pour the custard around the fruit. Depending on how much juice has accumulated and how much space you have between the fruit, you may not be able to pour all the custard into the galette, but even 2 tablespoons can give the right effect. Pour in as much custard as you can, then carefully return the pan to the oven.

Bake for another 12 to 15 minutes, or until the custard is set—it shouldn't jiggle when you gently shake the pan. Cool the galette on the baking sheet on a rack for 10 minutes.

Very carefully slide a small baking sheet or a cake lifter under the galette and slip the galette onto a rack to cool. The galette can be served when it is just warm or—my preference—when it has reached room temperature. Dust with confectioners' sugar just before serving.

# FRENCH PEAR TART

........................................................................................................................

**A VERY** simple tart, composed of an almond-and-butter crust and a few pears, this one has been a classic in our home ever since I was taught to make it more than twenty years ago.

My husband and I had eaten pear tarts like this every chance we got in France. The pears were always thinly sliced, fanned out and arranged like spokes in the crust, and the almond cream was always golden brown, puffed and cushiony around the pears. I was elated to discover how easy the tart was to reproduce, although I was astonished to learn that it was usually made with canned pears! My source for this bit of information was my pastry teacher, a Frenchman who had worked in the palaces of haute cuisine in Paris and was at the time of my class the executive pastry chef in a French restaurant that had received the *New York Times*'s highest rating.

Over the years, I did a little sleuthing and discovered that indeed canned pears were the fruit of choice. And you know what? They're a fine choice—pears take very well to canning in syrup. But fresh pears—if they're ripe—are a step up, and fresh pears poached in a little sugar syrup are even better. I know, because I make this tart all three ways, depending on how much time I have, and it is always good and always very special.

**MAKES 6 SERVINGS**

**SERVING:** This tart goes very well with aromatic tea.

**STORING:** Although you can make the almond cream and poach the pears ahead, once you've baked the tart, you should serve it the same day.

*Playing Around*

The almond cream is a great companion for a variety of fruits. It's as good with summer fruits like apricots or peaches as it is with autumn's apples. I have a soft spot for this tart made with plums. For a treat, use the wine-steeped dried prunes and fresh Italian prune plums from the Puffed Double Plum Tart (page 378).

**FOR THE PEARS**

6 canned pear halves, drained, or 3 ripe but firm medium pears, such as Bartlett or Anjou

**FOR POACHING THE FRESH PEARS (OPTIONAL)**

4 cups water

1¼ cups sugar

Juice of 1 lemon

Fresh lemon juice (if using unpoached fresh pears)

**FOR THE ALMOND CREAM**

¾ stick (6 tablespoons) unsalted butter, at room temperature

⅔ cup sugar

¾ cup ground blanched almonds

2 teaspoons all-purpose flour

1 teaspoon cornstarch

1 large egg

2 teaspoons dark rum or 1 teaspoon pure vanilla extract

1 9-inch tart shell made with Sweet Tart Dough (page 444) or Sweet Tart Dough with Nuts (page 444), partially baked and cooled

Confectioners' sugar, for dusting, or ¼ cup apple jelly mixed with ½ teaspoon water, for glazing

**TO POACH THE FRESH PEARS:** Peel the pears and leave them whole. Bring the water, sugar and lemon juice to a boil in a saucepan just large enough to hold the pears. Add the pears to the boiling syrup, lower the heat so the syrup simmers and gently poach the pears until they are tender when pierced with a knife, about 15 minutes.

Cool the pears to room temperature in the syrup. When you are ready to use the pears, discard the syrup. (If you want, you can refrigerate the syrup for up to 1 week and use it to poach another batch of pears.)

TO MAKE THE ALMOND CREAM: Put the butter and sugar in a food processor and process until the mixture is smooth and satiny. Add the ground almonds and process until well blended. Add the flour and cornstarch and process to blend, then add the egg. Process for about 15 seconds more, or until the almond cream is homogeneous. Add the rum and process just to blend. (If you prefer, you can make the cream with a mixer fitted with the whisk attachment or in a large bowl with a hand mixer.) You can either use the almond cream immediately or scrape it into a container and refrigerate it until firm, about 2 hours. (The cream can be refrigerated for up to 2 days or packed airtight and frozen for up to 2 months; defrost before using.)

GETTING READY TO BAKE: Center a rack in the oven and preheat the oven to 350 degrees F. Line a baking sheet with parchment or a silicone mat.

If you are using unpoached fresh pears, peel them now. Cut the poached or unpoached fresh pears in half from blossom to stem and core them. Rub the unpoached pears with lemon juice. Pat the fresh or canned pears dry so that their liquid won't keep the almond cream from setting.

Fill the baked crust with the almond cream, spreading it evenly with an offset metal icing spatula. Thinly slice each pear half crosswise. Lift each half on a spatula, press down on the pear to fan it slightly and place it over the almond cream, wide end toward the edge of the crust. The 6 halves will form spokes. Put the tart pan on the baking sheet.

Bake the tart for 50 to 60 minutes, or until the almond cream puffs up around the pears and browns. Transfer the tart to a rack to cool to just warm or to room temperature before removing the sides of the pan.

Right before serving, dust the tart with confectioners' sugar or warm the apple jelly with the water and brush this glaze over the surface of the tart.

# ROSY POACHED PEAR AND PISTACHIO TART

**PUT THIS** tart in the middle of your table, and you won't need any other decoration. Because the pears that form the tart's crown have been gently poached in spiced red wine, then sliced, they are rosy red at the edges and ivory in the center. Underneath the pears is a pale green pastry cream that gets both its flavor and its color from pistachio nuts. The pairing is as seductive as the look is alluring. And there's a little flavor bonus—if you save the pears' poaching syrup and boil it down with a bit of honey, you'll have a wonderful syrup to drizzle over each slice of tart. I often serve it to cap special meals or holiday dinners.

MAKES 8 SERVINGS

**SERVING:** The tart is festive enough to serve with a dessert wine or a port. It's also just right with strong coffee or light tea.

**STORING:** While the tart's components can be made ahead, the tart itself should be put together no more than 3 or 4 hours before serving.

### FOR THE PASTRY CREAM

- ⅔ cup shelled pistachios (do not use red nuts)
- 7 tablespoons sugar
- 1⅓ cups whole milk
- 4 large egg yolks
- 3 tablespoons cornstarch, sifted
- ¾ teaspoon pure vanilla extract
- ¼ teaspoon pure almond extract
- 2 tablespoons cold unsalted butter, cut into 4 pieces
- ¼ cup sour cream (if you do not strain the nuts out of the pastry cream)

### FOR THE POACHED PEARS

- 3 cups fruity red wine, such as Shiraz, Syrah or Zinfandel
- Zest of 1 orange—removed in wide strips
- Zest of 1 lemon—removed in wide strips
- ¾ cup sugar
- 5 ripe but firm medium pears
- Small lemon wedge

### FOR THE CARAMELIZED PISTACHIOS

- 3 tablespoons sugar
- 2 tablespoons water
- ½ cup shelled pistachios, slightly warm or at room temperature

### FOR THE SAUCE
### (OPTIONAL BUT DELICIOUS)

- Poaching syrup from the pears
- 2 tablespoons honey

- 1 9-inch tart shell made with Sweet Tart Dough (page 444), fully baked and cooled

**TO MAKE THE PASTRY CREAM:** Put the pistachios and 3 tablespoons of the sugar in a food processor and process until the nuts are finely ground, about 1 minute. Turn the nuts into a medium heavy-bottomed saucepan, add the milk and bring to a boil.

While the milk is heating, whisk together the remaining 4 tablespoons sugar, the yolks and the cornstarch in a bowl. When they are well blended, whisk in the vanilla and almond extracts. Whisking constantly, drizzle in one quarter of the hot milk—to temper, or warm, the yolks so they don't cook—then add the remaining milk in a steady stream. Pour this mixture back into the saucepan, put the pan

370 BAKING From My Home to Yours

over medium heat and, whisking energetically, bring to a boil. Boil, whisking, for 1 minute, then remove the pan from the heat.

You can scrape the pastry cream into a clean bowl, in which case it won't be smooth or, if you want a smooth cream, you can press the cream through a strainer, leaving the nuts behind; I usually leave the nuts in. Piece by piece, stir the butter into the pastry cream.

If you'd like to cool the cream quickly, place the bowl in a larger bowl filled with ice cubes and water and stir occasionally. Scrape the cream into a container, press a piece of plastic wrap directly against the cream's surface, cover and refrigerate for at least 4 hours or for up to 4 days.

TO POACH THE PEARS: Put the wine, citrus zests and sugar in a large narrow pot, one that will hold the pears snugly, and bring to a boil.

Meanwhile, peel the pears and immediately rub them with the lemon to keep them from darkening. Reduce the heat under the pot so that the wine simmers gently and lower the pears into the pot. Cut a circle of parchment or wax paper to fit inside the pot and press the paper against the tops of the pears. Partially cover the pot and simmer, turning the pears if needed so they are evenly colored by the poaching syrup, for about 30 minutes, or until tender—test the pears by poking them with the point of a paring knife. Remove the pan from the heat.

Transfer the pears to a heatproof bowl or storage container and pour over the poaching syrup; cool to room temperature. (When cool, the pears in the syrup can be covered and kept in the refrigerator, still in the syrup, for up to 3 days.)

TO CARAMELIZE THE PISTACHIOS: Place a piece of parchment paper or a silicone baking mat on the counter near your stove. Put the sugar and water in a small nonstick skillet or saucepan over medium-high heat and stir with a wooden spoon to dissolve the sugar. Then bring to a boil and cook without stirring until the sugar becomes an amber-colored caramel. Add the nuts and stir, without stopping, until the sugar becomes a dark caramel color and coats the nuts. Turn the nuts out onto the parchment or baking mat, spreading them out as best you can.

When the nuts are cool, coarsely chop them. Keep them in a cool, dry place until needed.

TO MAKE THE OPTIONAL SAUCE: About 30 minutes before you assemble the tart, remove the pears from the poaching syrup, pour the syrup into a saucepan and bring to a boil. Add the honey and boil until the syrup is thick enough to coat a metal spoon. Pour the syrup into a container and chill until needed.

TO ASSEMBLE THE TART: Cut the pears lengthwise in half, scoop out the cores and trim the stems and center veins as needed. Place the pears cut side down on a

triple thickness of paper towels. Cover with another triple thickness of towels and pat the pears dry. Leave them between the paper towels (change the towels if they are very wet) until the excess liquid is absorbed. When the pears are dry, cut each pear half lengthwise into 4 to 6 slices.

If you did not strain the pistachios out of the pastry cream, mix in the $\frac{1}{4}$ cup sour cream to thin it a little. Spread the pastry cream in the baked tart shell. (You may have some cream left over.) Top the pastry cream with the pear slices, arranging them in slightly overlapping concentric circles. Scatter the caramelized pistachios over the tart and, if you'd like, serve each slice with some of the wine sauce or pour the sauce into a small pitcher and pass it at the table. (The tart can be covered lightly and kept in the refrigerator for up to 4 hours.)

# HONEY-ALMOND FIG TART

MAKES 6 TO 8 SERVINGS

WHENEVER I'M lucky enough to have figs to bake with—they're not an everyday treat in the Northeast—I pair them with honey and nuts. The lusciousness of the trio can never be underestimated. Whether included in a recipe for a cake (see A Fig Cake for Fall, page 198) or baked into this tart, the individual ingredients have a way of keeping their flavors while bolstering those of their partners. That's why the combination is found in just about every region where figs are grown in abundance. I think of this tart as having a French Provençal personality, but with a change of honey, the addition of an herb, a different kind of nut, you can almost take a taste tour of the Mediterranean.

**SERVING:** You can serve this tart with whipped cream, crème fraîche (page 459), Crème Anglaise (page 451) or even a little ice cream, but I serve it plain (oh, okay, sometimes I dust it with confectioners' sugar).

**STORING:** Although you can make the almond cream and the tart shell ahead, the tart should be eaten the day it is baked.

### FOR THE ALMOND CREAM

- 1 stick (8 tablespoons) unsalted butter, at room temperature
- ⅓ cup honey (your choice of flavor)
- ⅔ cup confectioners' sugar
- 1 cup ground almonds
- 4 teaspoons cornstarch
- 1 large egg
- 1 large egg yolk

- 1 9-inch tart shell made with Sweet Tart Dough (page 444), partially baked and cooled
- 16 ripe figs (Kadota figs are very nice)

  About ⅓ cup red currant jelly mixed with 1 teaspoon water, for glazing

*Playing Around*

If you can't get figs, think about topping the almond cream with apricots or peeled and sliced peaches or nectarines. As the mood strikes, you can add the grated zest of a lemon or half an orange to the almond cream, or, if you're feeling more adventurous, mix in 1 tablespoon finely chopped fresh thyme or 2 teaspoons finely chopped fresh rosemary.

Combine the butter, honey and confectioners' sugar in a food processor (a great tool for this job) and process until smooth. Add the ground almonds and process to blend. Add the cornstarch and process to blend, then add the egg and yolk. Keep whirring for another 15 seconds, or until the almond cream is homogeneous. (If you prefer, you can make the almond cream with a mixer fitted with the whisk attachment or with a hand mixer.) Scrape the filling into a bowl and refrigerate for at least 2 hours (or for up to 3 days).

**GETTING READY TO BAKE:** Center a rack in the oven and preheat the oven to 375 degrees F. Put the tart pan on a baking sheet lined with parchment or a silicone mat.

**TO ASSEMBLE:** Cut the figs in half from blossom to stem. Spoon enough of the almond cream into the crust to come about ¼ inch shy of the rim. Arrange the figs cut side down in an attractive pattern over the cream.

Bake the tart for 30 to 35 minutes, or until the cream is puffed and browned; a thin knife inserted into the cream should come out clean. Pull the pan from the oven and transfer the tart to a rack.

Bring the currant jelly and water to a boil—you can do this either in a pan on the stove or in a microwave oven. Using a pastry brush, very gently paint the top of the tart with the glaze. Allow the tart to cool to just warm or to room temperature before serving.

**FRANCE-MEETS-FLORIDA HONEY-ALMOND TART:** The almond filling is also lovely with Florida's Ruby Red grapefruits. Peel 2 grapefruits, removing the rind and the white cottony pith beneath, and cut out the segments (leaving the membrane behind). Put the segments between two triple thicknesses of paper towels. Let the fruit drain for at least 1 hour—or up to 6 hours, if you've got the time. Arrange the segments in a pretty pinwheel pattern over the filling before baking.

# LA PALETTE'S STRAWBERRY TART

MAKES 6 SERVINGS

THE PARISIAN café La Palette counts among its assets the wall-to-wall artists' palettes and paintings that give it its name; its location, just steps from the Seine in a neighborhood chockablock with galleries; its sprawling leafy terrace; and its servers, each of whom has perfected a particular style of gruffness to mask a proverbial heart of gold. As endearing as these characteristics are, I think La Palette's greatest draw might be its strawberry tart, a dessert that, sadly, doesn't turn up on the menu in any predictable way. We got lucky one summer afternoon and, to guard against the disappointment of not being so fortunate on subsequent visits, I immediately took to making it at home.

The first time we had the tart, we were sitting at a wobbly table on the terrace, half under an umbrella and close to a tree, so that the sun played on the table and made on-again-off-again dapple patterns. It was the ideal setting for this dessert, which was simply a slice of well-baked buttery crust brushed with jam and strewn with cut and sugared strawberries. Because the wedge of crust had no sides and the berries had just been spooned over it, the fruit tumbled across the plate. The tart was accompanied by a small pottery bowl filled with crème fraîche, and it was as beautiful as any elaborate dessert crafted by a master pastry chef. Since that day, I have made this tart dozens of times, sometimes making it just as we had it at La Palette, sometimes embellishing the fruit with a little black pepper and eau-de-vie. It's a brilliant way to show off good berries and turn something simple and spare into something alluring and romantic.

| | |
|---|---|
| Best-quality strawberry jam | Sugar (optional) |
| 1 9-inch tart shell made with Sweet Tart Dough (page 444) or Sweet Tart Dough with Nuts (page 444), fully baked, cooled and removed from the pan | Splash of kirsch, a drop of fraise or framboise eau-de-vie or a spoonful of crème de cassis (optional) |
| | Freshly ground black pepper (optional) |
| About 1 quart ripe, fragrant strawberries | Crème fraîche (first choice) or whipped cream |

SERVING: If you'd like, you can top each portion with some crème fraîche or whipped cream, but I think it's more fun to do as they do at La Palette and just put a pot of it on the table and let everyone take a share.

STORING: While you can bake the crust early in the day and keep it at room temperature, and you can also halve and sugar the berries an hour or so in advance, this dessert should be assembled just before serving.

### *Playing Around*

This idea of crust-jam-and-fruit can be adapted to any berry (it's great with blueberries) or any soft fruit such as peaches, apricots, plums or nectarines (fresh or poached). When the season changes, you can use sautéed apples, pears or quinces. Omit the pepper and eau-de-vie and add whatever flavorings you want.

If you are going to be serving the whole tart at once, spread a generous layer of jam over the entire bottom of the crust, then cut it into wedges. If you are serving fewer people, just cut as many portions of the tart as you need and spread the jam over the cut pieces.

Halve as many strawberries as you need (quarter them if they are very large) for the number of people you'll be serving—be generous—and, if you think the berries need it, toss them with sugar. If you want to add a teensy bit of liqueur, stir it in now (but go easy—you want the liqueur to enhance, not take over, the flavor of the berries) and add a bit of the black pepper, if you'd like.

Put each piece of crust on a plate and spoon over the berries and their juice. Don't try to stay within the outline of the crust, just spoon the berries onto the center and let them tumble over either side. And if the point of the crust peeks out from the berries, so much the better.

Decorate or serve with the cream.

NO MATTER where in France you travel, you'll see a version of this fruit tart given pride of place in the window of just about every pastry shop. It's simple but unbeatable. The magic trio is a crust made with a sweet shortbread-like dough, a smooth pastry cream richly flavored with vanilla and a crown of perfectly ripe berries. You can use a mix of berries or just one kind—it is gorgeous with ever-widening circles of whole raspberries, blueberries or blackberries, tiny whole wild strawberries, if you're lucky enough to find them, or cut cultivated strawberries. Or you can use slices of lightly poached fruit—think about peaches, nectarines, apricots or plums. And it is spectacular with a combination of berries and fruits. In Paris, the pâtissier Gérard Mulot has stopped strollers in their tracks with his tarts made with fruits so fancifully arranged that every time I see one, I am reminded of a horn of plenty painted by Caravaggio. If you've a touch of the artist in you, you couldn't find a tastier palette to work on.

MAKES 6 TO 8 SERVINGS

SERVING: The tart needs nothing but a little espresso or some tea to accompany it.

STORING: Eat the tart as soon after it is constructed as possible, certainly on the day it is made. If you must keep it for a few hours, store it in the refrigerator, making sure to keep it away from any foods with strong odors.

About 1½ cups Pastry Cream (page 448), cooled or chilled

1 9-inch tart shell made with Sweet Tart Dough (page 444) or Sweet Tart Dough with Nuts (page 444), fully baked and cooled

2 pints fresh raspberries, blueberries, blackberries or strawberries, or an assortment of berries

⅓ cup red currant jelly mixed with 1 teaspoon water, for glazing

Smooth the pastry cream by giving it a couple of strong turns with a whisk. Spoon enough of the pastry cream into the tart crust to come almost to the rim, then even the surface with a rubber spatula. Carefully lay the berries on the cream, arranging them in any pattern that pleases you. If you are using strawberries, either halve them from top to bottom or slice them, depending on the size of the berries and your whim.

Bring the jelly and the water to a boil in a microwave oven or on the stovetop. Working with a pastry brush or pastry feather, dab each berry with a spot of jelly. Or, if you like, you can glaze the entire surface of the tart, including the bit of pastry cream that peeks through the berries.

# PUFFED DOUBLE PLUM TART

A SIMPLE puff pastry block with billowy borders encases spiced wine-steeped dried plums (aka prunes) and fresh autumnal Italian prune plums. Because I alternate the dried and fresh plums and put some of the fresh plums dark side up and some dark side down, the tart comes out of the oven looking like the picture of fall, its fruit purple and yellow, its base tinged with red wine and its border golden. It somehow looks both lunch-in-the-country casual and, particularly when you thicken the leftover spiced wine and pour a drizzle of it around each portion, dinner-party-in-the-city dressy.

FOR THE TOPPING

½ cup hearty dry red wine, such as
  Chianti, Rioja or Cabernet
  Sauvignon
2 wide strips orange zest
  Juice of ½ orange
2½ tablespoons sugar
½ piece star anise (or one 1-inch piece
  cinnamon stick)
  About 18 pitted prunes (dried
  plums)
  About 10 Italian prune plums,
  halved and pitted

FOR THE PASTRY

1 8-ounce sheet frozen puff pastry,
  preferably all-butter (see Note, page
  315), thawed
½ tablespoon unsalted butter, at room
  temperature
  Sugar
1 tablespoon heavy cream or whole milk

MAKES 4 SERVINGS

SERVING: Serve the tart with a drizzle of syrup over each portion and top, if you'd like, with vanilla ice cream or a spoonful of whipped cream or crème fraîche (my favorite).

STORING: The tart is at its prime when the fruit is still warm, so plan on enjoying this soon after it comes out of the oven—it's not a keeper.

*Playing Around*

The plum duo, complete with wine syrup, can be used as the fruit in the French Pear Tart (page 368)—it's a natural with the almond cream filling.

TO MAKE THE TOPPING: Bring the wine, zest, orange juice, sugar and star anise to a boil in a small saucepan. Boil for 1 to 2 minutes, then add the prunes and boil for 3 minutes more. Remove the pan from the heat, cover and let steep for 15 minutes.

Using a slotted spoon, transfer the prunes to a bowl. Return the saucepan to medium heat and boil for another 5 minutes or so, until the syrup is reduced a bit and slightly thickened. Remove from the heat, cover and set aside.

GETTING READY TO BAKE: Center a rack in the oven and preheat the oven to 400 degrees F. Have a baking sheet at hand, as well as a sheet of parchment paper or a silicone mat.

TO MAKE THE PASTRY BASE: Working on the parchment paper or silicone mat, roll the puff pastry into a 9-x-10-inch rectangle, or a 9- or 10-inch square—the dimensions are up to you, although if you change the size too much, you may have to adjust the amount of fruit. Lift the pastry, still on its paper or mat, onto the baking sheet. Smear the butter over the surface of the dough, leaving a 1-inch border bare. Sprinkle the buttered area with about 1 teaspoon sugar.

Arrange the prunes and fresh plums in rows across the pastry, leaving the un-buttered border bare. I like to alternate dried and fresh plums and to alternate cut side up and cut side down fresh plums. Using a pastry brush, lightly dab the fresh plums with a bit of syrup. Brush the border of the puff pastry with the cream and sprinkle with about 1 tablespoon sugar.

Bake the tart for 10 minutes, at which point the borders will have puffed some. Reduce the oven temperature to 350 degrees F, and bake for another 15 minutes (total baking time is about 25 minutes), or until the fresh plums can be pierced easily with the tip of a knife.

Cool the tart on the baking sheet for about 5 minutes before cutting it into quarters and serving with the poaching syrup.

# SPOON DESSERTS
## Puddings, Custards, Crisps and Ice Creams

# PUDDINGS
# AND CUSTARDS

PUDDINGS AND CUSTARDS can be as retro as a roadside diner's rice pudding, as modern as a four-star chef's herbed crème brûlée, as sophisticated as a pot de crème or as time-tested as Grandma's bread pudding, but they share a treasured trait: a soft, tender, savor-it-from-a-spoon texture.

An offer of a pudding is as good as a declaration of love. It's that soothing.

The key to perfect texture is careful mixing and just the right amount of heat. While I've given you clear instructions with each recipe, here are a few more helpful hints.

• PROCESS THE PUDDING. Using a food processor to mix the ingredients for a cornstarch-thickened pudding and then giving the cooked pudding a final blending in it is unorthodox but highly effective. Processing ensures a lump-free pudding and it also incorporates a small amount of air, which produces a slightly lighter and noticeably more velvety texture. Aerating is particularly good for chocolate puddings—it lessens their density and increases their sensuousness.

• MAKE A FIGURE EIGHT. Warming eggs over direct heat, which is the way you thicken many puddings and custards, can be a tricky business, since too much heat can curdle or scorch the eggs. The safest way to coax eggs into thickening without mishap is to cook them over low to medium heat and to stir them constantly with a small whisk or spatula. My technique is to use a combination of figure-eight and circular motions. Just put the tip of the whisk or spatula against the bottom of the pan and trace a few figure eights, follow by circling the edges of the pan a couple of times and then repeat until the mixture is thickened and velvety.

• USE A WATER BATH. Delicate cup custards, pots de crème and bread puddings turn out best when they are coddled in a water bath. Baked this way,

they are sheltered from harsh direct oven heat and cook evenly. Simply put the custard cups in a roasting pan, first lining the bottom of the pan with a couple of sheets of paper towels to keep the cups from sloshing around, and half fill the roaster with hot water.

• LOOK FOR A JIGGLE. Use the jiggle test to decide when your custards and creams are baked. Reach into the oven and very lightly tap a cup or two—if the custard doesn't jiggle or if it jiggles only a tad in the center, it's ready to come out of the oven. You can use the standard knife test—inserted into the center of the custard, it should come out clean—but you'll leave a slash mark. That's no problem, though, when you'll be decorating the top with whipped cream.

• COOL THE CUSTARD. While cornstarch puddings can be tasted as soon as they are cooked and many can be served just warm or at room temperature, baked custards need a cool-down period, and often a good chilling. If you're told to let a custard sit in its water bath for a few minutes after it comes out of the oven, to leave it on a cooling rack or to put it in the fridge, resist the temptation to taste it too soon. Patience will bring you a dessert with better texture and deeper flavor.

# CHOCOLATE PUDDING

I GREW up on My-T-Fine boxed pudding and was sure that, like Cheerios or ketchup, chocolate pudding was a food that could be bought but never made from scratch. I've since learned that Cheerios are, indeed, best left to industry; that ketchup can be made at home, but that it will never be like Heinz; and that homemade chocolate pudding—especially this one—is so much better than anything from a box or plastic container that calling the two by the same name should be a bookable crime.

While this pudding has the fine texture and refined flavor of a sophisticated European dessert, it is, at heart, a traditional American cornstarch pudding, albeit one made in a completely untraditional way: it's blended in a food processor and then given a final spin. While the pudding will work with almost any kind of chocolate, it should really be made with bittersweet, which has enough power to hold its own after a good chill.

MAKES 6 SERVINGS

SERVING: I think these are best served with a small spoonful of lightly sweetened whipped cream or crème fraîche, but when I was a kid, My-T-Fine was often topped with a layer of unwhipped cold heavy cream.

STORING: Covered, and kept away from foods with strong odors, the puddings can be refrigerated for up to 2 days.

| | |
|---|---|
| 2¼ cups whole milk | 2 large egg yolks |
| 6 tablespoons sugar | 5 ounces bittersweet chocolate, melted |
| 2 tablespoons unsweetened cocoa | and still warm |
| powder | 2 tablespoons unsalted butter, cut into |
| 2 tablespoons cornstarch | 4 pieces, at room temperature |
| ¼ teaspoon salt | 1 teaspoon pure vanilla extract |
| 1 large egg | |

*Playing Around*

If you'd like to add a little crunch to these puddings, your options are myriad. You could fold Schariffen Berger cocoa nibs (see page 479) into the hot pudding, or you could sprinkle some over the whipped cream topping. Another choice is to borrow the crunchies from another dessert—for instance, the spiced nut, raisin and chocolate swirl from Nutty, Chocolaty, Swirly Sour Cream Bundt Cake (page 182)—and make them the middle layer of the puddings.

GETTING READY: Have six ramekins or pudding cups, each holding 4 to 6 ounces (½ to ¾ cup), at hand.

Bring 2 cups of the milk and 3 tablespoons of the sugar to a boil in a medium heavy-bottomed saucepan.

While the milk is heating, put the cocoa, cornstarch and salt into a food processor and whir to blend. Turn them out onto a piece of wax paper, put the remaining 3 tablespoons sugar, the egg and egg yolks into the processor and blend for 1 minute. Scrape down the sides of the bowl, add the remaining ¼ cup milk and pulse just to mix, then add the dry ingredients and pulse a few times to blend.

With the machine running, very slowly pour in the hot milk mixture. Process for a few seconds, then put everything back into the saucepan. Whisk without stopping over medium heat—making sure to get into the edges of the pan—until the pudding thickens and a couple of bubbles burble up to the surface and pop (about 2 minutes). You want the pudding to thicken, but you don't want it to boil, so lower the heat if necessary.

Scrape the pudding back into the processor (if there's a scorched spot, avoid it as you scrape) and pulse a couple of times. Add the chocolate, butter and vanilla and pulse until everything is evenly blended.

Pour the pudding into the ramekins. If you don't want a skin to form (some people think the skin is the best part), press a piece of plastic wrap against the surface of each pudding to create an airtight seal. Refrigerate for at least 4 hours.

# SPLIT-LEVEL PUDDING

**IN AN** effort to make all the people happy all the time, I offer this duo: chocolate ganache on the lower level and vanilla pudding one level up. It's fun to have the silky pudding give way to the heavier chocolate—delicious too. It's also fun to play with flavoring the upper-tier vanilla (see Playing Around for ideas).

**FOR THE CHOCOLATE LAYER**
2 ounces bittersweet chocolate, finely chopped
⅓ cup heavy cream

**FOR THE VANILLA LAYER**
2¼ cups whole milk
6 tablespoons sugar
3 tablespoons cornstarch

¼ teaspoon salt
3 large egg yolks
2 tablespoons unsalted butter, cut into 4 pieces, at room temperature
2½ teaspoons pure vanilla extract

Chocolate shavings (page 471), for decoration (optional)

**GETTING READY:** Have six ramekins or pudding cups, each holding 4 to 6 ounces, (½ to ¾ cup), at hand.

**TO MAKE THE CHOCOLATE LAYER:** Put the chocolate in a 1- or 2-cup glass measuring cup. Bring the heavy cream to a boil. Pour the cream over the chocolate and let it sit for 30 seconds, then gently stir to blend. Divide the chocolate ganache among the cups and set aside.

**TO MAKE THE VANILLA LAYER:** Bring 2 cups of the milk and 3 tablespoons of the sugar to a boil in a medium heavy-bottomed saucepan.

While the milk is heating, put the cornstarch and salt into a food processor and whir to blend. Turn them out onto a piece of wax paper, put the remaining 3 tablespoons sugar and the egg yolks into the processor and blend for 1 minute. Scrape down the sides of the bowl, add the remaining ¼ cup milk and pulse just to mix, then add the dry ingredients and pulse a few times to blend.

With the machine running, very slowly pour in the hot milk mixture. Process for a few seconds, then pour everything back into the saucepan. Whisk without stopping over medium heat—making sure to get into the edges of the pan—until the pudding thickens and a couple of bubbles burble up to the surface and pop (about 2 minutes). You don't want the pudding to boil, but you do want it to thicken, so lower the heat, if necessary.

Scrape the pudding back into the processor (if there's a scorched spot, avoid it as you scrape) and pulse a couple of times. Add the butter and vanilla and pulse until everything is evenly blended.

Pour the pudding into the cups—depending on how warm the chocolate ganache in the bottom of the cups was, you might find that it runs up the sides of the cups and forms a lacy circle around the pudding. If it does, it's pretty; if it

**MAKES 6 SERVINGS**

**SERVING:** For a special treat, offer these with a plate of cookies—they're especially good with Mini Madeleines (page 172) or World Peace Cookies (page 138).

**STORING:** Covered, and kept away from foods with strong odors, the puddings can be refrigerated for up to 2 days.

*Playing Around*

Here are some suggestions for changing the flavor of the vanilla pudding:

**CINNAMON PUDDING:** Add 2 teaspoons ground cinnamon to the cornstarch and salt; reduce the amount of vanilla extract to 1 teaspoon.

**COFFEE PUDDING:** Make an espresso extract by dissolving 4 teaspoons instant espresso powder in 4 teaspoons boiling water. Reduce the vanilla extract to 1 teaspoon, and, after you've pulsed in the vanilla, add 2 teaspoons of the coffee extract. Taste the pudding and if you want a stronger coffee flavor, pulse in as much additional extract as you'd like.

**PEPPERMINT PUDDING:** Reduce the vanilla extract to 1 teaspoon and, after you have added it to the pudding, add a little pure peppermint extract or peppermint oil. Start with ¼ teaspoon of the peppermint extract (or ⅛ teaspoon oil) and add additional extract to taste, but add it by drops. Peppermint is a strong flavor, so go easy.

doesn't, the chocolate will be a surprise. Press a piece of plastic wrap against the surface of each pudding to create an airtight seal and prevent a skin from forming. Refrigerate the puddings for at least 4 hours.

If you'd like, scatter chocolate shavings over the tops of the puddings just before serving.

# REAL BUTTERSCOTCH PUDDING

**HERE'S THE** real deal—butterscotch pudding made with real butter and real Scotch whisky. It is, as all good puddings must be, smooth, creamy and comforting, but it's also got a little kick, making it anything but a nursery sweet.

½ cup (packed) light brown sugar

3 tablespoons water

1¾ cups whole milk

½ cup heavy cream

¼ cup cornstarch

¼ teaspoon salt

3 tablespoons sugar

3 large egg yolks

3 tablespoons unsalted butter, cut into 4 pieces, at room temperature

2 teaspoons pure vanilla extract

2 tablespoons Scotch whisky (preferably a strong single malt)

Whipped cream and Buttered Pecans (page 470), for topping (optional)

MAKES 6 SERVINGS

SERVING: One good buttery thing deserves another, so I like topping the puddings with the Buttered Pecans. Even better is topping the puddings with whipped cream and then topping the cream with the pecans.

STORING: Covered, and kept away from foods with strong odors, the puddings can be refrigerated for up to 2 days.

GETTING READY: Have six ramekins or pudding cups, each holding 4 to 6 ounces (½ to ¾ cup), at hand.

Put the brown sugar and water in a medium heavy-bottomed saucepan, put the pan over medium heat and bring to a boil, stirring to dissolve the sugar. Stirring and lowering the heat if necessary, boil for 2 minutes. Add 1½ cups of the milk and the cream and bring to a boil—don't worry if, as it's heating, the mixture curdles.

While the milk is heating, put the cornstarch and salt into a food processor and whir to blend. Turn them out onto a piece of wax paper, put the sugar and egg yolks into the processor and blend for 1 minute. Scrape down the sides of the bowl, add the remaining ¼ cup milk and pulse just to mix, then add the dry ingredients and pulse a few times to blend.

With the machine running, very slowly pour in the hot liquid. Process for a few seconds, then pour everything back into the saucepan. Whisk without stopping over medium heat—making sure to get into the edges of the pan—until the pudding thickens and a couple of bubbles burble up to the surface and pop (about 2 minutes). You don't want the pudding to boil, but you do want it to thicken, so lower the heat, if necessary.

Scrape the pudding back into the processor (if there's a scorched spot, avoid it as you scrape) and pulse a couple of times. Add the butter, vanilla and Scotch and pulse until everything is evenly blended.

Pour the pudding into the ramekins. If you don't want a skin to form, press a piece of plastic wrap against the surface of each pudding to create an airtight seal. Refrigerate the puddings for at least 4 hours.

# LEMON CUP CUSTARD

**CUSTARDS DON'T** come simpler than this one—and they don't come more satisfying either. I've often thought this should be called "after-school custard" because it makes a great welcome-home offering. This is a basic lemon custard, but in Playing Around, you'll find suggestions for other flavorings. Whether you go for the plain vanilla or opt for something a little more exotic, like orange-anise, what you'll get with any of these is a texture so silky and lithe you'll need a steady hand to keep the custard from wiggling its way off your spoon.

2¼ cups whole milk
    Grated zest of 1 lemon
4 large eggs

½ cup sugar
Pure lemon oil or extract (optional)

**GETTING READY:** Have six (6-ounce; ¾-cup) custard or coffee cups at hand. Put the milk and zest in a saucepan and bring just to a boil. Remove the pan from the heat, cover and set aside for 30 minutes so the zest can infuse the milk with its flavor. Reheat the milk before mixing the custard.

**GETTING READY TO BAKE:** Center a rack in the oven and preheat the oven to 325 degrees F. Line a roasting pan with a double thickness of paper towels and put the custard or coffee cups in the pan. Have a fine-mesh strainer at hand. Fill a teakettle with water and put it on to boil; when the water boils, turn off the heat.

In a 1-quart glass measuring cup or a heatproof bowl, whisk the eggs and sugar together until well blended. Still whisking, strain in about ¼ cup of the hot milk little by little—this will temper, or warm, the eggs so they won't curdle. Whisking all the while, slowly strain in the remaining milk. Discard the zest remaining in the strainer. If you'd like a stronger lemon flavor—I usually do—stir a few drops of lemon oil or extract into the custard. (Don't go overboard—⅛ teaspoon extract, less if you're using oil, is about the most you'll need.)

With a spoon, skim the foam off the top of the custard, then pour the custard into the cups. Very carefully slide the roasting pan into the oven, then pour enough hot water from the teakettle into the roasting pan to come halfway up the sides of the cups.

Bake the custards for 40 to 45 minutes, or until they jiggle only in the center when you tap the cups lightly. Transfer the custards to a rack and cool to room temperature, then cover and refrigerate for at least 2 hours before serving.

MAKES 6 SERVINGS

SERVING: Serve just as is.

STORING: Well covered and away from foods with strong odors, the custards will keep in the refrigerator for up to 2 days.

*Playing Around*

Here are just a few suggestions to get you started:

**VANILLA CUP CUSTARD:** Omit the lemon zest and oil or extract, and after the hot milk has been blended into the eggs, add 2½ teaspoons pure vanilla extract. (I often add ⅛ teaspoon pure almond extract too.) Alternatively, you can steep the milk with 1 split and scraped vanilla bean (see page 494) instead of using extract.

**LEMON-CLOVE CUP CUSTARD:** Add 4 whole cloves to the milk along with the lemon zest.

**ORANGE–STAR ANISE CUP CUSTARD:** Omit the lemon zest and oil or extract and add the grated zest of 1 orange and 3 points from a star anise to the milk before heating it.

**ESPRESSO–CINNAMON CUP CUSTARD:** Omit the lemon zest and oil or extract and add a cinnamon stick to the milk before heating it. Whisk 2 teaspoons instant espresso powder into the egg-sugar mixture.

**POT DE CRÈME,** or literally, pot of cream, is the French name for what we Americans have loved for centuries and known for equally long as baked or cup custard. In this recipe, most of the sugar is cooked in a skillet until it caramelizes and turns a deep mahogany color. Once caramelized, sugar is transformed from its well-known sweet self into a liquid that is slightly bitter, here just bitter enough to give a little edge and a lot of interest to the rich custard.

If you've got a pot de crème service (a set of dainty china cups with lids), by all means, use it—there's nothing more elegant. If you haven't, you can use Pyrex custard cups (the kind sold in most supermarkets), ramekins or espresso cups (actually, espresso cups are my favorites for this recipe).

Don't be alarmed when you see that the custards are cooked in the oven in a roasting pan covered with plastic wrap. This is a chef's trick and it's one that translates easily to the home baker. You needn't worry about the plastic wrap burning—the oven heat is too low for that. Just be certain to poke airholes in the plastic as directed, and all will be perfect. If you are using pot de crème cups, though, skip the plastic wrap—the lids are all you need.

| | |
|---|---|
| 2  cups heavy cream | 2  large eggs |
| 1  cup whole milk | 5  large egg yolks |
| ¾  cup sugar | |

**GETTING READY:** Center a rack in the oven and preheat the oven to 300°F. Line a large roasting pan with a double thickness of paper towels, then put eight 4-ounce (½-cup) custard cups, ramekins, espresso or pot de crème cups in the pan. Fill a teakettle with water and put it on to boil; when the water boils, turn off the heat.

Stir the cream and milk together and warm them in a microwave oven or in a saucepan over medium heat; set aside.

Measure out ¼ cup of the sugar and set it aside.

Put a medium heavy-bottomed saucepan (a nonstick pan works well) over medium-high heat and sprinkle in 2 tablespoons of the remaining sugar. As soon as the sugar melts and starts to caramelize, stir. When the color is uniform, stir in another 2 tablespoons sugar and continue to stir until it is melted and colored. Continue with the remaining ¼ cup sugar, adding it 2 tablespoons at a time. When all the sugar is deep amber, almost mahogany colored, stand away from the pan, so you don't get splattered, and stir in the warm liquid. The mixture will bubble furiously and may seize—don't panic, just keep stirring, and it will smooth out. Pull the pan from the heat.

Put the eggs, yolks and reserved ¼ cup sugar in a large glass measuring cup or a small bowl and whisk until pale and slightly thickened. Still whisking, drizzle in a little of the caramel liquid—this will temper, or warm, the eggs so they won't cur-

---

MAKES 8 SERVINGS

**SERVING:** The pots de crème are most elegant served at cool room temperature, but still irresistible chilled. If they've been in the fridge for several hours or overnight, let them sit on the counter for about 20 minutes before bringing them to the table. These custards need no embellishments—they're perfect just as they are—but I find that a swirl of very lightly whipped cream makes a nice finishing touch; a light, cool, refreshing counterpoint to the luxurious custard.

**STORING:** The pots de crème can be kept covered in the refrigerator for up to a day. Like all creamy concoctions, they will quickly pick up refrigerator odors, so keep them tightly covered.

dle. Whisking all the while, slowly pour in the remaining liquid. If there is foam at the top of the custard, skim it off with a spoon (foam isn't fatal, but it will turn into little craters on the top of the baked custards). Pour the custard into the baking cups.

Pour enough hot water from the teakettle into the roasting pan to come halfway up the sides of the cups. Cover the pan snugly with plastic wrap, poke two holes in two opposite corners and very carefully and steadily slide the setup into the oven.

Bake the custards for 35 to 40 minutes, or until the tops darken and the custards jiggle a little only in the center when tapped or lightly shaken.

Gingerly remove the roasting pan from the oven and place it on a cooling rack. Allow the custards to rest in their warm bath for 10 minutes, then peel off the plastic wrap and transfer the cups from the water (careful—they're still hot) to the cooling rack. Refrigerate when they reach room temperature. When the pots de crème are cool, cover them tightly with plastic wrap or their little lids.

## Playing Around

**COFFEE CARAMEL POTS DE CRÈME**: Warm the cream and milk as directed. Put 1 cup (about 3 ounces) coffee beans, preferably of the he-man espresso-roast variety, into a food processor and pulse to coarsely chop (not grind) the beans. Instead of caramelizing the sugar little by little, put the entire ½ cup of sugar and the chopped coffee beans into the saucepan over medium heat and stir until the sugar starts to melt. Continue to cook, stirring constantly, until the sugar is deep amber colored. Pour in the warm milk and cream and stir to smooth everything out, then remove the pan from the heat, cover it and allow the mixture to infuse for 20 minutes.

Strain the liquid into a measuring cup, discard the beans and, if necessary, add additional cream to bring the liquid up to 3 cups. Rewarm the mixture, beat the yolks and eggs with the remaining ¼ cup sugar and gradually whisk in the 3 cups of warm milk and cream. Continue as directed.

# CHOCOLATE POTS DE CRÈME

••••••••••••••••••••••••••••••••••••••••••••••••••••••••••••••••••••••••••••••••••••••••

**CHOCOLATE PUDDING** and chocolate pots de crème are often thought of as culinary siblings when they're really more like cousins from opposite sides of the family. The big difference between them is how they're cooked: the pudding is stirred on top of the stove and gets its thickening from cornstarch, while the pots de crème are baked and depend entirely on eggs and heat to set them. And, although the crèmes seem lighter than pudding, they are actually considerably richer. What both desserts deliver is comfort, even if pudding is homey and pots de crème elegant enough to serve at a dress-up dinner.

The custards, arranged in the water-filled roasting pan, need to be covered during baking. If you have pot de crème cups with lids, great; if not, use custard cups and a professional technique—cover the roaster with plastic wrap. There's no risk, because you'll be baking at a very low temperature. Just follow the directions, and don't forget to poke holes in the plastic.

| | |
|---|---|
| 4 ounces bittersweet chocolate, finely chopped | 1 large egg |
| 1½ cups heavy cream | 5 large egg yolks |
| 1½ cups whole milk | ¼ cup sugar |
| | Pinch of salt |

MAKES 8 SERVINGS

SERVING: While you can serve pots de crème at room temperature, I prefer these chilled. I usually serve them with a little lightly sweetened whipped cream or a dollop of crème fraîche.

STORING: The pots de crème can be kept covered in the refrigerator for up to a day. Like all creamy concoctions, they will quickly pick up refrigerator odors, so keep them tightly covered.

GETTING READY: Center a rack in the oven and preheat the oven to 300°F. Line a large roasting pan with a double thickness of paper towels, then put eight 4-ounce (½-cup) custard cups, ramekins, espresso or pot de crème cups in the pan. Fill a teakettle with water and put it on to boil; when the water boils, turn off the heat.

Put the chopped chocolate in a 2-quart glass measuring cup or a large heat-proof bowl. Bring ½ cup of the heavy cream to a boil. When the cream is just at a boil, pour it over the chocolate and wait for 1 minute. Using a rubber spatula and starting in the center of the bowl, gently stir the cream and chocolate in ever-widening concentric circles until the ganache is smooth; set aside.

Stir the remaining 1 cup cream and the milk together in a small saucepan and bring to a boil.

Meanwhile, in a large glass measuring cup or bowl, whisk the egg, yolks, sugar and salt together until pale and slightly thickened. Still whisking, drizzle in a little of the hot liquid—this will temper, or warm, the eggs so they won't curdle. Whisking all the while, slowly pour in the remaining liquid. Finally, slowly whisk the egg mixture into the ganache, stirring gently to incorporate.

With a spoon, skim the foam off the top of the custard, then pour the custard into the cups. Pour enough hot water from the teakettle into the roasting pan to come halfway up the sides of the cups. Cover the top of the pan snugly with plastic wrap, poke two holes in two opposite corners and very carefully and steadily slide the setup into the oven.

Bake the custards for 35 to 40 minutes, or until the tops darken and the custards jiggle a little only in the center when tapped or lightly shaken.

Gingerly remove the roasting pan from the oven and place it on a cooling rack. Allow the custards to rest in their warm bath for 10 minutes, then peel off the plastic wrap and transfer the cups from the water (careful—they're still hot) to the cooling rack. Refrigerate when they reach room temperature. When the pots de crème are cool, cover them tightly with plastic wrap or their little lids.

# CRÈME BRÛLÉE

EVERY ONCE in a while a dessert becomes so popular that it teeters on the brink of becoming a cliché, and that's what happened with crème brûlée. Familiarity toppled the great dessert from its pedestal. Lucky us: less crème brûlée in the outside world only makes it more special in the cozy world of our own homes. And, as luxe as this dessert is, it is a simply made baked custard that relies on eggs and cream for its goodness and caramelized sugar (*brûlée* means burnt in French) for its dash.

The most efficient way to caramelize the sugar topping is to use a blowtorch (see page 475). If you don't have a torch, you can chill the custards very, very well, then set them in an ice-cube-filled roasting pan and run them under the broiler. You won't get as even a coating with the broiler as you would with a torch, but you'll still get the flavor and the pleasure of a crackly sugar crust over creamy custard.

Note: The best baking dishes for crème brûlée are shallow, ideally just an inch high, about 4 inches in diameter and holding about ³/₄ cup of liquid. Porcelain, pottery or glass gratin or baking dishes are perfect, but if you don't have them, you can use ramekins or even disposable aluminum foil pans, an unglamorous but effective solution.

MAKES 6 SERVINGS

SERVING: Serve the crème brûlée when the crème is really cold and the brûlée is still warm. You can serve the whole dessert chilled, but the sugar topping won't have its characteristic crackle. And while I think crème brûlée should be served with nothing more than a spoon, you could offer berries and cookies as accompaniments.

STORING: The custard for crème brûlée must be made ahead so it has plenty of time to chill, but once you've caramelized the sugar on top, your storage time is over if you want the sugar to have crunch.

| | |
|---|---|
| 1¼ cups heavy cream | 2 teaspoons pure vanilla extract |
| ½ cup whole milk | |
| 3 large egg yolks | About 6 tablespoons sugar or sifted |
| ⅓ cup sugar | light brown sugar, for topping |

GETTING READY: Center a rack in the oven and preheat the oven to 200 degrees F. Put the six baking dishes (see Note above) on a baking sheet lined with parchment or a silicone mat.

Bring the cream and milk just to a boil.

In a 1- or 2-quart glass measuring cup or in a medium bowl, whisk the egg yolks, sugar and vanilla together until well blended but not airy. Still whisking, drizzle in about one quarter of the hot liquid—this will temper, or warm, the yolks so they won't curdle. Whisking all the while, slowly pour in the remainder of the cream and milk. Give the bowl a good rap against the counter to de-bubble the custard, then strain it into the baking dishes.

Bake the custards for 50 to 60 minutes, or until the centers are set—tap the sides of the dishes, and the custards should hold firm. Lift the dishes onto a cooling rack and let the custards cool until they reach room temperature.

Cover each custard with plastic wrap and refrigerate for at least 3 hours, preferably longer. (The custards can be kept covered in the refrigerator for up to 2 days.) For the sugar to be successfully caramelized, the custards need to be thoroughly chilled.

To caramelize the sugar topping with a blowtorch, work on one dish at a time. Sprinkle the top of each custard evenly with sugar—about 1 tablespoon for each dish—then brown the sugar, cooking it until it bubbles and colors. Wait until the bubbles subside before serving the crèmes.

To caramelize the sugar in a broiler, preheat the broiler and fill a shallow roasting pan with ice cubes. Sprinkle the custards with the sugar, put the baking dishes on the bed of ice and run the custards under the broiler. Don't move away from the oven—depending on your broiler, it can take seconds or minutes to caramelize the sugar, and you don't want to miss the moment and ruin the topping. When the sugar bubbles and browns, pull the custards out, remove them from their ice bed and let them settle down before serving.

## Playing Around

In any recipe in which milk or cream is heated, you have the opportunity to infuse the liquid with flavor.

**CINNAMON CRÈME BRÛLÉE**: Toss 2 cinnamon sticks into the saucepan with the cream and milk. Bring to a boil, remove the pan from the heat, cover and let infuse for at least 30 minutes or for up to 1 hour. When you are ready to make the custard, discard the cinnamon and rewarm the cream and milk.

You can use this same technique to infuse the crème brûlée with other herb and spice flavors.

**LAVENDER CRÈME BRÛLÉE**: Add 1 tablespoon edible lavender flowers to the hot cream and milk and continue as for Cinnamon Crème Brûlée.

**GINGER CRÈME BRÛLÉE**: Peel and chop a 1-inch-long chunk of fresh ginger, add to the hot cream and milk and continue as for Cinnamon Crème Brûlée.

**CARDAMOM-ORANGE CRÈME BRÛLÉE**: Add 4 crushed cardamom pods and 3 fat strips of orange zest to the cream and milk and continue as for Cinnamon Crème Brûlée.

**ESPRESSO CRÈME BRÛLÉE**: Line a fine-mesh strainer with a double thickness of damp cheesecloth. Bring just the milk to a boil, remove the pan from the heat and stir in 3 tablespoons finely ground espresso-roast beans. Let infuse for just 1 minute, then strain and discard the espresso grounds. Return the milk to the saucepan, add the heavy cream and continue with the recipe.

**TEA CRÈME BRÛLÉE**: Line a fine-mesh strainer with a double thickness of damp cheesecloth. Bring just the milk to a boil, remove the pan from the heat and stir in 1 tablespoon loose tea—I like Earl Grey. Let infuse for 4 minutes before straining the milk and discarding the tea leaves. Return the milk to the saucepan, add the heavy cream and continue with the recipe.

**RASPBERRY CRÈME BRÛLÉE**: Before you pour the custard into the baking dishes, put 3 or 4 raspberries in each dish.

# CARAMEL-TOPPED FLAN

**YOU'D BE** hard-pressed to find a dessert with a sexier, slinkier texture than this one. In classic flan style, the voluptuous vanilla custard is baked in a caramel-lined pan, so that when it is turned out, it is crowned with a shiny burnt sugar top and surrounded by swirls of bittersweet caramel syrup.

Depending on where you are, this upside-down custard might be called crème caramel, crème renversée or flan, and it might be served in individual portions or as a family dessert, as it is here. Wherever you have it and no matter its size, it will always have that great play between the caramel and the cold vanilla custard. And, even in the small Latino restaurants in my Manhattan neighborhood, where flan is brought out in aluminum foil cups and unceremoniously turned over on your plate, the dessert will always have an air of sophistication about it. That it is remarkably simple and very quick to make is a surprise as well as a bonus.

The only step in making the flan that can be the teeniest bit tricky is spreading the caramel evenly over the bottom of the pan, but you can nail it the first time if you follow my directions and pour the hot caramel syrup into a warm pan.

I think the flan looks more dramatic when it is made in a cake pan, but you can turn the recipe into individual servings: use six 6-ounce (³/₄-cup) or seven or eight 4-ounce (¹/₂-cup) ramekins, pudding cups, coffee cups or foil containers. Skip warming the containers before pouring in the caramel and start checking for doneness around the 25-minute mark.

**MAKES 6 TO 8 SERVINGS**

**SERVING:** Bring the flan to the table and cut it into wedges, like a cake. Serve it with some of the caramel syrup spooned onto each plate.

**STORING:** Covered with plastic wrap in its baking pan, the flan will keep in the refrigerator for up to 2 days. However, once you've unmolded it, it's best to enjoy it the same day.

*Playing Around*

**CARAMEL-TOPPED CO-CONUT FLAN:** For a more tropical flan with a somewhat lighter texture, replace the heavy cream with a 15-ounce can of unsweetened coconut milk (not sweetened cream of coconut) and reduce the amount of milk to 1 cup.

**FOR THE CARAMEL**

- ¹/₃ cup sugar
- 3 tablespoons water
- Squirt of fresh lemon juice

**FOR THE FLAN**

- 1¹/₂ cups heavy cream
- 1¹/₄ cups whole milk
- 3 large eggs
- 2 large egg yolks
- ¹/₂ cup sugar
- 1 teaspoon pure vanilla extract

**GETTING READY:** Center a rack in the oven and preheat the oven to 350 degrees F. Line a roasting pan or a 9-x-13-inch baking pan with a double thickness of paper towels. Fill a teakettle with water and put it on to boil; when the water boils, turn off the heat.

Put a metal 8-x-2-inch round cake pan—not a nonstick one—in the oven to heat while you prepare the caramel.

**TO MAKE THE CARAMEL:** Stir the sugar, water and lemon juice together in a small heavy-bottomed saucepan. Put the pan over medium-high heat and cook until the sugar becomes an amber-colored caramel, about 5 minutes—remove the pan from the heat at the first whiff of smoke.

Remove the cake pan from the oven and, working with oven mitts, pour the caramel into the pan and immediately tilt the pan to spread the caramel evenly over the bottom; set the pan aside.

TO MAKE THE FLAN: Bring the cream and milk just to a boil.

Meanwhile, in a 2-quart glass measuring cup or in a bowl, whisk together the eggs, yolks and sugar. Whisk vigorously for a minute or two, and then stir in the vanilla. Still whisking, drizzle in about one quarter of the hot liquid—this will temper, or warm, the eggs so they won't curdle. Whisking all the while, slowly pour in the remainder of the hot cream and milk. Using a large spoon, skim off the bubbles and foam that you worked up.

Put the caramel-lined cake pan in the roasting pan. Pour the custard into the cake pan and slide the setup into the oven. Very carefully pour enough hot water from the kettle into the roasting pan to come halfway up the sides of the cake pan. (Don't worry if this sets the cake pan afloat.) Bake the flan for about 35 minutes, or until the top puffs a bit and is golden here and there. A knife inserted into the center of the flan should come out clean.

Remove the roasting pan from the oven, transfer the cake pan to a cooling rack and run a knife between the flan and the sides of the pan to loosen it. Let the flan cool to room temperature on the rack, then loosely cover and refrigerate for at least 4 hours.

When ready to serve, once more, run a knife between the flan and the pan. Choose a rimmed serving platter, place the platter over the cake pan, quickly flip the platter and pan over and remove the cake pan—the flan will shimmy out and the caramel sauce will coat the custard.

# RASPBERRY BLANC-MANGER

**I WAS** tempted to change this recipe's name for two reasons: (1) many people might not know what a blanc-manger is; and (2) those who do might not want to make it. Over the years—and the blanc-manger has been around for many years, maybe even a millennium or two—the sweet has managed to make either no name or a bad name for itself. But I do love it—maybe because I never had it in America, where it has devolved into a kind of cornstarch pudding, but learned to make it in Paris, where it is light, pretty and beloved, particularly, I'm told, by newlyweds with no kitchen experience, because it is positively foolproof.

The ancient blanc-manger (pronounced "blah-mahn-jhay") was a nut cake, and today's sweet still has the nuts, usually almonds; but the crushed bones that culinary historians believe may have once provided the thickening have been replaced by gelatin. Used with a light hand, it makes the blanc-manger seem like panna cotta's kissing cousin. In my rendition, the dessert is speckled with raspberries, but you can use an assortment of berries or tiny pieces of peeled soft, ripe peaches.

I make the blanc-manger in a plain round cake pan and do nothing but unmold it before serving. Because of its ivory color and its polka dots of fruit, you don't have to do a thing to it to make it look like a fancy sweet. However, if you want an even more polished finish, look at Playing Around for a couple of additions that will make your blanc-manger more like the cakes displayed in Parisian pâtisseries.

MAKES 6 SERVINGS

**SERVING:** The blanc-manger, which must be served cold, can be presented plain with no accompaniments, but it is particularly attractive and extra delicious when it is served with the raspberry coulis. It can also be served with additional fresh berries or a spoonful of fruit salad. Pineapple goes well with the sweet, shimmery cake, but because fresh pineapple reacts with gelatin, put it on the side of the serving plate, if you want to use it, not in the dessert.

**STORING:** The blanc-manger can be kept in the refrigerator overnight. Keep it well covered in its pan and unmold it at the last minute before serving.

---

| | |
|---|---|
| 1½ cups cold heavy cream | 2 teaspoons pure vanilla extract |
| ¾ cup whole milk | 1 cup raspberries (or assorted berries), |
| ¾ cup ground almonds | or soft fruit cut into small pieces |
| ½ cup sugar | |
| 1 ¼-ounce packet unflavored gelatin | Raspberry Coulis (page 467), for |
| 3 tablespoons cold water | serving (optional) |

---

Have an 8-x-2-inch round cake pan at hand. Fill a large bowl with ice cubes and cold water, and set out a smaller bowl that fits into this ice-water bath.

Working with a stand mixer fitted with the whisk attachment or with a hand mixer in a large bowl, beat the cream until it holds soft peaks. Refrigerate while you prepare the rest of the dessert.

Put the milk, almonds and sugar in a small saucepan and bring to a boil over medium heat, stirring occasionally to make certain the sugar dissolves.

Meanwhile, put the gelatin and cold water in a microwave-safe bowl or a small saucepan. When the gelatin is soft and spongy, about 2 minutes, heat it in the microwave oven for 15 seconds, or cook it over low heat, to dissolve it. Stir the gelatin into the almond milk and remove the saucepan from the heat.

Pour the hot milk into the smaller reserved bowl and set the bowl in the ice-water bath. Stir in the vanilla and continue to stir until the mixture is cool but still liquid—you don't want the milk to jell in the bowl.

There are two little things you can do to make your blanc-manger a dead ringer for a pâtisserie offering. One is to glaze the top of the cake with a thin gloss of jelly. If you want a clear gloss, use apple or quince jelly; for a pink glow, use red currant jelly. Whatever jelly you choose, bring a couple of table-spoons of the jelly to a boil with a splash of water—you can do this in a microwave oven or in a small pan over direct heat. Using a pastry brush, spread a very thin layer of the jelly over the very cold cake (the cake must be fully set and cold before you put hot jelly on it). Then, if the cake looks as if it may have melted a tad, just put it back in the fridge to chill a while before serving. The second thing you can do is put the blanc-manger on a base: The traditional base is a thin disk of sponge cake—slices of cake like Perfect Party Cake (page 250) are just right, but any white or yellow cake, home-made or store-bought, would be good; just remember that you want a round that's be-tween ¼ and ½ inch thick, not a whole layer. You could also put the cake on a thin disk of fully baked Sweet Tart Dough (page 444). If you decide to use a base, you should build the blanc-manger in a springform pan. Put the cake or baked dough layer on the bottom, then pour in the blanc-manger mixture and chill.

When you've cooled down the milk mixture, use a large rubber spatula to very gently fold in the cold whipped cream, followed by the berries. Spoon the blanc-manger into the pan and refrigerate until set, about 3 hours. (If it's more conven-ient, you can keep the blanc-manger in the refrigerator overnight; just make sure it is not near anything with a strong odor.)

To unmold the blanc-manger, dip the cake pan up to its rim in hot water for 5 seconds, wipe the pan dry and invert the blanc-manger onto a serving plate. Serve with the raspberry coulis, if desired.

## Mastering Meringue

**MERINGUE** is nothing more than egg whites and sugar and nothing less than magical. You start with a bowl of jiggly egg whites and some sugar, and you beat air into them, and, presto-chango, you have swirls of glossy, billowy meringue. Not that there aren't pitfalls. Anyone new to beating egg whites—or even a veteran who has answered the phone while the whites were beating away in a stand mixer—has probably had the billows turn into clumps and balls; overbeating does that. Just keep the following rules in mind, and keep your eye on the bowl, and your whites are bound to peak beautifully every time.

• Strange as it may sound, old egg whites beat better than fresh ones. If you've been lucky enough to get still-warm-from-the-hen eggs, give them a few days so their whites will start to thin a bit, making them better for beating.

• While eggs separate most easily when they're cold, whites whip to their fullest when they are warm, so separate the eggs as soon as you take them from the refrigerator, then allow the whites to sit on the counter until they come to room temperature, about 15 minutes. In fact, because warm whites accept significantly more air than chilly ones, some pastry chefs go the extra step and warm the whites before beating them. If you want to ensure maximum puff—or you want to warm the whites faster—put the whites in a microwave-safe bowl and place them in a microwave oven set to the lowest power. Heat the whites for just 10 seconds, stir, then heat them in 5-second spurts until they feel warm to the touch. (If you've got an instant-read thermometer, the ideal temperature is 75 degrees F, but a little warmer is okay.)

• Always use a bowl that is super-clean and dry, with nary a speck of fat. Even a bit of egg yolk can upset your whites' puff power.

• Add a pinch of salt to the whites to liquefy them a bit at the beginning and to stabilize them a bit at the end. A pinch of cream of tartar or a squirt of fresh lemon juice is also a good stabilizer.

• A heavy-duty stand mixer with the whisk attachment or a handheld beater will help you get the most volume out of the whites. If all you've got is elbow grease, choose a metal bowl (copper is best for whites—the chemical reaction between the copper and the whites increases the amount of air you can get into the whites) and a balloon whisk.

• Start whipping with only the whites in the bowl. Whip the whites until they form medium-soft peaks, then, still whipping, gradually add the sugar.

• Don't get carried away. Properly whipped whites are smooth and glossy. If the whites start to lose their gloss and break up into little puffs, you've overdone it. (The sugar in the meringue goes a long way to safeguarding the eggs from overzealous beating.)

• Meringue is a use-it-or-lose-it preparation. Once you've got the whites whipped to perfection, use the meringue immediately—or as soon after immediately as possible.

# FLOATING ISLANDS

........................................................................................................

**FOR THE** French, this dessert is not only a classic, but often a childhood touchstone. In a country where people are more likely to buy their desserts from a neighborhood pâtisserie than prepare them at home, *îles flottantes* remains a mainstay in the make-at-home repertoire, in some part because it is so easy and in some part because it's a naturally showy dessert. The islands, soft poached meringue puffs, float in a smooth crème anglaise, which is even better when refrigerated overnight. Served in a large bowl (the dessert looks great served in a grand footed bowl) or in individual portions, the islands can be presented unadorned or given their traditional decoration—caramelized sugar strands. Making the strands is a last-minute job, but it takes only a couple of minutes and adds more than a couple of minutes' worth of oohs and aahs.

MAKES 6 SERVINGS

**SERVING:** Once the dessert has been assembled, it should be served immediately.

**STORING:** You can make both the crème anglaise and the meringue puffs in advance and keep them chilled, but the assembled dessert won't keep.

**FOR THE CRÈME ANGLAISE**

2 cups whole milk

6 large egg yolks

½ cup sugar

1½ teaspoons pure vanilla extract

**FOR THE ISLANDS**

2 cups milk

4 large egg whites, at room
  temperature

Pinch of salt

¼ cup sugar

**FOR THE CARAMEL (OPTIONAL)**

½ cup sugar

⅓ cup water

**TO MAKE THE CRÈME ANGLAISE:** Bring the milk to a boil.

Meanwhile, put the yolks and sugar in a heavy saucepan and whisk vigorously until thick and pale, 2 to 3 minutes. Still whisking, drizzle in a little of the hot milk—this will temper, or warm, the yolks so they won't curdle. Whisking all the while, slowly pour in the remaining milk. Put the saucepan over medium-low heat and, stirring constantly with a wooden spoon, cook until the custard thickens, lightens in color and coats the spoon (this can take 10 minutes or so)—if you run your finger down the spoon, the track should remain. For this recipe, the crème anglaise should be cooked until it reaches 180 degrees F on an instant-read thermometer.

Immediately remove the pan from the heat, strain the custard into a bowl and stir in the vanilla extract. Press a piece of plastic wrap against the surface of the custard to create an airtight seal and refrigerate until thoroughly chilled, or for up to 3 days. (The crème anglaise will improve with at least an overnight rest.)

**TO MAKE THE ISLANDS:** Spread a clean kitchen towel on the counter near the stove and have a large slotted spoon at hand. Put the milk in a wide saucepan and bring it to a simmer over low heat.

Meanwhile, put the egg whites in the clean bowl of a stand mixer fitted with the whisk attachment, or use a large bowl and a hand mixer. Beat the whites on medium speed just until foamy, then beat in the salt. When the eggs turn opaque, increase the mixer speed to medium-high and add the sugar about 1 tablespoon at a time. Whip until the meringue is firm but satiny and still glossy.

You have two choices in shaping the islands: you can just scoop up some meringue—specifically, an amount about twice the size of an egg—in which case you'll have the equivalent of a rocky volcanic island, or you can smooth the meringue to get a manicured island. For the smooth look, use a large oval spoon to scoop up the meringue, then use another large oval spoon to very gingerly transfer the meringue from spoon to spoon a couple of times to form a smooth oval.

Either way, one by one, lower the islands into the simmering milk, adding only as many islands as you can fit into the pan without crowding. Poach the meringues for 1 minute, gently turn them over and poach 1 minute more, then lift the islands out of the milk and onto the towel. Repeat until you've poached 12 islands. Put the puffs (which will have inflated when poached and will deflate when cooled) on a wax paper–lined baking sheet and chill them for at least 1 hour, or for up to 3 hours.

TO MAKE THE OPTIONAL CARAMEL: Decide whether you want to serve the meringues in one large bowl or six individual bowls, and have the bowl(s) at hand.

Right before serving, stir the sugar and water together in a small heavy-bottomed saucepan and cook over medium heat, stirring, until the sugar dissolves. Increase the heat, bring the sugar to a boil and cook without stirring, swirling the pan occasionally, until the caramel turns a pale gold color, 6 to 8 minutes or so. Pull the pan from the heat and let the caramel cool just until it is thick enough to form threads when it is dropped from the tines of a fork. (If the caramel hardens, rewarm it slowly over low heat.)

Either pour the crème anglaise into a large serving bowl and top with the meringue islands, or make six individual servings. If using the caramel, working quickly, dip the tines of a fork into the caramel and wave the fork over the floating islands to create threads that will quickly harden.

INCLUDING MARSHMALLOWS as a spoon dessert may seem like cheating—after all, they're eaten with fingers (or, by campers, from sticks picked up in the forest)—but making them at home is too much fun to miss. And in fact this dessert is related to others in this chapter: the base is meringue—sweetened and strengthened by a cooked sugar syrup and fortified by gelatin.

There's nothing difficult about making the marshmallows, but the meringue does need a long beating. While you can use a hand mixer, a stand mixer makes the job easier.

I'm giving you the recipe for a basic vanilla marshmallow. See Playing Around for raspberry, chocolate, cappuccino and pumpkin marshmallows.

About 1 cup potato starch (found in the kosher foods section of supermarkets) or cornstarch

¾ cup cold water

1¼ cups plus 1 tablespoon sugar

2 tablespoons light corn syrup

2 ¼-ounce packets unflavored gelatin

3 large egg whites, at room temperature

1 tablespoon pure vanilla extract

GETTING READY: Line a rimmed baking sheet—choose one with a rim that is 1 inch high—with parchment paper and dust the paper generously with potato starch or cornstarch. Have a candy thermometer at hand.

Put ⅓ cup of the water, 1¼ cups of the sugar and the corn syrup in a medium saucepan over medium heat. Bring the mixture to a boil, stirring until the sugar dissolves. Once the sugar is dissolved, continue to cook the syrup—without stirring—until it reaches 265 degrees F on the candy thermometer, about 10 minutes.

While the syrup is cooking, work on the gelatin and egg whites. In a microwave-safe bowl, sprinkle the gelatin over the remaining cold water (a scant 7 tablespoons) and let it sit for about 5 minutes, until it is spongy, then heat the gelatin in a microwave oven for 20 to 30 seconds to liquefy it. (Alternatively, you can dissolve the gelatin in a saucepan over low heat.)

Working in the clean, dry bowl of a stand mixer fitted with the whisk attachment or in another large bowl with a hand mixer, beat the egg whites on medium-high speed until firm but still glossy—don't overbeat them and have them go dull.

As soon as the syrup reaches 265 degrees F, remove the pan from the heat and, with the mixer on medium speed, add the syrup, pouring it between the spinning beater(s) and the sides of the bowl. Add the gelatin and continue to beat for another 3 minutes, so that the syrup and the gelatin are fully incorporated. Beat in the vanilla.

Using a large rubber spatula, scrape the meringue mixture onto the baking sheet, laying it down close to a short end of the sheet. Then spread it into the corners and continue to spread it out, taking care to keep the height of the batter at 1 inch; you won't fill the pan. Lift the excess parchment paper up to meet the edge of the batter, then rest something against the paper so that it stays in place (I use custard cups).

MAKES ABOUT 1 POUND MARSHMALLOWS

SERVING: Put the marshmallows out and let everyone nibble as they wish. Sometimes I fill a tall glass vase with the marshmallows and put it in the center of the table—it never fails to make friends smile. You can also top hot chocolate or cold sundaes with the marshmallows.

STORING: Keep the marshmallows in a cool, dry place; don't cover them closely. Stored in this way, they will keep for about 1 week—they might develop a little crust on the outside or they might get a little firmer on the inside, but they'll still be very good.

**RASPBERRY MARSHMAL-
LOWS**: Fruit purees are excellent for flavoring these candies.
For raspberry marshmallows,
you'll need a generous ⅓ cup of
puree; reduce the vanilla extract to ¼ teaspoon. After the
batter is mixed, gently fold in
the puree with a rubber spatula. You can use the same
measurements and technique
for other purees, such as strawberry, mango and passion fruit.

**CAPPUCCINO MARSHMAL-
LOWS**: Sift ¼ cup unsweetened cocoa powder, 2 tablespoons instant espresso
powder and ½ teaspoon ground
cinnamon together into a small
bowl. Stir in ⅓ cup boiling
water and mix until smooth. Reduce the vanilla extract to ½
teaspoon, and add it to the
espresso mix. After you add the
sugar syrup and gelatin to the
meringue, beat in the espresso
mixture and continue.

**LIGHT CHOCOLATE
MARSHMALLOWS**: Melt 3
ounces bittersweet or semisweet chocolate and stir in 2½
tablespoons unsweetened
cocoa powder. Reduce the
vanilla extract to ¼ teaspoon,
and after the marshmallow batter is mixed, fold in the chocolate mixture with a large rubber
spatula.

**PUMPKIN SPICE MARSH-
MALLOWS**: Whisk together
½ cup canned unsweetened
pumpkin puree, 1 teaspoon
ground cinnamon, ½ teaspoon
ground ginger, a pinch of
freshly grated nutmeg and a
pinch of ground allspice. After
the marshmallow batter is
mixed, fold in the spiced pumpkin with a large rubber spatula.

Dust the top of the marshmallows with potato starch or cornstarch and let the marshmallows set in a cool, dry place. They'll need about 3 hours, but they can rest for 12 hours or more.

Once they are cool and set, cut the marshmallows with a pair of scissors or a long thin knife. Whatever you use, you'll have to rinse and dry it frequently. Have a big bowl with the remaining potato starch or cornstarch at hand and cut the marshmallows as you'd like—into squares, rectangles or even strips (as they're cut in France). As each piece is cut, drop it into the bowl. When you've got 4 or 5 marshmallows in the bowl, reach in with your fingers and turn the marshmallows to coat them with starch, then, one by one, toss the marshmallows from one hand to the other to shake off the excess starch; transfer them to a serving bowl. Cut and coat the rest of the batch.

# CHOCOLATE SOUFFLÉ

**FEW DESSERTS** are as dramatic as soufflés and fewer have such an unde-
served reputation for finickiness. No less a culinary luminary than Marie-
Antoine Carême, who almost single-handedly invented pastry as we know it
today, was making soufflés in the early 1800s—and chronicling all the catastro-
phes that could befall the confection. It's my guess that soufflés earned their reputation for fragility at a time when ovens were unreliable, electric mixers were not
even a dream and the distance between the kitchen and the dining room was
long, cold and drafty. Hardly ideal conditions for allowing a soufflé to live up to
its name, which, translated from the French, means puffed up.

Today we've got the technology—good ovens, mixers and central heating (if
not the staff). All you need to succeed is a proper soufflé mold, a straight-sided
porcelain or heatproof glass dish and a batch of well-beaten egg whites. Simple—
you can get the mold just about anywhere and learn the rules for whipping whites
(see Mastering Meringue, page 400).

Otherwise all you need is a sense of adventure and an audience. After all, if
Carême made a big deal out of sugar and air, why shouldn't you?

6 ounces bittersweet chocolate, finely
  chopped
½ cup plus 2 tablespoons sugar
⅓ cup whole milk, at room
  temperature

4 large eggs, separated and at room
  temperature
2 large egg whites, at room temperature

Confectioners' sugar, for dusting

GETTING READY: Position a rack in the lower third of the oven and preheat the
oven to 400 degrees F. Give the inside of a 6- to 7-cup soufflé mold a thick coating
of butter, sprinkle it with sugar and tap out the excess. Refrigerate until needed.
Line a baking sheet with parchment or a silicone mat.

Put the chocolate and ½ cup of the sugar in a heatproof bowl over a saucepan
of simmering water and heat, stirring often, until the chocolate is melted. Transfer
the bowl to the counter and whisk in the milk. Let the chocolate cool for about 5
minutes, then, one by one, whisk in the yolks.

Working in the clean, dry bowl of a stand mixer fitted with the whisk attachment or in a large bowl with a hand mixer, whip the 6 egg whites until they just
turn opaque and start to hold peaks. Still beating, add the remaining 2 tablespoons sugar in a slowish, steady stream and continue to beat until the peaks are
glossy and almost firm. Stir one quarter of the whites into the chocolate to lighten
it, then use a rubber spatula to gently fold in the remaining whites.

Delicately turn the batter into the prepared mold and lightly sprinkle the top
with confectioners' sugar. Put the mold on the baking sheet.

Bake—it's better not to open the door and peek until you think the soufflé is
almost done—for 40 minutes, or until the soufflé is beautifully puffed and a thin
knife inserted into the center comes out clean (find a noncrusty part of the soufflé
and gently insert the knife at an angle). Remove the soufflé from the oven and
serve immediately, dusting the top with more confectioners' sugar if you'd like.

MAKES 4 TO 6 SERVINGS

**SERVING:** This soufflé has enough flavor and, of course, enough drama to go it alone, but it's awfully good with Crème Anglaise (page 451). Pour the custard sauce into a pretty pitcher and pass it after you've spooned out the soufflé, so guests can help themselves.

**STORING:** If you have any left-over soufflé, hold on to it. It won't be pretty, but if you top it with whipped cream and call it what it is—a fallen soufflé cake—you'll enjoy it.

*Playing Around*
Just for fun and a little crunch, you can add about 1 cup toasted almonds to the soufflé. Pour about a third of the soufflé batter into the mold, scatter toasted sliced almonds over the batter, add another third of the batter, scatter some nuts over it, and then pour in the rest of the batter and top with nuts.

# BOURBON BREAD PUDDING

**ADDING BOURBON** to bread pudding is a Creole custom and a good idea. An American whisky made from corn and aged in oak barrels, bourbon has a sweetness and more than a hint of vanilla, two qualities that mesh impeccably with an egg-and-cream pudding. I like to make this pudding in a loaf pan and use a French baguette, but, like all good bread puddings, it's a treat made with brioche, challah or chunks of cinnamon-raisin bread.

MAKES 8 SERVINGS

| | |
|---|---|
| 8 ounces baguette (or egg-rich bread), preferably stale | ½ cup sugar |
| | ½ teaspoon ground cinnamon |
| 1½ cups whole milk | Pinch of freshly grated nutmeg |
| 1½ cups heavy cream | 1 tablespoon bourbon |
| 4 large eggs | 1½ teaspoons pure vanilla extract |
| 2 large egg yolks | ⅛ teaspoon pure almond extract |

**SERVING:** I like serving this pudding at room temperature—the texture is best then and the flavors most pronounced. You can refrigerate the pudding, but I think it loses its lusciousness as its temperature drops. Cut the pudding into thick slices and use a pie server to lift the pieces from the pan. My own preference is to serve the pudding plain, with a big spoon. But you can serve it with fruit such as berries or caramelized apples (pan-roast apples as you would for the filling of Apple-Apple Bread Pudding, page 408).

**GETTING READY:** Have a nonreactive 9-x-5-inch loaf pan on hand (a Pyrex or pottery pan is perfect here), as well as a roasting pan big enough to hold the loaf pan. Line the roasting pan with a double thickness of paper towels. Fill a teakettle with water and put it on to boil; when the water boils, turn off the heat.

Cut the bread into 1-inch cubes. If the bread is stale, put it in the loaf pan. If it is not stale, spread it out on a baking sheet lined with parchment or a silicone mat and bake in a 350-degree-F oven to "stale" it for 10 minutes, then put it in the pan.

Bring the milk and cream just to a boil.

Meanwhile, whisk the eggs, yolks, sugar, cinnamon and nutmeg together in a bowl. Still whisking, slowly drizzle in about one quarter of the hot milk mixture—this will temper, or warm, the eggs so they don't curdle. Whisking all the while, slowly pour in the remaining milk. Add the bourbon and vanilla and almond extracts and whisk gently to blend. Rap the bowl against the counter to pop any bubbles that might have formed, then pour the custard over the bread and press the bread gently with the back of a spoon to help cover it with liquid. Cover the pan lightly with wax paper and leave it on the counter, giving the bread the back-of-the-spoon treatment now and then, for 1 hour.

**STORING:** The pudding is best the day it is made. You can keep it covered in the refrigerator for up to 1 day, but even if you bring it to room temperature before serving, the texture won't be the same.

**GETTING READY TO BAKE:** Center a rack in the oven and preheat the oven to 350 degrees F.

Discard the wax paper and cover the pan snugly with a piece of aluminum foil; poke about 5 holes in the foil. Slide the pan into the oven and very carefully pour enough hot water into the roasting pan to come halfway up the sides of the pudding pan. Bake the pudding for 30 minutes, then remove the foil and bake for 15 minutes more, or until the pudding is puffed and golden and a knife inserted deep into the center comes out clean. Transfer the baking pan to a rack and cool the pudding until it is just warm, or until it reaches room temperature.

**I LOVED** bread pudding even before I ever tasted it. I didn't grow up on it—my mom didn't make desserts—but I was intrigued by its cozy name. Later, when I actually saw a recipe for it, I was won over by its simplicity, and it became one of the first things I made as a new cook. Michael, my husband, didn't like bread pudding, a fact he never forgot—until I made this one of apple-buttered bread layered with caramelized apples. He loved it. Our son loved it. And, when I sent one off to my husband's office, everyone there loved it and three people (including a guy who'd never even scrambled eggs) asked for the recipe.

It's rich—sumptuous even—a dessert to make not only when you've got leftover bread but worthy of buying bread for the express purpose of having it left over.

**SERVING:** Cut into squares and serve the pudding at just about any temperature—slightly warm, room temperature or even chilled. If you want to gussy it up a bit, serve it with a pitcher of Crème Anglaise (page 451) or top each portion with a scoop of ice cream.

**STORING:** Bread pudding is best served the day it is made, but this pudding is still delicious served at room temperature the following day.

*Playing Around*

**JAM AND FRUIT BREAD PUDDING:** Use the same good bread and the same rich custard, but substitute a chunky premium-quality jam or a different fruit butter for the apple butter and a nice soft fruit for the apples (look for a fruit so soft it won't have to be caramelized first). Here are some combinations to get you started: peach preserves and peeled and sliced peaches; apricot jam (or apricot butter) and apricot halves or mango slices; or cherry jam and pitted and halved cherries.

FOR THE CARAMELIZED APPLES

3 medium apples, peeled and cored
  (Fujis or Galas work well)
3 tablespoons unsalted butter
3 tablespoons sugar

12 ounces egg bread, such as challah
  or brioche, or good-quality white
  bread, preferably stale, sliced
  ½ inch thick

  About 1 cup store-bought spiced
  apple butter

3 cups whole milk
1 cup heavy cream
3 large eggs
5 large egg yolks
¾ cup sugar
1 teaspoon pure vanilla extract

  Confectioners' sugar or apple jelly
  (optional), for finishing

GETTING READY: Butter a 9-x-13-inch baking pan (a Pyrex pan is perfect here), dust the inside with sugar and tap out the excess. Line a larger roasting pan with a double thickness of paper towels.

TO CARAMELIZE THE APPLES: Cut each apple in half from top to bottom, cut each half lengthwise into 6 to 8 slices and then cut each slice in half crosswise.

Put a large skillet (preferably one that's nonstick) over medium-high heat, add the butter and, when it melts, sprinkle over the sugar. Cook the butter and sugar for a minute or so—you want the sugar to caramelize but not burn, so adjust the heat accordingly. Toss in the apple slices—don't worry if the caramel seizes and lumps, it will melt and smooth out as you work—and cook, carefully turning the apples once or twice, until they are tender but not soft, 3 to 5 minutes. They should be golden, and some might even be caramelized. Transfer the apples and the buttery liquid to a plate.

If your bread is not stale, spread it out on a baking sheet lined with parchment or a silicone mat and bake at 350 degrees F to "stale" it for 10 minutes.

Spread one side of each slice of bread with the apple butter, then cut each slice on the diagonal to get 4 triangles. Cover the bottom of the baking pan with half of the bread, arranging the triangles, buttered side up, so that they overlap slightly (don't worry about spaces between the slices). Spoon over the apples and their liquid and finish "the sandwich" with the rest of the bread.

Bring the milk and cream just to a boil.

Fill a teakettle with water and put it on to boil; when the water boils, turn off the heat. Meanwhile, in a medium bowl, whisk together the eggs, yolks and the ¾ cup sugar. Still whisking, slowly drizzle in about one quarter of the hot milk mixture—this will temper, or warm, the eggs so they won't curdle. Whisking all the while, slowly pour in the remaining milk. Add the vanilla and whisk to blend. Rap the bowl against the counter to pop any bubbles that might have formed, then spoon off any foam that has risen to the top. Pour the custard over the bread and press the bread gently with the back of a spoon to help it absorb the liquid. Leave the pan on the counter, giving the bread the back-of-the-spoon treatment now and then, for about 30 minutes.

GETTING READY TO BAKE: Center a rack in the oven and preheat the oven to 325 degrees F.

Put the baking pan in the roasting pan, slide the setup into the oven and very carefully pour enough hot water into the roasting pan to come halfway up the sides of the pudding pan. Bake the pudding for about 1 hour and 25 minutes, or until a thin knife inserted deep into the center comes out clean. Transfer the baking pan to a rack and cool for at least 20 minutes before serving.

The pudding can be served as is or dusted with confectioners' sugar just before serving. Or, if you want to give the pudding a little gloss, put about ½ cup apple jelly in a small pot with a splash of water. Heat until the jelly liquefies, then brush a thin layer over the top of the pudding.

# FOUR-STAR CHOCOLATE BREAD PUDDING

**HOW CAN** something you'd be happy to serve at the end of a fancy dinner party also be something you'd be happy to make when you're hassled? This is the kind of culinary conundrum I'd like to come up against more often. Thanks to its ample amount of fine chocolate, this pudding transcends its homey origins and belies the fact that all you have to do to prepare it is heat some milk and cream, beat some eggs, soak some bread and slide the pan into the oven. I like to use a pan large enough to create a pudding that's only about an inch high. Cut into generous squares and topped with Crème Anglaise (page 451), chocolate sauce (pages 463 and 464) or snowy whipped cream, it looks classy.

If you'd like a deeper pudding, you can make the pudding in a 7-x-11-inch baking pan or in something deeper, like a soufflé mold. Alternatively, you can make individual puddings—depending on the size of the cups you use, you'll need 8 to 10. Of course, with any change of pan, you'll have to change the baking time, which is not difficult since, as you'll see, it is easy to tell when the pudding is properly baked.

MAKES 12 SERVINGS

**SERVING:** You could serve this pudding warm, but it is better at cool room temperature or even chilled—it also cuts better when it is cold. Serve the pudding simply with a dusting of confectioners' sugar or less simply with vanilla (or rum or Grand Marnier or brandy) Crème Anglaise (page 451), chocolate sauce (pages 463 and 464) or whipped cream or crème fraîche (page 459).

**STORING:** Covered, the bread pudding will keep in the refrigerator for up to 2 days.

| | |
|---|---|
| 12 ounces bread (brioche, challah or white), preferably stale | 1 cup heavy cream |
| ½ cup moist, plump raisins (dark or golden) or dried cherries (optional) | 3 large eggs |
| | 4 large egg yolks |
| | ½ cup sugar |
| 3 cups whole milk | 6 ounces bittersweet chocolate, finely chopped |

**GETTING READY:** Have a 9-x-13-inch baking pan at hand (a Pyrex pan is perfect here), as well as a roasting pan big enough to hold the baking pan and hot water. Line the roasting pan with a double thickness of paper towels.

Cut the bread into 1-inch cubes. If the bread is stale, put it and the raisins or cherries, if you are using them, into the baking pan. If it is not stale, spread it out on a baking sheet lined with parchment or a silicone mat and bake in a 350-degree-F oven to "stale" it for 10 minutes, then toss into the pan (with the fruit).

Bring the milk and cream just to a boil.

Fill a teakettle with water and put it on to boil; when the water boils, turn off the heat. Meanwhile, whisk the eggs, yolks and sugar together in a bowl. Still whisking, slowly drizzle in about one quarter of the hot milk mixture—this will temper, or warm, the eggs so they don't curdle. Whisking all the while, slowly pour in the rest of the hot milk. Add the chocolate and whisk it in gently until it is melted and the custard is smooth. Rap the bowl against the counter to pop any bubbles that might have formed, then pour the custard over the bread and press the bread gently with the back of a spoon to help cover it with liquid. Leave the pan on the counter, giving the bread the back-of-the-spoon treatment now and then, for 30 minutes.

**GETTING READY TO BAKE:** Center a rack in the oven and preheat the oven to 350 degrees F.

Slide the pan setup into the oven and very carefully pour enough hot water into the roasting pan to come halfway up the sides of the pudding pan. Bake for 35 to 45 minutes, or until the pudding is uniformly puffed, the top is dull and dry and a thin knife inserted deep into the center comes out clean. Transfer the baking pan to a rack and cool to room temperature.

# ARBORIO RICE PUDDING, WHITE, BLACK (OR BOTH)

**IF YOU** love rice pudding—and, hard as it is for me to believe, I have been told that there are people who don't—then you'll love this pudding, as much for what it is as for what else it can be (see Playing Around). It is a creamy but not unusually rich rice pudding made with Arborio rice, the round, short-grained Italian rice most famously used in risotto. Although you can make this pudding with a different kind of rice, I prefer Arborio because it holds a touch of its texture even after being cooked for half an hour.

The basic version is made with milk (please use whole milk), sugar and rice and flavored with vanilla, and, while I make that one often, you're more likely to find the pudding's chocolate twin chilling in the fridge at my house. Because rice pudding is so elemental, it can be vanilla or chocolate, and it can be enriched with whipped cream, studded with dried fruit, swirled with jam, served with fruit or left as it is, to be spooned out into a little cup and eaten at midnight as sustenance, comfort or indulgence, depending on the kind of midnight you're having.

MAKES 4 SERVINGS

**SERVING:** If you'd like, top the pudding with whipped cream, jam, Raspberry Coulis (page 467) or fresh fruit.

**STORING:** Covered, the rice pudding will keep in the refrigerator for up to 3 days.

¼ cup Arborio rice

2 cups water

3¼ cups whole milk

¼ cup sugar

1 tablespoon pure vanilla extract (for vanilla pudding)

3 ounces bittersweet chocolate, very finely chopped (for chocolate pudding)

Put the rice and water in a medium heavy-bottomed saucepan and bring to a boil. Lower the temperature and cook the rice, uncovered, for 10 minutes. Drain the rice in a strainer and rinse it; set aside.

Rinse out the saucepan, then pour in the milk, stir in the sugar and set the pan over medium heat. When the milk boils, stir in the parboiled rice. Reduce the heat to low and let the mixture bubble away gently, stirring occasionally, for about 30 minutes. As the pudding gets close to done, the rice kernels will be visible in the boiling milk—you'll see them floating just under the top layer of milk. The pudding won't be thick—that's okay (it will thicken in the refrigerator)—but the rice will be soft and it will have absorbed 80 to 90 percent of the milk.

Remove the pan from the heat and decide what flavor you'd like the pudding to be—add either the vanilla or the chocolate and stir gently until it is fully blended into the pudding. Or, if you'd like to make half vanilla and half chocolate, divide the pudding between two serving bowls and add 1½ teaspoons vanilla to one bowl and 1½ ounces chocolate to the other.

Pour the pudding into a serving bowl or into individual bowls or cups. Press plastic wrap against the surface of the pudding to keep it from forming a skin, and refrigerate for at least 6 hours, until thoroughly cold.

## Playing Around

With a palette as pristine as this pudding, there are several possibilities for embellishment and variation, among them:

**CREAMIER RICE PUDDING**: Whip ⅓ to ½ cup heavy cream until it holds firm peaks, and gently fold the cream into the cold pudding. Serve immediately.

**DRUNKEN FRUIT RICE PUDDING**: Steep ½ cup dried fruit in a liqueur or eau-de-vie for a few hours, then stir the fruit into the pudding. Possibilities include raisins (dark or golden) or dried currants and dark rum; chopped prunes and Armagnac; snipped dried apricots and amaretto or vodka; dried cherries and kirsch; and dried strawberries and Chambord or framboise.

**RICE PUDDING RING**: As soon as the pudding is cooked, pour it into a bowl, cover with a piece of plastic wrap and let the pudding cool to room temperature on the counter. Soften ½ packet (about 1½ teaspoons) unflavored gelatin in 2 tablespoons cold water. Put the spongy gelatin in a microwave oven and heat for 15 seconds, until it is dissolved (or do this in a saucepan over low heat). Mix the gelatin into the cooled rice pudding. Whip ½ cup heavy cream until it holds firm peaks, and fold the cream into the pudding. Spray a 3-cup metal ring mold—if you don't have a ring mold, you can use whatever you have, including a round cake pan—with vegetable cooking spray and spoon the pudding into the mold. Rap the mold on the counter to settle the pudding, cover with plastic wrap and refrigerate for at least 3 hours. Release the pudding by heating the mold with a hairdryer or by dipping the mold briefly in hot water, and turn the pudding out onto a serving plate. Serve with sugared mixed berries and, if you'd like, Raspberry Coulis (page 467).

# COBBLERS, CRUMBLES, CRISPS AND SHORTCAKES

FRUIT CRISPS, CRUMBLES, cobblers and shortcakes are good-no-matter-what desserts—no matter what fruit you use, no matter what topping combo, no matter what pan, no matter how neat the construction, no matter how messy, they are always delicious. When first-time bakers ask me where they should begin their adventures, I always point them in the direction of these uncomplicated sweets.

On a technical level, crisps are the easiest to make. The fruit—and it can be any fruit from soft berries to firm apples and pears—is mixed with sugar and, if you'd like, a little spice, turned into an oven-going pan and topped with a crisp mix. The mix always has butter and sugar and something to bind the two together, sometimes just flour, but often flour and oatmeal—which gives the dessert a wonderfully pebbly look and great texture. Since any of the toppings can be tasted before baking, even neophytes can personalize these recipes.

A crumble is really a crisp with a slightly different texture. The fruit may be the same you would use for a crisp, but you top it with a streusel, a mix of butter, sugar, flour and chopped nuts. Over the years, I've found that the easiest way to make a streusel that is crunchy on the outside and tender within is to blend the ingredients (I do this by hand), spread the mixture out on a piece of wax paper and put it in the freezer. After about 20 minutes, the mixture will be firm enough to break into chunks and strew over the fruit. But because there is nothing set-in-concrete about crumble recipes, you can replace the streusel in the recipe with a crumb topping from a coffee cake (try the toppings on pages 38 and 192) or muffins (see page 16) and, of course, the choice of fruit is always up for grabs.

When you come to shortcakes and cobblers, you tiptoe into the realm of dough. True, making biscuit dough requires a bit more attention than putting together a crisp or crumble mix (see page 2 for pointers), but I'll let you in on a secret: when you use the dough in a cobbler, any little mistakes go unnoticed. That's because the warm bubbling fruit softens the bottom of the biscuit and the generous amount of baking powder in the dough just about guarantees an impressive rise. It's another recipe that's good no matter what.

# CHERRY RHUBARB COBBLER

**WHEN I** told my friend the fabulous pastry chef and cookbook author Nick Malgieri about this dessert, he said, "It's a great idea to use rhubarb with cherries, since cherries can be so bland when baked." It made me think of Katharine Hepburn's line about Fred Astaire giving Ginger Rogers class and her giving him sex appeal. In any event, the give-and-take is deliciously evident in this dessert, in which the stars give each other sparkle and the brown-sugar-and-whole-wheat biscuit topping brings them together.

**SERVING:** The cobbler can be served as soon as it is not mouth-searingly hot, or you can wait until it reaches room temperature. You can even serve it chilled, but the texture of the topping isn't as nice when it's cold. It almost goes without saying that the cobbler is great with whipped cream or vanilla ice cream. Cherry vanilla would be even better.

**STORING:** This is best eaten the day it is made—in fact, soon after it is made.

### FOR THE FILLING

- 1 pound sweet red cherries, pitted and halved
- 12 ounces (about 4 long fat stalks) rhubarb, trimmed, peeled and cut into 1-inch pieces
- ⅓ cup sugar
- 1 tablespoon cornstarch
- 1 teaspoon ground ginger

### FOR THE TOPPING

- ¾ cup all-purpose flour
- ¾ cup whole wheat flour
- 3 tablespoons (packed) light brown sugar
- 2 teaspoons baking powder
- ½ teaspoon salt
- ¼ teaspoon ground ginger
- ¾ stick (6 tablespoons) cold unsalted butter, cut into about 18 pieces
- ½ cup whole milk

*Playing Around*

This biscuit topping is a great crown for almost any kind of cobbler or crisp, whether you're using summer or winter fruits. Try it over any of your favorite cobbler or crisp fillings, or use the filling in Depths-of-Fall Butternut Squash Pie (page 328) as the cobbler bottom.

**GETTING READY:** Center a rack in the oven and preheat the oven to 375 degrees F. Butter an 8-inch square baking pan (I like a Pyrex pan) and place it on a baking sheet lined with parchment or a silicone mat.

**TO MAKE THE FILLING:** Mix the cherries and rhubarb together in a medium bowl and stir in the sugar, cornstarch and ginger. Stir the fruit from time to time while you make the topping.

**TO MAKE THE TOPPING:** Put both flours, the brown sugar, baking powder, salt and ginger in a food processor. Pulse a couple of times just to blend. Scatter the pieces of butter over the dry ingredients and, using 1- to 2-second-long pulses, mix in the butter until the dough looks like very coarse meal with a bunch of pea-size pieces tossed in. Continuing to pulse the machine, add the milk, then pulse until the dough forms moist clumps and curds. Try not to process the dough so long that it forms a ball on the blade. Turn the dough out onto a very lightly floured work surface.

Cut the dough into 20 pieces and gently shape each piece into a ball. Don't worry about making the pieces perfectly round—the important thing is to not handle the dough too much or too roughly.

Pour the fruit and its syrupy liquid into the buttered pan and top it with the biscuit puffs, making 4 rows of 5 puffs each. Bake for 35 to 45 minutes, or until the biscuits are golden and the fruit is bubbling away. Remove the pan from the oven and cool the cobbler on a rack for at least 20 minutes.

THE NAME cobbler probably came from the idea that biscuit-topped fruit can be cobbled together with ingredients that are usually at hand. I almost always had everything needed to make the dough but rarely had enough fruit for the bottom layer—until I discovered those bags of good-for-cobbler frozen berries: wild blueberries, red raspberries, even mixed berries. In case you've never used frozen berries, I think you'll be pleased to find that, if frozen individually and not in syrup, they can be used with admirable results. You might also be pleased to know that you don't have to defrost them before cobbling them. (If you've got lots of fresh berries, though, you can certainly use them in this recipe.)

FOR THE TOPPING

- 2 cups all-purpose flour
- 1 tablespoon baking powder
- 3 tablespoons sugar
- ½ teaspoon salt
- ¾ stick (6 tablespoons) cold unsalted butter, cut into little bits
- ¾ cup cold heavy cream

FOR THE FILLING

- About 5 cups mixed berries (go light on the strawberries, they're a bit too watery for a cobbler)—frozen, not in syrup (no need to defrost them), or fresh
- 4–5 tablespoons sugar (depending on your taste)
- 1 tablespoon cornstarch
  Grated zest of ½ lemon or lime
- ¼ teaspoon (or more, to taste) freshly ground black pepper (optional)

Vanilla ice cream, for serving

GETTING READY: Center a rack in the oven and preheat the oven to 375 degrees F. Butter a 9-inch deep-dish pie plate and put it on a baking sheet lined with parchment or a silicone mat.

TO MAKE THE TOPPING: In a large bowl, whisk together the flour, baking powder, sugar and salt. Drop in the butter and, using your fingers, toss to coat the pieces of butter with flour. Quickly, working with your fingertips (my favorite method) or a pastry blender, cut and rub the butter into the dry ingredients until the mixture is pebbly. You'll have pea-size pieces, pieces the size of oatmeal flakes and pieces in between—and that's just right.

Pour the cream over the dry ingredients and toss and gently turn the ingredients with a fork until you've got a very soft dough. When the dough comes together, you'll probably still have dry ingredients at the bottom of the bowl—just use a spatula or your hands to mix and knead the dough until it's evenly blended. Don't overdo it; it's better to have a few dry spots than an overworked dough. Even with all the flour mixed in, the dough will be soft and sticky.

Turn the dough out onto a sheet of wax paper or plastic wrap, cover with another sheet of paper or plastic and gently press or roll the dough into a circle that is a scant 9 inches in diameter. Don't worry about getting the size exact or about

MAKES 8 SERVINGS

SERVING: As the cobbler cools, the berry juices will thicken a bit; cool it longer, and the biscuit will absorb the lion's share of the juices. Happily, the cobbler is great at any temperature and at any stage of juiciness. In order to get biscuit, fruit and juice in each serving, use the side of a big kitchen spoon to crack the cobbler's topping, then spoon out some of the biscuit along with some fruit and liquid into each bowl. Top each serving with a big scoop of vanilla ice cream and serve the cobbler with spoons.

STORING: Once the cobbler cools, you can keep it lightly covered for a few hours at room temperature, but you really should enjoy it the day it is made. Don't refrigerate it—the biscuit will lose its appealing texture.

*Playing Around*

Cobblers, like crisps and crumbles, are very free-form, so, if you'd like, use this topping over other fruit fillings—just keep in mind that this kind of biscuit does best with fruits that produce lots of juice. If you want to use it instead over an apple crisp filling, for instance, or another filling that is quite thick, you might want to think about pouring a little maple syrup or fruit syrup over the cobbler before topping it with ice cream.

seeing that the edges are even—this is a very homey dessert, and a rough-around-the-edges biscuit adds to its charm. Set the dough aside while you prepare the fruit. (If it's more convenient, you can refrigerate the dough on a baking sheet for up to 6 hours before baking it—just make sure it's well covered.)

TO MAKE THE FILLING: Toss all the ingredients into a large bowl and stir to mix.

Turn the fruit into the buttered pie plate and top with the biscuit. Using a small sharp knife, cut about 6 slits in the dough, just as you would for a piecrust. Then, using either the knife or a large piping tip, cut a circle out of the center of the dough.

Bake the cobbler for 60 to 75 minutes, or until the top is puffed and golden brown and the fruit is bubbling steadily up through the center steam hole and all around the scallopy edges of the biscuit. Transfer the pie plate to a rack and let the cobbler cool for at least 30 minutes before serving.

Serve the cobbler warm or at room temperature, with ice cream.

TROPICAL CRUMBLE

THERE'S AN adage in the food world, "what grows together, goes together," but some matches are more obvious than others. It's my guess that the bananas and mangoes in this pecan-streusel-topped crumble would fit squarely in the category of less-obvious combos. Yet once the fruits are baked, their textures take on a pleasing similarity and the softer, sweeter sides of their flavors perk up and dominate. Think of this in the dead of winter, when a taste of the tropics can be as warming as a cashmere throw.

FOR THE FILLING

½ stick (4 tablespoons) unsalted butter

2½ tablespoons (packed) light brown sugar

2 ripe but firm mangoes, peeled, pitted and cut into ½-inch cubes

4 ripe but firm bananas, peeled and sliced ½ inch thick on the diagonal

1 teaspoon finely chopped peeled fresh ginger

½ teaspoon ground ginger

Grated zest of ¼ lime

FOR THE STREUSEL

1 stick (8 tablespoons) unsalted butter, at room temperature

½ cup (packed) light brown sugar

½ teaspoon salt

3 tablespoons all-purpose flour

½ cup chopped pecans

SERVING: Set out spoons rather than forks, spoon out portions of the crumble into dessert bowls and top with whipped cream, runny crème fraîche, sour cream or vanilla ice cream.

STORING: This is best eaten the day it is made. If you do keep it, cover it, stow it in the fridge and serve it slightly chilled.

TO MAKE THE FILLING: Melt the butter in a wide nonstick skillet over high heat. Sprinkle the sugar over the butter, and when it bubbles, add the mango cubes. Cook the mango for about 2 minutes, without stirring, then turn the cubes over and add the banana slices. Cook for another 3 minutes, turning the bananas after a minute or two, until both the mangoes and bananas are browned. Keep the heat high and don't move the fruit around too much—you want the fruit to hold its shape and its texture.

Transfer the fruit and whatever juices remain in the pan to a heatproof bowl. Gently stir in the chopped ginger, ground ginger and lime zest. Set aside while you make the streusel.

TO MAKE THE STREUSEL: You can make the streusel in a food processor or with a mixer, but I like to make it by hand. Toss the butter into a bowl and, using a rubber spatula, work it until it is smooth. Work in the brown sugar and salt, and then, when the mixture is smooth, stir in the flour, followed by the pecans. Spread the streusel mixture on a piece of wax paper, fold over the paper and freeze for 20 minutes while you preheat the oven.

GETTING READY TO BAKE: Center a rack in the oven and preheat the oven to 400 degrees F. Butter a 9-inch pie pan (regular or deep-dish) and place it on a baking sheet lined with parchment or a silicone mat.

Spoon the fruit and its liquid into the pie pan. Remove the streusel mix from the freezer and, using your fingers, break the mixture up into topping-size chunks. Don't make the pieces teensy and don't try to make them even—higgledy-piggledy is the way to go. Scatter the pieces over the fruit.

Slide the baking sheet into the oven and lower the oven temperature to 350 degrees F. Bake the crumble for about 35 minutes, or until the topping is richly golden and the fruits are bubbling steadily. Transfer the baking sheet to a rack and allow the crumble to cool to your preferred serving temperature—just warm or at room temperature.

WHO DOESN'T love an oatmeal crisp? Especially when, like this one, it's got a few spoonfuls of extra sharp, spicy crystallized (or candied) ginger stirred into it. Part of the crisp mixture is pressed into the bottom of the pan to serve as a kind of crust for the chunks of super-tart rhubarb and a quickly made strawberry filling. Then the rest is strewn across the top in traditional crisp-crumble fashion. It's a cinch to put together, a pleasure to behold—nothing beats the homey look of berry-red jam bubbling around the borders of a crisp—and, not surprisingly, really great tasting.

For this recipe, you want to use the sugared ginger that is most often found in the dried-fruits-and-nuts section or sometimes the spice section of specialty stores and good supermarkets. Unfortunately, it has a tendency to become very dry and unpleasantly hard. If it has, put it in a strainer over a pan of simmering water and steam it for a few minutes, just until it softens.

MAKES 9 SERVINGS

SERVING: You can try to be neat about cutting the crisp into squares, but it's pretty hopeless; better to cut pieces in the baking pan and lift them out with a spatula or big spoon into shallow bowls. Have the crisp with ice cream.

STORING: This is best the day it is made, but if you keep it covered at room temperature overnight, you'll make a bunch of breakfasters happy the next day.

### FOR THE CRISP MIX

- 1 cup all-purpose flour
- 1 cup (packed) light brown sugar
- ¾ cup old-fashioned oats
- ½ teaspoon ground ginger
- Pinch of salt
- Tiny pinch of ground cinnamon
- ½ cup finely chopped walnuts
- ¼ cup very finely chopped crystallized ginger (see above)
- 1 stick (8 tablespoons) unsalted butter, melted and cooled

### FOR THE FILLING

- 1 pound (4–5 medium stalks) rhubarb, trimmed and peeled
- 3 tablespoons cornstarch
- ½ cup cold water
- 3 cups (about 12 ounces) strawberries, hulled and sliced
- 1 cup sugar
- ½ teaspoon ground ginger
- 1 teaspoon pure vanilla extract

GETTING READY: Center a rack in the oven and preheat the oven to 350 degrees F. Put a nonreactive 9-inch square baking pan (I like Pyrex or porcelain) on a baking sheet lined with parchment or a silicone mat.

TO MAKE THE CRISP MIX: Put the flour, brown sugar, oats, ground ginger, salt and cinnamon in a large bowl and sift the ingredients through your fingers to blend them—be on the lookout for lumps in the brown sugar. Mix in the nuts and crystallized ginger, then pour over the melted butter. Using a fork, stir the ingredients until they are thoroughly moistened.

Spoon half the mixture into the pan and pat it down lightly to form a thick crust; set aside the remainder for the topping.

TO MAKE THE FILLING: Slice the rhubarb into ½-inch wide pieces and scatter them over the pressed-in base. Dissolve the cornstarch in the cold water; set aside.

Put the strawberries, sugar and ginger in a medium saucepan and, with a fork, pastry blender or potato masher, crush the berries. Place the pan over medium heat and, stirring occasionally, bring the mixture to a full boil. Pour the dissolved cornstarch into the pan and, stirring with a whisk, bring everything back to a boil. Keep cooking and stirring until the strawberry filling is thick and no longer cloudy, about 3 minutes. Pull the pan from the heat, stir in the vanilla and pour the filling over the rhubarb. Scatter the remaining crisp mix over the filling, breaking it up with your fingers so you can scatter it evenly.

Slide the crisp into the oven and bake for 60 minutes, or until the topping is golden and the strawberry jam is bubbling up all around the edges. Transfer the pan to a rack and cool until only just warm or at room temperature.

# CRAN-APPLE CRISPS

**I PARTICULARLY** love making this crisp in October, when cranberries come into the market. It's a rite of fall that seems to brighten the prospect of shorter, cooler days. The topping is a mix of oats and coconut, one that is great with fall fruits. The crisp is also surprisingly good at room temperature and even the next day.

I like to make this dessert in eight individual servings, but you can make one family-size crisp if you'd like: just put the ingredients in a 2-quart soufflé dish or a 9-inch deep-dish pie pan and bake until the topping is brown and the fruit is bubbling up around it.

**SERVING:** These are good with whipped cream or ice cream, but I like them plain, the better to highlight the contrast between the sweet topping and the not-as-sweet fruit.

**STORING:** These should be eaten the day they are made, but if you've got some left over, store them covered in the refrigerator and serve them chilled the next day.

### FOR THE TOPPING

- ¾ cup all-purpose flour
- ½ cup (packed) light brown sugar
- ½ cup old-fashioned oats
- ½ cup shredded sweetened coconut
- 1 teaspoon ground cinnamon
- ¼ teaspoon ground ginger
- 1 stick (8 tablespoons) cold unsalted butter, cut into 4 pieces

### FOR THE FILLING

- 4 medium apples, peeled, cored and cut into ½-inch chunks
- 1 cup fresh or frozen cranberries (if frozen, don't thaw)
- ½ cup moist, plump dried cranberries or raisins (dark or golden)
- ⅔ cup sugar
- 1 tablespoon all-purpose flour

**GETTING READY:** Center a rack in the oven and preheat the oven to 375 degrees F. Lightly butter eight ovenproof cups or bowls, each with a capacity of about 1 cup. Put the cups on a baking sheet lined with parchment or a silicone mat.

**TO MAKE THE TOPPING:** Put all the ingredients in a food processor and pulse just until the mixture forms big curds, about 1 minute. (You can make the topping up to 3 days ahead and refrigerate it in an airtight bag.)

**TO MAKE THE FILLING:** Toss all the ingredients together in a large bowl.

Divide the fruit evenly among the cups, then spoon an equal amount of topping over each portion of fruit. Bake the crisps for 40 to 45 minutes, or until the topping is golden and the fruit juices are bubbling up around it. Transfer the cups to a rack and let them rest for at least 10 minutes (15 to 20 minutes if you've made one large crisp) before serving.

*Playing Around*

Feel free to add or subtract fruits for this crisp. I like using bits of dried apricot as an addition to the crisp—and I sometimes add chopped walnuts too. Pears are an easy replacement for the apples, and you can, if the spirit moves you, toss in a few small wedges of fresh pineapple with either the apples or the pears.

Or you can make a rather exotic **PINEAPPLE BANANA CRISP**: Cut 6 to 8 firm bananas into ¼-inch-thick rounds and toss them with very thin slices of pineapple—figure about 1¾ pounds pineapple, or about 2 cups of slices. Add raisins or apricots or even dried pineapple snippets if you'd like.

IT'S NOT too much to call these quintessential shortcakes. They are pale, golden, cracked and cratery, raggedy and round, but not perfectly so and a touch sweet. I don't like the shock of an unsweet biscuit against sweet berries, and I don't think cream and butter should show up for dessert without a little sugar to round them out fully.

If you are a died-in-the-wool chocolate lover, take a look at the recipe for Devilish Shortcakes (page 425). Of course, if you want to be all things to all dessert lovers, you could make a splash by serving black-and-whites: a tray filled with half coal-black Devilish Shortcakes and half pale shortcakes.

Shortcakes are members of the biscuit family, so if you're new to making them, take a look at page 20. Just remember, biscuits thrive on the principle of "less is more": the less you handle them, the more tender they'll be.

FOR THE BISCUITS

- 4 cups all-purpose flour
- 2 tablespoons baking powder
- ¾ teaspoon salt
- 6 tablespoons sugar
- 1½ sticks (12 tablespoons) cold unsalted butter, cut into small pieces
- 1½ cups cold heavy cream

FOR THE FILLING

- Berries (about ½ cup per shortcake), hulled and sliced if using strawberries
- Sugar
- Lightly sweetened softly whipped cream

GETTING READY: Center a rack in the oven and preheat the oven to 425 degrees F. Line a baking sheet with parchment or a silicone mat.

TO MAKE THE BISCUITS: Whisk the flour, baking powder, salt and sugar together in a large bowl. Drop in the butter and, using your fingers, toss to coat the pieces of butter with flour. Quickly, working with your fingertips (my favorite method) or a pastry blender, cut and rub the butter into the dry ingredients until the mixture is pebbly. You'll have pea-size pieces, pieces the size of oatmeal flakes and pieces in between—and that's just right.

Pour the cream over the dry ingredients and toss and gently turn the ingredients with a fork until you've got a very soft dough. When the dough comes together, you'll probably still have dry ingredients at the bottom of the bowl—just use a spatula or your hands to mix and knead the dough until it's evenly blended. Don't overdo it; it's better to have a few dry spots than an overworked dough. Even with all the flour mixed in, the dough will be soft and sticky.

Spoon out about ⅓ cup of dough for each shortcake onto the baking sheet, leaving about 3 inches of space between the mounds of dough. Pat each mound down until it is between ¾ and 1 inch high. (The shortcakes can be made to this point and frozen on the baking sheet, then wrapped airtight and kept in the freezer for up to 2 months. Bake without defrosting—just add at least 5 more minutes to the oven time.)

MAKES ABOUT
10 SHORTCAKES

SERVING: Serve the shortcakes when they are just slightly warm—their peak moment—or at room temperature.

STORING: The shortcakes are best soon after they are made, but you can freeze the unbaked mounds of dough before baking. Baked shortcakes can be frozen for up to 2 months; reheat them, still frozen, in a 350-degree-F oven before serving.

*Playing Around*

Take a look at some of the suggestions for fillings on page 425. To play with the biscuit, consider whisking some spice into the bowl along with the flour: 1 teaspoon ground ginger and a pinch of ground cinnamon. Or whisk 1 teaspoon ground ginger into the dry ingredients, then, after the dough is mixed, fold in some teensy bits of candied ginger (either crystallized ginger or stem ginger in syrup, available in Asian or specialty markets). Or add 1 teaspoon ground cinnamon and a pinch of freshly grated nutmeg, in which case you might want to add ½ teaspoon pure vanilla extract along with the cream. For something very different, you could whisk ⅓ to ½ cup very finely chopped nuts into the dry ingredients. To bring out their flavor even more, add a drop of pure almond extract to the cream.

If you have more dough, repeat, cooling the baking sheet first.

Bake for 15 to 18 minutes, rotating the sheet from front to back at the midway point, until the shortcakes are puffed and give just a bit when prodded. Pull the sheet from the oven and transfer the shortcakes to a cooling rack.

TO MAKE THE FILLING: Put the berries in a bowl, sprinkle with sugar to taste and let sit for about 10 minutes, until they are juicy.

The cakes are tender and really pretty fragile, so go easy with them. Use a serrated knife and not much pressure to cut each cake in half horizontally. (Alternatively, you can use the tines of a fork to prick a ring around the middle of the shortcake, then use your fingers to gently pry the halves apart.) Put the bottom halves on plates, top with the berries—make sure to include some of the sweet juices— and spoon over some whipped cream. Put the tops on the shortcakes or lean them against the cream, my preference. If you decide to go for the open-faced shortcakes, you'll get two textures—moist and moister.

# DEVILISH SHORTCAKES

THOSE OF us who adore chocolate love these cocoa shortcakes with a chocolate flavor that flirts with devil's food's depth and fancies red berries, as well as peaches, cherries, poached pears and even gobs of jam (see Playing Around).

If you need a short tutorial on working with biscuit dough, turn to page 20.

**FOR THE BISCUITS**

1⅓ cups whole milk

1½ teaspoons pure vanilla extract

1 large egg

3⅓ cups all-purpose flour

⅔ cup unsweetened cocoa powder

2 tablespoons baking powder

½ teaspoon baking soda

½ teaspoon salt

½ cup sugar

1½ sticks (12 tablespoons) cold unsalted butter, cut into small pieces

**FOR THE FILLING**

Berries (about ½ cup per shortcake), hulled and sliced if using strawberries

Sugar

Lightly sweetened softly whipped cream

MAKES ABOUT
10 SHORTCAKES

SERVING: Serve the shortcakes warm or at room temperature.

STORING: The shortcakes are best eaten soon after they're made, but you can freeze the unbaked mounds of dough before baking. Baked shortcakes can be frozen for up to 2 months; reheat them, still frozen, in a 350-degree-F oven.

*Playing Around*

Any go-with-chocolate berry or combination of berries is good with this shortcake, as are halved and pitted cherries with a splash of kirsch or brandy, peaches poached in a sugar syrup (equal parts water and/or sugar) with a bit of vanilla and or rum, pears poached in a sugar syrup with ginger and/or star anise, apricots poached in a sugar syrup with split vanilla beans, or fresh mango (poached or not) with a squirt of lime. You can also opt for ice cream in place of whipped cream. You can even make the shortcake biscuits for brunch—serve them warm with jam and butter, softened cream cheese, yogurt or sour cream.

GETTING READY: Center a rack in the oven and preheat the oven to 425 degrees F. Line a baking sheet with parchment or a silicone mat.

TO MAKE THE BISCUITS: Whisk the milk, vanilla and egg together.

Sift the flour, cocoa, baking powder, baking soda, salt and sugar into a large bowl. Drop in the butter and, using your fingers, toss to coat the pieces of butter with flour. Quickly, working with your fingertips (my favorite method) or a pastry blender, cut and rub the butter into the dry ingredients until the mixture is pebbly. You'll have pea-size pieces, pieces the size of oatmeal flakes and pieces in between—and that's just right.

Pour the milk mixture over the dry ingredients and toss and gently turn the ingredients with a fork until you've got a very soft dough. When the dough comes together, you'll probably still have dry ingredients at the bottom of the bowl—just use a spatula or your hands to mix and knead the dough until it's evenly blended. Don't overdo it; it's better to have a few dry spots than an overworked dough. Even with all the flour mixed in, the dough will be soft and sticky.

Spoon out about ⅓ cup of dough for each shortcake onto the baking sheet, leaving about 3 inches of space between the mounds. Pat each mound down until it is between ¾ and 1 inch high. (The shortcakes can be made to this point and frozen on the baking sheet, then wrapped airtight and kept in the freezer for up to 2 months. Bake without defrosting—just add at least 5 more minutes to the oven time.)

Bake for 15 to 18 minutes, rotating the sheet from front to back at the midway point, until the shortcakes are puffed and give just a bit when prodded. Pull the sheet from the oven and transfer the shortcakes to a cooling rack.

If you have more dough, repeat, cooling the baking sheet first.

TO MAKE THE FILLING: Put the berries in a bowl, sprinkle with sugar to taste and let sit for about 10 minutes, until they are juicy.

Cut each cake in half horizontally. Put the bottom halves on plates, top with the berries—make sure to include some of the sweet juices—and spoon over some whipped cream. Put the tops on the shortcakes or lean them against the cream (my preference). If you decide to go for the open-faced shortcakes, you'll get two textures—moist and moister.

# ICE
# CREAMS

**MY SON REMEMBERS** that often when he was very young, he'd get into bed and realize he hadn't had his ice cream for dessert, and that I would say, "That's okay, you can have it with breakfast." Then he claims that the next day, when he'd open the freezer, he'd find no trace of the ice cream, because I had eaten it. That wasn't true—at least, it wasn't *always* true.

Ice cream is really the only food that I love so immoderately that I might take the food from the baby's bowl. There's something about the chill and the texture and the taste and the way it slides down my throat that makes it almost impossible for me to resist its delights. And I resist only rarely, which explains why I have not only given you recipes for making your own ice cream, but for making ice cream sandwiches and cakes and pies too.

But I have one more scoop on ice cream for you. Although many ice cream shops will mix your favorite ingredients into one of their ready-made flavors, you don't have to leave home to get custom-blended ice cream. Start with a premium-quality ice cream in a flavor that can serve as a good base, then choose your add-ins: in addition to crunchies like chocolate chips, nuts and pieces of candy, pretzels, cake or cookies, think about fruit purees, extracts, syrups, sweet or savory flavor pastes (curry ice cream can be fun with chocolate or mango desserts), herbs and spices. Remove the ice cream from its container, cut it into hunks and put the hunks into a food processor or a mixer bowl. Give the ice cream a few whirs in the processor, or beat it in the mixer until

it is smooth using the paddle attachment (or the whisk, if you don't have a paddle). Toss in the add-ins, whir or beat to get them mixed in and then, depending on what you plan to do with your new flavor, either use it now or spoon it into a container and pop it into the freezer to firm up.

So, if you want chocolate-peanut ice cream, for example, just add gobs of chopped peanuts—dry-roasted, salted or honey-roasted—to good chocolate ice cream. Want it to have a little cinnamon flavor? Make a little paste by moistening ground cinnamon with water and beat it in. Want it to be rockier? Add some mini marshmallows and some chunks of chocolate too.

Want raspberry ice cream? Puree a package of berries in syrup and beat it into vanilla ice cream. For a little more pizzazz, add some raspberry liqueur—try framboise eau-de-vie or Chambord.

Once you get started, it's easy to go a little wild—also easy to imagine how Ben & Jerry might have come up with flavors like Chunky Monkey. (For monkeying around at home, try pureed bananas in coffee ice cream—add a little dark rum and a pinch of nutmeg too.) Play around enough, and you could have your own "house" flavor.

# VANILLA ICE CREAM

**PURE, FRESH,** creamy, full flavored, and it's better than anything store-bought—not only because when you make ice cream yourself you can use the best ingredients available, but because when you make it at home, you can lick the just-churned ice cream off the paddle.

This ice cream can be made using a plump, pliable fresh vanilla bean or pure vanilla extract. If you use a bean, you should split and scrape it, and then allow it to infuse the hot milk and cream with its flavor—give yourself an extra 30 minutes for this.

If you'd like to make a pint rather than a quart of ice cream, use the following proportions: 1 cup milk, 1 cup heavy cream, 3 large egg yolks, 6 tablespoons sugar and ½ vanilla bean or 2 teaspoons pure vanilla extract.

MAKES ABOUT 1 QUART

SERVING: If the ice cream is very firm, allow it to sit on the counter for a few minutes before scooping or warm it in a microwave oven using 5-second spurts of heat.

STORING: Packed tightly in a covered container, the ice cream will keep in the freezer for about 2 weeks.

2 cups whole milk

2 cups heavy cream

1 moist, plump vanilla bean, split and scraped (see page 494), or 1 tablespoon pure vanilla extract

6 large egg yolks

¾ cup sugar

Bring the milk and cream to a boil in a large heavy-bottomed saucepan. If you are using a vanilla bean, put the seeds and pod into the pan, cover and set aside for 30 minutes, then bring the milk and cream back to a boil before continuing. If you are using vanilla extract, wait until later to add it.

Meanwhile, in a medium bowl, whisk the yolks and sugar together until very well blended and just slightly thickened. Still whisking, drizzle in about one third of the hot liquid—this will temper, or warm, the eggs so they won't curdle. Whisking all the while, slowly pour in the remaining liquid. Pour the custard back into the pan and cook over medium heat, stirring without stopping, until the custard thickens slightly and coats the back of a spoon; if you run your finger down the bowl of the spoon, the custard should not run into the track. The custard should reach at least 170 degrees F, but no more than 180 degrees F, on an instant-read thermometer. Immediately remove the pan from the heat and strain the custard into a 2-quart liquid measuring cup or clean heatproof bowl. Discard the vanilla pod or if you are using vanilla extract, stir it in now.

Refrigerate the custard until chilled before churning it into ice cream.

Scrape the chilled custard into the bowl of an ice cream maker and churn according to the manufacturer's instructions. Pack the ice cream into a container and freeze it for at least 2 hours, until it is firm enough to scoop.

## Playing Around

You can flavor the custard before it gets churned into ice cream and/or toss crunchies and other goodies into the ice cream a minute or so before it is fully churned. Here are some ideas for both.

**MINT CHOCOLATE CHUNK ICE CREAM:** Before you refrigerate the custard, stir in ¾ to 1¼ teaspoons pure mint extract or oil. Start with ¾ teaspoon of extract (or just a few drops of oil), taste and then add more a little at a time, remembering that freezing will tone down the flavor. Just before you finish churning the ice cream, toss in up to 6 ounces of semi- or bitter- sweet chocolate, coarsely chopped (or use up to 1 cup store-bought mini chocolate chips).

**HONEY-VANILLA ICE CREAM:** Heat ⅓ cup honey with the milk and cream; reduce the sugar to ½ cup.

**CINNAMON ICE CREAM:** Reduce the vanilla to ½ vanilla bean or 1 teaspoon extract and whisk 1 tablespoon ground cinnamon in with the yolks and sugar. Or, if you'd like to use stick cinnamon, toss 2 cinnamon sticks into the milk and cream and infuse for 30 minutes.

**CRUNCHY ICE CREAM:** You can add up to 1 cup chocolate chips, caramel bits, chopped-up candy bars, chopped toasted nuts, Candied Nuts (page 469), Buttered Pecans (page 470) or liqueur-flamed or steeped dried fruit, such as rum raisins (page 92), Armagnac prunes or vodka or amaretto or Frangelico apricots. If you add dried fruits that have not been steeped in liqueur or at least plumped (see page 481), they will freeze too hard.

**SWIRLED ICE CREAM:** After the ice cream has been churned, you can spoon it into a big bowl, pour over swirlables—for instance, jam, chocolate syrup or dulce de leche—and marble them into the ice cream with a sturdy rubber spatula or wooden spoon.

# CHOCOLATE GANACHE ICE CREAM

**I GO** for dark, dark bittersweet chocolate in this ice cream, but it is good made with semisweet as well. (You could even use milk chocolate, but the flavor will be very mild.) It's also good with chocolate chunks, rum raisins (page 92) or both, tossed in at the last minute of churning.

| | |
|---|---|
| 6 ounces bittersweet chocolate, finely chopped | 1 cup whole milk |
| 1½ cups heavy cream | 4 large egg yolks |
| | ⅓ cup sugar |

Put the chocolate in a 2-quart liquid measuring cup or a large heatproof bowl. Bring ³/₄ cup of the cream to a boil. Pour the cream over the chocolate and let it sit a minute, then, using a rubber spatula and starting in the center of the mixture, slowly stir the cream into the chocolate in ever-widening concentric circles. When the ganache is smooth, set it aside.

Bring the milk and the remaining ³/₄ cup cream to a boil in a medium heavy-bottomed saucepan.

Meanwhile, in a medium bowl, whisk the yolks and sugar together until well blended and just slightly thickened. Still whisking, drizzle in about one third of the hot liquid—this will temper, or warm, the yolks so they won't curdle. Whisking all the while, slowly pour in the remaining liquid. Pour the custard back into the pan and cook over medium heat, stirring without stopping, until the custard thickens slightly and coats the back of a spoon; if you run your finger down the bowl of the spoon, the custard should not run into the track. The custard should reach at least 170 degrees F, but no more than 180 degrees F, on an instant-read thermometer. Immediately remove the pan from the heat and slowly and gently stir the custard into the ganache.

Refrigerate the custard until chilled before churning it into ice cream.

Scrape the chilled custard into the bowl of an ice cream maker and churn according to the manufacturer's instructions. Pack the ice cream into a container and freeze it for at least 2 hours, until it is firm enough to scoop.

**MAKES ABOUT 1 QUART**

**SERVING:** If the ice cream is very firm—as ice cream made with premium-quality chocolate often is—allow it to sit on the counter for a few minutes before scooping or warm it in a microwave oven using 5-second spurts of heat.

**STORING:** Packed tightly in a covered container, the ice cream will keep in the freezer for about 2 weeks.

# CREAMY DARK CHOCOLATE SORBET

IT'S HARD to imagine, I know, but this sorbet offers the same satisfaction as its richer sibling, ice cream, does. It has all the same creaminess, the satiny melt-in-your-mouth pleasure and the full, no-holds-barred taste, yet it has no eggs or cream and contains just a cup of milk—which can even be nonfat, if you'd like. I adapted this recipe from one taught me by the Parisian pastry chef Pierre Hermé.

1 cup milk

1 cup water

¾ cup sugar

7 ounces bittersweet chocolate, coarsely chopped

Stir all the ingredients together in a 3- to 4-quart heavy-bottomed saucepan. Put the pan over medium heat and bring the ingredients to a boil, stirring frequently. Lower the temperature and boil for 5 minutes, stirring occasionally and keeping a close eye on the pan—as the ingredients bubble and roll, the potential for boil-over is high.

Pour the mixture into a heatproof bowl and refrigerate until chilled before churning the sorbet.

Scrape the chilled sorbet mixture into the bowl of an ice cream maker and churn according to the manufacturer's instructions. Pack the sorbet into a container and freeze for at least 2 hours, until it is firm enough to scoop.

MAKES ABOUT 1½ PINTS

SERVING: Unlike ice cream, which could be served as soft custard straight from the churn, this sorbet needs time in the freezer to firm.

STORING: Packed tightly in a covered container, the sorbet will keep in the freezer for up to 2 weeks.

*Playing Around*

CHOCOLATE PEPPERMINT SORBET: Just like chocolate ice cream, chocolate sorbet takes happily to add-ins and flavorings, but the chocolate-peppermint combination is my favorite. When the chocolate mixture is tepid, add 1 teaspoon pure peppermint extract (or a few drops of peppermint oil). Don't add more—peppermint extract can go from delicious to medicinal by droplets. If you'd like, churn some finely crushed candy canes into the sorbet a couple of minutes before it is fully churned.

# BURNT SUGAR ICE CREAM

THE CARAMEL in this ice cream has a slightly bitter tang, with a touch of the sugar's original sweetness. It's a complex, interesting flavor and it's intense, so you can serve this ice cream on its own or with a docile and doting partner. If you're looking for supporting players, consider plain butter or sugar cookies like Grandma's (page 146), Sablés (page 131) or Lenox Almond Biscotti (page 141).

| | |
|---|---|
| 1 cup sugar | 4 large egg yolks |
| 3 tablespoons water | Pinch of salt |
| 2 cups whole milk | 1½ teaspoons pure vanilla extract |
| 1 cup heavy cream | |

MAKES ABOUT 1½ PINTS

SERVING: If the ice cream is very firm, allow it to sit on the counter for a few minutes before scooping or warm it in a microwave oven using 5-second spurts of heat.

STORING: Packed tightly in a covered container, the ice cream will keep in the freezer for up to 2 weeks.

Stir the sugar and water together in a medium heavy-bottomed saucepan. Place the pan over medium-low heat and cook until the sugar dissolves. Increase the heat and boil, without stirring, until the syrup turns a deep amber color—from time to time, brush down the sides of the pan with a wet pastry brush and swirl the pan. (Depending on the size of your pan and the intensity of the heat, it could take about 8 minutes for the caramel to color properly.)

Stand back—things can get a little wild—lower the heat and add the milk and cream. Don't be concerned when everything bubbles and seethes and the caramel hardens; it will calm down and smooth out as you heat and stir. Continue to heat and stir and when the mixture is smooth, remove the pan from the heat.

In a medium heatproof bowl, whisk the yolks and salt together until blended and just slightly thickened. Still whisking, drizzle in about one third of the hot liquid—this will temper, or warm, the yolks. Whisking all the while, slowly pour in the remaining liquid. Pour the custard back into the pan and cook over medium heat, stirring without stopping, until the custard thickens slightly and coats the back of a spoon; if you run your finger down the bowl of the spoon, the custard should not run into the track. The custard should reach at least 170 degrees F, but no more than 180 degrees F, on an instant-read thermometer. Immediately remove the pan from the heat and pour the custard into a 2-quart liquid measuring cup or clean heatproof bowl. Stir in the vanilla extract.

Refrigerate the custard until chilled before churning it into ice cream.

Scrape the chilled custard into the bowl of an ice cream maker and churn according to the manufacturer's instructions. Pack the ice cream into a container and freeze it for at least 2 hours, until it is firm enough to scoop.

# UNBELIEVABLY GOOD CHOCOLATE BLUEBERRY ICE CREAM

**I'M NOT** proud to admit this, but many years ago, when I was young and silly, I stopped dating a perfectly nice guy because he ordered a slice of blueberry pie with a scoop of chocolate ice cream on top. It didn't seem like such a bad idea to me when he ordered it, but then, as the blueberry filling started to sneak out of the pie and the ice cream started to melt over it, I decided I couldn't spend the rest of my life with a man who could eat blue and brown foods together.

So, given my strong feelings about the combination, it seems ludicrous that I made this ice cream. Yet there I was, alone in my house with a craving for chocolate, an ice cream maker at the ready and, right there on the counter, a jar of blueberry jam. I made the custard for the ice cream (a custard so delicious you can chill it and use it as a sauce), chilled and churned it and then I dropped in some blueberry jam at the last minute. And you know what? It was fabulous! The color is actually pretty—the blueberry jam turns the chocolate a more beautiful shade of brown. The taste is terrific—the blueberry brings a gentle edge to the rich chocolate. And the texture—wow! It's extra-creamy, like a frozen mousse.

**SERVING:** If the ice cream is very firm, allow it to sit on the counter for a few minutes before scooping, or warm it in a microwave oven using 5-second spurts of heat. Serve the ice cream on its own or over the equally luscious Double-Crusted Blueberry Pie (page 361).

**STORING:** Packed tightly in a covered container, the ice cream will keep in the freezer for about 2 weeks.

5 ounces semisweet chocolate, finely chopped

1 cup whole milk

½ cup heavy cream

3 large egg yolks

3 tablespoons sugar

5 tablespoons premium-quality blueberry preserves

Put the chocolate in a 1-quart glass measuring cup or a heatproof bowl.

Bring the milk and cream to a boil in a medium heavy-bottomed saucepan.

Meanwhile, in a medium bowl, whisk the yolks and sugar together until very well blended and just slightly thickened. Still whisking, drizzle in about one third of the hot liquid—this will temper, or warm, the yolks so they don't curdle. Whisking all the while, slowly pour in the remaining liquid. Pour the custard back into the pan and cook over medium heat, stirring without stopping, until the custard thickens slightly and coats the back of a spoon; if you run your finger down the bowl of the spoon, the custard should not run into the track. The custard should reach at least 170 degrees F, but no more than 180 degrees F, on an instant-read thermometer. Immediately remove the pan from the heat and pour the custard over the chopped chocolate.

Let the mixture sit for 1 minute, then, using a rubber spatula, starting in the center of the measuring cup and working in ever-wider concentric circles, stir until the custard is smooth.

Refrigerate the custard until chilled before churning it into ice cream.

Scrape the chilled custard into the bowl of an ice cream maker and churn according to the manufacturer's instructions. When the ice cream is thickened and just about ready, spoon in the blueberry preserves and churn to blend. Pack the ice cream into a container and freeze it for at least 2 hours, until it is firm enough to scoop.

# BLUEBERRY-SOUR CREAM ICE CREAM

**THIS IS** the summeriest of summertime ice creams. The romantic in me thinks it should be made only in a hand-cranked machine—and then only on a back porch. The color isn't really blue at all, more raspberry, in fact, and the texture is firm and creamy with bits of blueberry here and there.

1 cup blueberries—fresh or frozen (if frozen, thaw and drain)

⅓ cup sugar, or more to taste

Pinch of salt

Grated zest and juice of ¼ lemon (or lime, as you prefer), or more juice to taste

¾ cup heavy cream

¾ cup sour cream

Put the blueberries, sugar, salt and lemon zest and juice in a medium nonreactive saucepan and cook over medium heat, stirring, until the mixture boils and the berries pop and soften, about 3 minutes.

Turn the berries into a blender and whir until you have a fairly homogeneous puree, about 1 minute. (It will never be completely smooth, and that's just fine.) Add the heavy cream and sour cream and pulse just to blend. Taste and, if you'd like, add a squirt more lemon juice or a tiny bit more sugar.

Pour the custard into a bowl and refrigerate until it is chilled before churning it into ice cream.

Scrape the chilled custard into the bowl of an ice cream maker and churn according to the manufacturer's instructions. Pack the ice cream into a container and freeze for at least 2 hours, until it is firm enough to scoop.

**SERVING:** If the ice cream is very firm, allow it to sit on the counter for a few minutes before scooping, or warm it in a microwave oven using 5-second spurts of heat. Serve the ice cream solo or with whipped cream or lightly sweetened fresh berries, or both. Or serve it on top of a slice of cake or pie, or with sugar cookies, shortbread or biscotti.

**STORING:** Packed tightly in a covered container, the ice cream will keep in the freezer for about 2 weeks.

*Playing Around*

**MINTY BLUEBERRY-SOUR CREAM ICE CREAM:** Pour the cream into a small saucepan, add 30 fresh mint leaves and bring to a boil. Allow the cream to infuse for 30 minutes before straining the cream and continuing with the recipe.

# HONEY-PEACH ICE CREAM

....................................................................................................................

**YOU KNOW** how people are always talking about "peaches as sweet as honey"? Well, here's the sweet that gives truth to the phrase. This is a wonderful height-of-summer ice cream that's great on its own and terrific scooped over warm pie or dished out with cookies (it's particularly good with Grandma's All-Occasion Sugar Cookies, page 146). Whether serving this alone or along with another dessert, be generous—this is not a one-lick-will-do-you ice cream; it's got the kind of flavor that keeps calling you back for more.

| | |
|---|---|
| 4 large ripe peaches (about 2 pounds), peeled and pitted | 1 cup heavy cream |
| ¼ cup honey | 3 large egg yolks |
| 1 cup whole milk | ½ cup sugar |
| | 2 teaspoons pure vanilla extract |

Coarsely chop half the peaches into ½-inch chunks and toss them into a small saucepan. Add the honey and bring to a boil, then lower the heat, cover the pan and cook, stirring occasionally, until the peaches are soft but not mushy, about 10 minutes. Scrape the mixture into a blender or food processor and whir to puree. (Alternatively, use a hand blender.) Set the peach puree aside while you make the custard.

Bring the milk and cream to a boil in a medium heavy-bottomed saucepan.

Meanwhile, in a medium bowl, whisk the yolks and sugar together until very well blended and just slightly thickened. Still whisking, drizzle in about one third of the hot liquid—this will temper, or warm, the eggs so they don't curdle. Whisking all the while, slowly pour in the remaining liquid. Pour the custard back into the pan and cook over medium heat, stirring without stopping, until the custard thickens slightly and coats the back of a spoon; if you run your finger down the bowl of the spoon, the custard should not run into the track. The custard should reach at least 170 degrees F, but no more than 180 degrees F, on an instant-read thermometer. Immediately remove the pan from the heat and pour the custard into a 2-quart glass measuring cup or clean heatproof bowl. Stir in the vanilla and the peach puree.

Refrigerate the custard until chilled before churning it into ice cream.

Scrape the chilled custard into the bowl of an ice cream maker and churn according to the manufacturer's instructions. While the ice cream is churning, finely dice the remaining 2 peaches, then, just before the ice cream is thickened and ready, add the peaches and churn to blend. Pack the ice cream into a container and freeze it for at least 2 hours, until it is firm enough to scoop.

MAKES ABOUT 1 QUART

**SERVING:** Alone, as part of a sundae or scooped over pie, this ice cream is best if it is allowed to soften a bit. Let it sit at room temperature for a few minutes or warm it in a microwave oven using 5-second spurts of heat—this will keep the peach pieces from feeling too hard under your teeth.

**STORING:** Packed tightly in a covered container, the ice cream will keep in the freezer for about 2 weeks.

*Playing Around*

You can replace the peaches with nectarines, which need no peeling, or apricots, which should be peeled, a fairly easy job if you use a serrated vegetable peeler.

# INDISPENSABLES

## BASE RECIPES

## Pointers for Perfect Pie and Tart Dough

EVEN IF YOU DIDN'T LEARN to make pie dough at your grandmother's elbow (and few of us did), you can make perfect dough with a bit of confidence, a little patience, a refrigerator (dough loves cold) and the following indispensable information.

- Fat is the key to a crust's flavor and texture. Crusts made with only butter are flavorful and crispy (just what you might want for tarts), but not flaky. Flaky crusts (the kind so good for pies) are the ones made with vegetable shortening. If you want both flavor *and* flake, use three-quarters butter and one-quarter shortening.

- Start with cold ingredients. Butter and shortening should be *really* cold (even frozen), as should any water or eggs called for in the recipe.

- A food processor is a dough genie. Because the processor is so quick, the ingredients stay cold. And, provided you're careful, they don't get overworked, the prime culprit behind a tough crust.

- When in doubt, err on the side of moistness—a moist dough is better than a dry dough, which can be tough and may crack as it bakes.

- In piedom, the refrigerator is king—use it early and often to keep dough at its peak of workability. Dough should be chilled for at least an hour after it is mixed and for 30 minutes or more after it has been fitted into the pie or tart pan.

- If, at any time, the dough feels soft (particularly while you're rolling it out), pop it into the refrigerator for a quick chill. Twenty minutes in the fridge—or 10 in the freezer—is usually just enough to bring the dough back in line.

- Roll the dough out either on a lightly floured smooth work surface or between two sheets of plastic wrap or wax paper, or use a flour-dusted rolling slipcover (see page 491). Of the between-the-sheets alternatives, my favorite is the slipcover, followed by plastic wrap and then wax paper. Rolling between sheets gives you more control, helps you use less flour during rolling and, in the case of the slipcover, increases your odds of rolling the dough into a circle.

- Lift and turn the dough from time to time to make sure it isn't sticking to the work surface. If you are rolling between plastic wrap or wax paper, peel away both the top and bottom sheets frequently so they don't get creased and rolled into the dough.

- Roll the dough from the center out, giving it an eighth of a turn with each roll to keep it round.

- Be gentle, very gentle, when you fit the dough into the pie or tart pan. Don't pull or stretch it to fit, because anything you pull will shrink back as it bakes.

- Save those scraps—they make good patches for any little cracks. To patch a tear, flatten a small piece of dough, moisten it lightly and paste it over the offending spot.

**THE NAME** says it all. You can use this flaky, flavorful easy-to-roll dough for pies, galettes, turnovers or even tarts. If—heaven forbid—you could have only one dough for crust in your repertory, this would be the one to choose.

You'll need a large-capacity food processor to make a double crust. If your machine isn't large enough, make the dough in two batches.

**FOR A 9-INCH DOUBLE CRUST**

- 3 cups all-purpose flour
- ¼ cup sugar
- 1½ teaspoons salt
- 2½ sticks (10 ounces) very cold (frozen is fine) unsalted butter, cut into tablespoon-size pieces
- ⅓ cup very cold (frozen is even better) vegetable shortening, cut into 4 pieces
- About ½ cup ice water

**FOR A 9-INCH SINGLE CRUST**

- 1½ cups all-purpose flour
- 2 tablespoons sugar
- ¾ teaspoon salt
- 1¼ sticks (10 tablespoons) very cold (frozen is fine) unsalted butter, cut into tablespoon-size pieces
- 2½ tablespoons very cold (frozen is even better) vegetable shortening, cut into 2 pieces
- About ¼ cup ice water

**STORING:** Well wrapped, the dough can be kept in the refrigerator for up to 5 days or frozen for up to 2 months. While the fully baked single crust can be packed airtight and frozen for up to 2 months, I prefer to freeze the unbaked crust in the pan, and to bake it directly from the freezer—it has a fresher flavor. Just add about 5 minutes to the baking time.

Put the flour, sugar and salt in a food processor fitted with a metal blade; pulse just to combine the ingredients. Drop in the butter and shortening and pulse only until the butter and shortening are cut into the flour. Don't overdo the mixing— what you're aiming for is to have some pieces the size of fat green peas and others the size of barley. Pulsing the machine on and off, gradually add about 6 table-spoons of the water if making a double crust, 3 tablespoons if making a single crust—add a little water and pulse once, add some more water, pulse again and keep going that way. Then use a few long pulses to get the water into the flour. If, after a dozen or so pulses, the dough doesn't look evenly moistened or form soft curds, pulse in as much of the remaining water as necessary, or even a few drops more, to get a dough that will stick together when pinched. Big pieces of butter are fine. Scrape the dough out of the work bowl and onto a work surface.

If making a double crust, divide the dough in half. Gather each half into a ball, flatten each ball into a disk and wrap each half in plastic. Or shape the dough for a single crust into a disk and wrap it. Refrigerate the dough for at least 1 hour before rolling. (If your ingredients were very cold and you worked quickly, though, you might be able to roll the dough immediately: the dough should be as cold as if it had just come out of the fridge.)

**TO ROLL OUT THE DOUGH:** Have a buttered 9-inch pie plate at hand.

You can roll the dough out on a floured surface or between sheets of wax paper or plastic wrap or in a rolling slipcover. (I usually roll this dough out on the floured counter.) If you're working on a counter, turn the dough over frequently and keep the counter floured. If you are rolling between paper, plastic or in a slipcover, make sure to turn the dough over often and to lift the paper, plastic or cover frequently so that it doesn't roll into the dough and form creases.

If you've got time, slide the rolled-out dough into the fridge for about 20 minutes to rest and firm up.

FOR A DOUBLE-CRUSTED PIE: Fit one circle of dough into the pie plate, allowing the excess to hang over. Trim to a $\frac{1}{8}$- to $\frac{1}{4}$-inch overhang. Fill the pie and moisten the edges of the bottom crust with water. Center the second piece of dough over the filling and press it against the bottom crust. Using a pair of scissors, cut the top crust's overhang so that it extends about $\frac{1}{4}$ inch over the bottom crust. Tuck the excess top crust under the bottom crust and flute or pinch the crust to make a decorative edge. Alternatively, you can seal the doubled-up crust by pressing it with the tines of a fork. Follow the pie recipe's instructions for baking.

FOR A SINGLE CRUST: Fit the dough into the pie plate and, using a pair of scissors, cut the excess dough to a $\frac{1}{4}$- to $\frac{1}{2}$-inch overhang. Fold the dough under itself, so that it hangs over the edge just a tad, and flute or pinch the crust to make a decorative edge. Alternatively, you can finish the crust by pressing it with the tines of a fork.

TO PARTIALLY OR FULLY BAKE A SINGLE CRUST: Refrigerate the crust while you preheat the oven to 400 degrees F.

Butter the shiny side of a piece of aluminum foil, fit the foil, buttered side down, tightly against the crust and fill with dried beans or rice or pie weights. Put the pie plate on a baking sheet and bake the crust for 25 minutes. Carefully remove the foil and weights and, if the crust has puffed, press it down gently with the back of a spoon. For a partially baked crust, return the pie plate to the oven and bake for about 8 minutes more, or until the crust is very lightly colored. To fully bake the crust, bake until golden brown, about another 10 minutes. Transfer the pie plate to a rack and cool to room temperature before filling.

# SWEET TART DOUGH

**IN FRENCH**, this dough is called *pâte sablée* because it is buttery, tender and sandy (that's what *sablée* means). It's much like shortbread, and it's ideal for filling with fruit, custard or chocolate.

The simplest way to make a tart shell with this dough is to press it into the pan. You can roll out the dough, but the high proportion of butter to flour and the inclusion of confectioners' sugar makes it finicky to roll. I always press it into the pan, but if you want to roll it, I suggest you do so between sheets of plastic wrap or wax paper or inside a rolling slipcover (see page 491).

| | |
|---|---|
| 1½ cups all-purpose flour | 1 stick plus 1 tablespoon (9 tablespoons) |
| ½ cup confectioners' sugar | very cold (or frozen) unsalted butter, |
| ¼ teaspoon salt | cut into small pieces |
| | 1 large egg yolk |

Put the flour, confectioners' sugar and salt in a food processor and pulse a couple of times to combine. Scatter the pieces of butter over the dry ingredients and pulse until the butter is coarsely cut in—you should have some pieces the size of oatmeal flakes and some the size of peas. Stir the yolk, just to break it up, and add it a little at a time, pulsing after each addition. When the egg is in, process in long pulses—about 10 seconds each—until the dough, which will look granular soon after the egg is added, forms clumps and curds. Just before you reach this stage, the sound of the machine working the dough will change—heads up. Turn the dough out onto a work surface and, very lightly and sparingly, knead the dough just to incorporate any dry ingredients that might have escaped mixing.

**TO PRESS THE DOUGH INTO THE PAN:** Butter a 9-inch fluted tart pan with a removable bottom. Press the dough evenly over the bottom and up the sides of the pan, using all but one little piece of dough, which you should save in the refrigerator to patch any cracks after the crust is baked. Don't be too heavy-handed—press the crust in so that the edges of the pieces cling to one another, but not so hard that the crust loses its crumbly texture. Freeze the crust for at least 30 minutes, preferably longer, before baking.

**TO PARTIALLY OR FULLY BAKE THE CRUST:** Center a rack in the oven and preheat the oven to 375 degrees F.

Butter the shiny side of a piece of aluminum foil and fit the foil, buttered side down, tightly against the crust. (Since you froze the crust, you can bake it without weights.) Put the tart pan on a baking sheet and bake the crust for 25 minutes. Carefully remove the foil. If the crust has puffed, press it down gently with the back of a spoon. For a partially baked crust, patch the crust if necessary, then transfer the crust to a cooling rack (keep it in its pan).

MAKES ENOUGH
FOR ONE 9-INCH CRUST

**STORING:** Well wrapped, the dough can be kept in the refrigerator for up to 5 days or frozen for up to 2 months. While the fully baked crust can be packed airtight and frozen for up to 2 months, I prefer to freeze the unbaked crust in the pan and bake it directly from the freezer—it has a fresher flavor. Just add about 5 minutes to the baking time.

*Playing Around*

**SWEET TART DOUGH WITH NUTS:** This dough has a slightly more assertive flavor than Sweet Tart Dough, but you can use the two interchangeably. For the nut dough, reduce the amount of flour to 1¼ cups and add ¼ cup finely ground almonds (or walnuts, pecans or pistachios).

TO FULLY BAKE THE CRUST: Bake for another 8 minutes or so, or until it is firm and golden brown. (I dislike lightly baked crusts, so I often keep the crust in the oven just a little longer. If you do that, just make sure to keep a close eye on the crust's progress—it can go from golden to way too dark in a flash.) Transfer the tart pan to a rack and cool the crust to room temperature before filling.

TO PATCH A PARTIALLY OR FULLY BAKED CRUST, IF NECESSARY: If there are any cracks in the baked crust, patch them with some of the reserved raw dough as soon as you remove the foil. Slice off a thin piece of the dough, place it over the crack, moisten the edges and very gently smooth the edges into the baked crust. If the tart will not be baked again with its filling, bake for another 2 minutes or so, just to take the rawness off the patch.

# CHOCOLATE SHORTBREAD TART DOUGH

**GOOD ENOUGH** to eat on its own, this crust is delicious filled with pastry cream and fruit, ganache or pudding. Choose it whenever you want the full, deep taste of chocolate.

1¼ cups all-purpose flour

¼ cup unsweetened cocoa powder

¼ cup confectioners' sugar

¼ teaspoon salt

1 stick plus 1 tablespoon (9 tablespoons) very cold (or frozen) unsalted butter, cut into small pieces

1 large egg yolk

Put the flour, cocoa, confectioners' sugar and salt in a food processor and pulse a couple of times to combine. Scatter the pieces of butter over the dry ingredients and pulse until the butter is coarsely cut in—you should have pieces the size of oatmeal flakes and some the size of peas. Stir the yolk, just to break it up, and add it a little at a time, pulsing after each addition. When the egg is in, process in long pulses—about 10 seconds each—until the dough, which will look granular soon after the egg is added, forms clumps and curds. Just before you reach this stage, the sound of the machine working the dough will change—heads up. Turn the dough out onto a work surface and very lightly and sparingly knead the dough just to incorporate any dry ingredients that might have escaped mixing.

Press the dough into the pan. To bake it, follow the directions for Sweet Tart Dough, beginning on page 444.

**MAKES ENOUGH FOR ONE 9-INCH CRUST**

**STORING:** Well wrapped, the dough can be kept in the refrigerator for up to 5 days or frozen for up to 2 months. While the fully baked crust can be packed airtight and frozen for up to 2 months, I prefer to freeze the unbaked crust in the pan and bake it directly from the freezer—it has a fresher flavor. Just add about 5 minutes to the baking time.

## SPICED TART DOUGH

**BASED ON** Linzer Sablés (page 134), this nut crust is simple to make and extremely good with fruit. Because it has so much personality, I think it's best with simple fillings like pastry cream and berries. It's also wonderful with chocolate.

MAKES ENOUGH
FOR ONE 9-INCH CRUST

STORING: Well wrapped, the dough can be kept in the refrigerator for up to 5 days or frozen for up to 2 months. While the fully baked crust can be packed airtight and frozen for up to 2 months, I prefer to freeze the unbaked crust in the pan and bake it directly from the freezer—it has a fresher flavor. Just add about 5 minutes to the baking time.

| | |
|---|---|
| 1 cup ground nuts (almonds, toasted and skinned hazelnuts, walnuts or pecans) | ¼ teaspoon salt |
| | Pinch of ground cloves |
| 1 cup all-purpose flour | 1 large egg yolk |
| 1 tablespoon unsweetened cocoa powder | 1 tablespoon water |
| | ¾ stick (6 tablespoons) unsalted butter, at room temperature |
| 1 teaspoon ground cinnamon | 6 tablespoons sugar |

Butter a 9-inch fluted tart pan with a removable bottom.

Whisk together the ground nuts, flour, cocoa, cinnamon, salt and cloves. With a fork, stir the egg yolk and water together in a cup.

Working with a stand mixer, preferably fitted with a paddle attachment, or with a hand mixer in a large bowl, beat the butter and sugar together at medium speed until smooth, about 3 minutes, scraping down the bowl as needed. Add the egg and water and beat for 1 minute more. Reduce the speed to low and add the dry ingredients, mixing only until they disappear into the dough. Don't work the dough much once the flour is incorporated. If the dough comes together but some dry crumbs remain at the bottom of the bowl, stop the mixer and finish blending the ingredients with a rubber spatula or your hands.

Put the dough between two sheets of plastic wrap or wax paper or in a rolling slipcover (see page 491). With your hands, flatten the dough into a disk, then grab a rolling pin and roll the dough, turning it over frequently, until you have a round that is about 11 inches in diameter.

TO FIT THE DOUGH INTO THE PAN: Remove the top sheet of plastic or unzip the slipcover and carefully turn the dough into the buttered tart pan. Very gently fit the dough into the pan, lightly pressing it over the bottom and up the sides of the pan. Don't be concerned if the dough breaks, as it may—just gently press the tears together with your fingers. Chill the dough, covered with plastic wrap, for at least 2 hours.

TO BAKE THE CRUST: Center a rack in the oven and preheat the oven to 375 degrees F. Line a baking sheet with parchment or a silicone mat.

Remove the plastic wrap and, using a small sharp knife, trim the excess dough flush with the edges of the pan. Butter the shiny side of a piece of aluminum foil, fit the foil, buttered side down, tightly against the crust and fill with dried beans or rice or pie weights.

Place the tart pan on the baking sheet. Bake for 20 minutes. Remove the foil and weights and bake the crust for an additional 8 to 10 minutes, or until it is browned, dry and firm. Transfer to a rack and cool to room temperature before filling.

# PASTRY CREAM

....................................................................................................

**MASTER PASTRY** cream—a simple feat—and you'll have at your fingertips a silky filling that can be spread in a crust, topped with fruit and used to cap the finest dinner (see Quick Classic Berry Tart, page 377). You can also press pastry cream into service as the filling between layers of cake or even a serve-along spread with cookies.

This is a recipe for vanilla pastry cream, the base for any other flavor of pastry cream. You can add liqueur to the cream, or herbs, spices or other extracts (see Playing Around). Because it is essentially plain, it welcomes variation.

| | |
|---|---|
| 2 cups whole milk | 1½ teaspoons pure vanilla extract |
| 6 large egg yolks | 3½ tablespoons unsalted butter, cut into |
| ½ cup sugar | bits at room temperature |
| ⅓ cup cornstarch, sifted | |

Bring the milk to a boil in a small saucepan.

Meanwhile, in a medium heavy-bottomed saucepan, whisk the yolks together with the sugar and cornstarch until thick and well blended. Still whisking, drizzle in about ¼ cup of the hot milk—this will temper, or warm, the yolks so they won't curdle. Whisking all the while, slowly pour in the remainder of the milk. Put the pan over medium heat and, whisking vigorously, constantly and thoroughly (making sure to get into the edges of the pot), bring the mixture to a boil. Keep at a boil, still whisking, for 1 to 2 minutes, then remove the pan from the heat.

Whisk in the vanilla extract. Let sit for 5 minutes, then whisk in the bits of butter, stirring until they are fully incorporated and the pastry cream is smooth and silky. Scrape the cream into a bowl. You can press a piece of plastic wrap against the surface of the cream to create an airtight seal and refrigerate the pastry cream until cold or, if you want to cool it quickly—as I always do—put the bowl into a larger bowl filled with ice cubes and cold water, and stir the pastry cream occasionally until it is thoroughly chilled, about 20 minutes.

**MAKES ABOUT 2 CUPS**

**STORING:** The pastry cream can be kept tightly covered in the refrigerator for up to 3 days.

## Playing Around

**LIQUEUR-SCENTED PASTRY CREAM:** You can flavor vanilla pastry cream with various liqueurs. Reduce the vanilla extract to 1 teaspoon and, after you've added it, add 2 teaspoons liqueur. If you want more flavor (and you might), add more liqueur 1 teaspoon at a time. There are many good choices for additions, among them: amaretto (almond liqueur) or Frangelico (hazelnut liqueur), in which case you might want to reduce the vanilla extract to 1 teaspoon and add ¼ teaspoon pure almond extract; Chambord (raspberry liqueur); anisette (licorice); brandy; cognac; Armagnac; and eaux-de-vie such as kirsch (cherry), framboise (raspberry) or poire Williams (pear).

**RUM-SCENTED PASTRY CREAM:** After you add the vanilla extract, add 1 to 2 tablespoons dark rum, to taste.

**CINNAMON PASTRY CREAM:** Put 2 cinnamon sticks into the saucepan with the milk and bring to a boil, then remove the saucepan from the heat, cover and steep for about 1 hour. Cook the pastry cream with the cinnamon sticks, then discard the sticks when you stir in the vanilla extract. Alternatively, you can beat 2 to 3 teaspoons ground cinnamon into the egg-sugar-cornstarch mixture.

**GINGER PASTRY CREAM:** Follow the directions for Cinnamon Pastry Cream, steeping 8 to 10 quarter-size pieces of peeled ginger in the milk or adding 2 to 3 teaspoons ground ginger to the egg yolk mixture.

**CITRUS PASTRY CREAM:** Follow the directions for Cinnamon Pastry Cream, steeping the zest of 1 large or 2 small lemons, 2 limes or 1 orange, cut from the fruit in wide strips (make sure you don't have any of the white cottony pith), in the milk. Reduce the vanilla extract to 1 teaspoon and if you think you'd like a stronger citrus flavor, after you've added the vanilla, add a drop of the appropriate citrus extract or oil. Add additional flavor by droplets.

**COFFEE OR ESPRESSO PASTRY CREAM:** Make a coffee or espresso extract by dissolving 2 tablespoons instant coffee or espresso powder in 2 tablespoons boiling water. Add 1 tablespoon of the extract to the pastry cream after you've added the vanilla extract, then, if you want more flavor, add additional coffee or espresso extract 1 teaspoon at a time.

# CHOCOLATE PASTRY CREAM

**FILL CAKES**, pies or tarts with this pastry cream.

2 cups whole milk

4 large egg yolks

6 tablespoons sugar

3 tablespoons cornstarch, sifted

Pinch of salt

7 ounces bittersweet chocolate, melted

2½ tablespoons unsalted butter, cut into bits, at room temperature

MAKES ABOUT 2½ CUPS

STORING: The pastry cream can be kept tightly covered in the refrigerator for up to 3 days.

Bring the milk to a boil in a small saucepan.

Meanwhile, in a medium heavy-bottomed saucepan, whisk the yolks together with the sugar, cornstarch and salt until thick and well blended. Whisking without stopping, drizzle in about ¼ cup of the hot milk—this will temper, or warm, the yolks so they won't curdle—then, still whisking, add the remainder of the milk in a steady stream. Put the pan over medium heat and, whisking vigorously, constantly and thoroughly (making sure to get into the edges of the pot), bring the mixture to a boil. Keep at a boil, still whisking, for 1 to 2 minutes, then remove the pan from the heat.

Whisk in the melted chocolate. Let sit for 5 minutes, then whisk in the bits of butter, stirring until they are fully incorporated and the pastry cream is smooth and silky. Scrape the cream into a bowl. You can press a piece of plastic wrap against the surface of the cream to create an airtight seal and refrigerate the custard until cold or, if you want to cool it quickly—as I always do—put the bowl into a larger bowl filled with ice cubes and cold water, and stir the pastry cream occasionally until it is thoroughly chilled, about 20 minutes.

# CRÈME ANGLAISE

**SOMETIMES CALLED** English custard, or pouring custard, crème anglaise is the base of the world's most luxurious ice creams, the sea on which Floating Islands (page 401) float and, on its own, a luscious accompaniment to cakes, tarts and puddings.

While you can test the readiness of crème anglaise with your finger, you can measure it more accurately with an instant-read thermometer.

| | |
|---|---|
| 1 cup whole milk | ½ cup sugar |
| 1 cup heavy cream | 2 teaspoons pure vanilla extract |
| 6 large egg yolks | |

MAKES ABOUT 2½ CUPS

**STORING:** Covered and kept away from foods with strong odors, crème anglaise can be stored in the refrigerator for up to 3 days.

*Playing Around*

See the suggestions for varying Pastry Cream (page 449) for ideas on how to flavor crème anglaise.

Fill a large bowl with ice cubes and set out a smaller bowl that can hold the finished cream.

Bring the milk and cream to a boil in a small saucepan.

Meanwhile, in a medium heavy-bottomed saucepan, whisk the yolks and sugar together until very well blended and just slightly thickened. Still whisking, drizzle in about one quarter of the hot liquid—this will temper, or warm, the yolks so they won't curdle. Whisking all the while, slowly pour in the remaining liquid. Put the pan over medium heat and stir without stopping, until the custard thickens slightly and coats the back of a spoon; if you run your finger down the bowl of the spoon, the custard should not run into the track. The custard should reach at least 170 degrees F, but no more than 180 degrees F, on an instant-read thermometer. Immediately remove the pan from the heat and pour the custard into a 2-quart measuring cup or a clean heatproof bowl. Stir in the vanilla extract.

Refrigerate the cream until it is very cold, then cover it tightly. If possible, refrigerate the cream for 24 hours before using it—the extra chilling time will intensify the flavor and allow the cream to thicken a bit more.

# ALMOND CREAM

A **CLASSIC** French preparation, almond cream is based on butter, sugar, almonds and egg. Really more a luxurious spread than a cream, it comes into its own when baked. Smoothed over the bottom of a crust, then topped with fruit (as it is in the French Pear Tart, page 368), used instead of pastry cream to fill Brioche Raisin Snails (page 56) or simply spooned into little ramekins, capped with berries and baked like a tart, almond cream puffs and develops a light crust. Inside, it remains soft and creamy and deeply flavored by its namesake ingredient.

- ¾ stick (6 tablespoons) unsalted butter, at room temperature
- ⅔ cup sugar
- ¾ cup ground blanched almonds
- 2 teaspoons all-purpose flour
- 1 teaspoon cornstarch
- 1 large egg
- 2 teaspoons dark rum or 1 teaspoon pure vanilla extract

MAKES ABOUT 1½ CUPS

STORING: Kept well covered in the refrigerator, the almond cream will keep for up to 3 days.

TO MAKE THE CREAM USING A FOOD PROCESSOR: Put the butter and sugar in the food processor and process until the mixture is smooth and satiny. Add the ground almonds and continue to process until well blended. Add the flour and cornstarch and process to blend, then add the egg. Process for about 15 seconds more, or until the almond cream is homogeneous. Add the rum or vanilla and pulse just to blend.

TO MAKE THE CREAM USING A MIXER OR BY HAND: You can use a hand or stand mixer (fit the mixer with the whisk attachment), or you can blend the cream in a bowl with a rubber spatula. Blend the butter and sugar together until smooth. Add the almonds, beating to incorporate them completely. Blend in the flour and cornstarch, then add the egg, beating until the cream is homogeneous. Stir in the rum or the vanilla.

Scrape the almond cream into a container and use it immediately, or refrigerate it until firm, about 2 hours.

# BITTERSWEET GANACHE

**WHEN ALLOWED** to cool and reach a spreadable consistency, this ganache is perfect for spreading between cake layers or frosting a cake. Or, if you use the ganache while it is still warm, it can be poured over a cake, in which case it will serve more as a glaze than a frosting.

8 ounces bittersweet chocolate, finely chopped

1 cup plus 2 tablespoons heavy cream

½ stick (4 tablespoons) unsalted butter, cut into 4 pieces, at room temperature

Put the chopped chocolate in a heatproof bowl.

Bring the cream to a boil, then pour half of the cream over the chocolate and let it sit for 30 seconds. Working with a whisk or rubber spatula, gently stir the chocolate and cream together in small circles, starting at the center of the bowl and working your way out in increasingly larger concentric circles. Pour in the remainder of the cream and blend it into the chocolate, using the same circular motions. When the ganache is smooth and shiny, stir in the butter piece by piece. Don't stir the ganache any more than you must to blend the ingredients—the less you work it, the darker, smoother and shinier it will be.

If you are using the ganache as a glaze or as a filling for a pie or tart, use it immediately. If you are using it as a filling or a frosting for a cake, let it sit on the counter until it thickens to the desired consistency. You can refrigerate the ganache until it reaches the consistency you want, but in that case, keep checking on it—refrigerate it for too long, and it will thicken enough to be rolled between your palms and turned into truffle bonbons.

MAKES ABOUT 2 CUPS

STORING: The ganache can be tightly covered and kept in the refrigerator for up to 5 days or frozen for up to 2 months. Let the ganache stand at room temperature to bring it back to the consistency you need; stir gently before using. Alternatively, you can warm it in very short spurts (that is, about 5 seconds each) in a microwave oven, or put the ganache in a heatproof bowl over a pan of simmering water and heat it, stirring gently, until it reaches the desired consistency. Whether you're using a microwave or a double boiler, take care to use minimal heat: you don't want to risk having the ganache separate.

# WHITE CHOCOLATE GANACHE

MAKES ABOUT 1 CUP

**FOR THIS** ganache to work, you must use premium-quality white chocolate. I use either Valrhona Ivoire or white chocolate from Guittard.

10 ounces premium-quality white chocolate, finely chopped

⅔ cup heavy cream

1½ tablespoons unsalted butter, cut into 3 pieces, at room temperature

Put the chopped chocolate in a heatproof bowl.

Bring the cream to a boil, then pour it over the chocolate and let it sit for 30 seconds. Working with a whisk or rubber spatula, gently stir the chocolate and cream together in small circles, starting at the center of the bowl and working your way out in increasingly larger concentric circles. When the ganache is smooth, stir in the butter piece by piece. Don't stir the ganache any more than you must to blend the ingredients—the less you work it, the better it will be.

If you are using the ganache as a glaze or as a filling for a pie or tart, use it immediately. If you are using it as a filling or a frosting for a cake, let it sit until it thickens to the desired consistency. You can refrigerate the ganache until it reaches the consistency you want, but keep checking on it so you don't pass the stage you're aiming for.

**STORING:** The ganache can be tightly covered and kept in the refrigerator for up to 5 days or frozen for up to 2 months. Let the ganache stand at room temperature to bring it back to the consistency you need; stir gently before using. Alternatively, you can warm it in very short spurts (that is, about 5 seconds each) in a microwave oven, or put the ganache in a heatproof bowl over a pan of simmering water and heat it, stirring gently, until it reaches the desired consistency. Whether you're using a microwave or a double boiler, take care to use minimal heat: you don't want to risk having the ganache separate.

# CHOCOLATE GANACHE GLAZE

**THIS SIMPLE** recipe produces a smooth, deeply chocolaty glaze that can be used anytime you want to dress up a simple cake. It's quick to make, pours easily and remains soft and creamy when set.

4 ounces bittersweet chocolate, finely chopped

½ cup heavy cream

2 tablespoons sugar

2 tablespoons water

Put the chopped chocolate in a heatproof bowl.

Bring the cream, sugar and water to a full boil, then pour the liquid over the chocolate and let it sit for 30 seconds. Working with a whisk or rubber spatula, gently stir the chocolate and cream together in small circles, starting at the center of the bowl and working your way out in increasingly larger concentric circles.

If you are pouring the glaze over a chilled cake, particularly a chilled cake that is already frosted, the glaze can be used as soon as it is blended. If you are pouring it over a room-temperature cake or a cake that is not already frosted, leave the glaze on the counter until it thickens just enough to pour in a ribbon.

**MAKES ENOUGH TO GLAZE ONE 9-INCH CAKE**

**STORING:** The glaze can be made up to 1 day ahead and warmed just a smidgen either over simmering water or in a microwave oven. If you use the microwave, use 5-second spurts to bring it back to pouring consistency. Alternatively, put the ganache in a heatproof bowl over a pan of simmering water and heat it, stirring gently, until it reaches the desired consistency. Whether you're using a microwave or a double boiler, take care to use minimal heat: you don't want to risk having the ganache separate.

AN ALL-PURPOSE treat: whip it lightly and use it to top or accompany myriad desserts; whip it until it holds peaks and fill, frost or decorate a cake with it.

Cold is what you need to whip cream. If your kitchen is warm, you might want to put your mixing bowl and beaters in the freezer until needed.

Cream whips to almost 2 times its volume. To fill and cover a layer cake with whipped cream, you should start with 2 cups heavy cream.

For Chocolate and White Chocolate Whipped Cream, see pages 457 and 458.

1 cup very cold heavy cream

1–4 tablespoons confectioners' sugar (to taste), sifted

½–1 teaspoon pure vanilla extract, to taste (optional)

Working with a stand mixer fitted with the whisk attachment or with a hand mixer or a balloon whisk in a large bowl, beat the cream and sugar together just until the cream starts to thicken. Start beating the cream slowly—don't rush the process—and increase the speed as the cream gains texture. Continue to beat until the cream reaches the desired consistency. Be certain not to overbeat—when cream is overbeaten, it becomes very thick and looks as if it's on the verge of separating; seriously overbeaten cream turns to butter. To get it right if using a mixer, you may want to whip the cream until it is just shy of the desired consistency and finish the job by hand with a whisk. I prefer cream that's served as an accompaniment or a topping to be softly whipped; cream meant to fill or frost a cake or needed to hold up a cherry or other decoration should be whipped firmer. When the cream is whipped to the just-so point, stir in the vanilla extract, if you're using it.

MAKES ABOUT 1½ CUPS

STORING: Whipped cream is best used soon after it is made; however, it will keep for up to 24 hours and, if you want a thicker cream, keeping it is a good idea. To store whipped cream, line a strainer with a piece of dampened cheesecloth, spoon the cream into the strainer, place the strainer over a bowl and wrap the bowl and strainer in plastic wrap; put the setup in the refrigerator. Stored like this, the cream will lose its excess moisture and thicken.

*Playing Around*

You can add more sugar or none at all; use brown sugar instead of confectioners'; sweeten the cream with a little honey (be careful not to use so much that you make the cream runny); substitute another extract for the vanilla or use a combination of extracts; spoon in some spice when you add the sugar; or spike the whipped cream with a liqueur.

COFFEE WHIPPED CREAM: Make a coffee extract by dissolving 1 to 2 tablespoons instant coffee or espresso powder in an equal amount of boiling water; let cool completely. When the cream is almost whipped or whipped completely, beat in some or all of the extract. Start light and work your way up to the taste you like.

# CHOCOLATE WHIPPED CREAM

USING FINE-QUALITY chocolate, not cocoa powder, gives chocolate whipped cream the perfect texture and depth of flavor, making it almost a dessert in itself. Plan ahead: the chocolate-cream mixture needs at least 4 hours of refrigeration (24 hours is better) before it is whipped.

| | |
|---|---|
| 3 ounces bittersweet chocolate, finely chopped | 2 cups heavy cream |
| | 2–3 tablespoons sugar, to taste |

MAKES ABOUT 3 CUPS

STORING: The chocolate-cream mixture can be kept covered in the refrigerator for up to 1 day. Once it's whipped, it's best served immediately, but it can be covered and refrigerated for about 3 hours.

Put the chocolate in a heatproof bowl large enough to use for whipping the cream.

Stir the cream and sugar together in a heavy-bottomed saucepan and bring to a boil. Remove the pan from the heat and pour the cream over the chocolate. With a whisk, beat the chocolate and cream together vigorously—you want to make sure you've got a smooth mixture. Refrigerate for at least 4 hours, or, better yet, 24 hours; cover the cream once it is cool to protect it from foods with strong odors.

If you've refrigerated the cream for only 4 hours, you might want to beat it in an ice-water bath—set the bowl in a larger bowl filled with ice cubes and water. With a whisk, beat the cream until it is almost thick; this will happen quickly—pay attention! You want the cream to be just firm enough to spread but not so firm that it loses its lightness and creaminess. The cream is ready to use as soon as it is whipped.

# WHITE CHOCOLATE WHIPPED CREAM

ADDING WHITE chocolate to whipped cream gives the cream more weight, more velvety smoothness and more vanilla flavor.

6 ounces premium-quality white chocolate (such as Valrhona Ivoire or Guittard), finely chopped

1½ cups cold heavy cream

MAKES ABOUT 2 CUPS

STORING: Kept covered and away from foods with strong odors, the refrigerated whipped cream will keep for about 6 hours. If needed, give the cream a few turns with a whisk before using.

Put the chopped chocolate in a heatproof bowl and set the bowl over a pan of simmering water to melt; stir occasionally. While the chocolate is melting, bring ½ cup of the cream to a boil.

Transfer the bowl to a counter, pour in the hot cream and let it sit for a minute, then, using a small spatula, stir gently until the chocolate is smooth. Let the chocolate sit until it reaches room temperature—the chocolate can't be the least bit warm when you add it to the whipped cream.

Working with a stand mixer fitted with the whisk attachment or with a hand mixer in a large bowl, beat the remaining 1 cup cream only until it holds the softest peaks. With the mixer on high speed, add the white chocolate all at once and continue to beat just until the whipped cream holds firm peaks.

Turn the cream into a bowl, press a piece of plastic wrap gently against the surface to create an airtight seal and refrigerate for at least 2 hours.

# CRÈME FRAÎCHE

CRÈME FRAÎCHE—the name is French for fresh cream—is more like American sour cream than heavy cream, because it is slightly tangy and thick enough to be spoonable. For the baker, crème fraîche trumps sour cream on one point: it can be whipped.

Imported crème fraîche can be found in specialty markets and crème fraîche from the Vermont Butter and Cheese Company is widely available. However, it's easy to make a more-than-respectable crème fraîche at home starting with heavy cream, you just have to plan ahead: you need about 2 days for the transformation.

1 cup heavy cream
1 tablespoon buttermilk or plain yogurt

Put the cream and buttermilk or yogurt in a clean jar with a tight-fitting lid. Cover the jar and shake for a minute or so.

Put the jar on a counter and leave it for 12 to 24 hours, or until the cream thickens slightly. How long this will take depends on how warm your room is—the warmer the room, the quicker the thickening.

When the cream is thick, transfer the jar to the refrigerator and let it chill for 1 day before you dip into it.

MAKES 1 CUP

STORING: You can keep the crème fraîche in the refrigerator for about 2 weeks; the longer you keep it, the tangier it will become.

## FAUX CRÈME FRAÎCHE

**USE THIS** when you want the tang of crème fraîche but don't have any on hand and haven't the time to make the real thing. Unlike real crème fraîche, which you can use for baking, faux crème fraîche should be used only as a topping or filling.

For a firmer, tangier cream, you can play with the proportions of heavy cream to sour cream. Start by reversing the amounts (using ³⁄₄ cup sour cream to ¹⁄₂ cup heavy cream), then adjust the proportions by adding more heavy cream to suit your taste.

STORING: You can keep the cream covered in the refrigerator for a couple of hours, but it is best soon after it is made.

| | |
|---|---|
| ½ cup sour cream | Sugar to taste |
| ¾ cup cold heavy cream | ¼ teaspoon pure vanilla extract (optional) |

Put the sour cream in a medium bowl.

Whip the heavy cream until it holds soft to medium peaks—you don't want it to be too firm. Scrape the cream into the bowl with the sour cream and fold the ingredients together gently using a rubber spatula. Fold in the sugar and vanilla extract, if you're using it.

# LEMON CREAM

**THIS LEMON** cream tastes less buttery than Lemon Curd (page 462) and a little tangier. Use it to make a tart (page 331), fill a cake (it's very good between the layers from the Black-and-White-Chocolate Cake, page 258) or serve it alongside cookies or bread (it's great with toast made from Golden Brioche Loaves, page 48).

For the story behind this lemon cream, see page 332.

1 cup sugar

Grated zest of 3 lemons

4 large eggs

¾ cup fresh lemon juice (from 4–5 lemons)

2 sticks plus 5 tablespoons (10½ ounces) unsalted butter, cut into tablespoon-size pieces, at room temperature

**MAKES ABOUT 2½ CUPS**

**STORING:** Well covered, the cream can be kept in the refrigerator for up to 4 days; packed airtight, it can be frozen for up to 2 months; thaw it overnight in the refrigerator. Stir before using.

Have an instant-read thermometer, a strainer and a blender (first choice) or a food processor at hand. Bring a few inches of water to a simmer in a saucepan.

Put the sugar and zest in a large heatproof bowl that can be set over the pan of simmering water. Off the heat, rub the sugar and zest together between your fingers until the sugar is moist, grainy and very aromatic. Whisk in the eggs, followed by the lemon juice.

Set the bowl over the pan and start stirring with a whisk as soon as the mixture feels tepid to the touch. Cook the cream until it reaches 180 degrees F on an instant-read thermometer, whisking constantly to keep the eggs from scrambling. As you whisk, you'll see that the cream will start out light and foamy, then the bubbles will get bigger, and then, as the cream is getting closer to 180 degrees F, it will start to thicken and the whisk will leave tracks. Heads up: the tracks mean the cream is almost ready. Don't stop whisking and don't stop checking the temperature, and have patience—depending on how much heat you're giving the cream, getting to temp can take as long as 10 minutes.

As soon as it reaches 180 degrees F, remove the cream from the heat and strain it into the container of the blender (or food processor); discard the zest. Let the cream stand at room temperature, stirring occasionally, until it cools to 140 degrees F, about 10 minutes.

Turn the blender to high (or turn on the processor) and, with the machine running, add the butter about 5 pieces at a time. Scrape down the sides of the container as needed as you incorporate the butter. Once the butter is in, keep the machine running—to get the perfect light, airy texture of lemon-cream dreams, you must continue to blend the cream for another 3 minutes. If your machine protests and gets a bit too hot, work in 1-minute intervals, giving the machine a little rest between beats.

Pour the cream into a container, press a piece of plastic wrap against the surface to create an airtight seal and chill the cream for at least 4 hours, or overnight.

Before using the lemon cream, stir it a couple times with a whisk to loosen it.

# LEMON CURD

**THIS CLASSIC** lemon curd is smooth, creamy and quick to make, since you just put everything in a pot and gently cook it until thickened, a matter of minutes. Once cooled, the curd is great as a spread for biscuits, scones and muffins and equally good as a filling for cakes or tarts. For something with slightly more tang and slightly less butteriness, turn to Lemon Cream (page 461), which can be used in exactly the same way as lemon curd.

STORING: Packed in a tightly covered jar, the curd will keep in the refrigerator for up to 2 months.

| | |
|---|---|
| 1¼ cups sugar | 1 large egg |
| ¾ stick (6 tablespoons) unsalted butter, cut into 6 pieces | 6 large egg yolks |
| | Freshly squeezed juice of 4 lemons |

Put all the ingredients in a medium heavy-bottomed saucepan and stir with a heatproof spatula to moisten the sugar. Put the pan over medium-low heat and cook, stirring without stopping, until the butter melts and the mixture thickens like custard, 4 to 6 minutes. Keep your eyes on the pan, because the curd can curdle quickly. It is cooked enough when you can run your finger along the spatula and the curd doesn't run into the track you've created. Don't worry if the curd looks thin at this point—it will thicken more as it cools. Remove the pan from the heat and scrape the curd into a heatproof jar or a bowl. Press a piece of plastic wrap against the curd to create an airtight seal and cool to room temperature before storing in the refrigerator.

# BITTERSWEET CHOCOLATE SAUCE

**WARM, THIS** deeply flavorful sauce can be poured over cakes or around tarts. Chilled, it can be spread onto cookies.

½ cup heavy cream

½ cup whole milk

½ cup water

6 tablespoons sugar

4 ounces bittersweet chocolate, finely chopped

MAKES ABOUT 1½ CUPS

STORING: The sauce can be kept in the refrigerator in an airtight container for up to 3 weeks. If you want to use the sauce warm, heat it gently in a microwave oven or in a bowl set over a saucepan of gently simmering water.

Put all the ingredients in a heavy-bottomed saucepan, put the saucepan over medium-low heat and bring the mixture to a boil, stirring occasionally to blend. Lower the heat and let the sauce simmer for 10 to 15 minutes, or until it is thick enough to coat a metal spoon: if you run your finger down the back of the spoon, the sauce should not run into the track you've created.

If you want to use the sauce in its pourable state, let it cool for about 10 minutes. If you want to save it for later, cool it, pack it into an airtight container and refrigerate it until needed.

# MILK CHOCOLATE SAUCE

A THICK ribbony sauce, like hot fudge, with the mild, round flavor of milk chocolate, this is good cold or warm over cakes or ice cream.

MAKES ABOUT ¾ CUP

2 tablespoons (packed) light brown
   sugar
Pinch of salt
2 tablespoons light corn syrup
¾ cup whole milk

4 ounces premium-quality milk
   chocolate, finely chopped
1 tablespoon unsalted butter, at room
   temperature
½ teaspoon pure vanilla extract

Stir the sugar, salt and corn syrup together in a medium heavy-bottomed saucepan. Pour in the milk and stir to blend. Put the pan over medium heat and bring the mixture to a boil, stirring frequently. Turn the heat to medium-low and cook, still stirring, for 3 minutes.

Remove the pan from the heat, add the chocolate and stir until it is melted and the sauce is smooth. Stir in the butter and vanilla.

Use immediately, or pour the sauce into a clean jar with a tight-fitting lid; refrigerate until needed.

STORING: Tightly covered, the sauce can be kept in the refrigerator for about 1 week. If you want to serve the sauce warm, heat it gently in a microwave oven or in a bowl set over a saucepan of gently simmering water.

# HOT FUDGE SAUCE

**OLD-FASHIONED,** dark, smooth and shiny, this hot fudge sauce is the kind that firms the instant it's poured over ice cream.

½ stick (4 tablespoons) unsalted butter, cut into 8 pieces

6 ounces bittersweet or semisweet chocolate, finely chopped

¾ cup heavy cream

3 tablespoons light corn syrup

2 tablespoons sugar

¼ teaspoon salt

Set a heatproof bowl over a saucepan of simmering water, put the butter in the bowl, top with the chocolate and heat, stirring once or twice, until the ingredients are melted. Keep the heat very low—you don't want the mixture to get so hot that the butter and chocolate separate. Transfer the bowl to the counter when the mixture is smooth.

In a small heavy-bottomed saucepan, stir together the cream, corn syrup, sugar and salt, then bring to a boil. Boil for 1 minute and remove the pan from the heat.

Pour about one quarter of the hot cream over the chocolate and, with a rubber spatula and starting in the center of the bowl, stir the two mixtures together in ever-widening concentric circles. When it is smooth, pour over the remainder of the cream in 2 additions, stirring gently until the sauce is shiny and smooth again.

Allow the sauce to cool for about 10 minutes before using.

**MAKES ABOUT 1¼ CUPS**

**STORING:** In a tightly covered jar, the sauce will keep in the refrigerator for up to 3 weeks. Before serving, warm it gently in a microwave oven or in a bowl set over a saucepan of gently simmering water. Heat just until the sauce is pourable.

**GOOD FOR** pouring over cakes, tarts or, best of all, ice cream.

MAKES ABOUT 1 CUP

1 cup sugar

3 tablespoons water

1 tablespoon light corn syrup

¾ cup heavy cream

1 tablespoon unsalted butter

**STORING:** The sauce can be kept tightly covered in the refrigerator for about 1 week. Before using, warm gently in a microwave oven or in a bowl set over a saucepan of gently simmering water.

Put the sugar, water and corn syrup in a medium heavy-bottomed saucepan and stir just to combine. Heat over medium-high heat, without stirring (if the mixture is coloring unevenly, swirl the pan as needed to blend), until the caramel turns deep amber, 5 to 10 minutes, depending on the size of your saucepan and the intensity of the heat. As the sugar is caramelizing, wipe down any splatters on the sides of the pan with a pastry brush dipped in cold water. To test the color of the caramel, drop a bit on a white plate. Don't be timid about the color—if it's too pale, it won't have much taste.

Lower the heat, stand back from the saucepan—because the caramel will bubble and spatter—and add the cream and butter. When the spatters are less vehement, stir to smooth and calm down the caramel. Remove the pan from the heat.

Pour the caramel into a heatproof jar and cool until it is slightly warm and still pourable before using, about 1 hour.

# RASPBERRY COULIS

**IT TAKES** just 5 minutes to make this raspberry coulis, but what you get packs a lot of flavor. Fresh raspberries will give you beautiful color and flavor, but frozen raspberries will also give you good results. Use berries that are frozen whole without syrup and defrost them enough to process them.

1 pint (2 cups) red raspberries —fresh or frozen, partially thawed if frozen

3 tablespoons sugar, or more to taste

Put the berries and sugar in a blender or food processor and whir until pureed. Taste and mix in more sugar if needed. Press the coulis through a strainer or a food mill to eliminate the seeds.

MAKES ABOUT 1 CUP

STORING: The coulis is at its best just after it is made, but it can be kept covered in the refrigerator overnight.

## Playing Around

Using the same technique, and adjusting the sugar to taste, you can make other fruit coulis. Instead of raspberries, use blueberries, strawberries or exotic fruits like passion fruit, mango or pineapple.

# CANDIED ORANGE OR LEMON PEEL

**IF YOU** keep the peels in their syrup, you can chop them and add them to whipped cream, mix them into a cake filling or spoon them over ice cream. Dried and tossed in sugar, the peels are a good accompaniment to coffee and dainty cookies.

3 thick-skinned oranges or 5 lemons

4 cups water

2 cups sugar, plus more if drying the peel

¼ cup fresh lemon juice

MAKES ABOUT 8 SERVINGS

**STORING:** Kept in the syrup in a tightly sealed jar, the peel will keep in the refrigerator for up to 3 weeks. Dried peel, packed in an airtight tin, can be kept at room temperature for up to 5 days.

Using a sharp knife, cut a slice off the top and bottom of each orange or lemon. Stand the fruit on a cutting board and, cutting from top to bottom, cut off bands of peel about 1 inch wide, making sure you include a thin layer of fruit with every band of peel.

Bring a large pot of water to a boil and drop in the peel. Boil for 2 minutes, then drain the peel in a colander and rinse under cold water. Refill the pot and repeat the boiling, draining and cooling twice more.

Rinse out the pot and pour in the 4 cups water. Stir in the sugar and lemon juice and bring to a boil. Return the peel to the pot, cover and reduce the heat so that the syrup simmers gently. Stirring now and then, cook the peel for 1½ hours, until it is soft and completely candied. Remove the pot from the heat and let the peel sit in the syrup at room temperature overnight.

The next day, spoon the peel and syrup into a jar with a tight-fitting lid; refrigerate.

If you want dried candied peel, remove the peel from the syrup and lay the pieces out on a rack. Once the peel is dry, coat the pieces in sugar—just toss them into a bowl of sugar and turn them around until they are coated, then lift them out of the bowl and shake off the excess sugar.

*Playing Around*

**CANDIED CITRUS SLICES:** To make candied circles of citrus fruit instead of strips of peel, cut the whole fruit, rind and all, into rounds as thick or thin as you please; remove any seeds. The rounds take less time to candy than peel—start checking 30 minutes after you've added them to the syrup.

# CANDIED NUTS

**NUTS COATED** with brittle-like caramel are handy to have in the house. Sprinkle them over a whipped cream topping or on top of a hot fudge sundae, or eat them out of hand as popcornless Cracker Jack. You can use the same candying technique for popcorn, Rice Krispies or Cheerios. While candied cereal may sound strange, it is delicious wherever you'd use candied nuts.

MAKES ABOUT 1½ CUPS

**STORING:** You can keep the nuts in an airtight tin for a couple of days. Their keepability depends on how dry the environment is.

⅓ cup sugar

3 tablespoons cold water

1½ cups nuts—whole, halved or sliced (you can use skinned salted or unsalted peanuts, blanched almonds, walnuts, pecans, macadamias, pistachios or skinned hazelnuts)

Line a baking sheet with parchment paper or, better yet, a silicone mat.

Put the sugar and water in a medium heavy-bottomed saucepan and cook over medium-high heat, stirring with a wooden spoon, until the sugar dissolves. Keeping the heat fairly high, cook the sugar, without stirring, until it just starts to color. (If some of the syrup splatters onto the sides of the saucepan, wash down the splatters with a pastry brush dipped in cold water.) Toss in the nuts and immediately start stirring. Keep stirring, coating the nuts with the syrup. Within a few minutes, the nuts will be covered with sugar and will turn white—keep stirring until the sugar turns into caramel.

When the peanuts are coated with a nice deep amber caramel, remove the pan from the heat and turn the nuts out onto the baking sheet, using the wooden spoon to spread the nuts out as best you can. Cool the nuts to room temperature.

When the nuts are cool enough to handle, separate them and break them into small pieces, or pulverize them in a food processor.

# BUTTERED PECANS

**GREAT OVER** puddings or ice cream or even buttered biscuits, these pecans are quick to make and so good to have on hand. You can multiply the recipe to meet your needs.

½ cup pecan halves, whole or
  chopped
1 tablespoon unsalted butter

Pinch of salt (optional)

MAKES ½ CUP
(ENOUGH
TO TOP 6 SERVINGS)

STORING: In a bowl at cool room temperature, the nuts will keep for about 3 days.

Line a plate with a double thickness of paper towels and keep it near the stove.

Put a small skillet over medium heat and toss in the pecans. Cook the pecans, stirring, for 1 minute, or until they are ever so slightly toasted. Add the butter and continue to cook, turning, until the pecans have absorbed almost all the butter, another 2 minutes or so.

Remove the pan from the heat, stir in the salt, if you're using it, and turn the pecans out onto the paper towels. Cover with another double layer of paper towels and pat the pecans gently to remove some of the excess butter. Cool to room temperature between the paper towels.

# CHOCOLATE CURLS AND SHAVINGS

**YOU CAN** decorate everything from simple cakes and puddings to fancy cakes with these chocolate curls or shavings. The technique for curling or shaving chocolate isn't hard, but it's rare to get it right the first time—it takes practice. Fortunately, any shavings or curls that don't pass muster can be saved for recipes calling for melted chocolate.

**A hunk of chocolate (white, milk or dark)**

To get curls and good-size shavings, start with a block of chocolate that is broad enough on one side to let you run a vegetable peeler down it. The chocolate should be at warm room temperature—75 degrees F is perfect. If your room and your chocolate are cold, you can turn on one of the burners on your stove and very quickly pass the block of chocolate over the heat. Wait 2 minutes, then do it again. Your chocolate should now be right for shaving.

Stand the chocolate up on edge, holding it at an angle, on a piece of wax paper or parchment paper. Using a vegetable peeler, scrape down the side of the chocolate with the tip of the peeler if you want short shavings, or with the peeler's blade if you want curls.

**STORING:** If your room is cool, you can cover the curls or shavings with a piece of parchment or wax paper and keep them at room temperature. If your room is warm, keep them in the refrigerator, where they will be fine for about 2 hours.

# DECORATIVE CANDIED PETALS AND LEAVES

**CANDYING ROSE** petals or leaves such as mint, lemon balm or scented geranium is easy. Use them as a decoration on cakes or as a little nibble with tea or coffee.

**STORING:** Kept uncovered in a cool, dry place, the candied petals or leaves will hold for 1 day.

Fresh edible flower petals or leaves, stemmed or not (little pieces of stem look pretty)

Egg white(s)

Sugar

Rinse the petals or leaves under cool water, shake them dry and dry them thoroughly between sheets of paper towels.

In a small bowl, whisk the egg white until foamy. Put some sugar in a small bowl and have a piece of wax paper or parchment paper or a silicone baking mat close by.

Working with one petal or leaf at a time, dip it in the egg white to coat, allowing the excess to drip back into the bowl; pass each side of the petal or leaf through the sugar, so that it is lightly coated; and put it on the paper or baking mat to dry.

Let the petals or leaves dry overnight.

# A Dessert Maker's Glossary
## of Ingredients, Tools
## and Techniques

**BAKING MATS:** These are sheets of silicone (with some fiberglass) sized to fit into rimmed baking sheets (see below) or to cover flat cookie sheets and capable of withstanding temperatures up to 500 degrees F. The mats are completely—and almost miraculously—nonstick and can be considered just about permanent, since they can be used more than two thousand times. They wash easily and are a blessing when you are baking anything sticky, sugary or buttery—which accounts for just about all of what we bake. At first blush, the mats might seem a little pricey—the cost is about $20 per sheet—but I think I've more than made up the price in savings on parchment paper and foil, which is what I used to use to line baking sheets. I find the mats so efficient that I have bought one for each of my baking sheets and store the mat right in its baking sheet, ever ready for the next cookie session.

**BAKING POWDER:** Baking powder is a double-acting leavener: it gives its first push when it comes in contact with liquids, releasing carbon dioxide (that's when you might see bubbles in your batter), and its second when the oven's heat goes to work. Baking powder provides the puff power for quick breads, like muffins, biscuits and scones, and for many butter cakes. If you're not a constant baker, buy the smallest tin of baking powder on the shelf. And, no matter how frequently you bake, keep the tin tightly sealed in a cool, dry place and replace it every six months or so.

**BAKING SHEETS:** Baking sheets can be rimmed or not. The rimmed sheets, referred to as sheet pans by the pros, are sometimes called jelly-roll pans, and the unrimmed sheets, which might be raised on the two short sides, are usually called cookie sheets. I own both, but these days I find that I use the rimmed sheets almost exclusively. In some part, this has to do with how perfectly silicone baking mats (see above) fit into them, but my preference is based in large part on their practicality—they double as trays. So I also use rimmed baking sheets to hold a recipe's ingredients (see mise en place, page 487) and to ferry cake and other baking pans in and out of the oven (see lining baking sheets, below). It is good to have at least two baking sheets.

**LINING BAKING SHEETS:** As you bake through this book, you'll notice that I often instruct you to put your baking pan on a lined baking sheet. For this job, I suggest a rimmed baking sheet and, for lining, parchment paper or a silicone baking mat. Lined undersheets are great levelers and transporters—they even out the heat that hits the bottom of your baking pan and give you a convenient, safe way to slide your filled baking pans in and out of the oven—and they will catch anything that might bubble up and over the baking pan.

**BAKING SODA:** Bicarbonate of soda, what we know as baking soda, is one of the ingredients in baking powder and a leavening agent on its own. Unlike baking powder, baking soda's rising powers are best released in the company of acidic ingredients, such as sour cream, buttermilk and yogurt. And, while you will see recipes that call for baking powder and baking soda in tandem, you cannot substitute one for the other. Baking soda should be kept in a cool, dry place, since even a tiny bit of water will cake it. Check the expiration date on the box. If your box has been open and sitting in the cupboard for at least six months, I'd suggest a new box, just to be on the safe side.

**BAKING TIMES:** One of the most difficult things to give with perfect precision is baking time, because everyone's oven is just a little different. Even if the oven thermometer you have dutifully put in your oven registers 350 degrees F when you set your oven to that temperature, your oven cycles on and off—it will go up to a certain temperature, then dip, then go up and down again to keep the oven at an average of 350 degrees F. How high or low it goes and how often it goes up and down will affect how long the oven remains at the set temperature. So, because your oven and mine probably don't hit the same highs and lows and even if they do, they may not do so with the same frequency, doneness can vary by a few minutes from my oven to yours. This is why I usually give you a range of baking times. For instance, I might say, "Bake for 35 to 40 minutes," in which case you should check at the earliest time, 35 minutes, or even 5 minutes before. In the same spirit, you should not be concerned if what you are baking takes a few minutes longer than I suggest. And you should always be on the lookout for the visual clues and other doneness tests I give you—for example, puffiness, dryness, a cake pulling away from the sides of the pan or, most telling, a knife inserted into the cake coming out clean. The more you bake, the better your feel for time, temperature and doneness will be.

**BATTER:** The (unbaked) mixture you put together for cakes is usually referred to as batter, while the mixtures for cookies, bread and pastry crusts are usu-

ally called dough. The difference has to do with how substantial the mixture is. A batter is usually liquid or semi-liquid, while a dough is thick and heavy.

**BISCUIT CUTTERS:** Because biscuit dough is rolled or patted out to a thickness of about ½ inch, a regular cookie cutter is too low to cut the dough effectively. What you need is a tall cutter and, while you're at it, one that cuts sharply so that you don't torture the dough and "glue" its cut sides down—do that, and you won't get a great rise. Cutters made specifically for biscuits are tall rings or squares, and often topped by handles. They are available at housewares shops.

**BLENDER:** In all cases in which a blender is stipulated here, you can use a food processor (although the reverse is not true). However, when it comes to beating certain preparations, such as the Lemon Cream (page 461), into extreme smoothness, the blender has the edge over the processor. In any case, if one machine is preferred over another, the recipe will tell you so.

**BLIND-BAKING:** Blind-baking means baking a crust either partially or completely before adding the filling. To blind-bake a tart crust, make sure it is very cold—I always freeze it before baking—then place a piece of buttered foil, buttered side down, over the crust and press it so that it fits snugly against the base and sides. If the crust is truly frozen, you can bake it as is, checking on it after 15 minutes and pressing down any puffy portions with the back of a spoon. If the crust is cold but not frozen, fill it with dried beans or rice (see pie weights, page 490, for more information), bake as directed, then carefully remove the foil and weights. At this point, the crust is partially baked. If you want to fully bake the crust before filling it, return the crust to the oven and bake until it is golden.

While you can go weightless when you're blind-baking a frozen tart crust, a piecrust usually needs weights (see above) to curb its enthusiasm. After the unbaked crust has chilled thoroughly—or, better yet, been frozen—butter a piece of aluminum foil and fit the foil, buttered side down, snugly against the crust, covering the base and sides and lightly covering the rim. Fill the foil with weights and bake as directed, then carefully remove the foil and weights. At this point, the crust is partially baked. If you want to fully bake the crust before filling it, return the crust to the oven and bake until it is golden.

**BLOWTORCH:** You don't absolutely need a blowtorch, but, boy, it's fun to have on hand when you're making the sugar topping on a crème brûlée or when you've got a meringue you want to color. While you can pick up a blowtorch at Home Depot, a more elegant tool is available—called the Chef's Torch, it is home-kitchen-size, reliable, easy to use and pinpoint-precise.

**BUNDT PANS:** According to most accounts, Bundt pans were invented in 1950 for a Minneapolis Hadassah group that wanted an aluminum alternative to the pottery Kugelhopf pans they were accustomed to using for their tall tube cakes with fluted sides. The women called the pan and, by extension, the cake, *Bund*, which, in German, means a gathering of people. However, given that it was just after World War II, the inventor put a "t" at the end of the word so that people wouldn't associate the pan with the *Bund* that supported Hitler in the 1930s. As popular as the pan became in the 1950s and '60s—it hit a high point in 1966 when Tunnel of Fudge, a cake made in a Bundt pan, won the Pillsbury Bake-Off—it seems to be even more popular today. And while you can still get the classic pan, nowadays you can also get pans that turn out cakes shaped like roses, sunflowers, cathedral towers or Hansel and Gretel's cottage. I use traditional Bundt pans that hold between 10 and 12 cups. If your pan has a wildly different capacity, just scale my recipe up or down and adjust the baking time accordingly.

**MINI-BUNDT PANS:** Individual-serving-size Bundts come six to a pan, like muffin or popover pans. Any recipe for a regular-size Bundt pan can be made in a mini-Bundt pan, but you'll need to adjust the baking time.

**BUTTER:** Butter is one of the great basics of baking, a prime mover in the taste and texture departments and the backbone of the majority of cakes, cookies and pastries in the American and European repertory. Please, please, please and please, again, when a recipe calls for butter, do not use anything else. I have a sign in my kitchen that was painted in the 1930s and its proclamation is still true: "There is no substitute for butter." You cannot use margarine or any other kind of "spread" in a recipe that calls for butter and expect to get the proper results.

In America, unlike Europe, salted butter is often more widely available than unsalted butter. Try to find unsalted butter for your baking. Using unsalted butter not only gives you control over the amount of salt in your recipe, it gives you a slight difference in taste and texture too, since salted butter has a lower percentage of butterfat and, therefore, a higher percentage of water.

All of the recipes in this book were tested with unsalted Land O'Lakes butter, a nationally available brand.

**Cultured butter:** All butters are churned from cream, but some select premium American and European butters are churned from cream that has been cultured—that is, ripened with natural cultures (like yogurt) over a period of about 18 hours. Once cultured, the cream tastes more like crème fraîche than sweet cream, and it is this cream that is then churned into butter. Not surprisingly, cultured butter has a tang that is missing in butter made with *crème ordinaire*. Culturing is a long and expensive process and it is reflected in the butter's retail price. However, if you are at all interested in butter, I urge you to seek out a cultured butter and do your own taste test, and perhaps a bake-off. In the butter bake-off I worked on with The Baker's Dozen East (see page 220), we preferred the cultured butters from the Vermont Butter and Cheese Company and from Echiré in France, both of which have very high percentages of butterfat (close to 86 percent).

**Buttering pans:** When a recipe calls for a buttered pan, the butter used to grease the pan is separate from the amount of butter in the recipe's ingredient list. The easiest way to butter a pan is to use softened butter and to apply the butter with a piece of paper towel, a piece of the butter's wrapper (that's the most efficient and economical method) or a pastry brush, which is great for getting into corners and curves. When I'm doing a lot of baking, I keep a bowl of softened butter and a pastry brush at hand.

**Measuring butter:** Butter is measured in tablespoons, sticks and ounces. Tablespoons and ounces are usually marked on the sticks. One stick of butter is 4 ounces, or 8 tablespoons.

**Melting butter:** Melt butter by warming it over gentle heat or in a microwave—don't be rough with it. You don't want to either give it so much heat or keep it over the heat for such a long time that it burns or separates.

**Room-temperature butter:** In order for butter to mix properly with other ingredients and for it to aerate properly when beaten, it must be malleable, a condition it reaches when it is at room temperature. Sadly for butter, the temperature of most houses is so high that the butter often ends up oily and mushy rather than malleable. Keep an eye on the butter that you put on the counter: you're looking for the butter to give easily, but not completely, when pressed; it should still hold its shape.

**Storing butter:** Butter is a magnet for strong odors, so it should always be well wrapped. If I know that I'll be keeping butter in the fridge for a while, I wrap unopened sticks in plastic wrap and then foil. It's good to know that butter freezes perfectly and that, well wrapped, it can remain in the freezer for months. Some butter producers claim that butter can be frozen for up to 2 years. I'm sure they are right, but I make a point of using it within 6 months.

**BUTTERMILK:** Buttermilk is cultured milk, usually low-fat milk, and, because of the culturing process, it has an acidic tang. Buttermilk makes biscuits, muffins, breads and cakes more tender. If you don't find buttermilk in the dairy section of your supermarket, you can substitute $2/3$ cup plain yogurt (nonfat or low-fat) and $1/3$ cup milk for each cup of buttermilk called for in the recipe. You can also use powdered buttermilk, usually available in the baking section of the supermarket. To reconstitute powdered buttermilk, follow the instructions on the package.

**CAKE PANS:** Each recipe will tell you the size and shape of the cake pan you need. Sometimes I mention that I like to use a Pyrex pan, but in general, cake pans are assumed to be metal. My preference for layer cakes or round cakes is for high-sided pans—I buy professional-quality cake pans with 2-inch-high sides—made of aluminum (a good conductor) or another light metal. While dark pans are nice for breads, where a dark crust is often what you're after, I don't like them for cakes because I don't want my cakes to develop a well-done, deeply colored crust. For the same reason, I don't have any dark nonstick cake pans. The sole exception is a Bundt pan—its interior is dark and I love the way cakes bake in it.

Basic pans: Here are the basic pans a baker should have on hand:

- Three 8-inch round cake pans (1½ to 2 inches tall)
- Three 9-inch round cake pans (1½ to 2 inches tall)
- Springform pans: if possible, one 8-inch, one 9-inch and one 10-inch; these can be nonstick (if you buy only one springform, buy a 9-inch pan)
- One 8-inch square cake pan (1½ to 2 inches tall)
- One 9-inch square cake pan (1½ to 2 inches tall)
- One Bundt pan (with a capacity of at least 10 cups)
- Two 8½-x-4½-x-2¾-inch loaf pans
- Two 9-x-5-x-2¾-inch loaf pans
- One 7-x-11-inch pan
- One 9-x-13-inch pan
- One or two 12-cup muffin tins (standard tins have molds that are 2½ inches in diameter)
- One 9-inch pie plate (can be Pyrex)
- One 9-inch deep-dish pie plate (can be Pyrex)
- At least one 9-inch fluted tart pan with a removable bottom
- One 10-inch fluted tart pan with a removable bottom

**CANDY THERMOMETER:** Unless you're an avid candy-maker, you probably won't get a lot of mileage out of a candy thermometer (often labeled a candy/deep-fry thermometer), but for making syrups and caramels, it's the right tool for the job. Candy thermometers either clip onto the side of a pan or have little feet that allow them to rest in the pan and lean against the side, convenient when sugar is bubbling away on its own and you need to check its temperature frequently. If you have a digital instant-read thermometer that registers above 300 degrees F, you can use it for the recipes in this book, though it isn't as convenient as a candy thermometer unless you have a clamp to attach it to the pan (see instant-read thermometer, page 485).

**CARAMELIZE:** To caramelize sugar means to cook it until it melts and browns and tastes bittersweet. How dark a caramel you make and whether you leave it liquid or cool it until you've got brittle, will depend on what you have in store for it. Each recipe using caramel gives you the specific instructions you need. One general caveat: be careful. Caramel gets very hot—it may go above 500 degrees F! And it's sticky—if you get some on you, it won't slide off. If you get hot sugar on your fingers (or anywhere else), don't stick them in your mouth—everyone's first reaction—instead, quickly run your fingers under very cold water. If you want to be on the safe side, keep a bowl of ice and water near the range. Caramel is fun to make and adds incomparable flavor to desserts, but you've got to approach it with respect.

**CARDBOARD CAKE ROUNDS:** These circles of corrugated cardboard are available in specialty baking shops and are convenient to have on hand, particularly when you are making cakes that will be filled and frosted. Slip a round under the bottom layer of cake, and you'll be able to hold the cake in one hand while you fill and frost it with the other. Rounds also make carrying and transporting cakes easier. Cake rounds come in many sizes, but the 9-inch size is most useful for home bakers.

**CHESTNUTS:** While I adore freshly roasted chestnuts, I save them for eating on their own. When I need chestnuts for a dessert, I buy peeled and cooked whole chestnuts in a jar. Available in many supermarkets (particularly around holiday time) and specialty stores, the chestnuts are unseasoned, unsweetened and ready to use. From time to time I find vacuum-packed chestnut pieces in the market—these are usually less expensive than jarred whole chestnuts and good for any recipe in which you are going to break, chop or puree the nuts.

**Chestnut flour:** Chestnut flour, a sweet, gluten-free flour milled from chestnuts, adds flavor and bulk, but not structure, to a dough. It's available in heath food stores, specialty markets and online (one source is chestnutsonline.com).

**Chestnut spread:** Sold in cans in specialty shops and often in supermarkets, chestnut spread, a French specialty, is made of pureed chestnuts sweetened with sugar and flavored with vanilla.

**CHOCOLATE:** For those of us who love chocolate, it is, as the Greeks believed, the fruit of the gods. In fact, that's the translation of the ancient Greek word *"Theobroma,"* which is the genus of cacao, the trees from which we make chocolate. The base of all chocolate, whether dark or light, bitter or sweet, is chocolate liquor (which, oddly, is not liquid) made from ground cocoa nibs (cacao beans minus their shells). Chocolate liquor is half cocoa and half cocoa butter, and it is the sole ingredient in unsweetened chocolate (which is so bitter that most people shudder if they eat just a little shard of it). To make bittersweet and semisweet chocolate, sugar and usually more cocoa butter are added to the liquor. Milk chocolate includes even more sugar and milk solids. The more liquor in a chocolate, the deeper its flavor.

**Types of chocolate:** My favorite type of chocolate is bittersweet, but you might prefer semisweet chocolate, which is a little sweeter. You can use bittersweet and semisweet chocolate interchangeably, but there are no substitutes for unsweetened, milk or white chocolate.

**Cocoa percentages:** It has long been the practice in Europe (in fact, it was the law) to list the percentage of cocoa on the chocolate package, and premium American chocolates, such as Scharffen Berger and Guittard, do that as well. But if percentages were all that mattered, choosing a chocolate would be easy—you'd just pick a number. However, as with coffee, the quality of the final product depends on the quality of the beans and the care with which they were handled from the time they were grown and picked through to their drying, roasting and processing. For this reason, the best advice on purchasing chocolate I can give you is the following: buy the chocolate that tastes best to you. My favorite chocolates are made by Valrhona, Scharffen Berger and Guittard, and I usually use chocolates that are between 55 and 70 percent cacao.

**Melting chocolate:** Chocolate should be melted slowly, gently and dryly—don't let it get near water. (If a recipe calls for melting chocolate with a liquid, then you're fine; it's the rogue drops of liquid that can cause problems.) The safest way to melt chocolate is to use an improvised double boiler—an uncovered metal bowl set over a saucepan containing simmering water. As long as the bowl fits snugly into the pan, so that you don't have a lot of steam rising up around the sides and depositing droplets of water on the chocolate, you're golden.

You can also melt chocolate in a microwave oven. I find it's safest to put the chocolate in a microwave-safe container—uncovered—and to work on medium or low power and in short intervals. Here's an important point to remember about melting chocolate in a microwave: the chocolate may hold its shape even though it is melted, so to avoid overheating and possibly scorching the chocolate, stir it frequently.

No matter how you melt your chocolate, it's best to start with chopped chocolate—the chocolate will melt more evenly and the process will go faster.

**Storing chocolate:** Chocolate should be stored in a cool, dry place, never in the refrigerator or freezer, where its enemy, moisture, can attack it. Properly stored, dark chocolate will last for years, milk and white chocolates for about 1 year. If your chocolate develops a cloudy, grayish "bloom," don't despair—it means that the cocoa butter has separated. It may look unattractive, but melt it and it will be fine.

**COCOA NIBS:** Cocoa nibs (also called cacao nibs), the cocoa bean minus its shell, are pure chocolate. Cocoa nibs have only recently been available in the United States and only more recently to home bakers. (Scharffen Berger sells cocoa nibs, and nibs are also available online from pastry suppliers.) The ground nibs are crunchy and can be used the way you'd use chopped nuts or chocolate chips. Because they have such a strong flavor and because they are unsweetened, I prefer to use them sparingly—they're great sprinkled over whipped cream toppings for puddings, cakes or brownies.

**COCOA POWDER:** Cocoa powder is cocoa liquor that has been pressed to remove the lion's share of its cocoa butter and then ground. Always use unsweetened cocoa for baking, not sweetened, and sift it before adding it to the bowl. The two kinds of cocoa powder available are Dutched, which means it has been treated with alkali, and natural. While Dutched cocoa is often used in recipes with baking powder and natural cocoa is used in recipes with baking soda, you will not see appreciable differences if you use the cocoas interchangeably in these recipes.

**COCONUT:** When coconut is called for, I usually use sweetened shredded coconut, the kind found in the baking section of supermarkets. I like this co-

conut for its chewy texture. However, if you'd like, you can use unsweetened shredded coconut from the health food store. Usually sold in bulk, this coconut is drier than sweetened and won't give you the same chewiness, but it will give you a deeper flavor.

**COCONUT MILK:** Coconut milk is available in cans, usually in the Asian products section of the supermarket. Be sure to choose the unsweetened kind—save the sweet stuff, usually referred to as coconut cream (it's located in the mixed-drink section), for piña coladas.

**CONVECTION OVENS:** All of my recipes were tested in a regular—not a convection—oven. You can use a convection oven, but you will need to make whatever adjustments to time and temperature your oven manufacturer suggests.

**COOLING:** Cooling should really be considered a part of baking, the finishing touch, since, when a sweet comes out of the oven, its internal heat continues to rise. Allowing it to cool allows it to finish baking and set its texture.

**COOLING RACKS:** Cooling racks are not just convenient for unmolding desserts, they are essential for lifting them up off the counter (you don't want condensation forming under them) and for keeping air circulating around them. Choose racks with closely spaced wire bands or mesh (so your desserts don't fall through the wires and so the wires don't cut into them) and, most important, with feet that are at least $1/2$ inch high. If you've got ample storage space, it's good to have three round cooling racks (they'll make unmolding two cake layers easy) and at least one large rectangular rack for cooling cookies.

**CORNMEAL:** If, like me, you like cornmeal that retains a little grittiness after it is baked, choose stone-ground cornmeal, cornmeal that still includes some bran and germ. Stone-ground cornmeal is available in health food stores and some supermarkets.

COULIS: "Coulis" ("koo-*lee*") is the French word for a sauce made from pureed fruit.

CREAM: Heavy and whipping cream can be used interchangeably in these recipes. It used to be true that heavy cream had a higher percentage of butterfat than whipping cream did, but these days it's hard to know which cream has what, since many supermarkets offer something called "heavy whipping cream." Whatever cream you buy, make certain it is fresh—check the sell-by date and always smell it and/or taste it before you use it—and keep it in the refrigerator until needed.

To whip cream: Cream whips best when it is cold. Don't rush the process—start whipping the cream slowly and increase the speed only when the cream starts to hold its shape. (For more detail, see the recipe on page 456.)

CRÈME FRAÎCHE: Crème fraîche is cultured heavy cream with a taste and texture reminiscent of sour cream. However, crème fraîche has more tricks up its sleeve than American sour cream—it can be heated without curdling or separating and it can be whipped. While crème fraîche is a common supermarket product in France, it's a specialty, and therefore an expensive, item here, but fret not—it can be made easily at home using regular heavy cream and buttermilk (see the recipe on page 459). If you don't have crème fraîche or don't have the time to make it, you can substitute heavy cream in most recipes—although you won't get crème fraîche's characteristic sourness and tang—or if it's a topping you're after, you can use Faux Crème Fraîche (see page 460 for the recipe).

CRUMB: In baking, this term refers to the inside of bread or cake.

DECORATING SUGAR: Also known as sanding, sparkle or dazzle sugar, this is the sugar of Sugar Plum Fairies' dreams. It looks more like flakes than granules, it comes in far more colors than the rainbow and it keeps its shape, texture and color when baked. I've got jars of decorating sugars—testaments to time spent decorating gingerbread houses and Christmas cookies—but the color I reach for most often is plain old white. I sprinkle it over the tops of piecrusts, over butter cookies and onto the sides of slice-and-bake cookie logs, all for the same reason: fun. Decorating sugar is available in some supermarkets and in specialty stores such as Williams-Sonoma.

DECORATOR'S TURNTABLE: Essentially a lazy Susan, a decorator's turntable is a flat revolving plate on a pedestal. (Often the plate and the pedestal can be separated, which is great for storage.) Being able to turn a cake easily makes the job of smoothing frosting across its sides and top a cinch. A turntable isn't a necessary piece of equipment, but one you'll enjoy if you're a regular cake maker. To fill and frost a cake without a turntable, see cardboard cake rounds, page 477.

DOUGH: A thick, heavy mixture used to make bread, cookies or pastry crusts. Unlike a batter (see page 474), a dough is usually rolled or molded.

DOUGH SCRAPER: A square of metal attached to a grip, the dough scraper is a great tool for lifting and turning dough and, yes, scraping it off a work surface. It's also good for cutting a dough into sections—use it, for example, when you want to divide the dough for scones into neat wedges and then to transfer them to a baking sheet.

DRIED FRUIT: Dried fruits—such as raisins, currants, prunes, apricots, cherries and the like—add both flavor and textural interest to baked goods, but they're an asset to a dessert only if they are moist and plump. Hard fruit won't get softer, moister or plumper in the oven. Happily, even shriveled fruit is salvageable. To bring dried-out dried fruit up to snuff, simmer it for a minute or two in, or steam it for a minute or two over, boiling water, then pat it dry between paper towels.

**DUSTING AND DUSTERS:** Sometimes all it takes to give a plain cake a little panache is a dusting of confectioners' sugar or cocoa powder. A dusting should be just that—a light, snowy covering. You can get a dusting by putting the sugar or cocoa in a fine-mesh sieve and shaking the sieve over the dessert, but give the sieve the first tap over a piece of wax paper—sometimes that first tap produces a blizzard rather than a shower. For a more reliable dusting, put the sugar or cocoa powder in a shaker designed just for that purpose. Small canisters with perforated lids are available in housewares stores. I keep sugar and cocoa dusters filled and ready to go at all times.

When you want to dust a work surface with flour, it's easiest to grab a small handful of flour and toss it lightly over the surface—precision and delicacy don't count here.

**EGGS:** All of the recipes in this book were developed using large eggs.

**Egg safety:** Egg safety has become an issue because of concern about salmonella, a bacteria that may be found in eggs, but that, fortunately, is not often a problem. Salmonella can cause flu-like symptoms and, while healthy people can normally fight off the bacteria, the very old, the very young, ill people, pregnant women and people with compromised immune systems can be at risk, so you should always make certain you serve only fully cooked eggs to at-risk people. To kill the salmonella bacteria, eggs must be brought to a temperature of 160 degrees F or kept at a temperature of 140 degrees F for 3 minutes.

There are certain basic rules you should follow when buying, storing and using eggs:

- Buy your eggs from a market that keeps them refrigerated.
- When you get the eggs home, store them in the refrigerator. If a recipe calls for room-temperature eggs, take the eggs out of the refrigerator about 30 minutes ahead of time.
- Do not use eggs with broken shells.
- Wash your hands after working with eggs, and clean any work surfaces well after they've been in contact with raw eggs.

**Egg whites:** When a recipe calls for egg whites to be separated from yolks, it is usually because the whites will be whipped. Eggs separate most easily when they are cold, but whites whip to their fullest volume when they are warm, so after separating, you should leave them at room temperature for a while before you beat them. And before you beat them, make sure that both the whisk and the mixing bowl are dry and impeccably clean. Even a little speck of fat will impede the whites' progress to peakdom. (For a fuller discussion of whipping egg whites, see Mastering Meringue, page 400.)

**Egg yolks and sugar:** Beating yolks and sugar together is commonplace in baking, but it is not without a pitfall: As soon as sugar comes in contact with yolks, it begins to "burn" the yolks. "Burn" is the term bakers use to describe the way sugar causes the yolks to develop small lumps. To keep the sugar from burning the yolks, make sure to whisk the two ingredients together as soon as they are put in the same bowl, and do not allow them to sit.

**EXTRACTS AND OILS:** I use only pure extracts, and you should too. Extracts made from artificial flavors will mask the true goodness of all your other ingredients. These days, in addition to pure extracts, many pure oils are available. I have a particular fondness for lemon and citrus oils. If you choose to flavor your desserts with oils, do so with a light hand—they can be pretty powerful. Add oils by drops, not spoonfuls. Extracts and oils should always be kept tightly sealed in a cool, dry cupboard. Give them a sniff test every once in a while to make sure they've still got their pow—replace them if their aromas have faded.

**FLEUR DE SEL:** Translated literally from the French, "fleur de sel" means flower of the salt, a poetic way of describing its preciousness. A type of sea salt that is larger-grained, moister and less salty than common salt, it is not washed, iodized or treated with antihumidity chemicals. It is natural, hand-harvested from special salt ponds along the coast of Brittany—the most prized fleur de sel comes from Guérande—and it is unusually rich in minerals. Because it is raked from the finest salts that float to the surface of the ponds and because its availability is in the hands of the wind and rain gods, it is expensive. This isn't the salt to use when you're boiling pasta—treat it as a condiment, and use it sparingly and when its taste can be most appreciated (as in World Peace Cookies, page 138). Think of it as the extra-virgin olive oil of the salt world.

**FLOUR:** With few exceptions, these recipes call for all-purpose flour, which is the bleached and enriched flour found in the supermarket. The exceptions are cakes made with cake flour, a finer-textured flour that is lower in protein than all-purpose flour.

**Substituting all-purpose for cake flour:** If you do not have cake flour on hand, you can substitute all-purpose flour using this formula: 1 cup all-purpose flour minus 2 tablespoons = 1 cup cake flour.

**Scoop-and-sweep measuring:** I measure flour using the scoop-and-sweep method, which I learned from Julia Child. To use this technique, first aerate the flour by tossing it with a fork or knife, then dip your measuring cup into the flour bin and scoop up enough flour to have it mound over the top. Finally, take a straightedge, such as the back of a knife, and sweep it across the top of the measuring cup to level it. When you scoop and when you sweep, you should not press on the flour and pack it down.

**Sifting—or not:** Unless instructed to do so, you do not need to sift all-purpose flour—however, you should always sift cake flour, since it is often lumpy.

In recipes in which sifting is required, the flour is always measured before sifting.

**Storing flour:** All flour, regardless of type, should be stored in tightly sealed containers in a cool, dry cupboard. I store my flour in canisters that are wide enough to allow me to dip a measuring cup into them.

**FOLDING:** When you have a light, airy mixture, for example, meringue, and you need to blend it into a heavy mixture, let's say a cake batter, the technique you should use is called folding. You need three things for successful folding: a sturdy rubber spatula, a large bowl that will give you ample room to move the ingredients around and the good sense to know when to call it quits.

In most cases, the heavier mixture will be in the big bowl and the lighter one will be folded into it. If a batter is particularly heavy, you might be told to stir in (not fold) about one quarter of the lighter mixture—doing this lightens up the heavyweight batter so that when you mix in the remainder of the light ingredients, you don't have to work hard and risk deflating them. For that first step, you just scoop up some of the airy stuff, plunk it on top of the batter and stir the two mixtures together, gently but not so daintily. Next, to fold, spoon the lighter mixture over the heavy one and cut through the two mixtures with the edge of the spatula. When the edge reaches the bottom of the bowl, twist your wrist so that you bring the flat of the spatula against the bottom of the bowl and up the side. As you're bringing the spatula up the side of the bowl, use your other hand to give the bowl a quarter turn, so that the ingredients the spatula brings up from the bottom are on top of the mixture and folded over on themselves. As you keep cutting into the mixtures, lifting them up and turning the bowl, you will fold the two mixtures into each other. This sounds more complicated than it is. In fact, once you get the hang of it, you'll find it so easy—and so satisfying (it's mesmerizing to watch the batters change and blend)—that you might overdo it and knock the air out of your lighter mixture. The when-to-say-when moment is earlier than this—it's better to have a few clouds of unfolded-in meringue or a few streaks of unfolded-in chocolate than to have an overworked batter.

**FOOD PROCESSOR:** For the longest time, I turned to the food processor when I needed power over finesse, using the processor to grind nuts, crush crackers or soften ice cream—and I still use the machine for these jobs. But, oddly, the processor's kinder, gentler side is the one I now find most useful—when it comes to making delicate pastry dough, the processor is a wizard. Because the processor is so powerful and so quick, it cuts dough ingredients into one another with such speed and efficiency that the toughening properties in the flour don't have a chance to go into action and the butter doesn't have a chance to warm, either of which would make the dough heavy. Of course, you can be successful making dough by hand or with a mixer, but if you have a processor, I think you'll be delighted with the results you get.

**FREEZING:** As you'll see when you look at the Storing information at the end of each recipe, many baked goods, particularly cookies, cakes and crusts, are freezable. The key to having what you pull out of the freezer taste as good as what you put in is packing it airtight—air is what causes freezer burn and off tastes. If you are freezing a cake, it should be wrapped in at least two layers of plastic wrap. If the cake is glazed, the easiest thing to do is to freeze the cake unwrapped, just to set the glaze, then wrap it. For cookies, disks of dough or odd-shaped treats like shortcakes or muffins, I use plastic bags of the old-fashioned non–zipper-lock variety. (I find it harder to remove all the air from zipper-locks and, therefore, to get a tight seal.) I pack the bag about three-quarters full, gather it at the top and then—here's the important part—before I wrap a twist tie around the bag, I suck the air out of the bag, a job you can do with your mouth or, if you'd prefer, by poking a straw into the opening and pulling the air out through the straw. Either way, keep the bag, which should now conform to the shape of its contents, closed while you grab the twist tie and seal it. For safe measure, tuck this bag into another, and draw the air out of that bag too.

**Defrosting:** If you've got the time, the best way to defrost desserts is to allow them to remain in their wrappings overnight in the refrigerator. Thawed slowly and still wrapped, they will be thoroughly defrosted and they will retain their moisture. If you're in a rush—as most of us are most of the time—just put the wrapped treat on the counter and poke it gently from time to time to see how it's coming along.

**GANACHE:** Ganache is a blend of chocolate and heavy cream, although some ganaches contain butter and some both butter and eggs. Depending on the proportion of chocolate to cream, a ganache can be thick enough to mold into truffle bonbons or thin enough to pour over a cake as a glaze. Regardless of the consistency you're aiming for, the technique for blending ganache is the same. The chocolate should be finely chopped and placed in a heatproof bowl, and the cream should be brought to a boil. Whether you pour a portion at a time or all of the cream over the chocolate (the recipe will tell you what to do), you should let the ingredients rest for a moment, so the cream's heat can melt the chocolate, then stir with a rubber spatula or a whisk. Start by stirring in a tiny circle in the center of the bowl and slowly and gently work your way out to the sides of the bowl in ever-widening concentric circles. Don't rush, and don't stir energetically—what you are really doing when you blend the chocolate and cream together is forming a delicate emulsion (think chocolate mayonnaise). When properly made, ganache is shiny, smooth and perfectly blended.

GELATIN: I created and tested these recipes using powdered gelatin. The easiest way to work with powdered gelatin is to sprinkle the specified amount over the (specified amount of) cold water and to allow the gelatin to sop up the water and turn spongy. Then either put the spongy gelatin in a microwave oven and warm it for 15 seconds (a little longer if you've got more than a tablespoon of gelatin) so that it liquefies, or warm it in a small saucepan over very low heat.

GRATERS: While I still have an old-school box grater somewhere, these days when there's grating to do, whether it's chocolate, carrots or the zest from a bunch of lemons, I reach for a laser-sharp grater from Microplane. For years, Microplane manufactured woodworking tools, including metal rasps. Then, one day, in a necessity-is-the-mother-of-invention moment, a woman in need of a grater found herself unable to put her hands on one, so she went into her husband's workshop, grabbed a Microplane rasp and used it as a grater. Excited by the fact that the rasp did a better job than her usual grater, she wrote to the company suggesting that they market a line of rasps-cum-graters for kitchen use. And they listened. I keep a bunch of these graters, which are now widely available in housewares stores, in a canister on the counter. I have a grater with very fine holes for grating citrus zest—the grater is so good that the zest flies off it in dainty curlicues—a medium-holed grater for cheeses and a large-holed one for fruits and vegetables, and often for chocolate.

HAIRDRYER: It's an odd thing to have in the kitchen, but nothing beats a hairdryer for unmolding anything creamy or frozen. Any unmolding job that you used to accomplish by dipping the pan into a sinkful of hot water can be accomplished on dry land with a hairdryer. Just shoot some hot air around the pan to unmold a cheesecake or an ice cream confection—it's quick, there's no mess and you've got more control than with the water-dunk. A hairdryer is also great for putting the shine back on glazes that have gone a little dull in the refrigerator or for softening up frosting if you decide at the last minute to dress up a sweet with sprinkles or chocolate curls or anything else that needs a slightly sticky surface to cling to.

HONEY: Deriving its flavor and color from the bees' choice of blossoms, honey gives a sweet-tangy flavor, moisture and a supple texture to desserts. While I may suggest a particular honey for a recipe, I encourage you to use the honeys you like best. In general, the color of the honey is a good indication of its strength: light honeys, like clover and orange blossom, have milder flavors, while darker honeys, like pine, have bigger flavors.

**ICE CREAM MAKER:** Homemade ice cream isn't a necessity, but it is fun to make and delicious too. If you think you are going to be making ice cream often and in quantity, and if you've got a chunk of counter free, then you might want to spring for a pro-type ice cream maker with a built-in compressor. This means that you just flip a switch and start churning—there's nothing to prechill, so you can make ice cream at whim. However, speed and power come at a price—these ice cream makers start at about $300 and go to above $1,000. They're great, but they're certainly not the only game in town. With $50 and the willingness to plan ahead, you can have an ice cream maker that uses an insulated canister that must be well frozen before you churn—no problem if you've got freezer space and can keep the canister in the freezer at all times, always ready. Insulated-canister machines come in two varieties: hand-crank, for which you just turn the crank every few minutes (Donvier makes a good machine of this variety), and automatic, for which you fit the canister into a base with a motor, set the timer and allow the machine to churn away merrily (Cuisinart makes such machines). There's also the old-fashioned fill-the-barrel-with-ice-and-crank-unendingly-by-hand machine. Machines like these make great ice cream, but they're best left to very sunny days, backyards and times when there are lots of people around to share in the cranking.

**IMMERSION BLENDER:** Also called a hand or stick blender, this is a neat tool because it accomplishes its task directly in the pot or bowl you're using rather than in its own (you'll-have-to-clean-it-later) container. While an immersion blender has more uses in the savory than in the sweet kitchen, you'll love having it for sauces and coulis and for smoothing out any mixing jobs that didn't go precisely as planned.

**INSTANT-READ THERMOMETER:** Very few recipes in this book require a thermometer—I've tried to give you visual clues for testing the readiness of things—but for ease and, even more important, for accuracy, it's great to have a digital instant-read thermometer on hand. To make it easier to measure the temperature of ingredients you are stirring on the stove, consider purchasing a clamp that holds your thermometer to a saucepan. (Clamps are available at restaurant supply shops and some specialty shops.)

**INSULATED BAKING PANS:** These pans are constructed with double metal bottoms separated by an air pocket. The air cushion means that the heat hitting whatever you are baking is gentler. I am not a fan of these pans—they don't produce cakes or cookies or crusts that are golden enough for my taste. Run a test for yourself and see if you like them, but keep in mind that if you decide to use insulated pans, you might have to make slight adjustments in baking times. Insulated baking sheets do serve one purpose very well—they are good undersheets for pound cakes and other loaf cakes that must spend a long time in the oven. In this instance, the insulated sheet tones down the heat that hits the bottom of the loaf and allows the loaf to bake more evenly. (If you don't have an insulated sheet to use as an undersheet, you can stack two regular sheets one on top of the other.)

**KNIVES:** Here's what I'd suggest as a basic-plus knife wardrobe:

- Paring knife, not only for paring but also for cutting small fruits and, most important, for testing the doneness of cakes (see Testing, page 494).
- Chef's knife, preferably 6 to 8 inches, for chopping nuts and chocolate, for slicing and dicing fruit and

for just about every miscellaneous cutting job that comes up.

- Long gently serrated knife, for cutting cakes into layers.
- Long sharply serrated knife, preferably offset (with the blade positioned below the handle), for chopping chocolate and for slicing pies and tarts. A serrated knife is good for pies and tarts because it cuts through firm, crisp crusts as easily as it cuts through soft fillings. This is really an optional piece of equipment, but, once you own one, you will appreciate how well it does its job. A bread knife with the more triangular shape of a chef's knife also works well.

**KUGELHOPF PAN:** A tube pan with a swirl pattern, sometimes called a Turk's turban, this pan was made originally of pottery, painted and decorated with flowers and used to make Kugelhopf, the yeast-raised cake that is traditional in France's Alsace region. The Bundt pan (see page 475) is the Kugelhopf's successor, and the two pans can be used interchangeably.

**MALTED MILK POWDER:** The base of old-fashioned soda fountain treats, malted milk powder, made from dried and ground barley, adds a subtle sweet-nutty flavor to batters or doughs. It is available in supermarkets.

**MASCARPONE:** A double- or triple-rich cow's milk cheese, meaning it's 60 to 75 percent fat, mascarpone is often used in conjunction with creams as a filling or solo as an accompaniment. Its texture is thick and its flavor is very mild—much more like cream than cheese—which is why it is so good mixed with heavy cream or even cream cheese. Mascarpone is easy to work with as long as you don't overbeat it—work it too long, and it will turn as thick as butter.

**MEASURING:** Forgive me while I state what may be obvious: the first step to success in baking is to measure accurately. In part the need for accuracy comes from the chemistry of baking, but it also comes from the reality of baking—once a sweet is in the oven, there's not much you can adjust, change or fix. Actually, the inevitability starts even sooner since, once a batter is mixed, there's usually no room for change: you've got to get it right at the start, and that means using the right measuring tools.

**Measuring liquids:** Liquid ingredients should be measured in transparent measuring cups, preferably glass, not plastic, with spouts and measurements that are clearly marked in ¼-cup (or less) intervals. Pour the liquid into the cup, then, to determine that you're up to the mark, bend down so that the cup is at eye level to check. Or, if you want to save your knees and still get an accurate measurement, purchase the ingenious measuring cups from Oxo—each has an angled band of clearly marked measurements inside the cup, so that you can see how much you've got simply by looking down. I like to keep four sizes of liquid measuring cups on hand: 1-cup measure (good when you're measuring in ¼-cups); 2-cup (probably the size I use most often); 1-quart (a handy size); and 2-quart (I often use it as a mixing bowl and then—washed and dried—as a cooling bowl when I'm making custard, crème anglaise or ice cream).

**Measuring dry ingredients:** Dry ingredients should be measured in metal measuring cups. (Plastic cups crack and sometimes lose their shape—and their accuracy.) The key to properly measuring dry ingredients is to get a level measure, and to do this, you must measure dry ingredients in the proper-size cup. For example, if you want ¼ cup sugar, use a ¼-cup measure—never put dry ingredients in a measure that's larger than the amount you need. If you are measuring flour, cocoa, sugar or the like, use the scoop-and-sweep method (see page 482), which means you dip your measuring cup into the bin, come up with enough of the flour or whatever to mound above the cup, and then, to get the right measure, gently sweep a straightedge across the top of the cup so that the ingredients are level with the edge of the cup. The exception to this method is brown sugar, which is always "packed." Fill the measuring cup with the sugar and tamp it down with your fingers. As with all other dry measurements, the brown sugar should be level with the top of the measuring cup. You'll know you've packed brown sugar properly if when you turn it out of the measuring cup, the sugar keeps the cup's shape.

A basic set of dry measuring cups includes $\frac{1}{4}$-cup, $\frac{1}{3}$-cup, $\frac{1}{2}$-cup and 1-cup measures. I also like to have $\frac{1}{8}$-cup (2 tablespoons) and 2-cup measures. Having a full set of measuring cups is a necessity for a home baker; a double set is not an indulgence and often a time-saver.

**Measuring spoons:** Measuring spoons, in $\frac{1}{4}$-teaspoon, $\frac{1}{2}$-teaspoon, 1-teaspoon and 1-tablespoon sizes, are used for both liquid and dry ingredients. When measuring in spoons, the ingredients should be level with the rim of the spoon. It's good to have a double set of spoons.

**MICROWAVE OVEN:** You can make all of these recipes without a microwave, but a microwave oven is handy for melting butter and chocolate, bringing small amounts of liquid to a boil and dissolving gelatin.

**MILK:** All of these recipes were developed and tested with whole milk.

**MISE EN PLACE:** This is a French term that is used in kitchens around the world. It translates to setting up, or putting in place, and it refers to the readying of ingredients. If you are not in the habit of doing a mise en place, of measuring out all the ingredients and having them on the counter before you start to work on a recipe, think about making it a habit. There are two primary advantages to doing so before setting to work: (1) you know that all of the ingredients are accounted for—there's never the surprise of discovering you're one egg short; and (2) the process of getting a recipe ready for the oven is faster and smoother. Oh, there's another reason for a mise en place: having all your ingredients in front of you, measured out into containers and arranged on a baking sheet, will make you feel like you're starring in your own Food Network show.

**MIXERS:** With very few exceptions (that is, recipes like brioche and marshmallows), you can prepare all of my recipes using a hand mixer with variable speeds. However, if you really love to bake, I'd suggest you save your money, take up a collection or hint like mad around holiday time or, especially, on your birthday to get a heavy-duty stand mixer. They are expensive—about $250—but good ones are almost indestructible. If you are buying a stand mixer, I'd suggest you get one with a 5-quart bowl (a $4\frac{1}{2}$-quart bowl is fine, but it can feel a little small if you are making bread, and a 6-quart bowl can feel a little big when you're making a small batch of something or even a one-layer cake) and look for one that comes with a paddle (or leaf) attachment, a whisk and a dough hook. My favorite mixer is a 5-quart KitchenAid mixer that I bought in 1971. It has been used endlessly and has never needed a repair. If I were to amortize the cost of the mixer over the batches of cookies I've mixed in it, I think I'd end up having to pay KitchenAid.

**MIXING BOWLS:** Some women collect diamonds, I collect mixing bowls. I prefer metal bowls because they can be put over heat or in the oven, and because they clean easily and can go into the dishwasher if necessary. You should have a small bowl (or two) that's just big (or small) enough to beat a pair of eggs, a couple of bowls of a size you can use to make a dozen biscuits and at least one big bowl that gives you the room you need to fold ingredients together. You'll need a heatproof mixing bowl that can be set over a medium saucepan of water to serve as a double boiler for melting chocolate. For easy storage, look for nesting bowls. And, if you are an avid baker and cook, consider investing in two sets of bowls. Like a double set of measuring cups and spoons, having duplicate bowls makes prep easier and faster.

**NUTS:** Because of their taste and texture, nuts are used frequently in baking. But what makes nuts so delicious, their oils, can also make them a problem—nut oil can go rancid, and it can go rancid quickly. To guard against this, try to buy your nuts from a supplier that does a lively business. (I buy most of my nuts from a local health food store or from Trader Joe's, where nuts—and dried fruits—are invariably fresh.) If you can taste before you buy, so much the better. When you get the nuts home, wrap them well and store them in the freezer—they'll keep better and longer there. Even with these precautions, I urge you to taste a nut from your batch before you begin baking—it's advice from the better-safe-than-sorry handbook.

**Toasting nuts:** Toasting brings out a nut's nuttiness. To toast nuts, spread them in a single layer on a baking sheet lined with parchment or a silicone mat and slide them into a preheated 350-degree-F oven. Bake the nuts, stirring them once or twice, for about 10 minutes, or until they are nicely browned and you catch their aroma when you walk into the kitchen.

**Ground nuts and grinding nuts:** Ground nuts provide flavor and texture in cakes and cookies. In fact, in many European cakes and tortes, ground nuts are used in place of flour, and they are referred to as nut flour or nut meal. While finding ground nuts used to be a problem for home bakers, it's no longer the case, thanks to markets like Trader Joe's and Whole Foods and online resources like bakerscatalog.com. If you want to make nut meal at home, you can do so successfully using a food processor; just make sure to add a little sugar or flour to the nuts—about 1 teaspoon per cup of nuts—and to pulse and process only until the nuts are ground and still fluffy. The only hazard in grinding nuts at home is going too far and turning them into nut butter—don't. If you're making a fine-crumbed cake, strain your home-ground nuts; if you're making cookies or something not so fussy, you don't have to bother straining (then it's a question of personal preference). Once ground, the meal can be packed airtight and kept in the freezer for up to 2 months.

**OATS:** The recipes were tested with old-fashioned rolled oats. It's fine to use quick-cooking oatmeal instead, but it's best not to use instant. And, please, never use steel-cut oats—they'll remain pebble-hard no matter how long you bake your cookies.

**OILS:** A few of the recipes call for vegetable oil or, in one case, olive oil. Before using any oil, smell it and, if it smells a little off, taste it. Oils, which should be stored in a cool, dark place, are sensitive and can go off with age and mishandling.

**OVEN THERMOMETER:** A truly indispensable piece of kitchen equipment. You probably think your oven is accurate, and that when you set it to 350 degrees F, that's the temperature it will be. And you might be right—or you might not be. Some ovens lose their calibration, and some ovens are not properly calibrated from the start. So that you never have to wonder and—more important—never have to end up with a cake that's ruined because it wasn't baked properly, invest in an oven thermometer, keep it in the oven and check it often. If your oven is not accurate, at least you'll know in which direction and by how much, and you'll be able to make the needed adjustments. (You can also have the oven recalibrated.)

**PARCHMENT PAPER:** Parchment paper, now readily available in supermarkets (Reynolds sells parchment in the same kind of box in which they sell aluminum foil), is good for lining baking sheets and cake pans. I always keep a roll of parchment paper in the house as well as a package of parchment rounds. These are precut circles—they come in all sizes—that you can quickly slip into buttered pans. Available in specialty shops and online, they are a nice convenience.

**PASTRY BAGS:** Also called piping bags, pastry bags are used to shape batters and doughs and to decorate cakes. They are cone-shaped bags made of nylon, plasticized canvas or plastic that come in many sizes and into which you can fit plain or decorative tips. While professional pastry chefs use piping bags for everything from making éclairs to filling a cake pan with batter, at home you're more likely to pull one out when you want to decorate a dessert—bags fitted with star tips can make a dollop of whipped cream look like a princess's crown. If you want to pipe something simple or write "Happy Birthday" but don't have a pastry bag, you can use a plastic bag—it's easiest to use a zipper-lock bag. Fill the bag with whatever you want to pipe, press the air out of the bag, seal it and then push the contents into one of the bottom corners. Snip off the corner on the diagonal, first cutting a very shallow slant and then deepening it if you

need a larger opening. Hold the bag at an angle, squeeze and pipe away.

**PASTRY BLENDER:** A set of curved parallel wires attached to a handle, a pastry blender cuts butter into flour. The blender will give you a crumbly mixture with pieces of butter of varying sizes, which is good for biscuits and scones, but most jobs that can be done with a pastry blender can be done with your fingers—always my first choice.

**PASTRY BRUSH:** Available in sizes from narrow to wide enough to paint a barn, pastry brushes are useful for brushing dough with egg wash, tarts with glaze or the inside of pans with softened butter. You can buy pastry brushes in housewares stores or use paintbrushes from the hardware department. To get started, I'd suggest a ½-inch-wide brush for delicate jobs and a brush between 1 and 2 inches wide for buttering pans or dusting excess flour off cookie and pie dough.

**PASTRY FEATHER:** This is a goose feather used to brush glaze on delicate pastries. Available in specialty shops, a pastry feather is particularly good for applying a thin coat of liquefied jelly over the top of a fragile tart. Handled with care, washed after each use and left to air-dry, the feathers can be surprisingly long-lived.

**PEANUT BUTTER:** All the recipes were developed and tested with Skippy peanut butter. As good as natural peanut butter from the health food store is for sandwiches and snacking, it doesn't bake well.

**PIE AND TART PANS:** While I have bought pie pans in just about every pie-pannable material, I always seem to come back to my old standby: Pyrex pie pans. I like the way crusts bake in Pyrex pans, and I can lift the pan up and see how the bottom crust is coming along. If you prefer metal or pottery pans, please, go right ahead and use them. However, when it comes to tart pans, I suggest you use metal pans with fluted sides and removable bottoms—all of the tart recipes were created and tested in these pans.

**PIE WEIGHTS:** When you are baking a crust blind, which means when you are partially or fully baking it without filling (see blind-baking, page 474), you need something to keep the crust from puffing up: weights. While you can buy metal or clay stones to weight the crust, I find them too heavy—they press down so hard on the crust that they keep the crust from developing its best texture. It is better to use dried beans or rice. Keep a supply that you use only for baking—after they've been used once for blind-baking, they are no longer fit for dinner, but they're fine for lots more baking.

**POLENTA:** Polenta is the name for both a coarsely ground cornmeal and the dish you get when you boil the meal into a mush. In any of my recipes specifying polenta, you can substitute ordinary cornmeal—the texture will be less pronounced, but you'll still get corn's sweet flavor.

**POTS AND PANS:** In all likelihood, you've already got all the pots and pans you'll need to bake your way through this book—most kitchens do. But if you need to fill in your stock, look for:

- At least one heavy-bottomed 2- to 3-quart saucepan for making puddings, crème anglaise and syrups and for using as the bottom of a makeshift (but very effective) double boiler
- A skillet, preferably cast-iron, for making Swedish Visiting Cake (page 197) and Tarte Tatin (page 312)
- A nonstick skillet or heavy saucepan for making caramel

**PUFF PASTRY:** Puff pastry is one of the most elegant doughs in the baker's repertory—and one of the most time-consuming to make. It is made by encasing a block of butter in a flour-and-water dough and then rolling the dough into a long rectangle, folding it into thirds like a business letter, giving it a quarter turn and then repeating this roll-fold-turn operation a total of six times so that there are almost a thousand layers of dough and butter, which cause the dough to rise—or puff—dramatically when baked. I used to make my own puff pastry, but I don't any longer because I have found a source for excellent frozen all-butter puff pastry (from Dufour Pastry). I urge you to do a little research and find a source in your neighborhood for all-butter dough. I keep saying all-butter dough because the butter in puff pastry is the dough's raison d'être. Unfortunately, and somewhat remarkably, the most popular brand of puff pastry available in supermarkets, Pepperidge Farm, is made without butter. It does puff beautifully, and if that's all you can find, of course you should use it. However, what you'll be missing is the taste of butter and the golden color that you get when you bake a butter dough. (That said, the flavors of the recipes that use puff pastry are assertive enough to carry the dessert, so don't pass them by just because you can't find an all-butter puff pastry.) Whether you are making your own dough or using frozen dough, it is very important to keep it cold. If the dough warms as you're working on it, take a break and slip it into the refrigerator to regain its chill. Unlike desserts made with other doughs, puff pastry sweets are usually delicious eaten shortly after they're taken from the oven, and desserts made with puff pastry should not be kept long—after a few hours they lose their puff and, because of their high butterfat content, tend to become soggy and heavy.

**RECIPES AND HOW TO FOLLOW THEM:** Lots of people say that recipes are chemical formulas, and to some measure they are, but I prefer to think of them as road maps to get you to your delicious destination. And while I know there are adventurous types out there who like to go off-road every chance they get, I would encourage you to rein in that urge until you've been down the designated route just once. After that, if you'd like to make a detour, it's up to you.

Before you do anything, you should read through the recipe in its entirety—then read through it again. By knowing what you will be doing as you proceed with the recipe, you'll know what equipment and ingredients you will need—you can do your mise en place (see page 487)—and you'll be able to gauge the amount of time you'll need for preparing the dessert, baking and cooling it and, if necessary, chilling it.

After you've made the recipe once, then you can play around with it—within reason. It is never a good idea to change measurements, certainly never the measurements for flour, butter, leavening or eggs. But there is room for putting your personal stamp on a dessert: you can add or subtract flavorings, such as extracts, oils and spices; you can change the form of a dessert, making a tart in a square pan, for example, cutting brownies into triangles rather than rectangles or deciding to double up on layers in a cake; or you can mix-and-match frosting and fillings and decorations. I've given you lots of options in the Playing Around sections of recipes. Have fun, but don't stray too far.

**ROLLING DOUGH:** The important word when rolling out dough is "cold." No matter what kind it is, dough should be cold, kept cold during the rolling process and refrigerated once it is rolled out. Soft doughs like the Sweet Tart Dough (page 444) can be difficult to roll because they have so much butter in them, so with these doughs it's best to either press them into the tart pan or roll them between sheets of plastic wrap or wax paper. Doughs like

Good for Almost Everything Pie Dough (page 442) can be rolled out on a lightly floured work surface or in a rolling slipcover (see below). Whatever material you choose to roll on or between, the technique for rolling is the same. Put the dough (which should be cool, but not so cold and hard that it cracks or breaks as soon as you start to roll it) on the work surface and position your rolling pin across the center of the dough. Roll the pin over the dough until it's almost to the edge, then roll it back to the center. (Don't roll over the edges, because they will get too thin—you can roll them to whatever thinness you want at the end.) Give the dough an eighth turn, and repeat. Stop rolling periodically to lift the dough off the surface and to make sure it's not sticking, to dust the rolling surface with a little more flour and to turn the dough over so that both sides get an even workout. If at any time the dough gets soft and sticky, chill it in the refrigerator, then carry on.

**ROLLING PIN:** My favorite rolling pin is the kind called a French pin—it's a narrow (2-inch diameter) cylinder sans handles. I like the control I can get by keeping my palms on the pin and feeling the thick and thin portions of the dough. Originally my favorite French rolling pin was made of tightly grained wood, but then I discovered a pin made of nylon, and it became my fave. (The pin I like is made by Matfer and is available at cooking.com.) Recently the silicone rolling pin came along. It has well-built handles on ball bearings and great maneuverability, and the silicone barrel rolls easily and nonstickily over everything. And it comes in great colors, including bright red. It's irresistible.

**ROLLING SLIPCOVER:** This should be called the Piecrust Maker's Cheat. A pair of clear flexible plastic circles held together by a zipper, it looks like a slipcover for a throw pillow. When unzipped, the circles open out completely and lay flat on the counter. To use the slipcover to roll a crust of uniform thickness and perfect roundness, you dust the inside with flour, place a disk of chilled dough in the center of one plastic circle and zip up the slipcover. When the dough is rolled out, you open the bag and flip the crust over and into your waiting pie or tart pan, using the plastic circle to help you settle the dough in place. Lift off the slipcover, and you're ready to go. I have two slipcovers, one that is 14 inches in diameter and good for making 10- to 14-inch pies and tarts, and one that is 11 inches in diameter and good for standard 9- to 9½-inch pies and tarts.

ROTATING PANS: When you've got two baking sheets or three cake pans in the oven, positioned on two racks, you should usually rotate the pans halfway through the baking period to compensate for any hot spots in your oven. Rotate the pans from top to bottom—moving the pan(s) on the bottom rack to the top and vice versa—and from front to back, so the side of each pan that was facing the front of the oven now faces the back. However, when your batch of cookies will be in the oven for only 10 minutes, whether or not to rotate is a judgment call. If you know your oven is really uneven (because the same patch always comes out browner than everywhere else), then you might want to rotate, but usually when the baking time is so short, I opt to leave the pans in place, since I hate to let the oven's heat escape.

RUM: Dark rum has a natural affinity for anything that has vanilla in it. And it's awfully good with anything that's got butter or brown sugar, or raisins, or chocolate, or coffee, or pineapple, or orange or so many other ingredients. In other words, it's a terrific partner to scads of sweets. But you've got to use great-quality rum. Relatively inexpensive large-scale-production dark rum will add more sweetness than flavor to whatever you're baking and, in the end, you'll be disappointed. It's worth investing in a good rum, preferably one that has been aged for a while—if you're feeling flush, look for vintage rum (starting at about $20 a bottle). The instant you open the bottle, you'll smell the difference between it and its lesser-quality cousins. And the profoundly rich perfume of aged rum might seduce you into doing what aficionados do—drinking it neat, the way you might cognac, Armagnac or single-malt Scotch.

SALT: You won't go through a lot of salt in your pastry kitchen, but every grain you use is important—as much as salt brings out the flavors in savory foods, it boosts flavors even more in desserts. This is true in part because its taste is somewhat unexpected, but it's also true because salt has such an affinity for butter, chocolate, caramel and nuts—all bakers' musts. If you like, you can reduce the amount of salt in these recipes, but please don't eliminate it entirely—without salt, even favorite flavors can be a little flat. For baking, I always use fine-grain sea salt.

SIFTING, SIFTERS AND SIEVES: Although for the most part you won't have to sift flour before using it in these recipes, cocoa, cornstarch, and cake flour do need to be sifted. You can sift with a sifter or a fine-mesh sieve, which is what I use. I like the large open area of the sieve rather than the confined area of a sifter. In addition, sieves are easy to clean.

SILICONE: Because silicone is nonstick to the max, flexible and heat resistant up to about 500 degrees F, it is the ideal material for baking mats (see page 473), spatulas, mixing spoons, hot pads and baking mitts, and really good for rolling pins (see page 491), muffin pans and whisks too. If you need to replace any of these small kitchen necessities, I'd suggest you take a look at the silicone versions.

**SPATULAS, FLEXIBLE AND FIRM:** You'll notice I say "spatulas" in the plural—that's because the baking life is easier if you've got a few on hand. Flexible spatulas made of either rubber or silicone (my new preference) are kitchen workhorses, the tools you will grab when you are mixing, scraping, folding or stirring over moderate heat. Look for spatulas with sturdy but flexible heads and with handles that feel good to your grip, and stock up. It's good to have a small slender spatula or two for scraping out the remains of the peanut butter and jam jars, for nabbing a little frosting or for scooping out chilled hot fudge; a couple of medium-size spatulas for working in small to medium saucepans or blending small batches of batters and doughs; and a few spatulas with broad heads and long handles for just about every other job.

You'll need two kinds of metal spatulas. The first is the kind you use to flip food in a skillet—these broad-faced spatulas are handy for transferring cookies from baking sheets to cooling racks. The other kind of spatula is narrow and is used for icing cakes and cookies. I prefer this type to be offset, meaning that the blade is angled just slightly below the handle (like a trough). When you need to nudge a glaze smoothly over the top of a cake or even out frosting, you get more control with an offset spatula. You should have a small metal icing spatula for cookies and a nice long (8- to 10-inch) spatula for working on cakes.

**SPICES:** Spices are the pick-me-ups of pastry, the little somethings that can change a sweet's character. To get the flavor, fragrance and color that you expect from dried spices, though, you have to use spices that are fresh. You can tell if a spice still has its oomph by checking that its color is still vibrant and its perfume still potent—if the fragrance is there, chances are the flavor will be too. If kept away from light, heat and humidity, spices should remain in peak condition for at least six months—make sure to check on them.

**SPRINGFORM PAN:** This two-piece pan just about guarantees a beautifully straight-sided cake or perfect cheesecake. What makes a springform so useful is its removable sides—a spring latch opens the sides of the pan enough to allow you to lift it off the base without touching the cake. And springform pans are excellent for fragile cakes because after you remove the sides, you can leave the cake on the base of the pan for serving and cutting. It is useful to have both a 9- and a 10-inch springform pan.

**SUGAR:** Added to flour, butter and eggs, sugar completes the baker's sine qua non quartet. Sugar adds sweetness to desserts, of course, but it contributes to a dessert's texture and color as well.

**Granulated sugar:** Whenever you see "sugar" listed in an ingredient list, I mean for you to use regular granulated sugar (not superfine). I use cane sugar, the sugar most commonly available in supermarkets.

**Confectioners' sugar:** A very white, powdery sugar that contains a little cornstarch, sometimes called powdered or 10X sugar, confectioners' sugar can be measured straight out of the bin, but, because it is invariably lumpy, it must be sifted or strained before it is mixed into a batter. Confectioners' sugar is measured with the scoop-and-sweep method (see page 482).

**Brown sugar:** Brown sugar is white sugar to which molasses has been added. It is soft and moist and, unfortunately, prone to lumps of the rock-hard variety. Put brown sugar through a sieve before you mix it into a batter, because the lumps won't break up by themselves. I use light brown sugar almost exclusively, but you can use either light or dark in any recipe without a problem.

**TAKING NOTES:** Until I got to college, the rule was never write in your textbooks. The first time I underlined something in a book, I thought I was going to have my knuckles rapped. Now I write in everything from novels and travel guides to cookbooks. Cookbooks, in fact, are my most scribbled-in books. I always review the recipes I make from cookbooks, writing a short opinion and noting who especially liked the recipe. I also note any substitutions I might have made or might want to make, and if there was any difference between the baking time in the recipe and what worked in my oven, I write that down also. I encourage you to keep notes too. It's another way of making cookbook recipes (including these) your own.

**TESTING FOR DONENESS:** I've tried to give you as many tests for doneness as possible for each dessert. Sometimes you'll feel a cake to see if it's springy, touch a cookie to see if it's firm, look at a crust to determine if it's golden or tap a pudding to discover if it's still jiggly in the center. For cakes and muffins, the most usual test is to insert a knife deep into the center of the cake—if it comes out clean, the cake is ready to be pulled from the oven. For so many years, the standard instruction was to stick a toothpick into the cake. I've traded in my toothpicks for a paring knife, which is what the pros use. A knife goes in deeper and has more surface area than a toothpick, so you can really get to the center of the cake and better judge if it is done. The drawback to testing with a knife is the slash that it creates. For me, the slash is not a problem with most cakes, but it can be unattractive in a pumpkin pie or a custard. For desserts such as these, I've also given you visual cues to note so you

need resort to the knife test only if you really can't decide if the sweet is done. And if you slash a custard, remember—that's why there's whipped cream in the world.

**TIMERS:** Kitchen timers are absolute musts in my house. While I've got a pretty good sense of when something should come out of the oven and usually get to it just as the timer is about to ring (the combination of years of experience and a good sniffer), I'd hate to have to depend solely on that sense, which can disappear if the phone rings or I'm distracted by anything from a news flash to a bird on the windowsill. My favorite timers are digital and they count down from the set time, ring like mad and then start counting up, so that if I've missed the ring, I can tell just how many minutes have elapsed. (I like the kitchen timers made by Polder, particularly the one you can sling around your neck.) If you don't have a timer, grab a piece of paper, write down the time at which your treat is supposed to come out of the oven and keep an eye on the clock.

**VANILLA:** Vanilla, from the seed pods of orchids grown in tropical climates, is the most basic flavoring in the baker's repertory and the most important. Vanilla softens any harshness in a recipe, rounds out the flavor of eggs and perfumes everything to which it is added. The two most commonly available forms of vanilla are beans and extract.

**Vanilla beans:** Vanilla beans should be wildly aromatic, plump and pliable. For most recipes, you need just the pulp of the bean. To get to the pulp, slice the bean lengthwise in half with a sharp knife, then use the back of the knife to scrape the pulp out of the pod. When you are infusing milk or cream with vanilla, you'll add both the pod and the pulp to the liquid. When you remove the pod, hold on to it. Wash the pod, dry it—either at room temperature or in a 250-degree-F oven—then put it in a food processor with granulated sugar and whir to pulverize the bean and make vanilla sugar. Or plunge the pod into a bin of sugar to flavor the sugar, or save it to steep in another liquid. Keep vanilla beans, tightly wrapped in several thicknesses of plastic wrap, in the refrigerator. Well wrapped, they will keep for more than a year.

**Vanilla extract:** I have tested these recipes using vanilla extract—always *pure* vanilla extract—because it is readily available and consistently good. I can't emphasize enough the need for the extract to be pure, since imitation extracts can leave a bitter aftertaste that can ruin your sweet. While both pure and imitation extracts contain vanillin, the imitation extracts contain a synthetic vanillin often derived from lignin, a by-product of wood pulp. Synthetic vanillin mimics the basic flavor of pure vanilla, but it does not deliver the complexity and nuances of the real thing. Vanilla extract is made by steeping cured vanilla beans in alcohol and, by law, must be 35 percent alcohol by volume. Although the proof is pretty high, you won't use very much vanilla and what you do use will be divided among portions. However, if you don't want to use an alcohol-based extract, substitute the pulp of a vanilla bean.

**Substituting vanilla extract for vanilla beans:** In general, figure 1 tablespoon pure vanilla extract for 1 vanilla bean.

**VEGETABLE COOKING SPRAY:** You can use vegetable oil spray, such as Pam, any time you are instructed to butter a baking pan. I rarely use spray on cake pans, but I often use it for muffin pans and sometimes for Bundt pans, which are fussy to coat evenly.

**WATER BATH:** The safest way to avoid overcooking custards or puddings, and some cheesecakes, is to bake them in a water bath. Line a roasting pan with a couple of layers of paper towels, put the baking pan or custard cups in the pan (the toweling will keep them from bobbing about) and fill the roaster with enough boiling water to come halfway up the sides of the baking pan or cups. Tucked into a water bath, your dessert will bake evenly and be protected from direct heat. It's often easiest and safest to put the baking pan in the roaster, get the roaster into the oven and then pour in the boiling water. That way, you don't have to carry a roaster filled with sloshing hot water.

**WHISKS:** Whisks are the tools to reach for when you want to combine dry ingredients, such as flour, baking powder, baking soda and salt; when you want to give eggs a beating; or when you want to blend cake batters or stir custards and creams. Long, narrow whisks are ideal for stirring; fat whisks, aptly called balloon whisks, are for beating air into ingredients.

**YEAST:** I use traditional, regular-rise dry granulated yeast for my recipes because it is effective and available in supermarkets (sometimes in the refrigerated dairy cases, sometimes on the shelves near flours and sugars). Before you buy packets of yeast, make certain that the sell-by date has not passed.

Traditional yeast needs to be proofed by soaking it for a few minutes in a little tepid water (don't use water that feels hot to the touch—it will kill the yeast). Stir the yeast until it dissolves, then follow the recipe. If you'd like the fun of having your yeast bubble—for some, this is proof of the yeast's power to puff—mix in a pinch of sugar with the yeast, so the spores have a little something to munch on.

Rapid-rise, or instant, yeast needs no proofing or dissolving. It can be mixed into a dough directly; follow the instructions on the packet. My favorite quick yeast is SAF brand, available in supermarkets or in bulk from bakerscatalog.com.

ZEST: Zest, the brightly colored rind of citrus fruits, is both flavorful and fragrant. Directly under the thin layer of zest is the white cottony pith, which is terribly bitter. So the trick to using zest is to get just the zest. I grate it using a very fine-holed grater (see graters, page 484), and if the recipe calls for sugar, I grate the zest directly onto the sugar. Then, to get the most flavor and aroma from the zest, I use my fingers to rub the zest and sugar together until the sugar is moist and aromatic. This is an excellent way of getting the zest's volatile oils into the recipe.

# Index

Page numbers in *italics* refer to photographs.

fillings. *See also specific cake recipes*
  almond cream, 452
  bittersweet ganache, 453
  faux crème fraîche, 460
  lemon cream, 461
  lemon curd, 462
  pastry cream, 448
    chocolate, 450
    cinnamon, 449
    citrus, 449
    coffee or espresso, 449
    ginger, 449
    liqueur-scented, 449
    rum-scented, 449
  whipped cream, 456
    chocolate, 457
    coffee, 456
    ginger-infused, 212
    white chocolate, 458
    white chocolate ganache, 454
flan, caramel-topped, 395–97, *396*
flan, caramel-topped coconut, 395
fleur de sel, 482
floating islands, 401–2, *403*
flour
  for biscuits, 22
  cake, substituting all-purpose for, 482
  chestnut, buying, 478
  measuring, 482
  sifting, 482
  storing, 482
flower petals and leaves, decorative candied, 472
folding technique, 482–83
food processor, 483
freezing food, 483
French toast, sugar-crusted, 60
frosting. *See also specific cake recipes*
  applying to cakes, 245
  bittersweet ganache, 453

whipped cream, 456
  chocolate, 457
  coffee, 456
  ginger-infused, 212
  white chocolate, 458
white chocolate ganache, 454
fruit. *See also* berry(ies); fruit, dried; fruit desserts; *specific fruits*
  and jam bread pudding, 408
  summer, galette, 366–67
fruit, dried. *See also* apricots; currant(s); prunes; raisin(s)
  apple cheddar scones, 32, *33*
  biscotti, 143
  cherry-fudge brownie torte, 284–85
  chockablock cookies, 86
  chocolate-cherry biscotti, 144
  cornmeal and fruit loaf, 43
  cran-apple crisps, 422
  crunchy ice cream, 429
  date-nut loaf, 228
  depths-of-fall butternut squash pie, 328–29
  drunken, rice pudding, 413
  fluted polenta and ricotta cake, 200–201
  great grains muffins, *8*, 9
  lots-of-ways banana cake, 204–5
  oatmeal breakfast bread, 44
  savory cornmeal and fruit loaf, 43
  softening, 481
fruit desserts
  cherry rhubarb cobbler, 415
  cran-apple crisps, 422
  devilish shortcakes, 425–26
  mixed berry cobbler, 416–17, *417*
  pineapple banana crisp, 422
  strawberry-rhubarb double crisp, 420–21

tender shortcakes, 423–24, *424*
tropical crumble, 418–19

G
galette
  cranberry lime, 364–65, *365*
  cranberry orange, 364
  summer fruit, 366–67
ganache
  bittersweet, 453
  chocolate, glaze, 455
  defined, 483–84
  white chocolate, 454
garnishes
  buttered pecans, 470
  candied citrus slices, 468
  candied nuts, 469
  candied orange or lemon peel, 468
  chocolate curls and shavings, 471
  decorative candied petals and leaves, 472
gelatin, 484
ginger
  candied, loaf cakes, 227
  -choco crackles, 74
  -chocolate crackles, 74
  creamiest lime cream meringue pie, 337–39, *338*
  crème brûlée, 394
  fresh, and chocolate gingerbread, 212–13, *213*
  gingerbread fruit cake, 212
  gingered carrot cookies, 162
  gingered lime and mango meringue pie, 337
  -infused whipped cream, 212
  -jazzed brownies, 101
  pastry cream, 449
  strawberry-rhubarb double crisp, 420–21
gingersnap cheesecake crust, 237
glaze. *See also specific cake recipes*

chunky peanut butter and oatmeal chocolate chip-
sters, 73
cran-apple crisps, 422
great grains muffins, 8, 9
oatmeal breakfast bread, 44
oatmeal nutmeg scones, 30
oatmeal-nutmeg scones, fruity,
30
oatmeal spice shortbreads, 125
pineapple banana crisp, 422
for recipes, 488
strawberry-rhubarb double
crisp, 420–21
oil, pure, and extracts, 482
oil, storing, 488
orange(s)
berry muffins, 3
candied citrus slices, 468
cheesecake, 237
citrus-currant sunshine
muffins, 7
citrus pastry cream, 449
coconut tea cake, 195
cream tart, cookie-topped, 334
fresh, cream tart, 334–35
loaf cakes, 227
or lemon biscotti, 143
peel, candied, 468
-star anise cup custard, 387
zesting, 496
oven, microwave, 487
ovens, convection, 479
oven thermometer, 488–89

P

pans
Bundt, 475
insulated baking, 485
Kugelhopf, 486
mini-Bundt, 475
for muffins, 2
pie and tart, 489–90
for quick loaves, 2
rotating, in oven, 492
saucepans, 490

skillets, 490
springform, 493
types of, 476–77
parchment paper, 489
pastry, puff, about, 490
pastry bags, 489
pastry blender, 489
pastry brush, 489
pastry cream, 448
chocolate, 450
cinnamon, 449
citrus, 449
coffee or espresso, 449
ginger, 449
liqueur-scented, 449
rum-scented, 449
pastry dough. *See* pie dough; tart
dough
pastry feather, 489
peach(es)
-honey ice cream, *436*, 437
summer fruit galette, 366–67
tart, crunchy and custardy,
346–47
upside-downer, summery,
206
peanut butter
chocolate chip cookies, 68
-cocoa crisscrosses, 78
crisscrosses, 78, *79*
kids' thumbprints, 163
melted chip thumbprints, 163
and oatmeal chocolate chip-
sters, 73
peanuttiest blondies, 119
for recipes, 489
torte, 282–83, *283*
peanut(s)
-caramel topped brownie cake,
*263*, 264–65
chocolate-crunched caramel
tart, 355–57, *356*
chocolate oatmeal almost-
candy bars, 114–15
cocoa–peanut butter crisscrosses, 78

granola grabbers, 82, *83*
kids' thumbprints, 163
melted chip thumbprints, 163
peanut butter chocolate chip
cookies, 68
peanut butter crisscrosses, 78,
*79*
peanut butter torte, 282–83,
*283*
peanuttiest blondies, 119
snickery squares, 120–22, *121*
pear(s)
brown sugar Bundt cake, 179
cornmeal and fruit loaf, 43
depths-of-fall butternut
squash pie, 328–29
rosy poached, and pistachio
tart, 370–72, *372*
savory cornmeal and fruit loaf,
43
tart, French, 368–69
tart, tourtely, 306
torte, fold-over, 348–49
pecan(s)
all-in-one holiday Bundt cake,
187
apple nut muffin cake, 37
applesauce spice bars, *116*,
117–18
Bill's big carrot cake, *253*,
254–55
-brown sugar shortbread
cookies, *126*, 127
buttered, 470
carrot spice muffins, 14
chocolate Armagnac cake–the
cake that got me fired,
279–81, *280*
cocoa chocolate chip cookies,
68
cocoa-nut puffs, 156
coconut chocolate chip cookies, 68
coconut-nut family cake, 214
double apple Bundt cake,
184–85, *186*